College Board Achievement Tests

Here's a list of some important test-taking hints to review as you complete your preparation for the exam:

1. Get adequate rest the night before the exam. Be careful of your diet. You'll need to be in good physical shape to perform to your top capacity.

2. Don't forget to bring all the supplies you'll need to the test center. Be sure to take your admission ticket, several sharpened No. 2 pencils, one or more pens, and a good eraser.

3. Read all directions carefully. Different sections of the test will have slightly different formats which may call for different approaches to the questions.

4. Budget your time. Calculate the time you should spend on each question, so that you have time for them all. Be sure you don't linger on questions you're not sure about.

5. Read through the entire question carefully and think through each part before attempting to answer it.

6. Consider all choices. You must pick the *best* choice, not just a good choice.

7. As a rule, the easier questions are at the beginning of each test section; the more difficult ones, toward the end. First answer all questions you are sure about. Then, if you have time, go back and work on the others. If you spend too much time puzzling over difficult questions, you may not have enough time to answer other questions that you do know. You are not expected to know the answers to all questions on a College Board Exam as you might in a classroom test. Many students who do well on the CBAT do not answer every question.

8. Use the process of elimination. At times, you will not be sure of the correct answer, even though you have some knowledge of the question. It may be to your advantage to eliminate one or more of the answers as definitely wrong. Then answer the question, even though you may have to make an "educated guess" as to which of the remaining choices is correct.

9. Avoid wild guessing. A great deal of blind guessing is unlikely to raise your score; if you are unlucky in your guessing, it can even lower your score. When your score is calculated, you receive credit for each correct answer. However, there is a penalty for guessing: one fourth of the number of wrong answers is subtracted from the number of correct answers.

10. Mark your answers clearly. Use the proper soft-lead pencil (No. 2), and blacken the appropriate space for the answer you have selected. The mark must fill the space completely and be kept within the space. If you have to change an answer, be sure to use a good eraser to remove the original mark cleanly and completely.

11. If you finish all parts of the examination before time is called, double-check your answers. When you feel sure that you have completed the exam to the best of your ability, turn in your paper.

How to Prepare for
College Board Achievement Tests in
EUROPEAN HISTORY and
WORLD CULTURES

Second Edition

by

Leonard F. James
Formerly Chairman of the Department of History
Phillips Academy
Andover, Massachusetts

Barron's Educational Series, Inc.
New York • London • Toronto • Sydney

All inquiries should be addressed to:
Barron's Educational Series, Inc.
250 Wireless Boulevard
Hauppauge, New York 11788

Library of Congress Catalog Card No. 75-45106

Paper Edition
International Standard Book No. 0-8120-0656-9

Library of Congress Cataloging in Publication Data
James, Leonard Frank.
    How to prepare for the College Board achievement test
in European history and world cultures.
    Published in 1968 under title: How to prepare for
the College Board achievement test: European history
and world cultures.
    Includes index.
    1. World history — Outlines, syllabi, etc.
I. Title.
D21.J33   1976   902'.02   75-45106
ISBN 0-8120-0656-9

PRINTED IN THE UNITED STATES OF AMERICA

01   510   16 15 14 13 12 11

Contents

1. **Early Civilizations**
   Introduction: Prehistory River Civilizations   1
   Egypt   3
   Mesopotamia   8
   China and India   12

2. **The Shaping of Western Civilization**
   Greece: History and Government   18
   Greece: Contributions to Civilization   26
   Rome: The Republic   31
   Rome: The Empire   36

3. **The Middle Ages: Decline and Revival of Western Civilization**
   The Church Provides Leadership   42
   The Empire of Charlemagne and the Holy Roman Empire   46
   Byzantium, Islam, The Crusades   50
   Feudalism: Decentralized Society   55
   Medieval Towns and Trade and Medieval Thought and Learning   57

4. **The Beginning of Modern Times**
   The Renaissance   64
   The Reformation   67
   Explorations and Discoveries   72
   Colonization of Latin America   77
   Growth of National States and National Rivalries   81
       France   85
       England   89
       Russia   92
       Prussia   95
   China (618 A.D.–1912) and India (320 A.D.–1848)   96

5. **Revolutionary Struggles for Rights and Freedom**
   England Establishes Representative Government   102
   The Age of Reason: The Intellectual Revolution   105
   The American Revolution   109
   The French Revolution   113
   Napoleonic France   121
   The Peace Settlement and Its Consequences   125
   Congress of Vienna   126
   Reaction and Revolution   128
   Latin America: Century of Independence   131

6. The Growth of Modern Nationalism

The Industrial Revolution   137

Russia in the Nineteenth Century   144

France: Second Empire and Third Republic, 1852–1946   149

Growth of Democracy in Great Britain and the Problem of Ireland   152

Ireland: Home Rule and Independence   154

Unification of Germany and Italy   156

Romanticism: Nineteenth Century Intellectual Movement   162

7. Imperialism and National Rivalries Lead to War

The New Imperialism   164

China, 1842–1949   169

Turkish and Austrian Empires   173

World War I   177

The Peace Settlement   182

8. The Search for Security Fails

European Domestic Affairs Between the Wars   186

Germany: The Totalitarian State   196

Italy: The Corporative State   200

Union of Soviet Socialist Republics: The Communist State   203

Attempts At Collective Security   208

World War II and the Peace Conferences   213

9. Europe and the Middle East Today

The United Nations   220

The Cold War   224

France, Great Britain, and Germany Since 1945   230

Communist Satellite Nations Today   239

The Soviet Union   242

The Middle East   246

Israel   251

10. Recent History of the Far East, Africa, and Latin America

Nations of South East Asia   260

The People's Republic of China   267

Japan   273

India, Pakistan, and Bangladesh   281

Sub-Sahara Africa   287

Latin America Today   299

Post-1945 Conferences, Pacts, Treaties, Organizations   306

Terms and Definitions   309

How to Make Effective Use of 11 Model Tests   321

Answers to Tests   414

Index   421

1

Early Civilizations

Introduction: Prehistory River Civilizations

Terms

Prehistory	Archeologist	Neolithic
Preliterate	Anthropologist	Neanderthal
Pleistocene Age	Artifact	Cro-Magnon
Geologist	Paleolithic	Age of Metals

Topic Outline
Prehistory
The Stone Age: Paleolithic, Neolithic
The Age of Metals

Introduction: Prehistory River Civilizations

Prehistory

History begins with man's record through writing, and is conveniently divided into three periods:

1. Ancient, 3000 B.C. to 476 A.D., fall of Rome.

2. Medieval, 476 to about 1500 A.D.

3. Modern, 1500 to today.

The period we call "history," in which written records trace man's development, is a comparatively short one extending back only about 5000 years. Early man was probably on this planet a million years ago.

Prehistory is the long period of man's existence before the use of writing and written records. The period down the centuries to 5000 B.C. is called the *preliterate* or prehistoric, since the past had to be recreated from various types of remains.

There have been four glacial periods of the Ice Age when glaciers came down from the North Pole and covered Europe, much of Asia and North America. Between these ice periods of intense cold were intervals of warmer temperature. The first glacial period began probably about 550,000 B.C., and the fourth began probably about 25,000 B.C. The last glacial period is known as the Pleistocene Age, that in which man's origin is believed to have started. Reconstruction of the past has been the work of *geologists* who reconstruct the climate and conditions of early man from fossilized remains from glacial deposits and river beds; of *archeologists* who search for artifacts, the products of human workmanship such as pottery, tools, and weapons; and of *anthropologists* who reconstruct the past by studying primitive peoples living today in Africa, Asia, Australia, and South America.

Prehistoric times are conveniently divided into periods which are based upon the type and age of tools and other remains.

The Stone Ages

Man's use of reason and ability to adapt nature gradually to his use set him apart from animals, and his artifacts show his progress. Scholars have divided history into ages based upon the tools man used: (1) *Old Stone Age* or *Paleolithic*, from about 25,000 to 8000 B.C., the age of rough weapons and tools of stone made by chipping, (2) *New Stone* or *Neolithic Age*, from about 8000 to 3000 B.C. in which men learned to sharpen weapons and tools with sandstone. Man had now discovered the use of fire, was making simple clothes, and was beginning to use the bow and arrow.

Fossil Man

The longer part of the Old Stone Age was inhabited by *Neanderthal* man whose remains have been found in various places and named after them, Java Man, Peking Man, Heidelberg Man, all "anthropus" from the Greek "anthropos" meaning man, almost as savage as the beasts they killed. They dominated Europe during the last glacial period, but were either rapidly replaced or dominated and absorbed by *Cro-Magnon* Man, so named after the caves in France where his remains were first discovered. He was clearly of the type *homo sapiens*, the first of modern man, the inventor of more tools, of flintheaded weapons such as the harpoon and spear, and probably the bow and arrow. Cro-Magnon Man discovered how to make fire and, in addition, he showed considerable skill in portraying animals on cave walls. He used bones, antlers, and ivory for specialized tools, invented the use of the awl and thread, and apparently gave some attention to burial ceremonies. He grew no food, domesticated no animals, and was necessarily a nomadic food gatherer.

New Stone Age

About 10,000 years ago the last ice glacier that covered much of Europe, Asia and North America melted and the climate grew warmer. New Stone Age Man improved tools and weapons by grinding and polishing stone, and piercing axe and hammer heads with holes into which wooden handles were fitted. He cultivated crops, domesticated animals, and instead of simply using nature as he found it, he adapted nature to his needs. Whereas Old Stone Age Man wove grasses and reeds, New Stone Age Man used wool and flax for weaving into cloth. Burial remains indicate belief in some higher power able to do harm and good.

Age of Metals

Men began to look for substitutes for stone; in Egypt the widespread use of copper began, to spread into Babylon and then to Europe. This marked the end of the Stone Age and the Beginning of the Age of Metals. The addition of tin to copper produced the harder bronze alloy. It appeared in Egypt by the year 3000 B.C., spread to Asia Minor, to Crete, and to Greece. Iron was called by the Egyptians the "metal of heaven," indicating perhaps the discovery of meteorites, and was first used in Egypt about 1500 B.C., but does not appear to have been used in Europe until around 1000 B.C.

The use of metals, the invention of the potter's wheel, the development of writing and man's organization into comparatively large political groups indicated that he was entering a new era of existence. Such changes and developments did not occur generally but were concentrated in a few river valleys where rivers overflowed and left behind a rich soil on which abundant crops could be grown and a larger population supported. This in turn led to the gradual rise of towns and developing civilization.

Egypt

Terms

Fluvial	Hyksos	New Kingdom
Thalassic	Book of the Dead	Intercalary
Oceanic	Hypostyle	Ideogram
Middle East	Pictogram	Hieroglyphic
Clerestory	Dynastic Period	Rosetta Stone
Dynasty	Hyksos Period	Menes

People

Thutmose	Tutankhamen	Aton
Amenhotep	Osiris	Cheops
Akhenaton (Ikhnaton)	Ra	Champollion
Rameses III	Amun-Ra	

Places to Locate

Nile River	Fertile Crescent	Thebes
Tigris River	Memphis	Karnak
Euphrates River		

Topic Outline

Why Civilization Began in River Valleys
Ancient Egypt
  Pre-Dynastic Period
  Dynastic Period
  The Middle Kingdom
  Hyksos Period
  The New Kingdom
Egyptian Society
Religion
Art and Architecture
Sculpture
Calendar
Science
Writing
Egypt

Egypt

Why Civilization Began in River Valleys

River civilizations developed at different times in Egypt along the Nile valley, in Mesopotamia along the Tigris and Euphrates, in India along the Indus river, and in China along the Yellow and Yangtse river valleys. Each of these civilizations developed independently of the others, but with striking similarities, and with some differences caused by local physical environment and social patterns.

The raising of greater harvests for growing populations necessitated the development of a network of interacting irrigation canals and ditches, and careful regulation of the use of water. Rivers also served as a means of transportation for people and goods, and for the exchange of products and ideas between settlements along the valleys.

In all the areas of river civilization the similarities of development were striking. Crafts and commerce grew, alphabets and calendars were developed, arts and literature were created, political systems organized, and religious beliefs and philosophies appeared.

The transition from "prehistory" to "history" occurred with the river civilizations where the growth of towns necessitated government organization and administration, methods of defense, and the division of labor in a society which became increasingly complicated. The history of man has shown how water has played a significant part in his expansion and growth.

Scholars sometimes divide civilization into three great distinctive types:

1. *Fluvial* (fluvius = a river), along the banks of rivers and in fertile valleys.

2. *Thalassic* (thalassa = sea), around great inland seas such as the Mediterranean.

3. *Oceanic* in which oceans bind land masses together and bring various parts of the globe closer.

The Middle East (used throughout the book to designate the area of Mesopotamia and Egypt) river valleys of the Nile and Tigris-Euphrates are the cradle of western civilization, for these regions first produced a system of states or independent political units which conducted formal political relationships with each other. These were Egypt, and the Mesopotamian nations of Chaldea, Babylon, Assyria, and Persia.

Along the Fertile Crescent, which stretched from Egypt to Mesopotamia, several small and medium-sized states like Phoenicia and Judea developed, in constant rivalry with each other, but in close contact with the larger political units at each end of the Crescent.

Inevitably two forces interacted upon each other:

1. The invasion of the civilized areas by nomadic groups.

2. The rivalry of nations of the valleys.

In turn Egypt, Assyria, and Babylon attempted to control the Middle East, and by 500 B.C. Persia controlled from Egypt to Persia.

The common pattern of the river civilizations was the bureaucratically-administered state, headed by a king, who was also priest, and sometimes a god. He ruled through a privileged class of nobles and priests, and commanded the army. He ruled despotically, but usually followed the customs of his predecessor.

The social classes formed a pyramid, with the king at the top, and successive groups of priesthood and nobility, merchant and craftsman, and peasants below, with slaves at the base.

Ancient Egypt

Ancient Egypt was the valley of the Nile, 800 miles long between the Second Cataract and the Delta on the Mediterranean, plus the vast delta which is another 100 miles long. It had contact with the Red Sea and the Fertile Crescent, but was protected against easy attack by the sea and the vast deserts. Historically, Ancient Egypt is divided into five periods during its life-span of 4500 years, from 500 to 525 B.C.

1. **Pre-Dynastic Period,** (10,000 to 3100 B.C.)

This was the time of the Old and New Stone Ages, consisting of small political units merged into Upper Egypt in the south and Lower Egypt in the north, nearer the Nile delta.

2. **Dynastic Period,** (3100 to 2200 B.C.)

The Greeks identified *Menes* as the man who united both kingdoms and established *Memphis* as the capital. During this period the Third to the Sixth Dynasties ruled, according to the reckoning of later Egyptian historians who gave the term *Dynasty* to each royal ruling family. This was the period of the Pyramids when the Pharaohs (Great House) had pyramids built as their tombs. The Pharaoh was God and Priest as well as Ruler, accepted as divinely inspired, responsible for the annual rising of the Nile through his divine power.

3. **The Middle Kingdom,** (2200 to 2000 B.C.)

After 2200 B.C. the central government weakened, local nobles ruled local provinces, royal absolutism collapsed; and the capital was moved to Thebes; defenses against invaders were so weakened that they took over the country.

4. **Hyksos Period,** (1800 to 1570 B.C.)

The invaders from western Asia took advantage of the weak government, but brought with them into Egypt the important contributions of the horse and the wheel.

5. **The New Kingdom,** (1570 to 1100 B.C.)

Never completely accepting the Hyksos as rulers, the Egyptians under *Thutmose III* expelled the "foreigners," expanded the frontiers eastwards to the Euphrates and southwards into the Sudan. During this period some notable pharaohs appeared, but failed to save Egypt from ultimate decline and conquest; *Amenhotep III,* (1413-1377 B.C.) brought law and order to Egypt and made Thebes the most famous city of its time; under his son *Akhenaton* (or *Ikhnaton*) the country declined; *Rameses III* (1301-1234 B.C.) tried to revive Egypt's glory, but under his son *Tutankhamen* it declined even more rapidly, until during the seventh century the Assyrians conquered it and made it a province of their empire. In sequence, Egypt became a Persian province (525 B.C.), a possession of Alexander the Great (336 B.C.), then was ruled by one of Alexander's generals Ptolemy, and finally a Roman province in 30 A.D.

Egyptian Society

Economic life was dependent upon irrigation and was therefore rigidly controlled from above. The land in theory belonged to the pharaoh who demanded complete religious and political obedience. To use a modern term, it could be said that the economy was one of state socialism, since all economic enterprise was planned and regulated by the government. Agriculture was the basic occupation, but craftsmen became famous for their leatherwork, furniture, glassware, ceramics, and enameling. They built sea-going ships and carried on trade with Phoenicia and Crete.

Religion

In primitive religions "vegetation" myths and sun worship were based upon the belief that there were cycles of crop growth and decay, and that the sun brought seasonal changes. These forces of nature became personified as gods and goddesses. Egypt accepted these beliefs and made *Osiris* the God of the Nile and its annual floods, and *Ra* the Sun God, their important gods because upon them the Egyptians depended for life. A remarkable feature of Egyptian religion was the extraordinary concern for immortality, which played a significant part in the history of Egypt. As long as the body of a man was preserved, the soul would continue to live. The god Osiris symbolized the continual death and rebirth of life that man saw about him. Legend had it that Osiris had been killed by his brother, that his sisters had wrapped the corpse in linen, performed certain rites, and so restored the corpse to life. As lord of the underworld, Osiris weighed the heart of a dead person, determined from the weight whether the person had been good or evil, and, according to the answer, either had his soul devoured by demons or had it sent on to perpetual happiness in the Land of the Blessed. Egyptians believed they could achieve immortality if their corpses were preserved. To ensure immortality the priests sold charms and magic formulas collectively called the Book of the Dead. For centuries there was little ethical quality about Egyptian religion, but in time eternal life was regarded as a reward only for those whose behavior on earth merited it.

Religion became complex in its worship of the several gods, in particular, Ra the Sun God and *Amun-Ra*, the combined god of the capital city of Thebes and of the Sun.

A later pharaoh, Amenhotep, unsuccessfully tried to substitute a one-deity sun god named *Aton*, but polytheism (the belief in many gods) persisted until the end of Ancient Egypt.

Art and Architecture

Kings and subjects were so concerned with life after death that tombs were more significant than palaces and houses, for they were regarded as "castles of eternity" where food and equipment were provided for the dead in the next world. The two great architectural contributions were tombs and temples. Typical of the Old Kingdom is the Pyramid of Khufu (or Cheops as the Greeks called him) at Gizeh. This vast tomb of the pharaoh is 13 acres at the base, 481 feet high, with 2,300,000 blocks of stone each weighing 2½ tons. The number of men and years required for its construction is not known, but Herodotus, 2000 years later, estimated 100,000 men for 20 years. True or not, it is apparent that a tremendous number of men was used, and that the administrative planning to feed and house the workers must have been highly efficient.

Typical of the Empire period were temples, the outstanding example of which is that at *Karnak*, a huge colonnaded or *hypostyle* hall, a ceiling resting upon columns. The two center rows of columns, taller than the others, had a separate ceiling, and in the wall spaces above the lower roofs were the windows called *clerestory* windows, that is, the highest story of the nave of a church with windows opening above the aisle roofs. The high middle aisle and clerestory windows were later used in the Roman basilica and in the Gothic cathedral. The style of architecture was the post and lintel.

Sculpture

The main development was from the two-dimensional relief-type to three-dimensional sculpture, with many statues standing away from the wall. A significant development was from the abstract and symbolic to the personalized, portrait-like sculpture.

Calendar

Early man devised a monthly or lunar calendar of twelve months in order to establish holy days, developing a month of 29½ days totalling a year of 354 days. From time to time a thirteenth month was added.

The next major step was from the lunar month to the solar year. The Egyptians developed twelve thirty-day months, adding 5 days at the end of the year; although they did not remedy the error, they recognized that the calendar year was 6 hours short of the solar year, which added one day every four years. Julius Caesar later added the intercalary day every 4 years, the modern "leap year."

Science

A practical people, the Egyptians made learning serve their needs, those of precise measurements for pyramids and for field work. They devised addition and subtraction, simple multiplication and division, simple geometry.

Writing

Writing developed because man needed a means of keeping records. The first form of writing was the *pictogram*, a simple picture representing an object. Several pictograms put together could tell a simple story. For example, a modern comic strip without words is a series of pictograms.

Then symbols, instead of actual pictures, represented an idea and told a story. That is *picture writing*. A symbol of a man with a spear in his hand could depict a hunter. An *ideogram* is more sophisticated, a picture representing an idea. The same symbolic man, with three marks beneath it could represent three hunters. Or a circle with five dashes could represent five suns, or perhaps five days, since the sun rises daily. Another form of ideogram could be the symbol of an eye with a tear to indicate weeping; two symbols of an eye could mean "to see."

The Egyptians then used a sign to represent the *sound* of a word or a whole word. The next step was the Egyptian development of signs, each standing for a consonant plus a vowel, such as da or ra. This was a further step towards an alphabet, in which a single letter stands for a vowel sound or a consonant.

Hieroglyphics or "priestly writings" were found on tombs and temple walls. Not until the early nineteenth century were they deciphered by *Champollion* by means of the *Rosetta Stone*, a stone found in Egypt and containing inscriptions in Greek, hieroglyphics, and a simplified Egyptian writing. Champollion assumed that the three inscriptions said the same thing, and, by using his knowledge of Greek, he deciphered them. The Phoenicians made the significant advance of developing an alphabet. They simplified Egyptian hieroglyphics into 22 signs, each representing the *sound* of a consonant or of a consonant and a vowel. The Greeks used this system and created a true alphabet by using signs to represent separate consonants and vowels. The word alphabet comes from the Phoenician Aleph and Beth, from the Greek Alpha and Beta, the letters A and B.

Mesopotamia

Terms

Cuneiform	Code of Hammurabi	Polytheism
Diaspora	Behistun Inscription	Satrapy
Ziggurat	Alphabet	Babylonian Captivity
		Eyes and Ears of the King

People

Sumerians	Hammurabi	Alexander
Akkadians	Hittites	Nebuchadnezzar
Assyrians	Arameans	Sargon II

Places to Locate

Mesopotamia	Phoenicia	Israel
Babylonia	Lydia	Nineveh

Topic Outline
Old Babylonia
  History
  Contribution: Code of Hammurabi
  Small Nations in Transition Period:
    Hittites
    Lydia
    Phoenicia
    the Arameans
    the Hebrews
    Assyria
New Babylonia (Persia)
  Contributions of Various Nations
    Architecture
    Economy and Society
    Religion
    Science
    Astronomy and Astrology
    Writing: Phoenician Alphabet
    Military and Political Organization

Mesopotamia

Civilization in the Fertile Crescent

The name *Mesopotamia* means "the land between the rivers," the broad plain between the Tigris and the Euphrates rivers. The most fertile region is the delta stretching hundreds of miles northwards from the Persian Gulf. This vast area, today called Iraq, took the name *Babylonia* from the capital city, Babylon.

Unlike Egypt, which was ruled by a succession of dynasties or families, Babylon was ruled by a succession of nations who in turn gave their names to the area.

Open to invasion from all sides, it was first inhabited by Sumerians and Akkadians from the north (today's Iran), then by Kassites in the southern part, then by Assyrians over the whole region, and further north and westward over the entire *Fertile Crescent*, later by the Chaldeans, and finally by the Persians whose empire was to stretch from the Greek cities of Ionia to the frontiers of India.

Old Babylonia

The Plain of Shinar is in an area that extends 170 miles north of the Persian Gulf and between the Tigris and Euphrates rivers. As in Egypt, there was little water except for the annual flooding of the rivers which necessitated cooperation among the people for the maintenance of irrigation. The *Sumerians* came down from the northern hilly country, probably around 5000 B.C., overwhelmed the inhabitants of the valleys, built irrigation canals, and by 3500 B.C. had developed cities and well-organized city-states, but not a strong central government. They brought with them a wedge-shaped writing called *cuneiform*, written with a stylus on a piece of clay, later baked to make a permanent record. This writing and their religion were to become the basis for those of all other empires that succeeded them until the Persians absorbed the whole area.

The Sumerians were gradually conquered by the Semitic groups from the grasslands of the Arabian peninsula. The term Semite refers to Arabs, Arameans, Assyrians, Hebrews, Phoenicians, Chaldeans, and other peoples who all spoke dialects of the language called Semitic, who had many habits in common, and who were apparently able to adapt themselves very quickly to whatever people they lived with. One group was the Akkadians, who moved south, intermarried with the Sumerians, accepted much of the culture and religion of the Sumerians, and around 1500 B.C. had replaced the Sumerian language.

In time another group, the Amorites from Syria, under King *Hammurabi*, conquered the land of Sumer and Akkad, and added to their possessions Assyria in the northeast corner of the Fertile Crescent. Babylon became the capital of the kingdom now called Babylonia. Although Babylon was to be conquered and ruled by other people, it remained a holy city for nearly 1500 years and the economic center of the land between the rivers.

Code of Hammurabi

Hammurabi set up his code of laws throughout the empire, a simple set of primitive rules and methods of justice that were important because they replaced local laws. The king's name has been handed down to posterity in the designation of his laws, the so-called *Code of Hammurabi*.

The civilization of Babylonia suffered from declines and recovery for nearly one thousand years, and during the period of transition to the Assyrian conquest of Mesopotamia in 750 B.C. many small nations were able to develop in the western section of the *Fertile Crescent*. In Mesopotamia itself a powerful new empire developed in north-central Asia Minor and reached its height as the Hittite Empire by 1500 B.C.

Period of Transition: Small Nations

Hittites   This empire, contemporaneous with the Hyksos in Egypt (1800-1570 B.C.) dominated the area from the sources of the Tigris and Euphrates westward to the Mediterranean, including Syria and much of Asia Minor. A struggle developed between the Egyptians and the Hittites, resulting in the collapse of both empires around 1200 B.C.

After 1200 B.C. no powerful single group dominated the Fertile Crescent until the rise of Assyria around 750 B.C.

Between 1200 and 700 B.C. a number of small nations developed; *Lydia* under King Croesus, whose wealth came essentially from commerce; *Phoenicia*, originally conquered in turn by the Akkadians and the Amorites, became a great trading and colonizing nation, settling in Africa at Carthage, and trading along the Atlantic coast of Spain and Africa; the *Arameans*, another Semitic group, established several small kingdoms including Damascus, important as the caravan terminus to Babylonia. Excellent businessmen and merchants, they developed the Phoenician alphabet and spread it throughout the Fertile Crescent, and made Aramaic the general language. The *Hebrews*, originally from the lower Euphrates valley, were a nomadic people in search of a homeland. Moving into *Canaan*, later called Palestine, they finally conquered the Canaanites, but were themselves driven into the hills by the Philistines, who gave their name to Palestine. About 1025 B.C. King Saul unsuccessfully led the Hebrews against the Philistines, and was followed by David who eventually established his kingdom in the Palestine-Syria area, with Jerusalem as its capital. King David's son Solomon taxed the people so heavily that in time the northern part of Palestine revolted and seceded, resulting in two kingdoms: *Israel* in the north and *Judah* in the south. In 586 B.C. *Nebuchadnezzar*, the Chaldean from Babylonia, carried the Judeans into captivity. In 536 B.C. the Persians defeated the Chaldeans and permitted the Hebrews to return to Jerusalem. In turn the Greeks and the Romans conquered the Hebrews. A later revolt by the Hebrews against the Roman Caesars led to the destruction of Jerusalem in 70 A.D. and the Diaspora, the scattering of the Hebrews across the earth. Not until 1948, with the creation of modern Israel, did the Jews get a homeland of their own.

Assyria   From the highland region north of Nineveh, the Assyrians, who had for one thousand years maintained predominance in their region, moved southwards. In 910 B.C. they captured Babylon, moved into the Mediterranean land of Syria, and by 700 B.C. under Sargon II (who took the name of the conqueror of the Tigris-Euphrates area nearly 2000 years earlier) were in possession of the entire Fertile Crescent, including Syria, Egypt, Phoenicia, and Israel, making *Nineveh* their capital.

The Assyrians were unskilled in administration, and, after only 150 years of rule, were conquered by the Chaldeans, whose king Nebuchadrezzar became the ruler of Chaldea in 604 B.C., restored Babylon and made it one of the most magnificent cities of its time. At his death forty years later the kingdom began to give way before the attacks of the Persians from the north.

New Babylonia

Cyrus the Great of Persia defeated the Medes and within twenty years created the vast Persian Empire which stretched from the Greek cities of Ionia to the frontiers of India. His successors Cambyses and Darius conquered Egypt, Macedonia, and Thrace. Persian attempts to conquer the Greeks led to defeat at the hands of *Alexander* the Great of Macedon.

Architecture Buildings were made of sun-dried brick and consequently did not last as did Egyptian structures. The lack of stone prevented the use of the lintel and post architecture of Egypt. Instead the Mesopotamians to some extent used the arch, the vault, and the dome, although not until Roman times were they widely used.

The architectural symbol of Mesopotamia was the *ziggurat* (pinnacle), a temple tower dedicated to the gods of the city. It consisted of several stories, each stepped back and smaller than the previous one. Gardens were built on the terraces, and a great triple stairway climbed to the shrine of the god.

Economy and Society Agriculture was the basis, and was dependent upon irrigation. Cattle were domesticated and foods such as barley, oats, and dates were grown. An important "first" contribution was the wheeled vehicle. Trade was carried on by caravans westward to Egypt, eastward to India. Social organization was similar to that in Egypt, but even more rigidly drawn.

Other Contributions They divided the week into days, the days into hours, and the hours into minutes; they used the water level and the square, invented numerical calculation based on a decimal system, developed a standardized system of weights and measures.

Religion played almost as important a place in life as in Egypt, but with the emphasis upon everyday affairs, and as a guide for activities on earth. Future life, ethical behavior, heaven or hell had no place in their religion.

Writing was done upon clay, the only available material, in the cuneiform style, with a system of about 600 syllable signs. This writing was deciphered by scholars by means of the *Behistun Inscription*, written in three languages: Persian, Susian, a Persian dialect, and cuneiform Babylonian. From a list of known Persian cuneiform signs it was possible to read the Persian and thus in turn the Babylonian.

An important written document was the *Code of Hammurabi*, one of the first codes of law set up for a nation. Harsh though these laws were, and unjust in the sense that penalties differed for social classes, the code was important because it set down the laws for all to see, and set a pattern for future codes.

Astronomy and Astrology They made a careful study of heavenly bodies, recorded eclipses, and gave great attention to astronomy. The Babylonians developed the false science of astrology which taught that study of the stars could foretell the future.

The Hittites Recent discoveries have revealed that the Hittites developed the refining and the use of iron, and supplied it throughout the Near East for tools and weapons. They were great horsemen and influenced other peoples to use horse-drawn chariots for hunting and warfare, and to develop mounted troops.

Phoenician Alphabet The Phoenicians were primarily responsible for an alphabet of 22 consonants, their first two signs *aleph* and *beth* giving us the word alphabet.

The Hebrews: Contributions to Western Civilization

RELIGION From the Israelite faith in God stemmed two great religions, *Judaism* and Christianity, and some influences upon Mohammedanism. Originally believing in *polytheism*, the worship of many gods, the Israelites developed the concept of one tribal God Javeh (Jehovah), whom the early Elijah regarded as a stern avenging God. Later prophets emphasized other characteristics of Jehovah, concern for the poor and the weak, a belief in forgiveness.

During the Babylonian Captivity (586-539 B.C.) the Israelites believed that Jehovah was the champion of the oppressed everywhere, was the one Universal God, and so made the beginning of a world religion.

The Assyrians

MILITARY   Their contributions were a highly-trained and efficient army, and a centralized system of political organization. The ancient world feared the Assyrian army with its iron-tipped arrows, heavy cavalry, and chariot formations.

POLITICAL   They developed a system of national roads to enable the ruler to keep in close contact with his local governors. However, this political skill was essentially in organization rather than administration, the actual running of the affairs of the nation. The people were ruled from above and had very little participation in government.

The Persians

carried further the efficient organization of the Assyrians. Cyrus the Great started the imperial system of dividing the empire into 21 provinces or *satrapies,* each under a provincial governor or satrap. In each satrapy the king installed his own secretary and a military official, and to each province were sent the "Eyes and Ears of the King," special inspectors to report back on local administration. The great imperial post-roads rivalled the later Roman roads and joined together the four main cities Susa, Ecbatana, Babylon, Persepolis. Every 14 miles stations were established where the King's Messengers could get fresh horses. This early "Pony Express" enabled royal officials to travel nearly 200 miles a day.

Another significant feature of the Empire was the attempt to give the various racial and conquered groups of people certain basic rights, and to respect their various local gods. Prosperity in all parts of the empire meant better taxes for the government.

China and India

Terms

Peking Man	Buddhism	Brahmins
Chou Dynasty	Caste System	Karma
Ch'in Dynasty	Untouchable	Nirvana
Han Dynasty	Hinduism	*Upanishads*
Confucianism	Jainism	Reincarnation
Siniticism	*Vedas*	Transmigration
Taoism	Caste	

People

Dravidians	Jina	Brahma
Vishnu	Buddha	Confucius

Places to Locate

Hindustan	Harappa	Yangtze-Kiang
Deccan	Mohengo-Darra	Yellow River
Tamil Land		

Topic Outline

China

Geography

Dynasties

Economic and Social Life

Religions

    Confucianism

    Siniticism

    Taoism

    Buddhism

India

Early History

Literature

Religions

    Hinduism

    Jainism

    Buddhism

China

Geography

Present-day China is over 4,000,000 square miles in area, with a population of over 750,000,000. The country has three natural divisions, the valley of the *Yellow* or *Hwang Ho* river in the north, the valleys of the *Yangtze-kiang* river in central China, and southern China.

The valley of the Yellow river is a vast fertile plain that benefits from the river except when floods bring destruction. Central China is more fortunate, with its 3000-mile long Yangtze river navigable by ocean-going vessels for 600 miles, by smaller ships for 1500 miles.

Man appeared in the Far East probably 1,000,000 years ago. Modern excavations unearthed skeletal remains of Peking Man near Peking, probably dating back nearly 1,000,000 years, more advanced than Java Man in Europe, certainly using fire and crude stone implements.

By 2500 B.C. the people of the Yellow river region had developed city-states, built roads, canals and irrigation systems. By 1000 B.C. China may already have had nearly one fifth of the world's total population of about 150,000,000, perhaps had cities of 100,000 people, several times the size of cities in Egypt and Mesopotamia.

Much of the history of China is that of powerful ruling families or dynasties, significant only because they gave China periods of orderly government, interrupted by internal conflict or invasions, and enabled China to develop into a comparatively unified country. There are three main periods and dynasties.

Dynasties

Chou Dynasty (1025 to 255 B.C.)   This was the longest dynasty in China, contemporary with the Assyrian, Chaldean, and Persian empires. It controlled the area from north of the Yellow river to south of the Yangtze river. It was noted for its political organization, essentially feudalistic, in which local lords and princes received fiefs or land holdings in return for homage and service to their overlord. In time the local rulers became virtually independent, and the ruler fulfilled two functions, that of legalizing titles and possessions, and that of high priest who mediated between heaven and earth and performed the necessary rituals.

Ch'in Dynasty,   which probably gave the name China to the land, was short-lived, 221 to 206 B.C., but significant, because it brought unification to the country. The emperors replaced loose federalism with centralized government in which the provinces were no longer administered by the owners of the land but were placed under departments responsible to the emperor. A network of military roads was built, and the Great Wall was pushed 1400 miles from the coast into the interior, a defensive system which was to protect China for centuries against barbarian invasion from the northwest.

The Han Dynasty (206 B.C. to 220 A.D.)   extended China's boundaries and built a vast empire as a means of keeping nomadic invaders in check, much as Rome was doing between 264 and 133 B.C. In time the Chinese Empire included much of Central Asia, South Manchuria, North Korea, and south of the Yangtze river into northeast Indo-China. It was equal in size to the contemporary Roman Empire.

Then from 220 to 618 A.D. the country was torn by four centuries of disorder and internal strife, to be brought under control finally by the T'ang Dynasty, one of China's greatest, sometimes called "most splendid."

Economic and Social Life

During much of China's history the lot of the peasants has been the same. Without political rights, mere workers on others' land, a source of taxation, subject to serve as soldiers in their masters' armies, they remained local people whose economic and political horizon was limited to the village. Their lot was that of grinding poverty, with a life rigidly controlled by custom and tradition. Out of this situation the philosophy of Confucianism developed.

Religions

Confucianism.   Confucius (551 to 478 B.C.) was born to a priestly family, served as a state official, and then became a reformer and a teacher of rules of social behavior. We consider his teaching less a religion and more a code of behavior or morals, based essentially upon the relationships of individuals. Confucius did not formulate theories about the nature of the universe, or the after-life, or immortality. He was concerned with the codes of behavior by which men could live together in peace. The universe was governed by laws which regulated the stars and the seasons and thus maintained a balance. It was the duty of man to act similarly, because order would prevail if all people, rulers and ruled, respected the laws, set good examples for each other, and tried to live together in harmony, expressed in the rule, "What you do not like when done to yourself, do not do unto others." The wise ruler would make laws which maintained harmony and balance, and had the good of the people at heart.

The family, through ancestor worship and respect for each person's position within it, is the foundation of the organization of society, since the state itself is simply part of society. The ideal government would work for the welfare of the nation.

The contribution of Confucius of a code of ethics and morals was of great significance to China, for it solved the problem of how an overcrowded population could live together in harmony. Nevertheless, Confucianism did restrict progress, in the sense that Confucian scholars gave too much attention to rehashing Confucian text, and too little attention to thinking along contemporary lines and adapting to changing conditions. Rulers could too easily use the emphasis upon traditional authority and ignore the needs of the people.

Siniticism   was a native religion of China. It probably dates back to pre-historic times, and certainly contributed to the profound belief in ancestor worship and in retribution for good or evil. It failed to meet man's religious needs in times of stress and political trouble, and it perhaps bred a scepticism which prepared the way for Taoism, itself an almost do-nothing philosophy.

Taoism   (tao, "the path" or "the way") is an old Chinese philosophy which taught that man is an individualist, and that he should withdraw from the group and ignore all forms of ritual and regulation. Man should be content with his lot and forego all worldly pleasures and honors.

Buddhism   came from India to China in the first century A.D., and appealed particularly to poor people who could not understand the scholarly teachings of Confucius, Buddhism taught that life was suffering, and that since suffering was caused by desire, then suffering could be avoided by giving up all human desires.

India

India of today is a vast subcontinent, slightly more than half the size of the United States but with a much greater population of some 532,000,000.

In ancient times it was inaccessible except by land, and that only through the mountain passes of the Himalayas. This fact has colored all Indian history, since invaders have come from the northwest. South of the mountains are three great river valleys, the Indus in the northwest, the Ganges almost in the center of the northern plain, and the Brahmaputra in the northeast.

India is divided into three geographical areas: Hindustan in the northwest, from the Arabian Ocean to the Bay of Bengal; the Deccan south of the Narbada river; and Tamiland or Far South, occupying the southern part of India.

The northern plain is the most fertile, and there live most of India's people, and there the history of India's invasions and conquests has been enacted, and her culture has developed.

The early history of India was influenced by geography and climate just as were other civilizations, but conditions in India differed markedly from those in Egypt and Mesopotamia. Whereas they were dry, India enjoyed a warm climate and a heavy rainfall, resulting in luxuriant vegetation. These conditions have made research difficult for the historian and the archeologist because buildings and other remains of civilization have been destroyed by climatic conditions.

The northwest corner of India has a climate much like that of Egypt and Mesopotamia, and there the Indus river was the site of a flourishing civilization between 3000 and 1500 B.C. Modern excavators have revealed the remains of two cities, Mohengo-Darro and Harappa, cities of substantial size, dependent upon the river, and carefully organized, probably on a religious basis. This Harappa civilization, as some historians label the Indus culture, was essentially agricultural, although like that of Egypt it knew also the use of metals. Who the people were, where they came from, what their language was is still unknown. Neither the age nor the fate of this civilization has been determined, but it is believed that it was overwhelmed by some great tragedy, perhaps disease or invasion.

At the opening of the historic period 5000 years ago, the population of India seems to have been Dravidian, a dark-skinned people. Their Aryan invaders, coming from the northwest, conquered the Indus valley and treated the Dravidians as an inferior people, prohibited intermarriage, and thus began what was to become the present caste system.

We are dependent upon Indian literature for our knowledge of early India, which from 1500 B.C. preserved the legendary accounts of Aryan exploits in a collection of hymns, prayers, and philosophical ideas in the *Vedas*, which do provide some information on their way of living. We know little about the Aryans because they were more interested in religion and philosophy than in administration and politics. Consequently the history of India consists of long periods of anarchy interspersed with short periods of strong rule.

One aspect of life learned from the Vedas is the division of social classes into priests, warriors, artisans and farmers, and serfs, rigidly maintained in the castes of which the priests or Brahmins were the highest. Outside these castes were those who had no caste, the war captives and the slaves, who were to become today's pariahs or outcasts, the 50,000,000 "untouchables" whose mere shadow supposedly defiles a Brahmin. Whatever the actual origin of the caste-system — and it may well have been the fusing of the Aryan and the Dravidian people — it was to receive religious support.

Literature

The *Vedas* or *Rigvedas* written in Sanskrit, the language of the educated, come from the word meaning knowledge, and were the essential religion, philosophy, and beliefs of the times, too sacred for the Surdas to know, and therefore not written down but handed from father to son in the Brahmin caste.

The *Upanishads*, written between 800 and 600 B.C., are philosophical ideas about the truth behind creation, emphasizing the importance of the spiritual values, denying material values. The philosophy is not humanistic since it is completely disinterested in worldly affairs, and is concerned only with the mystery of life.

The Brahmins believed in reincarnation, or the transmigration of souls, and endless birth and rebirth of the soul in bodies of animals or men. A man's level of existence in the next life depended upon his deeds in this life.

Because all life belongs to one universal life force, no life must be destroyed, not even the cow, which is sacred to the Hindus.

Religions

Hinduism.   The history of India is so linked inevitably to the history of Hinduism that one cannot be understood without the other. Not only is Hinduism a religion, it is also a complete rule of life in which literally every act of the orthodox Hindu's life is regulated by precise ritual. Therefore since every task and occupation in society is assigned a social status within the caste system, violations of the caste organization would be religious heresy.

The Hindu believes that human life and happiness are governed by moral law, and that man's every act and thought shapes his character. The law of *Karma* or "deeds" holds every person to account for every action. After his death his soul will be re-born to a higher or lower existence or caste, if he is reincarnated in human form. Therefore the caste system is essentially a part of the Hindu religion, not simply a social stratification. Hinduism is polytheistic; and three important gods are *Brahma* the Creator, *Vishnu* the Preserver, and *Shiva* the Destroyer, symbolic of creation, preservation, and destruction, the three life processes. India's present beliefs are an inheritance from the distant past, for the concept of passive resistance, or more accurately non-violent non-cooperation, comes from an idea nearly 3000 years old.

Two contestants, or rebel groups, did not accept Hinduism, the Jains and the Buddhists.

Jainism. The followers of Jina believe in salvation in this life, to be attained by following certain precepts. Strict vegetarians, they believe in non-injury to living creatures, carrying their convictions to the point of begging for cooked vegetables. According to them everything has a soul, humans, animals, and plants. They regarded all material things as evil. The sect did not have widespread influence, partly because they had no system of teaching to attract the numbers of people.

Buddhism. The other rebel to Hinduism was Buddha, whose experience with asceticism, the renunciation of all earthly pleasures, convinced him that salvation was attainable in this life.

The Brahmins had controlled religious beliefs and ceremonies from Vedic times, maintaining their hold by their insistence upon ritual. Salvation was a reward to adherence to Brahmin teachings rather than a matter of individual effort. Many people opposed such an attitude, and found their champion in the great reformer Gautama Buddha (c. 560-483 B.C.). Born a prince, happily married and the father of a son, he became profoundly disturbed by the sorrow and misery he saw in towns. He protested against the increasing power of the Hindu clergy and its organized religion. At the age of 29 he renounced his worldly possessions and family, and for seven years meditated, led an ascetic life, and almost died from fasting and self-torture. "Enlightenment" convinced him that every man could work out his own destiny by being reasonable and moderate, without having to follow Brahmin rituals, and regardless of caste. He brought a message of hope and moderation through a religion which had no Supreme Being, no personal God, no immortality, but simply the belief that living the good and reasonable life would help man to achieve utter bliss and peace called Nirvana.

By 800 A.D. Buddhism had been almost driven out of India by the Brahmins, and was replaced by the old Hinduism. But missionaries spread Buddhist beliefs from Syria to Burma, so that today at least 30 per cent of the people of the world are Buddhists.

CHAPTER 2

The Shaping of Western Civilization

Greece: History and Government

Terms

Acropolis	Boule	Pnyx
Iliad	Strategoi	Ostracize
Odyssey	Helot	Delian League
Asty	Krypteia	Prytaneum
Polis	Apella	Dicastery
Areopagus	Ephor	Oligarchy
Archon	Phoros	Peloponnesian War
Ecclesia	Metics	Parthenon
Heliaea	Democracy	Geronsia
Tyranny		

People

Homer	Darius	Themistocles
Draco	Miltiades	Pericles
Solon	Xerxes	Philip of Macedon
Pisistratus		

Places to Locate

Crete	Marathon	Plataea
Cnossus	Thermopylae	Issus
Thrace	Salamis	Persepolis
Miletus		

Topic Outline

Influence of Geography
Early Greek Civilization: Crete; Mycenae
Colonization
Athenian City State: Institutions
Doric City State: Institutions
Persian Wars
Golden Age of Athens: Institutions
Peloponnesian Wars
Empire of Alexander the Great

Significant Dates

621 B.C.	Draconian Code
492–479 B.C.	Persian Wars

490 B.C.	Battle of Marathon
480 B.C.	Thermopylae
480 B.C.	Battle of Salamis
431–404 B.C.	Peloponnesian Wars
338 B.C.	Conquest of Greece by Macedonia

Greece: History and Government

Hellenic Greek civilization was never tightly organized like that of Egypt or Persia. It consisted of a series of city-states, a city and the surrounding countryside. The average city-state had a population of about 5000 people; Corinth had perhaps 75,000, and Athens, the largest, about 300,000 inhabitants.

To be a citizen of a city-state, a man and his ancestors before him must have lived there. Outsiders, or Greeks from other city-states, could not become citizens of another; slaves had virtually no rights whatever, and certainly were not citizens.

Rather narrow in outlook, the inhabitants of one city-state had nothing in common with citizens of another, except that they were Greeks. Each state was independent, owing allegiance to no other state, except through conquest. And yet these fiercely separate communities, who regarded themselves as Hellenes and their country of Greeks as Hellas, were able collectively to contribute profound ideas of human behavior and human rights.

Influence of Geography

The world of Hellas consisted of hundreds of islands in the Aegean Sea, colonies on the coast of Asia Minor, and the mountainous peninsula of Greece, some 25,000 square miles in area.

This was a *thalassic* civilization, because the sea played so significant a role in its development. The heavily-indented coasts of Greece and Ionia and the numerous islands provided protection for ports and cities, and stimulated navigation. Greek civilization spread eastward because ports and harbors were numerous on the east coast of the peninsula, but few in number on the west coast. It should be noted that the opposite was true of the Roman peninsula, so that Greece and Rome developed "back to back," Greece facing eastward, Rome facing westward. Geography and topography affected communication between Greek city-states, and influenced their size. Mountain ranges isolated states from each other, and the size of agricultural plains and their productivity determined the size of the city-states. Geography might frequently determine the location of a city, which usually had its *acropolis* or citadel on a rocky outcrop, with dwellings and shops below. One authority has written that the history of ancient Greece is "largely a record of successive thalassocracies, and Greek civilization was mainly the product of cities with a seafaring tradition."

Geographical fragmentation resulted in political fragmentation.

Origin and Early Development of Greece

Probably around 2000 B.C. Indo-Europeans from the Danube area began to move southward in successive waves, Acheans and Aeolians in 2000 B.C., Ionians in 1400 B.C., and Dorians in 1100 B.C. The Dorians brought with them the Iron Age, occupied most of the Peloponnesus, crossed over to Crete, and then to Asia Minor. They found the area already inhabited in three main areas: the island of Crete; the area around Troy, strategically located on the seaway from the Aegean through the Hellespont to the Black Sea; and on the peninsula of Greece at Mycenae and Tiryns.

Cretan Or Minoan Culture   On the island of Crete the barbaric Greek invaders found a highly developed pre-Hellenic culture, known to us through archeological remains. In the royal palace of the Minos dynasty at the capital city of Cnossus, remains indicate that the Cretan ships traded with Egypt and Syria, and sailed through the Straits of Gibraltar. A highly developed civilization is revealed through architecture, decorations, furniture, and a system of plumbing. Although Cretan dominance of the Aegean area apparently ended about 1450 B.C., presumably at the hands of the Achean invaders, its culture had already spread through the region.

The Mycenaean Civilization   from approximately 1400 to 1100 B.C. was less advanced than the Cretan, but with many evidences of that culture. The Dorian invaders destroyed part of this culture, although the next several centuries from 1100 to 800 B.C., called the Age of Darkness, was probably one in which old and new were synthesized.

Meanwhile a civilization had been flourishing at Troy at the Hellespont. Excavations begun by Heinrich Schliemann in 1870 and continued down to the 1930's have shown that the Troy of the famous Trojan Wars was the seventh city on that site. Homer, ninth century, wrote about the Trojan Wars of the 1100's, but his *Iliad* and *Odyssey* give a picture of the Aegean world of his time. Economic life was agricultural and simple; political life was tribal, with small states ruled by local kings. By the middle of the eighth century political power was in the hands of the council or nobles.

Colonization

During the period 750–500 B.C. Greek colonization expanded along the coasts of Asia Minor, around the Black Sea and westward into Sicily and Southern Italy, collectively called Magna Graecia, and westward into Spain. Growth of population, scarcity of food, need for markets, and political subordination of the people by nobles and merchants were the main causes of colonization. Settlements were carefully planned; each colony was politically independent but tied by sentiment and commercial interests to the mother city-state. The chief competitor was Phoenicia, which settled colonies along the greater part of the northern African coast and along the Spanish coast. Colonization led to the growth of specialization in Greece itself, from a domestic or local economy to an expanding trade throughout the Mediterranean and Asia Minor.

The City-State evolved from a combination of the citadel which provided refuge during attacks, the *asty* or area where people traded and lived, and the neighboring agricultural area. The unit was the *polis*, a political, religious, economic, and social entity, its inhabitants classed as citizens. The size of the *polis* differed; some were 50 square miles, others were occasionally several times that, but most were small enough to give the citizens direct participation in political life.

In general all city-states evolved along the same lines, with power passing from the hands of the all-powerful king-autocracy, to the wealthy group of aristocracy, and finally to the people, the democracy. By 500 B.C. there were some 300 Greek city-states.

Athens

Early kings were replaced by an aristocracy of leading landowning families, the Council of Elders or *Areopagus*. Opposition by middle class and peasant farmers resulted in revolts which were put down with great severity. Existing laws were codified by *Draco* in 621 B.C., and harsh though they were, they established "Rule by Law" and not a class or group. Economic unrest continued to trouble Athens, chiefly because debtors and their families could be enslaved and because government remained in the hands of a relative few.

Solon was appointed *Archon* or civil magistrate in 594 B.C., with extraordinary legislative powers. His several reforms have made his name synonymous with wise statesmanship. The first reform concerned debts and debtors. No man could remain or become a slave for debt; mortgaged lands were free of the mortgage; it was forbidden to export wheat; sons must be taught a trade; skilled craftsmen were encouraged to come to Athens, which became a trade center through these reforms.

In politics the holding of office was still limited to property owners, but all citizens, property-owners or not, could vote in the *Ecclesia* or Assembly. Solon instituted a new system of jury-courts, called *Heliaea*, in which all citizens could serve on panels of judges. The upper classes resented these changes, and civil strife persisted until *Pisistratus* in 560 B.C. usurped power and made himself supreme. His tyranny — a word that simply indicated the unconstitutional seizure of power and not necessarily a harsh rule — advanced the cause of the people. His basic contributions were:

1. The extension and protection of foreign commerce.

2. The appointment of local judges.

3. The weakening of the aristocracy by banishment, and the distribution of their lands among the peasantry.

In 509 B.C. another reformer, *Cleisthenes*, made a significant contribution to democracy by replacing family tribal political divisions with 10 new electoral districts from each of which 50 members were chosen by lot annually to constitute the Council of 500, or *Boule*, which handled the long-range problems of foreign policy, finance, and war. A Board of *Strategoi*, or Generals, was elected annually, one by each of the ten tribes. This system assured the political equality of all citizens.

**Sparta:
Dorian City-State**

While Athens was developing into a democracy, Sparta was becoming a military totalitarian state. At the southern end of the Peloponnesus, Sparta expanded its territory in Messenia, engaged in two wars against it, and finally conquered and enslaved it, instead of making a treaty with it. Since the Messenians were more numerous than the Spartans, they had to be kept under firm control. Sparta became a military state, a one-sided civilization, drilled in the art of war, superb fighters, completely inartistic, with no interest except soldiering. Its population of some 25,000 dominated a conquered population of nearly 500,000. The Spartan people formed a military state, since the citizen was devoted to the service of the state and was freed from the necessity of providing for himself and his family. Therefore the conquered inhabitants, or *Helots*, were obliged to work for their masters. This system of enforced slavery necessitated a secret police, the *Krypteia*, alert to the danger of revolt. Each year the *Ephors*, or guardians of the rights of the people, upon entering office declared war against the Helots, thereby permitting Spartan youths legally to kill any Helot they might consider dangerous.

The political organization of Sparta consisted of two kings, each a check upon the other; a Senate, or *Geronsia*, of 30 leading citizens, including the kings, 60 years old and elected by the citizens for life, who prepared legislation for the Assembly, or *Apella*, of all Spartan citizens over 30 years of age, which ratified the laws and determined all matters of state. The Spartan citizenry was actually an aristocracy of the few. Elected annually by the assembly were the five *Ephors*, or Watchers, whose responsibility was to protect the interests of the people against encroachments by the kings or the Senate. They became the guardians of the constitution, exercised executive and judicial powers, could call other officials to account, and supervised Spartan discipline and training. From their decisions there was no appeal.

The Spartan elders examined each child at birth, condemned weaklings to exposure and wild animals. At the age of seven each boy was taken from his parents and publicly trained for military life. He was taught to endure hunger, pain, to steal in order to survive. At 18 he was enrolled in a military company, but not until age 30 could he live at home, and then only on condition that he report for military service until age 60. This military caste of some 10,000 owned land which could be worked only by helots, who belonged to the state. All organization in Sparta had one objective — military efficiency for the supervision and suppression of the helots. Spartans were the garrison of their land and their slaves.

The Persian Wars 492–479 B.C.

During the sixth century the kingdom of Lydia conquered all the Greek cities in Asia Minor, except Miletus, but was in turn conquered by the Persians under Cyrus the Great in 546 B.C. The conquered Greek cities revolted and received assistance from across the Aegean Sea, especially from Athens, which sent 20 ships.

Darius the Persian, a successor of Cyrus, decided to crush the Hellenic cities, crossed the Hellespont and in 492 B.C. subjugated Thrace before moving southwards. A storm destroyed the accompanying fleet, and the invasion was postponed until 490 B.C. when an expedition sailed across the southern Aegean and met the Greeks on the Plain of Marathon, 26 miles from Athens. Sparta, asked to send aid against the 20,000 Persians failed to appear in time and left the problem to the Athenians who, under *Miltiades,* won a decisive victory. The news was sent to Athens by a courier who ran the 26 miles and 385 yards, commemorated today in the Marathon race.

In 480 Xerxes, son of Darius, led 250,000 men across the Hellespont, across Thrace, and southward into Greece. At *Thermopylae* the Spartans under

Leonidas made up for their earlier tardiness and held up the Persians, who nevertheless eventually reached Athens and burned it. But the Athenians, long ready with a navy and led by *Themistocles*, destroyed the line of communications by defeating the Persian fleet in the bay of *Salamis* in 480 B.C. A combined army of Athenians and Spartans defeated the retiring Persian army at *Plataea* in 478 B.C.

Greece was saved from conquest, and during the next century, but particularly between 479 and 431 B.C., was to make its great contribution to western civilization.

The Golden Age of Athens

This describes the half-century after the defeat of the Persians, the fruition of earlier centuries and the inspiration for mankind for centuries to come.

Athens had become prosperous through its expanding Mediterranean trade, its silver mines at Laurium, and the funds of the *Delian League*. The significance of the naval victory at Salamis in 480 B.C. persuaded several of the city-states to form the defensive alliance, called the Delian League, an association of Greek sea-states each contracting to supply ships for the common defense. Some could contribute only part of the cost of a ship, while others could make larger contributions. In time the smallest states were allowed to contribute money instead of ships, a *Phoros*, as the contribution was called. The treasury of the league was on the island of Delos, but by 454 B.C. the league was actually an Athenian Empire, with funds instead of ships contributed by its members. Athens undertook to provide the ships, moved the treasury to Athens, and used the funds to build the Acropolis.

Government of Athens

Athens developed the most democratic government of ancient times (*demos* = people, *kratos* = rule) and although it was originally limited to property-owners, by the time of *Pericles*, 461-429 B.C., all male citizens over 18 years of age participated directly in government. Slaves and resident foreigners or "metics" had no share in government. Of the entire population of around 300,000 only about 40,000 adult males could take part in government.

The Assembly of male citizens met 40 times a year on the *Pnyx*, and was the ultimate source of all political authority. Any citizen could speak and vote on any matter submitted to the Assembly by the Council of 500, and all such proposals could be passed, rejected, or amended by the Assembly. Of course, it was not to be expected that all "voters" would be present, but in this "town-meeting" type of government 6000 were necessary for an official decision. The Assembly exercised legislative power for the state, and could *ostracize* or exile any Athenian by a secret ballot recorded on pieces of clay called ostraka. By this method it could banish a self-seeking politician, and sometimes an eminent citizen whose views happened to be unpopular.

Council of 500 or Boule really directed public affairs. The Assembly was too large to be well-informed on all issues, so 50 men of at least 30 years of age were chosen by lot from each of 10 districts of Athens. They met four times a month, and the delegates from each district served as a continuous body for one month in sequence, with smaller committees in continuous operation. They exercised the executive and administrative powers, and lived in a public building, the

Prytaneum, named after the presiding group called Prytanes. While the Council could pass laws that did not conflict with the Assembly, its chief functions were seeing that laws of the Assembly were put into operation, the supervision of public festivals, the maintaining of the grain supply, and responsibility for public finances.

The Courts or Dicasteries

Legal cases were tried by large juries drawn from the citizens, usually of 201 or more, in the belief that bribery would be more difficult with a large jury. All citizens, that is, adult males over 18, could apply for the jury list, made up of 6000 citizens divided into 10 sections or *dicasteries* of 500 members each, leaving the other 1000 to be drawn upon when needed. Jurors were paid for their services, which included deciding the question of guilt and also the penalty. Each citizen could at some time share in the administration of justice.

The Magistrates or Generals

These *strategoi* were 10 in number and were elected by the Assembly, who came to be the most important magistrates in the city-state. They not only commanded the army, but had charge of all defense installations, the making of foreign policy, negotiation of treaties, the receiving of ambassadors, and the power to call extra meetings of the Assembly when the public interest demanded.

Political Parties developed because of group interests in Athens. In general the democratic group favored the new constitution which gave more power to the ordinary citizen, and was regarded as the patriotic party since it opposed all foreign influence.

The more conservative or *oligarchical* party (oligarchy = rule by a few) opposed the new constitution of Pericles because it had deprived its followers of their exclusive privileges. It sympathised with the aristocratic ideas of Sparta and sometimes was ready to side with outsiders if its own interests could be served.

In general, Athenian democracy was the outstanding example of wide and direct participation by citizens in government. Its weaknesses were its denial of voting rights to a large body of slaves and resident "foreigners," and its rather narrow parochial outlook of fierce loyalty to Athens that prevented a federation with other Greek states against common dangers.

Once the Persians were defeated, the Athenians set about the religious duty of restoring the temples destroyed by the enemy. The gods must be thanked for assisting in the defeat of the Persians, and the thanks must be on a grand scale. So a colossal statue of the goddess Athena was wrought in bronze and housed in a magnificent temple called the *Parthenon.* Temples to other gods and goddesses were restored and built, but the cost gave the opponents of Pericles the opportunity to criticize him.

The Peloponnesian Wars, (431–404 B.C.)

As we have seen, some 200 city-states in the peninsula of Greece, the Aegean islands, and along the coast of Asia Minor, organized together in the Delian League. When Athens forcibly prevented the dissolution of the league and removed its funds to Athens, opposition was soon headed up by Sparta and

Corinth. This was an unfortunate situation, for the Delian League might have been the beginning of effective collaboration between the Greek city-states. Unfortunately the Athenians failed to attempt to make the league a Greek federal system. The ensuing war was a tragedy of stupidity and pride. The economics of colonization and trade and the politics of defense both demanded the recognition of inter-dependence. Individual Greek city-states insisted upon their complete independence and pursued their separate rivalries. When the Island of Mylos refused to support Athens, that city captured the island, slaughtered the men, enslaved the women and children, and colonized the island. By 429 Sparta and Corinth pillaged Attica, the plague carried off one third of the population of Athens, and Athens then committed the folly of not concentrating upon its chief enemy, Sparta. Instead, the Athenians sent an unsuccessful expedition to Syracuse where the survivors were sold into slavery. The Spartans then called in Persia to help them, and finally in 404 B.C. destroyed the Athenian fleet, tore down part of the walls of the city, and took over all its foreign possessions.

Sparta proved to be an even harsher leader, so that continued rivalries and conflicts led to the supremacy of Thebes in 371 B.C., to be followed in turn by Macedonia, which defeated Thebes in 362 B.C. and conquered Greece by 338 B.C.

**Empire of
Alexander the Great**

While the Greek states were engaged in suicidal wars and failing to heed the warnings of Demosthenes, the great Athenian statesman and orator, that the Macedonian menace was threatening, *Philip* of Macedon was consolidating his country. When Athens and Thebes finally attempted to check him, Philip defeated them at Chaeronea in 338 B.C. He called all the Greek city-states together at Corinth, with each city free and under a Council, with Philip as king, with authority to declare war and make peace. He then revealed his great project — to conquer Persia which had subdued the Greek cities in Asia Minor.

After Philip's assassination in 336 B.C. his son Alexander decided to carry out his father's project. In 334 B.C. he took the land route to the Hellespont, defeated one Persian army at Granicus in Asia Minor, liberated the Greek cities in Asia Minor, defeated another Persian army at *Issus* in 333, liberated Egypt, and founded the city of Alexandria. He then marched across Asia Minor, defeated Darius and occupied *Persepolis*, the capital city of the Persian Empire. Darius was murdered, Persia made peace with Alexander, who then marched to the borders of India and won the battle of Hydaspes.

Alexander did not live to see the inevitable collapse of his vast artificial empire, and after his death in 323 B.C. his generals divided his empire between them: Cassander took Macedon and part of Greece; Ptolemy took Egypt; Seleucus took Persia. For two centuries the whole area was the scene of rivalries, until Rome made them her own provinces and established the Pax Romana in 146 B.C.

The death of Alexander marks the beginning of the *Hellenistic Age*, the period down to 146 B.C., resulting from the conquests of Alexander, in which Hellenic culture was spread to non-Greeks, the culture of the non-Greeks acted upon the Greeks, and the capital of the pre-Roman world was transferred from Athens to Alexandria in Egypt.

Greece: Contributions to Civilization

Terms

Philosophy	Antigone	Corinthian
Nous	Oedipus	Frieze
Socratic Method	Trojan Women	Hellenistic
Academic School	Alcestis	Pediment
Dialogues	Politics	Peristyle
Republic	Cynics	Parthenon
Realist	The Clouds	Propylaea
Logic	The Frogs	Erechtheus
Ethics	Architrave	Olympic Games
Sophists	Entasis	Epicureans
Sophistry	Ionic	Stoics
The Persians	Doric	pan-hellenic games

People

Thales	Sophocles	Hippocrates
Heraclitus	Euripides	Eratosthenes
Democritus	Aristophanes	Ptolemy
Anaxagoras	Herodotus	Euclid
Socrates	Thucydides	Archimedes
Plato	Praxiteles	Aristarchus
Aeschylus		

Greece: Contributions to Civilization

Philosophy

The word philosophy is derived from the Greek, meaning "love of wisdom," more precisely, the study of the causes and relations of things and ideas. The early Greek philosophers were puzzled about creation and existence, and they studied the universe in order to explain its origin, its function, and its meaning. The "father of philosophy" was probably Thales of Miletus who, around 600 B.C., tried to answer his own question, What is the universe made of? He decided that water exists in different "states" and was indispensable to growth and the maintenance of organisms.

Successive philosophers had different theories about what was the true earth-substance, but their essential importance is that they started the quest to understand the nature of the universe. Heraclitus (540–475 B.C.) believed that life was in constant transition. Democritus (460–370 B.C.) developed the theory that the universe was composed of atoms which could not be seen, which differed in shape, size, position, and arrangement, but moved about continuously and combined to create objects. Anaxagoras (500–428 B.C.) looked for one basic controlling agency which he called nous (mind), a pervasive force that ran the universe.

The basic questions which came to be of chief concern to philosophers were a natural rather than a supernatural explanation for happenings, and the problems of knowledge, political theory, logic, and ethics. Under the great philosophers, Socrates, Plato, and Aristotle, men began to study the human mind, how to reason correctly, how to discover truth.

Socrates (469–399 B.C.) was a practical philosopher who wrote no books but by constant questioning tried to make men think clearly, to take nothing for granted, to challenge every idea. This method of making people think by answering questions is the Socratic method. The Athenian elders, not liking to have their beliefs and their prejudices challenged, condemned Socrates to death by drinking hemlock.

Plato (427–347 B.C.) was the most distinguished disciple of Socrates, and was known as the Father of the Academic School because he took students to a public park in Athens called the Academy. He developed a system of idealistic philosophy. The world, he said, is governed by divine universal ideas, and man should try to discover these ideals and live by them, and so conform to ideal principles of justice and virtue in harmony with the divine Idea. His most famous writing are the Dialogues in which ideas, government, education, justice, virtue are examined in an imaginary series of dialogues. His *Republic* set up an ideal state to serve as a model for statesmen and citizens to strive for. The intelligent should be trained to govern the others; warriors should defend the state; and the rest of the people, presumably relatively unintelligent, should work and farm. In Plato's perfect community, government is simply the operation of rules for the benefit of all.

Aristotle (384–322 B.C.) was a follower of Plato but differed by being a *realist*, using facts to try to discover the laws which govern nature. He became the founder of Logic, the laws of thinking clearly; of Biology, the science of living things; of Politics, the science of government; of Psychology, the science of the human mind. His best known works are *Politics*, a study of over 150 constitutions of Greek city-states and the principles of government, and *Ethics*, an examination of the beliefs of men to find out the origin of happiness and virtue.

Sophists were teachers who studied men and their relationships with each other, a Greek approach to "making friends and influencing others." While some were brilliant thinkers, others used tricky arguments to win a point, sometimes descending to *sophistry* or clever attempts to deceive, perhaps an earlier version of modern propaganda.

Literature

Greek drama originated in local religious festivals, songs, and dances given by Athenians in honor of Dionysus the wine god; they became plays when plots and characters were added.

Epic poems and philosophical dramas are concerned with the eternal themes of man's fate in the universe. Tragedians brought out the great power of nature. Nature's law could not be evaded, so tragedy struck when men failed to take it into account. Man was master of his fate but was sometimes caught in circumstances. Comedies were tributed to human intelligence, since humor could be relished when incongruities were perceived by man.

Aeschylus (524–456 B.C.) wrote tragedies, one on the great victory at Salamis in 480 B.C. where he had fought, and another the story of Agamemnon, a Greek leader of the Trojan War, *The Persians, Oresteia*.

Sophocles (496–606 B.C.), who lived in Athens in the Age of Pericles wrote the famous *Antigone, Oedipus the King*.

Euripides (480–406 B.C.) lived through the Peloponnesian War and was the most popular of the tragic dramatists. His *Trojan Women* tells of the Trojan women captured by the Greeks. *Alcestis* is the story of the wife who offers to die to save her husband.

Aristophanes (444–380 B.C.) was the most famous comic writer, who made fun of many aspects of Athenian life, its leaders, and its assemblies in *The Clouds* and *The Frogs.*

Herodotus (485–425 B.C.) was the father of history, whose famous book was on the Persian Wars.

Thucydides (471–401 B.C.) was the first "scientific" historian, who tried to be accurate because he believed that men should learn from the lessons of history.

Architecture

The chief building in a Greek city was the temple, rectangular in shape, supported by windowless walls, with the porch, or extension of the roof, supported by columns. The Greeks did not use the arch, but connected the tops of columns by the *architrave* of plain stones. The columns were deliberately made slightly convex so that they were thicker in the middle — a technique called *entasis* — in order to appear perfectly cylindrical to the eye. They were of three types, all fluted: *Doric* with a simple capital top, and no base; *Ionic* with an ornamented capital and base; *Corinthian,* a more slender column with a base similar to Ionic but with a much more elaborate capital. The roof of the temple was gabled, with a ridge pole, and around the top of all four sides was the *frieze,* usually decorated. At each end was the *pediment,* formed by angles of the roof, usually decorated to show stories, incidents in Greek history, and processions. Temples were shrines for deities, not meeting places for worshippers.

The Acropolis was rebuilt after the Persian Wars, and the buildings were all dedicated to public use: the assembly and theaters under the sponsorship of the state, and, on the highest point, the temples to the gods. The finest of these was the Parthenon, both a temple to Athena, the patron goddess of Athens, and a symbol of the glory of the city. The Parthenon has two rooms; in the smaller one facing west, the temple treasures were stored, and in the larger one, facing east, was the statue of Athena. At each end was a porch whose roof was supported by a *peristyle,* or row of columns, of eight columns on each end and seventeen along each side. Another famous building was the *Propylaea,* a monumental gateway at the entrance to the sacred area on the Acropolis. During the Peloponnesian War the Athenians built the *Erechtheum,* another temple noted for its Porch of the Maidens whose roof is supported by sculptured figures of maidens instead of columns.

Under the guidance of Pericles, first citizen of Athens for 32 years (461–429 B.C.), the best talents were employed to beautify the city.

Sculpture

The basic interest of sculptors was in people, who were usually represented, although equally dramatic work was done of animals in friezes. In the Age of Pericles sculptors were realistic in depicting figures in action, such as the famous Discus Thrower by Myron. Sculptors tried to endow the human form with ideal beauty; they did not reproduce individuals so much as represent people and gods performing some characteristic act; they were not bound by tradition, and later became more factual and more realistic. Outstanding sculptors were Phidias, famous for his statue of Athena, and Praxiteles, noted for his Faun.

Medicine

At first, gods were asked for the boon of health; Aesculapius, god of medicine, spent his whole time keeping people healthy. Temples were built to him, and a priesthood was organized to maintain the proper ritual to the god.

Hippocrates (460–357 B.C.) is the Father of Medicine, the most celebrated physician of antiquity, from the family of the priesthood of the god Aeschulapius. He approached the problem of disease from the viewpoint that it resulted from natural, not supernatural causes. He emphasized the value of observation, careful interpretation of symptoms, and a high code of professional ethics. He was the author of the famous Hippocratic Oath, still taken by doctors, as a professional code of ethics.

Religion

It is not possible to separate early Greek beliefs from those of the Periclean Age because traditional ideas were perpetuated. For example, the Olympic Games were held in honor of the ancient god Zeus, the father of all gods; the Panathenaea held in Athens in honor of Athena, patron goddess of Athens, consisted of symbolic sacrifices, feasts, games, and poetic contests. Festivals in honor of Dionysus, god of vineyards and the theater, were theater performances of tragedies and comedies.

The Athenians persisted in the belief of the Homeric gods of Mount Olympus, but regarded the gods much like humans, with their sorrows, conflicts, jealousies, and joys. Seldom did a Greek city-state start a war without seeking the advice of the great God Apollo, through the priestess of the Delphic Oracle.

The Olympic or Panhellenic Games

Great public games or contests were religious in nature because they were celebrated in honor of the gods, and included art and literature contests as well as athletics. These games, with their religious aspects, were one force which tended to promote a national Greek pride and unity. The chief contest, held at Olympia every four years, featured physical contests such as running, jumping, discus-throwing, wrestling, and boxing under rigid rules of discipline and sportsmanship. The reward was a laurel wreath for the victor, who was specially honored with a public statue and the use of his name for the Olympiad, the succeeding period of four years. Today's Olympic games are modelled upon the Greek games.

The Hellenistic World

Although the Greek city-states had been seriously weakened, and although Greece was conquered first by Philip and then by Alexander of Macedon, these two men so admired Hellenic culture that they spread it through the Middle East, and so inaugurated a second phase of Greek culture and influence called Hellenistic.

Athens might have recovered some of its leadership had the people listened to Demosthenes who warned that the country of Macedonia to the north was a serious threat. Philip of Macedon was determined to add the Greek city-states to his empire, and in 338 B.C. at Chaeronea he and his son Alexander defeated a force of Athenians and Thebans. Philip then formed the Hellenic League of Greek city-states, except Sparta which refused to join, permitted them self-government, and organized his strength to fight Persia. In 336 B.C. he was assassinated and his brilliant son replaced him, carried out his father's plans, and, by 323 B.C., pushed the eastern boundary of his empire to the Ganges river in India.

His successors divided his empire into Egypt, Syria, and Persia, Macedon and Greece, and to these empires the Greeks brought their civilization, founded new cities throughout Asia Minor, Egypt, Mesopotamia, such as Alexandria and Antioch with 500,000 citizens each, and Seleucia on the Tigris with a population of 600,000. Once again local rivalries prevented unity against a common front, and the rising power of Rome to the west gradually absorbed parts of the old Greek empire, and in turn benefitted from Greek culture and achievements.

The Hellenistic Age was essentially a commercial one, with the growth of towns, including the incredible Alexandria with its magnificent palace, its library of 750,000 books, its theaters, concert halls, and parks, a truly cosmopolitan city. Trade centers of the Hellenistic world were Alexandria, Rhodes, the Asia Minor coast.

Contributions of the Hellenistic Age

Geography

Eratosthenes (276–195 B.C.) was the scientific geographer whose greatest achievement was his calculation that the earth's diameter was 7850 miles, less than 100 miles off the true figure. He described the geography of the known world, and suggested that men might reach India by sailing westwards.

Ptolemy (2nd century A.D.) was famous for his map of the world, still in use at the time of Columbus.

Science

Euclid (4th century B.C.) is famous for his precise textbook on geometry, in use down to today.

Archimedes (287–212 B.C.) was the foremost mathematician and physicist of the age. He showed the ratio of pi, 3.1416, of the diameter of a circle to its circumference, invented pulleys, the lever, the law of specific gravity, and the spiral screw inside a cylinder to raise water.

Aristarchus (310–230 B.C.) of Samos determined that earth and planets revolve around the sun, measured almost exactly the solar year and lunar month. Mistakenly he believed that the earth was the center of the universe, an error accepted until Copernicus (1473–1543) proved the contrary.

Philosophers

Internal dissension and expanding conquest affected philosophical thinking. The ideal society was no longer so important to men as the search for individual safety and behavior.

The Epicureans, led by Epicurus (342–270 B.C.) taught that pleasure and permanent happiness was a virtue, and that the simple life led to happiness. It fortified men against the blows of circumstance.

The Stoics, followers of Zeno (3rd century B.C.) meeting in the Stoa, stressed reason as the guide to conduct. Emotions were to be avoided. The highest good consisted in cooperating with nature or God. Moral wrong is the greatest evil. Stoicism later influenced Roman conduct and Christianity.

The *Cynics*, followers of Antisthenes (5th century B.C.) believed that virtue alone can bring happiness. Wealth, honors, and pleasure were unworthy of serious man. The modern meaning of cynic is one who believes that human conduct is based on self-interest.

Sculpture

Sculptors of the Hellenistic Age were realistic and factual in their work. They did not so much reproduce individuals as represent people and gods doing something typical and characteristic.

Rome: The Republic

Terms

Comitia Curiata	Pontifex Maximus	Delenda Est Carthago
Imperium	Plebs	Latifundia
Consul	Hortensian Law	Rubicon
Dictator	Pyrrhic Victory	Triremes
Twelve Tables	Punic Wars	Praetor
Quaestor	Quinquiremes	Censor
Tribune	Carthaginian Peace	

People

Etruscans	Scipio Africanus	Philip of Macedon
Pyrrhus	Hannibal	Octavian (Augustus)
Tarquin	Tiberius Gracchus	Gaius Gracchus
Xanthippus	Massinissa	Marius
Fabius Cunctator	Marcus Cato	Caesar

Places to Locate

Latium	Sicily	Cannae
Rome	Sardinia	Macedon
Carthage	Corsica	Cynoscephalae
Straits of Messina	Mylae	Rubicon river

Significant Dates

509 B.C.	Beginning of Rome
264–146 B.C.	Punic Wars
260 B.C.	Battle of Mylae
216 B.C.	Battle of Cannae
215–168 B.C.	Macedonian Wars
197 B.C.	Battle of Cynoscephalae
146 B.C.	Destruction of Carthage

Topic Outline
Early Geography
The Roman Republic: Institutions
Geographical Expansion: Punic Wars, Eastern Expansion, Macedonian Wars
The Late Republic
Decline of the Republic

Rome: The Republic

Early Italy and Rome

Geography

The Roman peninsula was more suited to farming than was Greece. With only few good harbors the Romans were farmers rather than traders, and what expansion did take place went westwards in the Mediterranean and for centuries did not go eastwards or interfere with Greek development.

Origins

Like the Greeks, the Romans were offshoots of a common Indo-European stock. About 2000 B.C. while one group was invading the Aegean world, another was invading Italy, where only a primitive culture existed. Later invaders brought iron implements and weapons, and came in three groups: Umbrians to the northern area of the peninsula; Latins to the Tiber valley, thus giving it the name Latium; Samnites to the south.

About 800 B.C. the Etruscans, whose origin is thought to be Asia Minor, conquered Latium, extended their power, conquered the settlement of Rome, and ruled the Latin population. A widespread rebellion by the various Latin tribes expelled *Tarquin*, the last Etruscan king, in 509 B.C., and the rise of independent Rome began. Rome occupied a central position, easy to defend, one which made it difficult for their enemies to unite.

Roman political development underwent somewhat the same process as that of the Greeks.

The Roman Republic

The Roman Republic was representative in government but limited to the patricians or aristocracy, who constituted the ruling class and were eligible for office. Some 30 families formed the inner circle within the patrician group.

The *Assembly,* or *Comitia Curiata,* consisted of free men who bore arms in defense of the state, grouped according to the districts or *curiae* in which they lived. It could not initiate laws, and did little more than give its assent to Senate decisions.

Consuls: The *imperium,* or power of life and death exercised by former Etruscan kings were now given two consuls, elected annually by the Assembly from the patrician class, and exercising their power in the interests of the patricians. They were commanders of the army, high priests, the police authority. Each could veto the proposals of the other and thus prevent one-man rule.

The Dictator was appointed for six months in an emergency, with absolute power over life and property during his term of office. It was always hoped that once the emergency was past, the Dictator would relinquish his office.

The Senate, the most important branch of government, consisted of 30 members of the landed aristocracy, chosen by the Consuls for life, with the power to conduct public affairs, to veto any act of the Assembly, and the right to "advise" the Consuls.

Two *Praetors* administered justice; two *Censors* assessed property values, took the census, and watched over public morals; two *Quaestors* ran the treasury, two (later 10) *Tribunes* protected the interests of the plebeians. The *Pontifex Maximum* was a layman who supervised the state religion, which was a department of government. None of these several offices was open to the plebeians.

What gains the plebeians did gradually win came about because the plebs, as soldiers, sometimes threatened to leave Rome and to form their own communities.

These "secessions of the plebs" were successful in winning rights for the plebeians in several instances:

1. In 470 B.C., the ten tribunes were elected by the plebs, with the authority to veto any illegal action of the other officials.

2. In 445 B.C. after a visit to Greece to study Solon's work, the Romans codified the laws by putting them in writing on the *Twelve Tables;* people now knew what the law was and what their rights were, limited in scope though they might be.

3. In 362 B.C., by the so-called *Hortensian Law,* one consul was a plebeian.

4. In 287 B.C. the Senate was empowered to veto decrees approved by the Assembly.

Nevertheless, Rome was not a democracy, because until the end of the Republic in 27 B.C. the wealthy group continued to control the government.

Expansion in Italy

Expansion was partly in self-defense and partly for the acquisition of territory. From the north the Gauls attempted to take Rome; in the south Rome subjugated the cities of Magna Graecia, which asked for help from King Pyrrhus of Epirus in northwestern Greece. Costly victories by Pyrrhus exhausted his resources, hence the name "pyrrhic victories," and finally cost him the campaign.

One reason for Rome's successful expansion was her farsighted policy of granting Roman rights and privileges to a conquered people, and of not interfering with local customs. Alliances were made with other peoples threatened by a common enemy. Rome's policy of "divide, conquer, and Romanize" proved its success when her allies remained faithful during her long struggle with Carthage.

Carthage was a former Phoenician colony founded in Tunisia in 800 B.C. By 264 B.C. when it first came into conflict with Rome, it was governed along much the same lines, but with the advantage of permanent military leaders instead of elected consuls. Her power was based on trade and commerce, for she became the greatest merchant of the Mediterranean, with colonies in North Africa, Spain, and western Sicily. Carthage posed a threat to expanding Rome, particularly when during a civil war in Messina, the northeastern tip of Sicily, the Carthaginians responded to an appeal by Messina for assistance. This incident was the beginning of the Punic Wars, so named from the Roman term for the Phoenician people of Carthage.

The Punic Wars   264–241 B.C., 218–201 B.C., 149–146 B.C.

Rome was a non-naval power at this time and was reluctant to engage in a war with the naval power of Carthage. But if Carthage should get control of Sicily, then Rome could be threatened with invasion across the narrow Straits of Messina. The Roman assembly insisted upon war, and was successful in the early campaigns in Sicily. But Carthaginian naval power proved successful in recapturing Sicilian ports, in attacking the coasts of Italy, and in preventing Roman reinforcements from landing in Sicily. Realizing that her *triremes* of three banks of oars were no match for Carthaginian five-bank *quinquiremes,* the

Romans copied a Carthaginian ship and built 100 in 60 days, equipping them with drawbridges for boarding parties.

At the battle of *Mylae*, 260 B.C., the Carthaginian fleet was decisively defeated, and another Roman fleet and army attacked the Carthaginian mainland. Carthage enlisted the help of *Xanthippus* of Sparta, who helped to defeat the Romans. The First Punic War ended in 241 B.C. when Carthage sued for peace, withdrew from Sicily, and paid a huge indemnity to Rome. But this war was simply a preliminary to the terrible struggle to come.

In the intervening years both sides consolidated their power. Sicily became a Roman province, a conquered territory outside Italy. Then Rome captured and fortified as bases the strategic islands of Sardinia and Corsica. Threatened by invasion from the north, Rome consolidated her boundaries by subjugating Cisalpine Gaul, the territory northward to the Alps. She was now ready for another contest with Carthage.

In the meantime Carthage had been building a huge empire in Spain, where new armies could be raised for an overland attack upon Rome. The Carthaginian leader *Hannibal* led his forces across the eastern end of the Pyrenees mountains, across southern Gaul, over the Alps and down into northern Italy.

At *Cannae*, 216 B.C., the Roman forces were literally annihilated, losing almost 90 per cent of the army. Rome itself was too strong to be attacked, and most of Italy remained loyal to her. The famous *Fabius Cunctator*, the Delayer, avoided all major engagements with Hannibal, and gradually wore down Hannibal's troops and supplies. In 204 B.C. Hannibal was recalled to defend Carthage against a Roman army under Scipio, later entitled "Africanus" in honor of his success.

Carthage became in reality a satellite of Rome, was obliged to surrender her Spanish possessions, had to pay a large indemnity, and was forced to permit Roman control of her foreign affairs, a "*Carthaginian Peace*." But the merchants of Rome were not happy to see a trade rival exist. In later years the Roman senator *Marcus Cato* thundered daily, "*Delenda est Carthago*," "Carthage must be destroyed." Her renewed prosperity led to her ruin, for in 149 B.C. when Carthage tried to defend herself against attack by king *Masinissa* of Numidia, an ally of Rome, her breach of peace was made the excuse for Rome to attack her. Carthage was forced to give up 300 youths as hostages, was ordered to surrender all arms and munitions, to give up the fortified city itself, and to remove her entire population ten miles up the coast. Carthage refused to comply with these demands to give up the city and remove her population, and for three years improvised weapons, attempted to defend herself, but was finally defeated in house-to-house fighting. The population was enslaved, the city burned, its stones ploughed under, and the fields ploughed up and sown with salt. The long contest with Carthage resulted in Rome's acquiring territory formerly held by Carthage, thus herself becoming a sea as well as a land power. Parts of North Africa, Spain, Corsica, Sardinia, and Sicily now came under Roman jurisdiction. The new province of Africa now had a new capital at Utica, and its people were completely Romanized.

Roman Expansion Eastwards   200–133 B.C.

During the course of the long struggle with Carthage, Rome was also expanding eastwards. As we recall, at the death of Alexander the Great in 323 B.C., his empire was divided between his generals into three kingdoms: Egypt under the

Ptolemies; Syria, covering a large part of western Asia, including the Euphrates valley, and portions of Asia Minor; and Macedonia, including parts of Greece.

Macedonian Wars 215–206 B.C., 200–197 B.C., 171–168 B.C.

Philip of Macedon unwisely gave assistance to Hannibal and attempted to expand into Greece. Two leagues of Greek states, the Aetolian in central Greece, and the Acheaen in southern Greece, requested and received Roman aid. At the great battle of *Cynoscephalae*, in Thessaly in 197 B.C. Philip was defeated and Macedonia became subject to Rome, although not a province.

The Late Republic, 127–31 B.C.

The republic's expanding boundaries and increasing wealth caused radical changes in the nation. Vast imperial commitments created problems that could not be handled by the old simple agrarian economy and the old republican constitution, with its tradition of service to the state. Overseas people in Africa, Spain, Macedonia, Asia were treated less than generously, were organized into provinces over which were placed governors or proconsuls appointed by the Senate. These officials were given complete authority, were responsible for the collection of taxes and grain tributes, and frequently made themselves private fortunes at the expense of the natives.

In Italy an economic revolution was paving the way for a political revolution. Large estates or *latifundias* were bought up in Italy by a new middle class of wealthy generals, governors, bankers, and contractors; small farmers were unable to compete with the slave labor of the latifundias and became landless unemployed who drifted to the cities to form a large proletariat ready to follow any popular leader. Service to the state was no longer a duty, and patricians and middle class preferred to live in luxury on their estates. Two groups were developing, the Optimates or wealthy aristocratic party and the Populares or popular party.

The Decline of the Republic

Reformers and strong men dominated the period from 113 B.C., until the establishment of the Empire in 31 B.C. The first reformers were Tiberius and Gaius Gracchus, two nobles who by adoption into plebeian families were eligible for the tribuneship. Each in turn attempted to introduce land reforms to limit acreage holdings, to break up large estates, and to distribute land to the poor. Each attempted illegally to hold office for a second term, and each was murdered at the instigation of the Optimates.

The Gracchi brothers were succeeded by two successful generals, Marius and Sulla, who led victorious campaigns in the East, held consular office for a number of years, killed off political opponents, and gave supremacy to the Optimates by reducing the power of the Assembly and the tribunate. Under Marius, 157–87 B.C., army commander and seven times consul, the army became professionalized and men served for 25 years, owed allegiance to individual generals rather than to the state, a condition that became a determining factor in the career of a successful head of state.

Julius Caesar, 100–44 B.C., an aristocrat, championed the people, was elected Pontifex Maximus and Praetor, and determined to win military glory. He became governor of Spain and in nine years of campaigning conquered Gaul, earned the fear of the Senate and was declared a public enemy. Instead of returning to Rome without an army, as he must officially do, with an army he crossed the Rubicon river, the southern boundary of his command of the province of Gaul, fought the Senate's champion Pompey in Spain, Greece, Macedon, and Egypt. The Senate, unable to oppose him effectively, named him dictator for life. During the remaining years before his assassination by Brutus he gave himself full authority as consul, tribune, dictator, and pontifex maximus, and transformed the Roman state. The Senate was enlarged with members from Italy, provincial governors made responsible to him, tax collections put in the hands of responsible officials, Roman citizenship opened to people in the provinces, unemployment reduced by the use of public works, and the Julian calendar introduced — to be in use still today. Fearful of threats to Roman liberty, self-appointed patriots murdered Caesar and threw the nation into further disorder until Octavian, Caesar's adopted son, in an empire-wide struggle, defeated opponents and became Augustus, technically *Princeps* or first citizen, actually the first emperor of Rome. While in actual fact he ruled as emperor, although not in name, from 31 B.C. on, the Senate officially conferred upon him the title Augustus in 27 B.C.

Rome: The Empire

Terms

Dyarchy	*Gallic Wars*	*Odes*
Coloni	*Orations*	*Germanina*
Justinian Code	*Georgics*	Pax Romana
Aeneid		

People

Nerva	Constantine	Livy
Marcus Aurelius	Ovid	Cicero
Horace	Severus	Vergil
Diocletian	Alaric	Tacitus

Places to Locate
Eastern and Western Empires
Byzantium

Significant Dates

31 B.C.	Beginning of Roman Empire
180 A.D.	Beginning of Decline of Roman Empire
410 A.D.	Rome Captured by Alaric
476 A.D.	Odoacer deposed last Roman Emperor. Traditional end of Roman Empire

Topic Outline
Administration of Augustus
Successors to Augustus
Temporary Stabilization of the Empire
Decline of the Empire: Causes
The Justinian Code
Contributions: Law, Architecture, Sculpture, Science and Engineering, Religion, Philosophy, Literature

Rome: The Empire

The Roman Empire   During the next 200 years Roman civilization achieved its fullest and greatest development, reaching from Britain to Mesopotamia, and enjoyed an almost unbroken era of peace.

Administration of Augustus,   31 B.C.–14 A.D.

The regime of Augustus could be regarded as a constitutional monarchy, since Augustus did not interfere with the elections of other officials, and claimed that he was not replacing the Republic but reforming it. He and his successors continued the reforms commenced by Caesar. Provinces were encouraged in self-government within the empire, corruption by governors was eliminated, justice was fairly administered, and all inhabitants of the empire, except slaves, were given Roman citizenship, with some provincials, such as Trajan the Spaniard, becoming Emperor.

Augustus' system is sometimes called a "dyarchy," or rule by two authorities, himself and the Senate. Actually, Augustus retained power through his wealth, his command of the army, his control of the Senate, which became subservient to his will. The provinces were divided between Augustus and the Senate, but the Emperor astutely included in his own provinces those bordering Rome, since there the military power was concentrated. Augustus won the support of the two important classes by deliberately separating the senatorial from the equestrian or middle classes, and the equestrian from the plebeian by property qualifications. To each group certain rights were given: to the senatorial class were open the higher magistracies, higher army commands, governorships of senatorial provinces; Equites were eligible for lower offices. Augustus could promote a man to either group by financial gifts, for as the richest man in Rome this was a useful technique for him.

Successors to Augustus,   14 A.D.–180 A.D.

The immediate successors to Augustus, Tiberius (14–37 A.D.), Caligula (37–41 A.D.), Claudius (41–54 A.D.), and Nero (54–68 A.D.) were generally incompetent, if not dangerous. In general these emperors followed the policy of Augustus. The boundaries were increased only to guard the flanks of the empire, Britain to protect Gaul, Dacia across the Danube in today's Rumania where Latin influence still remains. Government ran smoothly, peace was maintained, and the empire prospered.

In 96 A.D. the emperor Nerva instituted a technique to guarantee a capable successor by adopting a man of proven talent and loyalty as his son. Each emperor used ability as his yardstick, and the method accounted for four very able emperors: Trajan (98–117 A.D.), Hadrian (117–138 A.D.), Antoninus Pius (138–161 A.D.), and Marcus Aurelius (161–180 A.D.).

One unfortunate characteristic of the period was the cult of emperor-worship, a compulsory rite which became a political obligation and a guarantee of the perpetuation of the emperors as an institution. Unfortunately the death of Marcus Aurelius in 180 A.D. marked the end of stability and the beginning of the decline of the Roman Empire. But its 200 years of peace and prosperity brought many contributions to western civilization.

**Temporary
Stabilization
of the Empire**

The military anarchy of the third century could have brought the empire to total collapse, but fortunately two strong emperors, Diocletian (284–305 A.D.), and Constantine (306–337 A.D.) helped to stabilize it for fifty years. They abolished the former rights of local governments, gave to the provincial governors absolute power over local government, and closely supervised the administration of the provinces.

Diocletian more than doubled the number of provinces to 101, grouped these into 13 dioceses, or administrative units, grouped into four Prefectures: Gaul and Britain; Italy, Spain and Africa; the Danubian provinces and the Balkans; the Eastern provinces. He divided the empire into two halves with two co-emperors and two subordinate assistant Caesars who would eventually succeed the Augustus or emperor. Diocletian himself took over the eastern half of the Empire and assigned the western half to Maximian. Upon Diocletian's retirement in 305 A.D., civil war disrupted the empire until Constantine made himself ruler of the western empire in 312 A.D., and then of a united empire in 324 A.D., but with the capital shifted to the site of an earlier city called Byzantium, which had lasted from 627 B.C. until 196 A.D. when the Emperor Severus renamed it Constantinople, to remain for more than 1000 years as the center of the Byzantine Empire.

**Decline
of the Roman Empire**

A marked decline began with the regime of the emperor Severus (193–211 A.D.) a career army man who gave the army higher pay, new privileges, and even many of the rights of senators. He and his successors, such as the notorious Caracalla, destroyed the foundations of urban civilization. Towns were plundered to strengthen the army; service in city government ceased to be regarded as a duty of the citizen. Rome's subject people learned Roman ways while her own citizens grew lazy with government hand-outs and were content to loaf. Wealthy citizens imported luxury goods that could not be paid for with ever-decreasing exports, and gold was drained from the city. Higher taxes and rising prices led to the depreciation of money and to increased poverty. Rome was fast becoming an empire without vitality or purpose, and was on the road to disaster. Civil war and anarchy hastened the process of a declining central authority and the impoverishment of the sturdy farmers. They were forced into the growing ranks of the *coloni*, serfs bound to the large farms of large landed proprietors. Unwise government taxation forced much land out of cultivation, since larger crops meant more work and income, which meant heavier taxation and declining incentive.

By 240 A.D. brigands were roaming at will in northern Gaul, civil war had broken out in North Africa, and the slaves had revolted in Sicily. During the third century, barbarians under pressure from Asiatic tribes moving westwards, pushed across the frontiers into the Roman Empire. Rome was able to hold them back for a while, but later, because she was short of her own soldiers, she hired them to fill the Roman army, and was obliged to allow others to settle inside the empire's boundaries.

These Teutonic groups of Franks, Lombards, Goths, Vandals, and others were in turn under pressure from the Huns who poured across Asia into Europe in the later fourth century. The Teutonic tribes fought with the Romans against the common enemy, and then in turn against Rome. Under their leader *Alaric* they rebelled against Rome, and in 410 A.D. captured and plundered the capital city itself.

Then a flood of Teutons overwhelmed the Empire, crossing the Pyrenees into Spain, then to Africa, with another wave crossing the Rhine, until in 476 A.D. their commander, Odoacer, replaced the Roman emperor.

One of the most famous of the Teutonic chieftains was *Theodoric* (489–526) who invaded Italy and founded the new kingdom of the Ostrogoths (East Goths). He acknowledged nominal allegiance to the Eastern emperor at Byzantium but regarded himself as an independent ruler and a successor to Augustus. Theodoric did much to restore prosperity to Italy and to compile Roman law for his subjects.

The Justinian Code

The man credited with codifying, or gathering into one collection the Roman law, was *Justinian* (527–565) Emperor of the Byzantine, or Eastern Empire. The Justinian Code was a great collection of laws which included:

1. A *Code* or compilation of all Roman laws.

2. A *Digest* of selected opinions of great jurors.

3. The *Institutes*, a textbook for law students.

These were collectively the *Corpus Juris Civilis*, or body of civil law. So thoroughly was the work done that centuries later scholars were able to revive Roman law, which became the basis of civil law for France, Germany, Italy, Spain, Latin America, Louisiana, and Quebec Province.

Causes of the Decline

Several long-range *economic* factors also contributed to the decline: a drop in the birth rate which, in the long run, reduced the number of citizens and taxpayers; prolonged droughts in North Africa which dried up many of the fertile grain lands; a backward domestic agriculture; an inadequate purchasing power of the masses, and a low standard of living.

Christianity played a part since its followers refused emperor-worship, did not participate in public functions, and so, in one sense, destroyed the civic spirit by being a protest group, more concerned with its faith in the after-life than with performing state and religious ceremonies.

Moral causes are those to be seen in any civilization that is more interested in personal comfort than with its obligations to the community. Wealth was acquired by corruption and war, and the extremes of luxury and poverty worked their evils.

The decline was in no sense a sudden collapse but a long process of deterioration and the "silent invasion" of the empire's boundaries by outsiders.

Summary of Causes of Decline

1. Military despotism and bureaucracy

2. Destruction of urban civilization through: overtaxation, refusal of citizens to serve in government; government "bread and circuses;" rising prices and increasing poverty.

3. Decline of agriculture through: overtaxation; inability of small farmer-owner to make a living; the rise of *coloni* and agricultural serfdom.

4. Inability to defend frontiers through: difficulty in recruiting soldiers; barbarian invasions; admittance into empire of barbarians and their increasing power; central control increasingly replaced by weaker local governments.

Contributions

Government of the Roman World The Pax Romana existed for 200 years and brought not only peace within the empire but also law and order. It provided its citizens with many of the benefits which we associate with democracy. The plebeians won the right to elect tribunes to protect their rights with the power of veto, to have written laws, and later, the right to make new laws by voting in the assemblies, and finally, to hold any office in Rome, even that of Senator. Orderly government encouraged the development throughout the empire of roads, aqueducts, sewers, public baths, and theaters.

Law One of Rome's greatest contributions was that of law, rule by properly constituted authority and rules. The first written laws were the Twelve Tables by which every citizen knew his basic rights. The legal system was enlarged and improved as the boundaries expanded and other people became part of the nation. During the reign of Justinian (527–565 A.D.) in the Eastern or Byzantine Empire, legal experts organized the law into the Code of Justinian or Body of Civil Law.

Rome contributed some very important legal principles:

1. That laws must be "naturally fair and just" and equally applied to all men, another way of saying that all men are created equal before the law.

2. Roman law protected private property and regarded contracts as binding upon the parties.

3. A man is innocent until proven guilty.

4. Circumstances must be considered when interpreting the law, which can be adapted to meet changing conditions.

Architecture The Romans used the arch rather than the Greek column (except for decoration), the vaulted roof, really a series of arches, and the dome, which on Hadrian's rebuilt Pantheon is one hundred and forty-two feet in diameter. Their buildings were seldom temples but were usually used for secular purposes. The Roman Colosseum, for gladiatorial combats, could seat 45,000 people, and the Baths of Caracalla suggested the plan for the former Pennsylvania Station in New York. Largest of the buildings was the Circus Maximus which could hold over 200,000 people.

Sculpture This was sometimes very realistic and was usually to commemorate the feats and lives of emperors in busts, statues, and triumphal arches.

Science and Engineering *Medicine* was substantially advanced; special instruments were invented for particular operations; surgeons were regularly attached to Roman legions; hospitals first appeared for the treatment of soldiers, later for civilians, and were the first public institutions of this type in Europe.

Sanitation systems, sewers, drainage ditches were the most advanced known in Europe until the nineteenth century. Aqueducts served pure water to cities, with at least eleven leading into Rome to supply 350,000 gallons a day to the citizens; magnificent public baths were a feature of Roman cities.

Engineering Skilled masonry, the making of concrete, and the building of roads were significant contributions. There were some 52,000 miles of roads in the empire, with foundations several feet deep and some 15 to 20 feet wide. These made travel unusually fast, and lasted over the centuries, to be duplicated only in the nineteenth century.

Religion Roman gods were very much like those of Greece, many being identical: Greek Zeus and Roman Jupiter, Greek Poseidon and Roman Neptune, Greek Ares and Roman Mars, Greek Aphrodite and Roman Venus.

The Roman government performed the task of placating the gods with suitable sacrifices, so that the average citizen had little to do with religion.

Philosophy Romans studied the teachings of Epicurus and the Stoic School of Alexandria. Epicureanism was declining because it was degenerating into justification for self-indulgence. Stoicism put its emphasis upon duty and responsibility to others. But neither philosophy won a large popular following because each was too intellectual. The ordinary man wanted to identify himself with a deity who would improve his lot, if not in this world, then in the next. As a result many Eastern religious cults were introduced, but eventually Christianity filled this need very successfully.

Literature Roman literature began to achieve distinction in the last decades of the Republic. Two of its great prose writers were Caesar and Cicero.

Caesar (100–44 B.C.) His *Commentaries on the Gallic Wars* relate the first seven years of the Gallic wars and were written as a political document to further his own political ambitions.

Cicero (106–43 B.C.) gave his name to the first great period of Latin literature. His *Orations* reveal the cross-currents of Roman politics and are a useful source of material for historians.

The next group of writers belong to the Golden or Augustan Age of Roman literature:

Vergil (70–19 B.C.) was the greatest of the Augustan writers, and was the official poet of the emperor. His *Georgics* dealt with farming and stockraising; his *Aeneid* is a monumental epic describing the mythical origin of Rome and glorifying Rome's greatness.

Horace (65–8 B.C.) wrote on moderation and the simple rural life. His *Odes* are famous.

Ovid (43 B.C.–17 A.D.), a Roman poet, most famous for the *Metamorphoses*, several legends from the time of the Creation to Julius Caesar.

Juvenal (55 A.D.–135 A.D.), was a satirist exposing the discontent and the disillusionment of his times, and the vices of contemporary society.

Tacitus (55–117 A.D.) was the greatest Roman historian whose *Germania* was less a history of early Germans than an attack upon contemporary Rome. He praised the simple life of Germans in order to emphasize the effete life of his own day. His writings are really sermons on the virtues of the Republic, the vices of the Empire.

Livy (59 B.C.–17 A.D.) was a historian whose great work was the history of Rome from the foundation of the city to within a few years of the Christian era. His style was a clear and pleasing narrative, less concerned with the truth of events than with gratifying Roman interest in their history.

3

The Middle Ages: Decline and Revival of Western Civilization

The Church Provides Leadership

Terms

Jaweh	Edict of Milan	Doctrine of Salvation
Christos	Episcopus	Seven Sacraments
Chiliastic	Petrine Theory	Transubstantiation
Polytheism	Eastern (Orthodox	Gnosticism
Vulgate	Greek) Church	Excommunication
Interdict	Patriarch	

People

Peter	Pontius Pilate	Gregory the Great
Paul	Gregory I	

Significant Dates

313 A.D.   Edict of Milan
392 A.D.   Christianity the Official Religion

Topic Outline
Origins of the Church
Christians in the Roman Empire
Organization of the Church
Increasing Role and Authority of the Church
Eastern or Greek Orthodox Church
Faith and Heresies
The Sacraments
Excommunication and Interdict

The Church Provides Leadership

Introduction

If we regard the year 500 A.D. as the beginning of the so-called Dark Ages, the implication is that all Greek and Roman civilization and culture was lost, that nothing of value was retained. This is incorrect, for although the process of advance was slow, sometimes retrogressive, a new civilization and a new culture appeared in Europe between 500 A.D. and 1500 A.D., partly an inheritance from the past, partly influenced by contemporary life.

**Origins
of the Church**

The Christian Church was the first bridge between the periods, an inheritance from the troubled history of the Israelites. During the centuries between 1300

B.C. and 600 B.C. the Israelites had developed an unshakable belief in one god Jehovah, who had evolved from early beliefs in a vengeful god, Jaweh, into a sympathetic one which the Israelites regarded as a universal god.

Their beliefs and codes of behavior, the teachings of their prophets, the basic laws of Moses were set down in the 39 books of the Old Testament which Jews regarded as their sacred scripture, and which Christians regard as the foundation of Christ's teachings.

Jesus, founder of the Christian faith, was born during the reign of Augustus, probably between 6 B.C. and 4 B.C., according to the Old calendar, in the Roman province of Judea. Over the past centuries the prophets had foretold the coming of a Messiah, a leader sent by God to fulfill the destiny intended for his chosen people by Jehovah.

Christians in the Roman Empire

The teachings of Jesus among the common people attracted followers from whom he chose twelve to be his apostles. His simple teachings appeared to influential Jewish groups to be radical, perhaps inciting to social change. The Roman administrators of the province may have seen in Christianity a threat of rebellion. Jewish leaders turned Jesus over to Pontius Pilate, Roman governor of Palestine, who permitted him to be crucified as a common criminal. His apostle missionaries spread the story of his life and teachings, later to be the contents of the New Testament. At Antioch the word *Christian* was first used, from the Greek *christos* or Messiah. Two leaders of this movement were Paul the Apostle who organized Christian groups in Asia Minor and Greece, and Peter, one of the original twelve apostles, who organized the Christians in Rome. The essential tenet of faith was *chiliastic* (meaning a thousand), a belief in the coming of Christ for the Millenium, a thousand years which would lead to the final judgment. Christians therefore must be ready for the Day of Judgment. Since the immediate Second Coming did not materialize, the belief had to be modified into a doctrine of salvation. Paul's great contribution was to expand Christianity from a restricted Jewish belief based upon faithful adherence to prescribed laws and even dietary habits into a broader belief in one righteous God.

Christians were inevitably to come into conflict with the Roman authorities, not so much for their religious beliefs — for Roman polytheism accepted many gods — but for their refusal to accept the divinity of the Emperor, and their unwillingness to pay him the official respect demanded by the State. They refused to serve in the Roman army, to appear at public feasts, or to be spectators at gladiatorial combats, since they believed human life to be sacred. Christians were regarded as a disloyal group that merited punishment.

Persecutions were sporadic; Nero conveniently charged them with the burning of Rome; a later emperor persecuted them because they would not pay taxes; Diocletian perpetrated the most severe persecutions between 303 and 311 A.D. by burning their holy books, confiscating their property, denying them citizenship, and sending them into the arena. Persecution failed to stamp out their faith, and the eastern emperor Galen permitted them to rebuild churches and to worship publicly.

In 64 A.D. when part of Rome was destroyed by fire, the Christians were blamed for it, but, despite persecution and death in the arena, they continued to worship secretly. Although regarded with suspicion, they were generally left alone until 250 A.D. when they were blamed for civil war and barbarian invasions. Nevertheless Christianity continued to spread, until, during the reign of Constantine, Christianity was given equal rights with the old Roman religion, and then made the official religion of the Roman Empire. Some scholars question whether this actually was done by the Edict of Milan in 313 A.D. However, Christian beliefs and bishops were certainly permitted, the clergy were exempted from taxation, and by 392 A.D. Christianity was the official religion of the state by a decree of the emperor Theodosius, making it the only legal religion of the Roman Empire. Heresy was a crime against the state, and since this included the teaching of any doctrine condemned by the Church, this was the beginning of the use of *political* power to establish religious conformity.

Organization of the Church

The organization of the Christian Church developed step by step. As little groups of the faithful were established, a local elder was appointed to take charge of each group; these groups amalgamated into a larger group headed by a bishop, from *episcopus* meaning overseer. As Church membership increased, the organization adopted techniques of the Roman government. The bishop appointed pastors or priests within his own *diocese* or district. The bishop of the provincial capital city, now an archbishop, had authority over the several bishops of the province. Rome's leading position in the Western Christian Church was determined largely by the *Petrine Theory*, that Christ bestowed his mantle upon Peter (from *petros*, a rock), his first disciple, "Thou art Peter and upon this rock will I build my church." Not until around 1100 A.D. did the Bishop of Rome exclusively take the title Pope (from papas, a father). Since Rome had always been the center of appeal in legal cases, it automatically became the center of appeal on issues of faith.

The Church gained prestige and power during the administrations of two bishops of Rome, Leo I (440–461 A.D.) and Gregory I (590–604 A.D.). Leo negotiated with Attila when the Huns swept across Italy in 452 A.D. and again with Gaiseric when the Vandals sacked Rome in 455.

Increasing Role and Authority of the Church

As the empire rapidly declined during the sixth century, the Pope was regarded as second to the emperor, and sometimes was obliged to make decisions during the reigns of incompetents. The "bread and circuses" technique was no longer a political device, for feeding of the poor of Rome was now a necessity, and the Church assumed that obligation. Gregory even established grain prices and punished violators. The Pope during Gregory's time became increasingly concerned with the management of lands willed to the Church. Thus during the first six centuries of its existence the Western or Roman Church became involved in secular government as well as missionary work in Europe. Inevitably, as the Roman Empire declined, the Church took over its administrative duties.

Eastern or Greek Orthodox Church

The *Eastern or Greek Orthodox Church* developed differently because no one city could clearly demonstrate its primacy. Alexandria, Antioch, and Constantinople all claimed seniority. The Emperor at Constantinople simply designated the *Patriarch* — as the Metropolitan or bishop-in-chief was called — of Constantinople as head of his church, actually as part of the government of the Eastern

Empire, and certainly a servant of the Emperor. The Church accepted the divinity of the emperor who, as head of the church, determined its doctrine.

Faith & Heresies

Rome accepted the Vulgate version of the Scriptures, a standard Latin work for use by the people, used throughout Latin Christendom down to present times in the Roman Catholic Church.

The *secular* clergy served the laity or faithful who worshipped; the *regular* (from *regula*, a rule) clergy were men and women who lived in communities, under strict rules in monasteries and nunneries, away from the world, but always self-supporting. The institutions were developed for those who wished to seek refuge from the world. Controversy developed between secular and regular clergy, each claiming to be following Christ's teachings more effectively. Monasteries became important centers of learning and the development of church law, but they became subject to Church discipline.

As a defense against possible political interference, the Church gradually took the elections of its officials out of the hands of laymen. Eventually a College of Cardinals elected the Pope without outside interference. Popes acquired increasing authority over the selection of bishops and archbishops. However, since these officials had great political influence in their districts, but were also responsible to the Pope, increasing conflict was to develop in countries between the king as chief landowner, and church dignitaries as landowners technically owing allegiance to their overlord the king, but also to the Pope, their spiritual leader.

The authority won by the Church over the laity was based upon the function of church officials as intermediaries between the physical world and the invisible world accepted upon faith by Christians. *Salvation* is the basic doctrine of the Church, salvation to be attained only if basic rituals are performed, rituals that demand an expert whose authority is handed down from Christ to Peter, to the Pope, and down to the clergy. Only they are capable of performing the miracle of the *Eucharist*, the Lord's Supper of Communion, says the Catholic Church. The Eucharist was the miraculous ceremony in which the priest, by transforming the ceremonial wine and wafer into the blood and body of Christ, cleansed man of original sin and offered eternal salvation. This ceremony is *Transubstantiation*, the miracle which only the clergy are able to perform. Complicated though the doctrine of salvation is, its basic belief is that the ceremony of the Mass can offer good Christians immortal happiness.

Heresy is any doctrine which challenges the accepted official doctrine or *orthodoxy*. If a person believes that salvation is a personal matter, this is heresy in the eyes of those who believe that the sacraments are necessary for salvation. To Catholics the authority and infallibility of the Pope are indisputable. Protestants reject the doctrine of papal infallibility.

An early example of heresy is *Gnosticism*, from the Greek word meaning knowledge, which taught that knowledge rather than faith was the key to salvation. Since this could lead to the questioning of the Seven Sacraments, it was therefore a questioning of the authority of the Church.

The Sacraments

The Church developed seven Sacraments: *Baptism*, which brings the infant into the Christian community and makes him or her a Christian for life;

Confirmation, which brings the young person into the discipline of the Church; the *Eucharist,* which recalls the death and sacrifice of Christ; *Penance,* the confession of a sin, the request for forgiveness, and the performance of an act as the outward sign of repentance; *Extreme Unction,* the last rites given to a person near death, to show that his sins have been forgiven; *Holy Orders,* the conferring of priesthood; *Holy Matrimony* or Marriage.

Protestants have accepted Baptism and Communion, modified into a symbolic ceremony, not a miracle.

Excommunication and Interdict

These two spiritual penalties were used against those who disobeyed the teachings and instructions of the Church. If a person were excommunicated, he was deprived of all his rights as a member of the Church by a bishop or higher authority. He could not receive any of the sacraments, attend Mass, or be buried in consecrated ground; and other Christians were urged to have nothing to do with him. He could, however, confess his errors, reform his ways, and be admitted back into full Church membership.

If a monarch were excommunicated, then his entire kingdom could be placed under interdict, and no Church services would be held and no sacraments administered. The interdict was a very effective method of organizing public opinion against the monarch, and probably forcing him to obey the Church in order to have the interdict lifted. In the thirteenth century, for example, King John of England seized the Church property, was excommunicated, and his country placed under interdict. Public opinion forced the king to return the land to the Church, and the Pope demanded John admit his vassalage to the Pope, his spiritual overlord.

The Empire of Charlemagne and the Holy Roman Empire

Terms

Marches	Treaty of Verdun	Sworn Inquest
Missi Dominici	Penance at Canossa	Investiture
Holy Roman Empire	Concordat of Worms	

People

Franks	Henry IV	Welfs
Clovis	Gregory VII	Guelphs
Pepin	(Hildebrand)	Ghibellines
Charlemagne	Hohenstauffens	Frederick Barbarossa

Significant Dates

732 A.D.	Battle of Tours
800 A.D.	Charlemagne crowned Holy Roman Emperor
962 A.D.	Otto crowned Holy Roman Emperor
1122 A.D.	Concordat of Worms: Lay Investiture Issue Resolved

Topic Outline
The Frankish Empire: Charles Martel, Pepin, Charlemagne
Origin of the Holy Roman Empire
Collapse of Charlemagne's Empire
Establishment of the Holy Roman Empire
The Investiture Issue
The Concordat of Worms

The Empire of Charlemagne and the Holy Roman Empire

The Franks, a Germanic tribe from the lower Rhineland, expanded their home base into most of modern France, with their political center at Aachen, modern Aix-la-Chapelle in Alsace-Lorraine. Their history is the best thread through the early Middle Ages in the West.

Under Clovis (481–511 A.D.) the Merovingian king, unification was achieved, partly through military and political skill but also because his conversion to Christianity won him the support of the Roman Catholic Church. Under succeeding Carolingian kings, who followed the Merovingians, the kingdom was expanded into an empire which by 800 A.D. included many former Roman territories.

Two distinguished rulers were *Charles Martel* (the Hammer, 714–741 A.D.) and his son *Pepin* (747–768 A.D.). Martel defeated a Moorish invasion across the Pyrenees at Tours in 732 A.D., regarded as one of the greatest victories of civilization, since it turned back the threat of expanding Mohammedanism. His son Pepin allied with the Popes, defeated the Lombards who threatened Rome, and upon his death in 768 left his realm to be divided between Carolus Magnus or *Charlemagne*, and Carloman, who died within three years.

Charlemagne (771–814 A.D.) expanded his empire until it included what is modern France, Holland, Belgium, Switzerland, Austria, West Germany, North Italy, North Spain, and some land farther eastwards. He created military districts called *marches* under *margraves* whose duty it was to keep out invaders.

Charlemagne aspired to exert the authority of the former Roman emperors, and tried to maintain personal control throughout his empire by *Missi Dominici*, men sent by the king, a layman and a clergyman who traveled in pairs as royal inspectors. These men also exercised judicial powers, instituted the "sworn inquest," forerunner of the grand jury that gave information under oath to traveling judges, later to become the basis of the English jury system. Charlemagne was a patron of learning and brought the famous English scholar and churchman Alcuin to conduct his school at Aachen.

Origin of the Holy Roman Empire

On Christmas Day, 800 A.D., Charlemagne was crowned by Pope Leo III as Emperor of the Romans, an astute action which implied that Charlemagne was officially Emperor by Church authority. After Charlemagne's death his empire broke up, and with it the revived Roman Empire. In 962 A.D. Otto I, a successor of Charlemagne, re-established imperial rule and made himself protector of the papacy. In 961 he became King of Italy, and in 962 the Pope crowned him Roman Emperor. This was the official beginning of what is known as the Holy Roman Empire, a continuation of the empire of Charlemagne and the empire of the Roman emperors.

The Holy Roman Empire, which was to last officially and with varying fortunes until 1806 was actually performing the function of policeman and guardian of a territory over which the Church claimed spiritual authority but over which it could not exercise political control. This "alliance" of Church and State was to lead to great controversy when King and Pope each claimed the loyalty of subjects, for a native churchman was also a native landowner, and could find himself in conflict of loyalty to king and religious superior.

The history of the Holy Roman Empire is that of a Pope who was constantly to remind the Emperor that authority came from God to Pope to Emperor, and that the emperor's power was simply delegated. Emperors were frequently to emphasize that they considered themselves senior partners, not inferiors. The issue was resolved in the Reformation when national monarchs refused to accept dictation in internal affairs from the Church, a "foreign" power.

There were now two emperors in Europe, that of the Byzantine Empire who claimed but did not receive precedence, and that of the Holy Roman Empire.

Collapse of Charlemagne's Empire

Charlemagne's empire, without his capable guidance, soon began to disintegrate, not only because Charlemagne's successors were weak but because it had no racial or political unity to hold it together, because of poor communications, local self-sufficiency, and the growth of power in the hands of local nobles. These all contributed to decentralization and local government that became typical of medieval feudalism.

Charlemagne's three sons divided the empire by the Treaty of Verdun, 843 A.D., into France under Charles, part of present-day Germany under Louis, and to the third son Lothair the title of Emperor and the territory which included present-day Holland, Belgium, Luxembourg, Alsace-Lorraine, Switzerland, and North Italy. A later agreement divided the middle portion of Lothair's kingdom between the other two.

New calamities accelerated the disintegration of Charlemagne's empire. Invasions from three directions completely fragmented what remained of Charlemagne's empire. From North Africa in the early ninth century a wave of Moslems occupied Sicily and southern Italy; in the late ninth century the Magyars invaded from Asia and overran the Rhone valley and Lombardy, but were finally limited to what is Hungary; and the Teutonic peoples from Scandinavia overran Britain and the remaining parts of the empire, and forced the area into the system of local organization called feudalism.

By the end of the ninth century Germany was not yet a nation but a collection of four groups of people of which the Franconians or Eastern Franks and the Saxons of northern Germany were the most important.

In 919 A.D. Henry I, the Fowler, a Saxon, was elected King of the Saxons and Franks, and within a few years founded the German state.

Establishment of the Holy Roman Empire

His son Otto I (the Great) (936–973) was crowned at Aachen, Charlemagne's capital. He vigorously asserted his authority by keeping all the semifeudal duchies in his own family, by organizing a central government, and by defending the Church. In 961 A.D. the Pope asked Otto for his assistance, and in return he was crowned Emperor at Rome in 962. This officially established the Holy Roman Empire. Succeeding emperors were crowned by the Pope, although an internal struggle was already developing between Emperor and Pope.

By the early eleventh century the German kings were beginning to attempt to appoint the popes, and claiming the right to appoint bishops and church officials because they were landowners, therefore technically vassals of the king. A bishop owed his spiritual master, the Pope, his spiritual allegiance, but owed temporal allegiance to his king.

The Investiture Issue

The issue came to a head during the reign of Henry IV (1056–1106 A.D.), and the papacy of Hildebrand, Gregory VII. Too many church positions were being sold to nobles who wanted the revenues from landed estates and church offices; too many clergy married and left church property to their families. The Church was losing both property and authority.

Gregory VII claimed the authority that earlier Popes had exercised. He was, he said, the representative of St. Peter, who spoke through him and gave him, as Pope, the power of excommunication and complete control over the destiny of any man. The German bishops, who were also German nobles, resented this threat to their power, and deposed Gregory. Gregory in turn declared Henry IV deposed and excommunicated from the Church, and freed Henry's subjects from allegiance to the emperor. Needing a free hand to put down the rebellion which the Pope had provided the German nobles, Henry was forced to capitulate to the Pope. He hastened to Rome, waited barefoot in the snow for three days outside the castle at Canossa until pardoned by Gregory and freed from excommunication. The significance of the Penance at Canossa in 1077 was that the Emperor acknowledged the authority of the Pope. Although Henry later deposed Gregory and set up his own pope, the precedent of papal authority had been reinstated.

The Concordat of Worms

In 1122 by the Concordat of Worms the problem of lay investiture was resolved by Henry V and the pope. The emperor agreed to permit the Church to elect church officials and to invest them with the spiritual church robes and emblems; the emperor must be present at the ceremonies, and he had the right to give to the new church officials their secular powers and fiefs, and to receive their homage as their temporal overlord. This division of authority was clearly not the final answer to the problem, which was not to be resolved so simply.

For some thirty years two German feudal families struggled for supremacy, the Welfs and the Hohenstaufens. The Welfs favored the papacy and its new spiritual authority, the Hohenstaufens supported imperial rule and centralized government. It Italy two similar parties developed, the Guelphs (from the Italianization of Welfs) and the Ghibellines (the Italianization of Waiblingen, the name of one of the Hohenstaufen possessions.)

The empire had almost disintegrated when Frederick I (Barbarossa, 1152–1190 A.D.) succeeded in stopping internal strife and reorganizing the empire, and was crowned Emperor, again establishing the title of Roman Emperor.

But by the beginning of the fifteenth century the controversy between emperors and popes resulted in the break-up of centralized government in the

German states, and the election of emperors by four electoral princes whose power was almost absolute in their own territory. This situation prevented the development of a national German state until well into the nineteenth century.

Byzantium, Islam, The Crusades

Terms

Icons	K'abah	Greek Orthodox Church
Islam	Koran	Allah
Hegira	*Rubaiyat of Omar*	Caliph
Kismet	*Khayyam*	*Arabian Nights*
Iconoclastic Controversy		

People
Emperor Leo III
Urban III
Mohammed
Genghis Khan

Places to Locate

Byzantium	Dardanelles	Mecca
Medina	Baghdad	Cordova
Cairo	Toledo	Kingdom of Jerusalem
Antioch	Tripoli	Edessa

Significant Dates

632	Death of Mohammed
732	Battle of Tours
1096	First Crusade
1453	Capture of Constantinople

Topic Outline
The Byzantine Empire
The Iconoclastic Controversy
Mohammedanism
Expansion of Mohammedan Empire
Contributions of the Moslems
The Crusades
Effects of the Crusades

Byzantium, Islam, The Crusades

During the thousand years after the collapse of Roman authority throughout the vast empire it had once ruled, Europe's culture declined and most of Europe relapsed into barbarism. Called the Middle Ages or Medieval Period, because it came between the Ancient and Modern periods, it did make contributions between 1000 A.D. and 1500 A.D., preparing the way for many advances after 1500 A.D.

In the eastern part of Europe the former Roman Empire in the East maintained its independence and the culture of the West for another several hundred years, resisting several barbarian attempts to destroy it.

From the Middle East, or Asia Minor, another empire, the Moslem, was influencing western traditions. In the seventh century the religious beliefs of Mohammed and his followers erupted out of the Arabian Peninsula and won spectacular successes throughout Asia and parts of Europe. By 750 A.D., in about one hundred years, the Moslems built up an empire that stretched across North Africa eastwards to India and westwards into Spain. By the fourteenth century Mohammedanism had spread throughout India to the East Indies, which is today essentially Moslem in religion.

In Europe the Franks invaded the area which is now France, and set up a strong state which became the Holy Roman Empire under Charlemagne, recognized as the revival after an interruption of three centuries of the former Roman Empire.

The Byzantine Empire

In 330 A.D. the Roman emperor Constantine dedicated his new eastern capital, Nova Roma, soon to be called Constantinople, which was to outlive the Western Roman Empire by a thousand years.

The reasons for the rise of Constantinople are that its geographical position made it strategic for trade and manufacturing, and that Rome's location was increasingly open to attack. Well situated on a peninsula of land, Constantinople was protected by water on three sides, and fortified by impregnable walls and towers on the land side. The strategic waterways of the Dardanelles, the Sea of Marmora, and the Bosphorus form a continuous water route that *connects* the Black Sea with the Mediterranean and *separates* Europe from Asia. The name Byzantium, given to this empire, came from the oldest, half-mythical city of the seventh century before Christ, built on the same site by Byzas, and given the name Byzantium. It was to be a citadel against repeated attacks of invaders: the Persians in the seventh century, the Arabs in the eighth, and the Turks in the eleventh century and later. Historians have speculated seriously that had it not been for Byzantium's resistance to the Arabs, all of Europe might have become Moslem.

Byzantium became enormously rich as the great center of trade from every quarter of the compass. From the Black Sea came furs, hides, salt, and grain; from India, Ceylon and Arabia came spices and silks; from Africa, ivory and slaves; from the west came merchants eager to buy these products. Envied for its great wealth, Byzantium maintained a carefully-recruited and well-trained army with its own medical ambulance corps, its highly skillful intelligence service, and skilled diplomats to negotiate.

The empire was Roman in its law and centralized organization, but Greek in culture, language, and emperors. The government was authoritarian and highly centralized. The church was headed by a Patriarch who was simply one of a number of bishops singled out and appointed by the emperor, and therefore always dismissable by the emperor.

The Iconoclastic Controversy

The Papacy attempted to exercise at least religious authority over the Patriarch and Byzantium. A controversy developed between Pope and Patriarch over the use of sacred pictures and images, collectively called *icons*. One Byzantine emperor, Leo III (717–741 A.D.), considering the Church to be too idolatrous, decided to purify it by ordering the icons to be destroyed. This resulted in a long *Iconoclastic* ("image-breaking") *Controversy* which finally resulted in the separation in 1054 A.D. of the Church into two separate Churches, the Roman Catholic Church in the West, and the Greek Orthodox Church in the East, which does not acknowledge the Pope as the leader of Christendom.

The cultural contribution of Byzantium was that of preserving, during the several centuries in which knowledge of Greek disappeared from Europe, Greek masterpieces and making copies of them, the printing of books, building of great libraries and a university, and the preservation of the works of Plato, Aristotle, Homer, and Sophocles.

A serious blow came with the Fourth Crusade in 1204 A.D. Instead of attacking the infidels in the Holy Land, the Crusaders, financed by Venice and assisted by 50 Venetian ships, sailed for Constantinople, defeated it, and put a pretender on the throne and cornered much of its trade for Venice. A rebellion against the pretender gave the Venetians the excuse to do what they wanted, to loot the city, carry off everything they could, and wantonly destroy priceless classical manuscripts. Byzantium became a fief of the Papacy, which officially did penance for the Crusaders' victory, but rejoiced over the uniting of the two Churches. The Greeks reconquered it in 1261 A.D., but the Byzantine Empire never fully recovered, and in 1453 was overwhelmed by the superior numbers of the Ottoman Turks — the so-called Fall of Constantinople.

Mohammedanism

Islam means "submission to God," and is the religion of the Moslems, "those who submit." A warlike faith, it used the sword to conquer and set up a religion which, since it was antagonistic to Christianity, resulted in centuries of intermittent warfare with the Church. Nevertheless, Mohammedanism was far from being merely destructive, for the Moslems adapted themselves to the civilization they found, assimilated it, and were to develop into one of the three major cultural units of the West: the Latin, the Greek, and the Moslem.

Arabia was inhabited by nomadic tribal people whose religion was essentially animism, the worship of trees, springs, and stones; Mecca was a holy city where a sacred black stone was protected in a rectangular building called the *K'abah* or cube. Population pressure forced the Bedouin nomads to raid surrounding territories, particularly Egypt, Syria, and Mesopotamia.

Mohammed Founds a New Religion

About the year 610 A.D. Mohammed, a merchant in the caravan trade, announced that he had been chosen as the prophet of God to preach a belief in one God, Allah. Mohammed and his followers, persecuted by the inhabitants of Mecca for attacks upon the traditional Moslem gods, fled secretly to Medina in 622 A.D., a flight called the *Hegira*, marking the beginning of the Moslem calendar.

Because Mohammed's conviction that he was the chosen reformer of Judaism and Christianity was unacceptable to those religions, the Moslems were to make war upon them in the name of the "true" faith. The Mohammedan Bible, the *Koran*, compiled by Mohammed's followers, reveals the creed and the ritual of the new faith. All three Semitic religions were monotheistic, and all three included ethical principles and social laws. Before his death in 632 A.D. Mohammed had brought Arabia under his control and urged further expansion.

His followers chose the next leader or *Caliph* (Successor), who was the religious and political head of the state. Desiring to extend the faith, Mohammed had preached predestination, or *Kismet,* that the time of a man's death was fixed, that death in the service of the faith earned the right to paradise.

The disciplined forces overran Syria, Palestine, Egypt, Carthage by 700 A.D., and crossed the Straits into Spain and up to the Pyrenees by 713 A.D. Attempts to take over France were repulsed in 732 at the battle of Tours, and by 761 the Moslems were completely expelled from France, and their advance further into Europe was halted. Eastward they spread victory and faith into Mesopotamia, Persia, and as far east as the Indus river. In time their influence spread as far eastward as the Philippines. The Moslems were tolerant of their conquered people, probably because, like the Romans before them, they found that toleration made much simpler the administration of distant possessions.

Over the centuries rival caliphates were set up in Baghdad, in Cordova in Spain, and in Cairo, Egypt. In 1258 invading Mongols, under a nephew of Genghis Khan, captured and destroyed Baghdad. These Ottoman Turks seized control of the eastern Moslem world, became themselves fierce converts to Mohammedanism, captured Constantinople in 1453, and threatened all Europe. The Turkish sultans in Constantinople retained their supremacy as Caliphs until 1908 A.D., since then there has been no recognized official head of the Moslem world. The Caliphate was officially dissolved in Turkey by the National Assembly in 1924.

Contributions of the Moslems

Since the Koran was not permitted to be translated by the Moslems, those who wanted to read it had to learn Arabic, a language which became standard in the Islamic world.

The Moslems irrigated the deserts, terraced the hills of Spain, cultivated vineyards and orchards, carried goods throughout their world — steel from Toledo, leather from Morocco, fine linen damask from Damascus, drugs, dyes, and perfumes.

In the world of learning they invented or advanced Arabic numerals borrowed from India, algebra, probably the use of zero; astronomy; compiled encyclopedias of foreign peoples; introduced the mariner's compass to Europe; established famous universities at Baghdad, Cordova, Toledo, and Granada; founded extensive libraries; did much to revive and spread Greek ideas and learning; supplemented the spirit of scientific enquiry with experimental techniques; learned the manufacture of paper from China and produced it themselves at Baghdad and Samarkand.

In attempting the pseudo-science of alchemy, the turning of base metals into gold, they discovered alkalis such as saltpetre, sulphuric acid, salammoniac, and others.

In literature the best known of their works are the *Rubaiyat of Omar Khayyam* and the *Arabian Nights,* some thousand stories of Persia from the eighth and ninth centuries.

The Crusades

One result of the rise of Mohammedanism was the occupation of the Holy Land by the Arabs. Generally the Arabs did not interfere with pilgrimages to the Holy

City, but in the eleventh century the Seljuk Turks occupied Asia Minor and seriously threatened the Byzantine Empire.

Called upon by the Byzantine Emperor to give assistance, Pope Urban II in 1095 called for a holy crusade against the infidel, and in 1096 the First Crusade of the total eight was launched. Religious enthusiasm, the blessing of the Church, the opportunity for obtaining landed estates, and the desire of the Church to reduce local fighting between groups of barons, all stimulated the crusading movement. The first expedition of enthusiastic but ill-trained and poorly-led people was a failure. But the official First Crusade in 1096 under trained leaders resulted in the capture of Jerusalem and Asia Minor, and the establishment of the Christian Kingdom of Jerusalem, a strip of land roughly 500 miles long and 50 miles wide, from the borders of Egypt to the Euphrates river. This Kingdom of Jerusalem, which was divided into the Kingdom itself and three great fiefs called Antioch, Tripoli, and Edessa, lasted for nearly one hundred years.

The Fourth Crusade was a complete degradation of the crusading spirit, for Venice, jealous of Constantinople, subsidized the Crusaders to attack Constantinople. A complete contradiction of the basic crusading principle of preserving the independence of the Eastern Empire, the Fourth Crusade resulted in the replacement of Constantinople by Venice as the center of Mediterranean trade.

Two centuries of Crusades did not achieve the basic purpose of retrieving the Holy Land from the infidels, although secondary influences were significant. Spain finally drove the Moslems out of the peninsula, and Christians in Eastern Europe were able to hold back subsequent attempted Moslem invasions.

Effects of the Crusades

It is almost impossible to assess accurately the effects of the Crusades upon western Europe, since the question resembles that of asking which came first, the hen or the egg. For example, direct influences between Christendom and Mohammedanism were stronger in Spain and Sicily. The trade in silks and spices from Asia Minor was accelerated but was not new; the Crusades stimulated an already existing trade enjoyed by Venice with Asia Minor. Certainly western Europe borrowed much from the philosophy, science and culture of the Moslem world; banking houses in Italy set up branches in the Kingdom of Jerusalem and thereby developed conditions that became the basis for increased trading. The Crusades stimulated the romanticizing in song and story of the Crusaders, such as the saga of the search for Richard Lionheart, captured during the Crusades by a rival, and held for ransom for a staggering sum.

Such a crusading movement could not but broaden men's outlook, as they came into contact with other lands and other customs. One decided result was the levying by the Church of tithes, a tax upon the clergy to help finance the expedition, a tax that was continued and extended long after the Crusades had ended.

Feudalism: Decentralized Society

Terms

fief	homage	demesne
feudalism	investiture	manor
vassal	escheat	villein
sub-infeudate	forfeiture	serf
relief	scutage	chivalry
aids		

Topic Outline
Origin and Nature of Feudalism
Life on the Manor
Order of Chivalry
Military Organization
Reasons for Disappearance of Feudalism

Feudalism: Decentralized Society

Origin

With the break-up of Charlemagne's empire, central government and administration was replaced by local control, usually in the hands of a landowner who enforced his authority by his own private army. Since there was no central government to maintain them, thousands of little communities had to depend upon whom they must repay service in return for protection. This was the basis of medieval feudalism. Transportation throughout the old world virtually collapsed; roads degenerated into rutted wagon tracks because there was no central government to maintain them. Thousand of little communities had to depend upon their own efforts for protection and even survival. Discipline, law, and order, in the Roman tradition, were gone; skills were lost, and living conditions became more primitive. Commerce and trade almost entirely disappeared, land became the main source of wealth, its products were consumed by those who raised them, and villages became self-sufficient units.

Nature of Feudalism

In theory the king was the chief landowner, who handed out various parts of his land to his nobles, who repaid for land and protection with personal and military services to the king, in proportion to the size of their estates. This grant of land was the *fief* (territory held in fee, i.e., in return for service). The fief was the basis of the feudal system. Holders of fiefs were of the upper class, and each landholder, whether large or small, was a *vassal* to his superior, owing him a service. A noble who held a large fief would usually *sub-infeudate*, or sub-let, part of it to lesser landholders, in turn down to the smallest fief, usually a self-contained village.

The relationship between overlord and vassal included definite obligations. A vassal must supply a stipulated number of armed men, and must pay certain *reliefs* and *aids*. Relief was the payment given by an heir to a fief; aids were special money payments either to ransom the overlord if taken prisoner, or to celebrate the knighting of the lord's eldest son, or the marriage of the daughter.

Fiefs were not hereditary possessions, but if the heir was considered capable, then the fief was handed down through the family. The actual ceremony of receiving the fief included *homage* in which the vassal knelt before his overlord, placed his hands between those of the other, and promised faithful service. The *investiture* ceremony then followed, with the lord giving formal possession of the fief to his vassal. Lord and vassal were now bound by mutual promises and obligations.

If there were no heir to a fief, the land *escheated*, it reverted, to the overlord who could grant it out as he chose. If a vassal did not live up to his obligations, the penalty was *forfeiture* of the fief. One factor which later on led to friction between kings and Popes was that fiefs held by churchmen produced no income from relief, escheat, and marriage. Sometimes the overlord permitted his vassal to pay his military obligations in the form of *scutage* or shield-money (scutum, a shield), not infrequently of more value to a lord than actual soldiers. The vassal did not supply any other kind of income to his lord, who lived on the income and the produce of his own *demesne*, which might be several manors run by his own personal servants.

Life on the Manor

The lord of any manor was a member of the fighting aristocracy, and did no work whatever on his estate. Around the manor house or the castle were clustered the peasants' huts, each with its small plot of land. In the village would be the church, the priest's house, and little shops of craftsmen. Around the village were the arable fields, meadows, and woodlands. On the common or public pasture, cattle and horses grazed. The part of the cultivated land reserved for the lord's use was demesne land. There were three arable fields: one for the spring planting, one for the fall planting, one kept fallow or idle for a season. The fields were rotated so that none was exhausted from constant use. The fields were divided into strips, so that each man had several strips in each field but divided up so that all shared in good and poorer land. The fields were without fences except to keep out cattle in the growing season; thus the designation of the "open field" system.

On the manor were two classes of men, the *villein* or villager who paid for the use of his land but not free to come and go, and the *serf* who was bound to the manor. Although not free to leave the manor, the serf did receive protection from his lord, had the use of land and the right to use the common pasture; in return he paid in *week work* of stated days of work on the lord's land, plus some incidental duties. In fact, the system gave the lord the labor he needed without the payment of money wages. The manor had its own system of justice based on accepted custom. Vassals were expected to contribute their services when the manorial court met.

Chivalry

Derived from the French word *chevalier*, horseman or knight, *chivalry* was a code of behavior identified with feudalism. It prescribed a rigid set of rules for the fighting aristocracy; the young man must learn the code of honor and rules of the tourney by serving his apprenticeship as a page, then rising to squire (from *ecuyer*, a sword-bearer) in service to his knight, then finally to his own knighthood.

Military Organization

The feudal landlord, whatever his rank, was a soldier, and it was both his duty and his privilege to fight. In fact his position and power depended upon his fighting skill. He was trained from early youth to fight and to pillage and plunder as reward for success. Consequently the medieval castle was essential to feudalism. Inside it the feudal lord might defy his overlord or even the king; from it he could attack his neighbors.

Once a man was knighted, after his long apprenticeship, he became a recognized member of the brotherhood of fighting gentlemen, regulated by what was an international Order of Chivalry, which established a code of conduct. According to the rules he was supposed to defend the weak against oppression, secure justice, keep his promises, but all these only to his social equals, for the peasantry was of no consequence. At its best, chivalry promoted good manners but little else. The protection of the weak became the obligation of the Church, which attempted to prohibit fighting on Holy Days and at other times in the year.

Reasons for Decline of Feudalism

By the end of the eleventh century Europe was developing beyond the narrow, self-sufficient economy of feudalism. As commerce revived, so feudalism became economically outdated and disappeared under the pressures and interests of the merchant class. Nation-states gradually developed, with a king at the apex, surrounded and supported by merchants, the middle class, whose interests demanded law and order.

Feudalism was not a "system" deliberately imposed and identical everywhere. It grew out of necessity and might differ from country to country and age to age, but the basic principle remained the same. All land had its lord; every man was another's vassal; each tenant owed his lord loyalty and service; each tenant received land and protection.

Since feudalism was essentially an economic system adapted to local conditions, it lasted only so long as it was economically sound. When towns and trade developed, when landowners could do better economically by hiring paid labor, by making land produce more than was consumed locally, then self-sufficient feudalism was on its way out.

Medieval Towns and Trade and Medieval Thought and Learning

Terms

Craft Guild	Merchant Guild	Banks
Capital	Capitalism	Checks
Gothic	Romanesque	Codes of Lubeck
Dogma	Theology	Scientia
Scholasticism	Deductive Reasoning	*Summa Theologica*
Universitas	*Chanson de Roland*	*Canterbury Tales*
Mystery Plays	Transept	Flying Buttress

People

Thomas Aquinas	Roger Bacon	Dante
Chaucer		

Places to Locate

Venice	Genoa	Pisa
Hanseatic League	Hamburg	Danzig
Lubeck	Cologne	

Topic Outline

Reasons for Rise of Towns
Craft Guilds
Interests of Middle Class
The Hanseatic League
Venice
Rise of Banking
Capitalism
The Medieval Church
Education and Science
Geography, Literature, Architecture

Medieval Towns and Trade and Medieval Thought and Learning

Reappearance of Towns

Town life did not completely disappear during feudal times, but since towns depended essentially upon trade, the break-down of central authority and protection adversely affected towns. Local communities were self-sufficient, barter replaced the use of money, and trade routes were subject to banditry. But in later feudal times, conditions became more stable, surplus farm products were available, needs were not always satisfied by local production. Crossroads, or river fords, even a lord's castle became meeting places for simple traders. Towns gradually developed, realized the need to protect themselves, and, in doing so, encouraged people to come within their walls. Here a variety of goods and services became available, with some towns becoming famous for certain products which attracted merchants from other towns and countries. Some towns became so famous that they held special fairs, the medieval forerunners of modern trading centers and world's fairs.

Craft Guilds

To protect the interests of merchants and towns, craft and merchant guilds were organized. Craft guilds were associations of employers working in the same trade, such as saddle-makers, shoemakers, tailors, and the like. The purposes of the craft guild were to:

1. Regulate the quality of goods produced.

2. Control the price and hours of production in order to prevent destructive competition.

3. Limit membership to meet local needs.

4. Keep out "foreigners" from other towns, who might take business from local employers.

Craft guilds were not associations of working-men but trade groups of little businessmen who had served their apprenticeship in learning the trade, had hired out for daily wages as journeymen, and now were admitted into the guild as employers.

Merchant Guilds were associations of men engaged in buying and selling goods, not in producing them. These organizations:

1. Regulated buying and selling prices.
2. Bought in quantity at wholesale.
3. Protected shipment of goods to and from foreign markets.
4. Established business rules and procedures for their members.

Not infrequently the merchant guilds virtually ran a town's government, since its members were the wealthy and influential citizens. Merchant guilds performed the useful function of protecting a town's interests against tyranny and unfair taxation.

Rise of a Middle Class

To maintain their freedom of action, towns frequently bought their independence from the landowner, king, or noble, upon whose land their town had grown. Town charters spelled out their rights, which they jealously guarded. Even today no English monarch may enter the mile-square City of London without official invitation of the city guild members, represented by the Lord Mayor. Usually each merchant group had its own Guild Hall, and many famous ones can be seen in several European countries.

The rise of towns and trade marked the emergence of a middle class, one between nobles and workers, a middle class jealous of its rights and interested in helping to develop a central government capable of maintaining the order and the peaceful conditions in which trade could flourish. Later on, it was the middle class which was largely responsible for the rise of independent national states.

Two important developments were the rise of the Hanse (trading association) or the Hanseatic League of towns of northern Europe, and the rise to trading pre-eminence of Venice, the city-state whose trading operations were to dominate the entire Mediterranean area.

The Hanseatic League

The Hanseatic League originated in northern Germany as an association of Hamburg, Danzig, Cologne, Lubeck, and expanded to other trading centers for the purpose of gaining trading rights for its members throughout northern Europe. Its wealth came principally from its monopoly of the Baltic herring fisheries, and its control of the trade of Russia and the Low Countries. It protected its members with its own fleet, its own flag, diplomats, and legal code, the *Code of Lubeck*. During the fourteenth and fifteenth centuries the League flourished almost as an independent power enforcing its own rights. Its basic weakness was that individual member towns or groups of towns could not be depended upon to cooperate in an emergency. As centralized monarchies developed in the sixteenth century, its usefulness lessened.

Venice

Venice, in contrast to the Hanse League, was to become a first-rate power, highly and tightly organized. Many Mediterranean cities, such as Genoa and Marseilles, were profitably engaged in trading ventures, but by the fourteenth century Venice was undisputed mistress of the Mediterranean, and had a monopoly on some products traded in northern Europe. The government of Venice regulated the trade, built and operated its ships in its own shipyard, the Arsenal, and resembled a modern corporation in its operations. The state supervised its fleets of galleys, from "cradle to grave," ordering their use, supplying them with trained crews and bowmen, with physicians, and regulating their sailings to Flanders, Alexandria, London, Beirut, and the Black Sea. Attacks by the Ottoman Turks on the Venetian Empire in the Aegean, the discovery of America and the water-route around Africa to the Indies were all causes and effects in providing cheaper trade routes which competed with Venice and her overland routes to Europe. Consequently, by the sixteenth century the influence of Venice in the trading world was waning.

Banking and Capitalism

As trade flourished, so the profession of banking increased in importance. A bank's functions are to borrow and to lend. Banks began as safe deposits for money. Traders sold goods in various cities in Europe and frequently preferred to leave their money in safe-keeping rather than risk the danger of theft by highway robbers or pirates. At first the goldsmiths and silversmiths kept such funds in their safes and charged a fee for the funds entrusted to them, giving one or several receipts for the money. These men became trusted and began to be regarded as bankers with branches in different countries. Their receipts for money entrusted to them could be used in business and exchanged for money upon proper authorization of the owner of the receipts. Funds could be transferred from city to city or country to country, or orders could be given by a bank to its branches to pay out money as ordered. In simple form there developed what is today a banking system which borrows and lends, pays out on demand, and transfers funds by one simple method of checking accounts.

As business grew larger, more money was needed and the system of capitalism developed, the lending of money or capital, or its investment, in return for a dividend or profit, which is simply the reward for lending funds to other people. So there developed what is called the capitalist class, banking families which acquired money to be invested in growing business enterprises. Modern companies can expand by borrowing money from banks, who get their funds from people who wish to save surplus money in a bank, or from people who invest in a company by buying shares of stock or ownership in companies.

A new society was developing and demanding law and order, proper rules to safeguard property, and therefore very much in opposition to feudal nobles whose life depended upon private rights to fight and plunder as they saw fit. These demands of the middle class led gradually to the rise of nation-states which could protect such business interests and also depend upon those businesses to contribute towards the national welfare and safety.

Medieval Thought and Learning

Medieval man was no different from others before and after him in attempting to understand his place in the world and the general problems of life. In general it is true that medieval man accepted rather than questioned matters of faith, that he did not experiment in science as the Greeks had done, and that education consisted of learning by rote rather than by questioning and proving. But it is also true that man never gave up attempting to find answers to problems that faced him, whether spiritual or practical. The Middle Ages did make contributions to thought and culture, and in so doing prepared the way for the Renaissance.

The Medieval Church

The vast institution of the Church gained control of much of the political as well as the religious life of western Europe. Its position was based upon the Scriptures and Church teachings which were accepted as *dogma*, basic doctrinal beliefs laid down by the Church, and not open to question. *Theology,* the science of religion, had as its basic purpose the explanation of the relationship of God and Man, and the place of man in the universe. Theology used all knowledge and branches of learning, and was the Queen of the Sciences (*scientia* meaning knowledge in general). It was used to explain religion and demonstrate how man could obtain salvation. The teachers were called Schoolmen or Scholastic churchmen whose teaching was generally called *Scholasticism.* Their purpose was expressed by St. Anselm, Archbishop of Canterbury, "I do not seek to know in order that I may believe, but I believe in order that I may know."

The discovery of Aristotle's writings, with their emphasis upon deductive reasoning (reasoning through experimentation from particulars to a general conclusion), obliged men to reason as well as simply believe, because, to the medieval scholastics, Aristotle was regarded as the "master of those who know."

The problem was that reason and revelation were sometimes difficult to reconcile. *Thomas Aquinas,* a Dominican friar and one of the great medieval scholars, determined to reconcile Aristotle's reasoning with Church faith. In his 22-volume *Summa Theologica,* a sort of encyclopedia of all theology, he set out to prove that all scientific knowledge agreed with Church beliefs, taking up each point in Church doctrine and proving it. Nevertheless, the spirit of reason made men question still further, and even today we still seek to reconcile religion and science, faith and reason.

Education

Stimulated partly by experiences of the Crusades, and partly by natural curiosity and inquisitiveness, young men began to meet to discuss ideas. They formed groups somewhat like any guild, or *universitas,* a group of men like tailors or shoemakers in the same profession. The early universitas or university was a group of teachers and learners, like masters and apprentices. The two early universities were at Paris, originating from the Cathedral School of Notre Dame, and at Bologna in Italy, where civil law was taught. Other medieval universities followed, at Oxford and Salerno, until by the close of the Middle Ages there were no fewer than seventy-five. Then, as now, the purpose of universities was to bring together teachers and students for the exchange of ideas.

Medieval Science

Science was restricted to assumptions rather than proven facts. Medieval scholars studied Aristotle's ideas rather than experimented for themselves, although Roger Bacon, regarded as the greatest medieval scientist, did experiment, and did cast doubts upon unquestioning acceptance of long-established custom. He is remarkable for his imaginative scientific predictions which included machines for navigation, land cars without animals, and even a flying machine with wings "which beat the air in the manner of flying birds."

Little advance was made in medicine, chemistry, or physics, because these branches of learning necessitated experimental thinking. Advance in mathematics developed from the Arabic numerals and the invention of zero, the trigonometry of the Arabs, and the geometry of Euclid.

Geography

The voyages of Christian pilgrims and Crusaders and European traders to India and China added to man's knowledge; the use of the magnetic compass facilitated seafaring.

Literature

During the Middle Ages, Latin was the international language of the Church, the State, and the educated. The majority of people spoke the vernacular, the language of a country or a locality, and gradually literature was written for the people. The great works of Dante, Chaucer, and others were written in the vernacular.

The famous poem *Chanson de Roland,* telling of the defense of Roncevalles Pass (against the Saracens) by Charlemagne's rearguard, is a good example of romanticized writing in the language of the country.

Dante Alighieri (1265–1321 A.D.) wrote the *Divine Comedy* in the Tuscan dialect for his beloved Italy.

Geoffrey Chaucer (1340–1400 A.D.), one of the great medieval writers, portrayed in his *Canterbury Tales* the people of the countryside of England, written in English and describing a cross-section of lower and middle-class people.

For those who could not read, the "mystery" plays dealing with Biblical characters and saints, and the morality plays or allegories brought entertainment and instruction.

Architecture

The architecture of the Middle Ages reflects and symbolizes man's great concern with religion. Until around 1100 A.D. the prevailing type of architecture was *Romanesque,* a heavy style of massive walls, horizontal lines, strong columns, and the rounded arch. Usually the Romanesque church was a rectangular building, with a high nave down the center, aisles on each side of the nave, and a *transept*, the section crossing the main body of the building to form a cross. Because of the construction, windows were few.

The later architectural style of the Middle Ages was the Gothic, originally a term of contempt meaning "barbarian," in reference to the tendency to use too much decoration.

The Gothic style was light, with pointed arches designed to lead the eye upwards. The inner walls were thin in comparison with their height, and had to be supported with an outside wall called a buttress, to which a leaning arch, or *flying buttress*, was attached to keep the inside wall from being pushed outwards by the weight of the lofty roof. The Gothic cathedral was delicate in appearance and soared upwards. It became very popular in Europe, where the magnificent Cathedral at Chartres is the perfect example of the style. In New York City, St. Patrick's Cathedral and Trinity Church are good examples of the Gothic.

4

The Beginning of Modern Times

The Renaissance

Terms

Scholasticism	Humanism	Copernican Theory
Last Supper	*Mona Lisa*	*Divine Comedy*
The Prince	Chiaroscuro	Ptolemaic Theory

People

Petrarch	Erasmus	Vesalius
Shakespeare	Copernicus	Cervantes
Raphael	Paracelsus	da Vinci
Newton	Montaigne	Galileo
Machiavelli	Michelangelo	Harvey
The Medicis	Kepler	

Topic Outline
Origin of the Renaissance
Humanism
Italian Renaissance
Humanistic Literature
Renaissance Painting, Printing
Mathematics and Science
Medicine
Characteristics of the Renaissance

The Renaissance

**Origin
of the
Renaissance**

Literally the word *Renaissance* means a rebirth, referring to a rediscovery of and a new interest in the writings and culture of Greeks and Romans. In a broad sense the Renaissance means a progressive breaking away from old traditions and restrictions to the more vital and individualistic ideas of modern times.

During the period 1300 to 1600 A.D., western Europe changed from the essentially restricted life of the Middle Ages, with its emphasis upon Scholasticism, Church authority, a repression of man's worldly interests, to that of the modern world with its broader views of life and man, with its new society breaking away from the restrictions of feudalism, to a more dynamic society of town life, middle class interests, and the emphasis upon skepticism and individualism.

This change of outlook was gradual, one that developed with and was partly caused by the development of town life, the rise of nations whose needs and attitudes broke down former narrow boundaries. The increase in trading brought wealth which was spent on the arts, through patrons who could support and encourage great writers and artists.

Humanism

One aspect of the Renaissance was the actual re-discovery of Greek and Roman writers, and a re-birth of European interest in their ideas. Educated people became enthusiastic over the "humane" literature of the classical writers who regarded man as a person living in a vital world. This interest in classical literature is called Humanism (from *humanitas,* culture), and its scholars, Humanists.

One result of the change in attitude can be seen by comparing Dante's superb *Divine Comedy* with Petrarch's writings. Dante was concerned with showing Christians how they could achieve divine salvation. Petrarch was interested in worldly affairs. The center of interest shifted from heaven and the next world to earth and this world.

Italian Renaissance

The Renaissance appeared in Italy first because here were independent towns, a growing middle class, and the wealth to pay for learning and intellectual pursuits. Men who were engaged in such trading as the Venetians gained new ideas and experiences from their travels. As the Moslems increasingly controlled trading routes so men decided to find sea routes that were safer from interference. In Italian cities the merchant princes paid humanists to discuss their ideas, paid painters and sculptors and architects to produce masterpieces for them. As a consequence, works of art depicted the individuality of Greek sculptures and paintings.

One of the great patron families was that of the Medicis of Florence, who so encouraged the arts that the city became the most famous literary and artistic center of its time.

Humanistic Literature

One of the early Renaissance writers was Petrarch who wrote great Italian poetry and also collected valuable Greek and Roman manuscripts that had long been forgotten. In France, Montaigne wrote about society around him; in Spain, Cervantes satirized feudal life through his hero Don Quixote who set out on a series of chivalric adventures; in England, William Shakespeare portrayed people as modern individuals. One of the great Renaissance writers was the Dutchman Erasmus who published a Greek version of the *New Testament* in the hopes that it would be better understood, and also to criticize the practices of churchmen.

Renaissance Painting

One of the dramatic developments of the Renaissance was in painting, represented by the great artists Michelangelo (1475–1564 A.D.) and da Vinci (1452–1519 A.D.). No longer was painting conventionalized but represented individuals, used proper perspective, and developed *chiaroscuro,* the arrangement of light and dark to create depth and dimension in painting. A great sculptor, Michelangelo is remembered for his magnificent paintings in the Sistine Chapel of St. Peter's in Rome; da Vinci, painter, sculptor, architect, and inventor, is known for his famous paintings of the *Last Supper* and the *Mona Lisa*. Raphael was a master portrait painter famous for his several paintings of the Madonna.

Development of Printing

A significant Renaissance contribution was the development of printing, for now books and ideas could be brought to thousands of people throughout Europe. Learning was no longer restricted to the educated and the wealthy; and the printing press encouraged writing in the vernacular language of the people.

Science and Medicine

Scientists of the Renaissance no longer accepted without question the teachings of Aristotle and others. They depended not upon opinion but upon *observation* and *experiment*. A succession of mathematicians and scientists demonstrated the proper relationship of the earth to the solar system.

Copernicus (1474–1543) was the founder of modern astronomy. His Copernican theory that the earth turns on its own axis and revolves around the sun met with opposition because it contradicted the long-accepted Ptolemaic theory that the earth was the center of the universe.

Kepler (1571–1630) discovered that the planets moved in ellipses with the sun as the focus.

Galileo (1564–1642) discovered the law of falling bodies and founded the mathematical science of dynamics and motion. He developed a telescope through which his observations convinced him that the Copernican theory was true, and the earth rotates.

Isaac Newton (1642–1727) continued the work of Kepler and Galileo and mathematically proved that the motion of the moon about the earth, and planets about the sun, was explained by the same law of gravity which causes an apple to fall to the ground.

Paracelsus (1493–1541) challenged the long-accepted teachings of Galen and studied disease in order to discover what he believed to be cures for each disease.

Vesalius (1514–1564) the "father of modern anatomy," contradicted former assumptions and errors about the human body, and established the modern study of human anatomy.

William Harvey (1587–1657) discovered the circulation of blood, a most important step in understanding human physiology.

These three men laid the foundations of an accurate knowledge of the human body and demonstrated how medicine should be studied intelligently.

Niccolo Machiavelli (1469–1527). Italy, long a divided country and subject to constant invasions, was greatly affected by its political condition. In the north were the republics of Venice, Florence, and Genoa, in the central part were the Papal States, and in the south the weak Kingdom of Naples.

Machiavelli personally experienced two decades of invasion and he became convinced that only scientific statesmanship might save Italy from further foreign attacks. He advocated reliance upon the old Roman statecraft. In his famous book *The Prince*, published in 1513, he defended power politics and the position that the end justifies the means, because Italy had been for decades "without a head, without order, beaten, despoiled, lacerated and overrun." His book therefore urged action to meet a specific condition. He was a realist who believed that citizens should be ready to fight and die for their country, and he wrote at a time when war seemed to be the only way to develop Italian nationalism. Machiavelli helped to found the modern study of political science, the way governments should operate to achieve certain goals.

The Characteristics of the Renaissance

1. The growth of towns, trade, the middle class, and accumulated wealth.
2. The growth of interest in the ideas of classical civilization.
3. Increasing concern with people and their activities and motives.
4. The development of critical minds and self-realization.
5. The growth of national feelings and the rise of nations.
6. The magnificent achievements in painting, literature and the arts, such as had not been known since the days of Athens.

The Reformation

Terms

Reformation	Protestant
Council of Pisa	Lutheran
Council of Constance	Peace of Augsburg
Great Schism	Calvinism
Simony	Predestination
Indulgence	Theocracy
Ninety-Five Theses	Act of Supremacy
Infallibility	Counter-Reformation
Transubstantiation	Society of Jesus
Consubstantiation	Inquisition

People

Wyclif	Zwingli
Tetzel	Luther
Loyola	Calvin
Hus	

Significant Dates

1417   Council of Constance
1517   Luther's Ninety-Five Theses
1555   Peace of Augsburg

Topic Outline
Earlier Threats to Church Influence
Abuses Within the Church
External Forces Weakening the Church
John Wyclif and John Hus
Martin Luther

Indulgences and Their Abuse
Luther's Protest
Origin of the Protestant (Lutheran) Church
Calvinism
The Reformation in England
The Catholic Reformation or Counter-Reformation

The Reformation

The *Reformation*, or the challenge to papal authority, was inevitable as conditions changed in Europe, as men's physical and intellectual horizons widened. The Catholic Church had performed great services for mankind, but it could not continue to be both a religious and a political institution, because rising nationalities would not accept political interference from outside their own boundaries. In an age when middle class interests of trade and profit could be better protected by strong national governments, men would criticize the loss of national wealth through money payments to Rome, and directives from Rome that might appear to conflict with national interests. There were other causes for the growing struggle between King and Church, many of them the natural results of a changing world, some because of internal differences with the Church itself.

Earlier Threats to Church Influence

The new movements in literature, the emphasis upon individualism, and the growing consciousness of nationalism, all, directly or indirectly, threatened the position of the Church. One of the most serious disputes occurred in the late thirteenth century, when the French king, Philip IV, objected to the Pope's contention that Philip could not tax the French clergy. The pope finally gave in, but the conflict resulted in Philip's securing the election of a French clergyman as pope, and the moving of the papal court from Rome to Avignon in France. For nearly seventy years (1309–1377) the popes lived in Avignon in what was called the *Babylonian Captivity*, in reference to the time when king Nebuchadnezzar of Babylon took the people of Judah as captives to Babylon.

Papal prestige suffered severely, and many people resented the demands for funds for the new papal court in France. Furthermore, a French pope could lead not only to religious interference in the affairs of other countries but also political interference. In 1378 an Italian clergyman was elected pope by the College of Cardinals, the French cardinals elected their man at Avignon, and a third one was finally elected in 1409 A.D. at the Council of Pisa where 500 prelates and delegates from the states of Europe attempted to resolve the problem. Finally in 1417 A.D. the Council of Constance was able to secure the election of a pope which ended the Great Schism in the Church.

Abuses Within the Church

But abuses had developed within the Church itself. Popes had become patrons of art as a consequence of the Renaissance, levied tithes of about 10 per cent on incomes, had permitted simony, the sale of church positions and offices, and even allowed the sale of indulgences to help the building of St. Peter's in Rome. This was the issue which Martin Luther was to criticize so severely.

**External Forces
Weakening
the Church**

There were other forces destroying the unity of the Church, forces outside the control of the Church, and largely the result of changing times and conditions:

1. The Church had too much political power.

2. It was taking too much wealth from European countries to Rome, a loss of money which hindered trade in those countries.

3. It weakened royal authority by threats of excommunication and interdict.

4. It was regarded by many people as a foreign influence interfering in national affairs.

5. In an age of rising middle classes and capitalism it frowned upon interest and profit.

6. There were outbreaks of so-called heresy in religious teachings and practices that did not conform to doctrines approved by the Church. Some of the "heretical" teachings were no more than attempts to maintain the prestige and power of the Church by trying to reform abuses.

**John Wyclif and
John Hus**

John Wyclif and his Lollards believed that the Church should be subordinate to the State, and that salvation was a matter between man and his God. Another heretic was John Hus who was burned at the stake for similar beliefs.

Martin Luther (1483–1546 A.D.)

The founder of the Protestant Reformation, the religious revolt by which the universal authority of the Church was destroyed, was Martin Luther.

The issue appeared to have been a simple one which the Pope could easily have resolved. Luther became a professor of theology at Wittenberg University, recently founded by the Elector of Saxony. Into the neighborhood came *Tetzel*, a Dominican friar granting indulgences in exchange for money to be used to complete St. Peter's in Rome. Indulgences properly used could serve a very sound purpose. If the sinner were genuinely sorry and performed some penitential act, such as contributing to a charity or going on a pilgrimmage, then other penances might be remitted or excused. Early indulgences had been issued to Crusaders who were excused from further penances. Unfortunately, lazy or corrupt churchmen abused indulgences by selling them as substitutes for penances.

Catholics like Luther did not at first deny the Pope's right to issue indulgences, but they did believe that if indulgences were wrongly used then people would believe that all penances were removed by the mere payment of money. Martin Luther wished simply to reform the abuse of indulgences because he could not reconcile the sale of indulgences with a statement in St. Paul's Epistle to the Romans, "The just shall live by faith." This, Luther believed, meant that only sincere faith could lead to salvation. Such a position threatened the authority of the Church, which taught that a priest was a necessary intermediary between man and God. Were Luther's point of view carried to its logical conclusion, then sincere faith would not need the services of the priest.

Luther's Protest

Luther invited public discussion by posting on the door of the Wittenberg Church his *Ninety-Five Theses* or propositions, in 1517. Luther was convinced that indulgences were harmful to good Catholics because people were putting their trust in an indulgence which by itself could do no good.

"An indulgence cannot remit guilt," he wrote, and found himself in direct conflict with the Pope. Luther had not intended to cast any doubt upon the authority of the Pope, but he had in fact done just that, since his arguments meant that he placed conscience and faith in the Bible above the infallibility of the Pope. If people believed that sincere faith was enough to achieve salvation, then they would no longer regard the intercession of the priest as necessary, or even recognize the Pope as head of the Church.

Origin of the Protestant (Lutheran) Church

Summoned to appear at Worms to explain his conduct, he refused the order to recant. Within a few days he was excommunicated from the Church and declared to be an outlaw. By this time he was busy on his translation of the Bible into German, so that the people could follow his arguments on the authority of the Bible. He denounced the wealth of the Church, urged that money contributed by the German people for religious purposes should remain in Germany, and organized a completely new church separate from Rome. Much of the Catholic doctrine remained, but the basic changes were the elimination of confession, and a radical difference in the communion service. The Catholic doctrine of *transubstantiation*, the miracle of the changing of the ceremonial wine and wafer into the blood and body of Christ, was changed to *consubstantiation* which holds that while the wine and wafer remain as such, they contain the real presence of Christ.

The early "protests" of Luther had now resulted in a separate church of his followers, the Protestant Church.

Unfortunately, the act of denying the authority of the Pope led to bloodshed, for some princely supporters of Luther took the opportunity to seize church lands and wealth for themselves. Support of Protestantism became in some instances an excuse for plunder. In Germany peasant leaders took the opportunity to demand better conditions, and attempted to overthrow serfdom. Uprisings against landlords threatened the religious revolt, and Luther felt obliged to advocate severe measures against the "thieving and murderous peasants."

The followers of Luther, known as Lutherans, organized local congregations, worshipped frequently in the same churches in which they had worshipped as Catholics, and translated the Bible into German and distributed thousands of copies to the people.

The Emperor was obliged to agree to the *Peace of Augsburg* in 1555 A.D. which provided that the ruler of each German state, and there were 300 of them, should decide whether his subjects should be Catholics or Lutherans. This was not religious toleration, since the people had no choice but to follow the religion their rulers dictated. However, Lutheranism was accepted by some German states as the official religion, and thus it became firmly established in parts of Germany.

In the Scandinavian countries of Norway, Sweden, and Denmark, Lutheranism became the official religion, and Roman Catholic church property was surrendered to the rulers. In Switzerland Zwingli broke with the Catholic Church and established Lutheranism.

Once a breach had been made, other religious groups developed, for if man could seek his own salvation then he could decide what form his religious worship should take.

Calvinism

Another famous Protestant leader was John Calvin (1509–1564 A.D.) who preached the doctrine of *predestination*, that God, who knows the past, the present, and the future, must always know which men will be saved and which shall be eternally damned. Calvin became the virtual dictator of the city of Geneva, which became a *theocracy*, a state ruled by a church, since only those whom Calvin regarded as the faithful could vote and hold office in Geneva. "There never was such a busybody in a position of high authority," wrote Preserved Smith.

Being a dictator, Calvin suffered no opinion but his own, with a consequence that during five years fifty-eight "heretics" were executed and over seventy were banished. Nevertheless, for both religious and political reasons Calvinism flourished and spread into England and into France, where Calvin's followers were known as Huguenots.

The present-day Presbyterian, Congregational, and other religious denominations contain the basic features of Calvinism laid down by Calvin in his *Institutes of Religion*: simple worship, Bible readings, a sermon, prayers, and hymns.

The Reformation in England

In England the Roman Catholic Church had long been criticized, and Englishmen demanded that the English church, retaining Catholic ritual, be controlled by the nation. Circumstances provided the opportunity for the break. Henry VIII (1509–1547 A.D.), who had received from the Pope the title of Defender of the Faith for denouncing Luther, now in turn denounced the Pope. Henry wanted an annulment of his marriage to Catherine of Aragon, whom he had married eighteen years earlier. He appealed to the Pope, but that dignitary, anxious not to offend Catherine's nephew Charles V, the Holy Roman Emperor and powerful king of Spain, hesitated to satisfy Henry, who decided to act himself. He persuaded an English court to grant the divorce, and Parliament to pass in 1534 the *Act of Supremacy* which declared the king to be the head of the official Church of England, which still accepted Catholic ritual. Later, it was to sever its connections with the Catholic doctrine and become a Protestant institution. Its practices were in time adopted by the Episcopal Church of the United States. It must be said that while many persons supported the English Reformation on religious grounds, others supported it because they were rewarded with some of the valuable church property seized by Henry VIII and judiciously shared with others.

The Catholic Reformation or Counter-Reformation

With much of northern Europe becoming Protestant, the Catholic Church set out to reform its own internal abuses and to wage an active fight on behalf of its basic faith. The Catholics refer to this as the Catholic Reformation; the Protestants call it the Counter-Reformation.

From Spain came the essential and necessary missionary spirit. *Ignatius Loyola* (1491–1556) a soldier, became a militant crusader for the Catholic Church and founded the Society of Jesus, a new monastic order which participated actively in the world. For two hundred years the Jesuits were the chief teachers of Catholic Europe, conducting hundreds of schools, acting as confessors to ruling families, and becoming involved actively in politics. They were the active missionaries of the Counter Reformation, prepared to intrigue and to use force whenever necessary.

The Holy Office, or Inquisition, was the chief agent of the Church for the repression of heresy. Holding secret trials, and turning condemned heretics over to the secular government to be burned, it maintained a brutal reign of terror and successfully stamped out all heresy in Italy and Spain. It had little success north of the Alps, and by the end of the sixteenth century both it and the Counter Reformation had spent their force. The religious map of Europe was clearly defined, and in each country, whether Catholic or Protestant, the church was closely identified with national interests.

Explorations and Discoveries

Terms

economics	joint stock company	Treaty of Tordesillas
mercantilism	monopoly	

People

Henry the Navigator	Cortez	Cartier
Diaz	Aztecs	Cabot
da Gama	Columbus	Pizzaro
Cabral	Incas	

Places to Locate

Cape Verde	Viceroyalties of:	New Amsterdam
Cape of Good Hope	Peru, New Spain	New France
Macao	Delaware	Jamestown

Significant Dates

	Explorer	Exploration	Sponsored by
1488	DIAZ, Bartholomew	AFRICA — sailed around the southern tip	Portugal
1492	COLUMBUS, Christopher	BAHAMA ISLANDS — named one San Salvador	Spain
1493	COLUMBUS	SANTO DOMINGO	Spain
1498	DA GAMA, Vasco	INDIA — around Cape of Good Hope, eastwards	Portugal
1497–1498	CABOT, John	MAINE to CHESAPEAKE BAY from Newfoundland	England

1499–1501	VESPUCCI, Amerigo	SOUTH AMERICA — sailed along greater of eastern coast	Portugal
1513	DE LEON, Ponce	FLORIDA — searched for fountain of youth	Spain
1513	BALBOA, Vasco de	PACIFIC OCEAN — saw it from the isthmus of Panama	Spain
1519–1521	CORTEZ, Hernando	AZTEC KINGDOM of Mexico — conquered it	Spain
1519–1522	MAGELLAN, Ferdinand	WORLD CIRCUM-NAVIGATION	Spain
1530–1536	PIZARRO, Francisco	INCA KINGDOM of Peru	Spain
1534	CARTIER, Jacques	ST. LAWRENCE RIVER to Montreal	France
1539–1542	DE SOTO, Hernando	GULF OF MEXICO — explored from Florida to Mississippi River	Spain
1608–1615	DE CHAMPLAIN, Samuel	GREAT LAKES to Lake Huron	France
1609–1611	HUDSON, Henry	HUDSON RIVER and BAY	Netherlands

Chapter Outline
The Commercial Age
Reasons for Explorations
Mercantilism: Theory and Practice
Colonial Empires: Portugal, Spain, France, England

Explorations and Discoveries

The economic history of modern times can be conveniently separated into two periods: that of the Commercial Age from 1500 to 1750 A.D., characterized by changes and developments in commerce; and the Industrial Age from 1750 to the present, typified by developments in industrial techniques and production.

The Commercial Age   Here we are concerned with the Commercial Age, which was itself characterized by three "revolutions," each contributing to and affecting it. The first is the *Political,* marking the breakdown of feudalism and the medieval church and the substitution of national states and national churches. The second is the *Intellectual* revolution as reflected in the Renaissance, the Reformation, and the development of science and rationalism. The third is the *Geographic* revolution which opened the world to unlimited expansion and in turn greatly affected the economic and social life of Europe.

During the sixteenth and seventeenth centuries European nations reaped the rewards of the age of exploration. Trading and colonization increased, and capitalism expanded until it encompassed all economic life. This period, which was little more than the extension of earlier developments but on a vaster scale, is usually referred to as the Commercial Revolution. Trade and commerce increased as new sources of raw materials and new markets opened. The growth of capitalism, the accumulation of funds to invest in large trading enterprises, brought a demand for money to keep up with growing business. Gold and silver poured into Europe from the New World, encouraged business and increased prices.

Reasons for Explorations

The causes of explorations, which resulted in the development of colonial empires, include:

1. The broadening influences of the Renaissance and some of the inventions and improvements of the Renaissance years.

2. Ship construction and sailing devices to explore far beyond the ability of man through his limited horizons. During the Renaissance period ships tripled in size, rigging was improved, the stern rudder replaced lateral steering devices, and the magnetic compass and the astrolabe for determining longitude and latitude helped to encourage voyages of discovery and the rise of maritime nations.

3. The rise of trade and towns which led in turn to the search for better trade routes to replace the overland routes controlled by the Moslems, and the Mediterranean trade monopolized by Venice.

4. The development of a middle class of entrepreneurs and merchants encouraged the development of central authority which could protect them abroad. (Spain, Portugal, England, and France were becoming increasingly politically important and economically active).

5. The activities of merchant adventurers helped the evolution of capitalism, and middle class interests and national strength combined to foster an economic theory called mercantilism, which in turn led to the acquisition of colonies.

Mercantilism: Theory and Practice

Economics, in simple terms, is the study of how people and nations make a living, whether by agriculture, trading, commerce, or other means. *Mercantilism* was the current economic belief in national self-sufficiency. Merchants looked to the state for protection, and the state in turn regulated many aspects of commerce and business for the public good. The doctrine of mercantilism had as its principles:

1. Tariffs should be levied to keep out foreign competition.

2. Wherever possible exports were to exceed imports in cash value so that the balance would bring in gold and silver.

3. The shipping trade should be kept in the hands of the nation's merchant marine.

4. Colonies were very valuable because they could serve the mother country as a

market for her finished products and as a cheap source of supply of raw materials.

If colonies could supply gold and silver, so much the better. Undoubtedly, capitalism contributed to national wealth, to the search for overseas trade routes and markets, and to the acquisition of colonial empires.

Joint Stock Companies

As voyages lengthened and trade increased, the former methods of financing by individual merchants became inadequate. In Spain and Portugal development remained in the hands of the government. But in many countries the need for capital was met by the establishment of joint-stock companies. Investors bought shares in various companies; these could be bought and sold in the open market, and the company paid dividends to shareholders who left their investments with the company for long-range operations. The joint-stock companies were forerunners of modern industrial corporations.

Monopolies

Since the nation was to benefit from trade, and because business was thought of as limited in total quantity, governments regulated it in order to bring in the greatest income. Monopolies were granted to companies which were privileged to operate exclusive enterprises. For example, England, Holland, and France each awarded to one of its companies the right to trade in the Far East. Such monopolies as the English East India Company excluded foreigners from that enterprise and its area of operations, removed domestic competition, and thus secured the best returns on investment by price maintenance.

Colonial Empires

Portugal led the way in her attempt to find new sea routes to the East. Its navigators were encouraged by *Prince Henry* (the Navigator) 1394–1460, who was anxious to promote Portuguese commerce and national power. They explored the west coast of Africa, doubled around Cape Verde in 1445; *Bartholomew Diaz* rounded the Cape of Good Hope in 1486, and in 1498 *Vasco da Gama* reached India and returned with one cargo of spice whose profits encouraged others to develop trade routes. These explorations were soon to break the Venetian monopoly of trade with the East.

Meanwhile *Christopher Columbus*, a Genoese citizen who had studied geography, was convinced that the East could be reached by sailing westwards. Rebuffed by Genoa and Venice, he was sponsored by Spain and commissioned Grand Admiral of the Ocean Sea, and returned with his discovery of the Bahamas and the Caribbean islands. The Catholic Church, anxious to further its religious beliefs, anticipated the shift of commercial gravity, and in 1494 issued the Treaty of Tordesillas which attempted to divide the New World between Spain and Portugal by a demarcation line running north and south 370 leagues east of the Cape Verde Islands. *Cabral*, blown off course for India, touched the easternmost point of South America and laid claims for Portugal to the land that was later Brazil.

By 1557 the Portuguese had established a trading post at Macao, another near Canton in China, and started trading with Japan. This was the beginning of a great Portuguese "trading" empire, but not a colonial settlement such as was being developed by Spain and England.

Spain

Through her "conquistadors" Spain established the first true colonial empire. Over vast areas of Mexico, Central and South America a Spanish culture was imposed. In 1519 Hernando *Cortez* found the ancient civilization of the Aztecs in Mexico and the gold he was looking for.

In 1532 *Pizarro* discovered the *Incas* of Peru, forced the Indians to work the gold and silver mines, and contributed to Spain's temporary wealth and political predominance. Spain, unlike France and England, did not invest her newly-found wealth in trade and commerce, and as a result the great influx of precious metals served to ruin the country through high prices caused by added supplies of money without a corresponding increase in national products. This inflation assisted those who acquired the new treasure, but ruined the people of Spain whose wages did not rise with the increased prices of goods.

The geography of Spain's overseas empire prevented the union of the two vast areas. Two Viceroyalties were set up, one called Peru, with Lima as its capital, the other called New Spain consisting of the mainland north of Panama, Venezuela, the West Indies, and the Philippines, with its capital at Mexico City. The great contributions of Spain were the introduction of grains, cattle, and horses into her empire. It was the horse which in time gave to the Plains Indians of North America their great mobility and their fighting capacity, and affected American westward expansion.

France

France adopted a deliberate imperial policy in New France or Canada, carefully screening her colonists, permitting no self-government, and expanding the potentially valuable fur trade, which was her major economic interest in her colonial empire. The St. Lawrence river and the Great Lakes gave her control of the heart of the continent, and her possession of New Orleans made possible the establishment of a line of forts northwards to join those from Canada. New France was essentially a "trading" empire, although it had many characteristics of a colonial settlement, particularly around Quebec and Montreal.

The voyage of *Jacques Cartier* into the mouth of the St. Lawrence river in 1536 started France on her control of Canada.

England

England, unlike the other powers, established a vast colonial empire of settlers and immigrants, to serve as suppliers of raw materials and buyers of England's goods.

English trading companies, encouraged by royal grants and charters, established trading posts at Jamestown and Plymouth. From these simple beginnings the large American colonial empire developed until by 1776 there were about 3,000,000 people in the 13 colonies. The Dutch in New Amsterdam and the Swedes in Delaware founded trading colonies that were absorbed by England in the seventeenth century.

Unlike the Spanish and French colonies which were bureaucratic and nonrepresentative, the English colonies were generally left alone to run their own affairs and developed local self-government. Interference by the British government with rights long enjoyed by the colonists led finally to the break with England and the establishment of the independent United States of America.

The voyage of *John Cabot* in 1497, in the service of England, gave that nation a foothold in the New World by discovering Newfoundland and Cape Breton.

Colonization of Latin America

Terms

Peninsular Spaniards	Creoles	Mestizos
Mulatto	Mameluco	Cafuso

People

Mayas	Incas	Aztecs
Montezuma	Hernando Cortez	Francisco Pizarro

Places to Locate

Rivers:	Tenochtitlan	British Guiana
La Plata	Cuzco	Jamaica
Amazon	Quito	Orinoco
Magdelena	Guiana	Haiti
Yucatan Peninsula	Dutch Guiana	

Topic Outline
Geography
Pre-Hispanic History to 1500 A.D.
Indian Civilizations: Maya, Aztec, Inca
Spanish Conquest and Administration
Brazil: Colony of Portugal

Colonization of Latin America

The history of the continent is clearly divided into:

1. Pre-Hispanic to 1500 A.D.
2. Conquest and Colonial, 1500–1800 A.D.
3. Wars of Independence, 1800–1825
4. National Period since 1825.

Geography

An important fact to remember is that Latin America was remote from Europe and its influences. For example, if one takes Chicago as a center, only one European capital, Athens, is farther away from Chicago than is Brasilia, the modern capital of Brazil.

The geography of Latin America has hindered and helped its progress. The deserts of northern Mexico, of southern Peru and north Chile have limited its development. The mountains have obstructed travel and communications. The Andes run north and south for 4000 miles, and are from 200 to 600 miles wide.

Latin America's rivers are her important avenues of trade. The La Plata system drains modern southern Brazil, Paraguay, northern Argentina, Uruguay. The Amazon River, the greatest in the world, drains Bolivia, eastern Peru, eastern Ecuador, southern Colombia, and northern Brazil. The Magdelena river connects the interior of Colombia with the Caribbean, and the Orinoco connects central and eastern Colombia and Venezuela.

Pre-Hispanic History to 1500 A.D.

Although some theories suggest that the American Indians came across land bridges to the western hemisphere, one significant fact would seem to contradict them. Their crops, Indian corn, beans, melons, squash were not known in the Old World; and the basic staples of the Old World, rice, barley, and wheat were not known to the American Indians before the Europeans arrived.

Three main types of Indians inhabited Latin America:

1. Food-collectors who were hunters and nomadic groups on the plains of Argentina.

2. Primitive agricultural tribes in the Amazon forest and other regions.

3. Those who on a basic crop of agriculture established the remarkable civilization of the Mayas in the Yucatan Peninsula, Guatemala, and Honduras.

Indian Civilizations

The Mayas

The most brilliant civilization of the New World in pre-Columbian times flourished between the fourth and the sixteenth centuries. The Mayas were superior to the Incas and Aztecs in architecture, sculpture, mathematics, hieroglyphic writing, and astronomy, but inferior in government and organization.

The Old Empire, from the fourth to the tenth century, consisted of several independent city-states in the southern part of the Yucatan peninsula, perhaps of some 25,000 people each, dependent upon a corn crop. In the tenth century the center of population moved to northern Yucatan, presumably because the soil became exhausted and ceased to produce enough food for the people, although earthquakes, epidemics, or climatic changes may have been partly responsible. On the dry plains of north Yucatan, the Mayas depended upon natural water holes and their corn crops. Naturally, a priesthood evolved, whose function it was to propitiate the gods to whom they erected vast pyramidic structures surmounted by temples.

The Mayas who by 500 B.C. were approaching the level of civilization of the Egyptians three thousand years earlier, had performed mathematical calculations that enabled them to build remarkable temples. Their study of mathematics and astronomy was of a high order, but it was fitted into their own peculiar religious system.

The Aztecs

The Aztec civilization was comparable in some respects to the highest civilization of Egypt and Mesopotamia. The Aztecs were the dominant people in the highlands of lower Mexico, just prior to the voyages of Columbus. In the fifteenth century they created a confederacy extending from the Gulf of Mexico to the Pacific, with their capital Tenochtitlan where Mexico City now stands, and by 1500 A.D. ruled over southern Mexico, an empire of several millions. Under their kings, the Montezumas, they organized their empire, with a priesthood that believed in human sacrifice in worship of their sungod Quetzalcoatl. Their dedication of a new temple to the god of war was celebrated with the massacre of 20,000 victims whose hearts were ripped out while they were still alive. It is understandable that subject peoples, who could well be the victims, were in revolt. In the early 1520's the Spaniards with their guns and horses easily overran a civilization which was little more than one hundred years old but already on the decline.

The Incas

High in the Andes mountains the small Spanish band under Pizzaro found a civilization that stretched for nearly 3000 miles from Ecuador to central Chile. Starting as a small tribe near Cuzco, which later became their great capital of 250,000 people, this huge empire of an estimated 6,000,000 people were unified and firmly governed, and with consideration for the citizens. A highly developed system of roads was built, one running north and south and others running across them. Neither Mayas, Aztecs, nor Incas had discovered the wheel, so the roads were for the use of couriers, (able to run 100 miles a day) who ran in relays to post houses along the way.

Religion, intimately related to agriculture, was far less brutal than that of the Aztecs, and some researchers doubt whether human sacrifice was permitted.

The weakness of the Inca empire was that its highly centralized government, organized on a rigid social caste system, could function effectively only from the top. When the Spanish army captured and killed the Inca leader Atahualpa, the civilization along the Andes simply broke up and disappeared.

Spanish Conquest and Administration

Between 1519 and 1522 Hernando *Cortez* destroyed the Aztec Confederacy by winning over to his side discontented subject-peoples of the Aztecs. He was received in Tenochtitlan, the Aztec capital, by *Montezuma* but realized that he could have walked into a trap, so outnumbered were his forces. Hearing that some of his garrison in Vera Cruz had been killed by Montezuma's officers, he persuaded that leader to come to the Spanish headquarters, kept him prisoner, burned alive in front of the royal palace the Aztec leaders responsible for the Vera Cruz massacre, and demanded treasure from the Aztec emperor. Two factors favored Cortez. Montezuma believed that Cortez was the avenging god Quetzalcoatl; Cortez believed that while Montezuma was alive the Aztecs would not imperil his life by attacking the Spaniards.

Later, while Cortez was away in Vera Cruz, his lieutenant *Alvarado* provoked the Aztecs into revolt, and it took Cortez a year to defeat them. Tenochtitlan now became the capital of New Spain of the Ocean Sea, and Vice-royalty of New Spain.

Alvarado set out in 1523 to conquer the Mayan civilization, founded the town of Santiago de Guatemala, and was superseded by the *Montejos* who finally subjugated the Mayans in 1545.

Meanwhile Francisco *Pizarro*, in the isthmus, heard of the Incas, raised an expedition in 1531 that finally succeeded in taking Cuzco the Inca capital, and a few years later the northern capital of Quito. But not until mid-century was the vast Inca kingdom conquered, and then renamed the Vice-royalty of Peru, with its capital at Lima.

The history of colonial Spanish America is that of these two viceroyalties which had sovereignty over Spanish America until 1717 when the southern part of New Spain became the Viceroyalty of New Granada, with jurisdiction over the region of modern Colombia, Ecuador, and Venezuela, and in 1776 when part of the Viceroyalty of Peru became the Viceroyalty of La Plata, with jurisdiction over modern Argentina, Paraguay, Bolivia, and Uruguay. Subsequent explorations went northwards into what are now Florida, Texas, and California.

The eastern part of the continent had been discovered by a Portuguese explorer in 1500 and, according to the papal Treaty of Tordesillas of 1494 which drew a demarcation line north and south dividing lands eligible for colonization, Brazil became Portuguese.

Minor possessions were claimed by France (Haiti, Guiana), the Netherlands (Dutch Guiana), and Britain (British Guiana and Jamaica).

Administration in the Colonial Period

In addition to the four viceroyalties there were less significant territories called Captaincies-General, for example, Cuba, Santo Domingo, Guatemala. Whatever the jurisdiction, whether viceroyalty, captaincy-general, or lesser division, the officials were all appointed from Madrid by the Crown. There was no self-government in the Spanish possessions, no experience in such types of government, and almost without exception the Spanish officials returned to Spain after their term of office was completed. A further factor in authoritarian government was the Roman Catholic Church. To her had been given earlier the task of driving the infidel Moors from Spain; she considered that one of her colonizing tasks was that of bringing Christianity to the natives wherever the Church should go. As in Spain, the Church in New Spain intended to Christianize completely, to stamp out all traces of heresy, that is, any belief not acceptable to and controlled by the Church. Even bishops were only temporary residents of the colonies. One of the striking features of the Church in New Spain was the founding of Missions, from California to southern Chile, teaching not only religion but the breeding of animals, the cultivation of crops, and the several skills and trades necessary in such communities.

Social and Economic Distinctions

Socially and economically the class distinctions were drawn very sharply, even between Peninsular Spaniards, born in Spain, and Creoles, Spaniards born in the colonies. At the top were the Peninsulars who monopolized the leading positions in State, Church, and Army, numbering about 300,000 by 1800 A.D. The next social group was that of the Creoles, who were landowners, merchants, doctors, lawyers, and men of other professions, numbering about 3,000,000. Under them were the *mestizos* of mixed European and Indian blood, some 5,000,000, and mostly farmers and craftsmen. At the bottom of the social scale were 7,500,000 pure-blooded Indians of whom the majority, although not legally subject to forced labor, were in fact not free.

The Spanish made distinct contributions to Latin American civilization, introducing the horse, such crops as wheat and oranges, and establishing two universities by 1550 in Mexico City and Lima.

Causes of Discontent

There were several sources of discontent, one in particular being the mercantile system which ran the colonies for the benefit of Spain. Colonists in general were forbidden to produce anything grown or made in Spain; Creoles resented their exclusion from office; and opposition was general against the highly centralized and repressive administrative policy of Spain.

**Brazil:
Colony of Portugal**

Portugal claimed Brazil in 1500 and did little with it until French interests and the increasingly large Spanish empire in the New World seemed to threaten Portuguese claims.

In 1549 the king of Portugal named Bahia as the capital of the colony and sent out 1,000 persons to settle and administer it. By 1580 Brazil had several sugar mills and a population of some 25,000 Portuguese and 14,000 imported Negro slaves and some 18,000 of "civilized" Indians.

Not until the eighteenth century were diamonds and gold discovered in Brazil, and by that time Portugal's hold upon her colony was firmly established.

Generally, Portuguese control was far less effective than was Spain's in her colonies, because distances between settlements were so great and because the huge colony was run by the owners of vast plantations (fazendas).

The "Brazilian" as a distinct individual did not exist originally. There were a few hundred thousand Indians, Europeans of several national origins, and a great number of Negroes. The mixtures of these races whether the mulatto of Negro and white, the mameluco of Indian and white, or cafuso of Negro and Indian were all Brazilians.

Negro slave importations began in the 1530's, and by the end of the colonial period the Negroes numbered more than a million, workers on sugar, cotton, tobacco and coffee plantations.

Independence came to Brazil without any of the liberation movements of the Spanish New World empire. Brazil became independent in 1822 when Dom Pedro, the royal regent of the colony, so proclaimed it when ordered back to Portugal. In 1829 he became Pedro I, King of Brazil.

Growth of National States and National Rivalries

Terms
Balance of Power
Spanish Armada
Electors

Treaty of Westphalia
Peace of Augsburg
Thirty Years' War

People
Charles V
Richelieu

Philip II
Gustavus Adolphus

Places to Locate
Empire of Charles V
Holland
Bohemia

Prussia
Switzerland

Significant Dates
1555   Peace of Augsburg
1588   Spanish Armada
1618   Beginning of Thirty Years' War
1648   Peace of Westphalia

Topic Outline
Policy of the Balance of Power
Contest for the Holy Roman Empire
The Thirty Years' War

Growth of National States and National Rivalries

**Policy of the
Balance of Power**

One of the significant areas of sixteenth century Europe is the vast empire of Charles V, Holy Roman Emperor, which included much of Europe and the vast acquisitions of Spain in the New World. As the champion of Catholicism, Charles waged war against heretic nations in what appeared to be simply wars of religion. However, broader issues were involved. Independent national states were developing and expanding; in so doing they developed rivalries which led to attempts to maintain a "balance of power" to prevent one nation from becoming so powerful that it could threaten to dominate over all others. Catholic France opposed the Catholic Holy Roman Empire over political rivalry and power.

The balance of power was to become a recurrent theme throughout history. The attempt of Charles V to dominate Europe in the sixteenth century was repeated by Napoleon in the nearly nineteenth century and by Germany twice in the twentieth century.

The rise of ambitious and powerful monarchs in Spain, France, and England led to rivalries in sixteenth century Europe.

**Contest for the
Holy Roman Empire**

In 1519 when Maximilian, Holy Roman Emperor, died, three candidates presented themselves for selection to the Seven Electors, or rulers of important states in Europe (Catholic: the Archbishops of Mainz, Cologne, Trier, and the King of Bohemia; Protestant: the Duke of Saxony, the Margrave of Bradenburg, and the Count Palatine). The three candidates were Charles I of Spain and the Netherlands, Francis I of France, Henry VIII of England. Francis entered the contest because he feared encirclement by the Hapsburgs, at the moment Charles I of Spain, who inherited from his grandparents Austria (from Maximilian), the Netherlands, and Burgundy.

England entered the contest in the hopes of keeping the balance of power in Europe.

With his election as Holy Roman Emperor, *Charles I of Spain* (now referred to as Charles V of the Empire) was the ruler of what appeared to be the first super-state. Charles' ambitions to consolidate his power were threatened by the struggle now going on within the 300 independent states of "Germany" between the supporters of Catholicism and Protestantism. Not until 1555, more than thirty years after his coronation, was Charles able to bring about the important Peace of Augsburg by which the religion of the Protestant states was recognized and the religion of the ruler was to determine the religion of his people. In 1556, exhausted with the burden of ruling so vast an empire, Charles abdicated and left to his brother Ferdinand the title of Emperor and the Hapsburg lands in Central Europe, to his son Philip the throne of Spain and its New World possessions, the Netherlands, and scattered lands elsewhere.

Philip II of Spain (1556–1598) was a sincere Catholic, dedicated to a past that was gone and anxious to unify the west and restore Catholicism. He became involved with the revolt of his Dutch possessions, attempted to invade England, and fought against France. The Dutch rebelled against his absolutism and Catholicism and in 1581 the seven northern provinces declared their independence (not officially recognized until 1648). Philip's attempts to replace the Protestant Elizabeth on the English throne provoked her into assistance to the Dutch, which in turn led Philip to send his famous Spanish Armada against England in 1588. Its defeat and final destruction by storm was the beginning of the decline of Spanish power, the decisive step in the independence of the Dutch, and the beginning of England's rise to a significant role in international affairs.

The Thirty Years' War (1618–1648)

Charles V had succeeded in 1556 in bringing about an end to the fighting between Catholics and Protestants. The terms of the Peace of Augsburg that obliged the people of a state to accept the religion of their ruler was not accepted wholeheartedly, and this uneasy peace was broken in 1618 when Bohemia, once a separate kingdom within the Holy Roman Empire, was declared to be a possession of Austria. Bohemia was the home of John Hus who had been martyred for his opposition to the Catholic Church and was divided between Protestants and Catholics. The Catholic Hapsburg monarch refused to permit Protestant worship by the Bohemians, who thereupon chose their own Protestant King. The net result was that it was defeated and remained a province of Austria until 1919 when it became part of the independent nation of Czechoslovakia.

Protestants everywhere were alarmed by this Catholic victory, feared for themselves, and sought assistance from Lutheran Scandinavia. However, other factors were contributing to the explosive situation:

1. Spain wanted to consolidate Spanish Hapsburg power by making a compact kingdom of the Dutch Republic, Spanish Netherlands, and land southwards. This meant that the Dutch Republic must be crushed.

2. Austrian Hapsburgs wanted to make the Holy Roman Empire into a united modern state.

3. France, now unified, became the rival of Hapsburgs.

4. Protestant Scandinavia supported the German Protestant states.

The first phase of the war was Swedish assistance under *King Gustavus Adolphus* to German Protestants, opposed by Austria and Spain. France, under her minister *Cardinal Richelieu*, a Catholic, helped German Protestants and Sweden, in order to weaken the Hapsburgs.

After bitter fighting in which the German states were raided and plundered by both sides, the *Peace of Westphalia* was agreed upon in 1648. This brought significant changes to Europe, whose boundaries were to remain almost unchanged until the French Revolution:

1. Switzerland was recognized as independent, as the Swiss Confederation.

2. Holland was recognized as the independent United Provinces.

3. Prussia became an increasingly powerful state.

4. Generally, religion ceased to be an issue in Europe; neither Protestantism nor Catholicism had become predominant by the war.

Growth of National States and National Rivalries
France and England

Terms

Nationalism	Curia Regis
Primogeniture	Common Law
Parlement	Magna Carta
War of the English Succession	Model Parliament
War of the Spanish Succession	Power of the Purse
Treaty of Utrecht	Politiques
Shire	Absolutism
Hundred	The Fronde
Witanagemot	Year Books
Defaute de droit	Moots
Babylonian Captivity	Tun
Huguenots	Hundred Years' War
Domesday Book	War of the Roses

People

Louis VI	Henry II
Louis XIV	Edward I
Brythons	Louis XI
William the Conqueror	Colbert
de Montfort	Canute
Louis IX	King John
Marlborough	The Tudor Monarchs
Alfred the Great	

Significant Dates

1066	Battle of Hastings
1137–1453	Hundred Years' War
1215	Magna Carta
1295	Model Parliament
1572	St. Bartholomew's Day Massacre

Topic Outline

France

Attributes of Nationalism
The Capetian Monarchs
The Hundred Years' War
Royal Authority Increases
New Monarchs of Europe
Louis XIV: Symbol of Absolutism
War of the Spanish Succession

England
Early Invasions
Henry II and "Common Law"
Magna Carta, The Charter of Liberties
The Model Parliament
Tudor Monarchs

France

Clear distinctions between "state" and "nation" as used at this time are necessary. A "state" is simply a political community that may be artificial, involuntary, a dictatorship. A "nation" is a group of people bound together by commonly-appreciated ties of history, language, customs. In feudal times the basic sentiment was localism, support for the local leader and protector. People who begin to feel bound together by common interests and a common government begin to call themselves a nation. The Greek states never became a nation because they could never rise above localism. The sense of "nation" comes to a people when a common heritage and common aspirations for the future take precedence over local interests.

Attributes of Nationalism

Nationalism develops slowly and only when certain conditions and factors are present. Since feudalism is the antithesis of nationalism, one primary and necessary factor is royal authority. The growth of a middle class of merchants and traders is hampered by petty feudal rivalries and the absence of central law. An ambitious middle class will support monarchy and in turn be supported because a middle class brings wealth to the royal treasury. A strong central government must be able to protect its merchants at home, on the high seas, and abroad. The danger of attack from outside can stimulate a feeling of patriotism, the support of one's own country. Improved communications, the stimulus of trade and education, the development of a national language and literature all assist the rise of nationalism.

The course of nationalism is not smooth, for royal power is gained at the expense of the power of nobles, central power at the expense of local towns and communities. Therefore the gradual rise of nationalism may mean internal conflict as rival groups and interests struggle for control.

Charlemagne's empire was temporarily successful because of the strength and ability of the ruler. Even before his death and the subsequent line of weak rulers, Charlemagne faced an external danger that threatened his authority — the invasions of the Norsemen from Scandinavia. Raids upon the northern coast of Europe and upon Britain commenced in the later years of the eighth century, and continued for more than a hundred years. Charlemagne's successors were too weak to resist, and, in order to spare Paris from attack, the Norsemen were encouraged to plunder Burgundy. In the early tenth century the Norsemen were given territory in northwest France, to be called Normandy after the invaders. Other waves of Norsemen swept eastwards into Russia and settled at Kiev and Novgorod, while still others invaded Britain and sailed into the Mediterranean.

Their depredations resulted in the breakdown of such central authority as existed, and led to the widespread development of feudalism.

The Capetian Monarchs

When the Capetians succeeded to the throne of France in 987 A.D., the royal possessions were modest in comparison with those of the Dukes of Normandy, Britanny, Aquitaine, Guienne, Champagne, and Gascony. Feudal obligations of these vassals to their king were little more than a gesture. The Capetian monarchs strengthened their possessions and power whenever the opportunity was favorable. They established *primogeniture*, the succession of estates to the eldest son, in place of election of a successor by the nobles. The earlier conquest of England by William of Normandy in 1066 resulted in a vassal of the French king becoming king of England. The Duchy of Normandy was handed on as a possession of English kings.

Louis VI (1108–1137) enhanced his authority by obliging the Duke of Aquitaine to render homage, and by marrying his son to Eleanor, daughter of the Duke. But when Eleanor's marriage was annulled and she married Henry II of England, the duchy of Aquitaine came under the control of England, just as other earlier marriages built up Henry II's possessions to include Britanny, Anjou, Touraine, and Maine.

Philip II of France (1180–1223) took back these and other possessions and incorporated some of them into his own royal domain. He instituted *seneschals* or *prevots* to supervise districts for revenue collection and local control, and placed above them a corps of bailiffs or inspectors to report back to the Crown. As business and trade flourished, the Crown used men from their new middle class as government officials, thus further undercutting the power of the feudal nobility.

Royal Authority Increases

Louis IX (1226–1270) further strengthened royal authority by establishing new departments of state. The *Curia Regis* or King's Council, of advisors from the nobility was given the duty of supervising finances (the *chambre de comptes*) and of recording and distributing copies of laws (the *parlement*) a purely judicial body which did not have the legislative functions of the English Parliament. He extended his control over towns, where the lesser tradesmen and merchants resented the oligarchy of the wealthier merchants, and insisted upon the annual rendering of accounts. He prohibited private warfare and insisted upon the use of royal money throughout France. Differences of opinion in feudal courts were referred to the parlement or to the royal courts, sometimes even to the king personally. So respected were his decisions that foreigners sought his arbitration.

Successors extended these techniques of royal authority, increased it in the courts by encouraging *defaute de droit*, the right of a man to appeal to a higher court; the duties of the *Curia Regis* were extended to those of a specialized court by sending out to all parts of the country travelling judges who substituted royal justice for local justice. A further extension of authority was the use of the Estates General in 1302 as a larger group of advisors to include with nobles and clergy the Third Estate, representatives of towns.

Philip IV (1285–1314) clashed with the Pope over two issues: the right to tax the clergy without papal consent, and the right to decide whether a clergyman charged with treason should be tried by the royal or the Church court.

On the first issue the Pope backed down, but on the second the king agreed to let the case go to Rome. Unwisely the Pope admonished Philip publicly in a Papal Bull, or *bulla* or decree, entitled, "Listen, Son." Philip answered in similar vein, and in due course obtained the election of French popes, who lived in Avignon instead of Rome, in the so-called Babylonian Captivity from 1305 to 1378, puppets of the French monarch.

The Hundred Years' War (1337–1453)

Unfortunately for France she became involved in a struggle known as the Hundred Years' War in which fighting occurred sporadically for a century. The English king claimed both French territory and the French crown. French nobles fought on whichever side served their interests, and the countryside was plundered by rival bands of soldiers. During this time the Black Plague swept across Europe with devastating effect. Finally France was united under the strong leadership of *Joan of Arc* who drove the English from Orleans, was instrumental in getting Charles VII crowned as King of France, and inspired the French with such patriotism that they were victorious over the English. By 1483 France was one of the most powerful states in Europe, where other national states were now developing.

The New Monarchs

The middle of the fifteenth century saw the beginning of a group of kings called the New Monarchs, who laid the foundation of new national states by restricting the power of the nobles and by enforcing law and order.

They generally won the support of the middle classes who were tired of marauding nobles and their private wars; they were even prepared to support hereditary monarchs against parliaments too frequently dominated by nobles.

The New Monarchy came into France with *Louis XI* (1461–1483) who continued to expand royal authority, to suppress nobles, levy taxes. By 1500 the New Monarchs were getting control over the clergy.

Other French kings carried on the tradition until the middle of the sixteenth century when Henry II left his kingdom to three sons, the oldest of whom was fifteen. His widow, Catherine de Medici, for 30 years attempted to govern for her sons. France fell apart as rival groups contested for power, and the country suffered a series of civil wars.

The Huguenots or French Protestants were one group contending for power, and in 1572 Catherine ordered, on St. Bartholomew's Day, the massacre of all Huguenots, who had gathered in Paris to celebrate the marriage of Henry of Navarre, one of their leaders; thousands were massacred. In revenge the Huguenots renewed civil war against Catholic leaders until reaction set in. The *politiques* or politicians were men who decided that continued civil war was damaging the country, and that law and order was necessary. A leading *politique* was Jean Bodin who developed the modern theory of sovereignty, that there must be one authority strong enough to enforce the law, and if possible to do so without the consent of the people.

Thus there developed the belief in a strong monarch, perhaps in an absolute monarch.

Louis XIV: Symbol of Absolutism

One distinguishing feature of the early years of *Louis XIV* (1643–1715) was the *Fronde* uprising (1648–1653), a revolt of nobles against royal authority, and briefly by the middle class against the heavy taxations of the long war against the Hapsburgs. The successful suppression of these protests and the refusal of the kings of France to consider other than their own views were to lead to the French Revolution. Without a safety valve, the increasing antagonism to autocratic rule had no choice but violence.

The very nature of political conditions during Louis' reign contributed to complete royal autocracy. There were no restrictions upon royal authority such as Magna Carta, there were no courts of law to guarantee the rights of the people, the king was above the law, and, in fact, the expression "I am the State" describes Louis' position accurately.

Under his financial minister *Colbert*, mercantilism was encouraged at home and in the French empire, taxes were systematically collected, Canada was developed, and Louisiana was settled with Frenchmen.

One technique of royal control of the nobility and their subjection to authority was the use of the palace at Versailles. A magnificent palace, it also served as the center of royal activities. All positions, patronage, and offices were handed out by Louis to those who attended him at Versailles. Close supervision by Louis virtually eliminated intrigue and revolt; a man could not afford to stay away if he wanted advancement.

Four wars occupied the major efforts of France in attempts to extend her boundaries and gain further influence in Europe. The first, the so-called War of Devolution (1667–68) was simply a device to gain rights of inheritance which had been given up by Louis XIV's wife, daughter of the Spanish king. The next was an attempt to suppress the Dutch who were Protestant and offered haven for Louis' opponents. A balance of power coalition prevented the defeat of the Dutch, but Louis did acquire Franche-Comte, the country of Burgundy, from Spain, together with some towns in the Spanish Netherlands.

The third war, the League of Augsburg or War of the English Succession (1689–1697) was essentially against William of Holland who had been offered and had accepted the English throne, and as such became the leader in opposition to Louis' expansionist policy. By the Peace of Ryswick in 1697 the *status quo ante bellum*, or condition that existed before the war, was maintained.

War of the Spanish Succession (1702–1713)

This serious war, which became world-wide in eighteenth-century terms, started France and England on a long struggle which ended only at Waterloo in 1815.

The cause of the war was Louis' violation of an agreement with European leaders that upon the death of his brother-in-law Charles II of Spain the Spanish inheritance would be divided between Hapsburgs and Bourbons. But Charles left a will giving his possessions to Louis' grandson Philip, and Louis backed him up. This threat to the balance of power brought about the Grand Alliance of England, Holland, the Empire, and several German states. The French were beaten in Europe in four great battles by the allied leaders Marlborough and Prince Eugene — Blenheim, Ramillies, Oudenarde, Malplaquet. Wishing to maintain a balance of power on the continent by "containing" France, but not so weakening her that another European power could dominate, England arranged a typical balance of power treaty, the *Peace of Utrecht*, 1713, by which:

1. Philip V was confirmed as King of Spain with its overseas possessions.

2. Austria, which had hoped to gain the Spanish succession, received the Spanish Netherlands (Belgium).

3. The Duke of Savoy received the island of Sardinia and founded the line that later was to unite Italy in 1870 under the crown of Savoy.

4. England received Newfoundland, Nova Scotia (Acadia of Longfellow's poem), the Hudson's Bay territories, and Gibraltar.

5. The Elector of Bradenburg was recognized as King of Prussia.

This peace was no more than a truce, for France and England were close rivals in North America and India, and the Austrian Hapsburg Charles VI still wanted to be King of Spain.

The *Treaty of Utrecht* is significant because it left European power generally balanced, and because it replaced long-term French-Spanish rivalry with a strong family alliance of the two thrones; two ruling families were to consolidate Italy and Germany into two nations in the latter nineteenth century. From now on Great Britain acted as a balance wheel in European politics, throwing its weight against any nation which threatened to become too powerful on the continent.

England

Early Invasions

Early invaders of Britain were the Brythons who gave the country its name, coming from across the Channel at least one hundred years before the birth of Christ. They traded with the Phoenicians and Greeks, were under the religious direction of Druid priests, with temples of stone circles, most important of which was Stonehenge. In 54 B.C. Caesar, victorious in Gaul, decided to punish the people who had sent help to the Gauls. Defeating the inhabitants near the Thames river, he imposed a nominal tribute and returned to Rome for political advancement. Nearly a century later Claudius launched a new campaign, then left his officers to finish the task of occupation. A revolt in 60 A.D. resulted in the loss of three towns to the Britons who slaughtered the garrisons, but were eventually defeated. For four centuries Rome ruled most of the island, building roads and the famous Hadrian's Wall to keep out the Picts and Scots to the north. As Rome's power weakened, her legions and her frontiers were gradually contracted, and the last legion left Britain in 407 A.D.

Saxon invaders pushed the Britons into the wilds of Cornwall and Wales and destroyed almost all traces of Roman occupation. In time the Anglo-Saxons established several kingdoms, were Christianized by missionaries from Ireland and Rome, and were in turn attacked by other invaders, the Danes. Under Alfred the Great (871–900) the Saxons limited the Danes to the northern half of the island, with the Saxon monarchy ruling the south. But by the early years of the eleventh century the Danish King Canute was ruling both Denmark and Britain.

Internal intrigue encouraged *William of Normandy,* first cousin to the English king *Edward the Confessor,* to invade and successfully win the Battle of Hastings, 1066. Loyal Norman followers replaced Anglo-Saxon landowners, and became direct vassals of William. To maintain his authority and evaluate his possessions, William ordered a census and a stock-taking, the *Domesday Book,* which facilitated the collection of taxes due.

Henry II and "Common Law"

One hundred years later Henry II (1154–1189) proved himself a far more capable administrator than his European contemporaries by establishing a national monarchy in England. Since feudal and Church judicial courts could undermine his authority, he determined to bring all judicial affairs under his jurisdiction. He subdivided the old Curia Regis, the feudal council of nobles, into three courts: The Exchequer to deal with the collection of taxes and financial matters; the Court of King's Bench to handle all criminal cases; the Court of Common Pleas to handle all other cases. Itinerant judges from these courts traveled around the country making the law uniform through their decisions. The Assize of Clarendon of 1166 which instituted these changes also introduced in elementary form the jury system. Henry II's judicial reforms constitute the basis for British and American legal systems and for their *common law*. Unlike Roman law, it is not codified, or explicitly written down. Decisions of royal justices were collected in Year Books as the basis or precedents for future decisions on similar issues, and thus became "common" to all parts of England, based not upon statutes but upon custom.

Had Henry's successors extended his royal authority, England might have been ruled by an absolute monarch, responsible to no one. But increasing government expenses, the cost of participating in the Crusades, and royal quarrels with Popes gave the feudal nobles opportunities to exact certain rights from the Crown. A simple form of representative government had existed in Anglo-Saxon times, an ancestor of the later parliamentary system. *Moots* or assemblies of elected officials, dealt with affairs of the *tun* or township, the *hundred* or unit of several townships, and the *shire* or county, and were called tunmoots, hundredmoots, and shiremoots, all capped by the *Witanagemot*, a council of "wise" men including representatives from the shires.

Magna Carta, The Charter of Liberties (1215)

In the early thirteenth century King John antagonized his feudal barons by exacting unlawful taxes, demanding more than the usual feudal services, and precipitating a civil war which John lost. In June, 1215 A.D. at *Runnymede* the barons forced the king to sign a feudal contract, the *Magna Carta* or Great Charter which laid down the vital principles that taxes must be levied according to custom, that no man may be deprived of life or property except by the law of the land, that justice must be fair, not "sold, denied, or delayed." These applied *only* to clergy and nobles, and they did *not* institute trial by jury, taxation with representation, or representative government.

The significance of the document is in two basic principles:

1. That the law is above the King.

2. That force may be used against the king if he breaks the law.

These are the basis of the seventeenth century struggle between Crown and Parliament, and they are a basic characteristic of the American Declaration of Independence and the United States Constitution, the "right to revolt" in the Declaration, the safeguards for the individual in the Bill of Rights.

Associated with the early development of parliament are *Simon de Montfort* and *Edward I.* De Montfort, successfully leading a revolt against an English king in 1264, found himself in need of support and so called two successive parliaments which contained, first, representatives from the small landowners, then added two representatives from each borough or burgh. The year 1295 is usually accepted as the beginning of Parliament, since de Montfort's was "illegal," not being called by a legitimate ruler.

The Model Parliament (1295)

In that year Edward I summoned the *Model Parliament* which contained the commoners or commons as well as lords, and the writs summoning members contained "what concerns all should be approved by all." Although probably only a very small proportion of the population was involved, the important fact is the principle of "approved by all" involved in paying taxes. In 1297, in need of more funds, Edward I agreed that the new taxes could not be levied without the consent of parliament. This assured the periodic summoning of parliament, which realized that since it was the main source of financial supplies it had the "power of the purse," that is, the power to demand that certain laws be passed or grievances remedied in return for taxes. This same power of the purse was the basic cause of the American Revolution; either the colonists controlled both how taxes were raised and also how they were spent, or else the British did.

During the Hundred Years' War (1337–1453) when England tried to retain possessions in France the English kings became increasingly dependent upon parliament for money supplies. During that long struggle the barons began to assert their power, and at the conclusion of the war rivalry between them broke out in an exhausting civil war called the *War of the Roses*, between the baronial families of Lancaster and York. After 30 years of fighting, Henry Tudor, a Lancastrian, married a Yorkist, resolved the struggle, and started the House of Tudor as Henry VII, in 1485.

Tudor Monarchs

Henry VII (1485–1509) put an end to private armies, and organized a new system of law courts, headed by *Star Chamber*, which dealt severely with recalcitrant nobles. Although later resented as an arbitrary court, Star Chamber served its purpose in helping to consolidate the monarchy in the interests of the middle class.

Henry VIII (1509–1547) was important for the course the Reformation took during his regime.

Elizabeth I (1558–1603)

Henry VIII was succeeded by his ten-year old son Edward VI under whom Protestantism made progress, only to be set back under Mary, daughter of Henry VIII and a staunch Catholic who married King Philip of Spain, a defender of the Catholic church. Protestants were persecuted during her short reign. Henry's daughter Elizabeth was technically illegitimate in the eyes of Catholics, who refused to recognize Henry's divorce or the second marriage to Anne Boleyn, who was Elizabeth's mother. Elizabeth therefore supported the Protestant cause, and England now became officially a Protestant country, with English Protestant services.

Growth of National States and National Rivalries – Russia and Prussia

Terms
Diplomatic Revolution
Treaty of Tilsit
Window on the Baltic

People

Ivan the Terrible	Catherine the Great	Maria Theresa
Peter the Great	Frederick the Great	

Places to Locate

Rivers	Seas	Ural Mountains
Dneiper	Caspian	Riga
Volga	Black	Kiev
Ob	White	Moscow
Yenisei	Azov	St. Petersburg
Lena	Baltic	Prussia
Amur		Poland

Topic Outline

Russia
Geography of Russia
Recurrent Themes of Russian History
Contributions of Russian Rulers: Ivan, Peter, Catherine
Russia Opposes, Then Joins Napoleon

Prussia
Frederick the Great Extends Prussia
Austrian Succession and the Seven Years' War

Russia

Geography of Russia
The geography of Russia has greatly affected its political history. With no natural frontiers to the west it has suffered numerous invasions and has attempted to defend itself by expanding westwards. Because its rivers are either landlocked or flow into the frozen Arctic Ocean it has attempted to secure warm-water port: and outlets into the Mediterranean Sea. Much of its past history shows clearly that in some respects Soviet Russia is continuing former Czarist traditions of autocratic government and expansionist foreign policy.

Russia covers nearly one sixth of the earth, and its vast Eurasian plain stretches from its western frontier to half way across the continent. Although the Ural Mountains divide the plain north and south they have not been a barrier to conquest or trade. Historically, whoever has controlled this plain has attempted to control all of it, and Russian history demonstrates the continuous struggle for political supremacy in Eurasia.

The important rivers have been centers of population and a means of communication in European Russia. Here they flow north to south, the Dneiper into the Black Sea, the Volga into the Caspian Sea, with a complex of canals forming a continuous water route between the Caspian, Black, White, Baltic, and Azov Seas. Three long rivers, the Ob, Yenisei, and the Lena, flow northwards to the Arctic, while the Amur flows west to east and forms the Russia-Manchuria boundary.

The only good harbor Russia controlled before 1940 was Riga, and that only intermittently. But since this is on the Baltic Sea, the outlets to the North Sea were dominated by the Scandinavian countries. These geographical conditions explain why Russia's attempted expansion has been by land.

Recurrent Themes of Russian History

To understand Russian history one must appreciate that two basic themes recur through the centuries:

1. The necessity of a strong central government.
2. Expansion by conquest.

The original inhabitants probably came from the west and from the east into the plains, with early settlements along the westernmost river, the Dneiper, along which trade moved from the Baltic to the Black Sea.

In the ninth century Scandinavian warriors and traders, called Varingians or Rus (from which Russia was probably derived), moved down from the north and controlled the Dneiper, making Kiev their capital. For four centuries this principality of Kiev, loosely organized, traded with Byzantium, adopted much of the culture of the eastern Mediterranean world and the Christianity of the Greek Orthodox Church. During the twelfth century the center moved from Kiev after the city was stormed, but in the thirteenth century a Mongol, under a descendant of Genghis Khan, conquered all Russian cities with the exception of Novgorod to the north near the Baltic. Mongol conquest meant isolation from the West and the great advances of the Renaissance. The result was an acceleration of fragmentation of Russia into local units, so that whatever nationalistic sentiment had existed was now shattered.

Kiev was on the steppes of Russia and open to invasion. Resistance to the Mongols must come from a less accessible quarter. Moscow, in the forest area to the north and on the Volga river system, became that center, and since its prince became the chief tax collector for the Mongol ruler it gradually came to dominate the entire north. In 1480 the prince of Moscow refused to pay the annual tribute, defied a Mongol army, and inaugurated the rise of Moscow as the capital of a powerful Russian state.

Contributions of Russian Rulers

Ivan the Terrible   (1533–1584) was the outstanding ruler of this period, established the absolute autocracy that continued to the present, and instituted the system of serfdom. Everyone now served the state according to Ivan's dictates; the nobles became the officials, and the peasants provided food, taxes, and military service. Ivan expanded his Moscow kingdom eastwards by driving the Mongols out of the two regions of Astrakhan and Kazan, almost doubling his territory.

A later Russian drove the Mongols from Siberia and thus opened the way to the Pacific.

Internal troubles, famine, and discontent led to such exhaustion that the contesting princes put on the throne in 1613 the Romanov family which was to rule Russia until 1917, when Nicholas II was forced to abdicate. The Czar and his family were assassinated by the Bolsheviks in July 1918.

Peter the Great (1682–1725) was the first effective Romanov. He made the monarchy absolute, made the Orthodox Church a department of the government, and broke the power of the nobles by making service and loyalty, not birth, the basis for advancement and office.

Ambitious for Russia, he travelled widely in Europe and attempted to Europeanize Russia by introducing the fashions and customs of Paris and Vienna, modernizing army and navy, and initiating more efficient government by centralizing the bureaucracy and dividing the empire into eight divisions or "governments." But he failed to encourage an independent middle class which could have taken Russia well along the road to economic development. He did "modernize" Russia in one respect. For nearly 20 years he fought the Great Northern War with Charles XII of Sweden and succeeded in securing his "window on the Baltic" by acquiring the Baltic provinces and Riga on the Gulf of Finland. Here he built his new capital, St. Petersburg, facing the west.

During the eighteenth century the throne became the center of a struggle for power, so that during this time the nobility was able to establish itself as a privileged group living upon the serfs who were now the property of their masters.

Catherine the Great (1762–1796) was without legitimate title to the throne but won over the nobility by exempting them from taxation and military service. Her foreign policy was predatory, expansionist, and politically unsound. By this time Poland was no longer the power it had once been. Enfeebled by political anarchy, and open to attack from all sides because it was a plain without defensive frontiers, it presented its neighbors with the opportunity to dismember it. In three grabs between 1772 and 1795 Russia, Austria, and Prussia dismembered it completely. While Russia added some 180,000 square miles to its own territory, it also brought 6,000,000 discontented Poles into the Russian empire, and at the same time obliterated the buffer state between Prussia and Russia. Land had been acquired at the expense of political safety.

Russia Opposes, Then Joins Napoleon

In 1798 Great Britain persuaded Russia to join in a coalition against France. Bonaparte's successes, particularly the defeat of Austria at Hohenlinden in 1800, persuaded Russia to withdraw temporarily until 1803, when she joined the Third Coalition against France. Later successes of Napoleon, at Jena and Auerstadt, persuaded the Czar *Alexander I* to come over to his side, by the *Treaty of Tilsit*, 1807. Alexander had cause to regret the friendship. Russia suffered from the French Continental System which attempted to cut off all trade with Britain. The Poles were encouraged to think they might win their freedom, and Russia feared French influence in Scandinavia where *Bernadotte*, a marshal of Napoleon, had been made king.

Napoleon decided to punish Russia for breaking away from the Continental System, and in 1812 marched eastwards, defeated the Russians at Borodino in 1812, moved on to Moscow to receive the Russian capitulation which never came, and then in the face of a bitter winter began a retreat which became the rout of an army which was brutally decimated by lack of food, bitter cold, and Cossack raids.

Russian officers served in the subsequent armies of occupation in France, where they learned something of the ideals of the French Revolution and brought them back to Russia in the hopes of liberalizing the government.

Prussia

Frederick the Great Extends Prussia

One of the results of the Thirty Years' War (1618–1648) was the rise of the German state of Prussia. Although the several German states had been disastrously ravaged by war, the territory of the ruler of Brandenburg, one of the Seven Electors of the Holy Roman Empire, whose possessions were enlarged by the war, became the nucleus of nationalism. Another factor was that the Duke of East Prussia, *Frederick William* (1640–1688) centralized his possessions and built up his military forces. With Brandenburg-Prussia now the strongest of the German states, the Great Elector's son Frederick called himself King of Prussia. It was the great grandson, *Frederick II,* also called the Great (1740–1786), who raised Prussia to the rank of a first-rate power, and played a significant role in European politics.

In 1740 the Hapsburg emperor *Charles VI* died without a male heir but had arranged that his daughter *Maria Theresa* should succeed him. Frederick the Great wanted Silesia and deciding accurately that some other power might want to take it, took it himself. Spain, France, and some German states joined Prussia against Austria. Great Britain, already at war with Spain, supported Maria Theresa who emerged from this so-called War of the Austrian Succession (Treaty of Aix-la-Chapelle, 1748) with her empire intact, except for Silesia.

Austrian Succession and the Seven Years' War

The success of Frederick the Great was also the cause of some concern for Austria and France, who saw the threat of a too powerful Prussia. As a consequence, these two old enemies effected a "diplomatic revolution" by joining forces. Already Britain and France were at war in Virginia by 1754, and Britain was concerned about possible attack upon Hanover, the original home of the Hanoverian kings now ruling in England. When Frederick offered to protect Hanover in return for a treaty of mutual defense, the diplomatic revolution was doubly one.

With Britain busy in the New World with the Seven Years' War (French-Indian War, 1756–1763), Frederick survived years of war, won permanent title to Silesia, and persuaded German princes to form a league against Hapsburg aggression. So began, unknowingly, the basis of a greater Germany that was to be established in the later nineteenth century.

China (618 A.D.–1912) and India (320 A.D.–1848)

Terms
Guild
Mongol Dynasty, 1279–1368
Manchu Dynasty, 1644–1912
Indian Mutiny
T'ang Dynasty, 618–907
Ming Dynasty, 1368–1644

Mogul Empire, 1526–1761
India Act, 1858
Nepotism
Gupta Empire
Taj Mahal

People
Kublai Khan
Marco Polo
Tamerlane

Places to Locate
Hindustan
Bengal

Topic Outline
T'ang Dynasty (618–907)
The Mongol Dynasty (1279–1368)
The Ming Dynasty (1368–1644)
The Manchu Dynasty (1644–1912)
Basic Chinese Institutions
Government in China: National and Local
The Gupta Empire
The Mogul Empire
European Influence
India Act of 1858
Life in India

China (618 A.D.–1912)

**T'ang Dynasty
(618–907)**

The *T'ang Dynasty* (618–907), represents the Golden Age of medieval China. The Empire was run by a bureaucracy of civil servants, was divided into provinces, and, so far as was practicable, the land was divided between many people rather than left in the hands of a few, in order to develop agriculture, which was the chief source of revenue. Taxes were levied in grain, a form of taxation whose later abuse by Chiang Kai-shek in the 1940's was to be one cause of his loss of power to the Communists.

Economic prosperity during the period was in large part due to land and tax reforms, to more efficient transportation, and to a thriving foreign commerce. During this dynasty scholarship advanced, encyclopedias were written, groups of scholars were hired to write accounts of preceding eras, and to write treaties on law, economics, and administration. The first printed books were made by blocks; movable type, paper money, and playing cards were invented. After a revolt in 755 the dynasty was increasingly weakened as provincial governors became more powerful, until it ended soon after 900 A.D.

**The Yuan
or Mongol Dynasty
(1279–1368)**

The great ruler *Kublai Khan*, a descendant of Genghis Khan, held as suzerain the Khanates of China and Mongolia, with his capital at Peking. He improved imperial roads, constructed canals, organized a famous postal system with stations every 25 to 30 miles, and built granaries to store surplus grains for the lean years.

Marco Polo, the Venetian, travelled widely in the Far East, and served Kublai Khan for 17 years between 1275 and 1292. He left a vivid account of Peking with its 12,000 stone bridges, its use of coal for heating purposes, its prosperous commerce in silks, rice, pepper, and sugar with Central Asia. But the prosperity was rather illusory because peasants were tenant-farmers working for landlords, taxpayers were diminishing in number, and paper money was replacing hard currency and depreciating in value.

Gradually the Mongol supremacy declined from its peak, when it stretched from the Danube to the Pacific. Its contribution was a valuable exchange of goods and ideas.

In retrospect the three centuries of the T'ang Dynasty (618–907) were those in which China attained prosperity and power. The disunity which followed was not so serious because the ideas of unity and a centralized state were becoming established. The re-unification of China after the collapse of the T'ang Dynasty was the work of foreigners, the Mongols, who provided a landmark in Chinese history. Unfortunately, the Chinese felt humiliated by the Mongol conquest, and this domination by outsiders left a legacy of hatred of foreigners. When the Mongols finally were driven out of China, the Chinese tended to overemphasize their past ways and values.

**The Ming Dynasty
(1368–1644)**

This dynasty brought good government and prosperity, and extended its authority to Annam and Upper Burma. During this period great maritime expeditions were encouraged; Chinese ships and traders visited the East Indies, the Indo-China peninsula, India, Persia, Arabia, and Africa. Unfortunately, such expeditions were discouraged by the authorities, and the ancient prohibition against overseas travel was re-enforced. As a consequence, throughout the greater part of the Ming Dynasty China faced backwards, and slumped to mediocrity.

**The Manchu Dynasty
(1644–1912)**

The Manchus were foreigners who had established a state of their own in eastern Manchuria. In 1644 the last of the "barbarian" conquests of China began when the Manchus established the dynasty which lasted for 250 years. Like other foreigners they had little effect upon Chinese institutions, and China remained closed to other influences until the middle of the nineteenth century when European nations "opened" China to foreign ideas and institutions. Since the basic Chinese institutions lasted for nearly 2000 years, we should examine them.

**Basic Chinese
Institutions**

We have seen that Confucianism was a set of rules of proper conduct between people. Unlike Hinduism in India, which attempted to find salvation, Confucianism was concerned with good government and harmony among men. These concepts had great influence upon China.

Buddhism was introduced into China from India about the beginning of the Christian Era, and became a religion based upon spiritual ideas, in contrast to Confucianism which was concerned with life on earth. Buddhism became popular for several centuries because its ritual appealed to the great masses of people.

**Government in China:
National and Local**

In China the educated class was the ruling class, and good government was based upon the teachings of Confucius. It is important to understand that China was a country of thousands of peasant villages, of little towns, with little communication between towns. The country was neither industrialized nor centralized, and government was therefore largely local in areas which were self-sufficient. China was a country which could not be greatly injured by the loss of a few towns or even a province. Although it was organized as a modern nation, it did not think as a nation; its people could not have a common purpose or even think in terms of common defense against an enemy.

Government was organized from the emperor downwards through a system of officials, but each locality saw only the local official who was charged with administering law and order and collecting taxes. The important functions of the locality were handled by the guild and the family.

The *Guild* was the local organization for protecting the interests of the village or locality and acted as the liaison between the government officials and the community. Each occupation in the community had its own guild — tailors, shoemakers, even beggars. Prices were regulated so that no artisan could undersell the others, otherwise, "rice-bowls" would be empty, people would starve and be dependent upon the community for help. In villages the clan performed the same functions.

When the district magistrate or local official wished to put measures into operation he had to seek the approval of the guild association. Resistance by the guild could bring reprimand from higher officials who would blame the local magistrate for incompetence.

The guilds fixed prices, wages, standards of work, credit facilities, and in general supervised the economic, political, and judicial operations of the locality.

Importance of the Family.   The family played a role in Chinese history that is found nowhere else. The family or the clan performed in the village the same functions as the guild in the town. Not only was the property of the family held in common, but the family decided the life, even the occupation and marriage of each member of the group.

Collective responsibility and collective obligation were practices for the welfare of each and all. Any member of the family could call upon the group to assist him, and in turn he was expected to contribute to the family and to care for the old people. In a simple sense the family guaranteed social security to all. A corollary of this was ancestor worship, or obedience and respect to elders, the spiritual force which bound the family together. This ancestor worship contributed, as did Confucianism, to two of the weaknesses of China. There was greater concern for the past and its rigid traditions than for the future.

The other was the tradition of *provincialism or loyalty to a local community* only. The Chinese did not develop the same sense of nationality as did western nations, and this provincialism made China an easier target for attack. Furthermore, nepotism, or the giving of jobs to members of the family, was common in China, and government offices and business positions were subject to family ties and favoritism, with resultant inefficient, sometimes corrupt, government. In the long run this contributed to the collapse of China.

India (320 A.D.–1848)

We have seen that the ancient period of civilization began about 3000 B.C. and that Aryan invaders started to come in about 2500 B.C. and were the masters of northern India by 1500 B.C. During the Classical Period, 1500 B.C. to 500 A.D., the Aryan-Dravidian elements developed a civilization in which Hinduism established its religious and social system. Temporary invasions occurred at various times, such as that of Darius I which penetrated to the Indus plain and made western Punjab a province of the Persian empire. Two centuries later, in 326 B.C., Alexander the Great of Macedon crossed the Indus river, but his reign was short-lived. The history of India continued to be that of periods of temporary empires interspersed with periods of chaos.

The Gupta Empire (320–535 A.D.)

The high point of the classical period was the *Gupta* empire, during which the Ganges and Indus valleys were united under the Gupta dynasty. During this period, sometimes likened to the Periclean Age in Athens, mathematics, astronomy, and medicine flourished, and some great universities were established, and attracted students from all over Asia. Arabic numerals and the decimal system appear to have come from India, although scholars do not yet know how much Indian mathematics and science were influenced by contacts with Greeks and Arabs.

By the end of the sixth century, barbarian invaders were overrunning India, just as they were overrunning the Roman Empire.

By the end of the eighth century, Moslems were invading India, and by the end of the thirteenth century, the Ganges-Indus valley was under their control. The most important phase of the Moslem invasions was the establishment of the Mogul Empire (from the word Mongol).

The Mogul Empire (1526–1761)

In the late fourteenth century Tamerlane invaded India, sacked Delhi, and destroyed what government there had been. In the sixteenth century a descendant of Tamerlane and Genghis Khan, named Babur, invaded India with 12,000 men and made himself ruler of Hindustan. His successor Akbar instituted an administration that established a highly efficient civil service and a well-organized system of taxation. Religious toleration won him support of the Hindus and provided the opportunity to develop cultural standards that produced the Taj Mahal, encouraged artists, writers, and architects. The Mogul empire was a center of culture that spread its influence over all of south Asia.

Unfortunately, Akbar's successors were less tolerant, and attempted to force the Moslem faith upon the country. Grinding taxation to pay for lavish public buildings bred increasing discontent. Gradually India was divided into two cultures which remained so distinct that when Britain gave India its independence in 1947 it split into two nations, Hindu India and Moslem Pakistan.

The *caste system* became the socio-economic skeleton of the Hindu way of life. A person was born into a particular caste and there he remained. He was born into an economic niche, could not marry outside the caste, and must follow the particular trade of his caste.

Despite its limitations, the caste system did provide the individual with some security. To the western mind the caste system may appear to be unfair. But to the Hindu, with his disdain for worldly success, it did not appear necessarily unjust. One of its severe limitations, however, is that it constituted a barrier to the unity of the Indian people.

European Influence

At the time when India was sinking back into anarchy, European explorers and traders were appearing in the Far East. The Portuguese, in the forefront of European maritime explorations, maintained a monopoly of trade until the seventeenth century. In the first quarter of that century the Dutch and British East India Companies were establishing trading posts (called factories because the factors or company agents lived there). Their motivation was commercial, they became powerful organizations, and they gradually drove out the Portuguese from India, except for the little possession of Goa on the west coast of India, which remained Portuguese until India occupied it in 1961.

The French came into India during the seventeenth century, but before the end of the eighteenth century they had been driven out of their posts. In the meantime, and partly as the result of British influence, the Mogul dynasty grew progressively weaker. The English East India Company under the successive governors Robert Clive, Warren Hastings, and Lord Cornwallis gradually conquered the entire sub-continent.

By the Treaty of Paris, 1763, which ended not only the French-Indian War in North America but also the Anglo-French rivalry in India, the French agreed to give up their claims and possessions in India. A year later Britain secured control of the province of Bengal, which became the base for further conquest.

Although British troops had assisted in the defeat of the French, the British possessions in India were not under control of King or Parliament. They were private possessions of the East India Company, paying handsome dividends to the stockholders.

The break-up of the Mogul empire, in mid-eighteenth century, resulted in hundreds of native factions warring against each other, with the powerful Mahratta race controlling a wide area across the center of the continent. This menace to British possessions, relatively small in area, had to be met by force. It became apparent also that the Company was now faced with the obligation of attempting to govern as well as to reap commercial profits. Evidence of mismanagement and plunder obliged Parliament to pass legislation requiring royal approval of all company appointments. Thus, responsibility for government was divided between Parliament and Company.

India Act of 1858

As western methods and ideas replaced native customs and traditions, Hindu and Moslem resentment grew until it resulted in the famous Indian Mutiny of 1857 in the northern provinces of India. As a result of the mutiny the India Act of 1858 abolished the powers of the Company and transferred them to the Crown and its troops to the British army. A British government department was created under the Secretary of State for India, Queen Victoria was entitled Empress of India, the Governor-General was now the Viceroy of India, and a large Indian Civil Service ran the affairs of what was now a vast British colony.

Life in India

Unlike western life, that of India consisted of some 500,000 villages, each a self-sufficient unit economically and politically, in which the individual was subordinated to the group. British institutions undermined this local existence. Centralized administration weakened the authority of local officials, imported British textiles competed with village products, and the British demand for payment of taxes in cash seriously upset the barter economy of the countryside. The British did bring some unity to the country and did give Indians increasing participation in government. By so doing they helped to give the Indians a sense of nationalism which led to demands by the Congress Party for independence. The increasing influences of Mohandas Gandhi brought him to the front as his country's leader, and his long fight against the British by means of non-cooperation and non-violence finally won independence for India.

5

Revolutionary Struggles for Rights and Freedom

England Establishes Representative Government

Terms

Divine Right

Long Parliament

"Glorious Revolution"

Petition of Right

Triennial Acts (2)

Habeas Corpus

Solemn League and Covenant

The Restoration

Bill of Rights

People

Oliver Cromwell

Significant Dates

1628   Petition of Right

1640   Long Parliament

1649   Beginning of the Republic

1660   The Restoration

1689   Bill of Rights

Topic Outline

Stuart Monarchs

The Long Parliament

Civil War & the Interregnum of Cromwell

The Restoration of the Monarchy

Parliamentary Gains of the Seventeenth Century

England Establishes Representative Government

The basic contribution of England to western civilization is parliamentary government. This is not necessarily democracy in the sense that everyone may vote, but rather the concept that the ruler is restricted by a constitution, whether written or a collection of laws or both, that people are governed by laws and not by a man who may decide to do as he chooses at any time.

Under the Tudor monarchs (1485–1603) a centralized system was developing in England, and it was during the reigns of the Stuarts (1603–1688) that the limited-representative parliament was able to restrict royal authority.

As we have seen, in the thirteenth century the barons had forced a king to sign

Magna Carta, and Edward I had called a Model Parliament in 1295. Edward's purpose was simply to get more money to fight the Hundred Years' War against the French. But these precedents persisted, and in time the House of Commoners or Commons represented the untitled land owners and the wealthy townspeople who jealously guarded their right to vote taxes, and used this right to win increasing power for themselves. One significant historical fact is that the Elizabethan Poor Law of 1601, which obliged local parishes to take care of their own poor, helped to develop local government in the hands of local officials who were not Crown appointees. This helped to develop a broad base of government and local experience in administration.

The Tudors had been expert in handling parliament for their own royal purposes, but their successors the Stuarts were singularly inept.

Stuart Monarchs

James I, (1603–1625) insisted that he was king by divine right, which meant that parliament had no choice; he argued from this that while he might choose to listen to Parliament he had no obligation to do so; he decreed that he was head of the Church and would determine the nation's religious practices. He insisted that he would accept not the slightest interference in religion, for once he let his own authority or that of his bishops be questioned, then parliament would start to question his political authority. His, "No bishop, no king," meant quite simply that if bishops had no authority, then the king would have none.

Charles I, (1625–1649) unwisely maneuvered England into a war against Spain, paid for it with a loan forced from wealthier subjects, saved money by obliging citizens to house and feed his troops, and generally managed to get public opinion against him. Forced to call a parliament, Charles signed the *Petition of Right* in 1628, which laid down some of the basic principles of constitutional government:

1. No taxation without parliament's consent.

2. No imprisonment except upon specific charge, proper trial, and proven guilt.

3. No military law upon citizens in peacetime.

4. No quartering of troops upon private citizens.

Charles foolishly tried to enforce his official religious beliefs upon the Scots, who had for some time been Presbyterians determining their own religious practices. Charles attacked the Scottish resisters organized in the Solem League and Covenant and finally had to buy them off with money he did not have.

The Long Parliament (1640–1660)

Forced to call what was to become the Long Parliament, he found himself obliged to agree to several reforms before he got his demands:

1. All disputed taxes were abolished, and only the regular, customary ones could be levied.

2. By the Triennial Act parliament must meet at least once every 3 years.

3. Parliament could not be dismissed without its consent. Two highly unpopular royal favorites Archbishop Laud and Lord Strafford were removed and executed.

Civil War and the Interregnum of Cromwell

Attempts by Charles to interfere with the members and the sessions of parliament finally led to civil war. On one side were supporters of royal authority and a Church run by authority; on the other were those who supported parliament as the major partner in government and a church run by the people. Charles lost the war, was executed — illegally — and was succeeded by the parliamentary leader *Oliver Cromwell,* who became even more dictatorial than Charles ever had been. Cromwell simply dismissed one parliament after another and ran the Church just as autocratically. The Republic or Commonwealth was such a failure that upon Cromwell's death the remnants of the Long Parliament met and invited Charles II, son of Charles I, to become king upon conditions:

1. He would observe the principles of Magna Carta.

2. Accept all the gains won by parliament to date.

3. Not interfere with the religious system set up by parliament.

The Restoration of the Monarchy

Charles II (1660–1685) was astute enough not to cross parliament openly, but his brother James II (1685–1688) lasted only three years before an exasperated parliament drove him out and invited in as king William of Holland, a son of the sister of Charles II, married to Mary the daughter of James II. This so-called "Glorious Revolution," certainly bloodless, established important rights for parliament and demanded others from William III.

Parliamentary Gains of the Seventeenth Century

One of the most significant rights for any people is that of:

1. *Habeas Corpus* (literally, "you have the person") and addressed to the jailer ordering him, under penalty of contempt of court to:
a. Tell the prisoner with what crime he is charged.
b. Bring him to court for trial within a specified time.

These guarantee a citizen the opportunity to prepare his defense and to be properly tried or set free. This right, popularly referred to as *habeas corpus,* is probably the most fundamental right of citizens in the United States and other parts of the English-speaking world.

The second important gain was the:

2. *Bill of Rights* of 1689 which established:
a. The Crown may not suspend the operation of any law.
b. The Crown could not have an army without parliament's consent.
c. The Crown could not interfere with parliament's rights of free elections, the right to debate any subject without fear of punishment, its right to hold frequent meetings.
d. The right of the people to petition for the remedy of grievances, and the right to fair punishments.

The third document was the:

3. *Triennial Act* which stipulated that a new parliament must be called at least every three years, thus preventing either a long-run parliament, or a long time between parliaments.

During the seventeenth century the English people won the fundamental rights of representative government:

1. Regular meetings of the legislature.

2. The power of the purse for the legislature.
3. Government by established laws.

The Age of Reason: The Intellectual Revolution

Terms

Scientific Revolution	*Spirit of the Laws*
Treatises of Civil Government	*Leviathan*
Critique of Pure Reason	Deism
Thesis, Antithesis, Synthesis	*Social Contract*
Deduction	Pietism
Philosophes	Induction
Methodism	Rationalism

People

John & Charles Wesley	Georg Hegel
Charles Montesquieu	George Fox
Jean Jacques Rousseau	Galileo
Immanuel Kant	Voltaire
Thomas Hobbes	Diderot
John Locke	

Topic Outline
Advance in Scientific Methods
Rationalism: Opinion Based on Reason
Deductive and Inductive Reasoning
The "Philosophes": Publicists of Reason
Political and Other Writers (Reason applied to Government and Politics)
Philosophy: Faith or Reason?

The Age of Reason: The Intellectual Revolution

The chief characteristic of the period of the latter seventeenth century through the eighteenth century is the tremendous development of scientific knowledge, much of it started earlier during the years of the Renaissance. Man's horizons were so widened that the period is called that of the "scientific revolution."

Earlier science, until the days of such men as Galileo and Kepler, had been based upon theories seldom tested; technicians had worked without quite knowing what they were looking for, and intellectuals frequently had ideas but lacked technical skills to further their theories. Galileo (1564–1642) expressed the situation when he said that those who had theories should watch people who used their hands. Francis Bacon (1561–1626) said, "Neither the hand without instruments nor the unassisted understanding can do much."

Advance in Scientific Methods

During this age of the scientific revolution four significant methods of procedure are evident:

1. The combining of theory and practice.

2. The testing of theories by experimentation.

3. The use of mathematical signs to state more precisely than can words the laws of science.

4. The widespread exchange of ideas and discoveries by scientists.

In England in 1660 the Royal Society "for Improving Natural Knowledge by Experiment" was founded, to be followed later by many more learned societies.

The intellectuals of the period were scornful of the Scholastics of the Middle Ages and those who perpetuated their attitudes, theories without experimentation to prove their beliefs or even the careful examination of their own theories. The Scholastics merely repeated the Aristotelian belief that the sun was a perfect unchanging body. When Galileo saw through his telescope spots that moved steadily across the sun's surface, he concluded that the sun had blemishes upon it, and that since they seemed to move, then the sun was revolving on its axis. His critics refused to question Aristotle's theory, and argued that the spots Galileo saw were simply defects in his telescope. The sun, they insisted, was a perfect, immovable body; therefore it could not have blemishes or rotate.

Galileo began what others did later; he formed an independent judgment based upon experiment, not simply on book learning handed down through the centuries. "Reasoning from the Authority of Books," wrote Thomas Hobbes later, "is not Knowledge but Faith." The scientific investigations of Isaac Newton, particularly his law of gravitation, led him to use mathematics instead of words to describe scientific ideas.

Rationalism: Opinion Based on Reason

Advances in the physical sciences profoundly affected man's thinking in the whole range of knowledge. Scientific investigations based on experiment and reasoning had widened the horizons of knowledge, sometimes disproved and often explained in understandable terms much that had previously been accepted. If reason could do this, could not everything be tested by reason, men asked. If reason had proved itself in science, then if reason is applied to government, laws, religion, economics, social customs, it should produce equally beneficial results for mankind. Some men believed that science had revealed order, law, and design in the universe. Since man had discovered this, then man was apparently gifted with the reasoning power to make him master of his own fate. So *rationalism*, the regarding of reason as the final authority, typified the period. This affected religious attitudes also, since religion is based on faith. As might be expected, men carried their beliefs in reason too far, claiming that beliefs and tradition were probably wrong. They also assumed that because reason could explain physical phenomena it could also explain human action and motivate it. Put simply, men claimed that one had only to reason out a remedy for errors and injustices in society and they would be changed; men had only to decide what laws and principles were wise and they could be put into practice. They were wrong in assuming that wisdom alone would or could be the only motivating force in man's actions.

The significance of this "Scientific Revolution," of this "age of reason" is that man changed his attitude from that of accepting what he was told to that of *thinking* independently. The mark of the free man was his ability and right to criticize.

Deductive and Inductive Reasoning

One basic difference in thinking was from the *deductive* thinking of earlier times to the *inductive* thinking of the seventeenth century. In deductive thinking the reasoning proceeds from general statements to particular and concrete application. Galileo's critics were deductive when they claimed that since the sun was a perfect immovable body it could not have blemishes or revolve on its axis. In inductive thinking the reasoning proceeds from a particular instance to a general rule, as Galileo reasoned when he concluded that the sun had blemishes and revolved on its axis. Of course, both types of reasoning are used; the seventeenth-century thinkers simply corrected the excessive acceptance of deductive thinking and added the inductive reasoning as necessary and important.

The "Philosophes": Publicists of Reason

Paris became the first important center of "reason," where writers called themselves *philosophes*, not really philosophers but publicists, political scientists and social reformers who popularized reason. French was the international language used in cultural and diplomatic circles. Their great work was the *Encyclopedie*, not like modern encyclopedias which give balanced accounts of knowledge. The Encyclopedie of which Diderot was editor, was propagandist, advocating beliefs which were sometimes more emotional convictions than balanced statements.

Political and Other Writers (Reason Applied to Government and Politics)

Voltaire (Francois Arouet) (1694–1778) was the great champion of toleration, personal liberty, freedom of the press, and supporter of *Deism*, the belief in a Deity which made the laws which scientists discovered, but an impersonal Deity. Voltaire and the Deists were not atheists, men who believed in no God, for as Voltaire said, "If a God did not exist, he would have to be invented."

Denis Diderot (1713–1784) was in one sense a rival of Voltaire, in spreading through his encyclopedia the belief in rationalism and deism. Although Deism encouraged a more moderate view of religion, it failed to attract the average person because it was too intellectual, more a matter of the head than the heart. As a result reaction set in. George Fox, founder of the Quakers, and John and Charles Wesley, founders of the Methodists, did much to counteract "reasoned religion." The Quakers were concerned with the "inner spirit," or personal experience of the individual. The Wesleys preached extemporaneously and emotionally, stressing methodical devotion — hence Methodism — and frequent prayer.

In politics three men made their contribution based on reason.

Charles Montesquieu (1689–1755) wrote on what makes a good society. In his *Spirit of the Laws* he claimed that laws must be *reasonable*; since a just law was a reasonable one, then men would obey it. He decided that England had the best government, that it resulted from the balance and harmony achieved by separation of the three branches of government, the executive, the legislative, and the judicial.

Thomas Hobbes (1586–1679) and *John Locke* (1632–1704) are two important men in political thinking, for although opposites in point of view they made very significant contributions to modern ideas of government, both totalitarian and democratic.

Hobbes published his famous *Leviathan* in 1651 at a time when England was experiencing great instability caused by the execution of Charles I and the republican rule of Oliver Cromwell. His remedy for political insecurity shocked many contemporaries because he advocated absolutism or dictatorship. He began with the proposition that men are basically selfish and antagonistic, and are constantly at war with one another. The only solution, said Hobbes, was to make a covenant or agreement among men and then, since words without power are useless, to give one man the power to keep order. This would be the great Commonwealth, or Common Good. This is the "Leviathan" which must have absolute and undivided power.

Locke wrote two *Treatises of Civil Government* in defense of the Glorious Revolution of 1688 which in effect deposed the unwise James II and invited in King William upon terms which greatly restricted his authority. Locke differed sharply from Hobbes because he believed that the people should regard the government as a trustee carrying out their wishes. Locke's arguments are:

1. Man in a state of nature, before organizing with his fellows, has basic rights of life, liberty, and property.

2. When men get together in society they must set up rules of behavior (a constitution) to safeguard these rights for each man.

3. They then set up a government which acts as trustee to enforce the laws.

4. This government is based upon the consent of those who created it, and it has no right to take a man's property without the general consent.

5. If men's rights are seriously threatened by the government they have the right of revolution.

Locke's ideas greatly influenced the leaders of the American Revolution and appear in the Declaration of Independence.

Thus these two men, Hobbes and Locke, stand at the opposite ends of political thought. Hobbes is the forerunner of the doctrine of totalitarianism, Locke the forerunner of the doctrine of democracy, although seventeenth-century England was not then democratic. The two men influenced their own generations and succeeding generations down to today.

Jean Jacques Rousseau (1712–1778) was a critic not only of the *ancien regime* but also of civilization in general, believing that although man was naturally happy, he was the victim of the society he had created. His *Social Contract*, called the Bible of the French Revolution, portrayed an ideal society in which the individual finds happiness by submitting to a central government chosen by all citizens for their mutual protection and guidance. However, the "social contract" which gives the sovereign the right to govern restricts that right to public usefulness. Echoing Locke but with much more fervor Rousseau summed up, "All the rulers of the earth are mere delegates of the people, who, when they are displeased with the government, have the right to alter or abolish it." The French Revolution began a little more than twenty-five years after the publication of this work.

Philosophy: Faith or Reason?

Two philosophers of some note are Immanuel Kant (1724–1804) and Georg Hegel (1770–1831).

Kant was one of the leaders in Germany in the intellectual revolt against reason as the sole guide, which generated a religious revival called *Pietism*, a belief which regarded religion as a matter of faith and which objected to the current dogmatism. Much like the beliefs of the Wesleys in England, those of the Pietists included emotional sermons and sudden conversions.

Kant was the founder of the idealist school of philosophers, and in his book the *Critique of Pure Reason* he attacked the belief in reason alone. Man, he said, can appreciate beauty and religion, neither of which can be explained by reason alone. Therefore, since we cannot by reason prove the existence of God or immortality, and because we live as though they were true we may be justified in thinking that they are true.

Hegel lived through the French Revolution and although he originally agreed with it he increasingly came to respect the nation created by Napoleon. He aspired to a German nation which would develop through the dialectic process, that is, from the *thesis*, German disunity, would come the opposite or *antithesis*, German unity, and from this would come the *synthesis*, the ideal German state. Later on Karl Marx used this Hegelian dialectic to "prove" his theory of the inevitability of communism.

The American Revolution

Terms

Treaty of Paris, 1763
Declaration of Independence
Treatise of Civil Government
Articles of Confederation
Constitutional Convention
Stamp Act
Internal Taxes

Townshend Acts
Tea Act
Common Sense
Declaratory Act
External Taxes
Writs of Assistance
Intolerable Acts

People

Frederick the Great
Townshend
Maria Theresa

Thomas Paine
William Pitt

Significant Dates

1763   British Proclamation
1765   Stamp Act
1776   Declaration of Independence
1778   Treaty of Alliance with France
1789   Federal Constitution

Topic Outline

Duel for Empire: England vs. France in North America
Taxation Without Representation
The Townshend Acts
The Intolerable Acts
Advocates of and Reasons for Revolution
The Articles of Confederation
The Constitutional Convention
Significance of the American Revolution

The American Revolution

One of the basic causes of war in the eighteenth century was commercial and colonial rivalry. According to the economic doctrine of mercantilism, a nation's safety and prosperity depended upon its self-sufficiency, its ability to control raw materials and markets. For example, colonies would relieve England of her dependence upon Scandinavian forests for timbers and masts for her navy and merchant marine, and she would not be dependent upon a foreign source of supply that could be cut off during a war.

Nations were also convinced that international peace could best be maintained through a balance of power between nations, by a policy of organizing an alliance of smaller states against a powerful one that threatened the interests, even the safety, of other nations.

England and France were the leading rivals for colonies, trade, and power, and whenever their interests conflicted there was danger of war. The prizes at stake in North America were sugar from the West Indies, tobacco from Virginia, and furs. Complications developed in Europe because great military power and prestige there could provide the forces to win victory in North America.

In 1740 the question of who should succeed to the Austrian throne precipitated a war which brought England and France into conflict for another 75 years. The King of Prussia died in 1740 and left the throne to his son Frederick the Great; that same year Charles VI of Austria left his throne to his daughter Maria Theresa. Frederick wanted and took Silesia from Austria. Great Britain was afraid that France, now an ally of Frederick, might become too powerful, and persuaded Holland and Hanover to join her against Frederick.

While the War of the Austrian Succession was in progress in Europe, England and France had begun their duel for empire. The American colonists captured Louisburg, the strategic fort controlling the St. Lawrence river, but in India the French took the British trading post of Madras. In the peace negotiations of 1748 Britain unwisely exchanged Louisburg for Madras, and aroused the American colonists who saw their interests sacrificed to those of Britain.

Duel for Empire: England vs. France in North America

Friction was developing in the Ohio valley, where British troops supported colonial attempts to take French strategic forts along the valley. In Europe friction between England and France broke out into the Seven Years' War, the European aspect of the colonial French-Indian War. William Pitt, prime minister of England developed a global strategy called the "Pitt System" of:

1. Supporting Prussia with men and supplies to keep France busy in Europe.

2. Sending out well-led, effective troops to North America and India.

3. Destroying French sea-power to deny reinforcements to the French.

The *Treaty of Paris* (1763) confirmed Prussia's occupation of Silesia, provided for:

1. The cession by France to England of Canada and Cape Breton, and all territory east of the Mississippi, and several Caribbean islands.

2. Spain gave Florida to England, and received from France as compensation New Orleans and all Louisiana west of the Mississippi.

England was now the greatest colonial power, but she now was to experience increasing resistance from her American colonists who, with French danger gone from the north, were to demand increasing rights for themselves.

With the expulsion of France from Canada, England determined to put her North American colonies to good use under the mercantile system. They should provide her exclusively with raw materials — already specified in the Navigation Acts — and be a market for British goods. Furthermore, since Britain had incurred a vast debt because of the wars with France, she thought that the American colonists should expect to pay part of the costs of the war and for the troops to be maintained in the colonies for their defense in case France should try to recover her former colony of Canada. A succession of Acts of Parliament increased the opposition of the colonists to a system which was enforced to suit England's interests, often at the expense of the colonial interests.

The *Proclamation of 1763* reversed a policy which Britain had formerly supported. Colonists were not to settle west of the Appalachian watershed line, and no furs could be trapped without license from England. Britain did this in order to control all trade with North America, fearing that if settlers moved across the mountains, then their trade would be carried down the Mississippi River and would go out of England's control. To the colonists this meant that the frontier was closed to further expansion.

Taxation Without Representation: Threat to Colonial Power of the Purse

The *Stamp Act* of 1765 levied taxes on legal documents and business contracts, all of which were illegal in the eyes of the law unless stamps were affixed. Newspapers and their advertisements were also taxed, and as a consequence many of the influential men of the colonies were aroused against England. The money raised by the tax would pay for British garrisons and the salaries of colonial officials, who would now have to answer to England, not to the colonists. Thus in 1765 the very important rights won for Englishmen by the Bill of Rights in 1689 were being denied Englishmen in the colonies, who were more interested in their own affairs than in English mercantile arguments.

The Stamp Act raised so much opposition, especially shown in the agreement not to buy English goods, that British merchants demanded the repeal of the Act. The Parliament repealed it but enacted at the same time the *Declaratory Act* which stated that England retained the right to pass and enforce any law it chose.

The Townshend Acts

Since the colonists had raised a great cry against "internal" taxes, money levied *inside* the colonies and without the consent of the colonists, a new Chancellor of the Exchequer persuaded parliament to enact the Townshend Acts, which placed a tax on goods imported into the colonies, therefore an "external" tax which the colonists would not object to. However, since this tax was on British goods, which were still kept cheaper than foreign goods, the colonists were being forced to pay a tax on British glass, tea, lead, paints — or go without them. British officials used *Writs of Assistance* or general search warrants which were bitterly protested by the colonists. A search warrant is necessary if a crime is suspected, but search warrants must state what is to be searched, what is being searched for, and the warrant has an expiration date. The British misused the warrants in all these respects. Agitation led to the repeal of the Townshend Acts, with the exception of the tax on tea. Colonial opposition died down, because good tea could be smuggled in from Holland, and at cheaper prices than British tea. But when England passed the Tea Act in 1773 which gave the British East India company the right to sell tea directly to the colonies, to appoint its own wholesale agents, and to collect a small tax on each pound of tea for the British government, the colonists protested. This was a monopoly, the grant to one company of the right to sell a product and also a tax measure. Massachusetts protested in the famous *Boston Tea Party*, the dumping into the harbor of more than 300 chests of tea.

The Intolerable Acts

Britain retaliated with the Intolerable Acts. The *Boston Port Act* closed down the port until the tea was paid for; the *Government of Massachusetts Act* gave the colonial royal-appointed governor the right to choose colonial officials and to determine when town meetings could be held; the *Administration of Justice Act* permitted a British official who had allegedly committed a crime against a colonist to be tried in another colony or England, where there would probably be no witnesses, where "justice" could be repeatedly delayed.

Tension resulted in the skirmish at Lexington and Concord, and a little more than a year later the *Declaration of Independence* formally proclaimed the revolt of the American colonies on July 4, 1776.

Advocates of and Reasons for Revolution

In 1690 an essay was published by John Locke in England to justify the "Glorious Revolution" of 1688. His reasons were simple, and provided the American colonists with excellent arguments.

In his *Essay of Civil Government* John Locke argued that men are born with "natural" rights to act as they please. When men get together in any group or society, however small or large, they must draw up rules of behavior so that no one person may interfere with another's rights. This contract is then to be carried out by a government, which is a trustee charged with certain responsibilities. If that government does not carry out the wishes of the governed, then they may replace it. These arguments the colonists used as justification for revolution, supported by Tom Paine who in *Common Sense* pointed out that Britain and the colonies had such widely different interests that they could not be reconciled, and that "common sense" demanded a complete break with and independence from Britain.

The Articles of Confederation (1781)

As the war against England progressed, the colonies saw the need for joint action, and ratified the *Articles of Confederation* in 1781, a loose alliance or league of independent states that gave the so-called "central" government no power to levy taxes and troops or to interfere with the affairs of any colony. During the "critical period" the war with England was won, and Britain surrendered all territory south of the Great Lakes and westwards to the Mississippi to the new United States of America, in 1783. The war had been won with the help of the French Alliance in 1778, which supplied money and troops, less to help the colonists than to weaken England and her colonial empire.

**Constitutional
Convention:
Federal Government
Inaugurated**

Victorious as the United States were, their future was very uncertain. Their loose confederation was in danger of collapsing, and the British expected to be able to take over the colonies one by one, from the military posts that they still illegally retained along the Great Lakes.

Fortunately, strong leaders such as Jefferson, Hamilton, Madison, and Washington were able to persuade the thirteen colonies to agree to meet to consider strengthening the constitution. At Philadelphia they sat from May to September 1787, and there, despite opposition from some states which were afraid of substituting for British rule an equally powerful central government, they persuaded the states to ratify a new Constitution which was unique. Its basic principles were:

1. Federalism, of a central government with specified powers, and state governments with the remaining or "reserved" powers.

2. Popular sovereignty which gave the *people,* not just the central government, the right to amend the constitution.

3. Separation of powers into three branches of government, the *legislative* to pass laws, the *executive* to carry out the laws, and the *judicial* to interpret and enforce their operation. No one branch can dominate another.

Congress may pass a law, the President can veto it, but a two-thirds majority of both Houses can override the veto; and the Supreme Court has the authority to declare a law unconstitutional if it contradicts the rights and the regulations laid down in the Constitution.

This governmental system has come to be the outstanding type of democracy in operation today, not immediately democratic in 1789, when first adopted, but providing the basis for complete democracy.

**Significance of the
American Revolution**

The United States was the first example of a republic of so great a size. It certainly influenced the course of the French Revolution, whose *Declaration of the Rights of Man* reflects many of the principles of the Declaration of Independence.

The American Constitution and its principles have been read and adopted in spirit by many of the emergent nations of the past decade.

The French Revolution

Terms

Ancien Regime	Taille
Corvée	Gabelle
Physiocrats	Tax-Farming
Cahiers	The Bastille
Assignats	Girondist
Jacobin	Commune
The "Mountain"	The Directory
Reign of Terror	The Consulate
Third Estate	Philosophes
Estates-General	*Spirit of the Laws*
Tithe	*Social Contract*

Tennis Court Oath
National Assembly
Legislative Assembly
Declaration of the Rights of Man

"Second French Revolution"
Brunswick Manifesto
Committee of Public Safety
Thermidorian Reaction

People

Montesquieu
Turgot
Danton
Rousseau

Necker
Robespierre
Voltaire
Calonne

Significant Dates

1789	Estates-General Convenes
1792	France Declares War on Austria
1793	Louis XVI Executed
1792–1804	First Republic

Topic Outline

Critics of Divine Right and Old Regime
Financial Problems of France
The Work of the Estates-General
The Work of the National Assembly
The Legislative Assembly
Louis's Threat to Constitutional Monarchy
The National Convention
The Reign of Terror
The First Republic (1792–1804)
The Directory (1795–1799)

The French Revolution

In 1789 France appeared to be in a strong position. Her trade had increased under the mercantile system; she had helped Britain's North American colonies to break away from the mother country; and her population was more than double that of Great Britain. On the face of it she was in an impregnable position. But basic weaknesses were already threatening her security.

The foreign policy of Louis XV (1715–1774) resulted in the costly War of the Austrian Succession (1740–1748), and the Seven Years' War (French-Indian War) of 1756–1763 in which Great Britain had acquired Canada from France. The expenses to France had been enormous, and the system of absolute monarchy seemed incompetent to deal with internal problems.

Critics of Divine Right and the Old Regime

The French Revolution is the historical watershed that marks the division between the system of government known as the *ancien regime* and modern constitutional monarchies.

The Old Regime was essentially one in which the monarch claimed to hold his office by divine hereditary right, whose rule was to be obeyed without question, or if questioned, only because he permitted it. The necessities of government meant that in practice the monarch depended upon subordinates to carry out his wishes, and he in turn gave them privileges and rights which they jealously defended. France of the eighteenth century is the evident example of such a monarchy with its faults and weaknesses, although contemporary monarchs in other European nations were scarcely less autocratic. Frederick II of Prussia, Catherine the Great of Russia, and the rulers of Austria and Spain were all contemporaries of Louis XV of France, and they all demonstrated in greater or less degree the absolutist ideas of the French monarchy.

In France the clergy and nobles, called the First and Second Estates, were privileged classes, virtually exempt from taxation, occupying the best and most profitable positions in the country, yet showing little sense of the obligation of service to the nation. The Catholic Church, with its vast income from untaxed lands and from the tithe of 10 per cent tax on the produce from land cultivated by laymen, was anxious to prevent any restriction whatever on its privileges. The nobility, exempt from taxation, and even in some cases "pensioned" by the king from public funds, joined with the clergy in running the country as a sort of private preserve for their own special benefit.

The Third Estate, the unprivileged citizens, who paid taxes in money, produce, and labor, consisted of the middle class and the peasantry. Peasant complaints, apart from those about personal obligations to their superiors, were particularly directed at the *Corvée* or forced labor, the *taille* or head tax, and the *gabelle*, the forced purchase of salt, sold by the state at monopolistic prices and substantially taxed. The middle class of banker, merchants, administrators, and businessmen paid taxes but were denied any political rights. They were very conscious of the injustices and inadequacies of French political life, resented the fact that they were being taxed without any sort of representation, that in effect their money was being used not for national purposes but for the king's personal benefits. They were determined to remedy the situation, and they were supplied with sound arguments provided by writers and critics of the ancien regime.

The examples of the English Revolution of 1688 and the American Revolution of 1776 were supported by the writings of John Locke in his *Treatises of Civil Government*. A government, he wrote, was set up by men to serve their interests. In a state of nature, when each man did as he chose, there was no need for organization. But as soon as men lived together in social groups they must designate some of their number to act as their trustees and run a government according to the rules set up by the people. If the government, the trustees, did not carry out their obligation, then they could be removed, and a new government substituted, to govern in the interests of the people.

Montesquieu, in his *Spirit of the Laws* believed that government functioned best when the three branches, the executive, the legislative, and the judiciary were "separated" so that a proper balance could be maintained between the three.

Jean Jacques Rousseau in his *Social Contract* advocated a pure democracy in which the government derives its powers from the consent of the governed.

Voltaire was one of the more famous of the "philosophes" who criticized existing traditions and conditions, and demanded that intelligent reforms replace antiquated tradition. Some of the *philosophes* were concerned with national finances, whose abuses were becoming increasingly evident. These men called themselves *physiocrats*, believers in the rule of nature, in an orderly state of affairs. They disapproved of business regulation and mercantilism. If businessmen were left alone, if agriculture were properly developed, then the nation would become wealthy. The injustice that most disturbed the philosophers, who were of the unprivileged Third Estate, was the inequality of the law, the special privileges offered to nobility and clergy. The philosophers were perhaps naive enough to believe that once they demonstrated these ideas then people and the government would accept them. Their influence was important, for they set people to thinking, and this was one step towards action which finally brought about the French Revolution.

Financial Problems of France

Louis XVI (1774–1793) was woefully incompetent for the task facing him. Lazy, mediocre, and surrounded by sycophants, he failed to understand the political and economic problems of France. The nation was on the brink of national bankruptcy, taxes were collected and dissipated by appointees who were not called to account for the money they collected, and in many instances taxes were "farmed out," that is, a tax collector paid for the privilege of collecting whatever he could squeeze out, usually much more than the state ever received. Louis appointed Turgot to straighten out the financial problem, but his methods interfered with privilege. He proposed to tax by ability to pay and planned to reduce royal expenses. Queen Marie Antoinette, beautiful but politically stupid, persuaded Louis to dismiss Turgot because that minister approached the problem sensibly. France had exhausted her resources in the series of wars since 1689, and was to go further into difficulties by supporting the American colonies against Great Britain in 1778.

Turgot's successor *Jacques Necker*, a Geneva banker, published a document proposing that the aristocracy should receive no further grants out of the public money, that taxes be levied by ability to pay, and that in each province of France an assembly representing the governed be set up. Not surprisingly, Necker followed Turgot in dismissal.

In desperation Louis acted upon the advice of another minister, *Calonne*, and called a meeting of the Assembly of Notables, the clergy and the nobility, to ask them to make financial contributions. They stubbornly refused to face facts, demanded Calonne's removal, and refused adamantly to surrender any privilege. They had thereby invited revolution and sealed their own doom. Louis had only one recourse remaining, and that was to call, for the first time since 1614, a meeting of the Estates-General which had traditionally cast three votes, one for each Estate, with the privileged First and Second Estates able to outvote the Third Estate by two to one.

The Work of the Estates-General

In 1789, it convened with 308 clergy, 285 nobles, and 621 of the Third Estate which demanded representation by head-count with the three estates meeting as one body, not as separate groups. The announcement of the convening caused a demand for reforms, listed in *cahiers* or notebooks for the delegates, from all over France, demanding a national legislature for law-making, personal liberty, fair taxation, and fair trials.

The Third Estate refused to be brow-beaten, invited delegates from the other

Estates to join them as the National Constituent Assembly, and in the building containing the tennis court where they met took the Tennis Court Oath not to disband until a constitution had been drawn up.

While these events were developing at Versailles, the Paris workers and the country peasants were excited by rumors that the king was gathering foreign mercenary forces to expel the Assembly. In Paris the mob attacked the Bastille, the royal prison which symbolized injustice. In the countryside the peasants destroyed the country mansions of their nobles and along with them the old records which listed peasant feudal obligations.

That August the nobility, fearful of the peasantry, renounced feudal dues and privileges, ended the Church taxes and fees, agreed to institute fair taxation, and promised to open official positions to all citizens regardless of birth. On that night of August 4, 1789 the Old Regime ended.

The Work of the National Assembly (1789–1791)

The first action of the National Assembly was the abolition of serfdom, special taxes and dues, and special privileges. The *Declaration of the Rights of Man* was a statement of democratic principles and rights, containing the basic ideas of John Locke and many of the principles stated in the United States Declaration of Independence and Bill of Rights. All officials were responsible to the people, who were to enjoy proper legal trials, the rights of liberty and property, and participation in lawmaking.

The Executive, officially titled the King of the French instead of King of France, was to govern according to a constitution, although retaining a temporary veto power. The Legislature was a single, elected chamber, and the Judiciary consisted of elected judges. The bourgeoisie or middle class wanted the revolution to stop short with political and legal reforms and the constitutional monarchy. But town workers and peasants expected a social revolution, with equal opportunity for all in education and wealth. Disillusionment with the revolution led them to support demagogues who led the moderate revolution into bloodshed and terror.

The Church owned lands almost equal in value to the national debt of some three billion livres. In November 1789 all church and monastic property was appropriated for the nation, and on the assessed value of the land the government issued *assignats* or paper money in payment of government obligations. The church lands were overvalued and too much paper money was issued, so that the circulation of more money than the equivalent amount of goods led to higher prices and inflation, so that in six years the assignats lost 95 per cent of their face value.

Since the Church had no income to pay out in salaries, and since the Church was "nationalized" the State paid bishops and clergy as State employees, who were elected by the diocese or parish and must take an oath of loyalty to the new government.

The Legislative Assembly (1791–1792)

This new assembly succeeded the previous assembly which declared itself ineligible for immediate re-election. Unfortunately the new deputies were politically inexperienced and allowed themselves to be controlled by extremists. In the Assembly the seating of the several groups labelled them Left, Center, and

Right as they sat facing the Speaker. To his left sat the *Jacobins*, so-named because their headquarters was a former Jacobin monastery. They regarded the 1791 Constitution as a temporary one and favored a Republic with an elected head, and based on universal suffrage. They were a well-organized group of 130 out of the total of 740 deputies, with branches throughout the country, and able to control the central and local governments. To the right were the more numerous, 267 deputies, Constitutional Monarchists favoring the present government. In the center were the remaining deputies, not committed wholeheartedly to either Monarchy or Republic. The *Girondists* were a small group of Jacobins from the Gironde country around Bordeaux, who specialized in public oratory and in due course got control of French diplomacy.

Louis's Threat to Constitutional Monarchy

Louis XVI, although he accepted the constitutional restrictions and wore the tricolor cockade in place of the royal fleur-de-lys, decided to flee secretly from Paris towards the north of France to join loyal troops, make himself master of the provinces and return to Paris as master. At Varennes his disguise was discovered and he was brought back to "protective custody" in the Tuileries Palace. His presence in Paris placed the bourgeois deputies in a quandary, for alive he could be the center of plots, but his removal could lead to a republic in which too many people would have power. In early 1792 the Emperor of Austria headed a League supported by several European monarchs and French emigres. On April 20, 1792 France declared war on Austria, and in retaliation the Duke of Brunswick, commander of the invading armies, issued the *Brunswick Manifesto*, warning that all Frenchmen who refused to lay down their arms would be treated as rebels.

Since October, 1789, the "revolution" had been relatively free from violence, but by the summer of 1792 renewed violence threatened. Discontent had been mounting for several reasons:

1. The National and Legislative Assemblies had done little to benefit peasants and workers.

2. Prices were rising and the buying power of *assignats*, almost the only money in circulation, was dropping.

3. The war could result in the restoration of the emigres and the Old Regime.

4. The King, identified with the nations fighting against France, was evidently not to be trusted.

5. The Legislative Assembly, part of the new government of constitutional monarchy, was also suspect.

On August 10, 1792 a detachment of recruits from Marseilles, with their fierce marching song, the Marseillaise, stirred up the Paris mob and joined it in storming the Tuileries Palace. They imprisoned the royal family, set up their own local government, the "Commune," suspended the monarchy and successfully demanded a new election by universal male suffrage. The resulting Constitutional Convention (similar to the American Constitutional Convention of 1787) was charged with drawing up a more democratic constitution.

In the "September Massacres" Jacobin-led mobs arrested all suspected "enemies" and "counter-revolutionaries," gave the prisoners so-called trials in impromptu courts, and in three days executed over one thousand political opponents. This insurrectionary action of August, 1792 is considered to be the "second" French Revolution, which was to become so extreme that in exhaustion and disgust the French were to welcome later the strong rule of Napoleon Bonaparte as First Consul.

The National Convention (1792–1795)

This new Assembly was completely "rigged" because Jacobin agents turned away from the doors anyone they conveniently labelled as "counter-revolutionary" voters. The result was obviously a landslide for the republicans who in turn split into Left, Center, and Right, with the Girondists now the Rightists, favoring a decentralized government. The other Jacobin group, sitting high up on the extreme Left and named the *Mountain* supported an all-powerful central government, executed Louis XVI, declared war on Great Britain and Spain, set up rigid price controls, arrested and guillotined Girondist deputies.

The First Republic (1792–1804) and The Reign of Terror (June, 1793–July, 1794)

Maximilien Robespierre, who had helped to set up the program of the Convention, took over as leader. Determined to win the war and to stamp out counter-revolution at home, he suspended indefinitely the Constitution, and substituted the "revolutionary" or emergency government of the Committee of Public Safety.

*France's First Republic of the five she was to have over the next two centuries ushered in a Reign of Terror for which Robespierre was essentially responsible. It is interesting to note that his viewpoint on government was to be re-iterated more than one hundred years later by Lenin in the U.S.S.R. "To establish and consolidate democracy, to achieve the peaceful role of constitutional laws, we must find . . . annihilate the enemies of the republic at home and abroad."

Robespierre and his friends would, of course, decide who were "enemies." But how could Robespierre impose a dictatorship on a people who had just removed one? Simply by ignoring a recent referendum which had decided upon universal manhood suffrage. Robespierre and his cronies comprised the real government of France, the Committee of Public Safety, which acted much as it chose. Another group of deputies constituted the Committee of General Security which turned suspected enemies of the Republic over to the new Revolutionary Tribunal of sixteen judges and sixty jurors divided into several courts to speed up the process of repressing political opponents.

What Robespierre called swift, severe, and inflexible "justice" was meted out to more than 20,000 some 2000 of whom were conveniently put aboard leaky boats to drown in the Loire river at Nantes. This was all in the good cause of establishing a republic in which all citizens would demonstrate high ideals and unquestioned patriotism.

Another "democratic" step was the decree requisitioning "all Frenchmen for the service of the army."

In social and cultural matters Robespierre went even further. "We desire to substitute all the virtues and all the miracles of the Republic for . . . all the nonsense of the Monarchy." The forms of address Monsieur and Madame were replaced by Citoyen and Citoyenne, men wore the clothing of the workers, the

*First Republic (1792–1804); Second Republic (1840–1852); Third Republic (1875–1946); Fourth Republic (1946–1958); Fifth Republic (1958–)

so-called sans-culottes who did not wear knee-breeches. Out went the old calendar to be replaced by a new one dating from the first day of the Republic, September 22, 1792, now the first day of Year I. The Revolutionary Calendar had new months:

Winter	Nivose	Snowy
	Pluviose	Rainy
	Ventose	Windy
Spring	Germinal	Seed
	Floreal	Flowering
	Prairial	Meadow
Summer	Messidor	Wheat Harvest
	Thermidor	Heat
	Fructidor	Ripening
Fall	Vendemiaire	Grape Harvest
	Brumaire	Misty
	Frimaire	Frosty

Each month had thirty days, and the extra five were special holidays dedicated to Noble Actions, Labor, and the like. The working week was nine days, with the tenth day one of rest.

Robespierre's appeal for further "purification" of the government threatened men who decided to get rid of him and his excesses. In what is called the *Thermidorian Reaction* (9th of Thermidor, or July 27, 1794) Robespierre was arrested and the next day executed. In saving their own heads his executioners were hailed as heroes who had ended the Terror. Obliged to prepare a new constitution, the National Convention ordered that two thirds of its members must be re-elected, or appointed, to the new legislature. The Paris deputies rebelled but were promptly suppressed by the army, in which a young Corsican lieutenant named Bonaparte took a prominent part.

The Directory (1795–1799)

The new government, the Directory, consisted of a legislature of two houses, the Council of Ancients of 250 members at least 40 years of age, and a Council of Five Hundred of men over 30 years of age, chosen by property owners; the Executive of 5 Directors was nominated by the Council of 500 and chosen from the list by the Council of Ancients.

The Directors were generally inefficient, guilty of corruption, and soon sank low in the public esteem, while the army demonstrated its successes and even won acclaim for its victories against France's enemies. The Directory was soon to disappear and be replaced by the Consulate of Three, of which young Bonaparte was to become the leader, and within a few years the self-appointed Emperor of the French.

Edmund Burke foresaw in 1790 what would in due course happen in France.

"Everything depends on the army in such a government as yours, for you have . . . destroyed all the opinions . . . which support government. Therefore the moment any difference arises between your

National Assembly and any part of the nation, you must have recourse to force.''

Burke foresaw that the country would await the appearance of a charismatic leader, "some popular general who . . . shall draw the eyes of all men upon himself . . . the person who really commands your army is your master."

Napoleonic France

Terms

The Coalitions	Continental system
Consulate	Blockade system
Code Napoleon	Battle of Leipzig
Concordat	Hundred Days
Treaty of Tilsit	Berlin Decree

Places to Locate

Austrian Netherlands	Trafalgar
Helvetian Republic	Jena
Cisalpine Republic	Batavian Republic
Austerlitz	Parthenopean Republic (Naples)
Tilsit	Ligurian Republic (Genoa)
Piedmont	Auerstadt
Ulm	

Significant Dates

1795	Bonaparte Made Commander in Italy
1802	Treaty of Amiens
1804	Napoleon Crowned Emperor & First Empire
1805	Battles of Trafalgar, Ulm & Austerlitz
1813	Battle of Leipzig
1815	Battle of Waterloo

Topic Outline

Early Career of Napoleon Bonaparte
The Consulate
Domestic Reforms
The First Empire
The Third Coalition
Napoleon Controls the Continent
Continental System vs. British Blockade
Invasion of Russia
Final Defeat of Napoleon

Napoleonic France

Early Career of Napoleon Bonaparte   Napoleon Buonaparte (later spelled the French way, Bonaparte) came into prominence as an officer in the service of Revolutionary France. The peaceful revolution threatened the safety of other crowned heads in Europe, who decided to re-establish monarchy in France. In late 1792 France decided to strike first, invaded the Austrian Netherlands, and in doing so threatened Britain's balance of power policy. The execution of Louis XVI resulted in a coalition of France's enemies, Austria, Prussia, Holland, Spain, and Great Britain. Within two years this First Coalition was disintegrating and France had occupied Belgium and Holland and Germany west of the Rhine, and Nice and Savoy, thus securing her "natural frontiers."

Deciding to attack the nearer of the two remaining opponents, Austria and Great Britain, the Directory assigned the task of attacking Austrian forces in Northern Italy to young Bonaparte. This young, ruthlessly ambitious opportunist had already taken advantage of conditions.

Born on the French island of Corsica in 1769 Bonaparte went to a French military school at the age of 10, was a second lieutenant at age 20 and because of his services in the recapture of the French naval base of Toulon from the British was made a general of brigade at the age of 25. Within six years he had become dictator of France, partly through military success and partly through his sense of political timing.

As a reward for defending the National Convention from the Paris mob with a "whiff of grapeshot" in 1795, he was appointed by the Directory to command the army in Italy. Successful in conquering the little republics in Northern Italy, and in forcing the Austrians to give the Austrian Netherlands (later Belgium) to France, he was then appointed commander of the Army vs. England. Unable to cross the channel, but unwilling to admit his inability to attack France's enemy, he decided to hit at England through her possessions in India. He led an army to Egypt, seeing himself "on the road to Asia," was successful in Egypt but then had his communications cut when Nelson destroyed his fleet at the Battle of the Nile in 1798. Meanwhile England had persuaded Austria and Russia to join a coalition, which succeeded in defeating French armies in Italy and in opening up the French frontier to invasion. Slipping through the British blockade Bonaparte arrived in Paris just when the Directory was discredited for throwing away Bonaparte's earlier gains in Italy. Conspiring with politicians, Bonaparte drove out the Council of 500, announced that a revised constitution would be drawn up, and promptly established a temporary government of three Consuls, in which he immediately became the dominant figure.

The Consulate (1799–1804)

His peaceful overtures to the Second Coalition of Great Britain, Austria, and Russia were rejected by Austria which sent an army into Northern Italy to recapture Genoa. Crossing the Alps in 1800 Bonaparte defeated one Austrian army at the battle of Marengo, then another one later in the year at Hohenlinden, and so broke the Second Coalition.

In 1802 a peace was negotiated with Great Britain by the *Treaty of Amiens* by which the French Republic retained political hegemony over much of western Europe. The Austrian Netherlands, the left bank of the Rhine, and Piedmont were annexed as part of France; Holland (Batavian Republic), and Switzerland (Helvetian Republic) were closely allied to France; and the three republics in Italy, Liguria (Genoa), Parthenopea (Naples), the Italian (Cisalpine) acknowledged French control.

Great Britain regarded this French control of western Europe as a threat to its commerce, especially since Bonaparte had recently acquired Louisiana from Spain and appeared ready to revive an empire in North America.

Domestic Reforms

At home Bonaparte consolidated his personal power as First Consul and instituted much needed reforms. By an almost unanimous vote of male citizens Bonaparte was given executive authority for 10 years as First Consul, assisted by two other consuls, a Council of State appointed by him, and a Senate of supporters. As a gesture towards popular sovereignty two elective houses were instituted, a tribunate to discuss laws but not to vote on them, a legislature to vote laws but not to discuss them, and with all legislation to originate with the First Consul.

Political liberty for the people was a myth, but the nation gained in administrative efficiency that provided fair taxation, equal justice, increased business activity, and honest government that put France on its economic feet. In 1802 the Constitution was amended by a vote of 3,568,885 to 8374, or 425 to 1, making Bonaparte First Consul for life, with the right to choose his successor.

The Code Napoleon was the official code of all the legal changes that had occurred since the beginning of the revolution, stating clearly personal and property rights of citizens and setting forth the civil, criminal, and penal codes. The code of civil laws became the basis of such law in Holland, Belgium, Italy, and Louisiana.

Government was highly centralized through a system of subdivided authority of personally-appointed prefects for the departments, sub-prefects for the arrondissements or districts, and mayors for each municipality, all authorized to enforce Napoleon's orders.

The Concordat was negotiated with the Pope, by which the Papacy gave up all claims to church property previously confiscated and sold by the government, and agreed to permit the French government to appoint all bishops, to be consecrated by the Pope, with lesser clergy appointed by the bishops. All clergy were to be paid by the state, and in return for this agreement the Roman Catholic faith became the official religion of France, and the spiritual authority of the Pope on all matters of faith was recognized.

Education   From the primary schools to the university, education was rigidly controlled to train good citizens and to serve the purposes of patriotic indoctrination.

The First Empire (1804–1814)

Several attempts on Bonaparte's life by French monarchists and British agents persuaded the French people that the efficient government of France should be perpetuated. The Senate offered Bonaparte the title of Emperor and the right to found a dynasty, his own ruling house. The Pope was invited to Paris to perform the coronation ceremony in 1804, but Bonaparte, not wishing to acknowledge any man his superior, crowned himself Emperor Napoleon, First Emperor of the French, and crowned his wife Empress. A new nobility of rank and titles was created by Napoleon, but this was a nobility based on service to the state, not one based on feudal titles and rights. In 1809 Napoleon divorced his wife Josephine for "reasons of state," because his wife had borne him no children, and married

Marie of Austria. A son was born in 1811, given the title of King of Rome, and was apparently in line to succeed to the imperial throne.

The Peace of Amiens with Great Britain could be no more than a truce because the entire continent was closed to British commerce, and Belgium in the hands of the French was a "loaded pistol aimed at the heart of Britain."

Napoleon's determination to extend French power in Europe met with sympathy and support from middle class groups in Europe who envied the rights enjoyed by French businessmen, but with opposition from kings whose rule was threatened, and especially from Britain which feared French domination of Europe and the consequent threat to her European trade and the balance of power.

The Third Coalition

Napoleon planned to consolidate the more than 300 petty states of "Germany" by encouraging the larger principalities to absorb the smaller ones, and thus of necessity become allies of France. Great Britain thereupon organized the Third Coalition with Austria and Russia which feared Napoleon's expanding power. The Emperor determined to break England, the heart of the coalition, by invading England. Once again, unable to get control of the English Channel preparatory to invasion, he decided to become master of the European continent and break England, that "nation of shopkeepers," by denying it any trade with the continent. His admiral Villeneuve was unsuccessful in attempting to draw the British fleet out to the West Indies and leave the Channel clear for Napoleon's projected invasion of the island, so Napoleon moved his army eastwards and defeated an Austrian army at Ulm in October 1805. A day later the decisive victory of Admiral Nelson at Trafalgar destroyed a combined French and Spanish fleet and assured England of control of the seas and safety from invasion. Two giants, one a sea power, the other a land power, now struggled for victory.

Napoleon Controls the Continent

Napoleon marched eastwards to establish his control over the continent. In quick succession he defeated the Austrians at Ulm (1805), the Russians at Austerlitz (1805), the Prussians at Jena and Auerstadt in 1806, and the Russians again at Friedland in 1807.

The Empire was now at its height, and the young Czar Alexander concluded the Treaty of Tilsit with Napoleon whereby Russia agreed that Russia would control Eastern Europe and parts of the Ottoman Empire whenever it was dismembered; in return for this Russia would cut off all trade with Great Britain, and would join in war against her. Russia had to surrender her Polish provinces, which became the Grand Duchy of Warsaw under French protection. Napoleon now had his *continental system* ready for operation across his vast empire. The military giant France and the naval giant Great Britain now engaged in a fight for victory which squeezed the neutral United States, and finally led the Americans to declare war on England.

Continental System vs. British Blockade

Since he was unable to weaken British power by sea or invasion, Napoleon decided to undermine British trade and economy by excluding all British goods from France and French-controlled countries of the continent. This policy he put into operation by his *Berlin Decree* of 1806, which announced that the British Isles were blockaded and that no British trade or goods would be allowed on the continent. The British retaliated, as they could with their predominant sea power, by stating that they would prevent any ships going into ports to which British ships were not allowed. Other decrees affected neutral ships to the point that a neutral could go into no European port without danger of confiscation by one side or the other.

Two "leaks" developed in Napoleon's Continental System. One was Portugal and Spain, where Wellington's army kept the French constantly trying to prevent invasion of France from across the Pyrenees. The other leak was Russia which refused to abide by the French restrictions after 1810.

Invasion of Russia

This defection caused Napoleon to march on Moscow in 1812, where he waited for negotiations that never took place. The Russians simply deserted Moscow, and Napoleon was caught in the fierce Russian winter. This was the beginning of the end for him. The Russian campaign not only weakened his forces but gave heart to nations which were compulsory allies and resenting the heavy "liberating" hand of the emperor. The Battle of Leipzig, or Battle of the Nations, in 1813, led to defeat, to the occupation of Paris by the allies, and to Napoleon's exile to the island of Elba.

Final Defeat of Napoleon

In March 1815 he escaped from Elba, landed at Frejus in the south of France, and during the next Hundred Days gathered an army of veterans resentful of the foreign armies of occupation, fought the battle of Waterloo, and there on June 18 finished his career as emperor and commenced his lonely vigil on the island of St. Helena, in mid-Atlantic, where he died in 1821.

The Peace Settlement and Its Consequences

The Congress of Vienna — Reaction and Revolutions

Terms

Legitimacy	Ultras
Quadruple Alliance	Legitimatists
Holy Alliance	National Workshops
Nationalism	Second Republic
Monroe Doctrine	Second Empire
Greek War of Independence	Zollverein
Emigres	Frankfurt Assembly

People

Louis XVIII	
Louis Blanc	Louis Napoleon (III)
Polignac	Philippe Egalité

Places to Locate
Navarino
Kingdom of the Two Sicilies
Belgium

Significant Dates

1825	Decembrist Revolt in Russia
1829	Greek Independence
1839	Independence of Belgium
1848–1852	Second Republic in France

Topic Outline
The Congress of Vienna
  Issues Facing the Congress
  Settlements of the Congress
  The Quadruple Alliance and the Holy Alliance
Reaction and Revolution
  Revolutions of the 1820's
  The Monroe Doctrine
  The Greek War of Independence
  The Revolutions of the 1830's
  Revolutions of 1848
  Second Republic and Second Empire
  Failure of Revolutions of 1848

The Peace Settlement and Its Consequences

Congress of Vienna

The twenty-three years of war during the era of the French Revolution and the Napoleonic Empire left serious problems to be faced by the victors after Waterloo. Thrones had been overturned, boundaries destroyed, and the map of Europe completely changed. In the process the peoples of many parts of Europe had experienced some of the ideas of the French Revolution such as political rights, equal justice, and freedom of religion.

Issues Facing the Congress

Four basic questions faced the representatives of the victorious powers when they met at Vienna:

1. Should the earlier pre-war boundaries be restored?

2. Should the former reigning families be restored to their thrones?

3. Should the old regimes and type of government be restored, or should the people be permitted to have the rights they wanted?

4. Could similar devastating wars be prevented?

   The victors believed that the long exhausting war was to be blamed upon what they regarded as radical ideas of the French Revolution. If a repetition of such ideas could be prevented, or at least held in check, then the peace of Europe could be maintained. The men who gathered together at Vienna were statesmen, rulers, and deposed monarchs. There were no representatives of the common people. These leaders had no intention of allowing the further spread of the Declaration of the Rights of Man.

Settlements of the Congress

Metternich, Chancellor of Austria, determined to restore the old conditions, and strongly advocated the doctrine of *legitimacy* advanced by Talleyrand, that monarchs who were legitimately entitled to their thrones be restored to them.

France was restricted to its boundaries of 1792, the Bourbons were restored in the person of Louis XVIII (the Dauphin who would have been Louis XVII had been executed with his family in 1793), and France was assessed a large indemnity. France was now accepted as a member in good standing of the European nations but with barriers against possible future expansion: the Kingdom of the Netherland (Belgium and Holland), the Kingdom of Prussia in the Rhineland, the Kingdom of Sardinia in the south, and the North Italian States under the jurisdiction of Austria.

Austria was restored, with the exception of its former possession of the Austrian Netherlands (Belgium), but was compensated with several Italian states and duchies — the Tyrol, the Illyrian provinces, Milan, Parma, Modena, Tuscany.

The Germanic States were reduced to a loose confederation of 38 states under the presidency of Austria.

Russia received much of Poland as an integral part of its territory, so that Poland, which had disappeared by 1795 under the successive seizures by Austria, Prussia, and Russia, now re-appeared, even if only as a province of Russia.

Great Britain retained the useful colonial outposts it had won during the war: Malta, Tobago in the West Indies, Cape Colony in Africa, Honduras in Central America, and Guiana in South America.

The Quadruple Alliance and the Holy Alliance

As a further guarantee for future peace, the four nations Great Britain, Russia, Austria, and Prussia formed the Quadruple Alliance, a political alliance designed to prevent another major war. In 1818 France was admitted, and it became the Quintuple Alliance until Britain decided that her interests were best served by getting out and acting independently. She feared that the other Great Powers might attempt to dominate Europe, and might in due course threaten her. Britain preferred to remain an independent agent, able to form an alliance with any nation against the threat of one nation or group that threatened to become predominant.

The Holy Alliance, sometimes mistaken for the Quadruple Alliance, was a curious notion of Alexander of Russia, who organized the group of Russia, Austria, and Prussia "to take for their sole guide the precepts of Justice, Charity, and Peace." From a practical point of view it had no effect whatever upon diplomacy, and the Quadruple Alliance completely overshadowed it.

On the surface, the peace of Europe was restored and the map of Europe remained unchanged for 35 years, and no major war occurred. But underneath this apparent calm the growing demand of the people of Europe for their own national states and for liberal governments caused several revolutions.

The agitation for more business and economic freedom from restrictions and the desire to enjoy similar political rights won by the American and French Revolutions could not be permanently denied. The long period of war proved what this and later wars proved, that peace does not come simply by ending the fighting. Wars create problems that are only temporarily postponed at the peace table.

Reaction and Revolution

Nationalism can be defined as the state of mind or emotional belief of a people that they have common interests, such as language, culture, tradition, which distinguish them from other groups, and that they have a right to become an independent nation with their own distinct boundaries.

The French Revolution was largely responsible for this widespread feeling, because for the first time a people, not just the upper classes, rallied together to fight the common invader. Nationalism took two forms:

1. The unity of people of the same race, such as Germany and Italy, which both became unified in 1870.

2. The struggle of racial groups such as the Greeks and the Serbians and the Poles who desired to throw off alien rule and win their sovereign independence.

Although we are here considering Europe, it must be remembered that in the British Empire and in Latin America this same desire for independence was manifest.

A different aspect of freedom is that of *democracy*, the right of a people to run its own affairs on the principles of the American Revolution, and not to be ruled by an arbitrary ruler who operates as he chooses, as did the earlier kings of France. Basic to democracy is the concept of free elections, free speech, and government responsible to the wishes of the people. Although democracy began as the extension of these rights to the middle class, it was in time to become the right of the workers also.

The Revolutions of the 1820's

The first outbreak occurred in Spain and Portugal and the Kingdom of the Two Sicilies, where the middle class resented the loss of rights suffered under the restored monarchies of the Vienna settlement. To complicate the situation for Spain, the Spanish-American colonies asserted their independence and broke away from Spain during the Napoleonic era. Ferdinand VII of Spain suspended a Constitution of 1812, providing for universal suffrage and a constitutional monarchy, and planned an expedition against the Spanish colonies.

The Quadruple Alliance was so disturbed by the revolutionary trend that Austria was authorized to send in an army to overthrow the revolutionary government in Naples in 1821, while France helped to restore Ferdinand to full authority in Spain.

The Monroe Doctrine

Britain objected to this interference in the internal affairs of nations, and had already resigned from the Alliance. Suspecting that France was planning to help Spain recover her lost American colonies, she suggested to the United States that the two nations issue a joint declaration against European intervention in the western hemisphere. Great Britain was afraid of losing her economic investments in the new Latin American republics, and the United States feared the establishment of a strong European power in the western hemisphere. Unwilling to associate herself too closely with Great Britain, the United States announced its own Monroe Doctrine which laid down two essential principles:

1. That no further European colonization could be allowed in Latin America.

2. That no European power could be allowed to interfere in any way with the established governments in the western hemisphere, in brief a "Hands Off" doctrine.

The Greek War of Independence

The Turks controlled the whole Balkan peninsula up to the southern frontier of Austria. Within this "Balkania" the Serbs, a Slavic people, had managed to win some rights from their Turkish overlords. The Greeks, proud of their ancient tradition, rebelled against the Turks, sought the aid of Russia, and then were promptly assisted by France and England, who thus foiled Russia's attempt to gain influence and possibly an outlet into the Mediterranean. The naval battle of Navarino in 1827 destroyed the Turkish fleet. In the subsequent Treaty of Adrianople (1829), a small independent Greece was recognized, and Russia was allowed to annex from Turkey the strategic provinces of Wallachia and Moldavia (much of modern Rumania) which controlled the mouth of the Danube river.

The Decembrist Revolt in Russia in December 1825 was an unsuccessful attempt by intellectuals and army officers to obtain a limited, decentralized monarchy which would give local rights to the several provinces. Its only immediate result was the severe repressive policy of the Czar, but it was the beginning of several later attempts that finally culminated in the radical Bolshevik Revolution of 1917.

The Revolutions of 1830

In *France* the restored Bourbon king Louis XVIII adhered to the principles of the constitutional monarchy which confirmed many of the rights won in 1789, religious toleration, equal justice, and the revolutionary property settlements. However, returned *emigres* opposed these liberal ideas, called themselves Ultras, and in 1824 with the accession to the throne of Charles X, brother of Louis XVIII, supported his pretensions to become a "divine-right" monarch. In 1830 Charles and his minister Polignac, whose defeat of the Dey of Algiers in 1830 established the possession of an empire in North Africa, attempted to rig elections to the Chamber of Deputies in their favor. A riot was staged in Paris, barricades were thrown up, and the leaders announced their intention of establishing a republic under the presidency of the Marquis de Lafayette, hero of the American Revolution. The moderate liberals preferred a constitutional monarchy, forced Charles X to abdicate, and set up Louis Philippe, nicknamed "Philip Equality," as a constitutional monarch.

In the *Kingdom of the Netherlands* the Belgian section believed itself to be under-represented in the government, resented Dutch as the official language, and demanded more rights for its Catholic Church. They declared themselves independent in 1830 as a constitutional monarchy, were assisted by France and Great Britain against the Dutch attempt to repress it, and in 1839 were recognized as an independent kingdom by Great Britain. The invasion of Belgium by Germany in 1914 brought Great Britain into the war against Germany in defense of the "scrap of paper" of 1839 by which Britain guaranteed Belgium's independence.

This successful revolution was the first actual breach of the settlements of the Congress of Vienna.

Revolutionary attempts at change in Italy and Germany proved unsuccessful.

Revolutions of 1848

The earlier revolutions in France and Belgium were successful because they were widely supported. By 1848 conditions were changed by the forces of nationalism and liberalism. Subject peoples were more determined to revive their cultures and traditions, and in consequence developed a strong feeling for common purpose. Where aspects of the Old Regime remained, liberals demanded constitutional monarchies or even republics. Two factors precipitated the agitation: one was the failure of the grain harvest in Europe in 1846, and the other was the accompanying industrial depression and rise in unemployment.

France

The industrial revolution brought prosperity to the middle classes but also unemployment and misery to the workers. Their leader Louis Blanc demanded state factories run by and for the workers, and the right to vote for the workers. Royalists or "legitimatists" wanted a divine-right monarchy, and the French people in general criticized government corruption and the dullness of Louis Philippe's administration. That monarch used repressive measures, banned labor unions, caused increased opposition and the barricades once again, and wisely decided to abdicate when a republic was pronounced. Louis Blanc's demand for National Workshops was met, although these became relief projects rather than worker-owned factories.

The provisional government held an election in April 1848 in which almost the entire adult population of France voted — a landmark in European history.

Second Republic (1848–1852); Second Empire (1852–1870)

The new National Assembly, politically moderate, abolished the national workshops because they attracted too many hungry men to Paris. The workers revolted in what was the first example of class warfare, and more than 1500 were killed before the revolt was put down by troops.

By November 1848 the new constitution of the Second Republic was instituted, with a President to be elected every four years by the people. Louis Napoleon Bonaparte, nephew of the former emperor, was elected President. When he was prohibited by the Assembly from a second term, on December 2, 1851, the anniversary of Napoleon's coronation of December 2, 1804, he became dictator by a *coup d'etat* and a year later proclaimed himself Emperor Napoleon III, and inaugurated the Second Empire of France.

Austria

The Hapsburg Empire of Austria consisted of a mixture of several nationalities, Germans, Hungarians, Czechs, Poles, Rumanians, Serbs, Italians, and others, many of whom aspired to national independence. The revolution of 1848 in Paris set off rebellions against the Austrians in Italy, Hungary, and in Bohemia. But the Austrian government, assisted by Russia, which was afraid of rebellion in Poland, was able to repress these incipient revolts.

Germany

In Germany liberalism and nationalism were supported by the bourgeois businessmen and intellectuals who wanted a stronger German Confederation and freedom from Austrian domination. The strongest tie for the Germans was the *Zollverein* or customs union which by abolishing tariffs between the German states encouraged tremendous economic growth. This economic unity encouraged the demand for political unity for the Germans. In 1848 a Convention met at Frankfurt, capital of the Confederation. This popularly elected Frankfurt Assembly drew up a constitution which closely resembled the United States federal system, with a lower house elected by universal male suffrage, and an upper house chosen by the legislatures of the several states, with a constitutional monarch. Austria resisted this development because it would weaken her control over the German states. King William Frederick of Prussia, elected by the Assembly as constitutional German Emperor, rejected the offer. The whole nationalistic effort collapsed through lack of sufficient authority and experience.

Failure of Revolutions of 1848

The basic reasons for failure of the several revolutions of 1848 were the indifference of peasants once feudal restrictions were removed, the inability of the middle class and the workers to find a common program of reform, and the impracticability of achieving success by ideals and aspirations unsupported by organization and force.

One result of these failures was the publication by Karl Marx of the *Communist Manifesto* which proclaimed the author's conviction that a class war existed and should be encouraged and organized on behalf of the working classes of the world. This was to have a tremendous impact on future history.

Latin America: Century of Independence

Terms

The Liberator	Clark Memorandum
El Gran Colombia	Good Neighbor Policy
Roosevelt Corollary	

People

Miranda	Simon Bolivar
Pancho Villa	San Martin
Drago	Maximilian
Huerta	Father Morelos
Father Hidalgo	Iturbide

Significant Dates

1806	Deposition of Ferdinand VII of Spain
1814	Restoration of Ferdinand VII
1816	Independence of Viceroyalty of Rio de la Plata
1822	Independence of Brazil
1824	Independence of Peru
1824	Independence of Mexico

1861	Maximilian, Emperor of Mexico
1865	French Withdraw from Mexico
1895	British Guiana-Venezuela Boundary Dispute
1903	Roosevelt Corollary

Topic Outline
The Winning of Independence
Mexican Independence
Latin America (1825–1914)
   Mexican War (1846–1848)
   The French in Mexico
   Venezuela and the Monroe Doctrine
   The Spanish-American War
   The Panama Canal
   Interference in Latin America by the United States
   Roosevelt Corollary
   President Wilson's Intervention in Latin America
The Clark Memorandum
The Good Neighbor Policy

Latin America: Century of Independence

The Winning of Independence

The example of the American and French Revolutions and the concept of "natural rights" expressed by Locke, Rousseau and Voltaire influenced the inhabitants of Spanish and Portuguese America. Men who were later to be heroes and leaders, such as Simon Bolivar of Venezuela, San Martin of Argentina, visited Europe and planned the overthrow of colonial rule when the time was ripe.

Simon Bolivar: Liberator of the North

In 1808 Napoleon invaded Spain and placed his brother Joseph on the throne. The Spanish Americans refused to recognize him as their sovereign, and set up independent juntas or revolutionary councils in each of the four viceroyalties, and declared their allegiance to Ferdinand VII, the rightful king. But the taste of self-government convinced some leaders that full independence should be achieved. *Francisco de Miranda*, a Venezuelan Creole who had spent years of study in Europe and had hoped to get European support for an independence movement, returned to his native land and persuaded the revolutionary Congress to declare Venezuela independent in 1811. Unsuccessful against Spanish troops, he was betrayed and his place of leadership taken by *Simon Bolivar*, the "Liberator," of Venezuela. In 1814 Ferdinand VII was restored to the throne of Spain, and he not only refused to consider any reforms for Spanish America but sent more troops from Spain to crush the rebellion. For eight years Bolivar resisted the Spanish, and finally freed Colombia, Venezuela, and Ecuador, made them the new nation of El Gran Colombia which in a few years broke up into the three separate countries.

San Martin: Liberator of the South

While Bolivar was freeing the northern part of the continent, *Jose de San Martin* of Argentina, for twenty years an officer in the Spanish army, tried to free the Viceroyalty of Rio de la Plata, and succeeded in winning its independence in

1816. Convinced that lasting success depended upon defeating the Spanish where they were strongest, in the Viceroyalty of Peru, he joined there with a patriot *Bernardo O'Higgins* and for three years trained an army in western Argentina. In 1817 he made his famous march across the Andes, freed the southern part of Chile, then marched northwards and occupied Lima.

Bolivar crossed the mountains and took Quito in northern Peru and met San Martin in 1822 to discuss joint operations. But the two leaders differed on the type of government for the liberated colonies. San Martin favored a royal government headed by a monarch; Bolivar preferred a limited constitutional republic run by an aristocracy until the people could be educated. San Martin turned over his command to Bolivar, issued a farewell address in Lima, and spent the remainder of his life until 1850 in voluntary exile in France. In 1824 Bolivar freed Peru.

Mexican Independence

In Mexico the revolt began in 1810 under a priest *Father Hidalgo*, whose support of poor Indians and mestizos was not popular with other groups. After his capture and execution by the Spanish, his place was taken by Father Morelos who won a victory over the royalists and declared Mexico independent in 1813. But he too was captured and executed, and not until 1821 did a successful leader appear. Then *Iturbide*, a Creole officer and formerly on the royalist side, finally won independence for Mexico but made himself Emperor of Mexico. His rule was short-lived, but Mexico was to suffer numerous upheavals for the next hundred years. Nevertheless, in 1824 Mexico was an independent nation, and soon was so recognized by other nations.

Bolivar's hopes for a united Spanish-American federation did not materialize, for Central and South America separated into twenty independent states. Within less than twenty-five years Spain lost her colonies in the New World except Cuba and Puerto Rico. In 1819 she sold Florida to the United States.

This separation into so many states was caused partly by political and partly for physical reasons. The people had not had any experience whatever in self-government; they were used to rule by dictators, and unfortunately the local caudillos, political or military leaders, were generally accepted. Vast distances, deep tropical forest, great mountain ranges made transportation and communication difficult, except by river systems which limited development to areas around rivers.

Brazil had been despotically ruled from Lisbon, whose sole interest was revenues from diamond and gold mines and plantations. When in 1807 Napoleon invaded Portugal, the king fled to Brazil. Upon his return to Portugal in 1822 King John VI left his son Dom Pedro to represent him, but in that same year Brazil broke away from Portugal, and became an independent limited monarchy under Pedro I, who was succeeded by Pedro II who ruled until 1889 when Brazil became a republic.

Latin America (1825–1914)

Simon Bolivar had dreamed of a great federal union of Central and South America similar to that of the United States. But by 1825 that hope had gone. The vastness of the land, some 8,000,000 square miles, three times as large as the United States, was a handicap to union, as was the lack of a common interest of a population of 20,000,000 compared with that of 9,000,000 in the United States.

They had no common heritage or language, the Indians flatly refused to be assimilated into the white man's world, and the system of land ownership gave the average inhabitant no stake whatever in the country in which he lived.

The nineteenth century is called the medieval period of Latin American history because the upper classes dominated the government and the professions; the Church supported the upper classes in order to keep its own influence and wealth; government was usually dictatorial, itself subject to revolution and coups d'etat.

Throughout the nineteenth century Latin America remained comparatively isolated; little foreign capital was attracted to the continent, and what was invested there seemed to be used for the benefit of the investor. Weak as these nations were and potential targets for intervention by European powers, they were protected by the United States Monroe Doctrine and the British navy.

Four of the republics were federal with power divided between national and regional governments: Argentina, Brazil, Mexico, and Venezuela. Very few became democracies, although Chile, Argentina, Costa Rica and Uruguay in recent years can be so labelled. The others were and have generally been military dictatorships, although not dictatorships in the European sense. The military takes a greater part in politics than do European armies, for it has been through the army that a poor man might rise to comparative affluence and social position. The military has acted to suppress political opposition and to prevent free elections rather than regiment people's everyday life.

Revolutions have been common and frequent in Latin America, although the term *revolution* also is differently used than in Europe where it indicates a fundamental change in a political system, usually a complete reorganization of the social and political order, as the example of the French Revolution. In Latin America revolutions have usually been simple replacements of one dictator by another, rarely with fundamental changes. Armed forces have frequently put into office presidents and leaders who are given the right to rule by decree in case of emergency, with the president usually deciding what constituted an emergency. Elections have frequently been limited to wealthy and educated voters, and they preferred a "dictator" who would not disturb the social and economic system.

Latin America has seen few responsible political parties with platforms and opportunities to legislate to meet needs and changing conditions. In the Anglo-Saxon experience a majority party always concedes to the minority the right to become the majority by peaceful means, by persuading the voters. But in Latin America a "party" consists of "ins" who have no intention of being ousted, and the "outs" who have little chance of being elected.

Mexican War (1846–1848)

United States relations with Latin America remained amicable until the annexation of Texas in 1845. This resulted in the Mexican War of 1846 in which Mexico was obliged to cede half of its territory to the United States. Other Latin American countries regarded the United States as the aggressor.

The French in Mexico (1861)

In 1861 when Mexico failed to pay its obligations to foreign creditors Great Britain, Spain, and France jointly occupied the port of Vera Cruz. The British and Spanish later withdrew, but Napoleon III of France supported Maximilian of Austria on the throne as Emperor of Mexico, a French puppet supported by

French bayonets. The United States was too involved in the bloody Civil War to attempt to enforce the principles of the Monroe Doctrine until 1865. Napoleon III was persuaded to withdraw his troops, and Maximilian ruled less than two years before he was shot by Mexicans.

Venezuela and the Monroe Doctrine (1895, 1902)

In 1895 a long-standing dispute over the British Guiana-Venezuela boundary, which Britain had refused to negotiate, became an issue between Britain and the United States, which requested the British to arbitrate the matter. Britain, at first denying that the issue in any way touched upon the principles of the Monroe Doctrine, finally grudgingly acquiesced, and a division of the territory was arranged.

In 1902 Venezuela defaulted on several foreign obligations. Great Britain, Italy, and Germany threatened to blockade its ports, with Germany persisting after the others had ceased such action. President Theodore Roosevelt brought pressure to bear upon Germany, since he regarded this action as an attempt to interfere with the government of Venezuela, therefore a violation of the Monroe Doctrine.

The Spanish-American War (1898)

Spanish misgovernment of her only American colonies Cuba and Puerto Rico led to repeated attempts by Cubans for reform. The United States sympathized with the Cubans, and the sinking of the U.S.S. *Maine* in Havana Harbor in 1898 led to hostilities with Spain, lasting for three months. The defeat resulted in Spain's giving up Cuba, Puerto Rico, Guam, and the Philippines. Cuba was given nominal independence, and the other three became United States possessions. Cuba was obliged by the Platt Amendment to permit United States intervention and to make no foreign treaty without the consent of the United States.

The Panama Canal

For more than half a century the United States had considered the possibility of constructing an isthmian canal. A French company which had commenced such a project in Colombia in 1883 went bankrupt, and the republic of Colombia agreed to negotiate transfer of French interests to the United States. Impatient of delay, President Theodore Roosevelt encouraged the Colombian province of Panama to rebel; Roosevelt prevented Colombian troops from crossing into Panama; Panama announced itself as a republic, was immediately recognized by the United States, and promptly negotiated a canal treaty.

Interference in Latin America by the United States

The majority of Latin American countries feared the Colossus of the North whose actions implied further interference in their affairs. Reflecting the indignation of many Latin American countries over European intervention in Venezuela in 1902, Argentinian diplomat *Luis Drago* pronounced what has come to be known as the *Drago Doctrine*, denouncing the use of force to collect debts.

The Roosevelt Corollary

Within a short time after Drago's pronouncement, the issue of default on debts by a Latin American country had to be faced squarely. The Dominican Republic was threatened with armed intervention from Europe. Roosevelt realized that failure to pay debts could lead to repeated crises. He therefore extended the Monroe Doctrine from its original "hands off" warning to Europe into what is called the Roosevelt Corollary, that of intervention by the United States in the affairs of those Latin American countries if their actions "invited" foreign intervention.

President Wilson's Intervention in Mexico

Wilson intervened in Latin American politics by refusing to recognize General Huerta who engineered a *coup d'etat* in Mexico in 1913 and subsequently established himself as dictator. Although the major European nations recognized the Huerta government, Wilson not only refused to do so but demanded that Huerta resign. Mexican opponents of Huerta were led by Carranza who rejected Wilson's offer of assistance against Huerta, claiming that the United States had no right to interfere in Mexican internal affairs.

In August 1914, Huerta arrested American sailors who had gone ashore at Tampico; the Mexicans apologized, but United States Admiral Mayo demanded a formal salute of the American flag. They refused, and Wilson ordered the seizure of Vera Cruz, and was bitterly criticized by Carranza, who became president of Mexico upon the abdication of Huerta.

In 1915 the bandit leader Pancho Villa, guerrilla leader opposed to Carranza, murdered some Americans he took from a train in Mexico, and then killed nineteen more in a raid on Columbus, New Mexico. Wilson sent an expedition into Mexico to punish Villa, who raided Texas; Wilson sent in more troops but without success. Finally Wilson negotiated a settlement with Carranza, whose government he recognized in 1917.

This action against Mexico incensed Latin Americans, who feared that the United States might interfere further in Latin American affairs.

The Clark Memorandum

In an attempt to remedy the growing ill-feeling, the Hoover administration issued the Clark Memorandum in 1930 which repudiated the intervention principle enunciated in the Roosevelt Corollary, and re-stated the basic principles of the Monroe Doctrine, that:

1. The Doctrine was unilateral.
2. It did not concern itself with purely inter-American relations.
3. It was directed against European intervention in Latin America.
4. It was not to be used against Latin America.

The Good Neighbor Policy

The Clark Memorandum was later implemented by the Good Neighbor Policy of President Roosevelt in 1933, "I would dedicate this nation to the policy of the good neighbor . . . who respects her obligations and respects the sanctity of agreements in and with a world of neighbors."

By 1936 Roosevelt's warm reception at the Inter-American Conference at Buenos Aires indicated a friendlier feeling of Latin American nations toward the United States.

6

THE GROWTH OF MODERN NATIONALISM

The Industrial Revolution

Terms

Flying Shuttle
Domestic System
Free Trade
New Harmony
Dialectic
Cominform
Utilitarianism
Communism
Comintern
Dictatorship of the Proletariat
Spinning Jenny
Laissez-faire
Iron Law of Wages
Surplus Value
Class Struggle

Fabian Socialists
Socialism
Political Party
The Internationals
Factory System
Wealth of Nations
Principles of Population
Principles of Political Economy
Scientific Socialism
Consumer Co-operatives
Economic Determinism
Social Christianity
Utopian Socialist
"Inevitability of Communism" — Marx

People

Kay
Hargreaves
Eli Whitney
Adam Smith
Malthus
Ricardo
John Mill

Bentham
Saint-Simon
Fourier
Robert Owen
Karl Marx
Engels
Kingsley

Significant Dates

1764   Hargreaves' Spinning Jenny
1769   Steam Power for Machinery
1793   Eli Whitney's Cotton Gin
1795   Steam Power Loom
1807   Robert Fulton's Steamboat
1814   George Stephenson's Steam Locomotive

Topic Outline

Nature of the Industrial Revolution
Textile Machinery

Steam Power
Smelting and Blast Furnaces
Agricultural Improvements
The Factory System
Problems of an Industrial Society
Supporters of Laissez-Faire
Challengers of Capitalism and Laissez-Faire
The Communist Challenge
Errors in Marxist Theory
The "Internationals"

The Industrial Revolution

Nature of the Industrial Revolution

The First Industrial Revolution occurred between 1770 and 1870 and was characterized by:

1. The invention and use of machines in place of hand labor.

2. The use of steam power.

3. The rise of the factory system with its reserves of capital, a pool of labor, and machines.

4. The development of better transportation.

5. The rise of capitalism, the system of investing money in private ventures to make a profit.

The Industrial Revolution began in England because she had many of the necessary conditions for industrialization: a labor supply, capital looking for investment, raw materials brought from abroad in her merchant marine, and coal deposits for steam power to drive machines.

Although past centuries had provided such inventions as the compass, the clock, movable type, gunpowder, very little progress had been made in manufacturing and transportation.

Textile Machinery

The introduction of cotton cloth into England led to increased demand for it and the incentive to develop ways to produce it faster than could be done by the old spinning wheel and hand loom. In 1733 *John Kay* invented the flying shuttle, which produced the cross-thread or warp in cloth. This speedy process created the demand for a faster way to spin thread, a technique invented by *James Hargreaves* in 1764 in his spinning Jenny which spun several threads from one wheel. In a few years first water power then steam power was applied to these techniques, and then to a power loom which could replace more than one hundred weavers. In the United States the invention of the cotton gin (engine) by *Eli Whitney* in 1793 met the demand for increased supplies of cotton thread by separating the fibres from the seeds very much faster than could be done by human labor. This in turn made cotton production in the United States so profitable that the extension of slavery into newly-created territories and states was such a political issue that it became a major cause of the Civil War.

Steam Power

The adaptation of steam to machines was first developed in England in stationary machines to pump water from mines, then adapted by *James Watt* in 1769 to drive machinery, by *Cartwright* in 1785 to the power loom, by *Robert Fulton* to steamboats on the Hudson river in 1807, and the steam locomotive by *George Stephenson* in England in 1814. Steamboats and locomotives were the industrial advances upon earlier developments in road and canal building.

Smelting and Blast Furnaces

Other significant developments in Europe and the United States were the smelting and processing of iron, the blast furnace to provide the hot coke fire for smelting iron, and the Bessemer process for steel making by removing carbon from molten iron, resulting in the reduction of the cost of steel by nearly 85 per cent.

Agricultural Improvements

In agriculture scientific breeding and crop raising increased production and quality. Inventions such as the reaper, the thresher, and harvesting combines raised the necessary food to supply the rapidly-increasing number of factory workers who could not feed themselves.

The Factory System

The rapid development in machines necessitated large sums of money to pay for them. Men with spare money were attracted by the promise of financial reward to invest in companies. The factory system, with its machines, its capital, and its labor supply, led to the development of capitalism, the investment of money for anticipated profit. This in turn led to the rise of business corporations which attracted capital by selling shares of stock to stockholders. This system of business enterprise replaced the former "domestic" system in which one man acted as middleman between the home worker with hand tools and the consumer, provided raw materials and capital, and took all the risks.

Problems of an Industrial Society

The shift from an agricultural and commercial economy to an essentially industrial economy brought with it social, economic, and political problems that are almost unknown to an agricultural economy. The factory system with its concentration of labor caused a population shift to new towns. Men who as farmers or domestic system workers had been able to grow their own food were now dependent upon others. Unemployment could become a serious social problem because no group of persons was responsible for the care of the needy. Closely associated was the problem of care for the aged, for orphans and other dependent people who had formerly been taken care of by the village community. The economic belief of the new capitalism was *laissez-faire*, or freedom from any government restriction at any level. Consequently no responsibility was expected or demanded. Poor factory conditions, long hours, low wages, child labor were the products of competition among factory owners who felt no obligations towards their employees, whose wages depended completely upon the law of supply and demand. Other problems of urbanization were those of accident and sickness, housing conditions, epidemics of disease, education, police and fire protection, which at first were no one's responsibility and caused critics of the factory system to demand remedies and reforms.

Workers determined to remedy their grievances by forming trade unions or associations to help better conditions by acting collectively. Hungry unemployed frequently defeated the objectives of unionists by taking jobs at almost any wage. Business interests refused to accept responsibility and attempted to resist any and every restriction upon their freedom of operation. One significant result of industrialization was the growth of imperialism or colonization, as an answer to the growing demand for more markets.

Supporters of Laissez-Faire

The classical economists supported laissez-faire, the policy of noninterference with private business.

Adam Smith, author of *The Wealth of Nations*, published in 1776, pointed out that mercantilist ideas which believed that a nation's wealth depended upon a surplus of exports over imports, and the amassing of bullion at the expense of neighbors, were outdated. The exchange of goods, he said, works to the benefit of the nations involved, and their wealth increases. The attempt by each person to improve his own condition results in general prosperity. Any restriction, whether by wage-fixing, trade unions, or tariffs interferes with and hampers trade.

Thomas Malthus (1766–1834) in his famous essay *The Principles of Population* formulated natural laws which attempted to prove that since population tends to outrun food supply, then any action which encourages population expansion is harmful. Food increased by arithmetic progression, he said, while population increases by geometric progression. That is, in any given period, say one hundred years, food increases at the rate of 2, 4, 6, 8, 10, while population increases at the rate of 2, 4, 8, 16, 32. Any remedial legislation, such as increased wages, would only increase population and aggravate the problem.

David Ricardo (1772–1823) contributed his "iron law of wages," in which he argued that wages gravitate towards the subsistence level. If higher wages than the prevailing rate are paid, families increase in size because of increased income, more workers compete for the better-paying jobs, the wage level is forced down by competitive bidding by the workers, this in turn leading to misery and starvation. Therefore wages should be left to the laws of supply and demand of the available labor force and should not be regulated by legislation.

The group of men who supported "free trade," with no tariffs levied on competitive foreign goods, were known as the Manchester School.

John Stuart Mill (1806–1876) was the foremost exponent of economic liberalism. In his *Principles of Political Economy* he defended private property and *laissez-faire* but suggested that social inequality could be remedied by a more equitable distribution of wealth by levying income and inheritance taxes, without changing the bases of private ownership.

Jeremy Bentham (1748–1832) expounded the theory of "utilitarianism," by which any practice or institution was measured by "the greatest happiness of the greatest number." He believed that monarchy should be abolished, and that literate adults should have the right to vote. Since each individual is concerned with his own welfare and happiness, the best interests of the community are served by individualism or complete *laissez-faire*, in which every person is left free to satisfy his self-interest.

Challengers of Capitalism and Laissez-Faire

The Socialist Challenge   came from the Utopian Socialists, *Saint-Simon*, *Fourier*, and *Robert Owen*, who all believed in placing the means of production and distribution in the hands of the government, chosen democratically by the people. This was essentially public, not private, ownership. It must be remembered that in the early nineteenth century the terms "socialism" and "communism" were interchangeable, and simply meant society-owned or community-owned, an economic system without the implications of dictatorship that communism reflects today. In present-day usage both advocate state ownership, but while the socialist believes that the political party supporting the program should not only be freely elected into office but should also be freely voted out of office, the communist does not accept the right of free elections once the so-called political "party" has gained power.

Here we might define the term *political party*. It consists of people who have generally the same political ideas, who join or leave the party freely, who organize to elect candidates in order to pass legislation in their own interests. In the democratic concept, the majority party must permit the minority party to try to become the majority party by peaceful means and by free elections. The communist "party," while demanding the democratic right of coming to power by free elections, would then deny the opposition parties the right to exist, certainly the right to engage in free criticism and free elections.

The Utopians believed that if only men applied reason to all problems of industrialism then Utopia would be attained.

Saint-Simon (1760–1825) believed that owners of property and workers must co-operate. To avoid a workers' revolution the new industrialists must consider the social welfare of the poor.

François Fourier (1772–1837) believed that reform of economic inequality could be achieved through small "phalanxes" of 100 people to work as a group and share the profits in a fixed proportion.

Robert Owen (1771–1858), a wealthy Scottish manufacturer, supported labor legislation and trade unions, and advocated co-operative stores owned and run by the members who should share the profits among themselves. He earnestly advocated co-operation in production, by means of small communities of people who would support themselves on the land and would communally produce necessities. He established one such community at New Lanark, Scotland, and another at New Harmony in Indiana. Both failed because practice did not measure up to theory.

His lasting contribution was the formation of consumers' co-operatives that succeeded in Great Britain and spread throughout the United States.

The ideas of the Utopian Socialists had little appeal in general to workers, and little chance of success. They were idealistic rather than practical, and offered no specific program.

The Communist Challenge   *Karl Marx* (1818–1883) differed from the Utopians because he offered what he regarded as a positive program to achieve the socialist state, a theory of what he called "scientific" socialism, not merely an intellectual ideal. This program was based upon three so-called "laws" of history:

1. Economic determinism, or the economic interpretation of history.

2. The class struggle.

3. The historic inevitability of communism. These are to be found in his brief *Communist Manifesto*. A collaborator and supporter of Marx was his friend *Friedrich Engels*.

Economic Determinism: Das Kapital

Marx believed that *conditions* affected history, that the most influential conditions were economic, and that significant changes in history were economic ones. The German philosopher *Hegel* believed that change in history did not happen by chance, but according to a determined pattern. This pattern he called *dialectic*, which means logical presentation, and has nothing to do with dialect. Since he applied this change or dialectic to economic or material changes, he used the term *economic determinism*.

This was closely related to the second "article of faith," so labelled because his beliefs could not be proved but were used by those who accepted them at face value.

The Class Struggle was the most important of the Marxian "laws," since it would be the means to achieve communism. It was based upon the *labor theory of value*, the assumption that the value of a product equalled the total amount of labor that went into its production. The next step was the theory of *surplus value*, by which Marx meant that the difference between the selling price of an article and the actual wages paid for it was the amount by which the worker was robbed. Wealth would become more concentrated, competition would result in cost-cutting and wage-reducing, competition would necessitate a search for new markets overseas, which would result in imperialism, there would be fewer wealthy people and increasingly more poor people. Increasing misery through low wages would lead the proletariat to revolt against their employers, they would take over all private property, and set up a *dictatorship of the proletariat*, which would crush all opposition and eliminate all middle-class bourgeois ideas, until only one class in society remained, the working class. There would be no need for further dictatorship, since there would not be any opposition class.

Historic Inevitability of Communism

History, said Marx, is the record of class struggles, of the have-nots against the haves, of the exploitation of one class by another. To support this contention he traced historic changes: from a slave society in which slaveowners control the means of production, to a feudal society in which the feudal lord controls the means of production, to the capitalist society in which a few owners of factories control the means of production. In each instance society changed because of economic conditions. For example, feudalism became less economically productive than hired farm labor. The last phase, when all change ceases, will come, said Marx, with the overthrow of capitalism, when the workers eliminate the owners of property, when the workers, through the state, own all means of production and distribution, and work for themselves. This claimed Marx, would be the ideal, classless society, when no man exploits another.

Although, according to Marx, this revolution was historically inevitable, it could be hastened by organized, violent action, not by political action through government or by economic action through trade unions. Its appeal was in the *Manifesto*, "Workers of the world unite, you have nothing to lose but your chains."

Errors in Marxist Theory

1. Workers could not unite as a world group,

2. workers had strong feelings of nationalism for their own country,

3. the workers preferred to work through political and economic rather than revolutionary means,

4. capitalism was prepared to make concessions, so that workers were more concerned with sharing in the rewards and gains of the free enterprise system,

5. Marx assumed that the communist state would be classless, and that it would be benevolent,

6. perhaps the greatest error was Marx's failure to recognize that human nature could not be changed, that material rewards must be given for initiative, that incentive will spur peasant or factory worker to greater effort.

Marx's contribution was his exposure of the inadequacies and injustices of a completely unrestricted capitalist system and laissez-faire point of view. In so doing he performed the service of obliging men to consider the needs of an industrial society and ways of improving it.

The "Internationals"

The First International Workingmen's Association was founded in 1864, largely through the efforts of Marx. It attempted to organize the workers of every country and of every variety of radical belief. It was not a coherent political party, and expired in 1876 largely because of the intolerance of leaders to any ideas but their own, and particularly because of Marx's intolerance.

Second International Workingmen's Association was founded in 1889 and lasted down to World War I in general, in Russia until 1917. It represented Marxiam Socialist parties. It collapsed because of internal factionalism, because the classes cooperated and did not develop the anticipated class warfare, and because workingmen supported their respective nations when World War I broke out.

Third International was founded by Lenin in 1919, and became known as the *Comintern*, the Communist International summoning communists all over the world to unite against the "bourgeois cannibals" of capitalism. In 1943 it was officially dissolved by Stalin to placate his allies who were supporting Russia against German invasion. However, in 1947 it re-appeared under another name but with the same purposes as the *Cominform*, the Communist Information Bureau to coordinate the activities of communist countries under the direction of Moscow. Foreign communists were ordered to demand revolutionary tactics abroad and to reject any cooperation with democratic political parties.

Utopian Socialists in England were a small group of English reformers drawn from the clergy who believed that the church should direct its efforts to remedying social abuses. *Charles Kingsley*, the novelist, was a leader. It was a movement that was more Christian than socialist, and relied more upon private philanthropy than on state intervention.

The *Catholic response* to Marxism was much like that of the Christian Socialists, but the Catholics called it Christian Democracy or Social Christianity. Pope Pius IX (1846–1878) was uncompromisingly against trade unions and democratic governments, and regarded it as an error for a Pope to reconcile himself and the Church with "progress, liberalism, and modern civilization."

The Fabian Society of Socialists, or Fabians, were originally a little group of middle-class intellectuals with humanitarian compassion, who adopted as their exemplar *Fabius Cunctator*, the Roman leader against *Hannibal* who won finally through a policy of attrition, of gradually wearing down his opponent. They proposed to convert to a state-regulated economy through the free consent of the people in free elections.

Russia in the Nineteenth Century

Terms

Decembrists
Russification
Emancipation
Zemstvos
Anarchism
Nihilism
Crimean War
Treaty of Paris, 1856
Congress of Berlin
Treaty of Portsmouth

Social Democrats (SD)
Social Revolutionaries (SR)
Constitutional Democrats (Cadets)
Treaty of Shimonoseki
Russo-Japanese War
Autonomy
Bloody Sunday
October Manifesto
Duma

People

Bakunin
Disraeli
Nicholas I

Alexander II
Alexander III
Nicholas II

Places to Locate

Danube River
Korea
Rumania
Serbia
Bosnia-Herzegovina
Wallachia-Moldavia

Formosa
Pescadores
Liaotung Peninsula
Manchuria
Port Arthur
Tsushima Straits

Significant Dates

1854–1856	Crimean War
1861	Emancipation of Serfs
1877–1878	Russo-Turkish War
1904–1905	Russo-Japanese War
1905	Treaty of Portsmouth
1905	October Manifesto
1905	"Bloody Sunday"

Topic Outline

Nicholas I: Russification
The Crimean War
Alexander II: Emancipation of Serfs
The Russo-Turkish War
The Congress of Berlin
Alexander III
Nicholas II
The Russo-Japanese War
"Revolution" of 1905

Russia in the Nineteenth Century

Russia emerged from the Napoleonic Wars with two important territorial possessions in Europe. In 1809 she had acquired Finland, and by 1815 Bessarabia and the Grand Duchy of Warsaw. By 1815 Russia occupied more than a half of Europe, counting European Russia as part of Europe.

Nicholas I (1825–1855): Russification

Upon the accession of Nicholas I the leaders of a revolutionary group in Russia attempted to force reforms upon the Czar. For the next 90 years, up to the outbreak of World War I in 1914 two themes constantly recur through Russian history: One was the Near East Question*, the persistent attempt of Russia to expand westwards through Turkish territory, which included the Balkan peninsula; and the other was the repeated agitation for internal reform.

Each time reform came it was the consequence of military defeat, after the Crimean War of 1854–1856, and after the Russo-Japanese War of 1904–1905. Unfortunately, reforms were temporary only, and were followed by periods of repression through strict censorship, through the secret police, called the Third Section, and by banishment to Siberia. Despite such autocratic rule, Russia experienced great literary achievements during the nineteenth century, in poetry, novels and plays, through such writers as Turgenev, Dostoyevsky, and Tolstoi.

The Decembrists of the reign of Nicholas I were reformers advocating a constitutional, decentralized monarchy, although one group went further and advocated a centralized republic, a foreshadowing of the successful revolution of 1917. The unsuccessful agitation only resulted in severe repression by the Czar.

Nicholas used the Russian language and the state-controlled Greek Orthodox Church as weapons of "Russification" for forcing Polish and other racial groups to use the Russian language and attempting to force all subjects into the approved religion. More than 700 unsuccessful peasant uprisings occurred during Nicholas' reign.

The Crimean War (1854–1856)

As the first half of the nineteenth century proceeded, it became apparent that the Turkish Empire was weakening, probably destined to collapse. Russia saw an opportunity to pursue its traditional aim of expansion westwards, and so championed the cause of all Christians under Turkish rule, with the objective of securing influence in the Balkan peninsula, and if possible control of the Straits of Bosphorus and the Dardanelles. Austria, whose empire included several racial groups, including Slavs, was afraid of a strong Russia on her flank and possible Russian intervention in her empire.

Neither Great Britain nor France wanted to see Russia expand into the Mediterranean. Furthermore, French protection, since the Crusades, of the Roman Catholic clergy in the Holy Places, now controlled by Turkey, cut across Russian championship of Christians under Turkish rule. Earlier crises had been resolved, but in 1848 open rivalry between France and Russia over this issue

---

*What shall be done with Turkey? The Great Powers of Europe decided to support Turkey against Russia.

finally resulted in the Czar's sending troops into the Turkish provinces of Wallachia and Moldavia (part of modern Rumania) on the Black Sea and consequent Russian control of the Danube river. France joined Britain in supporting Turkey, the "sick man of Europe," by sending fleets through the Dardanelles into the Black Sea in 1854. The Crimean War, perhaps insignificant in importance, was one aspect of Britain's traditional balance of power. By the *Treaty of Paris* (1856):

1. Wallachia and Moldavia were to be autonomous under Turkish suzerainty.

2. The Danube river was to be open to all ships.

3. No nation, including Russia, could have fortifications or maintain a fleet on the Black Sea.

This was not a permanent solution, and the issue was to be revived in the Russo-Turkish War of 1877–1878.

Alexander II (1855–1881): Emancipation of Serfs

For some years prior to Alexander's accession, the problem of food shortages had concerned the government. Population had grown rapidly but food supply had remained almost static under the economically unproductive system of serfdom. Defeat in the Crimean War led to demands for reform, and in 1861 agitation from factory owners who wanted more workers, and from intellectuals who saw the need for reform, persuaded the Czar to emancipate the serfs.

Emancipation of the Serfs: The Limitations

The serfs were proclaimed to be free citizens, no longer the personal possession of landowners. They received sufficient land to maintain themselves; landlords were compensated for the loss of part of their land and the personal former services of their serfs; peasants were to redeem the land they received by payments to the government over a period of 49 years. However, the land became the *collective* property of the village or community, to be re-distributed periodically among the households according to the size of families. It is important to note that by the time of the Russian Revolution of 1917 the peasant had not become an individual land proprietor.

Because of these reforms and the removal of the administrative control of the landlords, some form of local self-government was necessary. So provincial district councils, called *zemstvos*, were created, representing landlords, townspeople, and peasants, and charged with the responsibility for roads, churches, schools, and other local matters.

Despite these reforms, discontent was by no means eliminated. The land allotments were generally too small; peasants resented the redemption fees they had to pay, claiming that those who worked the land ought to own it; and over the decades peasant production failed to keep pace with the demands of an increasing population. An attempt to assassinate Alexander II led to curtailment of the privileges of the *zemstvos* and other institutions, and consequent increase in the pace of revolutionary tactics.

Mikhail Bakunin accepted the earlier theories of the Frenchman *Jacques Proudhon* that private property favored a few at the expense of the many, and that it must be eliminated. He preached the doctrine of *anarchism*, in theory the complete absence of governmental restrictions and compulsions, but in practice a doctrine of force and revolt against existing institutions.

Among the intellectuals or intelligentsia another type of opposition took the form of *nihilism*, the acceptance of no authority, the refusal to take anything on faith, and the denunciation of all government, tradition, and, because it was controlled by the state, of all religion. Nihilism was more a philosophical idea than an active political program. The activists were the believers in *anarchism*. In its purely theoretical concept it was a belief that man was so inherently good that rules were completely unnecessary, and that each man should act for himself. In its actual form in Russia (and in other countries as exemplified by the Haymarket Riots in Chicago, in May, 1886) anarchism was individual, not an organized program, violent action against political opponents and governments. Extremists used terror in the belief that they were justified since the government refused to permit the real remedy, a representative parliament with the authority to legislate reforms. They organized secret revolutionary societies, plotted assassinations and destruction of property, and in 1881 succeeded in assassinating the Czar.

The Russo-Turkish War (1877–1878)

In foreign affairs the Near East Question again resulted in war. In 1875 insurrections against Turkish rule occurred in the Balkans provinces, and Russia used the opportunity to send in troops against the Sultan. The Russians advanced on Constantinople in 1877, initiating the Russo-Turkish War. British prime minister Disraeli sent a fleet to guard the Dardanelles, and Alexander signed an armistice and the *Treaty of San Stefano* with Turkey by which:

1. Turkey was to dismantle all fortifications on the lower Danube.

2. Russia was to receive Turkish territory on the Black Sea.

3. Turkey was to recognize the independence of Rumania, Serbia, and Montenegro in the Balkans.

4. Turkey was to grant autonomy to Bulgaria, a move which would clearly mean Russian influence there.

The Congress of Berlin (1878)

Neither Austria-Hungary, Great Britain, nor the recently-created German Empire was prepared to permit Russia to gain such an influence in this part of Europe as "protector" of these nations. Consequently Bismarck acted as the "honest broker" at the Congress of Berlin (1878), and the European powers and not Russia became the "protectors" of a new settlement:

1. Rumania, Serbia, Montenegro were recognized as independent nations.

2. Greece was enlarged.

3. The "Big Bulgaria" was divided into three parts.

a. The Principality of Bulgaria, the part along the Danube, with autonomy or home rule,

b. East Rumelia, the part south of the Black Mountains, also with autonomy.

c. The third part was returned to Turkey, and all these separate parts were to remain under the suzerainty of Turkey.

4. Austria was compensated with the right to occupy Bosnia and Herzegovina (today a part of Yugoslavia).

5. Britain received the right to control Cyprus, which became an important British naval base.

Turkey, deprived of half of her European possessions by her "friends," imported German military experts to train her army, and Russia had to await a more auspicious opportunity to pursue her expansionist policy.

Alexander III (1881–1894)   Russian defeat in the war led to increased pressure at home for reforms, and just as Alexander II was about to call for a consultative assembly elected by the zemstvos and municipalities, he was assassinated by a bomb.

Alexander III determined to avenge his father's death and to ensure autocratic rule, through the techniques of the secret police, press and university censorship, and persecution of non-Orthodox Church citizens.

Nicholas II (1894–1917)   determined to follow in his father's footsteps, and so failed to understand the pressing problems of industrialization, the agrarian crisis, and the need for constitutional and political reforms. His persistence in repressive measures and the Russification of minorities, who actually outnumbered the Russians, resulted in the rise of three political parties:

1. The DS or *Social Democrat* party (workers) which wished to remove the czarist regime by strikes and mass action.

2. The SR or *Social Revolutionary* party (peasants) which was dedicated to the use of violence to remove czardom and the aristocracy.

3. The KD (or Cadets) the *Constitutional Democrat* party (middle class) proposing a program of constitutional monarchy and a representative parliament.

In the meantime foreign affairs resulted in a defeat for Russia which led to the revolution of 1905.

The Russo-Japanese War (1904–1905)   In 1895 Japan had defeated China in Korea, gaining in the Treaty of Shimonoseki, (1895), Formosa and the Pescadores Islands, the Liaotung Peninsula on the China mainland, and the recognition by China of the independence of Korea. Russia, France, and Germany "persuaded" Japan to return the Liaotung Peninsula; subsequently in 1898 Russia "leased" it from China. This brought Japan and Russia into conflict, since both nations planned to acquire Manchuria.

Russia had built the Trans-Siberian Railroad, was constructing a base at Port Arthur, on the Liaotung Peninsula, and through its increasing influence in Manchuria was threatening Japanese expansion northwards from Korea. In the ensuing war Japan destroyed a Russian naval squadron at Port Arthur, landed armies in Manchuria, defeated the Russians in a series of battles, and in Tsushima Straits destroyed the Russian Baltic fleet which had sailed from the Baltic Sea to the Pacific.

President Theodore Roosevelt, not wishing to see either side become too powerful and perhaps upset the balance of power in Eastern Asia, negotiated the *Treaty of Portsmouth* in 1905:

1. Russia surrendered its Liaotung Peninsula to China.

2. Russia got out of Manchuria.

3. Russia ceded the southern half of Sakhalin Island to Japan.

4. Russia acknowledged Japan's "special interests" in Korea, a step in the expansionist program of Japan which no doubt led towards Pearl Harbor in 1941.

"Revolution" of 1905 At home in Russia the defeat was bitterly criticized, demands for reform increased, and on "Bloody Sunday," January 22, 1905, a crowd of unarmed workers, led by a priest, marched to the Czar's palace in St. Petersburg to ask for an 8-hour day, a representative assembly, the right to strike, and other liberal measures. Nicholas II ordered the troops to fire upon the workers; a thousand were killed, revolutionary sentiment swelled, the moderates joined the revolutionaries, and the workers called a general strike and established a council to coordinate their efforts, the Soviet of Workers' Delegates, led by Lenin.

In October, 1905, the Czar issued the *October Manifesto* promising a *duma* or legislative council to be elected by universal male suffrage and to be paramount in legislation. Supporters of czardom organized their own troops, who were joined by returning soldiers from the Russo-Japanese War, and successfully denounced the Manifesto.

Amid these disturbances the first Duma was indirectly elected, through an electoral college, but was immediately deprived of any power over foreign policy and finances, and was subject to dismissal by the Czar. This Duma was soon dissolved, and although others, the third (1907–1912) and the fourth (1912–1917) ran their course of time and introduced reforms for peasants and workers, their manipulation by controlled elections resulted in their becoming reactionary bodies. When World War I broke out in 1914, extremists were organizing for revolution.

France: Second Empire and Third Republic, 1852–1946

Terms

Ems Despatch

Communards

Treaty of Frankfurt

Constituent National Assembly

People

Napoleon III

Dreyfus

Clemenceau

Maximilian

Esterhazy

Boulanger

Zola

Significant Dates

1852   Establishment of Second Empire
1870   Franco-Prussian War
1871   Paris Commune
1875   Third Republic

Topic Outline

Second Empire
Franco-Prussian War
Third Republic
The Dreyfus Case: Monarchists vs Republicans

France: Second Empire and Third Republic, 1852–1946

Second Empire

After declaring himself Emperor Napoleon III in December 1852, Louis Napoleon conducted affairs increasingly as a constitutional monarch, in 1860 allowing the Assembly to debate his programs, and in 1869 giving it the further power of proposing laws and vetoing the budget. Napoleonic legend appealed to Frenchmen who wished to see their country play a larger role in European affairs, and to the bourgeois who remembered the barricades of 1848. Prosperity benefitted France as railroads, factories, steamship lines and other financial endeavors expanded, even though political freedom did suffer. Candidates for office were selected by the government, the legislature could do little but agree to measures submitted to it by the Emperor, and the government suppressed newspapers which criticized it.

In foreign policy the Emperor at first was successful. In 1854 he participated with Great Britain in the Crimean War against Russia, and presided at the peace conference in Paris. For his assistance to Sardinia against Austria he received Nice and Savoy. In North Africa he finished the conquest of Algeria and started the acquisition of French-Indo-China in Southeast Asia.

Prussia's victory over Austria in 1866 alarmed Napoleon, who attempted unsuccessfully to get territory along the Rhine and in the Low Countries as barriers against possible attack by Prussia. His unwise backing of the Austrian Maximilian as Emperor of Mexico—supported by French bayonets—offended the United States by challenging the Monroe Doctrine.

Franco-Prussian War (1870–1971)

In 1870 the liberals in Spain, who had successfully revolted, offered the throne of Spain to a relative of the King of Prussia. Napoleon promptly informed King William that acceptance of the offer would mean war with France, and demanded a promise that William would never allow a relative to accept the throne. William refused to agree, sent a copy of his message to Bismarck his chancellor, who promptly used the opportunity to provoke France into war. Bismarck edited the *Ems Despatch*, as William's telegram was named, so that William appeared to have snubbed the French ambassador, who in turn appeared to have insulted the Prussian king. This incident, designed by Bismarck to have the effect of a "red flag on the Gallic bull," provoked France into a declaration of war. Within less than two months the French emperor and his army were captured at Sedan, revolt broke out in Paris, a provisional government was announced in Paris, soon to be joined by other French cities. For several months the republican government resisted the Germans, but finally Paris fell to the invaders, and the French people elected a National Assembly which agreed to the terms of the *Treaty of Frankfurt* (1871):

1. France to cede Alsace-Lorraine to Germany.

2. To pay an indemnity of nearly one billion dollars to Germany in three years.

3. To support a German occupation army until the indemnity was paid. France never reconciled herself to the loss of Alsace-Lorraine, and was finally to be revenged in 1919, after World War I.

Third Republic

In January, 1871, the King of Prussia was crowned Emperor of the Germans in the Hall of Mirrors at Versailles, and a few days later the gates of Paris were opened to the besieging Germans. Technically, with the surrender of the French emperor Napoleon III, there was no French government to make terms with the Germans. Bismarck insisted on the election of a Constituent Assembly by universal male suffrage, in effect making the French nation accept his peace terms.

The Constituent National Assembly was only gradually able to institute the Third Republic. Elections were held in February, 1871, but out of more than 600 deputies only 200 were republicans. The Paris republicans refused to recognize the new government, and a civil war broke out between the Paris Commune and the National Assembly meeting at Versailles. The supporters of the Commune were generally radical republicans and socialists, labelled *Communards* because they demanded a decentralized government with local self-governing units called communes to be run by the people. The Commune lasted only from March to May, 1871, but it typified to many people the Marxist threat to the middle class and capitalist society. The National Assembly regarded the movement as that of revolutionism, and with determination moved against Paris and through the barricades, at a cost of thousands of casualties for the Paris republicans. The government arrested some 38,000 people, executed 20,000 of them, and deported some 7500 others. The newer republic was born in discord and hate which was to persist until it officially ended in 1946.

In 1875 the National Assembly enacted a constitution setting up the Third Republic. The Chamber of Deputies was chosen by direct election for four years, the Senate by indirect election by organizations in the departments for 9 years, and a President elected for 7 years by both Houses. The real political head of the government was the cabinet of ministers which was responsible for its policies to the Chamber of Deputies.

**The Dreyfus Case:
Monarchists vs
Republicans**

Since there were many parties in the Assembly, socialists to the Speaker's left, republicans in the center, monarchists to the right, no government could be formed without the support of several parties. One group under General Boulanger, "the man on horseback," impatient with republican government, was almost successful in seizing dictatorial power. The bitter rivalry between republicans, monarchists, and clericals almost tore the country apart over the celebrated *Dreyfus* case. Captain Dreyfus, a Jew, was convicted by court-martial of selling French military secrets to Germany, and sent to the French penal colony of Devil's Island. Against Dreyfus were monarchists, clericals, and the army, and anti-Semites. On his side were republicans and intellectuals led by *Emile Zola*, whose open letter "J'Accuse," exposed the "framing" of Dreyfus by the army, one of whose officers, Major *Esterhazy*, had sold the military secrets. The army, sensitive over the defeat of 1870, refused at first to reconsider the evidence. France split over the issue, the Dreyfusards defending the republic, the anti-Dreyfusards attacking it, so that the controversy resolved itself into that of France of the Republic against France of the Monarchy. Finally Dreyfus was rehabilitated, and the republic triumphed as *Georges Clemenceau* emerged as the strong republican leader and prime minister. The republic, watching the growth of socialist representation in the Chamber of Deputies, instituted reforms to win over the socialist support. Old age pensions, regulations to safeguard working and health conditions, limitations of working hours, all helped to heal up the old wounds and to give increasing strength to the Third Republic.

Growth of Democracy in Great Britain and the Problem of Ireland

Terms

Chartists	coalition government
two-party system	responsible government
social security	universal male suffrage
Reform Bills of 1832 and 1867	Parliament Act, 1911

Topic Outline
Political Reform
Restrictions on the House of Lords
The Two-Party System
Welfare Measures for the Workers

Growth of Democracy in Great Britain and the Problem of Ireland

Peace with France in 1815 brought with it economic readjustment that caused temporary depression. Transition from war meant a loss of orders for wartime goods, competition from the continent, returning veterans clamoring for jobs, heavy national debt and inflation.

Demonstrations and strikes were met with force as in the "Peterloo Massacre" in Manchester in 1819. The government of the day was barely representative, the right to vote was restricted to landowners, and seats in the House of Commons had not been redistributed in 200 years, despite the growth of industrialization and the rise of completely new towns.

Political Reform

In 1832 England embarked upon a program of political reform that was to transform it eventually from an oligarchy, or rule by a few, to a democracy. Real authority for government already rested in the legislature, which chose its own political leader, the prime minister, but the House of Commons was representative only of the landowning class. By the 1832 Reform Bill:

1. The voters were increased by nearly 50 per cent.

2. The vote was given to the middle class, on property qualifications.

3. So-called "representation" of "rotten" boroughs, towns now deserted or little more than ruins, was eliminated.

4. Representation was given to industrial towns.

5. In summary, these changes began to put power in the hands of the industrial towns.

The working class was in general excluded from the vote, and as a result the

Chartist movement was organized. The Chartists, regarded as radical agitators because of their dangerous program, were workers and some middle-class who demanded six major reforms:

1. Universal suffrage.
2. Secret ballot.
3. Equal voting districts.
4. Elimination of property qualifications for members of parliament.
5. Payment of members.
6. Annual elections.

These demands were bitterly opposed by parliament which shuddered at these threats to "ancient and venerable institutions."

Conservative prime minister Disraeli decided in 1867 that further extension of the franchise was necessary, and in that year succeeded in getting through parliament a Reform Bill that doubled the number of voters by extending the suffrage to "householders" in towns, men who either owned a house or paid rent. With passage of the Reform Bill of 1884, three out of four male adults could vote. In 1918 universal male suffrage became law; and in 1928 the vote was extended to women.

Restrictions on the House of Lords

By the Parliament Act of 1911 the power of the House of Lords over legislation was limited to a 2-year veto. Any bill passed in three successive sessions over a 2-year period by the House of Commons would become law despite adverse votes by the House of Lords. In 1946 the delaying action was limited to one year.

The Two-Party System

Great Britain is a political democracy today with a two-party system, a significant type of government that is operative as well in the United States and the British Commonwealth nations.

A two-party system is important because one party is the majority and generally strong enough to be able to carry out its policy. In a multi-party system, as in several European countries, no one party can be sure of getting a majority. Government then is run by a coalition of several parties whose basic platforms and interests may be so different that the temporary "alliance" of parties may break down and force the formation of another patchwork government.

A significant difference between Great Britain and the United States governments is that the British government is *responsible,* that is answerable to the wishes of the House of Commons. An election is held and one party is the majority, which chooses its leader, almost invariably a member of the House of Commons. The monarch then "sends for" this chosen leader and asks him to "form a government," which simply means that he chooses his ministers to be heads of the various departments. These ministers must be members of Parliament, with the great majority from the House of Commons. As members of the majority party these leaders must carry out the policy of that party and must "answer" to that majority for every aspect of policy. If a minister acts contrary to the wishes of parliament, which means the majority party, the members may request the prime minister to remove him, and even in extreme cases, vote "no confidence" in the prime minister, and replace him with another leader from their group. By this means the government is held "responsible" to parliament.

**Welfare Measures
for the Workers**

Factory Acts, 1833 to 1918 progressively limited child labor at a minimum of 9 years of age in 1833 to 14 years in 1918, restricted female employment, fixed hours of work for women and children, later for men, and improved conditions of work in mills.

Trade Unions and Social Security.   Socialist and Marxian philosophies gained very little headway. The extension of the franchise, the acceptance of capitalist economy modified by welfare legislation and the legislation of trade unions remedied many of the earlier grievances. Peaceful picketing and strikes were legalized in 1875; in 1906 trade unions were exempted from damage claims from peaceful striking; in 1913 union funds could be used for political purposes.

Economic crises persuaded some middle class intellectuals that neither the Conservative nor the Liberal party was facing realities, so they formed the Fabian Society which proposed to bring about gradually, by discussion and education and parliamentary methods, a state-regulated economy.

The Fabians encouraged the formation of the Labor Party, which originated in 1900 and became by 1945 the majority party. The Liberal Party, supported by the small Labor Party, won the election of 1906 and initiated in 1911 the "welfare state" by establishing workmen's compensation for accidents in 1906 and by compulsory insurance, paid for by workers, employers, and the government, for illness or injury-and-illness, and for unemployment, similar in general to the 1935 Social Security Act in the United States.

Ireland: Home Rule and Independence

Terms

British Commonwealth	Northern Ireland
Catholic Emancipation Act	Irish Free State
The Ulster Question	Statute of Westminster
Republic of Ireland	Home Rule
Easter Rebellion	Eire
Government of Ireland Act	Dail Eireann
Irish Republican Army	Sinn Fein

People
Parnell
de Valera

Places to Locate
Belfast and Northern Ireland
Dublin and Irish Free State

Significant Dates

1916	Easter Rebellion
1920	Government of Ireland Act
1922	Irish Free State Act
1937	Eire, "sovereign, independent State"
1949	Republic of Ireland

Topic Outline
Subjugation of Ireland
Movement for Home Rule
Creation of the Irish Free State
The Statute of Westminster
Republic of Ireland

Ireland: Home Rule and Independence

Although Great Britain had given its "white" colonies responsible government, one "colony" remained an increasing problem, Ireland.

Subjugation of Ireland

English rule over Ireland had begun in the twelfth century, but the Irish constantly opposed English rule, especially after England became Protestant. In the 1650's Cromwell ordered the evacuation of Irish people from the northern counties (now known as Northern Ireland) and their replacement by Protestant English and Scots. In the rest of Ireland nearly three-quarters of all land was taken over by Protestant landlords, often absentee landlords who were concerned with squeezing the highest possible rents from the oppressed Irish tenants. Not until the twentieth century did Great Britain take effective measures to remedy the situation.

More "plantations" of Protestants settled, and in the late seventeenth century repressive laws denied Irish Catholics political, religious, or property rights. In 1801 the Irish Parliament which, because of religious qualifications, represented Protestants only, was abolished, and representation to Parliament in London was substituted, still limited to Protestants. Between 1800 and 1840 the population of Ireland doubled, peasants were unable to find work on the land, and in 1845 a severe potato famine resulted in the death of 500,000 people and the beginning of a great stream of emigration from Ireland to the United States. By 1890 the population of Ireland had dropped nearly fifty per cent.

Movement for Home Rule

During the nineteenth century the Home Rules or Irish Nationalists demanded a separate parliament for Ireland. Led by *Charles Parnell* the Irish members of Parliament, now including Catholics since the Catholic Emancipation Act of 1829, which permitted Catholic representation, deliberately obstructed business in Parliament in their attempt to force through a Home Rule Bill granting self-government in internal affairs to the Irish. Despite the defeat of Home Rule Bills, the British government finally enacted one in 1913 which would have given self-government in most domestic affairs to the whole of Ireland. But the predominantly Protestant North Ireland, the province of Ulster, refused to accept separation from Britain under a general Irish government and threatened to resist by force. The Home Rule Bill became law, but with the proviso that it should not go into force until the Ulster question was settled.

In 1916 a group of Southern Irish Nationalists, the *Sinn Fein*, meaning Ourselves Alone, staged an armed rebellion in Dublin. This *Easter Rebellion* was put down, some of its leaders executed, but the movement was far from crushed. The

Sinn Feiners were only more determined to get complete independence from Great Britain. The years 1919–1921 were grim ones of violence, ambush, and murder, with the British-controlled Royal Irish Constabulary (the Blacks) and British ex-army officers (the Tans), derisively called the "Black and Tans," trying to put down a rebellion which by now was gaining momentum.

In 1920 the Government of Ireland Act was enacted by Parliament, providing for two parliaments, a Northern Ireland Parliament at Belfast and a Southern Ireland Parliament in Dublin. This was resisted by the Sinn Fein who formed the rebellious Irish Republican Army (the I.R.A.) which claimed to be the army of the Irish Republic, by which they meant the whole of Ireland.

Creation of the Irish Free State (1922)

An illegal Irish Parliament, the *Dail Eireann*, moved into full revolution, obliging the British to repeal the 1920 Act and substitute the Irish Free State Act of 1922 which recognized the Irish Free State as a dominion with the same rights of responsible government enjoyed by Canada. Ulster preferred to remain outside the Free State, and chose to remain joined with Great Britain in the official United Kingdom of Great Britain and Northern Ireland.

The Irish Republican Army was to persist, even to recent years, to demand the Union of all Ireland, and to commit terroristic acts against the British and Northern Ireland.

The Statute of Westminster (1931)

In 1931 the British government enacted the Statute of Westminster granting independence to the Dominions:

1. No law of the United Kingdom could apply to the Dominions unless they so wished.
2. No law of any Dominion could be overruled by the British parliament.

The old British Empire was renamed the British Commonwealth of Nations and Empire, the Commonwealth consisting of former dominions, Canada, Australia, New Zealand, South Africa, and the Empire consisting of other parts which were not yet fully independent. The members of the British Commonwealth were independent countries, choosing to recognize the same monarch, and free to "associate" and free to "dis-associate" if and when they may choose.

Eire (1937); Republic of Ireland (1949)

In 1937 the popular leader *Eamon de Valera* introduced a new constitution which changed the name Irish Free State to Eire, "a sovereign, independent democratic State."

In 1949 the Irish set up a republic outside the Commonwealth, the Republic of Ireland.

Unification of Germany and Italy

Terms

German Confederation	Social Security
Carlsbad Decrees	Kulturkampf

Zollverein

Frankfurt Assembly

"Blood and Iron"

Dreikaiserbund

Triple Alliance

Black and Red

Carbonari

Young Italy

Risorgimento

Red Shirts

People

Bismarck

Mazzini

Cavour

Garibaldi

Victor Emmanuel

Significant Dates

1864   The Danish War

1866   Seven Weeks' War

1870   Franco-Prussian War

1870   Kingdom of Italy Established

1871   German Empire Established

Topic Outline

Background of the Unification of Germany

Frankfurt Assembly (1848): Attempt at German Unification

Rise of Prussian Leadership

Political Wars of Prussia:

   Danish War, The Seven Weeks' War

   The Franco-Prussian War

Bismarck's Foreign Policy

Bismarck's Domestic Policy

Germany under Kaiser William II

Unification of Italy

Union of Northern and Central Italy under Sardinia

Kingdom of the Two Sicilies Liberated by Garibaldi

The Kingdom of Italy

Unification of Germany and Italy

Background of the Unification of Germany

When France secured her "natural frontiers" she acquired the German states west of the Rhine. The German princes were encouraged, by the Treaty of Campo Formio of 1797, to compensate themselves from church territories east of the Rhine. The number of states of the Holy Roman Empire was greatly reduced, and in 1806 Napoleon, now emperor, declared the Holy Roman Empire dissolved and the former Holy Roman Emperor to be styled Emperor of Austria. States on the Rhine were brought under French control as the Confederation of the Rhine, which included almost every German state except Austria and Prussia. But Austria resisted Napoleon again, only to be forced to sue for peace for the fourth time, in 1809. Prussia's earlier defeat at Jena in 1806 had aroused a feeling of nationalism against the French. Her opportunity for revenge came after Napoleon's disastrous Russian campaign. In 1813 the opportunity for "national liberation" came. The Prussians joined Russia and Austria, and at Leipzig, in

October 1813, Napoleon's army was defeated in the "Battle of the Nations" and forced back across the Rhine. Finally, at Waterloo in 1815 the Prussians under *Blucher* assisted *Wellington* in the final defeat of the Emperor.

At the Congress of Vienna Prussia was given possessions on the lower Rhine, so that she might keep a "watch on the Rhine" and protect herself against future possible French attack.

In 1830 the French, disappointed at the unfulfilled promises of their king, Charles X, replaced him with their "citizen-king" Louis Philippe. News of this encouraged liberals in other countries to demand constitutional rights. In Germany, while some princes made concessions, Prussia stood firm. But underneath the apparent calm, unrest was getting stronger in the demand for nationalism and German political unification.

Frankfurt Assembly (1848)	**Attempt at German Unification** As in Italy so in Germany a patriotic society was organized for the purpose of accomplishing the unification of the 38 states of the German Confederation created by the Congress of Vienna. The Carlsbad Decrees of 1819 had established throughout the Confederation strict control of university student societies (Burschenschaften), the center of agitation, and strict censorship of the press and all publications. However, one step towards the thwarting of Austrian attempts to "divide and rule" was the creation of a customs union, the zollverein, which by 1844 had virtually eliminated all tariff barriers between the German states.

In 1848 the Frankfurt Assembly, elected by direct manhood suffrage from several states attempted to set up a constituent body for all Germany. But Austria refused to participate, and the King of Prussia refused to accept the position of constitutional monarch of the proposed federal state.

Rise of Prussian Leadership	The kingdom of Prussia developed a prestige and administrative capabilities, and its ruler became convinced that the future of Germany depended upon military power. In 1862, he appointed *Otto von Bismarck* as chief minister of state, a man whose policy was to influence European affairs for the next twenty-five years. Bismarck's first problem was to persuade the independent states of Germany to unite, give up their sovereignty, and accept the leadership of Prussia. He was also convinced that Austria was Prussia's rival for control of Germany, and knew that sooner or later a show-down would take place between the two. Would Prussians be willing to fight Austrians, their fellow-Germans, if the situation so demanded? Bismarck needed Russian neutrality in any conflict that might arise between Prussia and Austria, since he was proposing a policy of "blood and iron." The great questions of the day, he said, are not to be decided by speeches. Between 1862 and 1866, despite opposition from German liberals, he built up the strength of the Prussian army, knowing that the spirit of nationalism would eventually be on his side. The blood and iron policy resulted in three wars, against Denmark, Austria, and France, each success contributing to final unification of Germany under Prussian leadership.

The Danish War (1864): The Seven Weeks' War (1866)	The two duchies of Schleswig and Holstein became an immediate issue because by agreement in 1848 they were ruled personally by the King of Denmark although still incorporated in the German Confederation. In 1863 Denmark annexed the two provinces; Prussia and Austria supported the Confederation's

protest, invaded Denmark and forced it to surrender the provinces in 1864. Bismarck cleverly persuaded Austria to administer Holstein, the southern of the two provinces and contiguous to Prussia, while Prussia administered Schleswig, to the north of Holstein. This situation led to friction between Prussia and Austria, with the latter challenging Prussia for leadership in Germany. The two met on the battlefield in the Seven Weeks' War in 1866.

Successful against Austria, Bismarck was statesman enough not to press his advantage. Prussia received Schleswig-Holstein and a small indemnity, and Austria agreed to the dissolution of the German Confederation and to withdraw from any new reorganization of Germany. Prussia proceeded to annex several former German states and organized a North German Confederation with the King of Prussia as its President.

The Reichstag, or Parliament, elected by universal manhood suffrage, would have no power over finances, and ministers were not responsible to it but to the Bundesrat, or Federal Council, whose delegates were from member states and voted as ordered by their sovereigns. The King of Prussia was in effect able to run Germany.

Bismarck then carried through a masterful stroke to unify the Germans under Prussia.

The Franco-
Prussian War (1870)

In 1868 the throne of Spain was contested by several candidates, one of whom was Prince Leopold, a Hohenzollern. Napoleon III of France, fearful of potential two-front attack from the Hohenzollerns, protested the candidacy and demanded that William of Prussia promise never to permit the candidacy to be renewed.

William sent a copy of a telegram explaining his courteous refusal to the French Ambassador to Bismarck, who so abridged it before publication that it appeared in the press as an affront to the Ambassador. The French reacted to this and other misrepresentations by Bismarck, as he hoped they would, by declaring war on Prussia on July 19, 1870.

After six weeks the French armies were defeated and Napoleon III captured at Sedan, and the lengthy siege of Paris began. By the Treaty of Frankfurt (1871), the French were obliged to pay a large indemnity and to cede Alsace and Lorraine to Prussia, which provided Prussia with a strategic defensive position against possible future attack by France.

In January 1871, in the Hall of Mirrors at Versailles Palace the King of Prussia was crowned Kaiser William I, Emperor of the Germans. One unfortunate result of Bismarck's "blood and iron" policy was that Germany had become unified by force and believed that war could be made to pay in terms of national greatness.

Bismarck, Chancellor of the German Empire (1871–1890) became the leading statesman in Europe, convinced that Germany's aims were now realized and that her basic foreign policy would be to prevent the formation of a European coalition against her.

Bismarck's
Foreign Policy

Realizing that France would almost certainly seek revenge for her loss of Alsace-Lorraine, Bismarck determined to isolate her. In 1873 he organized the *Dreikaiserbund*, or Three Emperors' League, of Germany, Austria, and Russia, in which the signatories agreed to consult upon common action in the event of war. The League was weakened in 1878 at the Congress of Berlin when Germany had to choose between the claims of Austria and Russia in the Balkans. Bismarck doubted the loyalty of the Slavs, and did not want Austria as an enemy.

The *Dual Alliance and Triple Alliance*

In 1879 he negotiated the Dual Alliance between Germany and Austria by which each would assist the other if attacked by Russia or by some other power supported by Russia. This was extended to the Triple Alliance in 1882 by the addition of Italy, outraged by French acquisition of Tunisia (at the deliberate encouragement of Bismarck) which Italy regarded as legitimately hers. The Triple Alliance was negotiated for five years, and was repeatedly renewed until 1915, when Italy backed out.

The terms of the Triple Alliance were:

1. If Italy were attacked by France without provocation, then Germany and Austria would assist her.

2. If Germany were attacked by France, then Italy would assist Germany.

3. If any one of the three were attacked by two or more Great Powers, the others must come to its assistance.

Bismarck's Domestic Policy

After the Franco-Prussian War Germany experienced a rapid industrial growth, accompanied by complaints from the workers of poor pay and long hours. Afraid of socialism and possible revolution, Bismarck at first prohibited socialist literature and meetings, then adopted the policy of "social security," providing the workers with such benefits as protection against losses caused by sickness, accident, and old age.

Unification was implemented through a common coinage, an imperial bank, an imperial Post Office, co-ordinated railroads, and imperial codified law. A legalized and guaranteed army made a military career attractive.

A great *kulturkampf*, "battle for civilization," was waged against the Catholic Church because it was not subordinate to the State, a fight to be duplicated by Hitler in the 1930's. The Center Party, second largest in Germany, defended papal infallibility and suggested restoration of the Pope's temporal power. Severe anti-Catholic measures aroused such bitter opposition that Bismarck finally had to "go to Canossa" in the sense that most of the measures were repealed, partly because even Protestants became alarmed at the religious restrictions imposed by Bismarck.

Opposed to the Social Democratic Party, far less radical than the Marxists but too liberal for his tastes, Bismarck legislated against them but compensated for the action and gained working class support through his social security legislation of compulsory insurance against illness and accident, and old age. Nevertheless Bismarck's crusades against the "Black (the Church) and the Red" (the radicals) were unsuccessful.

Germany under Kaiser William II

Differences between Bismarck and William II, who was determined to be his own master, led to Bismarck's dismissal in 1890, immortalized by the famous *Punch* cartoon "Dropping the Pilot." Unskillful in domestic and foreign affairs the Kaiser embarked upon an expansionist colonial and naval program that embittered relations with other nations, especially Great Britain, and resulted in the Triple Entente of Great Britain, France, and Russia.

Germany planned a Berlin to Baghdad railroad to the Middle East, encouraged the Boer President in the Boer War with the British, and started a large naval program for Germany's "future on the waters," which was regarded as a threat from what was now Europe's greatest military power.

The Unification of Italy

Napoleon I had encouraged the Italians to expect to become a united nation one day, but after 1814 the princes of the dozen principalities came back to rule, and Italian nationalism remained only a distant hope.

At the Congress of Vienna in 1815 Italy was treated as a pawn, because the delegates distrusted both nationalism and republicanism, and so Italy was to remain no more than a "geographical expression" until 1870. The several states of Italy came under the domination of Austria, an opponent of Italian nationalism. They were nine in number: the six kingdoms of Sardinia (Piedmont), Modena, Parma, Lucca, Tuscany, Naples, the two republics of San Marino and Monaco, and the Papal States.

In the peninsula secret societies such as the Carbonari, the Charcoal Burners, plotted and sometimes revolted sporadically against their rulers. Austria rushed in to repress all revolts, one of which had been organized by *Guiseppe Mazzini* (1805–1872) who also organized *Young Italy*, a society of patriotic Italians dedicated to uniting their country into a democratic republic. Impracticable though his idealistic aims were, for he lacked both the force to defeat the Austrians and the political skill and experience to organize a government, his ideals promoted the *risorgimento*, the movement for the resurrection or revival of Italy.

The Italians needed a leader who could make them sink their local prejudices and also claim their firm allegiance. One plan proposed a federation with the Pope as president.

In 1948 the revolts in other parts of Europe encouraged the Italians to attempt unification under *Charles Albert* of Piedmont-Sardinia, but the Austrians put down this revolt, and the Italian "Italy will do it herself" movement seemed to be illusory.

Union of Northern and Central Italy under Sardinia

But in Piedmont-Sardinia was a man who was to become the founder of Italian unification. *Count Cavour* (1810–1861), chief minister of the Kingdom of Piedmont, founded a magazine called *Il Risorgimento*, and brought Piedmont into the Crimean War against Russia simply because he believed he needed friends to help the Italians resist the Austrians.

In 1859 revolts broke out in Parma and Modena, and in Romagna which was part of the Papal States. Napoleon III agreed that Piedmont annex these two states if in turn she would cede Nice and Savoy to France. Italy now consisted of three parts: the enlarged Kingdom of Piedmont-Sardinia, the Papal States in the center of the peninsula, and in the south the Kingdom of the Two Sicilies.

The Kingdom of the Two Sicilies Liberated by Garibaldi

National enthusiasm encouraged *Guiseppe Garibaldi* to lead his Thousand Red Shirts from Genoa and attack the island of Sicily. Two months later the island was his. He then led his Red Shirts to Naples, forced the Bourbon king to flee, and then proposed to march on Rome and force the Pope to give up the Papal States. Cavour, fearing that an attack on Rome might bring in French troops to defend the Pope, sent a force of Piedmontese to complete the conquest of the Kingdom of the Two Sicilies, and to take command away from the impetuous Garibaldi.

The Kingdom of Italy (1870)

Popular plebiscites in various parts of Italy indicated that Italians wished to be part of the growing Italian nation. In March 1870 *Victor Emmanuel* of Piedmont was proclaimed King of Italy, an Italy that was not complete without the Papal States. At Rome the Pope refused to give up this territory and France promised to support him against any attack. But with the defeat of France in the Franco-Prussian War of 1870 the Pope was left without allies. Victor Emmanuel asked the Pope to agree to a settlement, and upon his refusal permitted Italian troops to enter Rome and overcome the token resistance of the papal forces. In 1870 King Victor Emmanuel entered Rome, now the capital of the united nation.

Risorgimento had been accomplished, although the Pope refused to recognize the legality of the new kingdom, and remained a "prisoner" in the Vatican, forbidding all Catholics in Italy to take part in politics. Not until 1929 was the problem resolved, when *Mussolini* agreed to recognize the Vatican as a sovereign independent state.

Romanticism: Nineteenth Century Intellectual Movement

Terms
Darwinian Theory
Social Darwinism

People

Wordsworth	Scott	Koch
Coleridge	Hugo	Darwin
Constable	Dickens	Spencer
Turner	Lister	Treitschke
Hegel	Pasteur	Nietzche

Topic Outline
Romanticism in the Arts
Advances in Science, Medicine, Technology

Romanticism: Nineteenth Century Intellectual Movement

The dominant intellectual temper of the period after Napoleon is summed up in "romantic." It resented industrialization, rebelled against mere reason, the eighteenth-century belief that the world was governed by unchanging laws, and against the formal type of literature. Romantic literature reflected:

1. The growth of national patriotism.
2. The spread of individualism and the belief in human rights.

Romanticism in the Arts

Characteristic of Romanticism was imagination and emotion in literature. *William Wordsworth* and *Samuel Taylor Coleridge* wrote a volume of verse called *Lyrical Ballads* in which they defined poetry as the "spontaneous overflow of powerful feelings," clearly illustrated in Coleridge's *Kubla Khan. Percy Shelley* championed liberty and freedom of thought.

In music the change was from the eighteenth century conventional and precise music of *Haydn* and *Mozart* to the more vital and romantic music of *Beethoven*, the German and Italian operas, and the light and satirist operettas of *Gilbert* and *Sullivan*.

Painting became freer, landscapes were represented more naturally by *John Constable*, and *William Turner* used colors vividly, almost in impressionistic style.

In *philosophy George Hegel* glorified the state, particularly that which gave the greatest freedom to the individual.

Novelists presented Romanticism in various aspects. *Sir Walter Scott* in *Ivanhoe, Kenilworth* and other novels portrayed the vividness of medieval times. *Victor Hugo* in his highly imaginative *Notre Dame de Paris* romanticized Paris and *Alexandre Dumas* entertained readers with his melodramatic *Three Musketeers* and the *Count of Monte Cristo*. *Honore de Balzac* and *Charles Dickens* each in his own way portrayed the contemporary scene, Balzac depicting French bourgeois life. Dickens was the champion of the underdog in such novels as *David Copperfield, Oliver Twist*.

Another phase of Romanticism was Humanitarianism, a concern with the injustices of the industrial age.

Advances in Science, Medicine, Technology

Advances were made in electricity, electromagnetism, theories of electrons and radioactivity. In medical science ether and chloroform alleviated the pain of operations; *Lister* introduced asepsis, the preventing of bacteria entering a wound, and antisepsis, the disinfecting of wounds. *Louis Pasteur* discovered the germ theory of disease. *Robert Koch*, who isolated the tuberculosis and cholera baccili, developed the science of immunology.

Charles Darwin formulated his theory of evolution which, based on scientific investigation, concluded that:

1. Man was descended from a lowly organism.

2. The evolution involves "natural selection," that in the struggle to survive in nature only the fittest survive.

3. That this "fitness" will be handed down to those capable of surviving.

This theory of the survival of the fittest was carried over by others into general affairs of man. "Social Darwinism" or the Darwinian theory applied to society supported the concept of laissez-faire in economic life. *Herbert Spencer* opposed any interference in business by the state, such as the regulation of monopolies or the establishing of minimum wages and maximum hours.

A further application of Social Darwinism attempted to justify war. Natural selection would mean that powerful nations would overcome weak ones, simply because only the fittest survived. Hence, *Treitschke*, the Prussian historian, asserted that "the grandeur of war lies in the annihilation of the puny man . . . in war the chaff is winnowed from the wheat." In the same vein *Friedrich Nietzche* concluded that only the man who had the power to attain authority was fit to exist. Both apparently failed to appreciate that in war the youngest and strongest were killed, that in the history of man, progress has been attained by cooperation not by antagonism.

In summary, while Romanticism reflected ideas of nationalism and humanitarianism, the scientific discoveries of the nineteenth century were one of its greatest achievements.

CHAPTER 7

Imperialism and National Rivalries Lead to War

The New Imperialism

Terms

Colonialism	Responsibility	Geopolitics
Imperialism	British North	Trek
Free Trade	America Act	Union of South Africa
Trusteeship	Reserved Powers	Dominion Status
	Social Darwinism	

People
Mackenzie
Rhodes
Durham
Papineau

Places to Locate

Ontario	Cape Colony	Algeria
Quebec	Transvaal	Southwest Africa
Australia	Angola	Orange Free State
New Zealand	Mozambique	Union of South Africa
Belgian Congo		

Significant Dates
1839   Durham Report
1867   British North America Act
1910   Union of South Africa

Topic Outline
Old Colonialism: White Settlements
The British Empire: Canada, Australia, New Zealand
Revival of Colonialism
Colonial Powers in Africa
Imperialism in China

The New Imperialism

Old Colonialism:
White Settlements

Imperialism is sometimes defined rather grandiloquently as the "spirit of empire," a vague term which might be more specifically defined as political mastery over economically backward areas. The term is usually restricted to the acquisition of non-European regions which were backward and which offered potential strategic bases, waterways, harbors, sources of important raw materials, and potential markets for the industrial nations.

This imperialism or colonialism was very sporadic during the greater part of the nineteenth century, because earlier colonialism, such as the British colonies in North America, had turned out to be a liability rather than an asset. Before industrialism had become competitive between nations, *free trade* was the popular demand, on the theory that trade anywhere and without restrictions of the mercantilist experience was far more beneficial than protectionist measures. Furthermore, European nations were too busy recovering from the exhaustion of the Napoleonic Wars and trying to unify under the incentive of nationalism. The example of Great Britain seemed to show that colonies would in course of time break away from the mother country. The "white" colonies of Great Britain were growing restive and demanding more rights.

The British Empire:

Canada

The Canada which Great Britain had acquired from France in 1763 had expanded into separate settlements, Upper Canada (later Ontario) and Lower Canada (Quebec); later expansion and settlement brought in the maritime colonies of Nova Scotia, New Brunswick, Prince Edward Island, each with a royal governor and an elected assembly. In 1837 revolts broke out in Upper Canada under *William Mackenzie* because old families denied new settlers equal rights, and in Lower Canada under *Louis Papineau* because the majority French resented British domination. The British government sent out as governor-in-chief of British possessions *Lord Durham* whose famous *Durham Report* of 1839 led to the establishment of *"home rule"* or responsible government for Canada. This document, sometimes ranked with Magna Carta, became the cornerstone of the new British *dominion status* for colonies. It proposed (1) that Upper Canada (Ontario) and Lower Canada (Quebec) be united, (2) that the legislative body be popularly elected, with *responsibility*, that is, with ultimate authority to run affairs unhindered by any interference from a British-appointed official, for domestic affairs.

In 1840 Upper and Lower Canada were united, and by 1850 the British governors were permitting the leader of the majority party to run Canadian affairs, Canada officially at this time being the two united provinces.

In 1867 the *British North America Act* established what is known as dominion status:

1. The 5 provinces (Upper and Lower Canada, New Brunswick, Nova Scotia, Prince Edward Island) were united as the Dominion of Canada in a federal government. Newfoundland remained a separate colony until 1949.

2. A royal government represented Great Britain, and was responsible to the Crown and Parliament in England for foreign affairs and defense.

3. The Federal Parliament at Ottawa consisted of a Senate appointed for life, and a democratically elected House of Commons based on universal male suffrage. The provinces (equivalent to the states of the United States) had their own separate parliamentary systems.

4. The federal and provincial governments had complete autonomy over domestic affairs in their own area. One difference from the United States is that the provinces have specified powers, and the federal government the remaining or reserved powers.

5. Other provinces were to be admitted as settled, and on an equality with the existing provinces. (Manitoba, 1870, British Columbia, 1871, Alberta, 1905, Saskatchewan, 1905, Newfoundland, 1949)

However, Canada's power over certain matters was not spelled out. Could Canada secede? What rights did she have in international affairs? Could she control her own armed forces? These questions were not resolved until the Statute of Westminster of 1931.

Australia

Interest in Australia was awakened by *Captain James Cook* who visited the area three times while on scientific investigations for the British government. In 1787 Britain decided to get a foothold in this corner of the globe and to get rid of convicts whose death sentence was commuted to transportation to the colonies.

This first settlement of a thousand people, convicts, marines, and families, in New South Wales was the beginning of Australia. Explorers went out, and during the nineteenth century the five mainland colonies of Queensland, New South Wales, Victoria, South Australia, Western Australia, and the island colony of Tasmania were settled. In 1901 they joined together in the federal Commonwealth of Australia, each state with local authority over its own affairs, and, as in Canada, with the prime minister responsible to the Commonwealth legislature, and dependent upon it for his tenure of office.

New Zealand

The earliest settlers on these islands, two of which were of significance, were convicts who escaped from Australia. By 1840 the British government was encouraging colonization, and in 1907 the islands secured dominion status.

Revival of Colonialism

The demand for raw materials was the essential reason for revised colonialism, but colonialism of a different sort. Unlike the sixteenth and seventeenth century practice of establishing settlers in a colony, the nineteenth century imperialism was the administration of native areas for the benefit of the colonial power.

One of the strongest arguments used in Europe and the United States in support of colonialism was that of the Social Darwinists, who adapted Darwin's thesis of the survival of the fittest in nature to the political and economic scene and justifying the acquisition of colonies. Survival was determined by fitness and superiority in nature, said Darwin. The Social Darwinists simply transferred the argument from nature to man, and justified the acquisition of backward areas by advanced nations, and even the subjection of weak nations to strong ones. The Anglo-Saxons defended their "superior" civilization as justifying expansion. Superior white men would bring civilization to inferior peoples. Others believed that imperialism was morally right but that imperialist nations had obligations gradually to teach backward peoples how to rule themselves and to run their own affairs. The first group believed in indefinite *ownership* of colonial areas, the second in temporary *trusteeship*, which would in due time turn back colonial areas to their educated and trained native leaders. History has shown that trusteeship was the actual development in the sense that, trained or not, the native populations have everywhere in the world been able, through the use of white political rivalries or white conscience, to take over their own administration.

Extremists used the threat of non-white domination as justification for imperialism. On the other side, vehement opponents of imperialism could show that colonies were costly in money and men killed in defending them, that subsidies had to be given to colonial areas in order to compete in world markets, that "free trade" was better served by world-wide markets and not by restricted colonial areas which each nation tried to keep for itself. Furthermore, nations committed to the principles of democracy were hard pressed to square democracy and colonialism in modern times. History has shown that the arguments of the anti-imperialists have prevailed.

Another reason for imperialism was *geopolitics*, the need for strategic geographical bases in order to carry out political objectives. Another was simply prestige, or, as Germany put it, "a place in the sun."

Of the several areas of imperialism—Africa, the Middle East, Southeast Asia, and China—Africa was the most spectacular, because except for the ancient kingdom of Abyssinia or Ethiopia and the young Republic of Liberia, the rest of the continent south of the Sahara was taken over by foreign powers.

Colonial Powers in Africa

Great Britain   displaced Holland in South Africa, and then acquired territories which gave her land stretching from the Cape to Cairo, interrupted only by the Dutch Republics of the Transvaal and the Orange Free State.

The Boer War (1899–1902) was the culmination of friction between the Dutch settlers in South Africa. In 1834 Britain had abolished slavery throughout the empire, including Cape Colony at the southern tip of Africa, acquired from the Netherlands in 1815, but inhabited by Dutch settlers called Boers or farmers since 1660. The Boers resented interference with their slave system of native Africans, and moved out from British jurisdiction in a vast *trek* across the Vaal and the Orange rivers to form two independent Boer republics, the Orange Free State and the Transvaal (South African) Republic.

Between 1852 and 1897 British policy fluctuated between recognition of the two republics and acquisition of them. In 1881 the Transvaal Republic was regarded, contradictorily, as being independent and under the suzerainty of Great Britain.

The discovery of gold and diamonds in the republics, essentially "farmer" republics uninterested in mineral wealth, led to a great influx of adventurers who expected Great Britain to protect and extend their rights and interests. *Cecil Rhodes*, the imperialist and diamond-mine owner, who became prime minister of Cape Colony, decided to use the discontent as a means to take over the Boer republics for Great Britain. His attempt to take over the Transvaal Republic led to the Boer War, in which the Boers were finally defeated, and agreed to accept British control for the time being in return for eventual self-government.

In 1910 the Union of South Africa — of Cape Colony, Natal, the Orange Free State, and the Transvaal Republic — was established with a central government to become another dominion within the British Empire.

In 1914 all the dominions fought on Britain's side against Germany.

By 1914 Britain had acquired many more colonial possessions in Africa, such as Rhodesia, Bechuanaland, Tanganyika, Kenya, Gold Coast, Uganda and others, most of which are today independent nations.

Egypt had long been technically a province of Turkey, but had come under foreign control in the nineteenth century. In 1869 the French-built Suez Canal opened, and in 1875 prime minister *Disraeli* of Great Britain bought from the Khedive of Egypt his bloc of 186,000 shares. Later a debt-ridden Egypt was occupied by its creditors, Great Britain and France, who then managed the country's finances. To control the tributaries of the Nile river, upon which Egypt's economy depended, Great Britain moved southwards into the Sudan. Meanwhile France moved eastwards, occupied Fashoda on the Blue Nile, in the Sudan, and an Anglo-French conflict threatened. By agreement in 1904 France agreed to acknowledge Britain's interest in Northeast Africa, and in return Britain recognized French interests in northwest Africa.

In 1915 Britain proclaimed Egypt and the Sudan as protectorates.

France.   The largest colonial empire in Africa was the French, one of more than 3½ million square miles, of which nearly one half was the Sahara Desert. France acquired her first African territory in 1824 as a result of an expedition against the Barbary pirates in Algeria. In 1881 with the blessing of Bismarck who wanted to isolate France from possible allies, France acquired Tunisia, thereby alienating Italy who wanted Tunisia. This drove Italy into the Triple Alliance with Germany and Austria.

As part of the 1904 agreement with Great Britain, France acquired influential control in Morocco, which resulted in two crises with Germany in 1906 and 1911. France regarded Algeria as a part of the French nation, with representatives in the Chamber of Deputies in Paris, and planned to "assimilate" the North Africans as Frenchmen. France expanded southwards in the Sahara, Equatorial Africa, and the Congo, and eastwards into Somaliland and the island of Madagascar.

Other Nations

Germany acquired Southwest Africa, the more profitable East Africa colony, the Cameroons, and Togoland on the west coast.

Italy had to be satisfied, until the days of Mussolini, with Tripoli and a piece of Somaliland.

Portugal acquired two widely-separated areas, Angola on the west coast and Mozambique on the east coast.

Belgium acquired a vast territory in central Africa, at first called the Congo Free State, then a personal possession of King Leopold II of Belgium until 1908, when it became the Belgian Congo, a colonial possession of the nation.

Imperialism in China

China, long isolated from the rest of the world, regarded itself as the Middle Kingdom, superior to all other nations. What trade it permitted to foreign nations was strictly limited to the port of Canton, where licensing fees and trading conditions were at the mercy of the Emperor's officials. In 1839 the Chinese decision to prevent further importation of opium resulted in the consequent Opium War of 1839–1842. By the subsequent Treaty of Nanking (1842), the "opening" of China began. Britain obtained the island of Hongkong and five "treaty" ports, including Canton, where concession areas were opened to British merchants, and the concessions to be administered by British laws.

During the remainder of the nineteenth century similar treaty ports and concessions were acquired by France (Kwangchow Bay), Germany (Kiaochow), Japan (Korea), and Russia (Port Arthur). As these encroachments on Chinese territory extended, the British persuaded the United States, at the turn of the century, to propose and support an *open door* policy.

By 1900 China had been forced to give foreigners so many political and economic rights that an anti-foreign feeling erupted in the Boxer Rebellion, a rising of secret societies officially recognized as gymnastic groups. So-called relief columns of foreign troops rescued embassy officials and nationals besieged in Peking, and Chinese territory was further impaired by demands for more concessions and a large indemnity.

Japan, anxious to forestall further Russian influence in Korea, "supervised" by Japan since 1895, provoked the Russo-Japanese War of 1904–1905, at the expense of China.

China, 1842–1949

Terms

Treaty of Nanking

Kuomintang

"most-favored nation"

Long March

Three People's Principles

People

Sun Yat Sen

Mao Tse-tung

Chiang Kai-shek

Chou En-lai

Places to Locate

Kiangsi

Canton

Hong Kong

Chunking

Shanghai

Formosa

Foochow

Significant Dates

1840–1842	Opium War
1842	Treaty of Nanking
1844	Treaty of Wanghsia
1911	Chinese Revolution
1937	Outbreak of Sino-Japanese War
1949	Republic of China
1949	Nationalist Government of China Goes to Taiwan

Topic Outline

The Opening of China

T'ai P'ing Rebellion and Sino-Japanese War

The Revolution of 1911

Rise of the Kuomintang Party and Chiang Kai-shek

The War with Japan

People's Republic (Communist) of China and Nationalist China (Formosa or Taiwan)

China, 1842–1949

**The Opening of
China**

In the eighteenth century China was as advanced as Europe in material prosperity, but the Industrial Revolution was to change the situation in Europe. China, now cut off from new techniques, could not keep pace with the changes in Europe. China's relations with the outside world had long been based upon the concept of the inferiority of foreigners. China had long been the center of civilization, the Middle Kingdom as it called itself. Missions from other nations were treated as no more than tribute-bearers; trade with China depended upon China's decisions, and was arbitrarily determined by the limited number of merchants allowed by the emperor to trade with foreigners.

The British East India Company, engaged in trade which included the very profitable importation of opium into China, refused to be treated as inferiors and to be subject to uncertain rules of trade. The opium trade, a highly questionable business, resulted in the loss of Chinese silver money to pay for the product. When the emperor ordered the trade to cease, and the foreigners refused to accept the order, the Chinese authorities seized more than 20,000 chests of British-owned opium, valued at $6,000,000.

While the destruction of opium was the immediate cause of the ensuing Opium War of 1840–1842, there were other basic issues. The British demanded fair trading rules, the establishment of diplomatic relations to protect their interests, and greater opportunities for general trade.

British success in the war resulted in the Treaty of Nanking in 1842 which gave foreigners the decidedly unequal trading terms forced from the Chinese. The main terms were:

1. Five "treaty" ports (Canton, Foochow, Shanghai, Amoy and Ningpo) were opened to British merchants and British consular officials.

2. The British were to trade with whomever they pleased.

3. The island of Hong Kong was ceded to Britain "in perpetuity."

4. China agreed to pay an indemnity of $21,000,000.

5. Until 1930 China could not levy more than a 5 per cent tax upon foreign imports.

In 1843 the "most-favored nation" clause was added whereby whatever concession was extended to any other nation must be granted to all nations having that clause in their treaties.

In 1844 the first treaty with America was signed at Wanghsia, including the most-favored-nation clause and the principle of extraterritoriality by which Americans, as other nations already had, remained free from Chinese law.

These restrictions remained down to recent times, and account in part for China's resentment of foreigners.

Unfortunately, the Manchu emperors and government officials failed to meet changing conditions and accept industrial society, which was necessary for national development and for military defense against further European encroachment. China lacked the capital and the skills for private industrialization; she attempted to achieve commercial success by monopoly instead of competition; and she retained the basic principles of Confucian ideals which, based upon local loyalty, failed to provide the sense of loyalty to a nation.

T'ai P'ing Rebellion and Sino-Japanese War

The T'ai P'ing Rebellion of 1850 to 1864 was a vast civil war which was partly economic and partly political, attacking many Chinese customs which seemed to contribute to China's helplessness, and which demanded the redistribution of land and equal educational opportunities. It is estimated that 20,000,000 people perished, and that many prosperous regions were laid waste.

A further great set-back for China was the Sino-Japanese War of 1894–1895 in which the recently-industrialized Japan forced China to cede Chinese territory to her.

The United States did not participate in the ensuing general "slicing of the Chinese melon," but through its Open Door policy did get commercial concessions from China. Chinese statesmen, convinced that Japan's success in the war and in the later Russo-Japanese War was the result of political reform in Japan, demanded reforms which the Manchu rulers promised by 1917. But discontent precipitated the revolution of 1911, led by Sun Yat-sen, which swept the Manchus off the throne and started China along the road which led to the Communist victory of 1949.

The Revolution of 1911

Several factors precipitated the 1911 Revolution:

1. The heavy indemnities paid to Japan after the Sino-Japanese War.

2. The failure of the anti-foreign Boxer Rebellion of 1900 with its heavy indemnities paid to foreign nations.

3. Economic disasters of floods and famine unrelieved by any government assistance.

4. Resentment of intellectuals with the slow pace of reform.

5. Revolutionary outbreaks in various parts of the country.

Rise of the Kuomintang Party and Chiang Kai-shek

Dr. Sun Yat-sen, the intellectual "father" of the Revolution, negotiated a republican form of government, with himself elected President of the Chinese Republic. Dissension developed, and a self-appointed emperor Yuan replaced Sun Yat-sen, the republic in turn was replaced, and ten years of internal dissension resulted in the establishment of the power of local warlords who dominated various sections of China.

Sun Yat-sen was elected President again in 1921, but in Canton a group organized the Kuomintang, or Nationalist Party, and took over Sun's Three People's Principles as its platform:

1. Nationalism, the liberation of China from foreign domination.

2. Democracy.

3. Livelihood, or economic rights and security for the people, generally along socialist lines.

Upon Sun's death in 1925 rival groups contended for power. The Kuomintang worked closely with Russia because both countries were anti-imperialist. Communists were admitted to membership in the Kuomintang, and although numerically weak were able to exert great influence. Outwardly committed to the Kuomintang program, they were actually planning for a communist China. Peasants were particularly receptive to communist promises of land reform, students and intellectuals were eager to have their talents recognized and used, and the communists played upon these interests. But one man was already coming to the fore as the potential leader.

Chiang Kai-shek had previously been sent to Russia for indoctrination and training as a revolutionary leader. As head of the Whampoa Military Academy, China's West Point, he was in a position to become an effective leader, particularly since he was interested in China's future and suspicious of Russia's doctrine and intentions. Within the Kuomintang party a split developed between the communists under *Chou En-lai* and the nationalist anticommunist group under Chiang Kai-shek, who got the jump on the communists and expelled them before they expelled him.

In 1927 Chiang Kai-shek launched his Northern Expedition against independent warlords. Meeting opposition from Chinese Communists, he instigated a shattering purge in Shanghai, Nanking, and other centers of Communist strength. The Communists then organized a soviet-type republic at Juichin in southeast China in 1931, where *Mao Tse-tung* first came into prominence. Between 1931 and 1933 Chiang launched four major but inconclusive "bandit-suppression" campaigns against Juichin, and in October 1933 combined an economic blockade and a military drive that killed or starved nearly 1,000,000 people. The Communists, forced to abandon their base, began the Long March northward, actually a mass migration. More than 90,000 communists left Juichin in October 1934, slipped through the Nationalist lines, and started the 6000-mile march across seven mountain ranges. Mao Tse-tung dominated the policy-making councils and led one column of Communists. During this Long March, *Lin Piao*, later to become Defense Minister, led another group. Finally in October 1935 some 10,000 men under Mao and Chou En-lai reached Yenan province in northern China, and established their new base.

The War with Japan

During the war between Japan and China, from 1937 to 1945, the Communist and Chinese Nationalist forces worked together occasionally against the Japanese, but more frequently fought each other in a continuing struggle for dominant position once the Japanese were defeated. Japan's objective was to keep China divided, prevent her industrialization and the threat of her competition, secure raw materials and markets, and develop the so-called Co-Prosperity Sphere in Asia to guarantee her own industrial predominance.

Chiang's refusal to submit, his evacuation of the coastal provinces, and the removal of millions of Chinese soldiers, students, and workers to the interior, with Chunking as its capital, had a profound effect upon Chinese customs and traditions. Old family ties were broken, free elections were scarcely possible; Chiang's government, under the stress of war, inevitably became reactionary and corrupt because it was not responsible to voters. The war against Japan was a revolution in itself, for the Communists could pose as the liberators of China and the champions of the peasants. In the ensuing internal struggle between Chiang and the Communists, after the defeat of Japan, the Kuomintang Party under Chiang became identified, not always justifiably, with failure and corruption, with foreign domination of China by American interests, with the economic disaster of terrible inflation, and with the perpetuation of the landlord class.

The suddenness of the Japanese surrender caught both Chinese Communists and Nationalists off balance. Mao and Chiang attempted to negotiate, or went through the motions, while their forces fought to secure control of northern China. By 1946 the entire country was torn by civil war. Although Nationalist forces outnumbered Communist troops, Mao Tse-tung inflicted a devastating defeat upon Chiang at Hsuchow where nearly half a million men were engaged on each side. Chiang's divisions were cut to pieces, and within months the Nationalist government fled to the island of Taiwan. In October 1949 Mao Tse-tung proclaimed the People's Republic of China.

People's Republic (Communist) of China and Nationalist China (Formosa or Taiwan)

Many Americans blamed the United States administration for the failure, but Chiang Kai-shek put much of the blame where it belonged, upon the Kuomintang itself. It was not so much the power of the Chinese communists that led to their victory, he said, but "the loose discipline and low spirit of the (Kuomintang) Party " which had "failed to enforce the Principle of the People's Livelihood."

What had happened was that the Chinese people, disillusioned with the lack of a positive program from the Kuomintang, had quite simply, in the Confucian Chinese manner, withdrawn their support from the Kuomintang and permitted the Communists to win.

Turkish and Austrian Empires

Terms

Autonomy	Pan-Hellenic	Pan-Slavic
Young Turks	Augsleich	Dual Monarchy
Magyars		

People

Sobieski
Kossuth

Places to Locate

Turkish Empire in 1815	Bosnia-Herzegovina	Serbia
Hungary	Montenegro	Bulgaria
Rumania	Danube River	Albania
Moldavia-Wallachia		

Significant Dates

1829	Greek Independence
1829	Autonomy for Moldavia-Wallachia and Serbia
1854–1856	Crimean War
1877–1878	Russo-Turkish War

Topic Outline

Background of Turkish Empire
People of the Balkan Peninsula
Independence Movements
The Crimean War

The Russo-Turkish War
Conflicting Interests in the Balkans
The Austrian Empire (Problem of Nationalities)
The Dual Monarchy: Austria-Hungary

Turkish and Austrian Empires

Background of Turkish Empire

With the capture of Constantinople by the Turks in 1453 the Byzantine Empire came to an end, and the great Justinian church of Santa Maria converted into a Moslem mosque. The Turks then turned their attention to further expansion, and conquered the areas of Greece, Serbia, Albania, Bosnia, and by the beginning of the sixteenth century took Hungary and came to the gates of Vienna. Meanwhile Turkish control was extended southwards through Mesopotamia, Syria, and Egypt, and along the southern shores of the Mediterranean, and across North Africa to the Atlantic. This vast empire was Moslem in religion and a complete autocracy in politics. It had one unique quality in that its administrative staff and the greater part of its army were composed of its Christian subjects forcibly converted to Mohammedanism. Europe made no attempt to combine against the infidels, and only Austria and the Republic of Venice resisted the Turkish advance. Venice retained its independence, although it was obliged to surrender its Aegean possessions in return for trading privileges in the Ottoman dominions and at Constantinople.

During the seventeenth century Turkey again attempted to expand westwards, successfully capturing Crete from the Venetians in 1669, and a few years later annexing the Ukraine from Poland. In 1683 a large Turkish army set siege to Vienna until overwhelmingly defeated by *Sobieski*, King of Poland. By a treaty in 1699 the Hapsburg monarchy regained most of Hungary. From this time on Turkish influence declined as dissatisfied subject groups and corrupt government weakened its power.

During the eighteenth century Catherine the Great of Russia acquired from Turkey the Crimean peninsula and land on the Dneister River, and what she claimed as the right to protect Christian subjects of Turkey, a claim which was later to be used as a pretext to make war on Turkey in the nineteenth century.

Although Turkey was unrepresented at the Congress of Vienna in 1815; she ruled over a large empire including most of Asia Minor, the Balkan peninsula, and the northern coast of Africa from Egypt to Algeria.

Because a significant part of the history of the nineteenth century involves the Balkan Peninsula, an understanding of racial issues there will explain in part the outbreak of the Russo-Turkish War of 1877–1878 and the outbreak of World War I in 1914.

People of the Balkan Peninsula

The Balkan peninsula is strategically located, since it is accessible from Europe and from Asia, and historically has been a battleground. The constituent racial groups, unwilling subjects of Turkey, created an explosive situation. The *Serbs* were of Slavic origin, inhabited what were the identifiable areas of Serbia, Montenegro, Bosnia, and Herzegovina, and were motivated by strong nationalist ambitions to create an independent nation of Serbians.

The *Rumanians* were of mixed origin whose ancestors were settlers and soldiers of the Roman army, who inhabited the provinces of Moldavia and Wallachia, strategically situated on the lower reaches of the Danube river, so as to control the traffic into the Black Sea.

The *Bulgarians* were originally a Turkish tribe from Asia which had become Slavic in language and culture, were located on the southern bank of the Danube, and were therefore potentially capable of strategic influence there.

Other racial groups under the Turks were *Greeks,* the most advanced of all the Balkan people, the *Albanians,* a nomadic people in a wild country, and the *Montenegrins,* a branch of the Serbs who had fled to the mountains in the fourteenth century and for nearly 500 years carried on a struggle that finally won them independence in 1799.

General opposition to Turkish control was caused by the subjection to Turkey of these Christian groups, forbidden to have firearms and obliged to contribute forced labor on the roads and fortifications, and by the indignity and harshness of official corruption.

Independence Movements

The Serbians revolted in a general uprising in 1804, and in 1829 by the Treaty of Adrianople were given autonomy but obliged to pay tribute to Turkey. In 1821, inspired by the nationalistic spirit of the French Revolution, two Greeks, the Ypsilanti brothers, started an uprising which resulted in the massacre of all Greeks in Constantinople and on the island of Chios, and the dispatching of a Turkish fleet to Greece in 1827. The Czar of Russia, Nicholas I, decided to weaken Turkey as a preliminary to seizing the Dardanelles, but was forestalled by Britain and France who, jointly with Russia, sponsored Greek independence, granted by the Treaty of Adrianople (1829), which also secured autonomy for Serbia and Moldavia-Wallachia. Not until 1878 did this area become independent as Rumania, and then only with the protection of Russia, which occupied the country for six years.

The Crimean War (1854–1856)

The Near Eastern Question developed in the mid-nineteenth century, and was essentially the attempt of Russia to expand in the Balkan area and Great Britain's opposition to Russia. As it developed during the remainder of the century it became an outstanding problem in European diplomatic affairs. Czar Nicholas I hinted at the granting of independence to all Balkan nationalities, of course under the protection of Russia, and used the pretext of the protection by Russia of the Holy Places under Turkish control as the claim to protect all Christians in the Ottoman Empire. France and Great Britain understood that this could lead to control of Constantinople and the Dardanelles by Russia, and opposed this move by sending fleets into the Black Sea, so precipitating the Crimean War. By the Treaty of Paris (1856), the integrity of the tottering Turkish Empire was maintained, the Straits were closed to foreign warships, and no nation was permitted to maintain warships or fortifications on the Black Sea. This was a distinct blow to Russian ambitions, which awaited only another opportunity.

In 1875 a crisis developed when Bulgarian and Serbian nationalists revolted in a declaration of war by Serbians and Montenegrins on Turkey. A massacre of 12,000 Bulgarians by Turkey led to strong protests from the other nations, especially Great Britain, and a declaration of war on Turkey by Russia.

The Russo-Turkish War (1877–1878)

The Russo-Turkish War ended in the Treaty of San Stefano (1878), by which Russia secured the independence of Serbia and Rumania, and a large Bulgaria nominally tributary to Turkey but really under Russian domination. This gave Russia too much power as the "protector" of the new nations in the Balkans, so at the Congress of Berlin (1878), other European nations forced Russia to surrender much of her victory.

Two nationalistic movements, the Pan-Hellenic or All-Greek, and the Pan-Slavic, precipitated further crises in the Balkans. Half the Greek people were still under Turkish domination in Crete, Thessaly, Epirus, and the Aegean Islands.

Various Slavic groups in the Balkans gave Russia the opportunity to extend her influence there under the guise of the Pan-Slavic movement which glorified the mission of the Slavic peoples and regarded Russia as destined to protect Slavs, including those in the Austro-Hungarian Empire.

But Germany and Austria quite naturally opposed the Pan-Slav movement. German motives were largely economic since Germany envisaged a large continuous economic area from the Baltic to the Persian Gulf which she wanted to exploit. Russian ambitions clearly cut right across Germany's.

Austrian opposition was basically defensive, since the Pan-Slav movement could lead to the break-up of her empire. As a counter-move Austria annexed to herself the Serbian-inhabited provinces of Bosnia and Herzegovina in 1908, and thus precipitated a series of Balkan Wars in which Greece, Bulgaria, Serbia, Montenegro fought Turkey, but then quarrelled over the spoils when Serbia and Bulgaria disputed each other's claims.

Conflicting Interests in the Balkans

Four interests were in conflict in the Balkans:

1. Austria-Hungary decided that it had to extend its influence to forestall Russia.

2. The South Slavs (later to form Yugoslavia after World War I) wanted to unite as Serbia.

3. Russia wished to reach the Mediterranean through the Balkans, since the Dardanelles were closed to her.

4. The *Young Turks*, a nationalist movement, wanted to strengthen Turkey and prevent the break-up of the extensive Turkish Empire.

The crisis that precipitated World War I occurred when the Austrian Archduke was assassinated at Sarajevo in Bosnia-Herzegovina by a Serbian in June, 1914.

The Austrian Empire (Problem of Nationalties)

After the Congress of Vienna and until 1848 Austria dominated politics in Italy and Central Europe. Nevertheless, it lacked unity, political and racial, for it consisted of Germans, Hungarians (Magyars), Czechs, Slovaks, Serbians, Rumanians, and Italians, and was to be increasingly theatened by the rising nationalistic feelings of its subject peoples, and by Russia's political tactics of encouraging such nationalism.

The first threat to autocratic rule came in 1846 in a revolt by Polish landlords, whose treatment of their serfs gave Austria a political weapon to crush the revolt.

Louis Kossuth became, in the mid-1840's, the spokesman for and leader of Hungarian nationalists. His demands in 1848 for parliamentary government and virtual autonomy for Hungary led to revolt by the workers, and the granting of virtual independence for Hungary, with the same emperor as Austria. The March Laws of 1848 instituted parliamentary government, and an elected assembly. Non-Hungarians within Hungary — Germans, Croats, Slavs, Poles, ad Rumanians — resented discrimination against them, rose in revolt and thus gave Austria the opportunity to intervene and, with the help of Russian troops, not only crush the revolt but also cancel all former concessions to Hungary.

The Dual Monarchy: Austria-Hungary

From 1850 the empire was unified and ruled from Vienna, although Hungary remained dissatisfied. The war with Prussia in 1866 over Holstein persuaded the emperor *Franz Joseph* that Hungary must be placated, so in 1867 he arranged the *augsleich* or compromise which restored to Hungary the 1848 Constitution and reorganized the Empire as a partnership, the Dual Monarchy. The emperor was crowned as King of Hungary, the two states had common ministers for finance and foreign policy, each country had a parliament for joint approval of budgets.

This situation of two separate states ruled by the same monarch was unique. The underlying problem was that of subject minorities. An increasing national consciousness of the minority groups and the opportunity afforded Russia to encourage Slav independence were to be a continuing source of trouble until the collapse of the Austro-Hungarian Empire in 1918, and the creation of new "self-determined" states at Versailles in 1919.

In the 1870's the center of disturbance was the region of Bosnia-Herzegovina, almost entirely Slavic in population and part of the Balkans ruled by the Turkish Empire.

Independence for Subject Nationalities

Rumanians, Bulgarians, Greeks, and Serbians were only awaiting an opportunity to revolt against Turkey. In the 1870's Serbia and Rumania freed themselves from Turkish rule; Bulgaria attempted independence in 1876 but was repressed with atrocities by Turkey, with the result that Russia then posed as the champion of these Christians and declared war on Turkey in 1877.

At the Congress of Berlin (1878), Rumania, Serbia, and little Montenegro were granted complete independence, but the Bulgaria issue was not resolved. Austria was given the right to occupy but not to annex Bosnia-Herzegovina. Since these two provinces were inhabited by Serbians the new nation of Serbians wished to include them within her boundaries, a desire that was encouraged by Russia, which wanted influence in the Balkans.

In 1908 the annexation of Bosnia-Herzegovina by Austria incensed Serbia, and in due course led to the assassination of the Austrian archduke in 1914 and World War I.

World War I

Terms

Three Emperors' League	Reinsurance Treaty
Dual Alliance	"Diplomatic Revolution"
Triple Alliance	Anglo-Japanese Alliance

Dual Entente

"Scrap of Paper"

Treaty of Brest-Litovsk

Schlieffen Plan

Sarajevo Affair

Triple Entente

Fashoda Incident

Drang Nach Osten

People

Marchand

Kitchener

Archduke of Austria

Princip

Places to Locate

Fashoda

Algeciras

Tangier

Tripoli

Morocco

Significant Dates

1879	Dual Alliance
1882	Triple Alliance
1894	Dual Entente (Entente Cordiale)
1905	Moroccan Crisis
1907	Triple Entente
1911	2nd Moroccan Crisis
1914, June 28	Assassination of Archduke of Austria
1914, Aug. 3	Germany Declares War on France
1917, April 16	U.S. Declares War on Germany

Topic Outline

Balance of Power Shift

Rival Alliances

Territorial Rivalries

Great Power Rivalries: Anglo-German

International Crises

The Balkans

The Sarajevo Affair

Events Leading to War

Whose Responsibility?

Course of World War I

World War I

The first general European war in a century started in 1914, a few weeks after the assassination of the Archduke of Austria on June 28th. This incident was not the cause of the war but simply the spark that started the conflagration. A series of crises that had commenced in 1870 built up increasingly to a tense situation which a minor incident could precipitate into a general war.

Balance of Power Shift

With the rise of two new nations, Germany and Italy, the old balance of power shifted. European powers had drawn the map of Europe in 1815 to suit their own interests. Consequently, when these two new nations came late upon the scene, through the consolidation of several states within their old boundaries, there was no room for their expansion in Europe.

European rivalry was intense, and as alliances developed there was no international body, such as the later League of Nations and the United Nations, to which problems could be referred. Not that either later body could make a final decision, but the opportunity for nations to discuss common problems could lessen tension.

The Three Emperors League of Austria, Germany, and Russia was strained after the Congress of Berlin (1878), when Bismarck negotiated the settlement after the Russo-Turkish War, and antagonized Russia by denying her the fruits of her victory.

Rival Alliances

Bismarck immediately arranged the Dual Alliance with Austria in 1879 in which the chief clause was that both would go to war if Russia attacked either. In 1882, Italy, angered at French acquisition of Tunisia, and anxious for the prestige of an alliance with Germany, joined the Dual to form the Triple Alliance, which guaranteed support to Italy by the allies if she were attacked by France, and obliged Italy to aid Germany if attacked by France.

The greatest weakness of the Triple Alliance was that Austria might assume that she would get Germany's assistance in any controversy between Austria and Russia. A further weakness was that France and Russia might decide to ally together, and that Great Britain could regard Germany as an increasing threat to the balance of power in Europe.

In 1890 the Russian-German Re-insurance Treaty, which replaced the Three Emperors' League, lapsed, and Germany did not choose to renew it. Russia needed capital for development, French investors were willing to lend capital, and in 1894 a secret convention between the two guaranteed the following while the Triple Alliance operated:

1. If Germany, or Italy supported by Germany, attacked France, then Russia would attack Germany.

2. If Germany, or Austria supported by Germany, attacked Russia, then France would attack Germany.

France wanted an effective counter-force to the Triple Alliance, and negotiated in 1904 an unwritten military understanding or *entente* with Great Britain. France and Britain had settled their differences which had been acute over the Fashoda incident. The French had dreamed of a solid French colonial empire from Dakar on the west coast of Africa to the Red Sea, and in 1898 sent *Colonel Marchand* to claim territory on the upper Nile in the Sudan still "open" for colonization. A British force under *General Kitchener* started up the Nile and came face to face with Marchand at Fashoda. The British forced France's hand, and earned the criticism of Frenchmen. Fortunately French interests in Morocco, which had not repaid French loans, presented England with the opportunity to support French influence in Morocco, and the crisis passed.

The alignment of Great Britain with her former adversary France was regarded as a "diplomatic revolution," occasioned largely by Germany's colonial activity and naval expansion program.

Territorial Rivalries

There were by 1900 several trouble spots in the world, where national rivalries could lead to war. In Europe France wanted revenge for the affront to her national honor and the loss of Alsace-Lorraine in the Franco-Prussian War. In the Balkans two future enemies, Austria and Russia, were contesting for influence in that area. Great Britain and Germany were rivals for influence in Turkey and for colonial possessions in Africa and in the Pacific. England regarded Germany as the threat to peace in Europe; Germany saw England as the one real obstacle to her expansion in Europe, because England would certainly attempt to prevent the rise of a predominant power that might in time threaten her. In North Africa French and German rivalry came close to hostilities over the two Moroccan crises of 1905 and 1911.

Anglo-German Rivalry

As Germany became industrialized she challenged Britain in world markets and with her merchant marine, and her claims that she needed a large navy to protect her commerce. She started a naval program that Great Britain regarded as a threat from so powerful a military nation.

An Anglo-Japanese alliance in 1902 enabled Great Britain to withdraw part of her Pacific squadron and station it in home ports to complement a naval building program of two ships to every one of Germany's. The entente between France and England provided that France would protect Britain's interests in the Mediterranean while Britain protected French interests in the North Sea. Germany regarded the subsequent Triple Entente of Great Britain, France, and Russia as "encirclement" and a block to her expansionist ambitions, which successive crises seemed to confirm.

International Crises

France and Italy had settled their differences by 1900, Italy accepting French predominant interests in Tunisia and Morocco, and France recognizing Italian interests in Tripoli (later Libya). Germany believed that her rights were ignored and, deciding that the Russo-Japanese War had seriously weakened Russia, chose to intervene in Moroccan affairs in 1905 by declaring that Morocco, which France had planned to control, must remain an independent country. The Kaiser visited the Sultan of Morocco in Tangier, hailed him as an independent sovereign, and demanded that an international conference be held on Morocco. Such a conference was held in Algeciras, Spain, attended by a representative from the United States, and while it was agreed that Morocco was to remain independent it was to be subject to French and Spanish control in the interests of the protection of foreigners. By 1911 France had sent troops to Fez to keep order, and the Germans countered by sending the gunboat *Panther* to the Moroccan port of Agadir. Great Britain announced its intention to support France, thereby increasing the tension between Great Britain and Germany.

The Balkans

Two issues created international incidents in the Balkans:

1. Germany's *Drang Nach Osten* or "drive to the East," through the Balkans to Turkey for economic development and therefore political influence, and

2. the increasing feeling of nationalism in the minorities parts of the Austrian empire, a movement encouraged by Russia.

The "protectorate" control by Austria over the former Turkish provinces of Bosnia and Herzegovina, peopled by Serbs, outraged Serbia, which wanted that territory for expansion and as an outlet to the sea. Austria knew that Russia supported Serbia, and feared that if Serbia were successful, then other national groups within her empire would attempt to break away. A Balkan war in 1912 against Turkey by Serbia, Greece, and Bulgaria, supported by Russia, alarmed Austria, which expected to be able to count upon German support. Austria was determined that Austrian Slavs, in Bosnia-Herzegovina, must be prevented from seceding.

The Sarajevo Affair

Of the 50,000,000 people in Austria-Hungary nearly one half were Slavs who had almost no political power. Some Austrian statesmen believed that if the Slavs were given autonomy within the Empire, they would not agitate for secession. The Archduke of Austria, heir to the imperial throne, supported this point of view, and in 1914 visited Bosnia-Herzegovina as probably a step in this direction. While on a state visit to Sarajevo he was assassinated on June 28, 1914, by a Serbian patriot, *Gabriel Princip*, who Austria believed had been aided and encouraged by Serbian officials. The incident gave Austria the excuse she needed to punish Serbia.

Events Leading to War

On July 23 Austria presented to Serbia an unconditional 48-hour ultimatum demanding:

1. Participation of Austrian officials in determining responsibility for the assassination.
2. The removal of school text-books unfavorable to Austria.
3. Suppression of all publications and societies unfavorable to Austria.
4. The removal of all military and civil officers guilty of "propaganda" against Austria.

Germany had already given Austria a "blank check" of support, and Russia felt obliged to encourage Serbia to resist Austrian demands. On July 28 Austria formally declared war on Serbia; Germany put pressure on Austria, but Russia now called for general mobilization instead of limited mobilization against Austria. Germany now believed she faced the danger of a two-front war, decided to make a fast and decisive attack on France, then be ready to face Russia. Her declaration of war on Russia on July 31 resulted in French mobilization, and on August 3 Germany declared war on France and attacked through Belgium, a violation of the neutrality pledge — the "scrap of paper" — signed by Great Britain and Prussia in 1839. In consequence, Britain declared war on Germany on August 4, to be followed by Austrian declaration of war on Russia on August 6th. Italy claimed that she was released from her obligations of the Triple Alliance because Germany provoked the war. Italy came in on the allied side in May, 1915.

Before the war ended, all the major powers were involved, the Central Powers of Germany, Austria, Turkey, and Bulgaria, against the Allies or Entente of Great Britain, France, Russia, Japan, Italy, Serbia, the United States and more than 20 other states.

Whose Responsibility?	Historians agree in general that Serbia and the major European powers were collectively responsible, that dynamic interests of economic and imperial rivalries, aggressive nationalism and rival alliances came into conflict, and that in the absence of an international mediatory organization, these conditions simply awaited an incident to erupt into war.

Course of World War I	Germany's strategy was the Schlieffen Plan of a fast drive through Belgium and France, and the encirclement and capture of Paris. By September 13 the Germans were only 30 miles from Paris and were already in possession of the industrial section of France. Then the war settled down into one of attrition and trench warfare.

The advantage was originally with Germany, with her central lines of communication and Russia's isolation from her Allies, for Germany cut off land supplies and Turkey closed the Dardanelles sea route, leaving only the North Sea route for supplies. Great Britain antagonized the United States by interfering with her neutral trade rights with the belligerents and with the neutral nations. Germany proved to be the greater menace because Germany's unrestricted submarine warfare resulted in the loss of American lives and ships. In April, 1917, the United States declared war on Germany, one month after a revolt broke out in Russia because of the lack of military equipment at the front and because of the almost complete breakdown of food and fuel supplies on the home front. Germany astutely arranged for Lenin to be brought through Germany by train from Switzerland and turned loose in Russia. Here he organized the Communist Party which took Russia out of the war in February 1918 by the Treaty of Brest-Litovsk, abandoning Poland, the Ukraine, Lithuania, Estonia, Latvia, Finland, and Transcaucasia.

With the release of armies from the Russian front, Germany made a tremendous drive on the western front where United States troops helped to stem the tide at Soissons, the Argonne Forest, Chateau-Thierry, and St. Mihiel. The exhausted Germans asked for an armistice, and on November 11, 1918, fighting ceased.

The war, which involved 65,000,000 troops, left 8,000,000 killed, 20,000,000 wounded, and millions of civilians dead from hunger and disease, cost more than $200,000,000,000, estimated at over $100 per person then living in the world. Four empires collapsed, the German, the Austrian, the Russian, and the Turkish. Significantly, the balance of power was completely destroyed in Europe.

The Peace Settlement

Terms

Self Determination	Collective Action
Peace Without Victory	Collective Security
Freedom of the Seas	Open Diplomacy
Weimar Republic	Mandate
Versailles Diktat	

Places to Locate

Alsace-Lorraine	Lithuania
Yugoslavia	Danzig
Latvia	Czechoslovakia
Finland	Poland
Polish Corridor	Estonia
Hungary	

Topic Outline
Problems of Peace
"Fourteen Points" of President Wilson
Compromises
Peace Terms for Germany
The League of Nations
Results

The Peace Settlement

Problems of Peace

The termination of the war brought problems of peace that were difficult to resolve:

1. The determination of the boundaries of Europe.

2. The issue of *self-determination* of the various national and racial groups in Europe which had been under the domination of Austria and Turkey.

3. The assessment of war damages and the means to make the losers pay them.

4. Measures to guarantee against another such devastating war.

"Fourteen Points" of President Wilson

No plans had been drawn up during the war except the general principles laid down in the Fourteen Points by President Wilson in January, 1918, based upon his belief that this was "the war to end all wars" and "to save the world for democracy." It must therefore be a "peace without victory," with no vanquished later seeking revenge on the victors. The Fourteen Points contained these basic principles which it was hoped would guarantee future peace by removing the causes of war.

The basic principles are:

1. Open Diplomacy, that is, no future secret agreements. This could never be enforced and was abandoned.

2. Freedom of the Sea, that is, complete rights of navigation in peace and war. This was an impossible ideal, since no nation in desperate straits in wartime would permit an enemy to get supplies without a struggle. This was abandoned.

3. Free Trade between nations, to avoid economic rivalries. This was too ideal to be accepted.

4. Reduction of national armaments.

5. Colonial claims to take into consideration the wishes of the native populations.

6. Settlement of the map of Europe on a basis of self-determination.

7. A League to guarantee the independence of all states, the League of Nations.

The Fourteen Points could be only a very general basis for settling the peace because:

1. Some principles were too idealistic to be practicable.

2. Secret agreements made during the war contradicted some of the Points.

3. During the final months of the war conditions changed. Russia had made a separate peace, and several subject groups within the Austro-Hungarian empire had already won their independence with the collapse of that empire.

However, the Fourteen Points did express Wilson's hopes for a peace based on justice and understanding, and a League of Nations that might eliminate the need for alliances and a balance of power system.

Compromises

The two contradictory concepts facing the peace conference were (1) the desire to found a new world order without force and war, and (2) the desire to punish Germany and so prevent a repetition of aggression, a condition that could be resolved only by force. Unfortunately, too little thought had been given to peacemaking, and at the peace conference nations attempted to resolve very complicated questions too quickly.

Peace terms were determined by the United States, Great Britain, and France, and were dictated to Germany. Wilson was so anxious to set up the League of Nations that he could be forced to compromise on other issues.

One of the tragic political errors of 1919 was to force the representatives of the new German Weimar Republic to sign the dictated peace, after a war for which the deposed Kaiser and his military leaders were responsible. Thus before Germany could become accustomed to the first republic in the history of the German people, that government was saddled with what the Germans were to label the "Versailles Diktat," later on to be the object of bitter denunciation by Hitler, and to no degree the cause of his rise to power in the early 1930's.

Lloyd George, prime minister of England, wished to make Germany "pay to the last penny," and *Clemenceau* of France, who as a young reporter in the United States in 1865 had watched the Reconstruction program being implemented, wanted to crush Germany in order to prevent another attack by Germany within another generation. The final peace terms were far from the ideal approach requested by Woodrow Wilson.

Peace Terms for Germany: The "Versailles Diktat" (Hitler)

Germany was obliged to accept the following terms without discussion by her representatives:

1. She was solely responsible for the war (the so-called "guilt clause" of Article 231).

2. All former German colonies were ceded to the Allies and set up as *mandates*, areas to be governed by specific nations but answerable to the League of Nations for their administration.

3. Parts of her territory were ceded to other nations: Alsace-Lorraine to France; Eupen and Malmedy to Belgium; part of West Prussia to Poland.

4. Her army and navy were to be rigidly restricted (although the restriction of 100,000 men for long-term enlistment furnished the later German army with highly-trained officers and non-commissioned officers.

5. She must make reparations in livestock, railroad equipment, merchant and fishing vessels, and other items to replace those destroyed or taken from allied countries during the war.

6. Reparations must be made to pay for all the costs of war, including civilian damages, pensions to widows and others in allied countries, to a total of $33,000,000,000 in 33 years.

7. Germany west of the Rhine and a 30-mile wide strip east of the Rhine was to be demilitarized, and subject to occupation by the Allies for 15 years.

Self-determination

1. Poland was to be revived, with an outlet to the sea, separating East Prussia from the rest of Germany by the *Polish Corridor*, inhabited almost equally by Poles and Germans.

2. Danzig was to be a Free City under the administration of the League of Nations.

3. Austria was obliged to recognize the independence of Czechoslovakia, Yugoslavia, Poland (including parts formerly in the empire), and Hungary.

4. Finland, Estonia, Lithuania, and Latvia on the Baltic were created as independent nations.

**The League
of Nations**

A League was organized, but the United States Senate refused to ratify the Treaty of Versailles which included the League. So the author-nation, the one nation which had asked for no rewards or compensation at the peace table, failed to join the League. This seriously weakened both the prestige and the efficacy of that organization.

Results

The peace settlement left a Europe in which the balance of power was gone. Austria was only a fragment of its earlier power, Russia had collapsed, France was exhausted, and though the "leader" on the continent, only a very weak one; the theory of *collective action* for *collective security* through the League of Nations, was to prove virtually ineffective; attempts to disarm and to eliminate war proved futile. In effect, neither collective action nor the alliance system was to work. As a consequence, Germany, seeking revenge and national honor, was to become the leading military power in Europe.

8

The Search For Security Fails

European Domestic Affairs Between the Wars

Terms

Inflation
Reparations
Maginot Line
Sympathetic Strike
Nationalization
Anschluss
Easter Day Rebellion
Irish Free State

Statute of Westminster
Treaty of Sevres
Treaty of Lausanne
Cortes
Expropriate
Curzon Line
Treaty of Riga
"Succession States"

People

Mahatma Gandhi
Kemal Ataturk
Alfonso XIII
General de Rivera
King Boris
Zamora
General Franco

Paderewski
Marshal Pilsudski
Dolfuss
Admiral Horthy
King Alexander
King Carol

Places to Locate

Syria
The Straits
Lebanon

Ankara
Iraq

Significant Dates

1916   Easter Day Rebellion in Ireland
1923   Turkey Declared a Republic
1931   Statute of Westminster
1936-1939   Spanish Civil War

Topic Outline

Post-War Economic Dislocation
Three European Problems
    Collapse of World Trade
    Rise of Totalitarian States
    Failure of Collective Security
Countries of the Middle East
Spain, Poland, Finland
Baltic and Scandinavian Nations

Switzerland and the Benelux Nations
The Succession States
Eastern Europe

European Domestic Affairs Between the Wars

Post-War Economic Dislocation

The end of the war brought economic hardship to all nations. Military demands had reduced the production of consumer goods, and in general European production in 1920 was little more than 60 percent of pre-war days. While at first this was believed to be a temporary dislocation, it became increasingly evident that for several European nations their overseas markets had been captured by the United States and Japan.

Another significant factor was money *inflation*, which meant higher prices for goods, which in turn meant that sales dropped, goods remained in stock, unemployment followed, and economic dislocation increased.

Another factor dislocating the flow of world trade was the attempt of many nations to be self-sufficient, and to keep foreign goods out by means of high tariffs. Had economic dislocation been limited to Europe the situation might have improved in time. Unfortunately there were world-wide forces at work. During the war the Allies had incurred a debt of $20 billion, over half of which was owed to the United States, a lesser amount to the United Kingdom, and a small proportion to France. It was expected that the three countries which owed the United States some $9½ billion — Great Britain, France, and Italy — would be able to collect their obligations from Germany reparations or money indemnity. The United States insisted that the allies pay their debts in full, so they in turn tried to collect from Germany. International debts — and reparations — could be paid in one of two commodities, either goods or cash. But since the United States had erected a high tariff foreign nations could not get funds by selling goods. If actual cash were to be paid, the day must come when there is no more cash left in the country, unless, of course, the government starts printing money. If the printed money has no solid backing, then it can soon become worthless paper.

A further complicating factor in world depression was the American stock market crash which reduced both American imports and American loans to foreign countries. Efforts had been made earlier to find a solution to the war-debts and reparations problems by postponing payments. In 1932 at the Lausanne Conference war debts and reparations were cancelled or went by default.

However, local national problems of unemployment and depression remained and affected European politics in two evident ways. In Germany, for example, a "strong" leader was regarded as desirable, one who by taking extraordinary measures could perhaps put a nation back on its feet. Hitler was such a leader promising jobs, orders to factories, an expanded army with increased professional careers, and the elimination of the hated Versailles treaty with its humiliating terms of national dishonor.

In other nations the chief concern was how to resolve the problems of economic slump and unemployment. Consequently, foreign affairs were of secondary importance, and nations wanted to avoid war, almost at any cost. This attitude gave Japan, Italy, and Germany the opportunity to expand, even by the use of force, without much fear of effective opposition from nations which had at one time supported the principle of collective action.

As the free enterprise system appeared to be collapsing, authoritarian ideas and organizations of the left and right — communism or facism and nazism — gained momentum. The world depression of the late 1920's and early 1930's was certainly a contributing factor to World War II because it encouraged the rise of dictatorships which believed and advocated that force could be used to advantage.

Three European Problems

The period between 1919 and 1939 was in fact a truce between wars rather than the anticipated period in which democracy would spread and international problems would be settled by negotiation.

Three problems faced Europe, where the balance of power had been upset and where the devastation of war left many countries economically exhausted. The first problem was the devastating international collapse of world trade and widespread unemployment that adversely affected the United States and Europe at a time when Europe appeared to be getting back on its feet.

The second problem was that of the rise of totalitarian states using force instead of negotiation to attain their objectives. The first instance was Japan's attack upon China in 1931 and its subsequent acquisition of Manchuria, another step in Japan's expansionist policy. Although far removed from European affairs, the Manchurian incident was a symbol of the unwillingness of nations to act collectively. Italy and Germany were no doubt encouraged to believe that force paid dividends.

The third problem was that of the failure of collective action through the League of Nations. If all nations had agreed to use force or the threat of force against any aggressor, the second world war might have been avoided. Unfortunately, each nation seemed to believe that by minding its own affairs it could avoid entanglement in foreign affairs. These were the years when international issues needed urgent attention.

A lesser problem, but one that became a financial drain and a distraction from more serious problems, was the stirrings of nationalism in many colonial areas. The democracies of Great Britain and France were challenged by growing demands for independence from their colonial possessions.

France had suffered severe losses in her young men and in the destruction of nearly one quarter of her productive industries and agriculture. Reconstruction taxed her resources, and the political stalemate caused by the system of numerous parties prevented the development of a systematic policy. Sceptical of the effectiveness of collective security, France built the very expensive Maginot Line of defensive forts on her eastern frontier, and developed the Maginot Line mentality of reliance upon concrete fortifications rather than a modern army.

In order to maintain her hold upon Algeria, France made it an integral part of the French nation, hoping that would prevent colonial trouble. In Syria force had to be used to keep the Arabs in line, and in French Indo-China demands for self-government foreshadowed the war which France was to fight between 1946 and 1954.

Great Britain as an industrial nation depended upon vast imports of raw materials which she processed into finished goods. She needed world-wide markets in which to sell these products in exchange for more raw materials and for much of her food. Post-war conditions were unfavorable, since competitors had captured some of her markets; much of Europe could not afford to buy her goods. This loss of markets resulted in increased unemployment which became a permanent feature from 1921, when 20 per cent of employables could not find work, until the outbreak of war in 1939 created demand again. A general strike in support of the coal miners who refused to accept a cut in wages and were locked out of the mines resulted in a law in 1927 which banned all general or sympathetic strikes. A Conservative government introduced protective tariffs in order to keep out foreign competitive goods, with the result that other nations retaliated with protective tariffs against British goods. Agriculture suffered competition from increased production abroad, and the government had to give subsidies or bounties to farmers. Twice the Labour Party, committed to *nationalization*, or state ownership of the means of production and distribution, came into office, in 1924 and 1929, but not until 1945 could it put its program into action.

In empire affairs Britain faced demands for complete independence for "white" colonies, armed insurrection in Ireland, and increased agitation in India and Africa for more self-government.

The Easter Day rebellion of the Irish in 1916 was repressed, but after 1919 a savage guerrilla war was fought until in 1922 a compromise was worked out, giving the Irish Free State—all of Ireland except the six northern Protestant counties— the same type of home rule enjoyed at this time by the white dominions of Canada, Australia, New Zealand, and the Union of South Africa.

In 1931 Britain enacted the Statute of Westminster which granted independence to the former home rule dominions.

The great opposition to Britain's colonial rule came from India, where Mahatma Gandhi advocated the policy of non-violent non-cooperation or passive resistance against British rule and actions.

In foreign affairs Great Britain depended too much upon the theoretical power of the League of Nations, did no more than verbally protest against Japan's attack upon China in 1931, and made no attempt to prevent Hitler's re-occupation of the Rhineland in 1936, acquiesced in Italy's conquest of Ethiopia, and engineered the incredible appeasement agreement with Hitler at Munich in 1938, in which Czecho-Slovakia was sacrificed to German ambitions. On Britain must be placed the blame for Hitler's expansionist success by 1939.

Countries of the Middle East

Egypt, long part of the Turkish Empire, was granted autonomy in 1841. The Suez Canal was completed in 1869, and in 1875 the Khedive of Egypt offered for sale his bloc of canal shares, which were purchased for England by Prime Minister Disraeli. A few years later Egypt defaulted on its international debts and in 1882 Great Britain established a virtual protectorate over Egypt. In 1914 Great Britain officially declared Egypt to be a British protectorate. Increasing Egyptian resentment at this condition led Great Britain to end—at least in name—the protectorate in 1922, allowed Egypt to set up its own constitutional monarchy, with reservations. The British proposed to secure the British "life-line" through Egypt in order to defend Egypt against "all foreign aggression," and because no Egyptian government would agree to this condition, Great Britain simply issued this as a unilateral declaration. Friction increased between the nationalist

WAFD Party and the British, until Mussolini's attack upon Ethiopia in 1935. Egypt now appreciated British support, and in 1936 accepted a treaty in which Britain agreed to defend Egypt, to maintain 400 pilots for the Suez Canal, and to evacuate all her troops from other places in Egypt.

Iraq, formerly known as Mesopotamia, was given to Britain as a mandate in 1919. However, the inhabitants, who had willingly accepted British help to throw out their Turkish masters, did not welcome the substitution of British control. When the ruler was proclaimed King of Iraq in 1921, the British withdrew their troops on the condition that their interests in the rich oil fields were protected. In 1930 the protectorate was replaced by a treaty of alliance between Great Britain and independent Iraq.

Palestine as a homeland for the Jewish people had in effect been promised in World War I by the British government, which had promised to support "the establishment in Palestine of a National Home for the Jewish people" without prejudice to "the civil and religious rights of existing non-Jewish communities in Palestine." This was in effect a contradiction, but when Britain received Palestine as a mandate in 1919 she did encourage Jewish people to settle there, with consequent opposition from the Arab inhabitants. The British were caught in an embarrassing position, since they could not afford to antagonize the large number of Mohammedans within the British Empire. The problem was complicated because an independent Arab kingdom of Transjordan was set up in 1928 within Palestine. Meanwhile other Arabs organized to form the Kingdom of Saudi Arabia, and this in turn led to an Arab demand to incorporate the whole area from Syria south to Yemen on the southern tip of the Arabian Peninsula.

Turkey, the western allies had decided, was to be deprived of all her non-Turkish possessions by the Treaty of Sevres in 1920. Turkey was obliged to give up Palestine, Syria, Mesopotamia, and Armenia, and to agree that Smyrna and its hinterland (the western part of Turkey) be under Greek administration for five years, and that the inhabitants, including a substantial Greek population, hold a plebiscite to decide to which country they wished to belong.

Some months before the Treaty of Sevres was drawn up, the Turks had revolted under *Mustafa Kemal*, overthrown the Sultan and established a republic in 1922. In that same year they attacked the Greeks in Smyrna and rejected the Treaty of Sevres. Next year the allies were obliged to negotiate—not dictate—a new peace with Turkey. The *Treaty of Lausanne* permitted Turkey to keep her ethnic boundaries, those in which Turks lived, but to surrender the rest—Arabia, Mesopotamia, Palestine, Syria. By so doing she regained her complete independence, and was guaranteed by the other powers that the strategic international waterway the Straits (Dardanelles, Sea of Marmora, the Bosphorus) would be open to all nations and guaranteed by the League of Nations.

In 1923 Turkey was officially proclaimed a republic with *Mustafa Kemal* as president. The government was a dictatorship controlled by *Kemal Ataturk* (Father of the Turks) through his position as president-general of the National People's Party, the only legal party in Turkey. Kemal instituted a ruthless policy of westernization; the capital was removed to Ankara in the middle of Asia Minor, the Turkish language was for the first time written in western letters, women received the right to vote, and many Islamic influences were removed.

Spain, Poland, Finland

Spain in the twentieth century was a paradox because an eighteenth century aristocracy of large landowners, the Church, and the army were faced with the increasing demands of a twentieth-century discontented peasantry and proletariat. Rural areas were overpopulated and suffering from endemic poverty, that is constantly present, while vast landed estates served the interests only of their possessors. Little progress had been made in industry, and a middle class was practically nonexistent. Unfortunately, the Church, instead of attempting to understand popular needs, chose to oppose any liberal movement. The industrial workers and miners of Catalonia and the peasants became adherents of syndicalism and anarchism, the literal destruction of their opponents, a far more radical program than those of socialism and communism. The government forbade unions, used strikebreakers and police spies against the workers, with the result that little attempt was made to face realistically the problems of hunger and poverty.

In Catalonia, of which Barcelona is the chief city, martial law was instituted in 1920, and *General Anido*, civil governor, simply shot labor leaders on sight. As a consequence, retaliation led to further murders.

Behind the facade of parliamentary government, *King Alfonso XIII* connived at a military dictatorship under *General de Rivera*, assisted by a directorate of eight generals. During his regime, whose slogan was "Country, Monarchy, and Religion," industrial enterprises were encouraged, but local governments were suspended and liberalism and any form of democracy suppressed. Despite such repression, discontent flared into open rebellion under Zamora, and was put down by de Rivera's successor.

Spain: Republican Government (1931)

Local elections for a new Cortes or Parliament were held in 1931 in order to draw up a new constitution. When the results indicated a republican landslide, Zamona threatened revolution unless the king abdicated. The next day Alfonso XIII fled, and in December 1931 a Republican government with a democratic constitution was established with Zamora as first president. The Cortes or legislature of one house was elected by universal male and female suffrage, with a responsible premier and cabinet, and a President elected by the Cortes and popularly-elected electors.

Two actions of the republican government antagonized landowners and Church. The lands of both were in many instances expropriated without compensation, and all schools, formerly under Church jurisdiction, were taken over by the republic. Spain seethed with discontent between the Right which thought reforms had gone too far, and the Left which regarded the reforms as inadequate.

Civil War (1936–1939)

Military men plotted to overthrow the government, and in 1936 General Franco led a revolt supported by most of the army. Atrocities were ferocious on both sides, and Spain became the site of a miniature international war, with Russia and France helping the Loyalists or official government, and Germany and Italy helping what were technically the rebels, Nationalists as they came to be called, under Franco's leadership. By 1939 Franco emerged the victor after a civil war which devastated the country and left bitter memories. The military losses, estimated at 400,000, were far outrun by the 800,000 who were killed by murder and execution.

Landlords, Church, and Army were again dominant, and the country slid back again under the rule of such men as an early minister of education, the *Marquis de Lazoya*, who could blame Spain's troubles upon "the stupid desire of the governments to teach the Spaniards to read."

Poland, in the eighteenth century, had been partitioned three times, and by 1795 had been swallowed up by Russia, Prussia, and Austria. During World War I Polish nationalists fought on both sides, not so much in support of either but in order to win recognition at the peace conference as an independent nation. On the basis of Wilson's principle of self-determination Poland was re-created and recognized as a republic, largely by the efforts of the pianist *Ignace Paderewski* and *Marshal Pilsudski*.

At the peace conference the Polish eastern frontier had been drawn at the *Curzon Line*, a line suggested by Lord Curzon and based upon racial facts. This was a fair boundary but it did not meet the demands of the Polish nationalist leaders, and in 1920 they attempted to extend their territory eastwards while Russia was engaged in a civil war. In 1921 the *Treaty of Riga* between Poland and Russia settled upon a new boundary line which made Poland the sixth largest state in Europe, but provided Russia in 1939 with the excuse to invade and occupy eastern Poland, at the moment when Hitler invaded Poland from the west.

The nationalism of Poland was weakened by divided opinions on foreign policy, since one group of leaders regarded Germany as the enemy, and another believed Russia to be the threat. Poland sought allies, and in 1921 France, also interested in preventing the revival of a powerful Germany, made an alliance with Poland, although it was to prove of little value when Germany attacked Poland in September 1939.

Despite attempts to industrialize, Poland remained essentially agricultural, and its peasantry remained at a subsistence level. During the 1930's Poland's chief concern was foreign affairs, since her main problem was the growing demand by Hitler's Germany for control of the German minority and the acquisition of the Polish Corridor which separated East Germany from the main part of the nation. As the 1930's drew to a close, Poland had reason to fear its two neighbors Germany and Russia, since both were awaiting the opportunity to take part of its territory.

Finland, for six centuries, had been ruled by Sweden. In 1809 it was ceded by Sweden to Russia as the Grand Duchy of Finland. Between 1809 and 1894 Russia permitted the Grand Duchy to run its own government and to enjoy its own institutions. Despite later attempts to Russify Finland, it retained its own identity, and in December, 1917, declared its independence and received recognition as a sovereign republic.

Baltic and Scandinavian Nations

Since the twelfth century the Esths and the Letts were ruled by foreign conquerors—Germans, Danes, Russians. The Lithuanians were originally part of Poland, but when that country was finally partitioned in 1795, Lithuania came under Russian control.

After the Bolshevik Revolution of 1917, Estonia, Latvia, and Lithuania declared their independence, were recognized in 1920, and became republics.

Theirs was to be an uneasy future, for Soviet Russia regarded them as a possible theater of invasion of her western frontier.

Denmark, Norway, and Sweden are of common Teutonic origin, and were collectively called Norsemen. In the fourteenth century Norway and Sweden came under the suzerainty of Denmark by the Union of Kalmar, with each kingdom retaining its own customs and traditions, and in some instances its own rule.

In 1523 Sweden became independent, gradually extended her influence over Finland, ceded it to Russia in 1809, and in 1815 received Norway, which had been an ally of Napoleon. Norway retained its own parliamentary institutions but was ruled from Sweden until 1905 when it became an independent monarchy.

Iceland, which had started its own local representative government in 930 A.D., became a possession of Norway in 1262, and when Norway became a subordinate province of Denmark in 1523, Iceland came under Danish control. In 1815 when Norway was joined to Sweden, Iceland remained with Denmark until 1918 when Iceland became an independent sovereign state united with Denmark through a common king.

In 1940 Germany invaded and occupied both Denmark and Norway. After the war the two nations became members of NATO, and suggested a Scandinavian Union of the three nations. Sweden refused to join NATO or the projected Scandinavian Union, claiming that to do either could be regarded as antagonistic to Russia, which might decide to counter allied influence in Scandinavia by occupying Finland.

Switzerland and the Benelux Nations

The Swiss Confederacy began in 1291 when three little mountain cantons, subjects of the Hapsburg Emperor, signed a Perpetual Compact and successfully resisted a Hapsburg army in the mountain passes. Other communities joined together in a Confederation pledged to joint action against a common foe, but to retain their own local institutions. Typical of their heroes is William Tell, perhaps mythical but symbolic of Swiss resistance. By the Treaty of Basel in 1499 the Emperor renounced all sovereignty over the thirteen cantons in the Confederation, and in 1648 Switzerland was recognized as an independent state.

The Confederation ended in 1789 with its conquest by France during the French Revolution days. Napoleon reorganized Switzerland on a federal basis in 1803 and added more cantons, one being the Italian-speaking canton of Ticino. In 1815 the Congress of Vienna added three more French-speaking cantons to it and arranged for international recognition of its neutrality.

Today nineteen of the twenty-five cantons are German-speaking with 72 per cent of the population, five are French with 21 per cent of the population, and one is Italian with six per cent of the population, and about 10 per cent speak Romansch, a local "Latin" language. All four languages are national, and Switzerland is the outstanding example of a nation in sentiment and national feeling without a common language spoken by all of its people.

An interesting note is that Switzerland broke off diplomatic relations with the U.S.S.R. in 1918, charging that a Swiss general strike had been caused by subversive Russian activities. She had originally refused to recognize the government of the U.S.S.R., strenuously opposed its entry into the League of Nations in 1934, and was in consequence charged with being a "Fascist" state by the U.S.S.R. which refused to attend a Civil Aviation Conference in 1944 since Switzerland was represented. Not until after World War II did Switzerland resume diplomatic negotiations with the U.S.S.R.

In 1648, by the Peace of Westphalia, the northern provinces of the territory which now comprises the Netherlands, Belgium, and Luxembourg received international recognition as the independent Netherlands. The southern part remained under Spanish rule until 1713, when it became Austrian. In 1815 the Congress of Vienna restored the monarchy to the Netherlands and added the former Austrian provinces. A revolt of the southern section in 1830 resulted in the establishment of an independent Belgium in 1839 with its neutrality guaranteed by the Great Powers.

Luxembourg, now officially the Grand Duchy of Luxembourg, remained united with the Netherlands until 1890 when it was given independence.

Succession States

Austria

The great Austro-Hungarian Empire was shattered in 1918, and from it were set up the "succession" states of: Yugoslavia and Czechoslovakia; parts were awarded to Rumania, Poland, and Italy; the remainder became the modern states of Austria and Hungary.

Austria became a little state one quarter its former size, with a population of 7,000,000 and a capital city of Vienna, with inadequate surrounding land. A republic was established, its economy was faced with unemployment and bankruptcy, but economic union with Germany, or *Anschluss*, was forbidden at Versailles. Unemployment and near-hunger in Vienna encouraged socialist leadership which aroused the fears of the conservative groups. The two political parties were of equal strength, the Social Democrats holding power among the workers of Vienna, and the conservative Christian Socialists getting their power from the peasantry in the provinces. Each group had its private army, the Schutzbund for the republic, and the Heimwehr under *Prince Stahrenberg* for the Christian Socialists.

Engelbert Dolfuss, head of the Christian Socialists, became prime minister, closed Parliament, censored the press, abolished trial by jury and habeas corpus, ordered the dissolution of all political parties and trade unions. Nearly 40,000 persons were arrested on suspicion, and over 100,000 residences illegally searched. Austria became the target for Nazi subversion. Dolfuss was assassinated by the Nazis, who agitated for the annexation of Austria to Germany. In March, 1938, Hitler simply marched in with his army and annexed Austria, and then conducted a plebiscite on the matter of annexation with a resultant 99 per cent vote suspiciously and conveniently in favor of what was already an accomplished fact.

Hungary

A very small Hungary set up a short-lived republic in 1918, but economic dislocation resulted in a communist rule under *Bela Kun*. This Hungarian Soviet Republic waged war upon Czechoslovakia and Rumania in order to communize them. Subsequently *Admiral Horthy* set himself up as dictator, of a country which was perhaps the most discontented of all the new Central Europe states because 3,000,000 Magyars or Hungarians had been "given" to Czechoslovakia, Rumania, and Yugoslavia.

Czechoslovakia

Bohemia became a fief of the German Emperor Otto the Great in the twelfth century, but was allowed to retain a government of its own. During the centuries Czech nationalism persisted and in 1918 the three former Austrian provinces of Bohemia, Silesia, and Moravia declared their independence under the leadership of Masaryk and Benes. The federated republic was born with the serious problem of some 3,500,000 Germans in a total population of 14,000,000, concentrated in the Sudetenland area. A Sudetendeutsch party under *Konrad Henlein* agitated for rights for the German minority, and in 1935 secured the greatest number of votes of the several political parties. The Czechoslovak government tried to win over its German minority by granting them cultural autonomy and granting them more government positions. The Sudetendeutsch Party was encouraged by the German and Austrian Nazis, and finally were successful in blackmailing Great Britain, France and Italy into the Munich appeasement arrangement of 1938.

Yugoslavia

The Kingdom of Serbia was the core of the new Kingdom of the Serbs, Croats, and Slovenes, with King Peter of Serbia as its monarch.

Within the kingdom discontent soon developed between the Serbians, the largest group with 45 per cent of the population and Great Catholics demanding a highly centralized government, and the Croats with 39 per cent of the population and Roman Catholics demanding a decentralized state with racial autonomy. Continued disharmony led *King Alexander* to set up a royal dictatorship in 1928, to restrict press and political parties, and to award to the largest single party two-thirds of the seats in the lower house. The assassination of Alexander in 1934, on a state visit in France, led to internal dissension that suggested a possible repetition of the 1914 crisis.

Eastern Europe

The states of southeastern Europe, Rumania, Bulgaria, Hungary were essentially agricultural. Little was done to remedy conditions, which deteriorated during the 1920's, and led to the establishment of authoritarian governments in an attempt to stave off disaster as world agricultural prices slumped.

In *Hungary* reactionary landlord interests modeled the government along authoritarian lines and accepted subsidies from the German Nazis. *Rumania* was dominated by *King Carol II* who between 1930 and 1940 used corruption and terror to consolidate power in his own hands, eliminated political opposition, and used the Iron Guard, a terrorist organization, as strike breakers and general toughs who were supported by the authorities in political murder. Carol made no contribution whatever to constructive leadership.

Bulgaria under *King Boris* was little different in the methods of operation from Rumanian techniques. Terrorist groups eliminated political opposition, and the government set up industrial methods much like the corporate techniques of Mussolini in Italy.

Greece began as a monarchy after the war, changed to a republic in 1924, returned to a monarchy in 1935. Whether republic or monarchy the basic issue was control of power. In 1936 *King George II* permitted General Metaxas to establish a dictatorship which did introduce social security and other reforms, although their implementation was not enforced. The monarchy and dictatorship were apparently sustained by a loyal army.

Germany: The Totalitarian State

Terms

Weimar Constitution	NSDAP
Proportional Representation	*Mein Kampf*
Initiative	Putsch
Referendum	Third Reich
Recall	Chancellor
Bundestag	Gestapo
Reichstag	Stresa Front

People

Friedrich Ebert	Goebbels
Hitler	Hindenburg
Stresemann	

Significant Dates

1928	Nazi Party in Reichstag
1933	Nazi Party Wins Plurality in Reichstag

Topic Outline
Weaknesses of the Weimar Republic
Inflation: Effects on German Economy
Constitution of the Weimar Republic
Hitler's Rise to Power
Political Success of the National Socialist (Nazi) Party
Domestic Policies of the Nazi Regime
Foreign Affairs

Germany: The Totalitarian State

Weaknesses of the Weimar Republic

The German experiment with democracy lasted from 1919 to the rise to power of Hitler in 1933, and although the *Weimar Constitution* was not officially repealed, for all practical purposes Germany was a dictatorship from 1933.

The German Republic took its name from the city of Weimar, a city long associated with Schiller and Goethe, hopefully to be a symbol of the peaceful character of the new republic. Unfortunately the constitution and the signing of the humiliating peace treaty were both the responsibility of the republican government. Whatever went wrong in Germany could be blamed upon the treaty, and the treaty blamed upon those who had signed it, the representatives of the republican government. The legend was cultivated that Germany was not really defeated in World War I but was "stabbed in the back" by radical elements inside Germany. The facts were that Ludendorff and Hindenburg, the military leaders, had insisted on surrender in 1918 because the German armies were beaten. But Germany chose not to believe the facts, and popular opinion increasingly criticized the Weimar Republic for having signed the "dictated peace," a matter in which they had no choice whatever. The "war guilt" clause was a rallying point for all who wished to prove that force had been right, The Social Democrats, led by Friedrich Ebert, did not favor nationalization although they were reformists. They were the largest single group in the Reichstag but with only 40 per cent of the seats, and they had the very difficult task of launching the new government and republic. Actions of the Independent Socialists, a small minority demanding a proletarian revolution of the Russian type, forced Ebert to call upon the army and a volunteer Free Corps of professional soldiers to suppress increasing violence. Later, both Free Corps and the Communists attempted to stage a *putsch* or *coup d'etat*.

Inflation: Effects on German Economy

Conditions were made almost chaotic as an incredible spiral of *inflation* developed. Briefly, the German government had expected to win the war and make the vanquished nations pay all Germany's costs. Consequently, Germany did not finance the war out of taxes. When the war ended, Germany borrowed money from banks to pay wartime debts, paid back with new printing-press money that had no solid backing of gold or silver, and so came to be regarded as worth no more than the paper it was made of, and so was not acceptable at its face value. Workers demanded higher wages, storekeepers raised prices, wage demands again increased—and the upward spiral continued upwards until it finally went out of control. Before it ended by wiping out all the old paper money, the German mark dropped from four to the United States dollar to literally trillions to the dollar. A family with a $50,000 life insurance policy or savings account had now no more than the price of a postage stamp. Not unnaturally the peace terms were blamed for the disaster, and Germans began to look for a strong leader to resolve all problems.

The United States tried to help with the Dawes Plan which recommended international loans as part solution. Over the period 1924 to 1929 economic recovery was accomplished, only to be given a setback by a depression which was to become world-wide.

Ebert's successor General Hindenburg was a monarchist and a conservative, who nevertheless supported the Republic.

Constitution of the Weimar Republic

The Constitution was in principle extremely democratic, embodying all the techniques favored by advanced democracies. It contained:

1. Universal suffrage, male and female, for all German citizens who had reached twenty.

2. *Proportional representation*, that is, representation for all political parties in proportion to their *total* nation-wide vote.

3. Initiative, referendum, and recall. *Initiative* is the process permitting voters to initiate legislation or to order the legislature to introduce legislation desired

by the voters; *referendum* is the process by which a political issue or a piece of legislation is referred back to the voters for their decision; *recall* is the process permitting voters to remove unfit public officials from their positions, without waiting for the expiration of a term of office.

4. The elective Reichstag was responsible for legislation.

5. The Ministry, under the leadership of the Chancellor, would hold office so long as it was supported by a majority of the Reichstag.

6. The official head of the Republic was the President.

a. Elected for 7 years by qualified voters.

b. Empowered in times of crisis to suspend civil rights and to issue emergency decrees having the force of law.

c. Authorized, upon the recommendation of the Ministry, to dismiss the Reichstag and to order a new general election.

Thus the President of the Republic could overrule parliamentary laws in a serious emergency — a term which was not precisely defined.

A striking feature of the Weimar Constitution was the declaration of rights which closely resembled the American Bill of Rights. It guaranteed to German citizens freedom of speech, press, assembly, and religion, and protected private property against seizure except by due process of law.

Democratic though the Constitution was, it was so radical a departure from past German experience that it could not succeed unless effectively and honestly supported by all groups in the country.

The weakness of the republic was not in the provisions of the constitution but in the lack of political experience of the Germans. Long used to guidance from above, the Germans were too ready to accept it again, especially in times of crisis. Furthermore, the restrictions of the Versailles treaty irritated the Germans, particularly the disarming of Germany, the only nation to be so limited. Conservatives, business leaders, professional army officers all resented the change from the ceremony and prestige of a monarchy to a drab republican government first led by the workingman *Ebert*.

Gustav Stresemann, foreign minister from 1923 to 1929, was responsible for improving German relationships in international affairs, for the Locarno Pacts, the admission of Germany into the League of Nations, and for the promise of the allies to withdraw from the Rhineland.

Hitler's Rise to Power

In 1932 Hindenburg was re-elected president for another term, but the support of militarists and monarchists declined. Hindenburg's chief opponent in that election was *Adolf Hitler*, born in Austria in 1889, a corporal in World War I, whose National Socialist German Workers' Party (National-sozialistiche Deutsche Arbeiter-partei, or NSDAP) or Nazi Party had not been successful over the years since 1921. With General Ludendorff he had attempted to overthrow the republic by a putsch in 1923. Sentenced to prison, Hitler spent several years writing *Mein Kampf* (My Struggle) in which he attempted to fuse nationalism and socialism as his political doctrine, believing them to be the strongest political forces of the day. His appeal was emotionalism based upon denunciation of the Versailles "Diktat," the "stab in the back" by pacifist traitors, the "guilt clause" of that treaty. Organized bands of National Socialist (Nazis) supporters used violence and terrorism to stifle political opposition, while Hitler's tirades appealed to German nationalists, businessmen, military men, the middle class who had suffered from inflation, and the workers who were suffering from a depression which was spreading across the world.

Political Success of the National Socialist (Nazi) Party

From twelve members in the 1928 Reichstag elections, the Nazi party increased its representation to 107 in the 1930 elections, to 196 in 1933, the largest single group, with 35 per cent of the Reichstag. Hitler was able now to force Hindenburg to grant him the office of chancellor or actual political leader of the Reichstag. New elections in March 1933 increased the Nazi lead to 288 out of 647 seats, or 44 per cent of the total which with the support of 52 Nationalist deputies gave Hitler the majority. Within a few days the Reichstag was set afire, blamed upon the Communists but regarded by many as a Nazi plot. Immediately the Communist party was ordered dissolved, and within a few weeks the same fate was meted out to the Socialist party with its 118 representatives. There remained finally only the Nazi party which had in March, 1933, received dictatorial powers from the rubber-stamp Reichstag for four years, and which by November 1933 had 92 per cent of the electoral vote.

Domestic Policies of the Nazi Regime

After the death of President Hindenburg in 1934 Hitler took over that office also, labelled himself Der Fuhrer and renamed Germany the *Third Reich*. (The First was that of Otto the Great in 962 A.D., and the Second was created by Bismarck in 1871.)

Religious groups and labor unions were completely subordinated to the State; Hitler's racial superiority concept led to the persecution of the Jews, a very convenient scapegoat on whom to blame anything the Germans disliked; education, newspapers, and all means of communication were put under the control of *Goebbels*, Minister of *Propaganda*, a term that now came to mean the deliberate withholding of vital information in order to mislead people. All opposition was subject to ruthless elimination by the dread Gestapo under Himmler.

The judicial system substituted "folk" justice for traditional legal principles, meaning that the individual was completely subordinated to the people, the volk, or quite simply, no one had any legal rights other than as determined by Hitler, who appointed all judges and established concentration camps for "enemies of the state" who had no appeal from arbitrary death sentences.

In economic matters the Nazis assumed complete control over agricultural production and prices, in an attempt to make Germany self-sufficient. The *Labor Front* replaced labor unions and employers' associations, professional people, and employers, and implemented the Four Year Plans of 1933 and 1936 designed to achieve economic recovery and re-employment.

Foreign Affairs

Determined to secure revision of the Versailles Treaty, Hitler knew that he could not successfully oppose Germany's former opponents Great Britain, France, Italy, and Russia if they presented a united front. He must therefore divide these powers while forging the nation into disciplined support of his leadership. Unable to secure immediate revision he defiantly took Germany out of the

League of Nations, then when his first attempt to annex Austria in 1934 was thwarted by the "Stresa Front" of Great Britain, France, and Italy at Stresa, he declared he had no intention of annexing Austria, and then was able to persuade Great Britain to permit the building of the German navy, which Hitler promised would be limited to 35 per cent of Britain's navy. His next move was to secure Germany's western frontier. While Mussolini was busy in Ethiopia, he reoccupied the Rhineland.

In March, 1938, he absorbed Austria as a province of Greater Germany. That same year he arranged the Munich Pact, and the next year took over the whole of Czechoslovakia.

It was now obvious that Hitler's purpose was unlimited aggression, and too late the western powers decided to act, by pledging assistance to Poland now threatened by Germany, assistance they simply could not give, even to attacking Germany on her western front while Hitler was engaged in the invasion of Poland. The western powers, despite all the events of the past few years, were totally unprepared for war.

Hitler offered the Russians his consent to the Soviet re-annexation of Latvia, Estonia, and Lithuania, proposed a division of Poland, and in August, 1939, negotiated a non-aggression pact with Russia. Hitler was now ready to strike, and did so with the undeclared invasion of Poland on September 1, 1939.

Italy: The Corporative State

Terms

Fasces	Totalitarian	Revisionist
Fascist	Corporative State	Syndicate
Fasci di Combattimento		

People
Mussolini
Haile Selassie

Places to Locate

Dodecanese Islands	Nice	Savoy
Italian Somaliland	Corsica	Eritrea
Ethiopia	Albania	

Topic Outline
Rise to Power of Mussolini
The Corporative State
Domestic Policies
Foreign Policy
Attack on France

Italy: The Corporative State

Italy emerged from the war that had been an economic calamity, resulting in financial chaos and widespread unemployment. Parliament seemed unable to settle strikes; open fighting in the country made matters worse, and the socialists, the largest party in the country, encouraged further disorder by inaction. The radical wing preached revolution and Russian-style dictatorship, and thereby helped to create an opposition which found its champion in a new party the *Fascist*, from the Roman word *fasces*, a bundle of rods bound around an axe, the symbol of the Roman lictor, therefore signifying authority.

Rise to Power of Mussolini

Mussolini, a former socialist, anti-militarist, and opportunist, came out of the war a revolutionary and an ardent nationalist. In March, 1919, he founded the *fasci di combattimento*, "groups for combat," demanding seizure of lands and property and the nationalization of mines. By mid-1922 the fascist groups were 300,000 strong; the parliamentary leaders decided that they could be used against communist groups, encouraged army officers to issue them arms and to train them. They roamed the countryside and terrorized labor union officials, radical newspapers and socialist party officers. In May, 1921, Mussolini and 34 of them had been elected to parliament, pronouncing themselves a political party. The so-called March on Rome in October, 1922, was simply the arrival of Fascists in Rome by free rides and on trains, and the summoning of Mussolini by the King to form a government. Within weeks Mussolini had established a dictatorship, and in 1926 was authorized to govern by decree, not by law; he coordinated the Italian state and the Fascist party by assuming the position of head of state, and *Il Duce*, the Leader of the Fascists, and occupying eight cabinet posts simultaneously.

In 1928 the Grand Council, or political bureau, of the Fascists took over the government, prepared lists of candidates for parliament, and in effect made parliament a rubber stamp of Mussolini. Italy was now a totalitarian state in which the individual served the state as ordered, a government in which, to use Mussolini's words, "the putrescent corpse" of democracy had no place. All parties other than the Fascists were suppressed, laws were used to serve Mussolini's purposes, and Italy was completely centralized from Rome.

The Corporative State

The basic difference in economic theories between communism and fascism is that communism believes in the elimination of capitalism, and fascism supported cooperation between labor and capital as operated by Mussolini. Independent labor unions were forbidden and were replaced by syndicates; the economy of the nation was organized into corporations through seven workers' associations and six employers' associations to supervise wages, working conditions, and prices, all responsible to the Minister of Corporations.

Businessmen approved the prohibition on labor unions, on the right to strike, and on new political parties, but they soon found that they too were controlled by the government. Agriculture, mining, and industrial business were all regulated by the government.

The Corporative State, as Italy was now labelled, ordered that only those could vote who were members of a workers' syndicate and paid taxes. All political districts were abolished, and deputies represented the country as a whole, not districts or parties. The choice of candidates for the Chamber of Deputies was completely rigged. The size of the chamber was reduced to 400, workers' and employers' federations nominated 800 candidates, professional associations another 200, and the total was reduced to a selected 400 by the Fascist Grand Council, another creation of Mussolini.

In the 1930's the Grand Council simply selected all deputies without going through the pretence of giving the people a say, it appointed all government officials, and in 1938 abolished even the rubber-stamp Chamber of Deputies. No vestige of even a pretence of democracy remained.

Domestic Policies

The government planned all economy, attempted to make Italy self-sufficient, but contradicted this by forbidding emigration and by subsidizing large families. Consequently, any anticipated rise in the standard of living was cancelled out by the increase in population. Textbooks, schools, youth movements were simply vehicles for fascist propaganda, extolling Italy's greatness and its strategy for expansion.

With the Church Mussolini made an agreement recognizing Vatican City as an independent State within Italy, Catholicism as the state religion. Religious instruction was increased in schools, and the Church agreed not to discuss politics in its official publications.

Foreign Policy

Italy was convinced that it had been cheated at the Peace Conference in 1919, and from the time of Versailles it became a "revisionist" nation seeking to revise the settlement in its favor whenever an opportunity presented itself.

The first incident occurred over the Dodecanese Islands which Italy had occupied since 1912, but had to surrender to Greece in 1920. The assassination of four Italian officials engaged in determining the Greek-Albanian border, led to the occupation of the Dodecanese Islands and Corfu. In subsequent negotiations, Italy retained the islands.

Mussolini then claimed that Nice, Savoy, and Corsica belonged to Italy, not to France, and annoyed the British by demanding participation in the operation of the Suez Canal.

In North Africa Mussolini determined to expand and to unite the Italian possessions of Eritrea and Italian Somaliland by conquering Ethiopia. Border incidents gave Mussolini the excuse to threaten Ethiopia, whose Emperor *Haile Selassie*, appealed to the League of Nations. In such a situation the League could and should have applied economic sanctions. The French regarded the League as protection against Germany; the British were unwilling to make commitments to assist France or to take any risks with Italy; and the two actions which could have halted Italy—oil sanctions, a blockade on oil shipments to Italy, and the closure of the Suez Canal to Italian vessels—were not put into force. Italy invaded Ethiopia, forced Haile Selassie into exile, and declared King *Victor Emmanuel* to be Emperor.

The significance of Italy's success was (1) the humiliation of the League and the implication that its members were not prepared to accept their obligations, (2) the humiliation of Britain and France, who had given in to blackmail by Italy, and had obviously appeased her, (3) encouragement to expansionist powers that they could act and expand with impunity.

In 1939, with practically no warning, Italy invaded Albania, and so gained for herself a better position on the Adriatic and the small oil deposits of Albania.

Britain and France accepted the *fait accompli,* and Hitler loudly applauded his Axis partner.

Attack on France   On June 10, 1940, with the Germans only a few days away from victory over France, Mussolini declared war on France, in the expectation of sharing the spoils, and so formally entered the war on Germany's side.

Union of Soviet Socialist Republics: The Communist State

Terms

Provisional Government	Kolkhoz
Brest-Litovsk	Sovkhoz
Political Party	Collectivization
New Economic Policy	Five-Year Plans
Kulak	Gosplan
Russian Soviet Federated Socialist	Supreme Soviet
Republics (RSFSR)	Soviet of the Union
Union of Soviet Socialist Republics	Soviet of Nationalities
(USSR)	Presidium
Leninism	Council of Ministers

People

Prince Lvov	Lenin (Ulyanov)
Alexander Kerensky	Stalin
Trotsky	

Significant Dates

1917 March	Czar Nicholas II abdicates
1917 October	Bolshevik Revolution
1918 March	Treaty of Brest-Litovsk
1918–1921	War Communism
1921–1928	New Economic Policy
1928	Inauguration of Five-Year Plans and Collectivization

Topic Outline

Background to Revolution
Provisional Government of Prince Lvov
Establishment of Dictatorship under Lenin
Periods of Russian Communism
   Period 1   (1918 to 1921) Communism Established
   Period 2   (1921–1928) New Economic Policy
   Period 3   Collectivization and State Industrialization
     Five-Year Plans
Structure of the Government
Constitution of 1936

Union of Soviet Socialist Republics: The Communist State

Background to Revolution

Nicholas II of Russia, nominally an autocratic ruler, was controlled by a small clique at court and greatly influenced by *Rasputin*, a monk whose claim to magic powers over the Czar's sickly son won him the support of the Empress.

Conditions in Russia grew worse as the war progressed; staggering losses were suffered by ill-equipped Russian troops, the drafting of millions of farmers created food shortages, and inadequate supplies of food and fuel to the cities created growing resentment against the government. The Czar took personal command of the troops, leaving the Czarina to gain increasing control of the government and to oppose all demands for moderate reforms. Scandals rocked the government as profiteers, black market operators, and speculators in military supplies were exposed.

Provisional Government of Prince Lvov

In March, 1917, a strike occurred at St. Petersburg, fighting broke out, and the Czar ordered the Duma to disband. The radicals organized a Soviet or Council of workers and soldiers, and *Prince Lvov*, a moderate liberal, organized a provisional or temporary government, which was to establish a constitutional government. The Czar was obliged to abdicate in favor of his brother the *Grand Duke Michael*, who refused to accept the throne.

The revolution was peaceful, and the new middle-class government expected to accomplish the necessary political reforms. Unfortunately several adverse factors prevented this: (1) the provisional government was inexperienced, was far removed from the lower classes, and continued to conduct a costly war, (2) the government failed to understand that the people wanted "peace, bread, and land," (3) the radical element of the Social Democrats was organized to use force to take over. The leader of this group was *Vladimir Ulyanov*—called *Lenin*— a revolutionary and leader of the radical wing of the Bolsheviks, in exile in Switzerland since 1908 but now brought back to Russia with the connivance of the German general staff.

The Social Democrats generally favored a bourgeois parliamentary republic as the first step towards a socialist society. Lenin, challenged on his more radical action, demanded the seizure of power, "then we will see what we can do with it." He demanded a "revolutionary-democratic dictatorship of the proletariat and peasantry."

Establishment of Dictatorship under Lenin

In July, 1917, Prince Lvov was succeeded by *Kerensky* as leader of the provisional government, which still delayed remedying the grievances of the lower classes. Local soviets or committees were running affairs in towns and villages, and on November 6, representatives of the Soviets led by Lenin carried out a *coup d'etat*, overthrew the provisional government, and set up a central executive Committee of the Soviets. The Bolsheviks had agreed to hold free elections, but when Lenin and his followers received only 25 per cent of the votes, his group dissolved the Assembly by force in January 1918 and set up a dictatorship under Lenin.

In March, 1918, Lenin negotiated the Peace of Brest-Litovsk with Germany, and could give full attention to internal affairs.

Civil war broke out in Russia, opponents of the revolutionaries, the White Russians (as distinguished from the Reds), assisted by the Allies in June 1918, attempted to crush local soviets and to halt the distribution of land to the peasants. *Trotsky* organized the Red Army which by November, 1920, had not only crushed all opposition within Russia but had also won back part of the Ukraine.

Periods of Russian Communism

The term *communism* is used in both an economic and a political sense, meaning (1) economically, ownership by the state of all the means of production and distribution, (2) politically, dictatorship which permits of no free elections of competing parties. Elections were held in Russia, but only handpicked communist candidates were eligible, and the voters chose Tweedledum or Tweedledee. *Socialism*, as distinguished from communism, believes in state ownership of the means of production and distribution, but accepts free elections of competing political parties. Thus a socialist country is usually regarded as having periodic and free elections, giving the opportunity to the voters to retain or to repudiate the socialists, as the British did in 1951.

The *First period of Communism*, between July 1918 and 1921, when complete communism was established.

The *Second period*, 1921 to 1928, of the NEP or New Economic Policy of a limited capitalism.

The *Third period*, from 1928, of Collective Farms and Industrial Five-Year Plans.

Period I (1918 to 1921)

1. Communism was thoroughly established.

2. Land was nationalized and given to the people to use rather than to own.

3. Businesses and banks were nationalized.

4. The "dictatorship of the proletariat" was established, the period during which the intellectuals, the middle-class, the believers in free enterprise, were to be deliberately and dictatorially eliminated.

The dictatorship of the workers was necessary until all "bourgeois" ideas had been eliminated. Then the classless society would have been achieved, and no further dictation would be necessary. That is the theory, whatever the practice.

Note: The Communist Party is not a political party in the western sense, which is a group of people with the same political ideas, who organize to get their representatives elected in order to enact legislation in their favor. To this must be added one important characteristic: a political party in office always acknowledges the right of any minority party to become the majority *by peaceful means*. This last is *not* accepted by the Communists, who do not agree to a free discussion of ideas and a free change in the government according to majority wishes.

Period 2 (1921–1928) New Economic Policy (NEP)

Criticism of pure communism became widespread. Peasants objected to having their produce taken by the government at whatever price the government chose to pay. Farm productivity consequently declined. Factory workers objected to "conscript" labor and complained of food shortages. Managerial and technical groups resented the loss of initiative and of rewards commensurate with skill and service. Lenin, who always was prepared to make a strategic retreat, realized that the communists had gone too far, and inaugurated the NEP of restricted capitalist enterprises. Peasants were permitted to sell whatever they had in surplus, retail trading for profit was allowed, graduated wage scales were revived, and small businesses were returned to private ownership.

Criticism was levelled by deep dyed communists at the new businessmen, the Nepmen, and the kulaks, the comparatively well-off peasant landowners, later to be brutally liquidated, were criticized for bourgeois attitude. In 1924 Lenin died, and a bitter struggle for leadership ensued.

Leninism

Just as Marxism was the doctrine of a class-struggle, so Leninism is essentially the doctrine of organizing a group dedicated to the actual physical aspect of the class struggle. Marxism was the theory; Leninism is the practice of the class struggle.

Marxism-Leninism was to be carried out by:

1. Totalitarian dictatorship.

2. Aggression against capitalist nations.

3. World-wide conspiracy by native communist parties following Moscow's leadership, and dedicated to the overthrow of governments by violence.

In domestic affairs Lenin believed:

1. That after the elimination of all other groups by the proletarian dictatorship there would be a classless society.

2. That the profit system would be replaced by the slogan "from each according to his ability, to each according to his needs" (ignoring the historical evidence of the effect of incentive and rewards for initiative).

3. That collective farming must replace private land ownership.

It is of interest to note that right up to the present the Russian authorities have had to make modifications in this last point, since peasants simply will not work to capacity without rewards for their greater effort.

Trotsky vs Stalin

These two men were the contenders for Lenin's position. Trotsky had been regarded by Lenin as too overconfident, Stalin as too brutal. Trotsky supported immediate agitation for world revolution and world communism as the only way to protect Russian communism: Stalin believed in first consolidating Russia as the base before embarking upon world communism. Stalin won out, and Trotsky went into exile, a bitter critic of Stalin, and was eventually killed in Mexico by what were presumed to be Stalinist agents.

Period 3 Collectivization and State Industrialization

Individual peasant farming did not produce enough food for the city workers upon whose industrial development the nation depended. Food prices were high, much produce was hoarded in hopes of better prices, and clearly the success of the revolution could depend upon how this problem was handled.

Kolkhozy and Sovkhozy: Collective Farms

Stalin ordered all peasants to join local collective farms, the Kolkhozy, where most of the land was owned by the collective, although each peasant was allowed to retain a small garden plot, a cow, and a limited number of chickens for himself. The kolkhoz was required to pay a tax in produce, the amount determined by the government. It must rent tractors from state-owned tractor stations placed strategically about the countryside. The next step was to transform the kolkhoz into a *sovkhoz* or State farm, owned and operated by the state, and with no peasant ownership whatever. Each sovkhoz was to specialize in a product, such as grain, or dairy produce, or stock-raising. Resistance to collectivization was met with force, so that by 1939 collectivization was virtually complete, although in the process millions of peasants had to be uprooted, and between one and three millions were starved to death.

Five-Year Plans

Five-year plans began in 1928, were repeated, sometimes extended, and were organized by *Gosplan*, the State Planning Commission, charged with the task of nationalizing, organizing, and planning production in industry and agriculture. The incentive was to be a higher standard of living for all.

The first Five-Year Plan hoped to increase industrial production by 135 per cent, agricultural production by 55 per cent, and oil, coal, and electric power by an average of about 150 per cent. The successive plans aimed at increasing production of consumer goods, and in 1938 concentrated upon moving industrial plants further into the interior as a defensive measure.

Despite all promises, the plans were implemented only at enormous cost in lives and at great hardship for all, since very little foreign capital was available. Raw materials and consumer goods were even sold abroad in order to purchase industrial equipment. Nevertheless, the nation was able to become sufficiently industrialized to put up strong resistance to German aggression in 1941.

Structure of the Government

In 1918 a constitution established the State known as the RSFSR, the Russian Soviet Federated Socialist Republics, changed in 1922 to the USSR, the Union of Soviet Socialist Republics, consisting of four republics, the original RSFSR, the Ukraine, White Russia, and Transcaucasia.

The Constitution of 1918 was based upon two main principles (1) the concentration of power in one body, the Congress of Soviets, (2) the revolutionary class nature of the electoral system.

Constitution of 1936

In 1936 the former constitution was replaced with a new one which would appear to give Russia a democratic form of government.

There are elections every four years to a parliament, the Supreme Soviet of two houses, the Soviet of the Union and the Soviet of Nationalities. But appearances are deceptive, and the actual administration of the U.S.S.R. is rigidly controlled by the Communist Party.

The *Supreme Soviet* has its two houses, and the representatives of the *Soviet of the Union* are chosen on a basis of approximately 1 for every 300,000 citizens; the *Soviet of Nationalities* represents the several nationalities roughly in proportion to their numbers. The Supreme Soviet meets several times a year, but normal routine business is conducted by the *Presidium*, or permanent committee, of 33 members. The Supreme Soviet selects the Council of Ministers, who are heads of departments. The head of the country is the *Chairman* of the *Council of Ministers*, a position held in sequence by Stalin and Khrushchev.

Each of the 15 republics which constitute the Union of Soviet Socialist Republics has a similar organization.

Paralleling the entire organization is the Communist Party. All candidates for election to the Supreme Soviet are carefully hand-picked Communist party members. At the head of the Communist Party is the Chairman of the Supreme Soviet's Council of Ministers. The Presidium of the Communist Party is the small permanent committee of the Central Committee, elected periodically by the All-Union Communist Party Congress. *This* Presidium of the Communist Party makes all decisions for the administration about every phase of Russian life. Through this tightly-knit organization of probably 500,000 full-time party officials the entire nation is governed by an elaborately-organized but autocratic dictatorship of one man who is leader of the Party and head of the government as Secretary-General of the Communist Party and Chairman of the Council of Ministers of the Supreme Soviet.

Attempts At Collective Security

Terms

Collective Security	Locarno Agreements
Washington Conference	Munich Pact
Kellogg-Briand Pact	Five-Power Pact
Germany-USSR Non-Aggression Pact	Four-Power Pact
Appeasement	Lytton Commission
Nine-Power Pact	Embargo

People

Neville Chamberlain
Samuel Hoare
Pierre Laval

Significant Dates

1921	Washington Conference
1925	Locarno Agreements
1928	Kellogg-Briand Pact (Pact of Paris)
1931	Manchurian Incident
1935	Italy Attacks Ethiopia
1936	Germany Occupies the Rhineland
1938	Austrian Anschluss
1938	Munich Agreement
1939	Germany Absorbs Czechoslovakia
1939	World War II Begins, September 1

Topic Outline

League of Nations Charter
The Washington Conference (1921–1922)
The Locarno Agreements (1925)
The Kellogg-Briand Pact

Aggression and Appeasement
  Japan Attacks China
  Italy Attacks Ethiopia
Germany Defies Western Europe
  The Rhineland
  The Austrian Anschluss
  The Munich Pact
  Germany-U.S.S.R. Non-Aggression Pact
Beginning of World War II, September 1, 1939

Attempts At Collective Security

The outbreak of World War II in 1939 and the involvement of the United States in 1941 were not caused simply by aggressive actions by Germany and Japan but essentially by the unwillingness of nations to face political facts and to act effectively and in time. Two methods were open. Nations could support the concept of collective action to protect and guarantee collective security. Or they could form alliances and attempt to maintain a balance of power against a potential aggressor. To use neither the collective action method nor the alliance system could encourage a potential expansionist nation and so threaten the peace. Unfortunately during the period between two world wars both policies were only half-heartedly adopted and very poorly implemented. Such nations as Japan, Germany, and Italy were increasingly convinced that other countries would avoid solid commitments, would prefer to remain neutral even in the face of aggression, and could be blackmailed into *appeasement*, the making of concessions to an aggressive potential enemy in the hopes of avoiding trouble, and usually made from weakness rather than strength. Events were to prove the truth of this belief.

League of Nations Charter

The basic principles of the League of Nations are contained in Articles 10, 11, and 16.

Article 10 "Members . . . undertake to respect and preserve as against external aggression the territorial integrity and existing political independence of all Members of the League. In case of any such aggression or in case of any threat or danger of such aggression the Council shall advise upon the means by which this obligation shall be fulfilled."

Article 11 "Any war or threat of war, whether immediately affecting any of the Members of the League or not, is hereby declared a matter of concern to the whole League, and the League shall take any action that may be deemed wise and effectual to safeguard the peace of nations . . ."

Article 16 "Should any Member of the League resort to war in disregard of its covenants . . . it shall *ipso facto* be deemed to have committed an act of war against all other Members of the League, which hereby undertake immediately to subject it to the severance of all trade or financial relations, the prohibition of all intercourse between their nationals and the nationals of the covenant-breaking State . . . It shall be the duty of the Council in such case to recommend to the several Governments concerned what effective military, naval or air force the Members of the League shall severally contribute to the armed forces to be used to protect the covenants of the League . . .''

The *intention* was that in the event of the threat of aggression all other nations would act collectively by taking economic or even military action against the potential or actual aggressor. This *collective* action was expected to be a deterrent and would safeguard all nations by presenting a united front. If war did occur, then it would be isolated and quickly ended by the overpowering force at the League disposal. No nation was obliged to take action but all were expected to be ready to do so. While the failure of the United States to join the League contributed to its weakness, the basic weakness was the reluctance of nations to act jointly and promptly against the aggressor, especially during the 1930's.

The Washington Conference (1921–1922)

Perhaps with a feeling of guilt over its refusal to join the League, the United States initiated the Washington Conference to prevent a naval armaments race and to take the first step towards disarmament.

By the terms of the *Five Power Pact* capital ships and aircraft carriers were to be restricted to a ratio of 5:5:3 for the United States, Great Britain, and Japan, with France and Italy to have a roughly 1.75 ratio. Japan received the German islands in the Pacific on the agreement that she would not fortify them. Great Britain agreed to erect no fortifications east of Singapore, and the United States agreed not to erect any west of Hawaii. The value of these terms depended upon Japan's willingness to abide by them. This naval agreement, the Five Power Pact, meant that Japan emerged as the strongest *one-ocean* naval power; she secretly fortified her new island acquisitions, and the Conference failed to set up any machinery to see that the terms of the agreements were carried out.

In the *Nine Power Pact* Japan agreed, along with the other signatories, to respect the Open Door, that is, essentially the territorial and political integrity of China. By the *Four Power Pact* she also agreed to negotiate with the United States, Great Britain, and France any differences of policy that might arise regarding the Pacific.

In actual fact Japan was already launched upon a policy of expansion in Southeast Asia. The Conference increased rather than decreased Japan's power, for although it was hailed as a great step towards maintaining peace, it was no more than a paper agreement without substance, since no means were taken to implement its terms.

The Locarno Agreements (1925)

In 1925 the Locarno Agreements between Germany and her neighbors France and Belgium were hailed as a tremendous step towards peace. They stated that Germany and France, and Germany and Belgium agreed that their common boundaries must not be changed, and that the contracting powers agreed not to wage war on each other. Great Britain and Italy guaranteed to assist whichever nation was attacked, if the agreements were broken.

This pact was nothing more than a local pact, which made no mention of nations on Germany's eastern frontier, Poland and Czechoslovakia. It weakened the basic principle of collective security.

The Kellogg-Briand Pact (Pact of Paris) (1928)

In 1928 the Pact of Paris was signed and also greeted as a great step towards the guaranteeing of peace. It was a completely illusory agreement of 54 nations to outlaw war as an instrument of national policy. To *outlaw* a person was to place him outside the law and permit anyone to kill him without fear of punishment. To outlaw war simply made no practical sense. It had no more than vague moral force, it had no machinery to enforce its principle, and since it permitted war for self-defense, then war was not outlawed. History shows that all wars can be rationalized as defensive wars, even by the aggressor who could claim that his offensive action was really defensive, since he was hitting before he himself was hit.

Disarmament attempts failed because:

1. No international police force was organized to replace national forces.

2. No nation could safely disarm unless its neighbors did. And who would force them to do so? With what force?

Aggression and Appeasment

Japan Attacks China (1931)

In 1931 Japan, which had joined the League of Nations and signed the Kellogg-Briand Pact, cynically attacked China on the flimsy excuse that China was not protecting Japanese interests on the South Manchurian Railroad. The final outcome of that attack was the establishment of Manchuria as an "independent" Japanese satellite called Manchukuo. The Lytton Commission, sent by the League of Nations to investigate, simply expressed regret at invasion of China, that Japan had been guilty of aggression, and that other nations not recognize the results of the aggression, that is, that Manchukuo was a separate nation. Non-recognition did not change the fact that Japan had proved that a powerful and determined nation would not be faced with collective action, only words. The incident showed that the League members were unwilling to support the principle of collective action. In Europe, Italy and Germany were to use the same techniques with impunity, having learned from Japan.

Italy Attacks Ethiopia

Mussolini, dictator of Italy, complained that Italy had not been given her fair share of colonies after the war, and proclaimed that he would recreate the old Roman Empire through the Mediterranean region. His first venture was against Ethiopia in 1935, a nation he hoped that no one cared about, one that was far away enough from European politics to be a safe gamble.

European statesmen hoped that Italy could be kept quiet if she were permitted to satisfy her ambitions in Ethiopia. The French foreign minister *Pierre Laval* persuaded Britain's foreign secretary Sir *Samuel Hoare* to accept a deal by which Italy be allowed to take over two-thirds of Ethiopia. Protests in France and Britain resulted in the replacing of the two ministers, but both nations refused to take such action as they had formerly agreed upon, to place an embargo on oil supplies to Italy. As a result, within a few months Ethiopia was in the hands of Italy, and political blackmail had brought dividends to Mussolini. Despite his threats to take action if oil were placed on the embargo list, the fact is that without foreign oil, and without permission of Britain and France to Italy to use the Suez Canal, Italy would have been unable to conduct a war. Aggression had once again paid off; appeasement had failed.

Germany Defies Western Europe

The Rhineland

By the Treaty of Versailles the Germans were forced to accept demilitarization of their territory west of the Rhine, the "left bank," and for 30 miles east of the Rhine. In 1935 Hitler denounced the clauses providing for German disarmament, and in 1936 he denounced the Locarno Pacts, and sent in troops to occupy the Rhineland demilitarized zones. Had the British or the French been prepared even to make a show of force, the very weak German troops would have been obliged to pull out. But Hitler had watched appeasement in action, and against the advice of his military experts sent in his troops successfully.

The Austrian Anschluss

In 1938, despite the Treaty of Versailles clause forbidding Anschluss between Germany and Austria, Hitler marched into Austria and annexed it to Germany. The example threatened the security of other nations, but Britain and France again did no more than raise their voices.

The Munich Pact (1938)

One threat to German expansionist ambitions was Czechoslovakia, a democratic nation created in 1918, well protected by natural and artificial defenses, with a first class army and a modern munitions plant. Germany wanted Czechoslovakia eliminated. Hitler's strategy was simple. Make sure that the German minority in the Sudetenland, just inside the defensive Sudeten Mountains, was mistreated, even to the point of having Germans in Czechoslovakia commit the brutality on their own people. In Czechoslovakia a Nazi group of Germans was organized. The German propaganda machine now turned out denunciation of the Czechs and made it apparent to other nations that unless the Germans inside Czechoslovakia were brought under the control of Germany, then war would ensue. Hitler reiterated publicly that Germany had no territorial ambitions in Europe, and that once this question was settled, then all would be peaceful. The fact was that once the outer defenses of Czechoslovakia were rendered useless, then the whole country was defenseless and would be ready for annexation to Germany.

Years earlier France had made defensive treaties with Poland, 1922, with Czechoslovakia, 1924, and with Rumania and Yugoslavia in 1926–1927, all directed against future threats from Germany.

In 1934 the U.S.S.R. had signed a Mutual Assistance Pact with Czechoslovakia promising aid if Germany attacked her, but only upon the condition that France gave assistance also. The U.S.S.R. was increasingly concerned with the expansionist moves of Germany and Japan; she strongly supported collective security; she had demanded League action against Italy's attack on Ethiopia; during the Czech crisis she demanded League action against Germany, and declared her intention of fulfilling her obligations to Czechoslovakia. How far her words could be trusted was of great concern, and of doubt, to Europe's statesmen.

Great Britain's prime minister *Neville Chamberlain* rebuffed Soviet overtures, fearful of getting involved in a war, and naively hoping that German expansion would be satisfied with the acquisition of the Sudetenland. In turn the U.S.S.R.

was convinced that the western nations were tacitly encouraging Germany to expand eastwards at Russia's expense.

At Munich in September, 1938, Chamberlain bought "peace in our time." France, Italy, and Great Britain, without permitting Czechoslovakia to be represented at the Munich Conference, agreed to permit Germany to occupy the Sudetenland, and notified Czechoslovakia that unless she agreed, then the signatory powers would not guarantee her new frontiers. This betrayal of an ally, without its having any say in the situation, was one of the most cynical acts of statesmanship in modern times. No nation could count on assistance after such an example of appeasement. Hitler had demonstrated that force did indeed pay off.

In early 1939 Hitler simply absorbed all of Czechoslovakia into Germany, and the allies who had promised to guarantee Czechoslovakia's new frontiers did nothing.

The march of events since 1931 had proven the hollowness of both collective security and the alliance system.

Germany-U.S.S.R.
Non-Aggression Pact
(1939)

The U.S.S.R., thwarted in its attempts to contain Germany, now decided that her best policy was to attempt to buy her own safety by allying with her. In August, 1939, a treaty between Germany and Russia was signed, the open clauses being the non-aggression pact between them, the secret clauses agreeing to a division of territory in the Baltic. Hitler could now count on no Russian interference with his attack on Poland.

Beginning of
World War II,
September 1, 1939

Britain and France, guarantors of Polish frontiers were unable to come to Poland's aid when Germany attacked her on the night of September 1, 1939. Their opportunity to stop Hitler had been in 1938. Two days later Britain declared war on Germany, almost exactly twenty-five years after the declaration of war against the Kaiser's Germany in 1914.

World War II and the Peace Conferences

Terms

Blitzkrieg	Vichy France	Atlantic Charter
Island Hopping	Yalta Declaration	Potsdam Conference

Places to Locate

Karelian Isthmus	Stalingrad	Okinawa
Dunkirk	Guam	Sakhalin Island
Coral Sea	Saipan	Kurile Islands
Midway	Iwo Jima	Port Arthur
Liaotung Peninsula		

Significant Dates

1941 June 22	Hitler Invades the U.S.S.R.
1941 August	The Atlantic Charter

1944 June 6	D-Day
1945 February	Yalta Conference
May 8	V-E Day
July	Potsdam Conference
August 14	V-J Day

Topic Outline
First Phase: To the German Attack on the U.S.S.R. (1939–1941)
   The Battle of Britain
Second Phase: To Pearl Harbor, December 7, 1941
    The U.S.A. Gradually Abandons Neutrality
    The Japanese Challenge to the "Open Door" Policy
    The Atlantic Charter
Third Phase: To the Invasion of Africa (1942)
Fourth Phase: Africa, Italy, and the Western Front
Final Phase: D-Day to V-J Day
   The Atomic Attack
The Yalta and Potsdam Conferences

World War II and the Peace Conferences

Because World War I was fought in a narrow area in France, it was expected that this war would be fought between the French Maginot Line and the German Siegfried Line. In fact, it was fought and decided across the world, in Europe, the Mediterranean, and in the Pacific, and was one of great mobility and new weapons, and on a vast scale never before experienced. The last few days of the war brought the use of the atomic bomb, a weapon that may, by its very potential in devastation, restrict future conflicts to conventional weapons and limited theaters.

First Phase: To the German Attack on the U.S.S.R. (1939–1941)

The absorption of Czechoslovakia by Germany in March, 1939, despite Hitler's earlier denials of that intention, convinced Great Britain and France that action must be taken. Great Britain made alliances with Turkey, Greece, and Poland, promised to send aid if they were attacked. The August, 1939, non-aggression pact between Germany and Russia sealed Poland's doom. On September 1, 1939, Germany invaded Poland after that nation refused to give up the Polish Corridor to Germany. Russia took the opportunity to seize eastern Poland and the Baltic states of Esthonia, Latvia, and Lithuania. Finland's refusal to give Russia naval bases in the Karelian Isthmus resulted in successful invasion by Russia.

The "phony" war of inaction by the western powers until April, 1940, was in fact preparation by both sides, the British and French preparing defensively, and Germany offensively. In another blitzkrieg or lightning attack, Germany took over Denmark and Norway, smashed through the frontiers of Holland and Belgium, drove the British army back to Dunkirk, turned on the French, and in less than three weeks had dictated peace terms to France. The French army was disbanded, 2,000,000 Frenchmen were sent as slave labor to Germany, the French fleet was interned, two-thirds of France was occupied, with the French paying all occupation costs, and the remaining third of France, with its capital at Vichy, was left "free" upon the condition of collaborating with Germany.

The Battle of Britain (1940)

With the collapse of almost the entire continent under German assault Hitler believed that Britain would agree to a compromise of acknowledging German domination of Europe in return for retention of her overseas empire. Despite the incredible feat of Dunkirk, in which 335,000 troops were rescued in a sea operation, Great Britain was in a desperate position. The odds appeared to favor Germany with its navy and the shorter distance for air attacks upon Britain and her factories. The one advantage that Britain held was a navy prepared to risk all rather than permit an unchallenged German landing on England's shores.

The Battle of Britain was the greatest air attack in history up to that time. On June 19 Hitler commenced air attacks that increased in intensity until 1000-plane raids were mounted daily. German strategic errors and British radar, plus the incredible work of an overworked air force, finally forced Germany to substitute submarine warfare in a series of attacks that threatened supplies of food and raw materials. By the early months of 1941 Britain was losing 500,000 tons of shipping each month. Only the assistance of the United States navy prevented defeat for Britain, since her merchant ships were being sunk faster than they could be replaced. Perhaps Hitler's greatest mistake was the belief that British resistance was almost ended when he invaded the Balkans to assist his ally Italy, which was suffering setbacks in North Africa. Hitler's campaign in Yugoslavia and Greece was successful but it fatefully delayed his projected attack on Russia, which had long been planned.

Second Phase: To Pearl Harbor, December 7, 1941

On June 22, 1941, without declaration of war, Hitler smashed into Russia on a 2000-mile front, and had advanced 500 miles into Russia by late November. German troops were surrounding Leningrad and within 30 miles of Moscow when an unexpected sub-zero winter set in and halted the German army in its tracks. The Russians began a counter-offensive, but the Germans consolidated for another smashing drive eastwards when the weather improved.

The U.S.A. Gradually Abandons Neutrality

In the mid-1930's the United States abandoned its former position about neutral rights and passed neutrality legislation to avoid any chance of becoming involved in war. But after war broke out in 1939 Congress in November modified her neutrality acts to permit belligerents to purchase munitions on a "cash and carry" basis in their own ships. The fall of France in June, 1940, brought to the United States the realization that Britain's possible collapse could have devastating consequences, and aid "short of war" became her policy. In September, 1940, the United States transferred 50 overage destroyers to Great Britain in exchange for eight naval and air bases from Newfoundland to the West Indies. When British funds ran low, Congress in March, 1941, passed the Lend-Lease Act which in effect gave vital supplies and munitions to Britain and her allies. At the request of Iceland and Denmark, the United States established a base on Iceland and Greenland, ferried supplies to those bases and, after suffering German submarine attacks, ordered the navy to shoot on sight. In November, 1941, Congress permitted Lend-Lease goods to be delivered and convoyed in American ships. These activities and the passage of the Selective Service Act of

1940 put American production into high gear, so that when the blow fell at Pearl Harbor the United States was not unprepared.

Japanese Challenge to the "Open Door" Policy

In 1937 Japan launched a full-scale attack upon China, forced Chiang Kai-shek into the interior, with his capital at Chunking, and in 1939 began an advance into Southeast Asia that overran French Indo-China and threatened the Netherlands East Indies. This expansion presented a clear challenge to the United States policy of the Open Door. Presumably Japan decided that her proposed Greater East Asia Co-Prosperity Sphere of expansion into all Southeast Asia would sooner or later meet opposition from the United States. Hence her decision to bomb Pearl Harbor in an attempt to remove whatever retaliatory force the United States had.

The Atlantic Charter

In August, 1941, the United States and Great Britain announced their basic aims for a peace settlement. President Roosevelt and Prime Minister Churchill met on shipboard off the Newfoundland shore in order to set down clearly their objectives for future peace. The United States was not in the war, and there was no evidence that she would be. However, this nation wanted to put its prestige and power behind the effort to encourage basic principles:

1. No territorial aggrandizement after the war.
2. No territorial changes except by consent of the people involved.
3. The right of people to select their own form of government.
4. Raw materials and trade opportunities should be open to all nations.
5. All nations should be assured of peace and of freedom from fear and want.
6. The use of force as a solution to disputes should be abandoned.

In later years the members of the United Nations supported these principles.

Third Phase: To the Invasion of Africa (1942)

On December 8, 1941, the day after Pearl Harbor, the United States Congress declared war on Japan, and in reply to the declaration of war by Germany and Italy, declared war upon the other two members of the Berlin-Rome-Tokyo Axis. The war now became global.

Six months after Pearl Harbor, Japan had possession of the Netherlands East Indies, the Malay Peninsula, the Philippines, New Guinea, and was threatening Australia and India. Two great naval victories saved Australia from invasion and turned away the threat to Hawaii. The first check to Japan's advance was the Battle of the Coral Sea, May 4–8, 1942, in which Japanese forces from the Solomon Islands were stopped by the United States navy as they headed towards the east coast of Australia. The second naval victory was the Battle of Midway in June, in which the Japanese suffered their worst naval defeat to date.

Fourth Phase: Africa, Italy, and the Western Front

In June, 1942, twenty-six countries signed the Declaration of the United Nations to fight until the Axis was defeated, to base peace upon the principles of the Atlantic Charter, and to coordinate their efforts through joint planning.

In North Africa the British fought German forces under *Rommel* who had driven them back within 60 miles of Alexandria. Under General *Montgomery* they consolidated their forces, broke the German line, and began the advance that carried them 1600 miles to the west. Meanwhile American forces under General *Eisenhower* landed at Casablanca, Oran, and Algiers and cornered Rommel between the American and British forces in Tunisia, capturing over 300,000 prisoners in May, 1943.

The allies then invaded Sicily, landed in southern Italy, and started the difficult fight north towards Rome, against stubborn resistance by the Germans.

In the spring of 1942, Hitler launched another massive offensive against the Russians in the Caucassus region, vital to Russia for oil supplies and the allied supply line through Iran. Not until the end of that summer was the German drive finally halted at Stalingrad (now Volgograd). This was the turning-point for Russia, for she steadily overran German forces until by the summer of 1944 Russian troops had penetrated into Poland, almost to the gates of Warsaw.

Final Phase: D-Day June 6, 1944 to V-J Day, August 14, 1945

The final phase of the war began on D-Day, June 6, 1944, with the allied invasion of the Normandy coast, followed in August, with another landing at Marseilles in southern France. By September the allies had landed 2,000,000 troops, liberated Paris and crossed into Germany. The Germans fought a bitter rearguard action to the Westwall, and then made a desperate counter-attack through Luxembourg, the famous Battle of the Bulge of December, 1944. While Russia continued its offensive through Rumania, Bulgaria, and Hungary and into Yugoslavia, the Americans massed their forces for an attack on the Ruhr region, the heart of industrial Germany. In February, 1945, the allies met at Yalta in the Russian Crimea to draw up concerted plans for the completion of the war.

In May, 1945, Germany capitulated after being completely overrun from east and west. On the basis of the "unconditional surrender" terms previously announced, the victors refused to negotiate with Germany, but divided the nation into military zones of occupation.

The Atomic Attack

After the Japanese naval defeats of the Coral Sea and Midway in 1942, the Japanese fortified island bases within their perimeter defense lines, from the Aleutians down to the Solomons, off the northeast corner of Australia. In July the Chinese Nationalist government, assisted by supplies flown in from India, defeated the Japanese in central China (Kiangsi province). The next month American marines landed at Guadalcanal in the Solomons and commenced the difficult and costly "island-hopping" to key Japanese islands, Guam, Saipan, Iwo Jima, and Okinawa, serving intermediate Japanese islands from a base of supplies. With the collapse of Germany in May, 1945, the allies drew up plans for mass landings on the Japanese home islands, anticipating very severe casualties if the Japanese should decide to defend every inch of their homeland in kamikaze fashion. Throughout June and July constant air attacks pounded Japanese cities, and during July the Russians massed their forces to invade Manchuria. On August 6, 1945, an American plane dropped an atomic bomb on Hiroshima; on August 8th Russia declared war on Japan and invaded Manchuria; on August 9th an atomic bomb was dropped on Nagasaki; and on August 14th Japan capitulated.

- The war had cost 22,000,000 lives of combatants and civilians, and over $3,000,000,000,000 in military expenditures and property damage.

The Yalta and Potsdam Conferences

Throughout the war the allied nations had met at various conferences to determine war-time policy and to consider possible peace settlements. The most significant war-time conference was held early in February, 1945.

The Yalta Conference (February 7–12, 1945)

This is one of the most controversial of the war-time conferences, probably because it is not considered in relation to significant circumstances.

Roosevelt and Churchill could never ignore the possibility that the Soviet Union would make a separate peace with Germany, with potentially fateful consequences for the western allies. As early as July 1942 Stalin had complained about the allied war effort and demanded a second front, "I must state in the most emphatic matter that the Soviet government cannot acquiesce in the postponement of a second front in Europe until 1943."

When the war-time leaders met at Yalta the strategic advantage certainly lay with the Soviet Union. Russian troops occupied all of Poland, were on German soil, and within 75 miles of Berlin. United States and British troops were still on the west bank of the Rhine river, 300 miles west of Berlin. Furthermore, the main campaign in the Pacific theater was yet to be mounted. Estimates by United States military advisors were that the war against Japan would take between twelve and eighteen months after the collapse of Germany, and would cost 1,000,000 American casualties. Therefore, it seemed absolutely necessary to seek Soviet assistance in the Far East.

The Yalta Declaration included:

1. Reaffirmation of the principles of the Atlantic Charter.

2. Promises of elections and guarantees of national freedom for liberated nations.

3. Plans for the occupation and administration of Germany.

4. Soviet participation in the war against Japan.

5. The establishment of a permanent organization for peace.

The agreements on free elections in Poland and other eastern European nations were based on hope rather than certainty, since the United States and Great Britain were in no position to force Russia to carry out her promises. Russia, despite her professed support of the principles of the Atlantic Charter, retained as part of her territory Estonia, Latvia, Lithuania, and parts of Finland, Poland, and Rumania. Russia created satellite "people's republics" of Poland, Hungary, Bulgaria, Rumania. Poland was given a part of Germany east of the Oder-Neisse rivers.

In order to persuade the Soviet Union to declare war on Japan, Roosevelt and Churchill agreed that the U.S.S.R. should recover all that she had lost to Japan in the Russo-Japanese War of 1904–1905:

a. The southern half of Sakhalin Island.

b. The lease of Port Arthur on the Liaotung Peninsula as a naval base.

c. The Kurile Islands.

d. Joint operation by China and the U.S.S.R. of the Chinese Eastern and the South Manchurian Railroads.

Even had the western allies not agreed to these terms, they were in no position to prevent the Soviet Union's taking these areas by force. Furthermore, the critics who claim that the United States should never have allowed the Soviet Union to declare war on Japan, when Japan was ready to capitulate after the dropping of atomic bombs on Hiroshima and Nagasaki, fail to explain how the United States could have prevented such a declaration of war.

Potsdam Conference, July 17–August 2, 1945

When the allied powers met at Potsdam, two new heads of state met with Stalin, President Truman and Prime Minister Attlee of Great Britain. The only basic settlement agreed upon was that Poland was allowed to extend her boundaries about 100 miles westwards into Germany as compensation for Russian expansion into Poland on her eastern frontier.

By the time the conference met there were serious disagreements between the allies over the treatment by Russia of eastern European nations, over German reparations, the administration of the Ruhr region, and other matters.

It was agreed that peace treaties would be signed as soon as possible with former German satellite nations. In 1947 peace treaties were signed with Rumania, Bulgaria, Hungary, Finland. In 1951 a peace treaty was signed with Japan, but neither Russia nor any of her satellites signed it. Germany still remained in 1966 without a final peace treaty, and divided.

CHAPTER **9**

Europe and the
Middle East Today

The United Nations

Terms

International Court of Justice | Assembly
The Big Five | The Third World
Security Council | Palestine Liberation Organization
Veto | Kangaroo Court

People

Dag Hammarskjold | U Thant
Count Bernadotte | Gamal Abdel Nasser
Trygvie Lie | Yassir Arafat
Ralph Bunche | Abdelaziz Bouteflika

Topic Outline

Aims of the United Nations
Machinery of the United Nations
Achievements
Effects of the Third World
Special Agencies

The United Nations

The Aims of the United Nations

As World War II progressed, the several states associated together in opposition to the Axis powers used the term *United Nations,* and from 1942 on laid down principles for a permanent organization. In May and June, 1945, delegates from 50 nations met in San Francisco to draft the Charter of the United Nations, which was ratified by 29 nations in October, 1945. The hope was that wartime cooperation could be continued through the United Nations to achieve two purposes:

1. An equitable peace settlement.

2. To make the United Nations a world organization through which all issues could be resolved peacefully.

The conclusion of the war left the Big Three, the United States, Great Britain, and Russia, the victors in a world that had changed drastically:

1. These three powerful nations would probably determine much future foreign policy.

2. The U.S.S.R. now found itself in a position to exercise great influence in Europe.

3. Two European powers — Germany and Italy — and one Asiatic power — Japan — had been completely defeated, and France was completely exhausted from German occupation and war devastation.

Unfortunately, wartime interests could no longer hold the U.S.S.R. and the Western allies together in peacetime. The widely divergent interests of Russia and the United States did not appear at first, and it was hoped that the machinery of the United Nations would provide the means for cooperation. Most of the postwar problems were resolvable if the major powers had as their sincere objective the solution of all international problems by peaceful methods. The strength of the United Nations was, of course, dependent upon the sincerity of its members. The United Nations was not intended to be a world government, but a meeting of nations for the discussion and peaceful solution of problems.

Machinery of the United Nations

The charter states the purpose of the organization: to maintain international peace and security; to take effective collective action for the prevention and removal of threats to the peace; to bring about by peaceful means the settlement of international disputes.

Several organizations within the United Nations were set up to carry out these high principles.

The Assembly

Each member nation was represented by its delegates with one collective vote. The Assembly was to meet at least once a year, more frequently if necessary, and to consider any issue of concern to its members.

The Security Council

This was to consist of 5 permanent members — the United States, Great Britain, the U.S.S.R., France, and China — plus 6 members elected for 2-year terms from the other members. Its functions were to investigate all issues that might lead to international friction, and to recommend action including collective armed action. This would require a 7-nation vote, including the unanimous agreement of the 5 permanent members. The veto of any of the Big Five would prevent action. Since all members were sovereign nations and would not allow themselves to be forced into action against their wishes, the veto power was essential, as much for the United States as for the U.S.S.R.

International Court of Justice

This is the third major organ of the United Nations. It was formed in 1907 as the Court of Arbitration at the Hague, then became the Permanent Court of International Justice in 1919 under the League of Nations. As the International Court of Justice it consists of 15 judges elected for terms of office by the Security Council and the Assembly, to settle any disputes brought to it by any nation. It had no authority to enforce its decisions, and nations could accept or reject its findings.

The Trusteeship Council had the task of administering regions, such as Africa, where the people wanted but were not ready for self-rule.

The Economic and Social Council was to secure economic development and security for all people, as promised in the Atlantic Charter.

The Secretariat, headed by the Secretary-General, was to carry on the routine work of the United Nations.

By 1950 the United Nations had a membership of 59 nations. Its annual budget was $50,000,000, two-thirds of which was subscribed by the United States. Its headquarters are in New York.

Achievements of the United Nations

Over the years the General Assembly has become increasingly important, partly because the veto has restricted action by the Security Council and partly because of the increase in membership of the Assembly from an original 50 signatories to about 145 in 1976. A recent significant role of the Assembly is that it has become a meeting-place for the more than 30 new nations of Africa.

The Secretary-General, ably led in turn by *Trygve Lie* of Norway, *Dag Hammarskjold* of Sweden, *U Thant* of Burma, and *Kurt Waldheim* of Austria, has played an increasingly important role in international affairs, acting almost as the ambassador of the United Nations.

The United Nations has, with general success, attempted to resolve issues of international tension.

1. Iran

During World War II Iran agreed to permit allied troops ot use its territory as a supple route between the Persian Gulf and the Russian front, via the Caspian Sea. After the war Russia attempted to retain and increase its influence through a puppet government in a northern province of Iran. In 1946 the United Nations used its influence to accomplish the removal of all foreign troops from Iran.

2. Palestine-Israel

In 1947 Great Britain, involved in the Palestine controversy between Jews and Arabs, submitted the issue to the United Nations, which appointed a commission to investigate and recommend a solution. The Assembly accepted the majority proposal to partition Palestine into two autonomous states of Jews and Arabs. The Arabs voted solidly against the resolution. When Great Britain withdrew from Palestine in May, 1948, the Arab states of Egypt, Syria, Lebanon, Transjordan, and Iraq were defeated when they invaded Palestine. *Count Bernadotte* of Sweden was appointed by the United Nations to mediate; after his assassination by Jewish terrorists, his place was filled by Ralph Bunche of the United States. The Jews not only refused to agree to his requests but added more territory and refused to readmit the 1,000,000 Arabs who had fled from Israel. The United Nations did not succeed in its objective because the Arabs were implacably opposed to the existence of Israel.

3. Korea

In June, 1950, the armies of North Korea crossed the thirty-eighth parallel, the frontier between the two Koreas, and attempted to subjugate South Korea. A United Nations commission in Korea confirmed the aggression. The United States immediately sent aid to South Korea. The Security Council met and in the absence of the Russian delegate recommended joint action, and created a United Nations Unified Command under United States direction. After three years of fighting the United Nations was finally able to secure a truce line of roughly the thirty-eighth parallel between North Korea and South Korea.

The United Nations   223

4. The Congo

In 1959 the Belgians were so shaken by riots in the Belgian Congo that they agreed to its independence within a year. Chaos resulted when natives rebelled against the new government. The Belgians sent in forces to maintain order. Russia appeared to be ready to intervene, and a showdown seemed possible between Russia and the West. The United Nations organized an international police force, mainly of Africans, and gradually was able to restore order to the country.

5. The Suez Canal

In 1956 the Egyptian leader *Gamal Nasser*, not willing to wait for the agreed-upon withdrawal of British forces from the Suez Canal zone, seized the Canal. The British and French, determined to punish Nasser and forestall further Arab action, sent parachute attacks against the Egyptians in the Canal zone. The United Nations condemned the action, sent in a special United Nations police force which replaced British and French troops, and finally resolved the problem by obliging the invading nations to leave. The United Nations proved its value as an instrument of international opinion.

6. Yom Kippur War, 1973

A very important task, and perhaps the most difficult one that the United Nations Special Forces has faced, has been in the Middle East — the patrolling of the United Nations' zones between Israel and Egypt, and between Israel and Syria since the Yom Kippur War of 1973 (see page 256 for this war).

The United Nations has had marked success in attempting to provide technical assistance and economic aid to underdeveloped nations, and in designating the decade of the 1960's as the "Development Decade" to use several agencies to try to attain its objectives:

1. The International Development Fund to provide capital for nations.

2. The World Bank to finance projects in some 60 countries.

3. The International Finance Corporation to encourage private industrial development.

4. The Special Fund for development projects.

These measures may, in the long run, give the United Nations added respect and greater success.

| The U.N. and the Third World | The U.N. today consists of more than 130 nations, of which the African and Asian nations form a very effective, and sometimes obstructionist, bloc. |

The value of the U.N. as an organization was seriously threatened in 1974 when the General Assembly permitted Yassir Arafat to represent the Palestine Liberation Organization and to address the Assembly. Arafat supposedly represented all Palestinians. This broke the precedent that only official *governments* — not groups — are represented in the U.N. Arafat and the PLO represent no one but their own organization. In the subsequent debate, that year's President of the Assembly, the Algerian Abdelaziz Bouteflika, ruled that

Israel could speak only once, no matter how many other nations spoke on the issue. This was a gross and biased violation of the tradition of the U.N., and a serious threat to its future value. The former Ambassador to the U.N. from the United States, John Scali, cautioned that when a majority rule became the "tyranny of the majority, the minority will cease to respect or obey it," and warned of the mood of the American people regarding the U.N.

Special Agencies of the United Nations

FAO, *Food and Agriculture Organization* to increase farm, fishery, and forestry products in order to improve food distribution and raise the level of nutrition.

UNESCO, *United Nations Education, Scientific and Cultural Organization* to stimulate international understanding by encouraging education and training groups in basic skills of sanitation and home economics.

WHO, *World Health Organization* to fight disease, survey world health conditions, and coordinate health information.

ILO, *International Labor Organization* to improve working conditions through cooperative efforts of management, labor, and government.

ICAO, *International Civil Aviation Organization* to aid international civil aviation through uniform safety measures and cooperative techniques.

WMO, *World Meteorological Organization* to establish worldwide networks of meteorological stations and the exchange of weather data.

ITU, *International Telecommunication Union* to promote international cooperation in radio, telephone, and telegraph, and to promote standardization of equipment.

UPU, *Universal Postal Union* to establish international postal rates and other regulations on international mail.

International Bank for Reconstruction and Development to assist economic development through loans for productive projects such as hydroelectric plants, railroads, ports, harbors, and similar establishments.

International Monetary Fund to promote stabilization of currencies, international monetary cooperation, and to improve credit funds.

UNICEF, *United Nations International Children's Emergency Fund* a specialized agency of recent years created to provide supplies and equipment for child health and welfare programs.

The Cold War

Terms

Satellite	North Atlantic Treaty Organization
Cold War	Containment
Truman Doctrine	Massive Retaliation
European Recovery Program	Brinkmanship
German Federal Republic	Sputnik
German Democratic Republic	Cuban Missile Crisis
Brussels Pact	Strategic Arms Limitation Talks

People

Anthony Eden   Nikita Khrushchev
Harry Truman   John F. Kennedy
Dwight D. Eisenhower   Fidel Castro
John Foster Dulles

Significant Dates

1947, March   Truman Doctrine
1948, March   Marshall Plan
1948, June   Berlin Blockade
1949   North Atlantic Treaty Alliance
1957   Sputnik Launched
1961   Berlin Wall
1962   Cuban Missile Crisis
1970   SALT, Strategic Arms Limitation Talks

Topic Outline

Background of the Cold War
The Truman Doctrine
The Marshall Plan
The Berlin Blockade
North Atlantic Treaty Organization (NATO)
"Brinkmanship" and "Massive Retaliation"
Sputnik and the Berlin Wall
Cuban Missile Crisis

The Cold War

Background of the Cold War

One basic problem that had previously not been foreseen developed with the defeat of the Axis powers. That was the Cold War, soon to be deliberately waged by the U.S.S.R. in its plan to undermine the West and establish communism on a worldwide scale. The term Cold War was used to explain the tension that developed between the United States and the Soviet Union for nearly 20 years after World War II. The term described the attempts of the Soviet Union to expand its influence, without "hot" war, into Western Europe, and the "containment" policy of the United States to prevent the spread of Soviet influence westward. Later, the term applied to any place where tension developed between the two nations.

In 1942, *Anthony Eden*, British Foreign Minister, had warned that difficulties of peacemaking might face the allies. "We must have no illusions about the future . . . To win the peace will be as hard a task as to win the war."

After years of bitter warfare people hoped that the forces of totalitarianism would be eliminated, that a better world would emerge, based on understanding and the end of rivalries that had caused past wars. But international politics are not easily reconstructed, and long-standing rivalries not easily resolved.

In Europe Nazism had been beaten; Germany could not be permitted to begin another war; Russia's prewar plans for the subversion of capitalist countries continued; hopes that the United Nations could resolve all international problems were soon dimmed; and the potential devastation of the atomic bomb threatened civilization itself.

One of the obstacles to the effective functioning of the United Nations was the polarization of power in the hands of the United States and the U.S.S.R. The former balance of power in Europe had completely disappeared, for no combination of European powers could equal Russia in actual or potential strength. When it became apparent that Communist Russia's plans were no different from the expansionist intention of Czarist Russia, the United States recognized and accepted its role of defender of democratic principles. The agreements of Yalta were not carried out, for Russia retained as part of its own territory Estonia, Latvia, Lithuania, parts of Finland, Poland, and Rumania, subverted and took over Czechoslovakia in 1948, created "people's republics" of Poland, Hungary, Bulgaria, Albania, Rumania, and Czechoslovakia, and annexed part of East Prussia. Poland was compensated with prewar Germany east of the Oder-Neisse rivers.

The only agreement that the wartime partners could arrive at on Germany was to divide the country into four zones of military occupation by the United States, Great Britain, the U.S.S.R., and France, supposedly to be administered as one economic unit. Berlin, one hundred miles within the Russian zones, was divided into four sectors of occupation by the same four nations.

The political vacuum left by the collapse of the Nazis necessitated temporary rule until Germany should be ready for unification. The objective was to carry out the 4 D's of the Potsdam Agreement: disarm, demilitarize, denazify, and democratize.

Russia deliberately kept Germany economically divided, and gradually made its zone a satellite under its complete control. Stalin's long-range purpose was to incorporate all of Germany into the communist empire by refusing to cooperate and by forcing the allies out of Berlin.

The first evident example of the *Cold War* in operation was Russia's attempt to bring Turkey and Greece under its control. These two nations had so far remained outside the Russian orbit, largely because Britain had provided them with economic and military aid. Early in 1947 Great Britain announced that economic conditions would oblige it to withdraw from Greece, where foreign-inspired attempts were being made to overthrow the government.

The Truman Doctrine   Greece and Turkey occupied a strategic position in the eastern Mediterranean, and President Truman resolved that they should not fall by default to Russian control. In March, 1947, he sent a special message to Congress, requesting $300 million for Greece and $100 million for Turkey in economic and military aid. "I believe that it must be the policy of the United States to support peoples who are resisting attempted subjugation by armed minorities or by outside pressures."

Congressional opposition was based on the argument that the "containment" of Russia was a matter for the Security Council. The President countered with the obvious reply that Russia, through its veto power, could paralyze action by the United Nations. Senator Vandenburg supported the measure provided it included a clause stating that United States unilateral aid would cease as soon as the Security Council could assume the responsibility. The Security Council never did assume this responsibility.

Congress passed the measure and, in so doing, it authorized a new direction for United States foreign policy: active participation abroad to contain Russia within its boundaries.

The Marshall Plan*

The United States recognized the fact that Europe was economically devastated and therefore a good target for communist doctrine. In a Commencement Address at Harvard in June, 1947, General George Marshall, now Secretary of State, proposed what was officially called the European Recovery Program (ERP), popularly known as the Marshall Plan. The security of the Western world depended upon the revival of European economy. The United States was ready to offer economic aid, upon certain conditions, to each nation wanting it:

1. Each nation requesting assistance must submit a program indicating what it could do for itself.

2. Each should submit its request for types of economic assistance.

3. No military aid would be given.

4. All European nations, including Russia, were invited to join the program.

While European nations were meeting in Paris to prepare estimates of their capabilities and their needs, the United States Congress debated what opponents of the program called "Operation Rat-Hole." In March, 1948, the communists seized the government of Czechoslovakia, and in doing so spurred Congress to enact the Marshall Plan, which called for the spending of $17 billion over a four-year period,** Russia refused to join the plan, brought pressure on Poland to withdraw, and set up its own so-called Marshall Plan. The United States sent rolling-stock, raw materials, and technical assistance to such an extent that the tremendous economic recovery of Europe thwarted communist purposes. The Soviet Union's attitude may be partially explained by an historical attitude dating back centuries — its fear of invasion from the West across its flat, "frontierless" western lands. Russian communist belief insisted that capitalist nations would have to eliminate the Soviet Union for their own safety.

The Soviet Union was convinced that the Truman Doctrine and the Marshall Plan were clear evidence of a deliberate attempt at "encirclement" by a capitalist world determined to destroy the Soviet Union and communism.

One reaction of the U.S.S.R. was the Berlin Blockade of 1948.

The Berlin Blockade

In June, 1948, Russia suddenly announced the closing of the rail, road, and water routes across the Soviet zone of Germany into Berlin. The Russians expected that the allies would be unable to supply the 2½ million inhabitants of West Berlin and would therefore have to get out of Berlin. This could well be the first step in forcing the allies out of western Germany. That in turn might convince the rest of Europe that the United States could be forced out of Europe by Russia.

---

*In June, 1967, H.R.H. Prince Bernhard of the Netherlands officially endowed a chair of Dutch Civilization at Harvard University, in commemoration of the initiation in June, 1947, of the Marhsall Plan, which Prince Bernhard referred to as "outstanding statesmanship," "politics without power."
**President Truman signed the measure on April 3, 1948.

Faced with this blockade the allies had three courses open to them:

1. Accept the situation and pull out of Berlin.

2. Force their way into Berlin and risk a serious confrontation with Russia.

3. Fly in needed supplies, and confront Russia with the choice of shooting down allied planes or letting them go through.

For nearly 11 months the allies ran an airlift that sent in an average of 30 planes an hour. They supplied the Berliners with food, fuel, and goods to maintain their economy.

In May, 1949, the Russians backed down and opened all routes to Berlin. Since the Russians would not agree to the reunification of Germany, the United States, Great Britain, and France merged their zones in 1949 to form one administrative unit. In 1954 they recognized the German Federal Republic of the three zones as a sovereign state and as an ally.

East Germany, agricultural and comparatively nonindustrial, was then organized by the U.S.S.R. as the German Democratic Republic under strict Russian control.

North Atlantic Treaty Organization (NATO)

Very obviously the U.S.S.R. was prepared to use various tactics to intimidate Europe, perhaps including force. Without actual fighting, the technique of the Cold War could result in expansion of communist control. Obviously, the European nations were too weak to resist a determined Russian attack, but if they were organized and supported by the United States they could deter Russian expansion westwards.

Russia had been able, through communist groups, to start a series of strikes in France and Italy, to have Marshall Plan aid boycotted at the docks, and had reorganized the old Comintern under the new name of Cominform, or Communist Information organization, to sovietize wherever it could.

Alarmed with these events, Britain, France, Belgium, Holland, and Luxembourg signed in March, 1948, a *Western European Union* agreement (the Brussels Pact) "to secure the principles of democracy, personal freedom, and political liberty." On the day the Brussels Pact was signed, President Truman praised it as a step towards European unity, and said that it was worthy of "our full support." The five nations could not muster the military or economic strength to counter Soviet aggression, and the next obvious step was support by the United States. On April 4, 1949, twelve nations signed the Atlantic Pact: the United States, Canada, Greenland, Iceland, Great Britain, Portugal, France, Belgium, Holland, Luxembourg, Denmark, and Norway. Later on, Greece, Turkey, and West Germany joined the original twelve.

The Atlantic Pact was not organized as a threat to the Soviet Union but as a deterrent to Russian expansion westwards. *Article 5* states the purpose of NATO clearly: "The Parties agree that an armed attack on one or more of them in Europe or North America shall be considered an attack against them all . . . and agree that if such attack occurs, each of them will assist the party or parties so attacked by taking . . . such action as it deems necessary, including the use of armed force . . ." NATO is a regional pact as permitted under the U.N. charter, organized to take immediate action.

"Massive Retaliation" and "Brinkmanship"

Tension between the two superpowers was increased by the conviction of the U.S.S.R. that it was being encircled by U.S. bases, from which nuclear bombs could be dropped upon the Soviet Union — bases in the British Isles, Morocco, Saudi Arabia, Libya, Turkey, and Okinawa.

The Republican Party went into the 1952 presidential campaign for Dwight D. Eisenhower by promising to "liberate" Central Europe from communism, "roll back" Soviet power in Europe, and "unleash" Chiang Kai-shek in Asia — all empty phrases in fact but believed by the Soviet Union to be real threats. In October, 1953, Secretary of State John Foster Dulles announced his "massive retaliation" concept, which stated that the United States was not to be lured into any more little wars, and that threats to American security would result in nuclear attacks. This threat of "brinkmanship," of going up to the very brink of war, not only increased the Cold War tension but threatened U.S. allies in Western Europe with annihilation in case of war.

Sputnik and the Berlin Wall

In October, 1957, the West was suddenly confronted with the successful launching of Sputnik I by the Soviet Union. According to the Gaither Committee appointed by President Eisenhower, this rocket-launched "earth satellite" could mean that by 1959 the Soviet Union could be able to launch a thousand intercontinental ballistic missiles upon American cities.

Whether or not the committee exaggerated, Sputnik gave Nikita Khrushchev, now the leader in the Soviet Union, a diplomatic weapon. He announced that the time had come for the Western allies to withdraw from West Berlin and hand it over to East Germany, which now called itself the German Democratic Republic. Khrushchev added that if at the end of six months, by May, 1959, an agreement had not been reached, the Soviet Union might be obliged to use force. The reason for these threats was apparently that the German Democratic Republic wanted to close the escape route to the West through Berlin. Between 1950 and 1958 more than 1,500,000 East Germans had fled, many of them professional people whose loss was a severe blow to East Germany.

In 1958 the German Democratic Republic had built a barrier of barbed wire, land mines, police dogs, and watch towers to seal off the entire frontier between East and West Germany. The only escape route from East Germany to the West was through Berlin. In the first nine months of 1958 more than 3000 doctors, dentists, and teachers had fled. Khrushchev insisted that the escape route through Berlin be closed. The West stood firm, despite Soviet threats, and for the moment the Berlin question was dropped. In 1961 Khrushchev reminded President Kennedy that the escape route had not been closed, and that by the beginning of August, 1961, more than 3,000,000 out of a population of 18,000,000 had fled to the West. Two weeks later the Soviet Union supervised the building of a concrete wall across Berlin, dividing East and West. The Western allies had the choice of using force to destroy the wall and confront the Soviet Union, or accepting the wall and a victory for the Soviet Union. They chose the latter.

The Cuban Missile Crisis, 1962

When President Kennedy entered the White House in January, 1961, he learned that former President Eisenhower had supported a plan to help Cuban exiles invade Cuba and overthrow Fidel Castro. Kennedy allowed the plan to continue, but without expected air support. The invasion at the Bay of Pigs in 1961 was a total failure, and the United States was soundly criticized by Khrushchev.

In October, 1962, United States reconnaissance planes photographed nuclear missile sites in Cuba, built and supplied by the Soviet Union, with medium-range missiles capable of hitting targets as far north as Hudson Bay. President Kennedy convinced Khrushchev that the United States would not tolerate Soviet missiles in Cuba, even if that meant nuclear war. Khrushchev agreed to remove the missiles if Kennedy guaranteed not to invade Cuba.

The "abyss of destruction" upon which the two superpowers had stood in the missile crisis proved to be the turning point in relations between them, and the Cold War began to decelerate.

The Summit Conference, 1972

President Nixon's meeting with the Soviet leaders at the Summit Conference in Moscow helped to improve relations, and *détente*, the relaxation of tensions, became a major foreign policy objective of both nations. Hopefully détente would lead to an expansion of trade and the limitation of nuclear weapons. The SALT (Strategic Arms Limitation Talks) Conference, which lasted from 1970 to 1972, led to agreement between the two nations to limit defensive and offensive nuclear weapons. Subsequent talks, called SALT II, have proceeded, but without precise limitation of weaponry. In fact, the Soviet Union has increased its offensive capacity by putting several independently directed nuclear weapons on each missile. These are known as Multiple Independently Targeted Re-Entry Vehicles, or MIRV's.

France, Great Britain, and Germany Since 1945

Terms

Fourth Republic

Popular Republican Movement

Viet Minh

Geneva Accord

Seventeenth Parallel

Fifth Republic

National Insurance Act

National Health Act

"Social Contract"

Commonwealth of Nations

Irish Republican Army, IRA

Ulster Vanguard

German Federal Republic

Oder-Neisse Line

Berlin Blockade

Allied Airlift

Ostpolitik

People

Charles de Gaulle

Ho Chi Minh

Georges Pompidou

Valery Giscard d'Estaing

Clement Attlee

Anthony Eden

Gamal Abdel Nasser

Edward Heath

Harold Wilson

William Craig

Konrad Adenauer

Willy Brandt

Helmuth Schmidt

Significant Dates

1944	Fourth Republic
1949	Adenauer, Chancellor of West Germany
1955	German Federal Republic
1957	Independence for Ghana
1958	Fifth Republic
1962	Independence for Algeria
1969	End of de Gaulle Regime
1969	Willy Brandt becomes Chancellor of German Federal Republic
1969	Ulster Riots

Topic Outline

France
Fourth Republic
French-Indo-China
Algeria
Fifth Republic

England
Limited Socialism
Social Security Legislation
Commonwealth of Nations
Suez Canal Crisis
Confrontation with Trade Unions
Who Runs the Government?
Ulster: Violence of Fanaticism

German Federal Republic
Division of Germany in 1945
Berlin Blockade: Allied Airlift
Adenauer Era
Willy Brandt: Chancellor

France, Great Britain and Germany Since 1945

France

When France fell to German invasion in June, 1940, General Charles de Gaulle fled to England with other Frenchmen and organized the Free French Movement. In London de Gaulle established the Free French National Committee to serve as a government-in-exile with himself as head.

Churchill gave de Gaulle his support, and in 1944, when allied forces were approaching Paris, de Gaulle led his troops into Paris as its liberator.

The Fourth Republic (1946–1958) The liberation of France marked the beginning of the new republic, although the first general elections were not held until October, 1945. This provisional government, with de Gaulle elected as president by the National Assembly, proceeded to write a new constitution for France. It was believed necessary to officially end the Third Republic, which dated from 1870. The Third Republic had proved ineffectual, with its 36 different governments in the 20 years between 1918 and 1938. It was also blamed for the ignominious defeat of France in 1940.

In this first election three major parties emerged: the Socialists, the Popular Republican Movement (MRP), and the Communists. With 26 percent of the vote and the largest single party, the Communists would be able to play a significant role in government if the other two parties could not collaborate.

President de Gaulle not only disliked working with the three parties, but believed in a strong executive. He refused to temporize with the leftists and in January, 1946, resigned office and retired to his country home.

Within a short time the Fourth Republic began to resemble the Third Republic. The prime minister had to depend upon the Assembly for his office. The Assembly lacked policy, direction, and the ability to implement a program. General elections in 1951 resulted in more chaos, for now there were six national parties, almost equally divided, in the National Assembly. Governments rose and fell as the several parties jockeyed for power, and the French people became increasingly cynical and indifferent. The Assembly reflected the divisive issues in France; it was unable to modernize French industry; inflationary prices reduced its foreign markets; and abroad it was plagued with the costly Indo-China war and the nationalistic demands of colonial Algeria.

Colonial Problems
French Indo-China

France had lost this colonial empire when Japan invaded it during World War II. Immediately after the war the Viet Minh, under Ho Chi Minh, fought the French for eight years, and finally defeated them at the disastrous battle of Dien Bien Phu in 1954. The Geneva Accord, signed by France and the Viet Minh, divided Vietnam at the 17th parallel, and promised properly supervised and free elections for the two parts by 1956. The defeated French army, already feeling itself disgraced in 1940 and now again in 1954, was sent to Algeria.

Algeria

The colony of Algeria, although represented in the Chamber of Deputies in Paris as an integral part of France, demanded independence. Algeria was more important economically to France than were Tunisia and Morocco, and was the homeland of a million Frenchmen, or *colons*. Some of the colons had been there for at least three generations.

Within four months of the loss of Indo-China, revolts broke out in Algeria, in the fall of 1954. The French settlers refused to consider independence for Algeria, since this would mean subjection to Moslem domination. The Algerians were insistent upon independence. Between the two groups a compromise was not possible. By 1956 France had 400,000 troops in Algeria, including most of its NATO divisions. The fighting became brutal on both sides and many Frenchmen were deeply troubled by its effects upon young conscripts. The government could not win, it censored all criticism, and after four more years of unsuccessful warfare was about to collapse. On May 13, 1958, dissatisfied French army leaders in Algeria set up a revolutionary authority in competition with the legal French government. Calling itself a Committee of Public Safety, it was committed to authoritarian government. The insurrection spread from Algiers to the island of Corsica, where French troops were based, and an attack on Paris to overthrow the Republic seemed imminent. At this point the followers of de Gaulle put him forward as a candidate, to the consternation of the revolutionary army leaders who wanted a man of their choice. On June 1, 1958, fearing a parachute attack on Paris, the National Assembly invited de Gaulle to become prime minister. It voted his government full authority to rule France as it wished for six months and requested that it draw up a new constitution for France.

The Fifth Republic

In a referendum to the French people the new constitution was accepted by an overwhelming majority, some 80 percent of the votes cast. A new Gaullist party, the Union for the New Republic, emerged as the largest party, and de Gaulle was elected president for a 7-year term, chosen by local "notables" (some 80,000 to 100,000 members of the Assembly, of councils, of assemblies of overseas territories, and local councils). He was to have the power to appoint and dismiss the prime minister, to dissolve the National Assembly, and to appoint all civil and military officials of the Republic. There were an Assembly and a Senate, with a prime minister in control of all business in the Assembly, but subordinate to the president.

In brief, all final decisions rested with de Gaulle. The government became little more than a bureaucracy run by the president. Against Algeria he conducted the war with vigor, but promised the Algerians independence, once a cease-fire agreement could be reached.

In April, 1962, a referendum in France resulted in a 90 percent vote in favor of independence for Algeria, and in July, 1962, de Gaulle handed over sovereign power to an independent Algeria. He had already granted independence to former French colonies in sub-Sahara Africa.

De Gaulle became the national "arbiter" of France, guiding its course to unify the nation and bring France to its natural destiny of "greatness" by a more independent foreign policy and by developing its nuclear capacity.

In 1965 the French people elected de Gaulle to a second 7-year term as president. They were fearful that without a strong leader France might again experience political chaos.

Resignation of de Gaulle

Charles de Gaulle's popularity declined, and in May, 1968, his political opponent, François Mitterand, called for the resignation of the government and new elections. More than 7,000,000 workers went on strike; this forced several more millions to stay home because public transportation stopped.

De Gaulle demanded a personal vote of confidence through a referendum. He insisted that unless he got a "massive 'yes' " he would resign and France would face the serious threat of civil war and communism. He then substituted an election for the referendum, and his party and pro-de Gaulle groups took 358 of the total 487 seats.

Less than a year later de Gaulle made a fateful decision. He demanded a referendum to support his demand for a new constitution which would reduce the power of the Senate. In an unusually heavy turnout, 53 percent of the voters rejected his proposal and therefore his continued leadership. He immediately resigned and went into seclusion until his death in November, 1970. He had saved France from anarchy, had twice successfully opposed the army when it threatened civil war in Algeria, had ended the costly and humiliating Algerian rebellion by granting independence to Algeria, and had restored the prestige of France. His greatest failure as a statesman was his unwillingness to recognize the need for cooperation with Western European nations. His dislike of American influence in Europe led him to expel NATO headquarters from France.

French Ambition for Leadership

Under President Georges Pompidou the Gaullist concern for the "grandeur" of France changed little, although France did ultimately agree to Britain's entry into the Common Market. During the oil embargo crisis of the winter of 1973–1974, France lined up separate deals with Arab oil nations, and in 1974 did its utmost to scuttle the Energy Conference in Washington.

Valery Giscard d'Estaing, who became president after Pompidou's death in 1974, showed that he had no intention of making any basic changes in de Gaulle's independent policy. In the Cyprus crisis of 1974 he deliberately tried to belittle NATO. He openly sided with Greece when it took its forces out of the organization because it resented United States policy on Cyprus. At the NATO meeting in Brussels in June, 1975, at which President Ford restated United States commitment to NATO, Giscard refused to send a delegate. However, he did attend, not as the French representative, but simply as the dinner guest of the Belgian monarch.

The basic issue has been the relationship of the United States and Europe, with France attempting to establish itself as the leader of Western Europe. The basic weakness of France's position is that it is not important or powerful enough to provide such leadership. The U.S. defense commitment to Europe is necessary, and Europe is well aware of this, as is the Soviet Union.

Great Britain

Limited Socialism

Immediately after the war, a general election was held which returned the Labour Party to power. This ended the coalition government and Churchill's premiership, which had brought victory. The voters of 1945 remembered the grim days of unemployment of the 1930's under successive Conservative governments. Unfortunately for his party, Churchill was concerned only with foreign affairs, and made little effort during the election campaign to understand the mood and needs of the people after five years of war and privation.

The large Labour majority of 393 out of 640 seats gave the party the opportunity to implement its policy of nationalization, the state ownership of the means of production and distribution, under the leadership of Prime Minister Clement Attlee. The government nationalized the Bank of England, coal mines, railroads, the trucking industry, and docks in 1947. People who held shares in these enterprises exchanged them for government bonds. These businesses were then operated by government boards, for the nation and not for private profit.

Social Security Legislation

The government enacted three significant major social security measures. The National Insurance Act combined health, old age, and unemployment benefits in a single weekly premium shared by worker, employer, and government. The

National Health (Industrial Injuries) Act provided compensation for industrial injuries for which the employer was not responsible. The National Health Service Act, so-called "socialized medicine," granted every citizen the right to free medical and dental services and supplies, hospital care, and nursing.

Commonwealth of Nations

The Labour Party initiated the policy of granting independence to nonwhite colonies with India and Pakistan in 1947. Previously, the British Empire had consisted of white "dominions" with self-government, and nonwhite colonies with limited self-rule. Ceylon — later to call itself Sri Lanka — received independence at the same time.

This policy of granting independence to former British colonies was later extended to African and other possessions. The Gold Coast was the first of Britain's black colonies to become an independent nation as Ghana in 1957. In the next ten years, twenty more British colonies became independent.

The Suez Canal Crisis, 1956

Labour won the election of 1950 with a majority of only 7 seats; it came under fire for its support of the U.S. and the U.N. in the Korean War, and for rising defense costs which threatened the social services. Attlee decided to test public opinion with an election, but lost to Churchill, who returned to power with a majority. Although Churchill reduced expenses and benefits of the National Health Service and denationalized the steel and transportation industries, the Conservative government did not interfere with the general Labour program. "The Welfare State is as much our creation as that of the Socialists," said the Conservatives.

Winston Churchill resigned in 1955, and his successor, Anthony Eden, soon faced an international crisis. In 1954 the British had agreed to withdraw their troops from the Suez Canal within two years, but retained the right of reentry if Egypt's control of the canal should be threatened. The offer by the United States to assist Egypt in the building of the Aswan Dam was abruptly dropped when Nasser, the Egyptian nationalist leader, made an agreement with the Soviet Union to purchase military equipment. Nasser seized the Suez Canal Company and possession of the canal — a financial blow to Great Britain and France, the majority stockholders in the canal. More than 115,000,000 tons of shipping had used the canal in 1955, and most of the income had gone to Great Britain and France. The tense situation was aggravated by the bitter enmity of the Arabs toward eight-year old Israel, and Israel's fear that Egypt would close Israel's vital water route.

Without warning, Israel invaded Egypt in October; Britain and France demanded a cease-fire. When Nasser refused to allow a Franco-British force to occupy key points, the two nations vetoed a U.N. Security Council resolution not to use force, dropped parachute troops into the Canal Zone, and bombarded Cairo.

The United States refused to give any support to the invasion; the Soviet Union sent an ultimatum to Britain and France to cease the attack; and the U.N. condemned the operation and sent a U.N. Special Force to replace invasion troops. Nasser emerged as the hero of Egypt; general world reaction condemned old-fashioned imperialism; Eden resigned; and Harold Macmillan became prime minister.

Confrontation with Trade Unions

Britain's economic position gradually worsened during the 1960's, and by the 1970's had reached serious proportions. Events were to prove that trade unions had become more powerful than the government. The first real confrontation was in October, 1973, when coal miners refused to work overtime unless the government — which operates the mines — considered their demand for a 30 percent wage increase. Failure to reach a compromise led the Conservative government under Edward Heath to order a "holiday" for industry from December 21 to January 2, and a 3-day work week after that. The miners' union won the showdown by refusing to accept Heath's terms. In February, 1974, Heath decided to call for a new election on the issue, "Who runs the government, the government or unions?" The voters gave the Conservatives 296 seats, Labour 301, and the rest to other parties. Heath could not get the 14 Liberals to support him, so Harold Wilson then formed a minority Labour government.

Wilson yielded to the miners, and in October, 1974, called for a new election, hoping to get a good majority. He won but with a majority of only 3, and by the smallest popular vote — 39.3 percent — for any majority party in British history.

Who Runs the Government?

Wilson's campaign issue was the "social contract" — an informal agreement between government and union leaders, who pledged to ask for wage increases only if necessary to maintain their members' standard of living. The "contract" did not work; inflation hit a record 25 percent, and unions made wage demands that could bankrupt the country. In March, 1975, the miners got a 30 percent wage increase, then indicated that they would later demand an additional 60 percent increase. Power workers received a 35 percent boost; police asked for a 40 to 50 percent hike; merchant seamen 80 percent. Union leaders and workers seem to ignore the fact that Britain must import at least 50 percent of its food, which has to be paid for with exports. Outrageous wage demands increase the price of British goods, and the income to pay for imports is lost.

A former Labour Minister has said, "Real power is moving away from the elected legislature and toward might nonelective bodies such as trade unions." Unions have successfully challenged the government in 1974 and 1974, and opinion polls show that only 10 percent of the British public feel that government has the real power, while 66 percent believe that trade unions have it.

In early 1976 trade union leaders realized the seriousness of Britain's economic plight. They agreed to accept for their workers a modest increase in weekly wages, and postponed earlier demands for substantial increases.

In March, 1976, Prime Minister Harold Wilson announced his retirement from office.

Ulster: Violence of Fanaticism

Ulster, or Northern Ireland, is torn by discrimination of one religious community by the other: deliberate discrimination is practiced against Catholics in employment, housing, and political rights. Every year the Catholics suffer the humiliation of the Protestant celebration of the Apprentice Boys Parade. This memorializes the apprentices who closed the gates of Protestant Londonderry against James II in 1689. James II had been forced to abdicate the English throne in 1688. He expected to raise enough support in discontented Ireland to invade England. His hopes were shattered when the Dutchman William of Orange, now

William III of England, defeated him at the Battle of the Boyne in 1689. The Protestant "Orangemen" of Ulster, who take their title to commemorate William's victory, annually reassert their dominance over the Catholics of Ulster.

During the late 1960's the 500,000 Catholics, outnumbered two to one by the 1,000,000 Protestants, attempted to win political and social rights by demonstrations and protest meetings. In 1969 brutal riots broke out when Protestants not only decided to break up Catholic demonstrations but also firebombed Catholic districts of Belfast.

The outlawed Irish Republic Army (IRA), which fought against the British in the 1920's, now assumed the role of defenders of Catholics against Protestants. The "Provisional" extremist guerrillas of the IRA criticized the "official" wing of the IRA as too passive and started a campaign of indiscriminate terrorism by killing and bombing Protestants. By 1972 the Protestants decided to retaliate against the IRA, whose Provisional leader, Sean MacStiofain — actually an Englishman, John Stephenson — promised "utmost ferocity."

British troops had been sent in to separate Catholics and Protestants, but were denounced by each side for "favoring" the other. The Ulster Protestants feared that the British would make such terms with the IRA that Ulster would eventually become part of the Catholic Republic of Ireland, where Protestants would be outnumbered three to one.

After 325 bombings in Ulster in the first three months of 1972, the British government suspended the Ulster parliament of Stormont, and placed Ulster under direct rule from London. This deprived the Protestant majority of the ability to control all local government in Ulster. William Craig, leader of the Ulster Vanguard, one of several armed Protestant organizations, denounced the action, called out 170,000 workers on strike, and threatened the use of force against any compromise from Britain.

Since 1972 the British government has made several proposals for compromise and peaceful settlement. However, extremists on both sides, whose shootings and killings have taken the lives of over 1000 men, women, children, and soldiers, have refused to compromise. The issue is what it has been for decades. The IRA wants to see Ulster become part of the Catholic Republic of Ireland. Ulster Protestants are quite prepared to wage a civil war that could spread to all of Ireland in order to force Britain to make Ulster an integral part of the United Kingdom, like Wales, or to give Ulster complete independence.

Peace in Ulster in 1981 seems no nearer than in 1970, for determined men on both sides are ready to use extreme violence to gain their ends. Religious fanaticism may prove too strong to accept a solution which moderate men might devise. One observer has said, "Northern Ireland has Protestants and Catholics but few Christians."

The German Federal Republic

Division of Germany, 1945

The Big Four wartime allies divided Germany into four zones of military government and occupation. The United States, Great Britain, and France intended to turn the country back to the Germans once it had been demilitarized, denazified, and prepared for democratic rule. Germany's economic situation was aggravated by the settlement at the Potsdam Conference of 1945, because the Soviet Union took land from Poland's eastern region for itself, and compensated Poland with a large area of Germany westward to the Oder-Neisse Rivers. Nearly 9,000,000 Germans were forcibly transferred from Eastern Europe to West Germany, 3,000,000 expelled from Czechoslovakia, and 500,000 from Hungary. About 10,000,000 of these people were absorbed into the three Western zones. Another problem was that Berlin, which had been divided into four sectors (one to be run by each of the Big Four) was 100 miles inside the Soviet zone of Germany.

Berlin Blockade and Allied Airlift

Because the Western allies would not let the Soviet Union interfere in their administration of the industrial Ruhr region, the Russians decided to force the allies out of Berlin. The Russians hoped that the allies might then decide to get out of Germany altogether; this would leave the field open for the Soviet Union.

In June, 1948, the Soviets announced the closing of road, rail, and water routes from West Germany to Berlin; this was a deliberate test of the Western allies. The 2,500,000 Germans in the Western allied sectors of Berlin would become dependent upon the Soviet Union for food, fuel, and all supplies. The Western allies responded with the airlift into Berlin, daring the Soviets to interfere with the operation. By the end of July, 1949, more than 274,000 flights had carried in over 2,200,000 tons of supplies; each month of the airlift, the U.S. Navy "sealifted" 12,000,000 gallons of gasoline to Bremerhaven, Germany.

The Western allies wished to hold free elections throughout the four zones, with hopes of unifying Germany. However, the Soviet Union refused to agree, intending to control East Germany as a satellite. Therefore, in 1955 the Western allies proclaimed their three zones the independent German Federal Republic.

The Adenauer Era, 1949–1963

Western Germany was now a federal republic, Bundesrepublik, and Konrad Adenauer, leader of the Christian Democrats, became its first chancellor. He had been mayor of Cologne from 1917, a member of the legislature of the Rhine province, had ordered Nazi flags removed from Cologne when Hitler visited it in 1933, was removed as mayor by Goering, and was twice jailed by the Nazis. At the age of 73 "der Alte," the Old One, was elected chancellor in 1949, and the Western allies replaced military governors with civilians.

Under Adenauer the defeated West Germany of 40,000,000 people had to absorb 10,000,000 refugees. At first an economic burden, they later became an invaluable labor force which helped to bring unparalleled prosperity to the Federal Republic.

Willy Brandt: Chancellor

Adenauer was succeeded upon his retirement by Chancellor Ludwig Erhard, under whom the republic suffered a temporary recession. In 1969 Willy Brandt, former dynamic mayor of West Berlin and foreign minister, became chancellor. He continued the policy he had initiated as foreign minister, that of *Ostpolitik*. This was the "Eastern Policy" of seeking normal relations with Eastern Europe, particularly with the Soviet Union. In Moscow he and Premier Kosygin signed an agreement which included:

1. A joint pledge to settle all disputes peacefully;

2. Recognition by the German Federal Republic of the German Democratic Republic and of the Oder-Neisse boundary line.

Although he received the Nobel Peace Prize for his *Ostpolitik,* Brandt met stiff opposition at home because by the agreement his nation:

1. Gave up claims to prewar territories east of the line;

2. Recognized the permanent division of Germany.

In May, 1974, Brandt abruptly announced his resignation, ostensibly because a close personal aide was arrested and confessed that he was an East German spy on Brandt's staff. But Brandt had been talking of resigning before this incident, because he knew that he was losing political support. The nation considered him erratic and indecisive, a poor administrator who had been unable to carry out his campaign promises of reform in education and taxation. The Social Democrats chose Helmuth Schmidt as his successor.

Communist Satellite Nations Today

Terms
Comecon
Warsaw Pact
German Federal Republic

People

Bela Kun	Edward Giereck
Imre Nagy	Eduard Benes
Janos Kadar	Klement Gottwald
Josip Broz (Tito)	Alexander Dubcek
Wladyslaw Gomulka	Walter Ulbricht

Significant Dates
1953   Rebellion in East Berlin
1956   Rebellion in Poland & Hungary
1968   Czechoslovakia invaded

Topic Outline
Rumania, Bulgaria, Albania, and Hungary
Yugoslavia, Poland, and Czechoslovakia
German Democratic Republic
Soviet Control of Satellites

Communist Nations Today

As the Russian armies advanced westwards in 1944, they helped local communist parties take over the governments of several Eastern European nations. It took some time to eliminate all opposition, but the established technique virtually guaranteed success. The communists gained control of the police, the courts, the press, and all other information media. Once this was accomplished, an opportune moment provided the final action.

Rumania, Bulgaria, Albania, and Hungary

Rumania, Bulgaria, and Albania were the easiest nations to communize because they were not industrialized and the peasants could not organize effective resistance. They provided agricultural supplies in exchange for Russian manufactured goods, on Russia's terms. *Albania* today is in the curious position of supporting Red China and loudly criticizing Russia, largely because Russia withdrew the aid which Albania needed for survival. It was in *Hungary* that the Russian attempted a revolution after World War I, under the leadership of the Hungarian radical *Bela Kun*, who at first succeeded but was later defeated. When the Russians advanced into Hungary in 1944 they brought with them Hungarian communists who established Rakosi as head of the communist regime. Harsh measures bred discontent, and in 1956 an internal revolt replaced Rakosi with the more moderate *Imre Nagy*. This revolt then expanded into full rebellion against communist dictation. The Russians sent in tanks and troops, repressed the rebellion after much bloodshed, installed a new leader, *Janos Kadar*, and kept 50,000 Russian troops in Hungary to maintain Russian control of the satellite. Today the regime is less repressive than before, although it still takes orders from Moscow.

Yugoslavia was occupied during the war by Italian, Bulgarian, and German troops. The Yugoslav patriot *Josip Broz* (later called Marshall Tito) led underground resistance against the Germans and established communist governments in the areas he controlled by 1943. The British and Americans sent him aid so that he was able to set up a government without Russian troops. As a result, Yugoslavia remains an independent communist country, successfully free of Russian control and receiving United States economic assistance. It is an example of a "nationalist" communist nation, not a satellite of Russia.

Poland lost much of its territory on its eastern boundary after World War II. Although it was compensated with part of East Prussia, Poland suffered severe hardship because of the removal of a large part of its population. In October, 1956, a revolt in Poznan brought to power the communist *Wladyslaw Gomulka*, who persuaded Khrushchev to permit him to moderate some of the communist practices. Poland, while remaining communist, has permitted private ownership of the majority of its farms, and is less rigidly controlled by Russia.

In December, 1970, Polish workers, students, and angry housewives demonstrated against a government announcement of up to 30 percent increases in the prices of food and fuel. The government had decided to export food to pay for imported machinery. Gomulka was replaced by *Edward Giereck*, who agreed to relieve the price situation.

Czechoslovakia, after being freed from German occupation forces, held elections in 1946 in which the communists emerged as the single strongest party. The prewar statesman, *Eduard Benes*, was president, but the communist leader, *Klement Gottwald*, became the political leader as prime minister. In a *coup d'état* in February, 1948, the communists gained control, Benes died (or was murdered), and the typical monolithic communist control was established. Czechoslovakia's hopes of being a "bridge" between Western democracy and Russian communism were extinguished.

In August, 1968, more than 200,000 Soviet troops and armored equipment crossed into Czechoslovakia to crush the "liberal" government of communist leader *Alexander Dubcek*. The Czech Communist Party had announced a program for its people that the Soviet Union could not tolerate in its satellites. The Czech Communist Party wanted socialism which corresponded to "our conditions and traditions":

1. Freedom of speech, press, assembly, and religion.

2. A production program to meet needs, not theories.

3. An independent judicial system.

4. Rehabilitation of Czechs who had been unjustly persecuted during the Stalinist years.

The Russians feared what they called "counterrevolution," but what was actually a move toward Western-style democracy. The Soviet Union could not allow its satellites more freedom than its own citizens had. The Soviet Union withheld necessary raw materials from Czechoslovakia, sent in Warsaw Pact troops to force the country into line, and made it clear that the Soviet bloc in Eastern Europe was a "Communist Commonwealth." Some observers considered this a "Brezhnev Doctrine" announcing the right of the Soviet Union to intervene in the internal affairs of any Soviet satellite.

German Democratic Republic

East Germany was occupied by the Soviet Union in 1945 as its zone of conquered Germany, and became a satellite of the Soviet Union. In 1953 a revolt against the communist regime was ruthlessly crushed by Soviet troops. In 1955 the Soviet Union declared East Germany a sovereign republic, the German Democratic Republic. The efforts of its fanatical communist leader, *Walter Ulbricht*, to industrialize East Germany have given its people the highest standard of living in the communist world. Fearful of the influence of its liberal communist neighbor, Czechoslovakia, it was Ulbricht who urged the stern measures taken against that country in 1968. In 1971 Ulbricht was replaced by *Erich Honecker*.

In 1970 Chancellor Willy Brandt of the German Federal Republic signed an agreement with the Soviet Union pledging recognition of the German Democratic Republic. This made it politically possible for Western nations to recognize the German Democratic Republic. Prior to this, the Western nations had avoided confronting West Germany with the fact that there were two Germanies.

Soviet Control of Satellites

There are three main means of control:

1. The leaders of these countries are supported in power by Russia in return for subservience to Russian interests and policy.

2. The *Comecon*, Council of Mutual Economic Assistance, was Russia's answer to the Marshall Plan and the European Common Market.

3. The Warsaw Pact is a military alliance of all Eastern European communist nations, except Yugoslavia and Albania, with the Soviet Union.

The Soviet Union

Terms

Comecon   SALT I
Cominform   Moscow Summit
Iron Curtain   Détente
Sino-Soviet Treaty of Friendship

People

Nikita Khrushchev
Leonid Brezhnev
Aleksei Kosygin

Significant Dates

1949   Sino-Soviet Treaty of Friendship
1962   Cuban Missile Crisis
1963   Sino-Soviet Breach
1972   Moscow Summit Meeting

Topic Outline

Post-War Stalinist Years
Sino-Soviet Treaty of Friendship
Nikita Khrushchev in Power
Rebellion in Soviet Satellites
Sino-Soviet Breach
Brezhnev and Kosygin Regime
SALT I and the Moscow Summit

The Soviet Union

Post-War Stalinist Years

As soon as World War I was over, Stalin reestablished his former policy of one-man dictatorship through the Communist Party. In 1946 he initiated the fourth Five-Year Plan for:

1. Farm collectivization in order to avoid dependence upon other nations for food.

2. Military preparedness, since he believed that war with "capitalist" nations would be inevitable.

He revived the old *Comintern* which had been, at least officially, dissolved as the official communist international in 1943, under the name of the *Cominform*, or communist information organization. Soon he was to isolate Russia deliberately from other nations by what Winston Churchill called the "Iron Curtain." This policy of isolation was deliberately imposed because of:

1. Russia's traditional suspicion of other nations.

2. The Russian people must be made to believe that their economic system was so much better than capitalism could provide.

Therefore the Russians could not be allowed to make comparisons based on facts.

Stalin not only developed a personal cult but also attempted to prevent others from increasing their personal power.

Economic conditions did not improve, and Stalin started a new wave of purges, presumably to shift the blame to scapegoats. He modified the 1936 constitution by seemingly liberalizing it. He permitted peasant groups and workers' organizations, all closely controlled by the Communist Party, to send in nominations for elections to the Electoral Committees, which then prepared the ballots.

Sino-Soviet Treaty of Friendship

In 1945, as a price for Russia's entry into the war against Japan, China was obliged to cede to Russia special rights over the South Manchurian Railroad, Port Arthur, and Dairen, and to accept military occupation of Manchuria.

Chiang Kai-shek charged that Russia meant to separate Manchuria from China, but Mao Tse-tung's victory over Chiang in 1949 brought about a new relationship between Communist China and the U.S.S.R. In December, 1949, Mao went to Moscow to sign the Sino-Soviet Treaty of Friendship, Alliance and Mutual Security by which:

1. Russia returned to China the territory and rights of 1945.

2. Each nation guaranteed the other mutual military assistance.

3. Neither would join any coalition directed against the other.

4. Port Arthur was to become a joint Sino-Soviet naval base, and Soviet troops were to evacuate Port Arthur.

5. The treaty was to last for 30 years.

Nikita Khrushchev, in power 1957–1964

At Stalin's death in 1953 a struggle for power ensued. First Malenkov took control, then the Bulganin-Khrushchev duumvirate held office, then Khrushchev alone took power as Chairman of the Council of Ministers and Secretary of the Communist Party. During his administration, the Stalinist policy of terrorism declined. In 1956 at the Twentieth Congress of the Communist Party of the Soviet Union, Khrushchev denounced Stalin. "The cult of the individual acquired such monstrous size chiefly because Stalin himself . . . supported the glorification of his own person . . . We must return to the main principle of collective leadership."

In 1961 the Twenty-Second Congress voted to remove Stalin's body to a plain grave, marked simply, "J.V. Stalin, 1879–1953." The citizens of the Soviet Union were permitted more freedom in changing jobs, in expression of opinions, and in working hours.

In foreign affairs the Khrushchev regime, while not repudiating the former communist policy of opposition to capitalist nations, expressed itself in favor of "peaceful coexistence." Evidences of this policy were:

1. Russian occupation troops were withdrawn from Austria in the 1950's.

2. Armistices ending the wars in Korea and Indo-China were made possible.

3. Yugoslavia, loudly critical of Russia, was officially "allowed" to remain an independent communist country under Tito, not taking orders from Moscow.

However, Russia continued its pressures on Berlin and Asia, and it could be said that peaceful coexistence was a unilateral policy, since the Western nations were afraid of provoking war with the U.S.S.R. Peaceful coexistence would continue until communism proved its superiority and conquered the world peacefully, claimed Khrushchev.

Rebellions in the Soviet Satellite Countries

Rebellions against tight Russian control broke out in East Berlin in 1953 and in Poland in 1956. As a result, in Poland pro-Stalinist members of the government were removed, workers received a wage increase and the Polish Communist Party under Gomulka was able to secure increased independence for Poland. Poland enjoys its own national existence, although its foreign affairs remain under Russian control.

A few months after the Polish outbreak, a revolution erupted in Hungary. The Hungarian Communist Party declared martial law and asked for Russian assistance. *Imre Nagy*, appointed prime minister, was a "national" communist, more concerned with the interests of his own country than with Russian interests. Successful in persuading the Russians to withdraw their troops, he offended the Soviet Union by:

1. Declaring that the one-party system of politics, dominated by the communists, was abolished.

2. Announcing the withdrawal of Hungary from the Warsaw Pact.

3. Asking the United Nations to consider Hungary's situation.

Since these actions indicated the end of Russian power in Hungary, Russian troops were sent in to crush the rebels. Nagy was captured and executed, and *Janos Kadar* was appointed to replace him as prime minister.

Sino-Soviet Breach

China became a communist nation in 1949, and supported world revolution, just as Soviet Russia had done during the early years of its revolution. By 1960 the Soviet Union had begun to enjoy the benefits of improved living standards, and wished to avoid a head-on conflict even with capitalist nations. Communist China, however, was still in a revolutionary mood in 1960, was advocating world revolution, and was clearly prepared to risk conflict, perhaps as justification for its harsh domestic policy. It had invaded Tibet in 1959, made claims to part of Kashmir, and invaded northern India in 1962.

Communist China showed itself increasingly opposed to the Soviet Union's continued policy of attempting to dominate all communist parties. China challenged Russia's position at the Moscow Conference of November, 1960. In essence, the Chinese delegates refused to accept a position inferior to the Soviet Union. This stand was not only a declaration of opposition to the iron discipline imposed upon communist countries by Moscow, but was also an announcement that eventually Communist China would become the leading and dominant communist nation.

By 1963 China indicated that a compromise between the two nations was impossible. In 1964 the differences were clearly irreconcilable. The main differences between the two communist giants were:

1. China charged the Soviet Union with bourgeois acceptance of peaceful coexistence.

2. China claimed that the Soviet Union was abandoning Marxism-Leninism and was restoring capitalism to Russia.

3. The Soviet Union accused China of using Albania to attack the Soviet Union verbally.

4. The Soviet Union accused the Chinese of a racist, anti-white policy, while the Chinese charged that the Soviet Union was supporting "colonialism" by not assisting "national liberation" movements in Africa, Asia, and Latin America.

Reduced to simple terms, the issue was that China, proud of its past long history, wished to become the dominant power in Asia, and believed that the Soviet Union challenged that position.

Khrushchev severed diplomatic relations with Albania, an ally of Communist China, and later suspended all economic and technical aid to China. In 1962 the United States confronted Khrushchev with the threat of nuclear war unless he removed the intercontinental missiles which the Soviet Union had secretly emplaced in Cuba. This gave Mao Tse-tung an excuse to accuse the Soviet Union of appeasement and to label the Cuban retreat another Munich.

In October, 1964, Khrushchev was deprived of his position of leadership in the Communist Party and Soviet government, after ten years of undisputed rule. The reasons given for his removal were:

1. The failure of his agricultural program.

2. His "cult of personality."

3. His disorganization of Soviet industry.

4. His undignified behavior, particularly at the United Nations.

5. His serious errors in foreign policy, particularly in Cuba.

6. The split between Communist China and the Soviet Union, which had degenerated into a personal feud with the Chinese leaders.

Brezhnev and Kosygin Regime

Leonid Brezhnev replaced Khrushchev as First Secretary of the Communist Party, and Aleksei Kosygin succeeded Khrushchev as premier. Both of these men are technicians; Brezhnev is a land utilization specialist and metallurgist, Kosygin a former textile commissar. Several changes have been introduced in Soviet life by the two men:

1. Industrial and agricultural planning were placed under centralized control.

2. Private farming and private ownership of livestock have modified Khrushchev's full farm collectivization.

3. The quality and quantity of consumer products have been increasingly influenced by consumer demand.

Relations with China have worsened since the Peking Summit Meeting between the United States and the People's Republic of China in February, 1972. Brezhnev has said that until Mao Tse-tung is replaced there is little hope of settling the differences. The Soviet fears of the People's Republic are based on some salient facts:

1. China has more than three times the population of the Soviet Union.

2. China is a nuclear power.

3. China claims that in the 19th century, Russia forced China to give up thousands of square miles of territory.

SALT I and the Moscow Summit

The purpose of the Strategic Arms Limitation Talks (SALT), begun in 1970 between the Soviet Union and the United States, was to limit the development and growth of defensive and offensive nuclear weapons by both nations. After 130 meetings, proposals were ready for consideration. President Nixon journeyed to the Soviet Union in May, 1972, to meet Chairman Leonid Brezhnev. The two leaders agreed in general to limit nuclear weapons and to consider trade relations. The Soviet Union needed technological assistance and improved trade. An indication of this was the wheat deal of 1972, at which time the Soviet Union bought a billion dollars worth of wheat. The easing of tension between the two nations, called *détente*, is a hopeful sign that the two superpowers can coexist peacefully despite differences in political systems.

However, economic *détente* is not paralleled by political *détente*. The Soviet Union has dragged its feet in SALT II, and has in effect indicated its intention to continue the arms race, charging the West with "preparing military adventures."

The Middle East

Terms
National Covenant
Phalangist Party
Baath Party
OPEC

People
Gamal Abdel Nasser
Shah Reza Pahlavi
Faisal of Saudi Arabia

Topic Outline
Turkey
Egypt
Lebanon, Syria, Jordan, and Iraq
Iran
Saudi Arabia
Kuwait, Yemen, and Southern Yemen
United Arab Republic

The Middle East

At the end of World War I the Arabs of the Middle East, recently emancipated from Turkish rule, came under the imperial rule of Great Britain and France.

Turkey

By the Treaty of Sevres, 1920, Turkey was obliged to give up Arabia, Palestine, Mesopotamia, and Syria, and to agree to the demilitarization and the internationalization of the Straits. Mustafa Kemal was sent by the Sultan to demobilize the troops in Asia Minor (after Sevres) but instead he reorganized the troops and prepared to defy the allies. He overthrew the Ottoman Empire in 1922, and proclaimed the Republic of Turkey, with himself as president. He moved the capital to Ankara, in the heart of Asia Minor, and started to westernize the country.

Egypt

In 1882 Great Britain placed Egypt under its paternalistic guidance, and by 1914 exercised almost complete sovereignty over the country. In 1922 Egypt became independent under King Farouk, but not until the Anglo-Egyptian Accord of 1936 was it agreed that eventually British control would be ended and troops withdrawn.

Personal extravagance by Farouk, corruption in public office, and delays in promised reforms led to an uprising in 1952 by the Society of Free Officers. This group ousted the monarchy and set up a republic, with Major-General Mohammed Naguib its first president and prime minister. He was removed by Lt.-Colonel Gamal Abdel Nasser in 1954, who was elected president by an overwhelming vote in 1956. Nasser challenged Britain and France over the Suez Canal in 1956, and won, but discouraged badly needed foreign capital. He also engaged in two disastrous wars against Israel. After his sudden death in 1970 he was succeeded by Vice-President Anwar Sadat.

Lebanon

During World War I Turkey lost Lebanon, which became a French mandate in 1919. Lebanon was promised full statehood in the near future. In 1926 it was recognized as an independent republic, but was under effective French control. Real independence came in 1945. Over the years it became the financial center of the Arab world.

The smallest country in the Middle East, only 4000 square miles, Lebanon was almost equally divided between Moslems and Christians. The "National Covenant" states that the president must always be a Christian, the prime minister a Moslem. Other high offices are similarly allocated. A long-outdated census shows an equal number of Moslems and Christians, but Moslems protest that no census has been held in recent years because the Christians fear it would favor the Moslems.

The fighting which broke out in Lebanon in April, May, and June, 1975, and caused at least 700 deaths, was between Christians and Moslems. The immediate cause was resentment by the rightist and basically Christian Phalangist political party. This group charged that the government has allowed Palestinian guerrillas to carry arms and thus to become an armed force, capable of influencing domestic politics which favor Moslems and leftists. Because the general Christian community of Beirut supported the Phalangists, the fighting has been between Christians and Moslems. The Moslems generally want Lebanon to join the Arabs in any conflict with Israel; the Phalangists do not want Lebanon dragged into a war which could destroy the small country. A complicating factor is that the Phalangists, and some conservative Moslems, fear that the left-wing groups which represent low-income Moslems are looking for support from the armed Palestinians for a social and economic revolution. Repeated fighting between Christians and Moslems continued throughout 1975 and into 1976. The Moslems, who are determined to have a greater share in Lebanon's government, have been assisted by Palestinian guerrillas. Syrian policy had been to support the claims of the Palestinian guerrillas. Warfare between Moslems and Christians broke out in Tripoli in early 1975 and spread to the capital city of Beirut. By mid-1976 more than 25,000 lives had been lost, the city of Beirut was paralyzed, and the nation was withoutj an effective government.

In April, 1976, Syrian troops were sent in to stop the civil war between Christians and Moslems and fought against Palestinian forces in Lebanon. Attempts at a truce within Beirut have been violated several times, and Christians in a coastal area nort of Beirut have formed what could become a state-within-a-state.

Syria

Syria, like Lebanon, was a Turkish possession until World War I, and was administered by the French as Lebanon was. Since 1945 its history has included some two dozen coups to seize power; half of them have been successful. In 1958 it joined Egypt to form the United Arab Republic, but dissolved the union in 1961.

Syria has been far more militant than Israel's other neighbors — Jordan, Egypt, and Lebanon. It has insisted that the issue of Arabs versus Israelis be settled by force; its armed forces have, over the years, repeatedly shelled Israeli villages from the Golan Heights; it insists that these Heights, which Israel took in 1967, be returned; and it has been a strong champion of the Palestinian guerrillas, providing them with arms and training.

Jordan

Jordan was part of the Turkish Empire until 1916, when the East Bank of the Jordan River became Transjordan, under British influence. In 1946 it became the Kingdom of Transjordan. After fighting against the new nation of Israel in 1948, Transjordan acquired the West Bank of the river and changed its name to Jordan; Hussein Ibn Talal was its king.

In 1970 inevitable civil war broke out between Arab guerrilla organizations and the Jordanian army. The guerrillas had practically become joint rulers of Jordan, carrying weapons in open defiance of the government and King Hussein. An August, 1970, assassination attempt on Hussein infuriated the Bedouins in the army. The army also suffered the humiliation of being ordered to take no action against Palestinian guerrillas who landed three hijacked international airliners in Jordan, burned them, and in effect taunted the Jordanian army. Faced with probable mutiny by his army, Hussein had no choice but to order his army chief to "act immediately to undo hostile planning." In the fighting which lasted for 10 days, Palestinian refugee camps were ruthlessly shelled and at least 20,000 people were killed. The guerrillas were driven out of Jordan and were not made welcome in Iraq and Syria. Thus they made tiny Lebanon their headquarters.

In the fighting between Irsael and Egypt and Syria, Hussein of Jordan has attempted, without success, to act as mediator in determining a settlement that could satisfy the Palestinians.

Iraq

Iraq is the area where the Sumerian Empire flourished in 5000 B.C. In more recent times known as Mesopotamia, it was taken from Turkey in World War I, made a British mandate in 1920, and given full independence in 1932 as a monarchy.

Iraq is a harsh police state where political coups have usually meant the execution of the ousted leaders. In 1958 the king and his family were executed in the royal gardens by republican revolutionaries. Oil exports are its chief source of income, which is spent on armaments rather than on the people, who are illiterate and poor. For years Iraq and Iran have argued over navigation rights of the Tigris-Euphrates estuary that forms part of a common boundary. Until early 1975 Iran had given the Kurds of Iraq — a non-Arabic people — assistance in their guerrilla war for independence. In 1975 Iran ceased giving aid to the Kurds, and relations with Iraq improved a little.

The Iraq Baath (Renaissance) Party, far leftist and ruthless, has spearheaded Arab opposition to Israel, refusing to recognize that country's right to exist and championing Palestinian guerrilla extremists. Iraq severed diplomatic relations with the United States because of U.S. policy toward Israel.

Deep hostility exists between Iraq and Syria because Iraq claims that Syria's diversion of water from the Euphrates River has ruined Iraqi crops and reduced drinking water supplies.

Iran

Iran is a Moslem but not an Arab country. The Iranians are Aryan, an Indo-European people whose ancestors were related to the Aryans of India. In this region, formerly called Persia, an agricultural civilization existed 6000 years ago. In 550 B.C. Cyrus the Great founded the Persian Empire here. In the 19th century Persia lost vast territories to Russia and Afghanistan; the discovery of oil in 1901 led to the division of the country into foreign zones of influence. In 1925 Reza Khan, an army officer, overthrew the government, was elected Shah, and founded the Pahlavi dynasty. In 1941 the British and Russians occupied Iran to prevent a German takeover, deposed Reza Khan because he was pro-German, and replaced him with his son, the present Shah, whose official title was Shahansha — King of Kings — Mohammed Reza Pahlavi Aryamehi — Light of the Aryans.

In 1961 the Shah launched the "revolution from the throne" or the "white revolution," calling for the end of serfdom and the distribution of land to the peasants; he personally distributed crown lands to peasants. In 1971 Iran, describing itself as the world's oldest monarchy, celebrated the 2500th anniversary of the first Persian Empire, the Archaemenid Empire of Cyrus.

Although professing to be pro-Western, it was the Shah of Iran who encouraged the Organization of Petroleum Exporting Countries (OPEC) to suddenly increase the price of petroleum fourfold; he has indicated that OPEC should further increase oil prices. He has spent billions of oil income on arming his country with modern weapons. Ostensibly a constitutional monarchy, Iran is in fact a one-party dictatorship.

Saudi Arabia

After World War I little was done to set up Arab states in the Arabian peninsula. *Hussein*, king of a region called the Hejaz (western Arabia), the champion of Arab independence, had little success because he was closely associated with Great Britain, which had done nothing to secure independence for the Arabs, despite past promises. His rival, *Ibn Saud*, became the leading Arab figure in the Middle East, and instituted the Kingdom of *Saudi Arabia*, formerly the Hejaz and Nejd. In 1953 he was succeeded by his son, *King Saud*.

Saudi Arabia is regarded with special reverence by the world's 500,000,000 followers of Islam because it contains Mecca, the birthplace of Mohammed. Its flag is green with a white sword below the inscription, "There is no God but God, and Mohammed is His Prophet." The country dates from the 18th century when the Saud family gained control of most of the Arabian Peninsula. King Faisal, assassinated in 1975, ousted his brother in 1964 and became king and a leading bitter opponent of the State of Israel. An important member of OPEC, Saudi Arabia produces 8,000,000 barrels of oil a day, and has about 25 percent of the world's known oil reserves.

Kuwait

Kuwait, situated between Saudi Arabia and Iraq, was freed from Turkish control during World War I, made a British protectorate, and recognized as an independent country in 1961. With an estimated population of 900,000, Kuwait has a per capita income of about $3000. This is largely from its vast oil income; Kuwait's reserves are estimated at 15 percent of the world's total. It is a capitalist welfare state which provides free education through the university level, free medical care, and subsidized housing and business enterprises. Its estimated oil income for 1974 was $6,500,000,000.

Yemen

Yemen — In classical times this desolate country on the Red Sea, now officially the Yemen Arab Republic, was the site of the rich mercantile kingdom of Saba or Sheba. Under Turkish domination for four centuries, it became independent in 1918. Yemen joined the United Arab Republic of Egypt and Syria in 1958 to form the United Arab States; when Syria withdrew, Yemen was thrown out by Nasser of Egypt. Civil war broke out in 1962 between royalists, backed by Saudi Arabia, and republicans, backed by Egypt. The war finally ended in 1970.

Southern Yemen

Southern Yemen, formerly the British colony of Aden and other territory in the southwest corner of the Arabian Peninsula, is now the People's Democratic Republic of Yemen. Southern Yemen is not to be confused with the Yemen Arab Republic, which is sometimes referred to as Northern Yemen. Primitive and poverty-stricken, the political ideology of the People's Democratic Republic of Yemen is Chinese Communism. After brief border fighting in 1972 between the two Yemens, both agreed to a future joining of the two into one nation.

United Arab Republic

In 1958 many Syrians, troubled by internal dissensions and threats from growing communist influence, decided that Syria should join Egypt and form a single state. That same year the two formed the United Arab Republic; they were soon joined by Yemen. Subsequently, Syria felt that Egyptian officials were exerting too much influence there and that Syrian revenue was being diverted to Egypt. In 1961 a group of Syrian army officers engineered a *coup d'état* and Syria separated from Egypt.

The United Arab Republic was dissolved when Syria withdrew and formed its own independent government. However, Egypt continues to be known as the United Arab Republic.

Arab League

Arab states united in hatred of Israel formed a league consisting of Syria, Lebanon, Iraq, Jordan, Saudi Arabia, Yemen, Egypt, Lybia, and the Sudan. Their common purpose was to further Pan-Arabic hopes of an organization based on common language and interests, almost with a sense of "race."

Israel

Terms

Ten Lost Tribes	Fedayeen
Babylonian Captivity	Al Fatah
Judea	Palestine Liberation Organization
Diaspora	(PLO)
Aliyot	Popular Front for the Liberation
Kibbutz	of Palestine (PFLP)
Moshav	Black September
Balfour Declaration	Yom Kippur War
Zion	Security Council Resolution 242
Haganah	Organization of Petroleum Exporting
Knesset	Countries (OPEC)

People
David Ben-Gurion
Levi Eshkol
Golda Meir
Yassir Arafat
Anwar Sadat
Yitzhak Rabin

Significant Dates
1917   Balfour Declaration
1920   British Mandate for Palestine
1948   Independence of Israel

1967   Six-Day War
1973   Yom Kippur War
1975   Egyptian-Israeli Interim Peace Agreement

Topic Outline
Historical Jewish Connection with Palestine
Beginnings of Israel
Balfour Declaration
U.N. Proposals on Palestine
Independence of Israel
Resources, Government, Defense
Arab-Israeli War, 1948
Six-Day War, 1967
Yom Kippur War, 1973
Egyptian-Israeli Interim Peace Agreement

Israel

Historical Jewish Connection with Palestine

More than thirty centuries ago, the tribal ancestors of the Jews migrated to Palestine and lived there for twelve centuries. Historical evidence shows that a group of tribes called Israelites entered Palestine from the Syrian desert. Under attack from common enemies, the several tribes of Israelites formed a kingdom under Saul, and extended their territory under David and Solomon. After the death of Solomon, who built the Temple of Jerusalem, the ten northern tribes formed their own kingdom of Israel. The two smaller tribes formed Judah; Jerusalem was its religious center. In 721 B.C. Israel was invaded by Assyria, and the "ten lost tribes" disappeared from history. In 586 B.C. the Chaldeans invaded Judah, destroyed the Temple, and carried off the people to Babylon. This is known as the Babylonian Captivity.

With the help of prophets Jeremiah and David the people preserved their religion, and were allowed by Cyrus the Great of Persia to return to Palestine in 538 B.C., where they built the Second Temple. During the next 400 years little is known about them except that during this time the Pentateuch (from Greek *pente*, five, and *teuchos*, book) the first five books of the Old Testament, were written.

Rome ruled this land from 63 B.C. as the province of Judea. Heavy taxation by Rome and a growing sense of their own nationalism led the Jews to revolt in 66 A.D. This resulted in the burning of the Second Temple, the slaughter of Jews, and their dispersal to other lands, the Diaspora. For centuries Jews were forced to live in ghetto areas of European cities, were isolated from other people, and restricted to specified trades. Consequently they practiced their own religion and culture.

Beginnings of Israel

The modern nation of Israel had its earliest beginnings in the later years of the 19th century, with the first of a series of *aliyot* (aliyah is the singular), waves of migration into Palestine. An existing Jewish community of about 25,000 was joined by another 25,000, who came mostly from Russia during a period of about twenty years. The new group became assimilated into the older group, which was opposed to the idea of a Jewish national homeland in Palestine. A few more emigrated to Palestine before World War I and established two distinctive institutions of today's Israel, the *kibbutz* and the *moshav*. The kibbutz (plural kibbutzim) is a communal agricultural settlement owned by the group; the moshav is a cooperative village of people who own land individually but work together for common interests.

The Balfour Declaration

During World War I the British captured Palestine from Turkey. The British Foreign Secretary, Arthur Balfour, issued a statement that was later referred to as the Balfour Declaration. Britain favored, he said, "the establishment in Palestine of a National Home for the Jewish people . . . nothing shall be done which may prejudice the civil and religious rights of existing non-Jewish communities in Palestine."

Great Britain received Palestine as a mandate under the League of Nations, with the understanding that Jewish people would be encouraged to settle there. But the Arabs, long under Turkish rule and now freed with the assistance of Lawrence of Arabia, wanted self-government and vigorously opposed Jewish immigration.

Between 1925 and 1939 another 35,000 Jewish immigrants came from Poland and Central Europe. Many were Zionists who believed that the Balfour Declaration meant the resettlement of Jewish Palestine. Zion referred to the hill in Jerusalem which was the residence of King David and his successors; to Zionists it signified the reestablishment of the Jewish nation.

The Palestinian Arabs, who had once welcomed the Jews, now felt threatened by some 380,000, or 30 percent of the total population. Arab extremists attacked Jewish settlements, which in self-defense organized the very effective military *Haganah*. Subsequent fighting threatened British oil interests in the Middle East.

British Proposals

In early 1939, Britain, unable to persuade Jews and Arabs to find a compromise, issued a policy statement which proposed the end of its mandate and the formation within ten years of an independent, Arab-dominated Palestine. Jewish immigration was to be limited to a total of 75,000 during the next five years.

After World War II the United States urged Britain to allow 100,000 Jews to enter Palestine. This proposal satisfied neither Jews nor Arabs.

U.N. Proposals on Palestine

Britain submitted the problem to the U.N., whose Special Commission on Palestine recommended:

1. By a majority, the partition of Palestine into Jewish and Arab states.

2. By a minority, a *federal* state including both Arab and Jewish communities.

The Arabs made an immediate tactical error by furiously denouncing both plans. Had they accepted the federal plan they could have controlled the Jews, who could not denounce either plan for fear of losing public sympathy. In November, 1947, the U.N. voted by a two-thirds majority for partition. Civil war broke out, and the United States unrealistically called on the U.N. to give up the partition plan, and urged Britain to continue its Palestine mandate. The British had had enough of using troops to turn back Jews who tried to enter Palestine, and to keep order in an increasingly tense atmosphere.

Independence of Israel, 1948

At 4 p.m. on May 14, 1948, David Ben-Gurion, long a believer in Zionism, read the Proclamation of Independence and the establishment of the Zionist State. "In the Land of Israel, the Jewish people came into being." Israel's independence was recognized almost immediately by the United States. Ben-Gurion, Israel's first prime minister, was born in Russia in 1886. He founded a Zionist movement in his home town, emigrated to Palestine in 1905, and was exiled from Palestine in 1914 because of his views. He spent several years in the United States, returned to Palestine, and served as secretary of the General Federation of Labor until 1935. From then on he was the leader of the MAPAI, the Israeli Labor Party.

Resources

Israel is relatively poor in natural resources, but those it does have — potash, phosphates, oil — are being intensively developed. Agricultural land is Israel's main natural resource, although it is somewhat handicapped by a shortage of water. Its project to harness and use water of the river Jordan is increasing tension between Israel and the Arabs, who fear diversion of vital water from their lands.

Government is a parliamentary republic; the *Knesset* or legislature, a single chamber of 120 representatives, is chosen for four year-terms by universal suffrage, on a proportional representation system. The country is divided into 120 political districts, and each party receives a number of seats in proportion to the total number of votes cast for it. The consequence is a fragmentation into some two dozen parties. In 1961 eleven parties returned one or more members to the Knesset.

Role of Government in Economic Life

Government plays a significant role in the economy of the country. It owns railroads, postal and communications systems, irrigation and drainage schemes, and over 50 percent of more than 100 corporations, totalling about 25 percent of the national product.

The Israel Federation of Labor, the Histadrut, owns about another 25 percent through businesses and farm cooperatives.

Internal Defense

Israel regards itself as a besieged state under constant threat of attack from the Arabs. Within hours of its independence in 1948 it was attacked by five Arab armies, although unsuccessfully. However, Israel knows that the Arabs have announced their intention to drive the nation off the map.

Israel's agricultural settlements serve not only for farm development but also as outposts of defense. In fact, some are deliberately chosen as military outposts rather than promising agricultural ventures. These kibbutzim, collective agricultural settlements, were (and many still are) operated by young men and women who perform the dual duties of farmer and soldier. Israel has no regular army, but has a professional core of 15,000 and 40,000 conscripts a year. Within three days it can raise a force of 250,000. In any emergency all civilian facilities, such as vehicles, hospitals, and personnel of all public utilities, are subject to military duty.

Arab-Israeli War, 1948

Arab reaction to Israel's independence was violent and immediate. "This will be a war of extermination and a momentous massacre which will be spoken of like the . . . Crusades." Simultaneously Israel was attacked by Egypt, Jordan, Iraq, Saudi Arabia, Lebanon, and Syria. Eight months later the Egyptians asked for a cease-fire, refused to recognize Israel as a nation, and swore revenge. However, Egypt had to accept the intolerable fact that Israel was now 50 percent larger than it had been in May, 1948. About 1,000,000 Arabs fled from Israel and the territory it had taken during the war; for nearly thirty years they have been living in refugee camps, where they are fed by a U.N. agency.

Six-Day War, 1967

The basic issue was the very existence of Israel as a nation, because to the Arabs Israel is illegally "occupied" land. Bitter opposition flared up in 1956 over the Suez Canal Crisis. As a result of this crisis Egypt denied the right of Israel to use the canal. The U.N. could neither enforce Israel's right to use the canal nor guarantee Israel's very existence.

The Arabs nursed their hatred, waiting only for the day when Israel would be driven into the sea. In May, 1967, Nasser demanded the withdrawal of the U.N. forces which had been stationed along the Egyptian-Israeli frontier, and began moving 80,000 Egyptian troops and armor into the Sinai. U.N. forces withdrew; three days later Nasser closed the Gulf of Aqaba and completely choked off Israel's southern port of Elath, announcing, "The Israeli flag will not pass through the Gulf of Aqaba . . . if the Israelis want to threaten us with war they are welcome." On May 24, Nasser placed mines across the four-mile wide Strait of Tirana, warning that an attack on Egypt or Syria would mean a war in which "the main objective will be the destruction of Israel."

On June 5, Israel struck without warning. Its planes flew below radar level in the darkness and bombed more than a dozen airfields in Egypt, Syria, and Jordan. Syria shelled Israeli towns; Jordan bombarded Jerusalem and shelled Tel Aviv. In six days Israel seized Jerusalem, Jericho, Hebron, and Bethlehem; took from Jordan the West Bank of the river; and occupied all of the Sinai Desert, including the fortress of Sharm-el-Sheikh, which blockaded the Gulf of Aqaba.

Israel's success in the Six-Day War was partly the result of its highly organized surprise attack and partly that of the inability of the Arab nations to cooperate effectively. A nation of fewer than 3,000,000 defeated its 40,000,000 neighbors, an area sixty times its size.

Background to the 1973 War

Prime Minister Levi Eshkol, who had led his country through the Six-Day War, died in 1967 and was succeeded by Golda Meir, who had worked for her people for fifty years. Born in 1898 in Kiev, in the Russian Ukraine, she and her family came to Milwaukee eight years later. After graduation from teachers' college she became a member of Poale Zion, a small Yiddish-speaking group of Labor Zionists. In 1921 she married, and she and her husband emigrated to Palestine.

She lived and worked for a time on a kibbutz, and then for the Histadrut, the General Federation of Labor which owns industrial plants and cooperatives. Mrs. Meir became a delegate on the Women's Labor Council, was one of the signers of the Proclamation of Independence of the State of Israel, and was the only woman member elected to the first Israeli legislature. Appointed minister of foreign affairs in 1956 by Ben-Gurion, she served until 1966, and became prime minister a year later.

Mrs. Meir immediately faced domestic and foreign problems. One domestic problem was Israel's political system of proportional representation in the Knesset, the 120-member legislature. Each party prepares a list of candidates and each party is represented in the Knesset in proportion to the number of votes it receives. Mrs. Meir was obliged to have six parties represented in her cabinet, including the United Workers' Party, which favored the rights of Arabs; the anti-Arab Freedom Party; and the pro-Soviet Union Communist Party. This was a virtually unworkable combination.

Golda Meir's attempts at negotiations for a peace settlement, not simply a prolonged cease-fire, always came up against the basic determination of most Arab nations to refuse to recognize the right of Israel to exist. Therefore the return of occupied land would bring the enemy to the very borders of Israel and threaten its very existence.

Two other factors complicated the problem for Israel. The first was that the occupied land increased Israel's Arab population by at least 1,250,000. This included more than 1,000,000 in the West Bank, half of whom were refugees; 250,000 in the Gaza Strip; and 15,000 in the Golan Heights. The increasing use of Arab labor contradicted the Zionist ideal of a truly Jewish state.

The second problem was the emergence of Arab guerrilla *fedayeen*, the "men of death," terrorists conducting their own Jihad or Holy War against Israel. Dedicated fighters from the more than 50 refugee camps throughout the Middle East, they had been generally ignored by the rest of the world for more than 25 years, and fed by the U.N. on a niggardly ration of 9 cents a day for dry food. The collective organization of moderate and extremist fedayeen is the Palestine Liberation Organization (PLO), of which *Yassir Arafat* is chairman. The most publicized and probably largest group is Al Fatah led by Arafat; the fanatical Popular Front for the Liberation of Palestine (PFLP), led by George Habash, gained its fame by its airliner hijackings in 1970. "What we want," announced Habash, "is a war like the war in Vietnam. We don't want peace. Peace would be the end of all our hopes." Another extremist group is Black September, which takes its name from September, 1970, when King Hussein of Jordan crushed the fedayeen movement in Jordan.

Yom Kippur War, 1973

On Saturday, October 6, 1973, during the celebration of Yom Kippur, the Day of Atonement, which is the holiest day of the Jewish year, the afternoon peace was suddenly shattered by tank and artillery fire. The suddenness of the attack across Israeli frontiers gave Egyptian and Syrian forces the initial advantage. President Anwar Sadat had decided to attack because his earlier attempts at negotiation had been rebuffed; therefore he saw no prospect of the return of lost Egyptian land through diplomacy. Sadat interpreted the U.N. Security Council's Resolution 242 of 1967 — "there should be no territorial gains by conquest" — to mean the return of all occupied land. However, Israel claimed that Egypt and Syria ignored the other part of Resolution 242, which stated that there must be "acknowledgement of the sovereignty and political independence of every state in the area." Israel interpreted this to mean that the Arab nations must recognize the right of Israel to be a nation.

Caught unprepared, the Israelis faced early defeat as 70,000 Egyptian troops and 500 tanks crossed the Suez Canal into the Sinai. The United States regarded with alarm a report that the Soviet Union was considering sending troops from two divisions stationed near the Black Sea into the fighting area. President Nixon ordered "Defense Condition Three," placing 2,000,000 U.S. troops at home and abroad on instant readiness to move anywhere. Tension relaxed and the two superpowers agreed to work to end the fighting and to organize a peace conference.

The early Arab advantage was lost when some Israeli forces came within 30 miles of Damascus. Others crossed the Suez Canal with 20,000 troops and 500 tanks and advanced to within 45 miles of Cairo. They trapped the Egyptian Third Army on the east bank of the Canal, and cut off food and fuel supplies.

Oil: A Political Weapon

The sudden fourfold increase in the price of oil by the Organization of Petroleum Exporting Countries (OPEC) was partly the result of the Yom Kippur War and certainly the result of the realization that oil could play a major role in the Arab-Israeli situation, particularly in the peace negotiations. Saudi Arabia's King Faisal, fiercely anti-Israel, had led in forming OPEC; its members had stated publicly on several occasions after the 1967 war that the production and price of oil could be used as political weapons against the United States to put pressure on Israel to return all the land occupied in 1967. The Shah of Iran, a member of OPEC, made it clear in early 1975 that oil prices would almost certainly be raised again. By mid-1975 the United States attitude toward Israel had become tougher, and Israel was openly blamed by the Ford administration for the failure of the recent peace negotiations.

Early Peace Negotiations

On October 22-23, 1973, cease-fire was proclaimed; in January, 1974, Secretary of State Kissinger negotiated a disengagement accord between Israel and Syria. Israel gave up the Egyptian territory it occupied west of the Suez Canal; Egypt reduced its forces on the eastern shore of the Suez Canal to a few thousand.

In April, 1974, Golda Meir resigned because she was blamed by some Israelis for failure to negotiate final peace agreements. She was replaced as prime minister by Yitzhak Rabin, the youngest prime minister in Israel's short history, and the first native-born. He had fought in three of the four wars against the Arabs; his mother was a Russian emigrant who became an early commander of the Haganah, the pre-independence, outlawed Jewish defense force which fought against British immigration restrictions before 1948. Rabin himself was a member of Haganah and became chief of staff of the Israeli army in the Six-Day War of 1967. He resigned as a general from the army when he was appointed Ambassador to the United States.

In May, 1974, Syria and Israel reached an agreement on one issue, thanks to the efforts of Henry Kissinger. For 28 days he flew back and forth between Damascus and Jerusalem, spending 85 hours in talks with President Hafez Assad and 40 hours with Golda Meir, not yet replaced. By the terms of the agreement, the Syrians regained 300 square miles of farmland, and Israel kept three strategic hills in the Golan Heights from which Syria had previously shelled Israeli kibbutzim. Between the military forces of the two nations the United Nations Disengagement Force of 1250 men policed the cease-fire. Syria considered this only the first step; it still insisted on the return of the Golan Heights, which Israel insisted it would not return.

The Rabat Conference, November, 1974

In November, 1974, twenty Arab leaders met in a summit conference in Rabat, the capital of Morocco. The purpose was to decide who should be the official Arab spokesman for the 3,000,000 Palestinians living in the Middle East from Lebanon to Kuwait, nearly half of whom were refugees from Palestine.

The Arab leaders gave Yassir Arafat and the Palestine Liberation Organization the responsibility for "liberating" the Israeli-occupied West Bank of the Jordan River, where more than 650,000 Palestinians live. This action by the Arab nations changed the Palestine Liberation Organization from clandestine guerrillas to a formidable political organization whose voice would have to be listened to in future negotiations about a Palestinian homeland.

Arafat Invited to the United Nations, November, 1974

That same month the United Nations, by a vote of 105 to 4 (some nations abstained) invited Arafat and a delegation from the PLO to represent the Palestinians in the debate on Palestine. This invitation to the leader of an organization responsible for commando raids and indiscriminate slaughter of Jewish civilians, gave Arafat the unofficial status of a head of state.

In his speech and later discussions he made it clear that his short-run objective was to get as much of the West Bank of the Jordan River and as much of the Gaza Strip as Israel could be persuaded or forced to give up. There he would start building a homeland for the Palestinians. His long-range objective is to create a nonsectarian state of Palestinians and Jews, in which the Jews would be in the minority. This would achieve his announced intention of eliminating the nation of Israel and absorbing it into an Arab-majority, independent Palestine nation. Arafat's purpose has given the "hawks" in Israel reason to argue that the surrender of any Israeli-occupied Arab land would lead to national suicide.

Egyptian-Israeli Interim Peace Agreement

Secretary of State Kissinger's "shuttle diplomacy" to arrange a peace agreement between Israel and Egypt collapsed in March, 1975. The hard line taken by both nations made a compromise impossible at that time. President Sadat of Egypt insisted that the essentials for an agreement must be the surrender of the strategic Gidi and Mitla passes in the Sinai Mountains and the return of the Abu Rudeis oil fields take by Israel in 1967. Prime Minister Rabin demanded a written guarantee of nonbelligerency, because to surrender the strategic passes without a guarantee that Egypt would not use force could mean the invasion of Israel.

As a consequence of the demands to which neither nation would agree, negotiations broke down and the danger of war in the Middle East seriously increased. Egypt said it could not promise nonbelligerency before it got control of the passes and the oil fields; Israel insisted that its very safety would be in danger if its troops withdrew without Egypt's guarantee not to use force.

Finally, several weeks of intense effort by Kissinger as mediator resulted in the second "interim" peace agreement. "Interim" indicated a step-by-step approach to eventual peace. Egypt and Israel agreed to the following basic terms:

1. The conflict between them shall be resolved "by peaceful means." The two agree not to "use force or military blockade against each other."

2. Israel will withdraw its forces up to 25 miles in occupied Sinai and give up the Gidi and Mitla passes and the Abu Rudeis oil fields.

3. Egypt will permit nonmilitary Israeli cargoes to use the Suez Canal.

4. The agreement for a United Nations Peacekeeping Force shall be renewed annually.

5. At the request of both nations the United States will supply 200 civilian technicians to operate two strategic early warning surveillance stations — one operated by Egypt, the other by Israel — and three "watch" stations in support.

Although Egypt signed the agreement, Israel at first only initialed it until the United States Congress agreed to the sending of technicians. On October 10, 1975, Israel signed the agreement immediately after Congress approved the sending of technicians. Part of the agreement included substantial economic assistance to Egypt and military hardware assistance to Israel.

Arab Reaction to the Agreement

Yassir Arafat publicly announced to a graduating group of women guerrillas in Damascus, "I say in your name and the name of new generations, in the name of our sacred soil, that this American solution cannot, cannot, cannot take place."

The head of the Syrian-supported guerrilla group said, "Palestinian relations with Egypt are very bad until further notice."

Syria officially condemned the agreement as a setback for the Arab cause since it ended the state of war between Egypt and Israel; it failed to refer to other Israeli-occupied territory; and it gave the United States a foothold in the region and made it a party to the conflict, "although Arab efforts in the past were aimed at keeping her out of the conflict."

CHAPTER 10

Recent History of the Far East, Africa and Latin America

Nations of South East Asia

Terms

Bandung Conference
Geneva Accord (Agreement)
Republic of Vietnam
Democratic Republic of Vietnam
National Liberation Front

Viet Cong
Tonkin Gulf Resolution
Khmer Republic
Khmer Rouge
Sri Lanka

People

Sukarno
Suharto
Bao Dai
Ho Chi Minh
Ngo Dinh Diem
Nguyen Van Thieu

Le Duc Tho
Henry Kissinger
Norodom Sihanouk
Lon Nol
Mrs. Sirimavo Bandaranaike

Significant Dates

1950   Republic of Indonesia
1954   Geneva Accord on Vietnam
1955   Bandung Conference
1963   Federation of Malaysia
1965   Singapore Independence
1973   Cease-Fire in Vietnam
1975   South Vietnam Collapses

Topic Outline
Geographical Units
S.E. Asia Since 1945
   Indonesia
   Vietnam
   Laos and Cambodia
   Thailand
   Burma
   Malaysia
   Singapore
   Sri Lanka
Problems Facing S.E. Asia Nations

Nations of South East Asia

Geographical Units

The Portuguese took control of the *Malay Peninsula* in 1511 and made it the center of a prosperous commercial empire. It was in a strategic geographical position, commanding the direct approaches from India and lands east to the Far East. The Malay Peninsula is an extension of the Indo-China Peninsula, itself an amalgam of Indian religious and artistic culture and Chinese political concepts.

The East Indies are three thousand islands which were a mixture of Indian and Chinese civilization. The Islamic religion was grafted onto the Hindu and Buddhist heritage.

The Philippines: Although geographically and racially a part of the East Indies, the Philippines were greatly affected by exposure to the Spanish conquest and other Western influences.

These lands of tropical South East Asia shared a common heritage of Indian, Chinese, and in some places, Moslem influences. They did not think of themselves as South East Asians, since they had no racial, national, linguistic, or social unity. Consequently they became a fertile field for European traders. By mid-17th century the Dutch had control over most of the East Indies through their East India Company; the British took over the Malay Pneinsula during the Napoleonic Wars. In the 1850's the French, through the excuse of the murder of a missionary, secured Cochin China, and by 1900 had extended their control through Indo-China.

During World War II the Japanese conquest of these colonial areas destroyed the myth of white supremacy. Japanese use of natives as administrators and troops gave further impetus to the aspirations of nationalism and independence. Nationalist leaders gained experience, and communist groups learned guerrilla warfare against the Japanese. When Japan surrendered, most of South East Asia was in its hands. Before the former colonial rulers could reestablish their control, the native leaders took over and declared independence.

South East Asia since 1945

Indonesia

The Dutch commenced operations against the native leaders immediately after the war, and launched an all-out drive in 1948. Settlement was finally reached, and in 1949 sovereignty over all the former Dutch East Indies, except New Guinea, was turned over to the Indonesians. In 1950 the islands were united as the Republic of Indonesia, with *Sukarno* as president. In 1963, after repeated demands by Indonesia, the Netherlands handed over Irian (Western New Guinea) to the Republic of Indonesia.

President Sukarno distrusted both Americans and Europeans. He feared that they wanted to exploit the country's national resources of oil, minerals, and spices.

In 1955 the *Bandung Conference* was held in Indonesia. This conference represented 29 Asian and African countries and nearly one and a half billion people, over half the world's population. However, the threat of old-style imperialism was overshadowed by the new threat of communism, which many delegates regarded as "super-colonialism."

The Bandung Conference made clear the position of its members. The newly independent states would form a Neutral Bloc and would remain neutral in the

Cold War. Prime Minister Nehru of India became the leading spokesman for the "neutralists" — a term referring to those nations which would take no side in the polarized world of the United States and the U.S.S.R. However, when Communist China occupied Tibet in 1959 and later invaded the northern borders of India, Nehru appealed to both the United States and Britain for assistance, and also accepted aid from Russia. Apparently the belief in neutralism was a one-way street.

Sukarno Replaced

The economy seriously declined under Sukarno. He attempted to make Indonesia the leader of the nonaligned nations, moved closer to Communist China, replaced elected members of parliament with appointed ones, and was declared "President for Life."

In September, 1965, Indonesia's pro-Communist party attempted to take over the government by a coup, which was put down by the military under General Suharto. Reportedly, several hundred thousand communists were executed, many of them Chinese living in Indonesia. Diplomatically the army eased Sukarno out of power and replaced him with Suharto. Suharto's contributions were the reduction of 600 percent inflation, and financial arrangements that attracted foreign capital to help develop Indonesia's great natural resources of tin, bauxite, manganese, nickel, and oil.

A serious problem is that Java, the largest of several thousand islands, is one of the most densely populated areas in the world, with 1500 persons per square mile. Indonesia's economic future will be greatly helped because it is the leading oil producer in South East Asia.

Vietnam: North and South

The original French colony was called Cochin China (later South Vietnam). Annam, Cambodia, Laos, and Tonkin were protectorates that retained some local authority, but the government was securely controlled by the French Governor-General in Hanoi.

After the fall of France to Germany in 1940, the Japanese secured control of the whole area. On the eve of their defeat in 1945 the Japanese proclaimed the Emperor Bao Dai of Annam the ruler of all Indo-China. He could not retain his position against a nationalist government proclaimed by Ho Chi Minh, an old revolutionary leader with communist ties, who proclaimed the independence of Indo-China as the Republic of Vietnam. The French attempted to set up a federation of Indo-Chinese states in what they called the French Union. This would leave some autonomy with the member states. Ho Chi Minh's government of the Republic of Vietnam refused to accept this limitation. Fighting continued and the French established a rival government to Ho Chi Minh's, which was distinguished by the name Republic of Viet Minh because it was run by the Viet Minh Party.

The Geneva Accord, 1954

The French fought the Viet Minh until 1954 when overwhelming support for Ho Chi Minh from China resulted in the defeat of the French at Dien Bien Phu. Despite Ho Chi Minh's victory, the French might have held on to their possessions had not Communist China supplied food, guns, and military training to his troops.

Meanwhile, truce arrangements were being drafted in Geneva, Switzerland by France, Great Britain, and the Soviet Union. The United States was represented but took no part in drafting the terms, which were signed in July, 1954, by the French commander in Indo-China and the Viet Minh defense minister.

By the terms of the Geneva Accord:

1. Vietnam was divided at the 17th parallel.

2. French forces were to evacuate North Vietnam within 10 months.

3. Viet Minh forces were to evacuate South Vietnam within 10 months.

4. Elections were to be held within two years throughout all Vietnam to set up a unified government for the two parts.

5. Cambodia and Laos were to be recognized by the Viet Minh as politically and territorially independent.

6. Civilians were to be allowed to move from one Vietnam to the other.

7. Truce terms were to be supervised by a commission from Canada, Poland, and India.

South Vietnam Refuses the Election

Over 1,000,000 refugees crossed from North Vietnam into South Vietnam, presenting the serious economic problems of feeding and housing them. Ngo Dinh Diem became the leader in South Vietnam and declared himself the first president of the Republic of Vietnam. The Assembly elected in March, 1956, denounced the Geneva Accord — nobody from South Vietnam had signed it — and stated, "We do not consider ourselves bound by the Geneva Agreement, which has been signed against the will and in contempt of the interests of the Vietnamese people."

Diem refused to permit the elections provided for in the Accord, claiming that free elections were not possible in communist North Vietnam. The International Commission for the Supervision of the Truce moved from Hanoi to Saigon in 1958 because it was being deliberately handicapped by the uncooperative attitude of the North Vietnamese. In October, 1958, the Republic of (South) Vietnam was established. This indicated that it would be impossible to form a unified Vietnam. Later, North Vietnam labeled itself the Democratic Republic of Vietnam.

U.S. Intervention in Vietnam

U.S. intervention included three stages:

1. President Eisenhower's "direct role" in the ultimate breakdown of the Geneva Accord by sending 600 U.S. military advisors to help train South Vietnamese troops — a "limited-risk gamble."

2. North Vietnam's announcement of the formation of the National Liberation Front (NLF) in both Vietnams, dedicated to the liberation of South Vietnam from the United States, led to President Kennedy's commitment to help South Vietnam "preserve its independence," and the sending of 4000 U.S. military to help

train South Vietnamese troops. Kennedy may have been influenced by his Vice-President, Lyndon Johnson, who urged him to either support South Vietnam or to pull back to San Francisco and a "Fortress America." By November, 1963, the month of Kennedy's assassination, more than 17,000 U.S. troops were in South Vietnam, casualties were mounting, and American helicopter crews were transporting South Vietnamese troops and bombing the Viet Cong and North Vietnamese troops. The "limited-risk gamble" of Eisenhower had become Kennedy's "broad commitment" to save South Vietnam. General Nguyen van Thieu was now president of South Vietnam, replacing Diem who had been assassinated.

3. The third stage was President Johnson's choice between withdrawal from a worsening situation and corruption within South Vietnam, and escalation of U.S. involvement.

The Tonkin Gulf Resolution (1964)

The decision to escalate the number of troops (ultimately to over 500,000) appeared to be forced by events. It was reported that two U.S. destroyers were attacked by North Vietnamese torpedo boats in the Gulf of Tonkin. Information revealed several years later indicated that the report was highly exaggerated, if not falsified. At the time (August, 1964) it offered Johnson the opportunity to demand support from Congress. By Joint Resolution the U.S. Congress declared, "Congress approved and supports the determination of the President, as Commander in Chief, to take all necessary measures to repel any armed attack against the forces of the United States and to prevent further aggression." A unanimous vote in the House, and an 88 to 2 vote in the Senate supported the President.

By January, 1968, General Westmoreland asked that the 550,000 troops be escalated to 730,000; he was removed from office. The continuation of the war, escalation of the number of troops, and mounting casualties during Johnson's administration aroused popular opinion against him and led him to announce in March, 1968, that he would not be a candidate in that year's presidential election.

The Nixon Administration

As a presidential candidate in 1968 Richard Nixon pledged to end the war, intending a systematic withdrawal of U.S. troops: 25,000 were out by August, 1969, 128,000 by September, 1970. At the same time the policy of "Vietnamization" was followed, whereby the fighting was turned over to the South Vietnamese, supported by U.S. logistical supplies and airpower. Nixon outraged Congress and much of the nation by sending troops into Cambodia in May, 1970, against communist forces there. Withdrawal of U.S. troops a few weeks later left the Cambodians to fight a devastating civil war. This led to complete control of the country by Cambodian communists in May, 1975.

Cease-fire in Vietnam

Peace talks with Vietnam proved fruitless for nearly four years. Finally in January, 1973, Le Duc Tho for North Vietnam and Henry Kissinger, secretary of state for the United States, agreed on a cease-fire arrangement. This was labeled by Nixon as "Peace with Honor." The longest war in the history of the United States had finally ended. However, 56,000 troops were killed or died in service, of whom 69 percent were under 22 years of age; 303,000 were wounded. An incredible 3,000,000 tons of bombs were dropped by U.S. planes, and the military costs alone were $140,000,000,000.

By the January, 1973, cease-fire agreement:

1. All U.S. troops were to be withdrawn.

2. South Vietnam was to determine its own future.

3. American prisoners of war were to be returned.

4. The implication was that both Vietnams would be peacefully reunited at some later date.

Prior to the cease-fire the United States rushed vast stores of military hardware to South Vietnam, and enough planes to make the South Vietnamese Air Force the fourth largest in the world. The Nobel Peace Prize was awarded to the two cease-fire negotiators. Le Duc Tho refused his; Kissinger accepted his. Between January, 1973, and April, 1975, hundreds of thousands of Vietnamese were killed in continued fighting. South Vietnam's leader, Thieu, and his corrupt government remained in power until the sudden collapse of the South Vietnamese forces in April, 1975, ended the fighting in favor of Hanoi.

Cambodia and Laos

These two former parts of French Indo-China received their independence within a decade of the end of World War II, by the terms of the Geneva Accord of 1954, which ended the French occupation of French Indo-China. Cambodia and Laos are what remains of the once great Khmer Empire, which by the 13th century stretched from the South China Sea westward into Burma. Invasions by the Siamese and the Vietnamese reduced Cambodia to its present size in the 19th century.

Cambodia unfortunately became involved in the fighting in South East Asia. In early August, 1965, Prince Sihanouk, Cambodia's chief of state, described the United States as Cambodia's "enemy No. 1." In 1967 the United States allowed secret infantry patrols into Cambodia to lay mines and reconnoiter communist forces. In March, 1969, U.S. B-52's secretly bombed North Vietnamese sanctuaries in Cambodia, and deliberately falsified official reports in order to prevent public knowledge of the facts. In early 1970 Prince Sihanouk was removed from his position while visiting China, and replaced by General Lon Nol, who proved himself incompetent. In addition to sending U.S. troops into Cambodia in May, 1970, President Nixon supplied Lon Nol with military and economic aid worth nearly $2 billion over the next five years. Since 1970 the civil war between the Lon Nol government and the Khmer Rouge has cost more than 700,000 civilians killed and 3,500,000 left homeless. The Khmer Rouge was the communist-led collection of groups opposing the Lon Nol government. It had no official leader. In April, 1975, the Khmer Rouge took control of the country, and began its program of "reeducation" of the people.

The agony of Laos has been less severe; there the communists took control of the country but retained the appearance of joint rule with the monarchy.

Thailand

Until 1939 this country was called Siam. It was never a colony of any nation and was not occupied by Japan during World War II. The word *thai* means free and indicates the pride of the people in their past and present freedom. It is one of the largest countries in South East Asia and has outstanding rice crops and agricultural abundance.

Thailand became a member of the South East Asia Treaty Organization (SEATO), sent troops to fight in Vietnam, and allowed American bases on its soil. As the United States began to withdraw from Vietnam in 1969, Thailand improved its relations with Hanoi and the People's Republic of China. In 1975 Thailand insisted upon the ultimate withdrawal of all U.S. forces. In May, 1975, relations between Thailand and the United States became strained because Cambodia, then communist, seized the U.S. merchant ship *Mayaguez* and its crew in international waters. Failing to receive a response to its requests for the release of ship and crew, the United States launched an attack upon Cambodian forces and bases, partly by naval vessels, and partly by U.S. Marines flown by helicopter from U.S. bases in Thailand, without notifying Thailand of its intentions. This was clearly a violation of the neutrality of Thailand and by Thailand, and threatened possible serious retaliation by Cambodia. In early 1976 Thailand gave notice to the United States that its troops must be withdrawn from Thailand within a few weeks.

Burma

Burma had been administered by Great Britain as part of India since 1886, but was given local autonomy in 1937. Its occupation by Japan in World War II united the various elements against the invaders. When the British returned after the defeat of Japan they were strongly opposed by revolutionary forces, and Britain finally granted Burma its independence in 1948. It chose to become an independent republic as the Union of Burma; it is not a member of the British Commonwealth.

Malaysia

In 1863 the Malay Peninsula was divided into the Straits Settlements, which was a Crown colony, and nine protectorates, to form British Malaya. Occupied by Japan during the war, it presented Britain with a problem because of the various elements of which it is composed. Forty percent of the population are Malays, forty percent are Chinese and most of the rest are Indians. One problem was that in 1949 China had become communist; the other was that Britains's proposal of a Malayan Union — a single government — displeased the Chinese, who wanted more power, and the Indians, who feared for their racial identity. In 1956 the British offered federation. The area became an independent member of the Commonwealth as the Federation of Malaya in 1957. In 1963 the federation initiated the Federation of Malaysia, which included Malaya, the island of Singapore, and two small British colonies, Sarawak and North Borneo, on the island of Borneo. The new federation was organized to provide greater political security, especially against the threats of Indonesia, and greater economic opportunity, with Singapore as its port.

Singapore

Long a British colony, Singapore became an independent state in 1958 as a member of the Commonwealth, and then an integral part of the Federation of Malaysia in 1963. However, the majority of the population are Chinese; they objected to being subordinated to the much larger Malay population of the federation. In 1965 Singapore became an independent state.

Sri Lanka

What was originally known as the island of Ceylon was acquired as a colony by Great Britain in the early 19th century. It was gradually given varying degrees of self-government. In 1948 Ceylon received its full independence, as a member of the British Commonwealth. Parliamentary democracy encouraged a radical movement of ultra-leftist students, particularly sons of peasants, who found no jobs after completing the free education offered by the state. Elections in 1960 brought to power Mrs. Sirimavo Bandaranaike, the world's first woman prime minister. During her first administration the country suffered from inflation and rising unemployment. She was ousted in 1965, but was returned to power in 1970. In 1972 Ceylon became a "socialist democracy" as the Republic of Sri Lanka.

Problems Facing South East Asian Nations

Since the winning of independence several Asian nations have attempted to resolve the problems which they all face:

1. Great poverty and low income.

2. The need to improve agricultural production.

3. The necessity of industrialization in order to raise the standard of living.

4. The development of education and administrative and technical skills.

The People's Republic of China

Terms

Kuomintang Party

People's Republic of China

Commune

Great Leap Forward

Great Proletarian Culture
  Revolution

Red Guards

Document 21

People

Chiang Kai-shek

Mao Tse-tung

Lin Piao

Chou En-lai

Confucius

Significant Dates

1949   People's Republic of China

1958   Great Leap Forward

1966   Great Proletarian Cultural Revolution

1971   Admittance to United Nations

Topic Outline

Defeat of Chiang Kai-shek

Communist Leaders

  Mao Tse-tung

  Lin Piao

  Chou En-lai

Chinese Communist Program

Communes and Industrialization
Maoism vs. Moderation
Sino-Soviet Conflict

People's Republic of China

**Defeat of
Chiang Kai-shek
by the Communists**

With the defeat of Japan in 1945 the rivalry between the Nationalist Kuomintang Party of Chiang Kai-shek and the Communist Party of Mao Tse-tung once again flared up. The United States assisted Chiang with weapons and military advisors, but when his campaign against the communists proved abortive, President Truman sent General George Marshall in 1946 with the mandate to attempt to effect conciliation between the two groups. The objective was to form a collaborative government. But Chiang was convinced that collaboration with the communists would play into their hands, and that the only way to deal with the communists was to defeat them on the battlefield. During the next few years Chiang's control slipped. Early in 1949 the Nationalist government, having lost its last stronghold in China, appealed to the governments of France, Great Britain, Russia, and the United States to act as intermediaries. Chiang Kai-shek, like leaders of past centuries, had lost the "Mandate of Heaven," and the Chinese people simply withdrew their support.

*Criticisms of the
Kuomintang
(Nationalist) Party*

General Wedemeyer of the United States Army had been sent to China earlier on a fact-finding mission, and had warned of this danger. He had told Chiang and his chief ministers that they would not defeat the communists unless they offered a program of reform which could win popular support. Wedemeyer warned them that morale was low in the army, that the country faced economic collapse, that devastating inflation was undermining confidence in the Kuomintang, and that ruthless grain collections in the face of serious food shortages were causing increasing resentment among the peasants. Despite more than $2 billion in United States aid, the Nationalist forces collapsed and Chiang was obliged to withdraw to Formosa (Taiwan). Unless other nations were prepared to get involved in a war on the Asian continent, there was nothing to do but recognize the fact that the communists had control in China, now called the People's Republic of China. Communist success must be attributed to disciplined organization, forceful leadership, the political vacuum created by the Nationalist government's failure, and the willingness of the Chinese people to support any group that seemed capable of bringing some order to the country.

**Communist Chinese
Leaders**

Mao Tse-tung was born in 1893 in Hunan province, the son of Mao Jen-sheng, a farmer who could not make a living on his two and a half acres. He joined a local general and in a short time had acquired enough money to enlarge his farm. In a few years he moved from the peasantry into the ranks of the rich farmers and moneylenders, a class which his son soon set out to destroy.

Mao Tse-tung's education consisted of brief periods at several schools, where his furious temper and obstinacy usually led to his expulsion. He acquired no systematic education and did not learn to become objective in his thinking. His early life on the farm gave him an acute insight into the mind and aspirations of the peasants. He never accepted the Soviet contention that the success of the revolution would depend upon the urban proletariat, but not until the days of the Long March of 1934 did his views predominate. He was then 41 years old, and during the more than forty years since he has taken orders from no man. In 1949 his three decades of struggle carried him to power and the leadership of 750,000,000 people.

Mao's career has shown that once he makes an idea his own, it cannot be wrong, and he will stubbornly defend it at all costs. This attitude is typical of the communist approach to problems. Disagreement cannot be permitted, and the Party cannot make mistakes. Too many past successes have apparently convinced Mao of his infallibility, so that he suffers from the inability to face facts realistically and objectively. Consequently, Mao and the Party may not be able to handle the tasks that face them. Both are efficient machines for straightforward tasks that demand single-mindedness, such as the destruction of a political or social institution. But since 1957 Chinese leadership has been unable to develop the economy of China to the advantage of its people.

This failure, which is blamed upon counterrevolutionaries and uncooperative nature, may be the force which impelled Mao to precipitate the Great Proletarian Cultural Revolution. Some observers believe that Mao senses that he cannot control the circumstances that shape people's lives, and that he is obsessed with the fallacious belief that no one nation can attain communism until all nations do. World revolution has apparently become a fixed objective and a basic cause of the split between mainland China and the Soviet Union.

The basic objectives of Chinese foreign policy have been:

1. To lessen the United States pressure on China, fancied or real, by reducing United States prestige and power in Asia.

2. To become the dominant power in Asia and, with the United States and the U.S.S.R., become one of the three great powers.

3. To organize and control a new and monolithic communist bloc.

4. To prove that "wars of liberation" by communists can be victorious anywhere.

Lin Piao   was the man who in 1966 was expected to become Mao's successor. A veteran of the Long March of 1934, he had studied military tactics with Ho Chi Minh, and later captured 40,000 of Chiang Kai-shek's troops. In 1966 he spoke of "power coming out of the barrel of a gun" as indicating policy. It is probable that he attempted a coup against Mao, because he disappeared on a flight. In 1971 it was officially announced that he had been killed in an airplane accident while trying to leave China.

Chou En-lai   emerged as Number Two man after Lin Piao's disappearance. In the 1920's he had served with Chiang Kai-shek against the warlords in an attempt to unify China. Chou became disillusioned with Chiang when he suddenly struck against the communists in Shanghai. Chou fled to communist headquarters and became an important official. A veteran of the Long March, he was appointed premier of the People's Republic in 1949. In 1971 Chou told an invited United States table tennis team that their visit "opened up a new page in the relations between the two nations." President Nixon's prompt response to this gesture was his "New China Policy," which resulted in his visit to China for the Peking Summit Conference in February, 1972.

In 1974 Chou En-lai became the leader of the moderates. He called for internal harmony and the modernization of every phase of the nation's economy. In January, 1976, Premier Chou En-lai died, and in September Mao Tse-tung died, leaving China in a condition for possible upheaval. The official successor to Mao, as chairman of the Communist Party, is Hua Kuo-feng.

The Chinese Communist Program

The first objective was to reunify a fragmented country into a socialist nation according to the beliefs of Karl Marx — a socialized economy and a totalitarian political dictatorship. This meant the elimination of some of China's traditional ways of life — the village organization, the family ties and ancestor worship, the guilds — and the substitution of organizations of types or classes of workers — farmers, laborers, and businessmen.

Between 1949 and 1952 large land holdings were broken up and redistributed to peasants. Tens of thousands of landlords were executed, and dissidents were removed on the charge of "counterrevolutionary" attitudes. This was the essence of Marxist class warfare, which was designed to use political power as the means to the end of reshaping society in the communist image.

In 1956 and 1957 Mao initiated the "Hundred Flowers" movement which permitted critics of the regime to express their views. The implication was that a Hundred Flowers should be allowed to bloom — a hundred points of view about the government and operation of China. The result was that critics were identified and eliminated for their temerity!

Communes and Industrialization

Although millions of landlords were killed and their land distributed to the peasants, the land was soon organized into state-owned farms cultivated with state-owned machines. In order to control the peasants and, hopefully, raise farm production, farm families were obliged to join the local commune which included common kitchen and dining rooms, collective living, and collective care of the very young and the old. Thus villages were organized and turned into great collectives, closely supervised by the Communist Party. By 1958 there were some 25,000 communes with several thousand peasants in each.

The original commune plan did not prove successful in operation. In recent years more land has been given to local farmer cooperatives, peasants are allowed personal plots of land, and the remaining communes aree administrative units.

Mao attempted to centralize industry through a series of Five-Year Plans similar to those of the U.S.S.R. In 1958 he inaugurated the Great Leap Forward under the slogan, "Twenty Years in a Day," in which little "backyard" furnaces were set up in hundreds of locations for the production of essential steel. Within a year the agricultural and industrial experiments were faltering. Backyard furnaces were a total failure, severe drought crippled the agrarian program, the commune system proved unsuccessful, and bureaucratic mismanagement brought disaster.

Great Proletarian Cultural Revolution

The operative technique of Communist China is under the control of the relatively small Communist Party of some 17,000,000 members, who are placed by the Politburo, or Policy Committee, in key positions throughout the country. The full force of the Red Army is behind them to govern the 750 million Chinese.

The period since 1961 has been a difficult one for China for several reasons:

1. Serious food shortages continued.

2. Population growth aggravated food shortages, and probably will continue to do so, for estimates were that by 1980 the population of China will be 1,000,000,000.

3. The anticipated success of the Great Leap Forward did not materialize.

4. China's worsening balance of payments (exports below imports, and therefore a difficulty in paying for the difference) provides insufficient cash to import much-needed tools and machines for industrial development.

There are indications that these problems may become worse before they get better, and may be a significant factor in determining China's foreign policy. One result of internal troubles was that the curious Great Proletarian Cultural Revolution that began in the summer of 1966 appeared to be getting out of control by May of 1967.

Mao decided that "permanent revolution" was being hindered by internal differences of opinion:

1. The wishes of the Chinese masses for better living conditions contradicted the communist theory of hardship and sacrifice of personal interests.

2. The age-old Confucian philosophy of social harmony and family life contradicted the Marxist-Leninist theory.

3. The managerial experts were more concerned with making China a great industrial power than with communist theories and ideology.

Therefore Mao launched the Great Proletarian Cultural Revolution. In simple terms this was an attack on educators, journalists, writers, and any group which could influence people's thinking, an attack against what Mao called the "disease of bourgeois ideology" and "evidences of the past." He organized the Red Guards, teen-agers from schools and universities, to be used to "arouse the masses." Hundreds of thousands traveled across the country, holding huge rallies to carry out Mao's slogans of "Down with the Old World," "Down with Evidences of the Past!" The Red Guards became a thorough nuisance and a serious threat to the nation. The Red Guards destroyed antiques and religious monuments, and intimidated and beat up even old-time communists who dared to criticize their vandalism and negative actions in Peking, Shanghai, Canton, and other cities. In October, 1967, Mao ordered them to stop the "armed struggle." They had performed Mao's purpose of intimidating any kind of opposition to him. Not until 1969 did the Red Guards really cease, and this was accomplished only with the help of local military commanders.

*Admittance to the
United Nations*

Once relations were established between the United States and the People's Republic, it was inevitable that the United States could no longer continue its policy of refusing to recognize the government and nation of nearly 800,000,000 people, and pretend that Chiang Kai-shek's government on Taiwan — called Nationalist China — represented the Chinese people. In October, 1971, Nationalist China was officially expelled from the United Nations and the

People's Republic of China was admitted by the United Nations General Assembly. The vote was 78 to 35, with 17 members not voting. By September, 1975, full diplomatic relations had not been established between the United States and the People's Republic of China. However, when the first envoy from the Republic arrived in the United States in 1973, his reception was that usually accorded to ambassadors.

Maoism v. Moderation

In 1974 several of the regional military commanders who had helped to end the excesses of the Red Guards suddenly found themselves shifted to new positions outside their own power bases. At the same time a very curious official attack began against the old sage Confucius "and his like," who were denounced as "buffoons who had a place only in the garbage of history." The real charge against Confucius is that his teachings, which the masses of China followed for centuries, are traditions that do not fit communist theory. The Maoists call these traditions the "four olds" — old thought, old culture, old customs, old habits. History shows that dictators from whatever century or country distrust everything which they cannot control, i.e., dictate. Confucius, born in 551 B.C., tried to restore order to a country torn by constant war among feudal warlords. His ideal was a ruler who was benevolent and believed in moderation and humanity. Mao prefers a more aggressive and combative nation.

In 1974 a secret document, later labeled Document 21, began circulating in Peking. This document showed a very disturbing industrial and agricultural slump. Chou En-lai suddenly emerged from seclusion to become the chairman of the first meeting in ten years of the National People's Congress, held in absolute secrecy. One reason for the meeting was fear by moderates that Mao was once again trying to encourage "permanent revolution" by urging people to "dare to go against the tide." The moderates were horrified at the possibility of another so-called Cultural Revolution. Document 21, prepared by the Central Committee of the Communist Party, showed that mining production, iron and steel, and the armaments industry were all underproducing, and that this was because of party policy and the radicals. Led by Chou En-lai, the moderates called for "comprehensive modernization of agriculture, industry, national defense, and science and technology," in the next "crucial" ten years. The economic task facing China, which is not even able to feed all its people, left no time for revolutionary campaigns by Mao, who was 81 years old and failing physically.

The Sino-Soviet Conflict

Although Chinese communism reflects many of the ideas of Russian communism, there are important differences, especially in relation to the recent Sino-Soviet conflict:

1. Despite assistance from Russia, the Chinese have relied essentially upon their own resources.

2. China has a long history of its own, and it intends to be the dominant power in Asia.

3. Russia, as the traditional leader of the communist world, does not welcome the Chinese challenge for dominance.

4. Russia is no longer so aggressive in methods; it wants to develop its own

resources and does not want the risk of a nuclear war. China may decide to divert attention from restrictions at home by aggressive words and actions abroad.

In July, 1975, leaders of 35 nations in Europe, plus Canada, the United States, and the Soviet Union, signed a European Security Agreement which emphasized the peaceful settlement of international disputes. The Soviet Union had been advocating this since 1954; once it was signed, the Russians proposed a similar collective security agreement for Asia. The People's Republic of China considered this suggested agreement an attempt to encircle and isolate mainland China.

At the beginning of 1977 foreign relations between the People's Republic and other nations were uncertain. Hua Kuo-feng's position as chairman of the Party was threatened by outbreaks of violence in some parts of the Republic. There is divided opinion between moderates who want the Republic to become a modern nation, and the radical group who are more concerned with Communist doctrine than with modern technology. There are indications that Hua's position is by no means secure.

Japan

Terms

Shogun

Kamikaze

Treaty of Kanagawa

Genro

Treaty of Shimonoseki

Twenty-One Demands

Tanaka Memorial

Komeito

Soka Gakkai

People

Tokugawa

Matthew Perry

Douglas MacArthur

Significant Dates

1854   Treaty of Kanagawa

1941   Pearl Harbor

1945   Occupation of Japan

1952   Independence of Japan

1960   Revised Security Treaty

1972   Okinawa returned to Japan

Topic Outline

The Old Japan

   Chinese Influence

   Early History

   Tokugawa Shogunate

The Meiji Restoration

Expansion of Japan

   Sino-Japanese War, 1894-95

   Russo-Japanese War, 1904-05

Manchurian Incident, 1931
War Against China, 1937-45
"New Order in Asia"
The New Japan
Post-War Occupation
The New Government
Independence
The Security Treaties
Return of Okinawa
Political Parties
Economic Changes
International Relations

Japan

The Old Japan

According to tradition, the first emperor of Japan, in 660 B.C., was descended from the Sun Goddess, and the ruling house continued from that origin. In fact, the origin of the Japanese people is unknown; some of the people have similarities to people in South China and Indo-China, others are similar to inhabitants of Korea and Manchuria. The most primitive are the aboriginal Ainu, who are probably a branch of the original inhabitants, whom the Japanese either absorbed or drove from the southern islands.

Chinese Influence

In the last 1000 years B.C. successive waves of immigration to Japan took place, probably from northeast Asia via Korea. Large numbers of Koreans brought Chinese culture, the Chinese script, and Buddhism to Japan. In 645 the Great Reform in government occurred. The emperor was in theory the owner of all land, and all persons, irrespective of position or birth, owed him allegiance.

Early History

The population of medieval Japan was divided into the free and the slaves. The highest members of the free class occupied important rank at court; the lesser nobility practiced the professions and warfare; the small landowners and peasants paid taxes in grain and labor. In the 12th century a military commander, the *shogun*, became the real ruler of Japan, controlling officials, law, justice, and finance. This situation continued until the revolution of 1867.

In the late 13th century the Mongols, who had overrun much of Asia, part of Europe, all of Korea, and most of China, demanded Japan's submission. Japan refused, and Kublai Khan, the Mongol leader, attacked. Because the weather was unfavorable, he stopped the fighting temporarily. In 1281 a fighting force of some 140,000 Mongols, Chinese, and Koreans, probably the greatest overseas expedition yet seen, attacked on a narrow beachhead. However, they were struck by a typhoon which destroyed most of their fleet and forced them to withdraw. The *kamikaze* or "divine wind" saved Japan. This was to be remembered in World War II when kamikaze pilots flew their bomb-laden planes into American ships.

The Tokugawa
Shogunate,
1603–1868

For 250 years the Tokugawa system, an authoritarian government which suppressed individual rights and creative abilities, gave peace to Japan.

Japan was a potentially centralized feudal society; the population was stratified into four classes: warriors, farmers, artisans, and merchants. The imperial court was isolated from the people and the country was divided into feudal possessions. The landed vassals were kept economically poor and politically controlled. They were obliged to maintain "alternate residence," spending some time each year in the new capital of Tokyo, which now replaced Kyoto. The vassals' families remained as hostages in the city while they returned to their estates.

When the Portuguese first arrived in the 16th century, they were welcomed, and many Catholic monastic orders converted thousands of Japanese to Christianity. But this new religion threatened to weaken the totalitarian state, since it demanded not only religious but also political allegiance.

In 1587 the shogun ordered the missionaries to leave immediately, and decided that all foreign influence must be removed. In 1638 a decree prohibited any Japanese citizen or ship to leave Japan and ordered the expulsion of all foreigners. Only the Dutch traders were permitted to continue a limited trade. This trade was under strict supervision on an artificial island, Deshima, less than one-fiftieth of a square mile, off Nagasaki.

The Meiji
Restoration

Japan's isolation was ended in 1854 with the negotiation of the Treaty of Kanagawa by Commodore Perry of the United States Navy. This was "the first formal treaty with any foreign country." The essential provision was the opening of two ports to American ships. This was soon followed with commercial rights to the United States, Great Britain, Russia, and Holland. The Japanese quickly appreciated that foreign power must be matched. "Let us have dealings with foreign countries, learn their drill and their tactics."

Japan decided that it must unite against Western threats by restoring imperial rule. In 1868 the Emperor Meiji (Enlightened Rule) determined to modernize Japan. Most feudal lords voluntarily transferred their feifdoms to the emperor. Feudalism was officially abolished in 1871, and the cash compensation subsequently paid to landowners became the capital for industrialization. However, the nature of industrialization created problems for Japan. Conservative tradition remained in the hands of the new capitalists; industrial economy was a forced one, more for military than consumer needs; the low wages paid to workers could not purchase consumer goods that were available; foreign markets became increasingly essential, even if it meant taking them by force.

Political reform was more apparent than real, since social classes rather than institutions or principles were the basis of government. The cabinet of government officials was responsible to the emperor, not to the Diet, or parliament. The Diet itself was elected by a limited number of property holders. Furthermore, the ministers of war and of the navy had to be an active general and an active admiral, appointed by their services, and removable by them. No cabinet could function without these two ministers. Finally, "the Emperor . . . is the head of the empire, combining in himself the rights of sovereignty . . . had supreme command of the army and navy." He became an object of national worship, an absolute ruler who could do no wrong, and without whose approval no law of the Diet was operative. By tradition, older statesmen who had been active in political life became members of the genro, the highest advisors to the emperor. This was an inner ring of great political power.

Expansion of Japan

The geographical position of Korea made it a pawn between Japan and Russia in the late 19th century. Because Korea pointed directly towards Japan, it could be an invasion route into Japan. Korea's ice-free ports could give Russia year-round access to the Pacific. Ideally, an independent Korea would keep these rivals apart. However, Japanese militarists intended to control Korea, which China regarded as an independent but "tributary" state under China's protection.

In Korea, an anti-Japanese and generally anti-foreign organization rebelled against the Korean government and defeated its troops. China sent in troops to assist its tributary state. The Japanese claimed this action was a threat to their interests and sent an army to Korea, insisting that Korea was not dependent upon China. While hostile Japanese and Chinese troops faced each other, China refused Japan's proposal of a joint administration of Korea. Japan then removed the Korean king and established a new government, which immediately requested Japan to expel the Chinese troops.

As a result of the **Sino-Japanese War of 1894-5** which followed, China had to sign the Treaty of Shimonoseki which:

1. Recognized the independence of Korea.

2. Ceded to Japan the Pescadores Islands, Formosa (Taiwan), and the strategic Liaotung Peninsula.

3. Opened seven Chinese ports to Japan on a most-favored-nation basis. This success made Japan the leading power in the Far East.

Japan suggested that in return for Korea as a Japanese sphere of influence, Russia take Manchuria as its own sphere of influence. Russia's contemptuous refusal convinced Japan that it should fight Russia before that country completed the railroad across Manchuria.

The Russo-Japanese War of 1904-5 resulted in the ignominious defeat of Russia — and the second major step in Japanese expansion. In 1905 the two combattants were persuaded by President Theodore Roosevelt — who was anxious to see that Japan did not become too powerful — to sign the Treaty of Portsmouth, in New Hampshire. Russia ceded its rights in the Liaotung Peninsula, but perhaps more important, Japan proved its ability to defeat a Western nation and destroyed the concept of white invincibility. Japanese ambitions were whetted.

The Twenty-One Demands on China

In 1915, while war raged in Europe, Japan, an ally of the Western powers, acquired German concessions on the mainland of China, the strategic German Pacific islands. Japan also presented China with the *Twenty-One Demands* which would have made China a satellite of Japan.

The basic points were:

1. China must agree to accept whatever arrangements Japan made regarding German rights and holdings in Shantung province.

2. In South Manchuria Japan's leaseholds and rights were to be extended for 25 years, and in South Manchuria and Inner Mongolia Japanese citizens could own land, travel wherever they wished, and engage in business.

3. Japan and China were to hold jointly the biggest mining and smelting corporation in China.

4. China could not lease or cede any harbor, bay, or island to any other power.

5. Japan must share in police administration, and China could not accept foreign loans without Japan's consent.

As soon as these demands became public knowledge, protests were sent to Japan. Nevertheless, Japan did in effect secure Chinese agreement on the first four points.

Demanding but not receiving equality at the peace conference in 1919, Japan made significant gains at the Washington Conference of 1921.

In the mid-twenties *Baron Tanaka*, a veteran of the Russo-Japanese War and now a general, became prime minister and minister for foreign affairs. Tanaka's "positive" policy anticipated further expansion on the Asian continent. A document attributed to Tanaka, but never authenticated, was supposed to have contained the program he presented to his emperor. The design for world conquest must follow this pattern: first Japan must take Manchuria, then China, Siberia, Central and Southeast Asia, Europe, and America. While the authenticity of the document, the so-called Tanaka Memorial, may be in doubt, its ideas seem to have been currently entertained by Japanese militarists, as the future was to indicate.

Manchurian Incident (1931)   In 1931 Manchuria became the target of Japanese expansion. An exceedingly fertile region of 380,000 square miles, its mineral resources were being developed, and its Chinese population had grown to 28,000,000. On the pretext that China had not prevented the destruction of Japanese property on the South Manchurian Railroad, leased to Japan after the Russo-Japanese War, the Japanese seized Mukden and other towns, took control of Manchuria, set up a puppet government, and renamed the area Manchukuo. League of Nations action was ineffectual, and Japan was ready to believe in its military leaders.

In the meantime the Chinese in Shanghai boycotted all Japanese goods; the Japanese navy and army shelled and occupied the port; and for the next few years Japan digested its conquest of Manchuria. The period between 1933 and 1937 was simply a period of uneasy truce that ended in 1937.

"Police Action" in China (1937–1945)   In July, 1937, fighting broke out near Peking between a Chinese garrison and a Japanese force conducting manuevers. The Japanese force was permitted there under the terms of the agreement after the Boxer Rebellion.

The reason for the attack was Japan's determination to prevent the unification of China, which would be an obstacle to Japan's intended continental expansion. In a brief time Japan had control of the coastal cities of China; China was trading space for time. After 1939 the war in China was essentially a stalemate: Japan held what it had while China was unable to mount a determined offensive.

"New Order in Asia"

Japan could not afford to stand still once its plans for expansion were under way. In 1941 Japan moved into southern Indo-China and announced its "New Order in Asia," later changed to "Greater East Asia Co-Prosperity Sphere." This meant nothing less than Japan's expansion further southwards and westwards on the Asian continent. Inevitably war would come to the Pacific, since the United States and Japan were on a collision course. Negotiations between the two nations in November and December, 1941, were unsuccessful, because each side was committed to an unchangeable policy. Japan insisted that the United States stop helping China. The United States demanded that Japan withdraw from China and agree to respect China's independence.

Japan had committed itself too deeply to withdraw and had become a prisoner of its own expansionist policy. Similarly, the United States could not back down from its historical support of the policy of China's independence. The attack on Pearl Harbor on December 7, 1941, was Japan's gamble to win all.

The New Japan

Postwar Occupation

American occupation of Japan between 1945 and 1952 was decisive in Japan's development. Changes were instituted that would not have occured had not Japan been occupied by a foreign power. Several Japanese cities were gutted, factories were destroyed, and the people were hungry and apprehensive of a cruel and vindictive occupation. Instead, they found the occupation constructive in a way that some Japanese writers have called the "second opening" of Japan.

In theory the occupation was operated by a 13-nation Far Eastern Commission in Washington and a four-nation Allied Council in Tokyo. Actually the occupation was American, under General Douglas MacArthur, who was Supreme Commander for the Allied Powers (SCAP), and whose Army of Occupation operated through the civilian Japanese administration. The military supervised to make sure that the Japanese officials carried out the laws.

The New Government

The position of the emperor was changed from that of a sacred person, whose word was law, to that of "the symbol of the State . . . deriving his position from the will of the people." By 1946 it had become evident to MacArthur that responsible Japanese officials were progressing very slowly with a new constitution for Japan, so he instructed his office to draw one up. Although it was criticized both inside Japan and elsewhere for its American origin and flavor, it gave governmental power to the Diet or Parliament. This was a measure which the Japanese may have been completely unable to initiate.

The constitution of March, 1947, established two elective houses. The House of Councillors consisted of 250 members, half running for election every three years. Sixty percent were chosen to represent districts and forty percent were elected on a single national vote. The House of Representatives consisted of 467 members for 118 electoral districts. Each electoral district chose 3 to 5 members. Like the British House of Commons, the House of Representatives elects its own prime minister, whose cabinet is in fact responsible or answerable for all its actions to the House of Representatives, although in theory it is responsible to the Diet of both houses. The House of Representatives can be dissolved if the government wants a new election. The House of Councillors is not dissolved. On almost all matters the final right of decision rests with the House of Representatives. If there is a disagreement between the two houses on a finance bill, it becomes law 30 days after the lower house passes it. If any other bill is rejected by the House of Councillors it becomes law if passed again by the House of Representatives by a two-thirds vote.

The only limitation upon the ultimate political power of the House of Representatives is that any revision of the constitution requires a two-thirds vote of each house and ratification by a simple majority in a national referendum. These changes not only gave political power to the Japanese people but also gave the emperor a completely new role. The emperor became the symbol of a loyalty based upon respect and affection, and thus did a great deal to stabilize politics in postwar Japan.

Independence

In July, 1950, a National Police Reserve of 75,000 men was established. This paramilitary force was to take over from the United States troops the responsibility for internal security in Japan.

Negotiations for Japan's independence culminated in September, 1951, in a treaty signed at San Francisco by most of the nations which had fought in the Pacific war. Three nations refused to sign — the U.S.S.R., India, and the People's Republic of China. However, because these three played no direct part in governing postwar Japan, the military occupation officially ended when the treaty was ratified in April, 1952. This did not mean the withdrawal of occupation forces, because other conditions had been imposed upon Japan in 1945.

The Security Treaties

The new constitution obliged Japan never to maintain "land, sea, and air forces"; Japan agreed to mutual security treaties by which the United States guaranteed Japan's safety and kept armed forces in Japan. To assist local police a National Police Reserve of 75,000 was organized in 1950. Two years later it was renamed the National Security Force, and a small naval force was added.

By the Revised Security Treaty of 1960, the United States, which had already withdrawn ground troops, retained numerous air bases and two naval repair depots. The Japanese National Security Force was renamed the Self-Defense Force. It consisted of 200,000 men, over 1000 planes, and a small destroyer-size naval force, all equipped with modern weapons.

The treaty aroused some anti-American protests because:

1. Some Japanese feared a revival of militarism, and believed that disarmament and nonalignment offered a better chance for survival in the event of another war.

2. The presence of U.S. personnel and the numerous American air bases meant the loss of cultivable land to runways. Incidents of friction occurred between Americans and Japanese.

By 1975 many Japanese showed less worry about the Soviet Union's and China's nuclear development, and complained of the presence of American forces 30 years after the war. Socialists and communists favor "unarmed neutrality," and disapprove of any possible involvement in war.

Return of Okinawa

One of the bloodiest battles of World War II was fought on Okinawa from April through June, 1945. It cost the lives of 12,000 Americans, 100,000 Japanese, and 62,000 Okinawans who were caught between the two armies.

As the Cold War between the United States and the Soviet Union escalated, Okinawa and other of the Ryukyu Islands became increasingly important to the United States, although most of the one million inhabitants wanted to be Japanese. The U.S. built a complex of military bases and nuclear installations; used Okinawa as a base for B-52 bombing missions in Vietnam; and took some of the best farm land for airfields, bases, military housing, six-lane highways, hamburger stands, and used-car lots.

In 1971 opposition to the Americans became so intense that the United States withdrew its B-52's and chemical weapons. In 1972 the official ceremony of returning Okinawa to Japan took place in the Imperial Palace in Tokyo.

Political Parties

Japan was supposed to become a political democracy under the new constitution. However, the sense of concern for the individual that characterizes the United States Constitution is not present in the Japanese one. In Japan political actions are taken not for the good of individuals but for the nation-family. In Japanese politics the individual is less important than the group. Consequently, Japanese political parties are combinations of groups that support men capable of leadership, who have political skill, and who have patronage to distribute.

The Liberal-Democratic Party

This is a curiously named Conservative Party. In power since Japanese independence in 1952, it was responsible for much of the economic rehabilitation of the country. It is supported by the business community, government employees, and a conservative trade union, and has managed to keep the Socialist Party out of power.

The Japanese Socialist Party

The Socialist Party is the major opposition party. It is Marxist in doctrine, opposes the Security Treaty, advocates government ownership of industries, and opposes the rearming of Japan. It is supported by the trade unions and has gradually but steadily won more seats in the Diet.

The Japanese Communist Party

The Communist Party resists any return to the "old order," and condemns the members of the Liberal-Democratic Party as fascists and traitors who are selling out to foreign capital. It controls the *Zengakuren*, the National Federation of Student Self-Government Associations, whose main tactic has been to demonstrate against the United States.

Komeito (Clean Government Party)

Sometimes known as the Fair and Bright Association, Komeito is the political force of the Buddhist sect, the Soka Gakkai or Value Creating Society, a "new religion." Teaching mutual assistance and faith healing, it gives a sense of community to the urban poor and peasants who have migrated to the cities from the countryside.

Economic Changes

The early occupation years contributed significantly to economic reform in Japan. The basic change was the land reform measure of October, 1946, which provided for compulsory sale of land by absentee landlords. Acreage limits were established for owner-farmers and resident-landlords. All other land was sold to the government, which then sold it to existing tenants and others at a fair price and with contracts that guaranteed tenure.

Other significant measures were the Trade Union Act of 1945 and the Labor Relations Act of 1946. Together these acts granted workers the right to organize and to strike. The Labor Standards Act of 1947 established better working conditions, accident compensation, and health insurance.

Japan's incredible economic recovery from the devastation of World War II has been termed the "most spectacular rise in economic power and living standards the world has ever seen." Japan is the largest shipbuilder in the world, and according to Lloyd's Register of Shipping, half the ships sailing in 1971 were Japanese built. It is also the world's largest producer of motorcycles and bicycles. Japan's industrial progress is the result of the attitude of its workers, and of the Ministry of International Trade and Industry, the MITI. In factories, workers work as a team to produce more to assist Japan's progress. The MITI, which has no equal in the United States, is a government bureau whose function is to supervise Japan's economy and to study the economies of other nations through the Japan External Trade Organization, JETRO.

International Relations

A basic principle of Japan's foreign policy has been open and peaceful world trading conditions. Japan enjoyed very favorable trade relations with the United States until 1971, when the United States demanded the right to export goods to Japan.

The Peking summit meeting between President Nixon and Chou En-lai in 1972 shocked the Japanese, who had not been notified of the plan. They wondered whether they would be the only major noncommunist power in the Pacific. Japan has fostered further cultural relationships with the United States to encourage a firm partnership between the two largest nations (in terms of economics) in the noncommunist world.

India, Pakistan, and Bangladesh

Terms

National Congress Party | Neutralism | Mukti Bahini
March to the Sea | Awami League | Andhra Desa

People

Mahatma Gandhi | Ayub Khan | Zulfikar Ali Bhutto
Mohammed Ali Jinnah | Mujibur Rahman | Indira Gandhi
Jawaharlal Nehru | Yahya Khan

Significant Dates

1935   Government of India Act
1947   Independence of India and Pakistan
1971   Independence of Bangladesh
1971   India-Pakistan War
1975   India's "State of Emergency"

Topic Outline
Mahatma Gandhi and Civil Disobedience
Pakistani Demands for Independence
Independence for India and Pakistan
Kashmir: Disputed Province
Unrest in Pakistan
Bangladesh: Independent East Pakistan
India-Pakistan War, 1971
Conditions in Bangladesh
India, 1975: "State of Emergency"

India, Pakistan, and Bangladesh

Despite the ability and the dedication of Britain's Indian Civil Service, the British lost sight of any long-range goal. They excluded Indians from senior civil service positions, and became increasingly divorced from an understanding of the needs of the vast population of India. The natives were accorded unequal political status and were not allowed to determine policy for their own country. Towards the end of the 19th century, men of the Hindu Renaissance, who were reviving interest in India's past, rejected Western culture as materialistic.

At the beginning of the 20th century, resistance to British rule stiffened. The defeat of Russia by Japan was a contributing factor. Moderate spokesmen in the India National Congress Party advocated self-government by constitutional means, while extreme nationalists, predominantly in Bengal, prepared to use force.

However, unity was hampered by conflicts between the Hindu majority and the Moslem minority. The Hindus wanted a proportional representation which would give the Moslems little voice, while the Moslems demanded representation which would be at the expense of the Hindus.

The Congress Party was built on too narrow a base to be effective. It was essentially a Western-educated, middle-class organization, ignorant of or uninterested in the economic needs of the lower classes. Participation by India in World War I, and the principles of "making the world safe for democracy" and self-determination spurred demands for home rule. This was the very least that would be acceptable to India.

Mahatma Gandhi and Civil Disobedience

Disillusionment led to the rise of *Mohandas K. Gandhi* (called Mahatma, the Saint) and his passive resistance method against Britain and British institutions. Passive resistance deprived the British of the cooperation they needed from Indians if their plans for gradual transference of power were to be carried out.

The India Act of 1919 provided for a dyarchy, or joint rule, of bureaucratic and responsible government. This kept such key departments as justice and police in the hands of the British.

Believing that the process of self-government was too slow, Gandhi in 1922 launched a campaign of massive civil disobedience, called nonviolent noncooperation. Unfortunately, this period had begun with a very serious incident in 1919. A local military commander, faced with a mob at Amritsar, ordered his troops to fire for 10 minutes. Four hundred people were killed, and this incident, which was not an isolated one, alienated nationalists. They formed the Congress Party and adopted Gandhi's teaching of deliberate civil disobedience. Gandhi believed that the refusal of Indians to obey the British government would put it in an intolerable position. When his followers resorted to violence, Gandhi went on a hunger strike in his home; when the British arrested him as the leader of civil disobedience, he fasted in their prisons. In 1930 he led a "march to the sea" and there deliberately and symbolically made salt from sea water as a protest against the British government's salt monopoly. British retaliation by mass arrests simply made the British position ridiculous. In 1935 the British compromised with Gandhi in his demand for Indian independence. The Government of India Act of that year provided that Indians hold ministerial positions in local governments.

Moslem (Pakistani) Demands for Independence

During World War II Indian demands for independence were incessant, and all half-way measures were rejected. When the Labour government came into power in 1945 it prepared to meet Indian demands, but the Moslem League under Mohammed Ali Jinnah demanded a separate state for the Moslem minority of India. Such a separation was difficult because Moslems formed majority groups in the northwest and northeast sections of India, while millions were scattered throughout other parts of India.

Independence for India and Pakistan

In 1947 the peninsula was partitioned into two self-governing parts, the Republic of Pakistan with its two widely separated sections, and the Republic of India. Both were self-governing members of the British Commonwealth of Nations.

Until 1971, when East Pakistan declared its independence as Bangladesh, Pakistan consisted of two parts, nearly 700 miles apart and separated by India. Pakistan's religion was Islam and its population was 94,000,000. India, called Bharat in its constitution, had a population of 450,000,000. Unfortunately Pakistan's separation from India was accompanied by the senseless massacre of Hindus and Moslems by each other, as Moslems left India for Pakistan, and as Hindus left Pakistan for India. More than 8,000,000 Indians were involved in these "migrations." At Lahore Station the Moslems went on a rampage, cutting the throat of every Hindu they met. In another station Sikhs ran through trains beheading Moslem men, women, and children. More than 1,000,000 people were slaughtered during the migrations. A year after independence Gandhi was murdered by a Hindu fanatic. *Jawaharlal Nehru,* educated in England, an intimate of Gandhi, and an outstanding leader in his own right, became prime minister. Nehru was a noncommunist, an anticolonialist, and a spokesman for "Asia for the Asians" and for the "neutralist bloc" which attempted to remain noncommittal to either side in the Cold War. Nehru's unrealistic neutralism was abruptly shattered when India was attacked by China in 1962.

Kashmir: Disputed Province

When India and Pakistan were established in 1947, some 500 prince-ruled states, ranging in size from 200 acres to 80,000 square miles, were surrendered to the two countries in return for financial grants. The one problem was the province of

Jammu and Kashmir, in the northwest of the Indian subcontinent. The ruler of Kashmir was a Hindu, but 80 percent of the people were Moslem. The maharajah of Kashmir wanted to remain independent; Pakistani troops invaded Kashmir and the maharajah requested aid from India. Prime Minister Nehru of India referred the issue to the United Nations, promising the people of Kashmir that they would be allowed to choose which nation they wanted to join. This promise was not kept, however. Fighting over Kashmir ended in 1948 with a United Nations' cease-fire, but friction continued. In 1964, after repeated border incidents, Nehru claimed that the "issue of Kashmir" was "an internal matter for India alone to settle." In 1966, after Nehru's death, President Ayub Khan of Pakistan and Prime Minister Lal Shastri of India signed an agreement at Tashkent, in the Soviet Union, to settle the matter peacefully.

Unrest in Pakistan

Unfortunately for Pakistan, Mohammed Ali Jinnah died in 1948 without having had time to name a successor or create a strong political party to carry out an effective government policy.

After years of bitter internal struggle by rival political parties, a constitution was adopted in 1956 which renamed the country the Islam Republic of Pakistan. General Mohammed Ayub Khan was soon to emerge from a military coup as the "strong man." He then suspended the constitution, declared martial law, assumed the title of president, and proclaimed a new constitution which gave him almost absolute power. The elections were fraudulent, and strong opposition came from East Pakistan, which was divided from West Pakistan by India.

East Pakistan claimed that it was treated like a colony, and demanded the ouster of Ayub Khan. At the head of the protest movement was Sheikh Mujibur Rahman, leader of the political Awami League, who demanded local self-rule. Although East Pakistan contained 57 percent of Pakistan's 128,000,000 people and contributed two-thirds of the nation's foreign earnings through its sales of tea and jute, it received less than one-half of the nation's investment and development funds.

Bangladesh: Independent East Pakistan

In 1969 Ayub Khan resigned. The Commander in Chief of the Army, General Yahya Khan, took control, proclaimed martial law, and called for a new constitution and elections. Although he was a Pathan from West Pakistan, he determined to be fair to Bengali East Pakistan which, with 75,000,000 people, would have 169 seats in the 313-member National Assembly. West Pakistan, with 54,000,000 people, would have 144 seats. Yahya Khan confidently believed that Mujibur Rahman of East Pakistan would win only 100 seats, and that the other 69 members from East Pakistan would line up with West Pakistan members for a majority of about 210 to 100. To Yahya Khan's consternation Rahman won 167 of the 169 seats, and Zulfikar Ali Bhutto, leader of the People's Party in West Pakistan, won only 83 of the 144 seats. Mujibur Rahman and his Awami League had a clear majority in the National Assembly, and a mandate from their supporters to demand self-rule for the people of East Pakistan.

Two events led to the independence of Bangladesh, the new name for East Pakistan. In November, 1969, a severe cyclone roared across East Pakistan, flooding the plains and killing more than 250,000 people. The government of

Pakistan in Islamabad was slow to provide relief for the thousands of flood victims, and the Bengalis blamed Yahya Khan, a Punjabi.

Dissatisfied with the unexpected results of the election, Yahya Khan postponed the meeting of the National Assembly. Immediately Rahman announced a six-point program which proposed that East Pakistan control the raising and spending of its own taxes and foreign trade. Opposition to this proposal by Yahya Khan resulted in a general strike in East Pakistan and the murder of hundreds of Pakistani government troops and civilians who were opposed to East Pakistan's independence.

On March 23, 1971, "resistance day," Rahman announced that he had taken over full control, and ordered the flying of the green, red, and gold flag of Bangladesh, the Bengali Nation. Rahman was arrested in West Pakistan on charges of treason. Yahya Khan's army deliberately and brutally slaughtered hundreds of thousands of Bengalis in East Pakistan, ruthlessly destroyed towns, irrigation pumps, tea plantations, and jute mills, and carried out a reign of terror that sent millions of refugees fleeing into India. Estimates indicated that the Punjabis of West Pakistan had deliberately attempted to destroy the economy of East Pakistan. By August, 1971, more than 8,000,000 Bengalis had become refugees in India. This was as though the entire population of Maine, Vermont, Massachusetts, and Rhode Island had become homeless. On April 12, 1971, East Pakistan declared itself the independent People's Republic of Bangladesh.

The India-Pakistan War, 1971

Pakistan's ruthlessness was costing India $2,500,000 each day to feed the refugees. India permitted the Mukti Bahini, Bengali guerrilla freedom fighters, to be trained on its soil. In December, 1971, Yahya Khan made a fatefully wrong decision. He ordered 200 bombers to fly through mountain passes into India to destroy the important air base at Agra. The surprise attack was bungled, and was denounced by Indian Prime Minister Indira Gandhi as a full-scale war against India. This gave India the opportunity to assist Bangladesh in achieving actual independence, and to humiliate its enemy, Pakistan.

India quickly occupied 1500 square miles of Pakistan and captured 60,000 Pakistani troops in Bangladesh. Two weeks after the bomber attack, 60,000 troops in Pakistan surrendered and Yahya Khan accepted India's cease-fire proposal.

Yahya Khan immediately resigned as president and appointed as his successor Zulfikar Ali Bhutto, whose Pakistan People's Party had been defeated by Rahman in the 1970 elections. Bhutto, a rabid anti-India, pro-Communist China politician, declared himself chief administrator of martial law and minister of defense, foreign affairs, and the interior. He insisted that East Pakistan "remains an inseparable and indissoluble part of Pakistan." In 1973 India returned 90,000 prisoners of war to Pakistan, and Pakistan allowed 200,000 Bengalis to leave for Bangladesh; Bhutto pledged to recognize independent Bangladesh.

Bangladesh

Mujibur Rahman was finally released from jail in Pakistan, and in January, 1972, was named prime minister of Bangladesh. In March, 1973, his Awami League won 292 out of 300 seats in the National Assembly of Bangladesh. After three years of independence Bangladesh is still a disaster area. With its population of nearly 80,000,000 in an area the size of the state of Wisconsin, the new nation has staggering statistics. It is the most overcrowded nation in the world, with about 1500 persons per square mile, seven births every minute, and a per capita income of $70. Although more than $3 billion was contributed by various nations to help rebuild the country, it is still not able to feed itself, and the steel, engineering, shipbuilding, and fertilizer industries have produced only 9 percent of the goal set by the government. Consumer prices have risen 400 percent, and corruption throughout the government, including charges against Rahman's family, is on a scale almost too large to be credible. It is believed that only 10 percent of the relief commodities ever reach the poor. The Awami League demands bribes for business permits, and it is alleged that up to 250,000 tons of rice, badly needed in Bangladesh, are smuggled into India, where rice fetches better prices.

Although a man of great personal charm and magnetism, Rahman proved to be an incompetent administrator. In December, 1974, he declared a state of emergency and put the press under censorship. In early 1975 he abolished the parliamentary system and declared himself president. These measures were useless remedies for economic deterioration. One official said that Rahman had taken Bangladesh "from poverty to ruin." A foreign observer considered Bangladesh "a basket case."

In August, 1975, Rahman was killed in a military coup which made Khandakar Moshtaque Ahmed the president. Ahmed inherited the same economic problems faced by Rahman.

India, 1975: "State of Emergency"

In 1966 Mrs. Indira Gandhi, daughter of former Prime Minister Jawaharlal Nehru, but no relation to Mahatma Gandhi, became prime minister. Reelected by a large majority in 1971, Mrs. Gandhi promised a program of garibi hatao, "abolish poverty," but did very little to carry out such a program. The declaration of independence from West Pakistan by East Pakistan (Bangladesh) in 1971 led to bitter repression by Pakistani troops in Bangladesh, and nearly 10,000,000 refugees fled into India. Their care and feeding cost India millions of dollars and added to the country's already severe financial problems. During the next few years economic conditions in India worsened, and Indira Gandhi's government failed to solve the problems.

In March, 1975, demonstrators in New Delhi charged the government with corruption and failure to improve the poverty level of 360,000,000 people who were living in semi-starvation.

In June, 1975, Indira Gandhi was found guilty of campaign irregularities in the parliamentary election of 1971 which had returned her for a second term of office. Under the law her conviction barred her from her seat in parliament, which she needed in order to hold office as prime minister, and disqualified her from holding any political office for six years. Unless the supreme court of India reversed the decision, her political career was virtually finished.

Mrs. Gandhi answered the court conviction by declaring a "state of emergency," but withoutoffering proof that an emergency existed. Under this ordinance all political freedoms were suspended, full censorship was imposed on the press, and Mrs. Gandhi had the right to order the arrest of anyone. The people of India were denied the right of freedom of speech, the right to criticize any government action, and the basic right of habeas corpus. Under this right a citizen must be told what he is charged with, in order to defend himself, and must either be brought to trial within a specified time or released. Under Mrs. Gandhi's "state of emergency" no arrested person is allowed to appeal to a court of law for release, and newspapers may not mention the name of any detained person or the place of detention. This is the essence of a "police state."

In August, 1975, parliament, dominated by Mrs. Gandhi's party, enacted a retroactive law — to be operative before Mrs. Gandhi's conviction in June, 1975 — which stated that her election to parliament could not be challenged by any court of law. This action put Mrs. Gandhi above the law.

Mrs. Gandhi ordered the arrest and imprisonment of prominent leaders of opposition political parties and even some critics in her own party. Thus she deprived other political parties of their leadership.

When asked why citizens could be imprisoned indefinitely without a specific charge of wrongdoing and without a trial, she answered, "Courts are so slow and individual guilt is difficult to prove."

It is probable that Mrs. Gandhi will face little political opposition, because when people live under conditions of semi-starvation they are more concerned with food than with freedom.

Sub-Sahara Africa

Terms

"White Man's Burden"	*UNITA	Apartheid
French Community	Yoruba	Afrikaner
Republic of the Congo	Ibo	Homelands
Zaire	Hausa	*UDI
*PAIGC	Biafra	African National
*FRELIMO	Kikuyu	Council
*FNLA	Uhuru	*ZANU
*MPLA	Mau Mau	*ZAPU

People

Patrice Lumumba	Jonas Savimbi	Jomo Kenyatta
Joseph Mobutu	Alhagi Balewa	Harold Macmillan
Antonio de Spinola	Yakuba Gowon	Ian Smith
Samora Machel		

Significant Dates

1957	Independence of Ghana
1965	Unilateral Declaration of Independence of Rhodesia
1974	Independence of Guinea-Bissau and Mozambique

Topic Outline
Physical Geography
Early History
Kinds of Colonialism
French Colonies

*See TERMS AND DEFINITIONS page 309.

Belgian Colonies
   Belgian Congo
   Rwanda and Burundi
Portuguese African Colonies
   Independence
   Guinea-Bissau
   Mozambique
   Angola
British Colonies
   Ghana
   Nigeria
   Kenya
   Tanzania
Republic of South Africa
Rhodesia
Backgrounds of African Nationalism
Problems of Independent Nations

Sub-Sahara Africa

In discussing Africa we must differentiate between Mediterranean North Africa and sub-Sahara Africa. The Mediterranean region is considered part of the Arab world, as it has been since the 8th century; the Arab language, tradition, and culture have predominated there. The Sahara Desert has been a barrier between the two parts of Africa.

Physical Geography

Sub-Sahara Africa is a great plateau rising from 3000 feet in the east to 6000 feet in the west. It has no area of great plains or farming country. The plains ares are along the coast; they are narrow in width and only occasionally 100 miles wide.

There are four great river systems:

1. The Nile in the northeast which rises in Lake Victoria and empties into the Mediterranean.

2. The Zambesi in the southeast.

3. The Niger in the northwest.

4. The Congo in the center of Africa, with its vast plateau covered in great part by a tropical rain forest.

These last three rivers cannot be easily used as inland highways because waterfalls and rapids prevent movement upstream. Compared with its arable acreage, Africa is overpopulated in some areas; the soil is poor; and productivity is low. Unlike parts of Europe and the Middle East, Africa does not have river systems which permit irrigation and the growth of towns.

Early History

The Africa which Europeans began to visit during the Age of Exploration was not a country or a seat of culture, but a massive continent three times the size of Europe.

Phoenician traders nearly 3000 years ago established Carthage, which ultimately dominated all of northwest Africa, and sailed down the east coast, 2000 years before Vasco da Gama. The Greeks founded Cyrenaica, between Egypt and Carthage. After the defeat of Carthage by Rome the area along the southern shores of the Mediterranean became a Roman province, Africa.

Subsequently the Arabs extended their influence across north Africa into Nigeria, leaving behind a great imprint, their Moslem religion. Today at least one-third of all Africans are Moslems.

Africa was generally bypassed by explorers and traders because it was difficult of access, had few harbors, and its mountain ranges and cataracts blocked progress into the interior by land and water. It remained the Dark Continent until the late 19th century. This name indicated Western ignorance about the continent. The industrial revolution with its need for raw materials and markets, and fields for investment, gave new impetus to interest in Africa. The industrial revolution also provided Europeans with the financial and technical means to conquer the African continent.

With the exception of the French acquisition of Algeria in the 1830's and the old Dutch settlement in South Africa, Europeans did not begin their colonization until after 1870. With their control over the Suez Canal and their authority over Egypt, the British began to expand, first into the Sudan and then into Nigeria. Belgium, France, Portugal, and Germany joined in the scramble for territorial possessions. By 1914 the entire continent was divided among European powers, with the exception of the independent nations of Abyssinia and Liberia. Under the guise of the "White Man's Burden," "Kultur," and other euphemisms, Africa was subjugated to foreign interests.

From 1900 to the early 1920's the influence of nationalism bypassed Africa, except for the Moslem lands along the Mediterranean.

World War II accelerated the process of change through native contact with outside influences. Not only did Africans acquire confidence in their abilities, but their colonial masters lost prestige. The natives began to appreciate their own strategic and economic importance, particularly their various resources of copper, tin, manganese, cobalt, gold, diamonds, and palm oil. The granting of independence to Libya in 1951 accelerated the demand for independence by other African colonies.

Kinds of Colonialism

Great Britain   For many years British policies were designed to grant ultimate independence, except for strategic bases such as Gibraltar and Aden. In many instances former British colonies have chosen to remain as independent nations within the British Commonwealth of Nations because financial and economic benefits work to their advantage.

Belgium   Belgian colonial rule was based upon increasing economic benefits for the natives. However, there was no self-government for anybody, including resident Belgians. Although there was no color bar, racial segregation was maintained in social life.

France   France claimed to support the policy of "assimilation," to make Frenchmen of all its colonial people. However, the French did not follow that policy for fear they would be assimilated by the Africans. The French did not practice segregation; they spent large sums of money to develop their colonies. Yet when the opportunity came, most French colonies preferred independence to assimilation.

Portugal and Spain Both nations, especially Portugal, ran their colonies as exploiters rather than as developers. While Portugal proclaimed nonsegregation, both nations practiced segregation and political control.

French Colonies

The French had trouble with their colonies immediately following the end of the war in 1945. The local revolt in Algeria, which lasted for eight years, and the serious revolt on the island of Madagascar, were resisted with sufficient brutality to discourage attempts at independence in other French colonies.

While the British were preparing their colonies for ultimate self-government and independence, the French were in theory ruling on the principle of French Identity, which stated that all colonial people enjoyed all the rights assured in the French constitution. This was the promise; the fact was that French rule was authoritarian and included the policy of forced labor. Despite postwar plans for granting universal adult suffrage and more mature participation in government, independence was far from a reality. Britain's granting of independence to Ghana in 1957 forced the French to act faster. When General de Gaulle returned to power in France in 1958, he ordered elections in all French Africa, in which every territory except Algeria could choose:

1. Complete independence.
2. To remain as a French colony or
3. To become a member of the French Community.

French Guinea chose independence; *French Somaliland* chose to remain a colony; and the other twelve became members of the French Community, which meant self-government, but the common concerns of foreign affairs, defense, and economic planning were administered by an executive committee of the heads of the member states. All were free to become fully independent at any time they chose.

France's hopes that African nations would remain within its jurisdiction were soon shattered. In 1960 the 13 member states of the French Community declared themselves independent republics, and in 1961 they were all recognized as such by the United Nations: Cameroon, Central African Republic, Chad, Congo Republic, Dahomey, Gabon, Ivory Coast, Malagasy, Mali, Niger, Senegal, Togo, and Upper Volta.

Belgian Colonies
Belgian Congo

The Belgians boasted that their colonial system was the best and the most enlightened. The Belgian Congo, one-third the size of the United States, was administered on the basis of economic and welfare development of the natives, but without any political rights of any kind for anyone, natives or Belgians. There were no representative institutions, no elections, and no voters. The Belgians were lulled into false security by believing that the high standard of living enjoyed by the natives was a substitute for political rights, and that the natives accepted the situation.

France's granting of independence to its possessions caused immediate reaction in the Belgian Congo, and shattered Belgium's concept of granting independence over the next hundred years. In 1958 the native manager of a Leopoldville brewery, *Patrice Lumumba*, heard de Gaulle speak in Brazzaville, in the French Congo. Leader of the radical wing of the Congolese National Movement, Lumumba attended an All Africa People's Conference in Ghana in December, 1958. On his return Lumumba spoke to a mass rally and demanded immediate independence for the Belgian Congo. Rioting broke out a week later in Leopoldville. The Belgians first tried repressive measures, then promised early reform, then suddenly panicked. On June 30, 1960, the Congolese received independence as the Republic of the Congo. After 5 days the Congolese army mutinied, the United Nations intervened, and the horrors of the massacres of and by natives were committed. The people had had absolutely no preparation for assuming the responsibilities of complete independence.

Parts of this Republic of the Congo (not to be confused with the Congo Republic), a country as large as the United States east of the Mississippi, declared their independence, and for five years the country was torn by civil war. In 1956 a tough paratrooper, Joseph Mobutu, staged a coup, seized power, and assumed dictatorial powers to give stability to the country. He renamed the country Zaire, the name by which the Congo River was formerly known. The word comes from the Bantu *nzari*, meaning river; in the 17th century the powerful Kingdom of the Congo controlled both banks of the river and called it the Congo.

Rwanda and Burundi In 1919 the former German colony of Ruanda-Urundi was given to Belgium as a mandate. Because of conflicts between the two main tribes, the Watusi and the Bahutu, Belgium divided the land in 1962 into the Republic of Rwanda and the Kingdom of Burundi. Although the Bahutu outnumbered the Watusi, they were traditionally the servants of the Watusi. Both nations were severely torn by internal strife. In Rwanda the Bahutus massacred thousands of Watusi, deliberately killing pregnant women; Watusi revenge was merciless. Educated Bahutus and their sons, many dragged out of schools, were shot, bayoneted, or beaten to death.

Portugal's Africa Colonies Worst run of all the colonial areas were the Portuguese colonies. The Portuguese claimed to follow a policy of *assimilation*, whereby the colonial areas were regarded as an integral part of Portugal and their inhabitants were considered Portuguese. An extraordinary point of view was that racial misunderstandings could be avoided by racial assimilation, a condition which only a small minority of natives could ever attain. If a native became literate in Portuguese, became a Christian, earned a stated minimum salary, and gave up all native customs, he could become an *assimilado* and enjoy complete social and political citizenship. Until he was allowed to become an assimilado he was an *indigena* or native, subject to completely different law and legally compelled to work for an employer for six months a year. According to the 1950 Portuguese census, fewer than one percent of the total population in Angola and Mozambique were assimilados.

In these "overseas possessions" — not colonies, Portugal claimed — guerrilla warfare continued into 1974. In that year General Antonio de Spinola, a former

Portuguese commander and military governor of Guinea-Bissau on the bulge of West Africa, recommended that Portugal's 500 years of colonialism in Africa be ended.

Independence for Portugal's Colonies

In 1974, General Antonio de Spinola proposed that Guinea-Bissau, Mozambique, and Angola be given a considerable degree of self-rule. For the pervious 13 years bitter guerrilla warfare had been fought in the colonies, costing a total of 5000 lives and $6 billion. At least 40 percent of Portugal's annual budget had been spent on the fighting, and 100,000 Portuguese youth fled from Portugal every year to avoid the draft. In April, 1974, the long years of dictatorship in Portugal ended with a coup by the military under General Spinola, and in August Portugal announced plans to begin the transference of power to its colonies.

The original plan had been to set up a federation of the three colonies, giving them a wide measure of self-rule but keeping them under the Portuguese flag. However, continued guerrilla fighting convinced Portugal to grant independence to these colonies.

Guinea-Bissau

Led by the African Party for the Independence of Guinea-Bissau and the Cape Verde Islands (the PAIGC) voters supported independence, which was granted in September, 1974. In 1975 the Cape Verde Islands voted to become part of Guinea-Bissau. Independence may not improve the country very much: it is very poorly developed; its 600,000 people are poorly educated; and it has virtually no industry or economic base.

Mozambique

The guerrillas who fought under the name of FRELIMO, Front for the Liberation of Mozambique, won independence on June 25, 1975 and set up a Marxist government. Its leader, Samora Machel, is a Marxist who intends to abolish capitalism and who denounces liberal democracy in any form. A new law permits the jailing of people for up to 8 years for the very vague crime of "sabotaging decolonization."

Thus, white-dominated, racist South Africa is bordered by a black Marxist regime, and Rhodesia may lose one of its last two outlets to the sea. However, Mozambique, which has a population of 8,000,000 blacks, is expected to provide 150,000 mineworkers for South Africa and to sell South Africa power from its giant Cabora Bassa hydroelectric plant. These two undertakings could earn Mozambique over $200 million a year. However, independence will almost certainly bring economic troubles. Mozambique's people already live at a subsistence level; Marxism has scared foreign capital away; and thousands of Portuguese technicans, teachers, doctors, and civil servants have fled the country.

Angola

This country, larger than Texas and California combined, but with only 6,000,000 people, is torn by fighting among the FNLA, MPLA, and UNITA. The Front for the Liberation of Angola (FNLA) has received help from Zaire, whose president is a relative of the FNLA's leader. The Popular Movement for the Liberation of Angola (MLPA) is Moscow-oriented and supported by the Portuguese Communist Party. The National Union for the Total Independence of Angola (UNITA) under the leadership of Jonas Savimbi, has wide popular support, including white Angolans who want to remain in the country.

All three colonies are ill prepared for independence because their people are largely illiterate and untrained in the difficult business of running an efficient government. A complicating factor is the tiny but potentially oil-wealthy enclave of Cabinda. A Portuguese protectorate since 1885, Cabinda was governed by the Portuguese from Angola. Only 2000 square miles in size, it is a wedge of land between Zaire and the Congo Republic. Its nearly 130 off-shore wells yield some 52,000,000 barrels of oil a year, which gives Portugal $400 million a year in royalties and taxes. Claims and counterclaims to Cabinda indicate future trouble.

British Colonies
Ghana

This was the first black African colony of a white nation to become independent. Formerly the colony of the Gold Coast, it was given independence on March 6, 1957; Kwame Nkrumah was its first prime minister. March 6, 1957 is a red-letter day for sub-Sahara Africa because Ghana's independence inspired other colonies to demand or seize independence. By the end of 1974 there were 35 black African nations south of the Sahara.

Nigeria

This former colony was hailed as the nation which could prove not only that Africans could rule themselves but also that several different tribes could live together as one nation. Its population of 60,000,000 was the largest of all colonial areas, and its city of Ibadan was the world's most populous all-black city.

The new nation of 250 tribes consisted basically of three areas and three dominant tribes, each jealous of and fearful of domination by the other two. The northern region is largely agricultural land belong to the Hausa tribe of 7,000,000. They are mostly Moslems who live under a semi-feudal system. The western region is an urban area of some 13,000,000 Yorubas. The eastern region is the home of some 8,000,000 Ibos, who were willing to spend nearly half of their public funds on education; they thus became the most educated people in Nigeria and filled important government positions and skilled occupations throughout Nigeria. Nigeria's first leader was Alhaji Balewa, a Hausa who formed a Hausa-dominated government which was corrupt, and unable to control inflation. Widespread discontent exploded in 1966 with the assassination of Balewa by Ibo army officers. A few months later the Hausas retaliated by killing the Ibo prime minister and scores of army officers. They savagely slaughtered more than 30,000 Ibos and maimed thousands more in the northern region. More than 1,250,000 Ibos fled in terror across the Niger River into their eastern homeland region, which they declared the independent nation of Biafra. For more than two-and-a-half years civil war reduced the Ibo region from 30,000 square miles to 3000 and its population to 3,000,000. Biafra surrendered in January, 1970, to General Yakuba Gowon, leader of the Federal Nigerian government, who declared general pardon "for all those misled into attempting to disintegrate the country." Oil discovered in 1966 is expected to yield $7 billion of income yearly within a decade. This money is necessary to remedy poverty, primitive roads, and the lack of professional people. In May, 1975, General Gowon was deposed by a coup d'état led by Brigadier Muritala Mohammed. In February, 1976, Mohammed was assassinated.

Kenya

In the 1950's a bitter conflict broke out between the natives and the white settlers, who had closed to the natives 5,000,000 acres of very fertile White Highlands. This area is the home of about 1,250,000 of the Kikuyu tribe, who bitterly resented the loss of their traditional lands. In 1953 the Kikuyus and other Africans organized the terrorist Mau Mau, whose slogan *Uhuru* is the Swahili word for freedom. This group forced Africans to kill white settlers. In two years of terrorist activities, 500 security officers, 7000 Mau Mau members, and 1300 civilians lost their lives. Only 50 European civilians were killed; the others were Africans who refused to cooperate with the Mau Mau.

In December, 1963, Kenya was given independence. Jomo Kenyatta, who had been accused of being the Mau Mau leader and who had been jailed by the British for several years, became Kenya's first prime minister, and later its first president. Kenyatta claimed that Kenya would become a multiracial country in which Africans, Europeans, Asiatics, and Arabs would live together as one nation.

Hopes have dimmed for Kenya's becoming a peaceful and successful multiracial nation. In 1970 over 1000 Asian businessmen were ordered to close their operations, and the requisitioning of the White Highlands has begun by orders to Europeans to sell their lands to the Ministry of Lands and Settlements. Kenya's problems are undoubtedly the reason for this change. The population growth rate of 3.3 percent a year will double the population in 21 years. In 1973, 48 percent of all Kenyans were under 15 years of age; this means that education costs are soaring. In addition, the "Kenyanization" of trade and businesses is clearly a divisive issue.

Tanzania

This nation is a union of what had been Tanganyika and Zanzibar. Tanganyika became independent in 1961, Zanzibar in 1963. In 1964 the two countries decided to form the single nation of Tanzania.

Other former British colonies which have become independent nations are Botswana, Gambia, Lesotho, Malawi, Sierra Leone, Somali, Sudan, and Uganda.

The Republic of South Africa

The former Union of South Africa, once a member of the British Commonwealth is now a completely independent and separate entity as the Republic of South Africa. This nation is the outstanding example of *apartheid* in action, the separation of the races politically and economically. South Africa is in effect a compartmentalized society in which each racial group, white and native, lives separately, has separate kinds of work, separate levels of wages, and separate standards of education.

In 1971 the population was estimated at 22,000,000, of whom 15,645,000 were Africans or natives, 4,000,000 were whites (40 percent "English-speaking" of English descent, and 60 percent *Afrikaners* of Dutch descent), and the rest were Coloreds of mixed blood, and Asiatics.

The policy of apartheid or separation is not a new one. The Dutch settlers of the 18th and 19th centuries believed in "baasskap" or boss-hood, simply white domination. The modern form of apartheid is the result of conditions that developed in the 1920's and 1930's. Most of the Afrikaners, who knew only Africa as their home, were farmers whose methods were traditionally to move on to new land when their soil was exhausted. By the end of World War I there was virtually no more free land, and a "poor-white" class developed, consisting of farmers who could no longer make a living from the land as owners or even as sharecroppers. By the early 1930's some 20 percent of the Afrikaners were unemployed. This situation made so deep an impression on Afrikaner political thinking that laws were enacted to ensure that the situation did not occur again. Between 1925 and 1940 great numbers of Afrikaners were absorbed into government jobs restricted to whites. The white man was made secure from black competition by receiving wages based upon his needs as a "civilized person," and not at the competitive market rate paid to Africans, sometimes a rate of 10 to 1 for the same work. Farming is conducted increasingly by black men on farms owned by white men who work for the government.

The Afrikaner believes, or at least practices, the principle that nationalism is white supremacy, and that compromise not only makes no sense, but would be a betrayal of principle. Against what he regards as the "black menace," the Afrikaner is ready to use any means necessary.

Complete apartheid would logically mean the separation of the country into two parts, one for the whites, the other for the blacks. But since native labor is needed, apartheid is racial rather than physical separation. This is achieved by (1) stripping the African of all political rights, (2) dictating where he may live, (3) determining what kind of work he may do, (4) denying him work completely if he resists restrictions, and (5) obliging him to carry at all times a "pass-book" which lists his personal details, restricts his movements unless authorized, prevents his leaving a job, and keeps him under very close control.

Various acts passed by parliament give the government complete control over all citizens. It can suppress all criticism, order a person under house arrest for months or years at a time and deny him the right to visit or have visitors, dole out to the natives whatever little education it may decide upon, and repress the natives to the point where outright rebellion may afford the only relief from a repression which must engender its own violent reaction.

Apartheid should not be equated with discrimination against blacks as in some communities in the United States, for at least blacks have the law on their side in the United States. In the Republic of South Africa complete segregation is enforced by every means at the disposal of the state. Riots by blacks occurred in Soweto, a black "dormitory" outside Johannesburg, and also on the outskirts of Cape Town. Some observers believe that these riots indicate growing impatience by the blacks, and the beginning of continued violence, particularly by the impatient young blacks. It is believed that Vorster is putting pressure on Ian Smith, Premier of Rhodesia, to give political rights to Rhodesian blacks because Vorster fears that violence in Rhodesia could spread rapidly to South Africa.

What does the future hold for South Africa? The independence of almost all of Africa will not make the situation any easier. South Africa is the symbol of everything to which the African objects, and it may be that action against white domination will come from outside the country. The whites cannot maintain a monopoly of power, yet they refuse to permit the Africans to participate. Ultimately only the possession of political power will satisfy the Africans. World opinion has become increasingly critical of this contradiction in a decade in which independence and political rights have been achieved by 35 African nations. In early 1960 British Prime Minister *Harold Macmillan* toured Africa and said at a meeting of parliament in the Republic of South Africa, "The wind of change is blowing through this continent. Whether we like it or not this growth of national consciousness is a fact."

The "Homelands" Policy

Although the independence of Portugal's black colonies may cause South Africa to become less racist, the issue of apartheid remains. Prime Minister Vorster's determination to retain apartheid and the increasing demands by blacks for a more effective role in the nation's affairs have simply speeded up the creation of more Bantustans, which are separate regions for the natives. South Africa still restricts blacks and silences potential political leaders by jailing them. The Terrorism Act of 1967 makes it a capital offense to "cause, encourage or further feelings of hostility between white and other inhabitants."

This so-called "homelands policy" is an attempt to consolidate 50 fragments of land given to the blacks into 9 "homelands," in effect 9 independent black nations within South Africa. This division reserves 86 percent of the land for the 4,000,000 whites and gives the remaining 14 percent — the poorest land — to the 15,000,000 blacks. This policy of separate "nationhoods" for blacks avoids giving equal citizenship and basic rights to nonwhites.

There is almost no danger of "liberation guerrillas" within South Africa because black nationalist leaders and organizations have been suppressed and the whites control a highly efficient security service of police and armed forces. What can threaten South Africa and Rhodesia — the only two white-controlled nations in sub-Sahara Africa — is black opposition from outside.

Rhodesia

Until 1923 Southern and Northern Rhodesia were two possessions of the British South Africa Company. After 1923 Southern Rhodesia (population 70,000 whites and 1,500,000 Africans) was given semi-dominion status; only whites were allowed to vote. Northern Rhodesia remained a crown colony (15,000 whites, 1,400,000 Africans) and Nyasaland was a protectorate (population 2000 whites, 1,300,000 Africans).

After World War II the Africans of Northern Rhodesia and Nyasaland began to demand freedom. The white population asked for assistance and the British suggested federation.

In 1953 the three areas became the Central African Federation. However, agitation for independence increased during the late 1950's and in 1963 the federation was dissolved. Northern Rhodesia became an independent Republic of Zambia; Nyasaland became the independent Republic of Malawi; and Southern Rhodesia became a self-governing member of the British Commonwealth as Rhodesia. Rhodesia was denied independence by the British government because its white minority of 275,000 refused to allow the black majority of 6,000,000 full participation in the government. In 1965 Prime Minister Ian Smith issued a Unilateral Declaration of Independence (UDI). Britain tried to persuade other nations to join it in an economic boycott on exports and imports to Rhodesia, but the boycott was only partially successful.

After years of agitation by blacks for participation in government, in 1971 the British government sent a special commission, which believed it had persuaded the blacks of Rhodesia to accept a program of gradual progress toward majority rule. But since "gradual" actually meant "in seventy years," the blacks not unexpectedly rejected the plan by 99 to 1. One significant consequence of the British Commission was that black political parties, previously banished, were allowed to organize as a means of gauging black opinion. The African National Council (AFN) became the "sole voice and instrument of the black masses." Ian Smith's reaction was to recommend to his white supporters separate economic development of white and black areas — a plan to segregate the races.

In December, 1973, Smith proposed a constitutional conference to discuss the issue of political rights for blacks. Later he arrested the leader of the AFN; this effectively scuttled the proposed conference.

The ANC consists of two major groups, the Zimbabwe African People's Union (ZAPU) and the more militant Zimbabwe African National Union (ZANU). Zimbabwe is the African name for Rhodesia. ZAPU supports a negotiated settlement with the government; ZANU favors continued guerrilla warfare. In June, 1975, both groups played into the hands of the government when they met to discuss tactics in future talks with Ian Smith. Supporters of the two rival groups clashed, fights broke out, and a crowd of ZANU's pelted police with stones. The police fired at the rioters and later at others who smashed cars and looted stores in other black townships.

In Geneva in October, 1976, a conference was convened between Ian Smith and Rhodesian blacks to discuss Rhodesia's political future. The purpose of the Geneva Conference is to find a formula for transferring political power from Rhodesia's 275,000 whites to its 6,000,000 blacks, a transfer which is supposed to occur within two years.

A serious stumbling-block to the transfer of political power from whites to blacks is the interim control of the important ministries of Defense and Justice, in effect the military and the courts. The British negotiator Ivor Richards has suggested four possible alternatives:

1. Direct control of both ministries by a Briton,

2. Control of the two ministries by a committee composed equally of Rhodesian whites and blacks, with a neutral chairman, presumably a Briton,

3. Control of one ministry by a black, the other by a Rhodesian white,

4. Control of both ministries by a Rhodesian white who is not a member of the governing Rhodesian Front.

Smith has consistently demanded control by whites of both ministries. Blacks do not trust Smith, whom they think is simply stalling for time. Prime Minister Vorster will probably continue to put pressure on Smith, fearing that violence in Rhodesia would spread to South Africa. Rhodesia is now a republic, with no ties to Great Britain, although neither Great Britain nor the United Nations recognizes it.

Backgrounds of African Nationalism

One of the causes of some of the problems of modern Africa is that colonialism carved out possessions without regard to geography, economics, or tribal boundaries. There was, of course, no sense of nationalism among the natives; they were bound only by tribal loyalties. The tribe was the political unit; law and simple government were run by tribal custom. Colonial administration was generally indirect and through existing chieftains who were allowed to retain some of their authority in return for support of the colonial power. In time colonial rule broke down tribal relationships because the authority of the chiefs was undermined, and no native form of government was substituted.

The British did attempt to train their colonial areas in participation in government, and left behind them a respect for legal procedures. One of the problems, vividly represented in the former Belgian Congo, is that tribal loyalties have tended to fragment areas and create disunity. Consequently, the emergent nations, about 35 since 1957, have faced problems of loyalty and nationalism. African nationalism has been anticolonial rather than pro-African; colonial areas wished to be free from European domination, whether political or economic. Recent experience has shown that mere independence is no guarantee of improvement for the natives. The emergent nations are eager to develop quickly, especially economically, because their people are motivated by the "revolution of rising expectations." This is the belief that independence would bring improved standards of living and educational opportunities.

It would be a mistake to assume that international communism will be successful in Africa. These new nations have not thrown off their colonial masters to accept dictation from other powers. Russian methods may attract them because Russia has made such great economic strides in only 50 years. African nations may decide that socialism is the best method of economic development, but that by no means indicates willingness to accept Russian influence.

Problems of Independent Nations

Some black leaders, especially Nkrumah, had hoped that Pan-Africanism, some type of federation of several black African nations, would be possible. But struggles for power among national leaders leave little hope for this in the near future.

Another difficult problem is the reconciliation of divisive tribal traditions and nationally unity. The savage civil war in Nigeria illustrates this. With few exceptions, ethnic group loyalties, religion, and language are stronger than nationalism in Africa.

Of the 34 former colonies which are independent black nations, 18 were under military rule in 1975. For example, Nigeria was promised a return to civilian rule, but this has been postponed on the grounds of "serious ethnic and regional discord." In Equatorial Guinea and the Central African Republic the leaders have been declared presidents for life.

Effective opposition parties — necessary for democratic parliamentary government — are rare in black African nations. In some, opposition parties are not allowed and in others they are so weak that they are ineffective. Political independence did not bring the great "new life" that new African nations expected, and the experience of corruption, favoritism, and incompetence has resulted in this realization expressed by a Zaire official, "Control and discipline are vital in Africa . . . Without these you have no government."

A critical factor is that developing nations have little capital to spend on industrial development and modern agricultural methods. Dictatorships and military rule do not encourage capital investment. The fourfold increase in the price of oil by the monopolistic OPEC nations seriously affected several developing nations, whose income from their exports could not pay for the oil so necessary for their industrial development.

One of the main issues that must be squarely faced by the industrial West and

OPEC is that they have not only the moral but also the economic and political responsibility for the development of the underdeveloped nations.

Latin America Today

Terms

Hacienda	Caudillo	Cientificos
Fazenda	Alliance for Progress	Mexicanidad
Campesinos	Bay of Pigs	

People

Juan Peron	Fulgenico Batista	Luis Echeverria
Salvador Allende	Fidel Castro	
Augusto Pinochet	Porfirio Diaz	

Topic Outline
General Trends
Social Structure
   The Hacienda
   Urban Workers
Politics and the Military
Economic Problems
Alliance for Progress
Argentina
Brazil
Chile
Cuba
Mexico

Latin America Today

General Trends

The 1950's saw revolutionary changes accelerate in Latin American politics and economics. Dictators in Argentina, Columbia, Peru, and Venezuela were thrown out, and in Cuba the revolution against Batista proceeded. When the decade ended, the great majority of the people in Latin America participated in elections, but the 1960's ushered in a period in which extremist groups appeared; Castro's revolt is one example. Only time will tell whether the United States can further democracy in Latin America by supporting the moderates, or whether Castro-type leaders have more appeal. Several factors may favor the radical groups. One factor is that of the "imperialism" charge against the United States. This is sometimes a device used to assign the blame easily instead of examining internal conditions. In many parts of the continent the wealth is held by a small proportion of the population. In some areas almost feudal conditions of land ownership survive. Land hunger is a bitter issue, since land reforms of the Mexican type — the distribution of haciendas or landed estates to the peasants — have been discussed but very rarely implemented. Too many people sense the "revolution of rising expectations," and realize that they do not have to accept conditions as they are. Unless moderate changes are introduced, radical ones may result; some observers believe that social and economic change cannot come about without revolution.

The United States is vitally concerned with the future of Latin America and realizes that a mature and thoughtful policy must replace the older policy of "keeping the Latin Americans in line."

A beginning was made by the United States during the Coolidge administration. The Clark Memorandum of 1928 specifically repudiated the Roosevelt Corollary of 1904, which sanctioned intervention in Latin American affairs when the United States thought it necessary. The United States now reverted to the policy of the Monroe Doctrine, which tried to keep Europe out of the Western Hemisphere. This was followed in the late 1930's by Franklin Roosevelt's "Good Neighbor" policy of respecting the rights of others, through which the United States hoped to improve relations with Latin America. The United States is obliged to recognize basic problems in Latin America and to establish its policy accordingly.

Social Structure
The Hacienda

The commanding figure in the political, social, and economic life of Latin America has been the great landowner, the *patron*. The farm worker has been (and is) a sharecropper who, in general, was allowed to cultivate a small piece of land sufficient, or nearly so, to feed his family. In return he had to work a certain number of days each week on the patron's land or in his house. The *hacienda* (*fazenda* in Brazil), was not only the large agricultural estate but was (and still is in some places) a self-contained community that determines the lives of its people. It is the home and the livelihood of the peasants, who see nothing of the outside world and have no contact with government or national politics. As Latin American nations are becoming more industrialized, the traditional hacienda system is declining. Landowners see greater opportunity in banking, mining, and other businesses, and peasants are moving into industrial towns.

The Urban Worker

Many of the unskilled workers live in vast shanty towns which ring the great cities. These include the *favelas* of Rio and the *barrios* of Caracas, into which people from the countryside have poured, hoping to find work. Grim though conditions may be, the people living there are better off than the *campesinos*, those living in the *campo*, the countryside. Many millions of these country people live in chronic hunger, almost never seeing such luxuries as meat, eggs, and milk.

Industrialization is a force for change. In general, the urban working class is increasing three times as fast as the rural population. Mexico City has more than 7 million people, and Saõ Paulo in Brazil, with over 6 million, is the fastest growing city in the world.

Politics and the Military

On a national scale and in government the *patron* system operates in much the same way as the hacienda. There can be little comparison with the party system of the United States, because Latin America has always followed the tradition of loyalty to a person, not to a party. Industrialization is changing this because the interests of different groups in an industrial society are not basically the same.

When Spanish control ended in the early 19th century, the very real threat of anarchy made loyalty to a leader necessary. The *caudillo,* the political boss or leader, expected devoted loyalty from his supporters, and in return he gave protection, jobs, and a generous share of the spoils. Landowners and business-men are generally less concerned with direct participation in politics as long as their interests are protected.

In a political sense the military has played an important role in Latin America. Historically the army has not been limited to military functions; in the early days of nationhood it helped to maintain order and helped carry out civic programs such as communications and transportation systems. Intervention by the milit-ary, armed coups, removal of civilian governments by generals, and rule by uniformed dictators have all been common experiences of most Latin American countries. By 1970 well over half of the people of Latin America were under military rule. Because the rank and file of the military are from the working and peasant classes, the army may play a larger part in politics in the future.

Economic Problems   Population growth is becoming increasingly a serious problem in Latin America, and elsewhere. Medical science has reduced infant mortality and extended life expectancy to the point where annual population growth has almost doubledd, to 2.7 percent. In 1973 the population of Latin America was 290,000,000. Since economic development is not keeping pace with population increases, both agricultural production and per capita income have declined in recent years.

Another serious factor is the widening gulf between lower and middle classes in regard to income. Brazil is attempting a breakthrough by developing its interior, but at a financial cost that few other Latin American countries can afford.

The economy of the *hacienda*, the large landed estate, has delayed economic progress throughout Latin America. A self-sufficient economic unit much like medieval European feudalism, the hacienda has been as "local" in outlook as was the feudal village.

The landowners, fewer than ten percent of the population, owned almost all the arable land of Latin America, and retained their hold through predominance in the national legislature, the military, and the professions.

Neither peasants nor urban workers have sufficient buying power to create demand for manufactured goods and to increase the productive power of the countries. Another handicap common to most of Latin America is that most of its nations depend upon raw materials — coffee, wheat, meat, minerals, and the like — and the sales of these materials upon the world market are affected by competition from other nations. The fall in price of a cent or two in a pound of coffee, for example, can result in the loss of millions of dollars a year for a nation such as Colombia.

Foreign businessmen have been reluctant to invest money in Latin America. This is partly because of frequent changes in government, sometimes by force, and partly because political instability and economic stress may result in the failure of Latin American governments to meet their obligations. Sometimes they may go as far as to expropriate foreign property.

Another basic problem of Latin America is its tremendous need for internal development and for some kind of common market arrangement. Industrial development will be limited until manufactured goods can be transported to consumers and until consumers can afford to buy them. The desperate need is for roads, irrigation projects, and improved agricultural techniques. When the peasant has capital in the form of surplus crops and surplus income then, but not until then, can he improve his condition, consume more goods, and create more demand for manufactured goods. Unless economic assistance can remedy these fundamental problems, it will be of little use to simply give monetary aid without careful organizing.

Attempts have been made for closer cooperation among the nations of the Western Hemisphere, from the Pan-American Union of 1910 to the Organization of American States of 1951. These groups have discussed matters of common interest and have attempted to coordinate diplomatic and military interests.

Alliance For Progress

The purpose of the Alliance, which was proposed by the United States during the Eisenhower administration and initiated under President Kennedy in 1961, was to help the Latin American countries emerge from their economic underdevelopment. It was to be "a vast effort unparalleled in magnitude and nobility of purpose, to satisfy the basic needs of the people for houses, work, and land." The intention was to make the wealthy pay the cost of necessary assistance. Estimates in 1961 were $100 billion for the next 10 years; 80 percent was to come from Latin America, 10 percent from the United States, and 10 percent from other sources. Unfortunately, results have disappointed hopes. By 1971 the economic growth of Latin America was only 1.5 percent instead of the modest 2.5 percent which had been hoped for. Critics of the United States charge that the Alliance was simply a new form of Yankee imperialism—perhaps a useful excuse for domestic failures.

Argentina

Argentina has the largest and most highly developed trade unions in Latin America, and they became the base of Colonel Juan Peron's political power. Peron had seen the political power of organized workers in Europe, and when the military in Argentina took power by a coup iin 1943, he asked for the modest position of secretary for labor and welfare. He secured increases in wages, bonuses, and welfare benefits for the workers. The General Confederation of Labor became a powerful political weapon. When Peron became minister for war and vice-president of the Republic, his opponents in the army and middle class dismissed and imprisoned him in 1945. His wife Evita, popular with the poor, and the peronista labor leaders threatened a general strike. The government yielded and in a new election Peron won 57 percent of the votes and became president, the caudille.

An exhausted post-World War II Europe needed vast supplies of beef and grain, and Peron sold these at exorbitant prices. He used the profits to boost workers' wages and welfare benefits and to finance the Five-Year Plan (1947-51) to extend industrialization.

Peron had the constitution amended to give him a second term, but galloping inflation and strong-arm police methods against his critics resulted in a coup which forced him into exile in 1955. Conditions worsened in Argentina, which was then without unified leadership. Rising unemployment and a threefold increase in the cost of living resulted in numerous coups. Nineteen years after he left for Argentina, Peron returned as president. He lived for a year, and was survived by his second wife, Isabel, who succeeded him as president. Faced with political terrorism among parties and increasing inflation, she was forced to yield to workers' demands for a wage increase of over 100 percent.

Brazil

Brazilians believe that if any Latin American country will ever reach "great power" status, it will be their nation. Portuguese-speaking, with a population of 100,000,000 and an area of 3,000,000 square miles, it is roughly equal to all the Spanish-speaking countries of South America combined.

The capital city of Brazilia, 600 miles from Rio de Janeiro, was built partly for the purpose of developing the interior of the country.

The turning point in Brazil's recent history came in 1964 with a military coup against President Goulart, who had tried to become Brazil's Peron. The military believed that social dissolution had been threatened by Goulart's policies. Congress was forced to change the constitution, and despite protests by urban terrorists, the military retained power and reduced inflation by 25 percent.

Chile

Chile's vast nitrate and copper resources led to the rise of a working class that could use its votes and its power to strike as a means to win some benefits for itself. Despite a welfare system of medical aid and old age pensions, Chileans workers remained poor. Their per capita income in recent years was less than $700 a year.

After World War II Chile suffered from a severe drop in the price of copper and nitrates, from rampant inflation, and from an out-of-date agricultural system based on the hacienda. Peasants left the land and came to the cities, where there were very few jobs. Consequently, the Communist Party had wide appeal and supported the socialist politician, Salvador Allende.

In the 1970 election, Allende campaigned on a Marxist platform of nationalization of major industries and the takeover of foreign businesses. He won with a plurality of only 36 percent, against the National Party's 35 percent and the Christian Democrats' 28 percent. The Christian Democrats joined with Allende's socialists and communists for a combined 64 percent of the vote. Under the constitution the legislature had to choose the president, because no party had a majority. It chose Allende, the first freely elected Marxist in the history of Latin America. However, he was actually elected by only one-third of the voting public. Despite this modest vote, Allende proceeded as though he had widespread support.

Foreign capital was scared away from the Marxist government, and the middle class feared a completely communist regime, for Allende hinted at replacing Congress with a single-chamber "Assembly of the People" as a new stage in "building socialism."

Military Takeover,
September, 1973

Searing inflation; shortages of food; and crippling strikes by trucking firms, shopkeepers, and copper miners threatened economic chaos that Allende could not control. An unsuccessful coup by the military in June, 1973, was followed by a successful one in September. When the military's demend for Allende's resignation was refused, the military attacked the presidential palace with tanks and planes, bombed factories held by workers, and arrested thousands of people with unnecessary brutality. Allende refused the army's offer of safe conduct out of Chile, and either shot himself or was murdered in the palace by the military. Allende was partly to blame for his own political downfall — not his death — because he made two serious mistakes. He ignored the fact that two-thirds of the country had not voted for him, and he assumed that the middle class would let him proceed with "Chilean socialism."

The military installed General Auguste Pinochet as president; however, more than a year later Chile's economic problems remained largely unsolved and the country was literally a police state. Copper prices dropped, and although inflation was reduced to 350 percent a year, nearly 20 percent of the population suffered from "extreme poverty," and the unemployment rate was 10 percent.

Cuba

In 1934 an army sergeant, Fulgencio Batista, led a revolt and set up puppet presidents. Batista set up a new constitution in 1940 and easily won the presidential election for a four-year term. He made a deal with the communists: they would support him in return for control of the labor movement. He gave the communists two positions in the government; this was the first time in Latin American history that communists held cabinet rank. Batista, the mulatto sergeant, was caught between two desires:

1. To be a man of the people and a great democratic leader.
2. To amass wealth and power in the caudille tradition.

Batista was sent into exile in 1944 but returned and organized his army followers, seized power, and became increasingly dictatorial, using brutal police tyranny against critics. Opposition to him grew, particularly from the University of Havana, where Fidel Castro was a law student. On July 26, 1953, Castro and a group of followers failed in an attempt to storm the Moncado barracks in Santiago. Castro fled, later gave himself up, received a 15-year sentence, and was pardoned in 1955. He left Cuba, trained his men in Mexico, and landed on the east coast of Cuba in December, 1956. Only a handful of his men escaped from Batista's troops. Those who did escape went into the Sierra Maestra mountains, where peasants supported them. Castro's followers gradually increased to 2000. Batista's 40,000 troops lost their morale in the mountain guerrilla fighting; Batista fled, and Castro entered Havana on January 8, 1959.

Castro's middle-class supporters, who saw him as a land reformer, believed that Cuba would now return to the democratic process, individual liberties, and social justice of the 1940 constitution. They soon found that Castro was a supporter of the political and economic system of the Soviet Union. Tenant farmers were given full ownership of the land they worked; house rents were halved; wages and salaries were raised by 25 percent; and prices were reduced. Castro won increasing popularity for raising the living standards of the poor.

Castro became the typical caudillo and took into his own hands all the reins of power — the army, the secret police, the judiciary, the press, and the nationwide groups known as Committees for the Defense of the Revolution. Cuba is a military dictatorship, although it claims not to be. The attempt of refugee

Cubans, with limited United States support, to overthrow Castro in 1961 resulted in the disastrous Bay of Pigs invasion. That same year diplomatic relations between the United States and Cuba were broken off after Castro took over U.S.-owned sugar estates, public utilities, banks, and refineries without compensating the owners, and declared that his revolution was "exportable." He called upon young revolutionaries in South America to "turn the Andes into the Sierra Maestra of Latin America."

By 1962, after the nationalization of agriculture, crop production decreased, food supplies declined, and there was a general drop in productivity and in living standards. Almost all foods — meats, fats, fish, eggs, milk, and bread — and clothing were rationed.

In recent years Castro has indicated that Cuba would consider renewing diplomatic relations with the United States.

Mexico

In 1910 a revolution changed Mexico from a dictatorship, which had shown no interest in the condition of the people, to a government which has attempted to remedy the inequities of the 19th century. In 1876 a mestizo, Porfirio Diaz, seized dictatorial power. For more than 30 years he ran Mexico on the theory that the nation's salvation would be the capital and skills of foreign investors. The *cientificos*, the managerial group that advised Diaz, believed in the superiority of whites over natives; Diaz, they said, "had the soul of a white man." The cientificos attracted foreign capital, which by 1910 totaled at least two-thirds of all Mexico's investments. Crops were produced for export rather than for domestic use. As a result, the peasants faced starvation; their life expectancy was 30 years, and more than 40 percent of all children died before their first birthday from malnutrition and disease.

The 1910 revolution was the result of a deep hatred for everything Diaz stood for. It consisted of a series of explosions that continued for 10 years and killed at least 2,000,000 people. The revolution was fought with the determination to replace "Diaz-potism" with:

1. The right to vote.

2. No reelection of a president.

3. The right of workers to organize with state protection.

4. The cult of *Mexicanidad*, whose purpose was to remove foreign privileges and control the nation's natural resources.

By the 1930's foreign oil concerns were expropriated, and in succeeding decades one-third of the land came under the control of Mexican villages. Industrialization increased so greatly after World War II that Mexico was no longer considered a "developing" country.

In 1970 Luis Echeverria was elected president and launched a vigorous drive to tackle corruption and rural poverty. On December 1, 1976, Hose Lopez Portillo was elected to serve a six-year term as president. But Mexico still suffers from a wide gap between the wealthy and the urban and rural poor. The one-party political system does not allow for a real implementation of popular opinion, and although the president has great executive power, he is restricted by the political system which elects him. He cannot make politically unpopular decisions which he might think are essential for the nation's economic well being.

Post-1945 Conferences, Pacts, Treaties, Organizations

AOP   **Alliance for Progress (1961)**
Some $20 billion of public and private financing for Latin America to provide economic growth. Instituted by President Eisenhower.

Baghdad Pact (1955)
The United States sponsored, but did not join, this group consisting of Great Britain, Turkey, Iran, Iraq, and Pakistan, in a military alliance to serve as a barrier against Russian aggression.

Bandung Conference (1955)
At Bandung, Indonesia, representatives of 23 African and Asian nations met to form a united front of peoples of these countries as a counterweight to the West. However, these nations soon realized that colonialism was far less an issue than was the relationship of Communist China with its neighbors.

CENTO   **Central Treaty Organization (1959)**
The name given to the former Baghdad Pact after the withdrawal of Iraq in 1959.

Colombo Plan (1950)   (Sometimes referred to as Point 4)
A plan to raise capital in the West, originally to assist Asian nations, later extended to other countries. Beneficiaries were India, Pakistan, Nepal, Burma, Thailand, North Vietnam, South Vietnam, Malaysia, Indonesia, the Philippines, Australia, Laos, and Cambodia.

EDC   **European Defense Community**
An unsuccessful attempt to form a common defense organization in which the armed forces suplied by member nations were to be under centralized control. France objected to such an army, which would include German officers and men.

EEC   **European Economic Community or Common Market (1957)**
By the Treaty of Rome the six member states of the Schuman Plan agreed to establish a customs union within 15 years to (a) gradually abolish all trade barriers among themsleves, and (b) establish common tariff policy with all other nations. Great Britain joined in 1973.

EFTA   **European Free Trade Association or Outer Seven (1959)**
Great Britain, Austria, Denmark, Norway, Sweden, Switzerland, and Portugal agreed to cut tariffs among themselves, although no agreement was made to have a common tariff policy with other nations. Finland joined in 1961.

European Coal and Steel Community (1951)
Coal and steel production of France, Italy, Belgium, the Netherlands, Luxembourg, and West Germany placed under the jurisdiction of the organization for 50 years.

IGY   **International Geophysical Year (1957–1958)**
An 18-month study by 66 nations of the environment of man — earth, oceans, and outerspace — particularly successful in joint projects in Antarctica, where 11 nations established many bases.

NATO   **North Atlantic Treaty Organization (1949)**
An association consisting of the United States, Canada, Great Britain, France, Belgium, the Netherlands, Luxembourg, Norway, Denmark, Iceland, Italy, and Portugal, to protect the principles of democracy and law and to protect the signatories from armed aggression by the U.S.S.R. Turkey, Greece, and West Germany joined later.

SHAPE, Supreme Headquarters of Allied Powers in Europe, is its operational body.

The forces of NATO remain under the control of the individual nations supplying them.

OAS   **Organization of American States (1948)**
This grew out of the earlier Pan-American Union. Members are nations of the Western Hemisphere. The Council can call meetings of ministers of foreign affairs to discuss issues of common concern. In 1964 the resolution of 20 OAS members called for mandatory sanctions against Cuba. Sanctions were lifted by the OAS in 1975.

Schuman Plan (1951)
Proposal by Robert Schuman, French foreign minister, that the entire production of steel and iron by France and Germany be placed under one authority, with no trade barriers between the two. Was to be open to other nations to join.

SEATO   **South East Asia Treaty Organization (1954)**
United States, Great Britain, Australia, New Zealand, the Philippines, and Thailand organized in defense against communist aggression in South East Asia. Headquarters were in Bangkok, Thailand. In October, 1975, Secretary of State Kissinger and representatives of the active SEATO members decided that "in view of the new situation in the South East Asian region [the alliance] should be phased out."

Tashkent Conference (1966)
This was called by the U.S.S.R. in that country to attempt to resolve the Indian-Pakistan controversy over Kashmir. A cease-fire was arranged and India and Pakistan agreed to attempt to resolve the issue peacefully.

Warsaw Pact (1955)
The communist countries of Eastern Europe (except Yugoslavia) — U.S.S.R., Poland, Bulgaria, Czechoslovakia, Hungary, Rumania, and East Germany, signed a 20-year mutual defense treaty.

UNRRA   **United Nations Relief and Rehabilitation Administration (1943–1947)**
A relief organization to assist suffering people, not nations as such.
Distributed $4 billion of supplies; 90 percent of the goods and 72
percent of the costs were paid by the United States.

Terms and Definitions

Absolutism   The doctrine or practice of government unrestricted by representation or another means.

AFN   See African National Council

African National Council   Political organization of the blacks of Rhodesia demanding political rights. See **Zanu, Zapu**

African Party for the Independence of Guinea-Bissau and the Cape Verde Islands   Those supporting independence for these two Portuguese colonies. Cape Verde subsequently declared itself independent.

Afrikaner   A member of the white race in the Republic of South Africa. The language, Afrikaans, originates from the early Dutch settlers. Natives are designated as Africans or Bantus.

Afro-Asian (Bandung) Conference   Held in April, 1955, it was the first international conference of African and Asian peoples. Participants were Ethiopia, Gold Coast (later Ghana), Egypt, Lebanon, Libya, Saudi Arabia, Sudan, Syria, Turkey, Yemen, Afghanistan, Iran, Iraq, Jordan, Cambodia, Ceylon, People's Republic of China, India, Indonesia, Japan, Laos, Nepal, Pakistan, the Philippines, Thailand, North Vietnam, and South Vietnam. The conference passed resolutions condemning imperialism, supporting self-determination, and economic and cultural cooperation.

Agency for International Development (AID)   A U.S. government agency to administer economic assistance schemes.

Alliance for Progress (Alianza para el Progreso)   A United States sponsored and assisted movement, supported by 20 Latin American countries to coordinate and develop Latin American economics and to raise the standard of living.

Amnesty   Pardon for political offenders, although the term is sometimes used to include tax violators.

Anarchism   Political doctrine of individualists who advocate the elimination of organized government. In pure theory, anarchists believe that people are so inherently good that rules are unnecessary. Anarchists have performed independent acts of violence. The term is derived from the Greek **anarchia**, meaning nonrule.

Anschluss   The union of Austria with Germany, resulting from the occupation of Austria by the German army in 1938. Austria was actually absorbed into Germany as Ostmark.

Anti-Clericalism   Opposition to organized religion. The name for any policy which wishes to subordinate the church to the state.

Apartheid   Pronounced apart-ite, it literally means "apart-ness." It is the policy of the whites in the Republic of South Africa of literal segregation of blacks from whites. The natives have no rights other than those granted by the whites. Apartheid is complete racial inequality.

Appeasement   The making of concessions to an adversary in the hopes of avoiding trouble. Usually a policy of acting from weakness. It is not synonymous with compromise, a policy in which each adversary makes concessions to the other but also wins gains.

Arab League   A loose confederation or association of Arab countries, reflecting Arab nationalist sentiments. Has consistently opposed the existence of Israel and French control of Algeria.

Atlantic Charter   A joint declaration made in August, 1941, by President Roosevelt and Prime Minister Churchill, stating common principles for the future of the world. Although the United States was not yet involved in the war, it expressed its support for all people of the principles of (1) self-determination, (2) the right of free choice of government, (3) equal opportunities for all nations for trade, and (4) a permanent system of general security and disarmament.

Autarchy, Autarky   Self-sufficiency, the ability of a nation to produce all its needs, without dependence upon other nations. It is derived from the Greek *autarkeia*, self-rule.

Authoritarian   A system of strong national government, essentially dictatorial.

Autonomy   Literally self-rule; in historical practice it has frequently meant virtual independence with some nominal subordination. For example, after the Congress of Berlin (1878) Bulgaria was divided into 3 zones, each with varying degrees of self-government, but still nominally within the Turkish Empire.

Baghdad Pact (Central Treaty Organization, CENTO)   A treaty of 1955 between Iraq and Turkey, joined by Great Britain, Pakistan, and Iran for common purposes of security and defense. In 1959, after the withdrawal of Iraq, it was renamed the Central Treaty Organization, with headquarters in Ankara.

Balance of Power   The foreign policy of two or more nations who cooperate in order to prevent one nation from becoming predominant over others. Under this policy, alliances are sometimes formed.

Balfour Declaration   A letter of November, 1917, from Arthur J. Balfour, British Foreign Secretary; to Lord Rothschild, Chairman of the Zionist Federation, stating that the British government favored "a national home for the Jewish people in Palestine." Resulted ultimately in the establishment of Israel in 1948.

Bandung Conference (Afro-Asian Conference), of 28 Afro-Asian countries at Bandung, Indonesia, in April, 1955. It was the first Afro-Asian conference, and while it passed resolutions opposing colonialism and supporting self-determination, it condemned communism as "super-colonialism."

Bantustan An area in the Republic of South Africa set aside for occupation by native Africans. There are 8 Bantustans, occupying 14 percent of the land area and containing some 70 percent of the population. Sometimes designated as native reserves.

Benelux A convenient abbreviation of Belgium, the Netherlands, and Luxembourg, used when these three nations are working together for common purposes.

Bipartisan Foreign Policy A foreign policy in which two opposing political parties agree upon common objectives and action in order to present a united national front in foreign affairs.

Blockade A system of preventing supplies from reaching another nation. Although it normally refers to wartime conditions in which one nation's navy prevents ships from entering another nation's ports, it can be used for a similar operation in peacetime.

Bolsheviks The radical faction of the Russian Social Democrat Party. It is derived from *bolshinstvo*, a majority.

Bourgeois The Marxists used this adjective to denote the attitude of the middle class (bourgeoisie), generally in contrast to the proletariat or workers.

Brinksmanship The term used by John Foster Dulles, secretary of state during the Eisenhower administration, to describe a policy in international relationships of being willing to go to the very brink of war.

British Commonwealth A free association of independent nations which were formerly colonies within the British Empire. The Commonwealth has no common head, no common government, and no member has authority over any other member. The existing colonies are included as "Empire" in the full title, British Commonwealth and Empire.

Brussels Treaty Organization (Western European Union) A military alliance originally formed in 1948 by the Benelux nations, France, and Great Britain. Renamed Western European Union in 1955. These nations joined NATO in 1949 but also retained their independent alliance, which is strictly European.

Capitalism The free enterprise system whereby individuals invest money to make a profit, which is payment for lending money. A person who owns a share of stock in a company is a capitalist. As a propaganda word, intending to convey a selective interpretation, it is used to denote ownership of property by a very small minority, supposedly at the expense of the so-called "propertyless" who form the great majority. It should be noted that communist countries have "capital" to be invested in economic enterprises, but the "profits" are used by the state as it determines. Competition which might benefit the consumer would be labeled "exploitation" if anyone made a personal profit.

CENTO See Baghdad Pact.

Central Treaty Organization See Baghdad Pact.

Coexistence Usually in the phrase "peaceful coexistence," a term used originally by Khrushchev to indicate the absence of war between the U.S.S.R. and its adversaries, but not the absence of ideological differences.

Cold War A policy and condition of opposition and tension without actual war. The condition has existed between the U.S.S.R. and the Western powers since 1947, and is responsible for the involvement of the United States in NATO, SEATO, etc.

Collective Action See Collective Security.

Collective Security The policy by which nations agree to guarantee each other's security, by force if necessary. Thus collective action is necessary to make collective security effective.

Collectivism An economic term which includes all types of central ownership by the state, i.e., socialism in Great Britain under the Labour Party, corporativism in Italy under Mussolini, and communism in the U.S.S.R.

Colombo Plan In January, 1950, the British Commonwealth members devised a plan for the cooperative development of South and South East Asian countries: Burma, Bhutan, Borneo, Cambodia, Ceylon, India, Indonesia, Japan, Laos, Malaya, Nepal, Pakistan, the Philippines, South Korea, Thailand, and Vietnam, totalling about one-quarter of the world's population. The British Commonwealth nations of Australia, Canada, New Zealand, and the United Kingdom cooperated to plan public administration, agriculture, industry, training of personnel, health services, and scientific research.

Colony An area of land completely subject to control by a nation, and not an integral part of that nation.

Comecon (Council for Mutual Economic Assistance) An organization set up in 1948 for the development and coordination of national economies in Eastern Europe — all communist countries.

Cominform In 1947 the Communist Information Bureau (Cominform) was established in Belgrade to coordinate the activities of communist parties under the leadership of Moscow. Officially dissolved in 1956, perhaps as a gesture by the U.S.S.R.

Comintern (Communist International) Originally the Third Workingmen's International founded in 1919 in Moscow as the headquarters of the organization dedicated to the overthrow of capitalism. Officially, perhaps only ostensibly, dissolved in 1943, and replaced in 1947 officially by the Cominform.

Common Law Unlike written or statute law, consisted of customs and judicial decisions which became precedents for future decisions on similar issues.

Common Market See European Economic Community.

Communism In theory the community (as opposed to private) ownership of all means of production and distribution. In practice, communism has also shown itself to mean political dictatorship and a revolutionary movement dedicated to the violent overthrow of capitalism. In recent years the U.S.S.R. claims to have rejected the use of violence.

Concentration, Theory of A Marxist theory that larger capitalists (property owners) absorb or destroy smaller ones until all capital and property is concentrated in the hands of a very few enterprises and bankers. According to Marx, at this time violent revolution will eliminate capitalism.

Concordat An agreement between popes and governments establishing the rights and duties of the Catholic clergy.

Condominium The rule of a territory by two countries. For example, the Sudan was ruled jointly by Great Britain and Egypt until it became independent in 1956.

Confederation An association or alliance of independent states working together for common purposes, but without a central government to control the constituent parts, as in a federation.

Containment As the Soviet Union attempted to extend its influence westward in Europe during the Cold War, the United States determined to confine, or contain, the Soviet Union.

Corporative State Sometimes corporate state; a country, such as Italy under Mussolini, in which corporations or associations of workmen and employers select members of the legislature, and institute rules for wages, hours, and conditions of labor. Not a free enterprise.

Council for Mutual Economic Assistance See Comecon.

Coup d'état A sudden change of government, usually started by a group within the existing government. Not a revolution, in which a great part of a nation may be engaged. Examples: Suharto in Indonesia, restricting Sukarno's power; the ousting of Nkrumah from Ghana.

Curzon Line A proposal, named after Lord Curzon, to settle the disputed frontier between Poland and Russia in 1920. It was an essentially fair proposal based on ethnic considerations. It was rejected by the Poles, who subsequently pushed their frontier farther eastward. In 1939, after Germany invaded Poland, the Curzon Line became the frontier in Poland between the Russian and Nazi troops.

Dardanelles The straits or channel in Turkey leading from the Aegean Sea to the Sea of Marmora, and on into the Black Sea. A very strategic waterway which Czarist and Soviet Russia have attempted to control for more than 125 years.

De Facto, De Jure Recognition A nation which receives *de facto* recognition is considered to have an effective government, even though it may have come to power by revolutionary means. Such recognition is "preliminary," sometimes only tentative, and simply accepts the situation that a government does *in fact* exist. This does not necessarily indicate approval or disapproval.

De jure recognition is full, legal recognition of a new state or government, and is usually accompanied by the exchange of diplomatic officials. Such governments have usually come into existence by peaceful, constitutional means.

Decembrists In St. Petersburg in December, 1825, some Russian officers wanted to institute reforms in the government. The movement was divided because some members wanted to force the czar to abdicate and set up a republic, others wanted to restrict the czar's powers, and still others wanted to free the serfs. Four leaders of the conspiracy were executed and 120 were exiled to Siberia. The conspiracy only confirmed Nicholas I's distrust of liberal ideas.

Deductive Reasoning Proceeds from general statements to particular application. For example, the Scholastics, who claimed that since the sun was an immovable object it could not rotate on its axis, (as Galileo claimed) were deductive thinkers.

Deflation An economic condition in which there is a reduction in the amount of available money, or a reduction in proportion to goods available on the market. Prices drop because less money buys more goods; wages drop, and unemployment may result. See Inflation.

Deism The belief in an impersonal deity which made the laws discovered by scientists.

Demarche In diplomatic language a proceeding, a step forward.

Detente A reduction in or a cessation of strained relations between nations.

Dialectical Materialism "Dialectic" is the art of logical argument; "materialism" is the belief that essential changes in history have been economic. Thus, according to the dialectical process, all things change in a prescribed pattern. Thus the class struggle is exemplified in the Bourgeois (thesis), and its opposite the Proletariat (antithesis), resulting in the Socialist Revolution (synthesis). According to Marx, all human history has developed as a dialectical process.

Dialectics   A process of reasoned argument based upon change, as stated by Hegel from the *thesis* (German disunity in the mid-19th century), and its opposite, the *antithesis* (German unity), comes the *synthesis* (the ideal German state).

Dictatorship   Absolute rule by one person or group.

Dictatorship of the Proletariat   In theory a temporary period of dictatorship by the working class in order to eliminate all opposing ideas. When such opposition was eliminated, the dictatorship would cease, since there would be only one class. This was Lenin's theory.

Dollar Gap   For the United States a dollar gap would be the difference between purchases abroad and smaller sales abroad. The U.S.A. would therefore spend more dollars than it received in the equivalent of pounds sterling from Britain or francs from France. The foreign government would then demand that the U.S. dollar bills be redeemed, or exchanged for gold. This could result in a "dollar drain" from the U.S., and therefore a dollar gap.

Dominion   The term as used by Great Britain referred to a colony which received the right of self-government in domestic but not foreign affairs. This policy was initiated by the British North America Act of 1867 (commemorated by Expo '67 in Canada in 1967). After the passage of the Statute of Westminster in 1931 the dominions became completely free and independent sovereign nations. They chose to remain associated with Great Britain in the British Commonwealth of (Independent) Nations.

Dreikaiserbund   Or "League of Three Emperors" of Germany, Austria, and Russia. Devised by Bismarck in 1873, it was simply an "understanding" of common interests among the three nations.

Due Process of Law   The use of the established procedure laid down in a constitution. For example, a citizen cannot be sentenced without a fair and proper trial.

Duma   A Russian parliament created by Czar Nicholas II after the 1905 Revolution. There were four Dumas between 1905 and 1916.

Dyarchy   A rule by two authorities. For example, the Roman emperor Augustus and the Senate technically had joint authority.

Dynasty   A succession of rulers of the same family.

Economic Determinism   Marx claimed that the conditions which most powerfully affected history were economic ones. Therefore, history was determined or changed by economic factors.

Eisenhower Doctrine   Proposed by President Eisenhower in 1957, that the United States assist any nation in the Middle East, which requested aid against communist internal subversion or overt external aggression. Example, the Lebanon incident in 1958.

Encirclement (Einkreisung)   Before both world wars Germany claimed that alliances to prevent German expansion were "encirclement," denying Germany the necessary right to get more "living-room" — *lebensraum*.

Encyclical   From the Latin *bulla encyclica*, meaning a circular letter, sent out by the pope to all bishops, dealing with questions of faith, morals, or behavior. It is usually known by its opening words, such as the 1963 *Pacem in terris*, On peace in the world.

Entente   An "understanding" in diplomatic language, rather than a written agreement. The *entente cordiale* of 1904 between Great Britain and France removed the obstacles to common action.

Euratom   European Atomic Energy Community. An organization established by France, the German Federal Republic, Italy, and the Benelux countries in 1958, to plan research on atomic energy and a market for nuclear products.

European Coal and Steel Community   In 1952 the Benelux nations, France, Italy, and Western Germany planned to control the production and marketing of coal and steel in their countries, and to modernize their industries.

European Defense Community (EDC)   An unsuccessful attempt by most of the NATO nations (not including the United States and Great Britain) to set up a supranational authority with common armed forces and budget, supposedly to be a tighter group than NATO.

European Economic Community (Common Market or Inner Six)   On January 1, 1958, France, the German Federal Republic, Italy, and the Benelux nations organized as a "common market" which by 1966 would eliminate all customs barriers among them, set up a common tariff policy on imports, and gradually remove all restrictions on the movement of workers and capital. In 1973, Denmark, the Republic of Ireland, and the United Kingdom joined.

European Free Trade Association (EFTA)   An association of western European nations agreeing to favor each other in respect to tariffs. Members are Denmark, Norway, Sweden, Austria, Portugal, Switzerland, and Great Britain. Sometimes referred to as the Outer Seven, i.e., outside the Common Market.

European Recovery Program (Marshall Plan)   In June, 1947, in a commencement speech at Harvard, the United States Secretary of State George Marshall, proposed a plan to assist European nations to "return to economic health in a world without which there can be no political stability and no assured peace." The basic concept was not charity but a joint operation of the United States to help European nations to help themselves. Communist countries, although invited to participate, were forbidden to do so by the U.S.S.R. Sixteen nations accepted the United States' offer: Austria, Belgium, Denmark, France, Great Britain, Greece, Iceland, Ireland, Luxembourg, the Netherlands, Norway, Portugal, Sweden, Switzerland, and Turkey.

Expropriate   To transfer private property to public government ownership, usually, but not always, with compensation to the private owner.

Fascism   The political and economic methods used under Mussolini in Italy. The name comes from the *fasces* or bundle of rods tied around an axe, the symbol of authority in Rome. Mussolini adopted this symbol as emblematic of the new corporative state.

Fertile Crescent   The fertile region that stretched through the valleys of the Nile, Euphrates, and Tigris rivers. In ancient times this was the site of several river civilizations.

Fifth Column   During the Spanish Civil War, 1936–1939, the rebels under Franco attacked Madrid with four columns of troops. Inside the city, Franco's supporters organized sabotage as the "fifth" column.

Fifth Republic   Established in France in October, 1958. The 1st Republic lasted from 1793 to 1804; the 2nd from 1848 to 1852; the 3rd from 1875 to 1945; the 4th from 1946 to 1958.

Flemings   The predominantly Flemish-speaking inhabitants of northern Belgium. They outnumber the Walloons, and are generally Catholic and royalist. See Walloons.

FNLA   See Front for the Liberation of Angola.

Free French   French supporters of General de Gaulle who refused to acknowledge the French armistice in June, 1940. In 1944 de Gaulle's French Committee of National Liberation was proclaimed and recognized as the French Provisional Government.

Free Trade   An economic theory or policy of the absence of restrictions or tariffs on goods imported into a country. There is no "protection" in the form of tariffs against foreign competition.

FRELIMO   See Front for the Liberation of Mozambique.

French Community   In 1958 the African colonies of France, except Guinea, voted under the Constitution of the Fifth Republic to become a community of independent states in association with France. Guinea voted to become completely independent of France. By 1961 all members of the community had voted to become independent sovereign nations.

Front for the Liberation of Angola   One of the three native organizations struggling to gain power before the granting of independence by Portugal in November, 1975.

Front for the Liberation of Mozambique   The successful guerrilla organization that fought for 13 years to win independence in 1974.

GATT (General Agreement on Tariffs and Trade)   Came into being in 1948, when several nations agreed to negotiate on tariff reduction. Usually negotiated between individual countries. Most of the world's trade is controlled by nations agreeing to GATT.

Geneva Agreement   The agreement between the French and Ho Chi Minh in 1954, which ended French occupation of French Indo-China and divided North and South Vietnam at the 17th parallel.

Genro   An inner circle of advisors to the emperor of Japan, before World War II, consisting of elder statesmen.

Geopolitics   The study of strategic geographical positions as important political objectives. For example, the Panama Canal is a strategic geographical waterway with obvious political importance.

German Democratic Republic   Usually known as East Germany. According to an agreement between it and the U.S.S.R. in 1955, the German Democratic Republic became a sovereign, independent state. Recognized as an indepenent nation.

German Federal Republic   A federation of West German states, established in 1949 by the United States, Great Britain, and France. It became an independent republic in 1955, with Bonn as its capital. Frequently referred to as West Germany.

Great Leap Forward   The attempt by the People's Republic of China to surpass other nations in the production of coal and iron, typified by unsuccessful "backyard furnaces."

Great Proletarian Cultural Revolution   The attempt by Mao to eliminate any influence that contradicted communist theory; an attack upon all "old ideas."

Heresy   Any doctrine which challenged the official Church doctrine or orthodoxy.

Holy Roman Empire   The empire was organized under Otto I, who was crowned emperor by the pope in 962 A.D. It consisted largely of German and Italian territory. The emperor represented the former tradition of European unity under an authority appointed by the pope. By the 15th century it was practically no more than a name. It was officially dissolved by Napoleon in 1806.

Home Rule Responsible government for the internal affairs of a former colony, although foreign affairs usually remain under the control of the mother country. Britain recognized such an area as a "dominion," which carried the connotation of internal self-government.

Imperialism The acquisition and administration of colonial areas, usually in the interests of the administering country. Only a few colonial areas, such as the Falkland Islands, exist today.

Inductive Reasoning Proceeds from particular instances and examples to a general rule; the accumulation of enough facts to establish a general position.

Inflation An increase in the amount of money in relation to available goods, or a drop in goods available in relation to the amount of money. Prices increase and sales may drop since prices are high in relation to wages. Governments like to avoid both inflation and deflation, since both may result in economic dislocation.

Initiative The process by which voters may start or initiate legislation themselves, or order the legislature to introduce legislation desired by the voters.

Inner Six See Common Market.

IRA See Irish Republican Army.

Irish Republican Army An illegal band of dedicated guerrilla fighters that originated in the 1916 Easter Rebellion in Ireland, and operates today in Ulster.

Iron Curtain The phrase coined by Winston Churchill in 1946 to designate the frontier dividing the communist states of Europe (U.S.S.R., Albania, Bulgaria, Czechoslovakia, Hungary, Poland, East Germany, and Rumania) from Western Europe. This frontier stretched from Stettin on the Baltic Sea to Trieste on the Adriatic.

Irredentism The demand to recover what a nation regards as lost territory. For example, Italy in 1870 considered Trieste, Nice, and Savoy, among other areas, as *Italia Irredenta*, unredeemed Italy, which must someday be incorporated within the nation.

Japan External Trade Organization An organization that evaluates foreign business and trade methods and passes the information on to Japanese businesses.

JETRO See Japan External Trade Organization.

Kellogg Pact (Kellogg-Briand Pact, Pact of Paris, 1928) "Outlawed" war as an instrument of national policy, except for "self-defense." It contained no machinery to enforce the agreement.

Kulturkampf "Battle of Ideas," a term describing the conflict between Bismarck and the Catholic Church in Germany. Bismarck objected to the influence of the Church upon the citizen in political affairs, particularly after the formation of the Catholic Center Party.

The Kulturkampf denied the right of priests to refer to politics in their sermons. Priests were imprisoned for ignoring Bismarck's orders.

Kuomintang The Chinese Nationalist Party founded by Sun Yat-sen, later under the leadership of Chiang Kai-shek. In 1949 it was defeated by the communists under Mao Tse-tung and withdrew to the island of Formosa (Taiwan).

Labor Theory of Value The Marxist belief that the value of an article is determined by the amount of labor put into it. Actually, those who provide materials, tools, goods, ideas, and marketing techniques also contribute to the value of an article.

Laissez-Faire The economic doctrine of the complete absence of government restrictions on any aspect of economy. Literally, "leave alone;" colloquially, "hands off."

Legitimists Advocates of the return to thrones of monarchs with claims of direct (legitimate) descent. Applied particularly to the Congress of Vienna, 1814–1815.

Manchukuo After the Japanese took Manchuria in 1931, they renamed it Manchukuo. Henry Pu Yi, the last Manchu emperor of China (deposed in 1911) was made the Emperor of Manchukuo. He was a puppet of the Japanese government.

Mandate An order from the League of Nations to a country to administer a territory and report back to the League. For example, Palestine was a British mandate.

March on Rome In 1922 Mussolini demanded the formation of a Fascist government, and urged his followers to go to Rome to demonstrate, after the Fascists had seized power in several cities. King Victor Emmanuel III dismissed the prime minister and invited Mussolini to come to Rome from Milan. Contrary to the Fascist myth that Mussolini "marched on Rome," he actually came by train.

Marshall Plan (European Recovery Program) A cooperative plan proposed by Secretary of State George Marshall in 1947, offering to help all nations help themselves back to economic recovery. Nations submitted proposals of what they could do for themselves and what they needed. The United States contributed $18 billion in four years; this represented 25 percent of the total cost of European recovry. The participating European nations contributed the other 75 percent.

Marxism-Leninism Marxism is the belief that a class struggle exists. Leninism is the organization of extremists to precipitate the class struggle into violent action. Thus the theory of Marx is implemented by the practice of Lenin.

Massive Retaliation   The policy suggested by U.S. Secretary of State Dulles to use nuclear force against "brush-fire" or conventional confrontations.

Mensheviks   The moderates of the Russian Social Democrat Party, opposed by the more radical Bolsheviks. The term is derived from *menshintsvo*, a minority.

Ministry of International Trade and Industry   A Japanese government department whose function is to assist and encourage Japanese businesses.

MITI   See Ministry of International Trade and Industry.

MPLA   See Popular Movement for the Liberation of Angola.

Narodniki   A secret Russian revolutionary society of 1873 which attempted to win the support of the peasants. University students dressed as peasants went out to the farms, but their socialist doctrines were not popular with the peasants. The movement not only failed completely but was savagely persecuted by the czarist government.

Nation   A group of people who are bound together by common ties of history, language, customs, and who probably have a clearly defined boundary.

National Union for the Total Independence of Angola   One of the three black guerrilla groups fighting for power before Angola became independent in November, 1975.

National Covenant   The agreement in Lebanese politics that the president must always be a Christian and the prime minister a Moslem.

National Liberation Front   Communist groups in both North and South Vietnam who were dedicated to freeing South Vietnam from the control of the United States.

Nationalism   The feeling of a people that they belong to one nation and should work together for the benefit of the nation.

Nationalization   The acquisition by the state of any means of production or distribution. For example, the British Labour Party believes in "common ownership of the means of production, distribution, and exchange." In 1945–1950 it nationalized railroads, coal, electricity, gas, and transportation. It exchanged government bonds for company shares held by citizens in the private businesses.

Neutralism   The policy of not siding with any group or country in peacetime. For many years India was neutralist and would not commit itself to the policies of the Western nations or the communist bloc.

Neutrality   Nonparticipation in war; the condition of remaining a neutral and of taking no sides.

Nihilism   A philosophical belief which accepts no authority and insists upon the sovereignty of the individual. It is not a political doctrine, as is anarchism. The term is derived from *nihil*, meaning "nothing."

Non-Aligment   The policy of not making agreements or treaties with other nations, of remaining uncommitted.

North Atlantic Treaty Organization (NATO)   An organization formed in 1948, consisting of the Brussels Treaty Organization (Belgium, Luxembourg, the Netherlands, France, and the United Kingdom) and the United States, Canada, Denmark, Iceland, Italy, Norway, and Portugal. The members agreed that an attack upon one would be regarded as an attack upon all, and that each would assist "as it deems necessary." The treaty declared its purpose "to safeguard the freedom, common heritage, and civilization of their peoples founded on the principles of democracy, individual liberty and the rule of law." The German Federal Republic, Greece, and Turkey joined later.

North Vietnam   In July, 1954, the French and the Viet Minh signed the Geneva Accord or Agreement. This recognized Vietnam as one state divided temporarily into two zones by the cease-fire line, and provided for a general election to unite the two zones. The southern zone, or South Vietnam, did not ratify the Agreement and refused to permit an election on the grounds that it would not be conducted fairly.

OAS — Organization of American States   Set up in 1948 at the Ninth International Conference of American States, in Colombia, to coordinate the work of its members, to attempt to settle disputes between members, and to protect its members against aggression.

Oder-Neisse Line   The boundary between Poland and East Germany, formed by the Oder and Neisse rivers. Accepted by the Allies at the Potsdam Conference of 1945. German territory east of the line was transferred to Poland. This totaled about one-fifth of Germany's prewar area.

OECD — Organization for European Economic and Cultural Development   Established in 1961 by the same nations as in OEEC, plus Canada, the German Federal Republic, Japan, Spain, and the United States It was to succeed OEEC. Purposes were: (1) to facilitate world trade, (2) to coordinate economic policies, and (3) to aid the economic expansion of nations.

OEEC — Organization for European Economic Cooperation   Set up in response to the Marshall Plan to coordinate the economies of the nations receiving aid under the European Recovery Program. Members were: Benelux, Austria, Denmark, France, Great Britain, Greece, Iceland, Ireland, Italy, Norway, Portugal, Sweden, Switzerland, and Turkey.

OPEC   See Organization of Petroleum Exporting Countries.

Orangemen   The Ulster Protestants, who take the name from William III of England, who was originally from the province of Orange in Holland. He defeated James II, who attempted to invade England with Catholic Irish support.

Organization of Petroleum Exporting Countries   This organization consists mainly of Arab oil-producing countries who, in 1973, arbitrarily raised the price of exported oil fourfold.

Outer Seven (European Free Trade Association)   Referred to as the Outer Seven in contrast to the original Inner Six of the Common Market. Members were originally, Austria, Denmark, Norway, Portugal, Sweden, Switzerland, and the United Kingdom. The members agree to eliminate tariff and trade restrictions among themselves over a period of time. Denmark and the United Kingdom joined the Common Market in 1973.

PAIGC   See African Party for the Independence of Guinea-Bissau and the Cape Verde Islands.

Peonage   The condition of being bound to the *patron* in the *hacienda* system of Latin America.

Philosophy   the study of the causes and relations of things and ideas. Greek philosophers attempted to explain the origin, the structure, and the meaning of the universe. General laws that provide the rational explanation of anything.

Pietism   A belief that religion is a matter of faith and not simply a matter of dogma and doctrine.

Plurality   The largest block of three or more blocs of votes, but less than a majority. For example, if in a three party election, Party A gets 40 percent of the vote, Party B 35 percent, Party C 25 percent, Party A has a plurality and wins the election.

Police State   A country in which individual liberties are not allowed. There is no freedom of the press, free elections, or free speech.

Political Party   Consists of people with the same political ideas, who organize to get their candidates into office in order to pass laws in their interests. A majority political party acknowledges the right of the minority party to become the majority by peaceful means. Any dictatorial party, such as the Nazi or Communist party, is not a political party in the accepted definition.

Power of the Purse   The power held by whatever body controls the levying and the spending of income. The power to spend money is the power to determine policy, i.e., what shall be done.

Propaganda   Originally the dissemination of information, from the word *propagate*. However, during the two world wars the word acquired a special connotation, in the sense that a desired purpose, other than simple information, was to be achieved. Today propaganda not infrequently means the withholding of vital information in order to achieve a desired purpose. If the vital information were not withheld, a different decision might have resulted.

Proportional Representation   Representation for all political parties entered on a ballot, in proportion to the votes won by each party.

Protectorate   A territory which is under the "protection" or jurisdiction of another state, although not annexed to it.

Rapproachement   In diplomatic language the reestablishing of good relations between nations.

Recall   The process by which voters may remove officials from public office before the expiration of their terms.

Referendum   The referring to the voters of a piece of legislation for their approval or disapproval.

Responsible Government   In British usage, the prime minister and his cabinet are responsible or answerable to the House of Commons for their actions, since they are leaders chosen by the majority party. As "responsible" ministers they are subject to removal by the wishes of the majority of the House of Commons.

Revolution   Usually a fundamental change in a political system, in which one government is replaced with an entirely different one, e.g., the American and French revolutions.

Risorgimento   An Italian word meaning "resurrection," it was applied politically to the Italian movement of the 19th century for the unification of Italy. Although Italy's acquisition in 1919 of the Trentino, Istria, and South Tyrol was regarded by many as the completion of Risorgimento, Mussolini chose to revive the term *Italia Irredenta* in his demands for Nice, Savoy, and Corsica.

SALT   See Strategic Arms Limitation Talks.

Sanctions   Economic restrictions or boycott. The League of Nations ordered sanctions on Italy after its attack upon Ethiopia in 1935. Since oil and steel were exempted from the sanctions, and since Mussolini could not have conducted the war without those vital materials, the whole purpose of imposing sanctions was nullified.

SCAP   See Supreme Commander for the Allied Powers.

Self-Determination   The ability of a group, usually ethnic, to determine how it wishes to be governed, as an independent nation or as an integral part of another. The "succession" states created from the Austro-Hungarian Empire after World War I are examples of peoples who chose independence.

Separatism A belief or movement advocating separation from a larger group. Many separatists in Quebec want that province to sever all connections with Canada and become independent.

Socialism 1. An *economic* belief that the means of production and distribution should be owned by the state, and 2. a *political* belief that this economic objective should be attained through the free choice of the electorate, which should have the opportunity to replace such an economic system if it so wishes. The *political* difference between socialism and communism is that communism has not yet permitted free and open elections.

Strategic Arms Limitation Talks These began in 1970 between the United States and the Soviet Union and have continued in attempts to limit nuclear weaponry.

Succession States Those states or parts of states which were formerly part of the Austro-Hungarian Empire and which became independent after World War I. Separate nations were Austria, Czechoslovakia, Hungary, and Yugoslavia. Some parts of the old Austro-Hungarian Empire were given to Italy, Poland, and Rumania.

Supreme Commander for the Allied Powers The title given to General Douglas MacArthur as commander of the Occupation forces in Japan in 1945.

Surplus Value According to Marx, the difference between the cost of an article and its selling price. The worker, according ot Marx, was "robbed" of this difference.

Theocracy A state ruled by a church. Usually the right to vote and to hold office is limited to those who are admitted to membership in the church.

Third Reich The name given to Germany during the Nazi regime between 1933 and 1945. The Nazis claimed that the First Reich was from 963–1806 A.D. (the Holy Roman Empire), and the Second Reich was between 1871–1918 (the German Empire of William I and II). Hitler claimed that the Third Reich would last for a thousand years.

Tonkin Gulf Resolution The authority given to President Johnson by Congress in August, 1964, to take necessary action against any aggressive actions by North Vietnam.

Totalitarian A stronger term than "authoritarian," since a totalitarian system extends its control over every aspect of a citizen's life and demands total subjection to the state.

Truman Doctrine The statement made by President Truman in 1947 when he asked for aid for Greece and Turkey, which were being subjected to communist pressure. He announced the need of supporting "free peoples who are resisting attempted subjugation by armed minorities or outside pressure."

Ulster Six counties of Northern Ireland that are technically under British jurisdiction for all but local affairs. The area contains a Protestant majority that does not want union with the Catholic Republic of Ireland.

Ulster Vanguard One of several militant Protestant organizations in Ulster that has used guerrilla tactics similar to those of the IRA, against Catholics and as reprisals for IRA actions.

UNESCO — United Nations Educational, Scientific and Cultural Organization An agency of the United Nations which contributes to peace by assisting education, the natural and social sciences, cultural activities, rehabilitation, mass communication, and technical assistance to various parts of the world.

UNICEF — United Nations Children's Emergency Fund Originally designed to help child welfare and health programs in countries devastated by World War II, it has been expanded to include the children of emergent countries. UNICEF provides milk, clothing, and medical assistance to children throughout the world.

UNITA See National Union for the Total Independence of Angola.

United Arab Republic Officially created in February, 1958, by the union of Egypt and Syria. In September, 1961, a *coup d'etat* in Syria dissolved the union, but Egypt retained the name of United Arab Republic.

UNRRA — United Nations Relief and Rehabilitation Administration Instituted in 1943 to bring relief to refugees and rehabilitation to the industries and economies of nations.

Vatican City Since 1929 these .16 square miles or about 100 acres of territory in Rome are the smallest independent sovereign state in Europe. In 1870 the Papal States in Italy were incorporated, over the pope's protest, into the Kingdom of Italy. From that date until 1929 the several popes refused to acknowledge Italy's action and refused to step outside the Vatican. Mussolini resolved the issue in the Lateran Agreement of 1929, which established the Vatican as a separate state within the city of Rome.

Viet Cong Members and supporters of the National Liberation Front, also known as VC, an abbreviation of Viet Nam Cong Sam. They are Vietnamese communists.

Viet Minh An organization started in 1941 by Ho Chi Minh to resist Japan in Indo-China. Later became active against the French, from 1946–1954, and succeeded in driving the French from Indo-China.

Walloons The predominantly French-speaking citizens of southern Belgium, generally anti-Catholic and anti-royalist. They inhabit the predominantly industrialized area of Belgium.

Warsaw Pact — Eastern European Mutual Assistance Treaty   A 20-year treaty of mutual assistance and cooperation between the U.S.S.R., Albania, Bulgaria, Czechoslovakia, German Democratic Republic (East Germany), Hungary, Poland, and Rumania, signed in 1955. Established unified military command, and each nation agreed to give assistance to any member attacked in Europe.

Weimar Republic   The name given to Germany's first federal republic, named after its capital, Weimar. Created in 1919, it lasted until 1933 when Hitler came to power. The Allies, after World War I, forced its representatives to sign the Versailles Treaty which, among other features, charged Germany with the sole guilt for the war. Thus Germany's first republican government started inauspiciously, since Germans were later to identify democracy with what they regarded as a dictated peace.

West Irian   Formerly the Netherlands New Guinea, it is the western part of the island of New Guinea, which became a province of Indonesia in 1963.

ZANU   See Zimbabwe African National Union.

ZAPU   See Zimbabwe African People's Union.

Zimbabwe   The native name for Rhodesia. Between the 11th and 19th centuries, Zimbabwe was probably the heart and capital of a great African empire. A search for gold began here and almost became a "gold rush."

Zimbabwe African National Union   The more militant of two black organizations in Rhodesia. It advocates continued use of guerrilla warfare.

Zimbabwe African People's Union   The second of two black political groups in Rhodesia which are demanding political rights. It supports a negotiated settlement with the Rhodesian government.

Zionism   The belief in the establishment of a separate homeland for the Jewish people. The movement was founded in the late 19th century by Theodor Herzl and was supported by Chaim Weizmann during World War I. Britain supported the general idea of a Jewish homeland in the official Balfour Declaration of 1917.

Independent Nations (former colonies) of Sub-Sahara Africa

Present Name	Date of Independence	Former Control	Former Colonial Name
Angola, Republic of	1975	Portugal	Angola
Botswana	1966	Great Britain	Bechuanaland Protectorate
Burundi, Republic of	1962	Belgium	Ruanda-Urundi
Cameroon, United Republic of	1960	France	French Cameroun
Central African Republic	1960	France	Ubangi-Shari
Chad, Republic of	1960	France	Part of French Equatorial Africa
Congo Republic	1960	France	French Congo
Dahomey, Republic of	1960	France	Part of French Equatorial Africa
Equatorial Guinea	1968	Spain	Fernando Po (an island)
Gabon Republic	1960	France	Part of French Equatorial Africa
Gambia, The	1965	Great Britain	Gambia
Ghana, Republic of	1957	Great Britain	Gold Coast
Guinea, Republic of	1958	France	Part of French Equatorial Africa
Guinea-Bissau, Republic of	1974	Portugal	Portuguese Guinea
Ivory Coast, Republic of	1960	France	Part of French Equatorial Africa
Kenya, Republic of	1963	Great Britain	Kenya
Lesotho, Kingdom of	1966	Great Britain	Basutoland
Malawi, Republic of	1964	Great Britain	Nyasaland
Mali Republic	1960	France	French Sudan
Mauritania, Islamic Republic of	1960	France	Mauritania
Mozambique, Republic of	1974	Portugal	Mozambique
Niger, Republic of	1960	France	French West Africa
Nigeria, Federal Republic of	1960	Great Britain	Nigeria
*Rhodesia			
Rwanda, Republic of	1962	Belgium	Ruanda-Urundi
Sao Tome e Principe	1974	Portugal	Sao Tome
Senegal, Republic of	1960	France	French West Africa

Continued

*Rhodesia was formerly known as Southern Rhodesia; it became a white-ruled, self-governing colony. In 1965 Rhodesia declared itself independent by the Unilateral Declaration of Independence (UDI). In 1970 it declared itself a republic, although neither Great Britain nor the United Nations recognizes it as an independent nation.

Independent Nations (former colonies) of Sub-Sahara Africa

Present Name	Date of Independence	Former Control	Former Colonial Name
Sierra Leone	1961	Great Britain	Sierra Leone
Somali Democratic Republic	1960	Great Britain	British Somaliland Protectorate
		Italy	Italian Trusteeship Territory of Somalia
Sudan, Republic of	1956	Great Britain and Egypt	Anglo-Egyptian Sudan
Swaziland, Kingdom of	1968	Great Britain	Swaziland
Tanzania, United Republic of	1964	Great Britain	Tanganyika (independent 1962), Zanzibar (independent 1964)
Togo, Republic of	1960	France	Togoland
Uganda, Republic of	1962	Great Britain	Uganda
Zaire, Republic of (formerly Republic of the Congo)	1960	Belgium	Belgian Congo
Zambia, Republic of	1964	Great Britain	Northern Rhodesia

How to Make Effective Use of 11 Model Tests

1. Always read the question carefully. Don't jump to conclusions without first understanding exactly what is asked. For example, in Test VIII, No. 28, the question is, "What was the Holy Roman Empire in the 16th century," and not simply, "What was the Holy Roman Empire in general." There is an important difference.

2. The multiple choice questions 21-45 in Tests I-X include several marked with an asterisk. Of each set of four statements, only one is incorrect and three are correct in fact and interpretation. The correct statements provide useful review material on the several topics.

3. Some questions ask for a decision on the truth or falsity of each statement. Do not be satisfied to test your accuracy. Know why each statement is true or false. The tests are designed as a teaching device as well as a means to measure the accuracy of knowledge.

4. Time relationship is important in history. Many questions ask for chronological organization. For example, if you know the time relationships you can immediately mark as False three statements about the Twenty-One Demands in Test VIII, Questions 61-65.

5. Test XI is a final chronological factual review of the material.

Test I

Associate the lettered person or item in Column II with the appropriate numbered statement in Column I.

COLUMN I   COLUMN II

	COLUMN I	COLUMN II
_____ 1.	I dismissed Turgot and Calonne, my finance ministers	A. Legitimacy
_____ 2.	Known as the "George Washington" of Latin America	B. Harrapa
_____ 3.	I discovered the ancient city of Troy	C. Louis XVI
_____ 4.	He wrote the Report which proposed a reorganization of Canada in the 19th century	D. New Harmony
_____ 5.	Invaders of early Egypt	E. Durham
_____ 6.	City which was an early center of civilization in India	F. Schliemann
_____ 7.	Emperor who moved his capital to Byzantium	G. Locke
_____ 8.	He said that population would outrun food supply	H. Huguenots
_____ 9.	French supporters of the Calvinist doctrine	I. Bolivar
_____ 10.	Attacked the belief in pure reason alone	J. Malthus
_____ 11.	He became the first president of the German Republic	K. Hyksos
_____ 12.	The Consulate was his first political office	L. Hippocrates
_____ 13.	Leader of England's only republic	M. Cromwell
_____ 14.	Father of medicine	N. Ebert
_____ 15.	He believed that men should be trained to rule others	O. Hitler
_____ 16.	He explained the law of gravitation	P. Kant
_____ 17.	He said he had won "Peace in our time"	Q. Newton
_____ 18.	He was the leader of the Pakistan independence movement	R. Galileo
_____ 19.	Refers to the restoration of rulers entitled to their thrones by heredity	S. Napoleon
_____ 20.	A communal settlement organized by Robert Owen	T. Constantine
		U. Jinnah
		V. Chamberlain
		W. Plato
		X. Cavour
		Y. Metternich

In the following multiple choice questions, place the appropriate letter in the blank space in front of the question.

_____ 21. The contribution of the Phoenicians to the Mediterranean area was
  A. The spreading of their ideas through trading
  B. Their distinctive language
  C. Their religious beliefs
  D. Their highly organized administrative system

_____ 22. The guardians of the Spartan Constitution were
  A. The Helots
  B. Ephors
  C. The Secret Police
  D. Two kings ruling jointly

_____ **23.** The term Hellenistic refers to
   A. The civilization that developed from the spread of Greek culture through the Middle East
   B. The civilization of Greece from earliest times
   C. The worship of Helen
   D. The culture brought to Greece from Macedon by Philip and Alexander

_____ **24.** The Roman Empire declined for the following reasons EXCEPT
   A. The decline of agriculture because the small farmer could not make a living
   B. Urban civilization was declining through overtaxation
   C. Christianity was spreading throughout the empire
   D. Romans were increasingly unwilling to serve in the government

_____ **25.** The Holy Roman Emperor was
   A. A second title and office of the Pope
   B. The ruler who defended the Church and Catholic lands for the Pope
   C. The title given to the Christian leader who recaptured Jerusalem from the Turks
   D. The leader of the Greek Orthodox Church in Byzantium

_____ **26.** The Ptolemaic theory was
   A. The Renaissance approach to scientific enquiry
   B. The law of falling bodies
   C. The belief that the earth revolved around the sun
   D. A pre-Renaissance belief that the earth was the center of the universe

_____ **27.** China in the 19th century was not a nation for the following reasons EXCEPT
   A. It was a country of thousands of self-sufficient communities
   B. People came into contact with local affairs only
   C. The Chinese people objected to the rule of the Manchus
   D. There was no representative system of government through which local interests could be communicated.

_____ **28.** The final partition of Poland during the reign of Catherine the Great was detrimental to Russia's interests for the following reasons EXCEPT
   A. It added 6,000,000 Poles as citizens of Russia
   B. It removed the threat of a powerful Poland
   C. The Poles strongly objected to "Russification"
   D. It removed a buffer state between Russia and Prussia

_____ 29. By his statement "No Bishop, No King" King James of England meant
   A. That a bishop did not need a king in order to be a bishop
   B. That England did not need a bishop or a king
   C. That if he allowed the authority of the bishop to be questioned, then his position as king might be questioned
   D. That he did not have to listen to bishops

*_____ 30. The Petition of Right, 1628, laid down the following rights EXCEPT
   A. Parliament had to agree to taxation
   B. Citizens could not be obliged to keep or pay for soldiers in their own homes
   C. Martial law could not be imposed in peace time
   D. A prisoner had the right to a trial by jury

*_____ 31. Oliver Cromwell did the following EXCEPT
   A. Illegally ordered the execution of the King
   B. Established a republic
   C. Became so popular that the monarchy was abolished during the remainder of the century
   D. Dismissed parliaments as he chose

*_____ 32. In 1789 the Third Estate did the following EXCEPT
   A. Invited the nobles to join them in the National Assembly
   B. Demanded the execution of Louis XVI
   C. Demanded voting in the Estates-General by heads, not by Estates
   D. Agreed not to disband before a constitution was drawn up

*_____ 33. Industrialization created the following problems EXCEPT
   A. Community responsibility for unemployed factory workers
   B. Care for the aged, the sick, and needy dependents
   C. The development of power to run the machines
   D. Sanitation, fire, police protection, and such public services

*_____ 34. Great Britain, France, and Austria fought against Russia in the Crimean War for the following reasons EXCEPT
   A. Austria feared that Russian policy might encourage racial groups in Austria to seek independence
   B. Great Britain did not want Russia to control the Dardanelles
   C. France feared Russian influence in the Mediterranean
   D. Britain wanted to force Turkey to give her control of the Dardanelles

_____ 35. The Government of Ireland Act of 1920 established one of the following
   A. A government for the whole of Ireland
   B. A government for Northern Ireland and one for Southern Ireland
   C. The Irish Republic
   D. The Dail Eireann as the government of Ireland

_____ **36.** The Boer War broke out because
    A. Diamonds and gold were discovered in the Dutch republics
    B. The British decided to protect Cecil Rhodes against Boer attacks
    C. The Boers always resented being a colonial possession of Britain
    D. Cecil Rhodes attempted to take over the republics for Britain

*_____ **37.** Social Darwinism justified 19th century imperialism for the following reasons EXCEPT
    A. Strong nations had the right to acquire backward areas
    B. The superior civilization of the Anglo-Saxons
    C. The obligation of advanced nations to teach backward people
    D. The white rulers were only temporary trustees

_____ **38.** Switzerland is an exception to the usual definition of a nation because
    A. It has distinctive boundaries
    B. It is an independent nation
    C. It has no common language
    D. It has been successfully neutral in several wars

_____ **39.** Hitler gained control of Germany early in 1933
    A. By suppressing all opposition parties
    B. By his party's winning a majority of seats in the Reichstag
    C. By winning a plurality of seats in the Reichstag
    D. Simply because Hindenburg appointed him as Chancellor

_____ **40.** The New Economic Policy was different from the previous period of communism because
    A. Land was nationalized for the first time
    B. Dictatorship was replaced with free elections
    C. The dictatorship of the proletariat was outlawed
    D. A limited amount of free enterprise was permitted

*_____ **41.** The United Nations has been successful in preventing or limiting aggression in the following EXCEPT
    A. Palestine
    B. Iran
    C. The Congo
    D. Vietnam

_____ **42.** Russia's long-range objective of the Berlin Blockade was to
    A. Cause the United States to take its forces out of Europe
    B. Starve out West Berlin
    C. Keep West Germans from reaching Berlin
    D. Force the Allies out of Berlin

_____ 43. One cause of the American Revolution was Britain's belief in the policy of
   A. Complete laissez-faire
   B. Exporting more than she imported
   C. Close regulation of all foreign trade
   D. Payment of a bounty on timber and naval supplies

_____ 44. Neutralism is
   A. The policy of remaining neutral during a war
   B. The right of a neutral to trade with a belligerent
   C. The insistence by a neutral nation that belligerents shall respect her rights
   D. The policy of remaining uncommitted or unallied during peace time

*_____ 45. The Latin American agricultural unit called the hacienda has hindered progress for the following reasons EXCEPT
   A. It is a moneyless economy and no capital can be saved by the farm workers
   B. Life is limited to local horizons and experiences
   C. Most Latin American countries have a "one-crop" economy
   D. Peasants have no purchasing power to spur the economy

Wars can be divided into the following types:
   I. Imperialist
   II. Balance of Power
   III. Aggressive
   IV. Civil
   V. Defensive
   VI. Collective Action

_____ 46. Which of the following wars illustrates Type I?
   A. Crimean War, 1854–1856
   B. Russo-Turkish War, 1877–1878
   C. Boer War, 1899–1902
   D. Franco-Prussian War, 1870–1871
   E. Korean War, 1950–1953

_____ 47. The Crimean War was essentially
   A. I   D. IV
   B. II   E. V
   C. III

_____ 48. The Sino-Japanese War of 1894–1895 was
   A. I   C. IV
   B. II   D. V

_____ **49.** The War in China, 1945–1949, was

     A. II   D. V

     B. III   E. VI

     C. IV

_____ **50.** Support given to South Korea in the Korean War, 1950–1953, was

     A. I   C. IV

     B. II   D. VI

Associate each of the persons in Column II with the appropriate statement in Column I.

COLUMN I	COLUMN II
_____ **51.** I put the sun in its place	A. Newton
_____ **52.** I explained the law of gravitation	B. Wyclif
_____ **53.** I defended the freedom of speech and thought	C. Erasmus
	D. Hobbes
_____ **54.** I translated the Bible into English	E. James II
_____ **55.** I was invited to become king in 1688	F. William III
	G. Copernicus
	H. Voltaire

56-70 For the following three topics indicate by T or F whether each statement is True or False.

The Ninety-Five Theses of Martin Luther

_____ **56.** Were posted on the church door at Wittenberg

_____ **57.** Condemned the Catholic Church on its dogma

_____ **58.** Criticized the sale of indulgences

_____ **59.** Were intended to bring about the Protestant revolt

_____ **60.** Although not intended to do so, were in part responsible for the Protestant revolt

The Franco-Prussian War, 1870–1871

_____ **61.** In effect ended the Second French Empire

_____ **62.** Was partly the result of the formation of the Triple Alliance

_____ **63.** Extended Germany's border west of the Rhine for the first time

_____ **64.** Resulted in the loss to France of Alsace-Lorraine

_____ **65.** Led to the creation of the German Empire

The Yalta Conference, 1945

_____ **66.** In the long run it proved advantageous to the Western allies

_____ **67.** Successfully settled the Polish border as that of 1919

_____ **68.** Agreed in principle to self-determination for the liberated nations of Eastern Europe

_____ **69.** Provided concessions in Manchuria to the U.S.S.R. if she would declare war on Japan

_____ **70.** Was the final peace conference after World War II

Questions 71 to 75 refer to the following types of government
   I. Hereditary Monarchy, unrestricted
   II. Republic
   III. Constitutional Monarchy
   IV. Dictatorship
   V. Military coup d'etat

_____ 71. Which type applies to the German Federal Republic?
         A. I
         B. II
         C. III
         D. V

_____ 72. Which type refers to France of 1965?
         A. II
         B. III
         C. IV
         D. V

_____ 73. Which type refers to India of 1966?
         A. II
         B. III
         C. IV
         D. V

_____ 74. Which type refers to the German Democratic Republic?
         A. I
         B. II
         C. IV
         D. V

_____ 75. Which type is applicable to Indonesia in 1966?
         A. II
         B. III
         C. IV
         D. V

Put the following persons in their correct chronological order.

_____ 76.   A. Nicholas I
_____ 77.   B. Frederick the Great
_____ 78.   C. Catherine the Great
_____ 79.   D. Lenin
_____ 80.   E. Karl Marx

Place the following persons in the chronological order of their discoveries or voyages.

_____ 81.   A. Magellan
_____ 82.   B. Columbus
_____ 83.   C. Leif Ericson
_____ 84.   D. Jacques Cartier
_____ 85.   E. Henry Hudson

In each of the following groups certain names are out of place because they lack an important characteristic common to the others in the group. Indicate the ones that do not belong, in the order in which they appear.

GROUP I

_____ 86.   A. Mazzini
_____ 87.   B. Mussolini
_____ 88.   C. Garibaldi
                      D. Cavour
                      E. Machiavelli
                      F. Pope Pius IX
                      G. King Victor Emmanuel II

GROUP II

_____ 89.   A. Mao Tse-tung
_____ 90.   B. Chiang Kai-shek
_____ 91.   C. Francisco Franco
                      D. Sun Yat-sen
                      E. David Ben Gurion
                      F. Lenin
                      G. Oliver Cromwell
                      H. Charles de Gaulle

GROUP III

_____ 92.   A. Louis Philippe
_____ 93.   B. Bismarck
_____ 94.   C. de Gaulle
_____ 95.   D. Shastri
                      E. Victor Emmanuel II
                      F. Adenauer
                      G. Suharto
                      H. Emperor Charles V
                      I. Napoleon I
                      J. Harold Wilson
                      K. Theodore Roosevelt

Test II   Associate the lettered person or item in Column II with the appropriate numbered statement in Column I.

COLUMN I	COLUMN II
____ 1. Sometimes referred to as the Land Between the Rivers	A. Babylonish Captivity
____ 2. Serfs who were bound to the soil in the Roman Empire	B. Walter Ulbricht
____ 3. The thousand years which would lead to the final judgment	C. Incas
____ 4. The period when the Popes lived in France	D. Colombia
____ 5. The term given to an alliance or association of equals	E. Surplus Value
____ 6. The difference between the selling price of an article and the price paid for it according to one writer	F. Mesopotamia
____ 7. Legislation which established British dominion status	G. Greece
____ 8. A plan for international loans for reparations payments in the 1920's	H. Induction
____ 9. The communist leader of East Germany since 1945	I. Coloni
____ 10. The Indian province which was the cause of dispute between India and Pakistan	J. British North America Act
____ 11. The belief in several gods	K. Risorgimento
____ 12. The Nation where the column and pediment were traditionally used	L. Monopoly
____ 13. They developed an elaborate road system in Latin America	M. Kashmir
____ 14. A grant of land in feudal times	N. Confederation
____ 15. An exclusive right to produce or sell goods	O. Fertile Crescent
____ 16. The place where a rebellion was assisted by Theodore Roosevelt	P. Dawes Plan
____ 17. The term describing reasoning from the general to the particular	Q. Apartheid
____ 18. A movement in 19th century Italy advocating the resurrection of the country	R. Polytheism
____ 19. Term meaning complete racial segregation	S. Fief
____ 20. The term describing reasoning from the particular to the general	T. Deduction
	U. Millenium
	V. Federation
	W. Venezuela

In the following multiple choice questions, place the appropriate letter in the blank space in front of the question.

____ 21. Egyptians used irrigation methods for production because
   A. They were excellent mathematicians
   B. Their political organization provided adequate labor

C. Since taxes were paid in grain, more grain had to be grown

D. Their important water supply came only from Nile floods

*____ 22. Important legal contributions by Rome are the following EXCEPT

A. A man must prove his innocence to the court

B. The law must be just to all men

C. Contracts are legally binding

D. The law must take into account changing circumstances

____ 23. Rome succeeded in finally defeating Carthage because

A. Hannibal committed suicide after his defeat by Scipio

B. Rome wanted the wealth of North Africa for herself

C. Rome had command of the sea

D. Cato demanded that Carthage be destroyed

____ 24. The Greek city-state developed because

A. The Greeks disliked the idea of forming a nation

B. The Spartans and Athenians had nothing in common

C. Geographical features isolated areas from one another

D. Greece was a thalassic civilization

____ 25. The interdict was more severe than excommunication because

A. It was a penalty imposed upon Kings and Emperors

B. It remained in effect over a whole country until the ruler was relieved of the sentence of excommunication

C. Priests and bishops were penalized by it

D. Once enforced it could not be lifted

____ 26. The Lay Investiture Issue was

A. A conflict between Emperor and Pope over the appointing of Church officials

B. The issue of whether or not priests should marry

C. The question of whether or not a priest could give property to the Church

D. The right of the Pope to choose his successor

____ 27. The main objection to Indulgences was

A. They were sometimes money payments as substitutes for penances

B. They were contributions to charity in addition to genuine penances

C. The Pope had no right to issue them

D. Martin Luther wished to reform their mis-use

*____ 28. Peter the Great helped to develop Russia as a nation by the following EXCEPT

A. He secured Riga as Russia's "window on the Baltic"

B. He rewarded the nobles for service and loyalty

C. He modernized the army, navy, and government administration

D. He encouraged the development of a middle class

*_____ 29. The Model Parliament of 1295 resulted in the following EXCEPT
   A. Representation of the non-nobles
   B. The principle that those who paid taxes should have a voice in the levying of taxes
   C. The establishments of annual meetings of parliament
   D. The right of representatives to demand certain laws in return for taxes

_____ 30. The Proclamation of 1763 aroused the colonists in America because it
   A. Enforced the mercantile system
   B. Consisted of Navigation Acts to restrict colonial trade
   C. Demanded that the colonists pay part of the cost of the French-Indian War
   D. Denied the colonists the right to settle west of the Appalachians

*_____ 31. The "Glorious Revolution" did the following EXCEPT
   A. Put William of Orange upon the throne of England
   B. Guaranteed the rights of free speech to parliament
   C. Provided for the position of prime minister in England
   D. Guaranteed the people the right to petition the Crown

*_____ 32. The Stamp Act resulted in the following EXCEPT
   A. The refusal of the colonists to import British goods
   B. The imposition of a tax on all legal documents
   C. The beginning of organized resistance to Britain
   D. The passage of the Declaratory Act

*_____ 33. The Committee of Public Safety in France did the following EXCEPT
   A. Ordered the execution of thousands of citizens
   B. Safeguarded the public against arbitrary arrest
   C. Became the real government of France with Robespierre at its head
   D. Was largely responsible for the Reign of Terror

_____ 34. Robert Owen's only success was
   A. The establishment of New Harmony as a successful experiment
   B. The organization of consumers' cooperatives
   C. The winning of widespread support for his economic theories
   D. The organizing of powerful trade unions

*_____ 35. By the Treaty of Portsmouth Russia suffered the following losses EXCEPT
   A. The northern half of Sakhalin Island
   B. The Liaotung Peninsula
   C. Her influence in Korea
   D. Her influence in Manchuria

*_____ **36.** The following are correct statements about the basic ideas of these authors EXCEPT

    A. Smith: *Wealth of Nations:* complete laissez-faire

    B. Malthus: *Principles of Population:* food supply increased more rapidly than population

    C. Ricardo: "Iron Law of Wages:" higher wages resulted in larger families, which in due course led to lower wages

    D. Mill: *Political Economy:* wealth should be more equitably distributed through income and inheritance taxes

_____ **37.** Chiang Kai-shek lost to the Chinese Communists because

    A. The United States failed to give him any assistance

    B. Japan was able to conquer the whole of China

    C. Chiang's Kuomintang Party failed to offer a program to win peasant support

    D. Russia assisted the Communists with armed forces

*_____ **38.** Opponents of 19th century imperialism advanced these arguments EXCEPT

    A. Colonies were costly to maintain, both in men and money

    B. Free trade was better served through world markets

    C. Colonies did not provide strategic bases

    D. Colonialism could not be justified in a democratic nation

*_____ **39.** Mandates which later became independent nations are the following EXCEPT

    A. Iraq

    B. Turkey

    C. Palestine

    D. Syria

*_____ **40.** Basic causes for discontent in Russia during 1914–1917 were the following EXCEPT

    A. Shortages of food caused by the drafting of millions of farmers into the army

    B. Inability of the Czarist government to supply cities with food and fuel

    C. The personal leadership of the troops by the Czar

    D. Refusal of the government to grant any demands for self-government

_____ **41.** Appeasement is the policy of

    A. Agreement between two powerful nations

    B. Compromise in which each side is willing to make a concession

    C. Alliance between small nations against a powerful nation

    D. Concessions given by one side only, in the hope of avoiding further demands

_____ 42. In 1966 the United Arab Republic consisted of
A. Syria and Egypt
B. Egypt, Jordan, Yemen
C. Egypt
D. Syria, Lebanon, Jordan, Egypt

_____ 43. Post-war threat to world peace by the U.S.S.R. was
A. That she believed in state ownership of the means of production
B. That she had helped to defeat Germany and wanted reparations
C. That she retained the historical ambition of Czarist Russia to expand westwards
D. That she was still a dictatorship

_____ 44. Chinese communes were organized to
A. Provide cheaper accommodations for farmers
B. Control the peasants and increase food production
C. Teach farmers how to increase food production
D. Satisfy peasant demands for better prices for their products

_____ 45. The basic cause for the division of India into two parts in 1947 was
A. That each side wanted Kashmir for itself
B. Religious differences of the two nations
C. Jinnah's dislike for Gandhi
D. The fact that the British empire was disintegrating

The following are types of political or social beliefs, or a point of view expressed by a political group. Indicate which each excerpt is

A. Nihilism
B. Social Revolutionary Party
C. The Tennis Court Oath
D. The Divine Right Oath
E. The Decembrists

_____ 46. An entire nation cannot be suppressed, and still less can the discontent of a nation be suppressed by rigorous measures . . . That is why the government in Russia has no moral influence over the people: that is why an event like killing the Czar excites sympathy among a great part of this very people. Pay no heed to flatterers, Your Majesty. Regicide in Russia is very popular.

_____ 47. All were of the opinion that the Assembly should meet for deliberation in a situation so delicate, and, consequently, should seek out a suitable place . . . There we made the following resolution, "Be it resolved that all members of this Assembly immediately take a solemn oath never to separate until the constitution of the kingdom shall be established."

_____ 48. Napoleon invaded Russia and then only, and for the first time, did the Russian people become aware of their power . . . The soldiers would say, "We freed the Fatherland from the tyrant and now we ourselves are tyrannized over by the ruling classes. Many cherished the hope that the Emperor would grant a constitution. We thought of creating a Senate of the oldest and wisest Russian men of the present administration . . . Then we thought of having a Chamber of Deputies composed of national representatives."

_____ 49. The fundamental principle was absolute individualism. It was the negation of the obligations imposed upon the individual by society, by family life, and by religion.

_____ 50. Kings are justly called gods, for that they exercise a manner or resemblance of divine power upon earth: for if you consider the attributes to God, you shall see how they agree in the person of a king. God hath power to create or destroy, make or unmake at his pleasure, to give life or send death, to judge and to be judged by none . . . And the like power have kings.

Associate each of the persons in Column II with the appropriate statement in Column I.

COLUMN I		COLUMN II
_____ 51. I was elected president, but I made myself emperor	A.	Mohammed
	B.	Herodotus
_____ 52. What I did was known as the Hegira	C.	Louis Napoleon
_____ 53. I favored Legitimacy	D.	Pasteur
_____ 54. I was called the Father of History	E.	Metternich
_____ 55. I developed a vaccine to prevent rabies		

56-70   For the following three topics indicate by T or F whether each statement is True or False.

The Triple Alliance

_____ 56. Was the "Encirclement" denounced vigorously by Germany

_____ 57. Was an offensive alliance designed to start aggression at the right time

_____ 58. Was partly organized out of the belief that France would seek revenge for the Franco-Prussian War

_____ 59. Was not supported by all the three members in 1914

_____ 60. Is sometimes referred to as the Three Emperors' League

The Lend-Lease Act

_____ 61. Provided assistance to any belligerent nation in World War II which asked for it

_____ 62. Offered assistance to any nation whose defense the President deemed vital to the defense of the United States

_____ 63. Was an agreement between the United States and Great Britain regarding the exchange of bases and equipment

_____ 64. In effect, ended the neutrality of the United States

_____ 65. By this Act the United States became the "arsenal of democracy."

The Truman Doctrine

_____ 66. Was joint action by the United States and European nations

_____ 67. Was unilateral action by the United States

_____ 68. Gave substantial economic aid to Turkey and Greece

_____ 69. Resulted from pressure by the U.S.S.R. on Greece and Yugoslavia

_____ 70. Announced a United States doctrine of willingness to assist any nation threatened by internal or external communism

During the period after the Second World War changes occurred in former colonial areas

   I. One split into two nations

   II. One formed a federation with one or more areas

   III. One developed a policy of racial separation

   IV. One suffered violent internal conflict resulting in intervention by the United Nations

   V. One was the first African colony to become an independent nation

The former colonies involved are included in the following

A. Ghana	F. Malaysia
B. Belgian Congo	G. Dutch East Indies
C. Republic of South Africa	H. Canada
D. India	I. Portuguese East Africa
E. Ceylon	J. Kenya

_____ 71. Which of the above was Type I?

_____ 72. Which was Type II?

_____ 73. Which was Type III?

_____ 74. Which was Type IV?

_____ 75. Which was Type V?

Associate the persons in Column II with the terms in Column I.

COLUMN I	COLUMN II
_____ 76. Window on the Baltic	A. Robespierre
_____ 77. Committee of Public Safety	B. Stalin
_____ 78. Iron Curtain	C. Peter the Great
_____ 79. Peace Without Victory	D. Darwin
_____ 80. Survival of the Fittest	E. Woodrow Wilson

Associate the periods in Column II with the wars listed in Column I.

COLUMN I	COLUMN II
_____ 81. Russo-Turkish War	A. 1890–1900
_____ 82. Opium War	B. 1870–1875
_____ 83. Sino-Japanese War	C. 1850–1860
_____ 84. Crimean War	D. 1875–1880
_____ 85. Franco-Prussian War	E. 1840–1845

Questions 86-88 refer to the following statement

"And covenants, without the sword, are but words, and of no strength to secure a man at all. Therefore, notwithstanding the laws of Nature, which every one of them hath kept . . . if there be no powers erected, or nor great enough for our security, every man will, and may lawfully rely on his own strength and art . . . The only way to erect such a common power, as may be able to defend them from the invasion of foreigners, and the injuries of one another . . . is to confer all power upon one man."

_____ 86. The author wrote this in defense of which of the following
   A. The belief in the divine right of kings
   B. That men are born with natural rights
   C. That the government is a trustee which must act as the people desire
   D. Absolute rule
   E. Constitutional Monarchy

_____ 87. Similar ideas are to be found in
   A. *Treatises of Civil Government*
   B. *Principle of Political Economy*
   C. *Common Sense*
   D. *The Prince*
   E. *The Communist Manifesto*

_____ 88. The excerpt could have been written by
   A. John Locke
   B. Thomas Hobbes
   C. Edmund Burke
   D. Adam Smith
   E. Jean Jacques Rousseau
   F. Karl Marx

Questions 89-90 refer to the following quotations.

Speaker I
"The real triumph is that it has shown that the representatives of four great Powers can find it possible to agree on a way of carrying out a difficult and delicate operation by discussion instead of by force of arms, and thereby they have averted a catastrophe . . . We must feel profound sympathy for a small and gallant nation in the hour of their national grief and loss . . . she has earned our admiration and respect for her restraint, her dignity, for her magnificent discipline in the face of such a trial as few nations have ever been called upon to meet."

Speaker II
"All is over. Silent, abandoned, broken (that gallant nation) recedes into the darkness. She has suffered in every respect by her association with the Western democracies and with the League of Nations, of which she has always been an obedient servant. She has suffered in particular from her association with France . . . We have sustained a defeat without war . . . we have passed an awful

milestone in our history, when the whole equilibrium of Europe has been deranged . . . And do not suppose that this is the end. This is only the beginning of the reckoning.''

_____ 89. Speaker II is regretting the failure of which policy?
      A. The balance of power
      B. Collective security
      C. The Alliance system
      D. The North Atlantic Treaty Organization
      E. The Warsaw Pact

_____ 90. Which are the "Four great Powers" mentioned by Speaker I?
      A. Germany, Italy, Japan, Russia
      B. Great Britain, Germany, France, Russia
      C. Great Britain, Germany, Italy, France
      D. Great Britain, France, Italy, Yugoslavia
      E. Great Britain, Germany, France, Czechoslovakia

_____ 91. Speaker I is defending
      A. The Russo-German Pact of August, 1939
      B. The Kellogg-Briand Pact
      C. The Hoare-Laval Agreement
      D. The Munich Agreement
      E. The Manchurian Crisis of 1931

_____ 92. Speaker I is probably
      A. Franklin Roosevelt
      B. Eduard Benes
      C. Mussolini
      D. Chamberlain
      E. Lenin

_____ 93. Speaker II is probably
      A. Hitler
      B. Churchill
      C. Truman
      D. Stalin

Questions 94-95 refer to the following excerpt.
"Behind that line lie all the capitals of the ancient states of central and eastern Europe, Warsaw, Berlin, Prague, Vienna, Budapest, Belgrade, Bucharest and Sofia, all these famous cities and the populations around them . . . and all are subject, in one form or another not only to Soviet influence but to a very high and in some cases increasing measure of control from Moscow."

_____ 94. The reference is to
      A. The Curzon Line
      B. The line from Stettin to Trieste
      C. The Oder-Neisse boundary

D. The Berlin Wall

E. The line separating East and West Germany

_____ **95.** The Speaker is

A. President Kennedy

B. President Truman

C. Winston Churchill

D. The mayor of Berlin

E. The German Chancellor

Test III

Associate the lettered person or item in Column II with the appropriate numbered statement in Column I.

COLUMN I	COLUMN II

_____ 1. The term meaning a sea civilization

_____ 2. The name given to Mohammed's flight to Medina

_____ 3. Name for state collective farms in Russia

_____ 4. A census of people and property held in England in the 11th century

_____ 5. Chinese philosophy and code of behavior

_____ 6. Sale of Church offices and positions

_____ 7. The name given to Spaniards born in a Spanish colony

_____ 8. Search warrants much criticized in the American colonies

_____ 9. Early 20th century Russian reformers advocating constitutional decentralized monarchy

_____ 10. The agreement which created the Dual Monarchy of Austria-Hungary

_____ 11. Belief in taking no sides, in remaining uncommitted

_____ 12. A religion which was a complete way of life

_____ 13. Twentieth century defensive fortifications in France

_____ 14. The policy used to keep the U.S.S.R. within her boundaries after 1945

_____ 15. In France this was the codification of civil, criminal, and penal law

_____ 16. Bismarck's crusade against the Church and radicals

_____ 17. The Permanent Executive Committee of the U.S.S.R.

_____ 18. The man who advocated world-wide revolution, and quarrelled with Stalin

_____ 19. A special United States envoy who attempted to work out a compromise between Mao Tse-tung and Chiang Kai-shek

_____ 20. The document which repudiated the Roosevelt Corollary

COLUMN II

A. Augsleich
B. Creoles
C. Code Napoleon
D. Clark Memorandum
E. Neutralism
F. Octobrist
G. Maginot Line
H. Thalassic
I. Hegira
J. Trotsky
K. Hinduism
L. Simony
M. Marshall
N. Domesday Book
O. Cold War
P. Confucianism
Q. Presidium
R. Writs of Assistance
S. Black and the Red
T. Anschluss
U. Sovkhozy
V. Mestizos

In the following multiple choice questions, place the appropriate letter in the blank space in front of the question.

_____ 21. Belief in the afterlife had no place in the religion of the

    A. Babylonians   C. Hebrews

    B. Egyptians   D. Confucians

*____ **22.** All the following EXCEPT ONE were gains made by the plebeians when they threatened to secede
    A. Election of the 10 tribunes
    B. The Twelve Tables of Law
    C. The Draconian Law
    D. The Hortensian Law

____ **23.** The term "pyrrhic victory" refers to
    A. Lengthy military campaigns in Pyrrhus
    B. Roman victories against Pyrrhus
    C. Costly victories which ultimately led to defeat for Pyrrhus
    D. Victories that are won with little effort

*____ **24.** Charlemagne's empire broke up for the following reasons EXCEPT
    A. It was divided between Charlemagne's three sons
    B. It was attacked by Teutonic peoples from Scandinavia
    C. Local nobles were unable to keep it intact
    D. Because it had no racial or political unity

*____ **25.** Byzantium's contributions to western civilization were the following EXCEPT
    A. Its important trade with the Far East
    B. Its resistance to continued attacks by the Turks
    C. The preservation of many Greek manuscripts
    D. Its Iconoclastic Controversy with the Pope

____ **26.** The Reformation in England resulted in
    A. The immediate establishment of Protestantism there
    B. The substitution of the King for the Pope as head of the Church in England
    C. The Pope's awarding Henry VIII the title of "Defender of the Faith"
    D. No change whatever in the position of the Pope in the Church in England

*____ **27.** The Renaissance was essentially the following EXCEPT
    A. A rediscovery of and interest in the writings and culture of the Greeks and Romans
    B. A re-emphasis upon Scholasticism and Church authority
    C. A breaking-away from the restrictions of feudalism
    D. The development of middle class interests, and an emphasis upon individualism

____ **28.** Despite improvements made by Kublai Khan, Chinese prosperity declined for the following reasons EXCEPT
    A. Too many peasants were tenant farmers
    B. Paper money was replacing coin money and depreciating
    C. Kublai Khan was a foreign conqueror
    D. The number of taxpayers was decreasing

*____ **29.** Geographical factors influencing the history of Russia are the following EXCEPT
  A. The need to secure warm-water ports
  B. Rivers that are dangerous roads for attack coming from the West
  C. The great Eurasian plain open to attack from the West
  D. The Ural Mountains dividing the Eurasian plain north and south

*____ **30.** Bolivar's dream of a federal union of Latin America was impossible because of the following EXCEPT
  A. The vastness of the continent
  B. Interference by European nations
  C. The lack of a common heritage and common interests
  D. The refusal of the Indians to be assimilated

____ **31.** Opposition to the Townshend Acts resulted from the essential fact that
  A. Townshend was the Chancellor of the Exchequer
  B. The colonists believed that neither king nor parliament could enact any law for the colonies
  C. The colonists objected to all aspects of mercantilism
  D. The Acts levied what the colonists knew were "internal" taxes

*____ **32.** The Articles of Confederation did the following EXCEPT
  A. Organized a government to conduct a war
  B. Gave full authority and power to a central government to conduct the war
  C. Left the states with the power to levy troops and taxes as they chose
  D. Appointed George Washington as Commander-in-Chief

*____ **33.** Significant scientific methods during the age of the "scientific revolution" were the following EXCEPT
  A. Treating theories by experimentation
  B. The use of mathematical symbols by scientists to express scientific terms
  C. The jealous guarding by scientists of their own discoveries
  D. The combining of theory and practice

____ **34.** Fabian Socialists believed in
  A. Immediate action to remedy industrial injustices
  B. A free enterprise system moderately regulated by the government
  C. A gradual adoption of their program through constant advocacy of it
  D. Using Marxian tactics if results were obtainable in no other way

*_____ **35.** The Chartists demands all eventually became law EXCEPT
     A. Universal suffrage
     B. Annual parliaments
     C. Secret ballot
     D. Payment of members of parliament

*_____ **36.** Italians opposed their several rulers through the following organizations or movements EXCEPT
     A. The Carbonari
     B. The Red Shirts
     C. The Octobrists
     D. The Risorgimento

*_____ **37.** The little territory of Bosnia-Herzegovina was significant in international affairs for the following reasons EXCEPT
     A. It was Slavic and wished to free itself from Austrian rule
     B. Serbia wanted to acquire it as an outlet to the sea
     C. The Russians were the conspirators who arranged for the death of the Archduke in Sarajevo
     D. The assassination of the Archduke gave Austria the opportunity to attack Serbia

*_____ **38.** China remained a backward nation compared with modern powers for the following reasons EXCEPT
     A. It lacked capital and industrial skills
     B. It attempted to modernize through monopolies rather than through competition
     C. It lacked the military power to defend itself
     D. It no longer accepted Confucian ideals of local loyalty

_____ **39.** The chief problem facing the Weimar republic was that
     A. It was a republic
     B. Its leaders had been obliged to accept responsibility for the "war guilt" clause in the treaty in 1919
     C. Ludendorff and Hindenburg had surrendered in 1918
     D. Germany had been "stabbed in the back" in 1918

_____ **40.** The Munich Pact marked the almost total collapse of collective security because
     A. Chamberlain thought he had "won peace in our time"
     B. Germany was able to get control of Germans in Czechoslovakia
     C. Several nations failed to live up to their guarantees to defend Czechoslovakia
     D. Czechoslovakia was not present when the Munich Agreement was negotiated

*_____ **41.** The Locarno Agreements seemed to guarantee future peace for the following reasons EXCEPT

    A. Germany agreed not to change her boundaries with France and Belgium

    B. Germany guaranteed not to go to war with France or Belgium

    C. Great Britain and Italy agreed to guarantee the boundaries of France and Belgium

    D. The western European powers avoided any commitments about Germany's eastern frontier

*_____ **42.** The Fourth Republic of France was replaced by the Fifth Republic for the following reasons EXCEPT

    A. The French army in Algeria revolted

    B. France feared that the French troops might send parachute troops against Paris

    C. France had 400,000 troops in Algeria

    D. The government of France was unable to resolve the Algerian problem

_____ **43.** The long-range policy of the Truman Doctrine was

    A. To assist Great Britain in giving continued aid to Greece

    B. To help Greece and Turkey against Russia

    C. To contain Russia

    D. A diplomatic move to persuade Russia to negotiate international issues

_____ **44.** The first African colony to receive its independence was

    A. The Belgian Congo   C. Madagascar

    B. Guinea   D. The Gold Coast

_____ **45.** Apartheid is designed to

    A. Force all native Africans to work for their colonial rulers

    B. Achieve complete political and racial separation of Africans and whites

    C. Revive tribal customs and organizations

    D. Provide eventual limited participation in the government by the Africans

In the following definitions, choose for each what is the Most appropriate definition and mark it after the M, and choose the Least appropriate definition and mark it after the L.

Anarchism

_M_ **46.** A. A belief in a gradual change of government to communism

    B. Regards government as a necessary institution, even if unpopular

_L_ **47.** C. Supports the violent removal of all rulers and forms of government

    D. Does not believe in government of any sort

Neutralism

_M_ **48.** A. The policy of being so self-sufficient that a nation can avoid any relationships with other nations, even economic ones.

    B. The policy of remaining neutral and taking neither side in a war

_L_ **49.** C. The policy of remaining uncommitted to any nation or group of nations in peace time

D. The policy of attempting to form a Third Force between two powerful nations or groups of nations

Associate the person in Column II with the appropriate statement in Column I.

	COLUMN I	COLUMN II
_____ **50.**	I ordered the kulaks to be eliminated	A. Freidrich Ebert
_____ **51.**	I became the president of the German Republic	B. Sukarno
		C. Kosygin
_____ **52.**	I was leader of the country just before Lenin	D. Clement Attlee
		E. Emile Zola
_____ **53.**	I drove the French out of Indo-China	F. Thomas Hobbes
_____ **54.**	I first advocated "peaceful co-existence"	G. Adam Smith
_____ **55.**	I replaced Churchill as prime minister	H. Voltaire
_____ **56.**	I was recently elected a leader of the U.S.S.R.	I. Jeremy Bentham
		J. Ho Chi Minh
_____ **57.**	I was associated with the Fashoda Incident	K. Stalin
		L. Kerensky
_____ **58.**	I wrote the _Leviathan_	M. Kitchener
_____ **59.**	I publicly defended Dreyfus	N. Khrushchev
_____ **60.**	I wrote the _Wealth of Nations_	

For the following three topics indicate by T or F whether each statement is True or False.

The Weimar Republic

_____ **61.** Hindenburg was the first president

_____ **62.** The first president was a workingman

_____ **63.** It was severely criticized for signing the Versailles Treaty

_____ **64.** Hitler praised this government for ending World War I

_____ **65.** It lasted until 1933 when Hitler replaced it with another form of government

Treaty of Brest-Litovsk

_____ **66.** It ended World War I

_____ **67.** It took Russia out of the war in 1918

_____ **68.** It deprived Russia of a great part of her European land area

_____ **69.** It was the cause of the Bolshevik Revolution in Russia

_____ **70.** It provided Germany with the opportunity to attempt a breakthrough on the western front

Magna Carta

_____ **71.** It stated that the king was above the law

_____ **72.** It stated that the law was above the king

_____ **73.** It guaranteed the citizens that there would be no taxation without representation

_____ **74.** It guaranteed that a man would be tried by his peers

_____ **75.** It established democratic government in England

Associate the wars in Column II with the topics in Column I.

	COLUMN I	COLUMN II
_____ 76.	Concessions and Treaty Ports	A. Russo-Turkish War
_____ 77.	Prohibition of forts and warships on the Black Sea	B. Opium War
_____ 78.	The "Sick Man of Europe"	C. Russo-Japanese War
_____ 79.	An emperor and his army captured	D. Crimean War
_____ 80.	The Liaotung Peninsula ownership was transferred	E. Franco-Prussian War

Associate the correct dates in Column II with the terms in Column I.

	COLUMN I	COLUMN II
_____ 81.	Munich Agreement	A. 1917
_____ 82.	NATO organized	B. 1919
_____ 83.	Korean War began	C. 1936
_____ 84.	Proclamation of the Republic of Israel	D. 1938
_____ 85.	Spanish Civil War began	E. 1947
_____ 86.	Khrushchev deposed	F. 1948
_____ 87.	Bolshevik Revolution in Russia	G. 1949
_____ 88.	Treaty of Versailles	H. 1950
_____ 89.	Truman Doctrine announced	I. 1957
_____ 90.	Ghana became independent	J. 1964

The following quotations are taken from five of the topics listed below. Indicate the source of each quotation.

A. Covenant of the League of Nations
B. Charter of the United Nations
C. The North Atlantic Treaty Organization
D. The Atlantic Charter
E. The Yalta Agreements
F. The Bandung Conference
G. The Rome-Berlin-Tokyo Axis Agreement
H. The Kellogg-Briand Pact

_____ 91. The three governments consider it the prerequisite of lasting peace that every nation in the world shall receive the space to which it is entitled. They have therefore decided to stand by and cooperate with one another in their efforts in Greater East Asia and the regions of Europe respectively.

_____ 92. The allied chiefs jointly declare their mutual agreement to concert during the temporary period of instability in liberated Europe the policies of their three governments in assisting the peoples liberated . . . to solve by democratic means their pressing political and economic problems . . . to reorganize the government of liberated Poland on a broader democratic basis, and to permit the government to hold unfettered elections as soon as possible on the basis of universal suffrage and secret ballot.

_____ **93.** They deem it right to make known certain common principles in the national policies of their respective countries on which they base their hopes for a better future for the world. They seek no aggrandizement . . . they desire to see no territorial changes that do not accord with the freely expressed wishes of the people concerned. They respect the right of all peoples to choose the form of government under which they will live.

_____ **94.** The parties agree that an armed attack against one or more of them in Europe or North America shall be considered an attack against them all; and consequently they agree that, if an armed attack occurs, each of them . . . will assist the party or parties so attacked by taking forthwith, individually and in concert . . . such action as it deems necessary.

_____ **95.** The conferees recognized the urgency of promoting economic development in the Asian-African region . . . The conference condemned racialism as a means of cultural suppression . . . The conference decared that colonialism is an evil which should be speedily brought to an end, and declared its support of independence for those people who are subjected to alien rule.

Test IV

Associate the lettered item or person in Column II with the appropriate numbered statement in Column I.

COLUMN I	COLUMN II
_____ 1. The area of which Nineveh was the capital	A. Subinfeudation
_____ 2. The official site of a Greek Alliance	B. Dyarchy
_____ 3. He inflicted a severe defeat on the Moslems in the 8th century	C. Statute of Westminster
_____ 4. He established the Society of Jesus	D. Dialectic
_____ 5. This guarantees the right of a fair trial	E. Nationalism
_____ 6. The term describing the logical presentation of an argument	F. Sarajevo
	G. Charles Martel
_____ 7. The ownership by the state of the means of production, or the act of taking over ownership	H. Cominform
	I. Loyola
	J. Sinn Fein
_____ 8. The God of the Jews	K. Tenochtitlan
_____ 9. Capital of New Spain of the Ocean Sea	L. Code of Lubeck
_____ 10. The sub-leasing of land to a vassal	M. Habeas Corpus
_____ 11. Legal rules applied to an association of North European trading towns	N. Babylon
	O. Balance of Trade
_____ 12. The term describing an excess of exports over imports, with the difference paid in money	P. Javeh
	Q. Nationalization
	R. Zollverein
_____ 13. A 20th century customs union in Europe	S. Propaganda
_____ 14. The site of the assassination in 1914 of the heir to the Austrian throne	T. Delos
_____ 15. This document granted complete independence to the former British dominions	
_____ 16. Joint rule by British and Indian officials	
_____ 17. A political party whose name means "Ourselves Alone"	
_____ 18. An agency of the 1950's for the spread of international communism	
_____ 19. The term describing the desire for independence	
_____ 20. A term that may be used to describe or mean the withholding of vital information in order to mislead people	

In the following multiple choice questions, place the appropriate letter in the blank space in front of the question.

*_____ 21. All the following EXCEPT ONE were different names for the same area of land or part of an area
    A. Palestine
    B. Judah and Israel
    C. Damascus
    D. Canaan

*____ 22. All the following EXCEPT ONE were applicable to the Gracchi brothers
   A. They were nobles adopted into plebeian families
   B. They attempted to limit the size of landholdings
   C. They were murdered by their political enemies
   D. They were successful Roman generals and consuls

____ 23. The Emperor Augustus claimed that he
   A. Was emperor by hereditary right
   B. Was a constitutional monarch and was only reforming the republic
   C. Had the right to exercise dictatorial powers
   D. Had been elected by the generals who defeated Caesar's assassins

*____ 24. The Emperor Henry IV was obliged to submit to the Pope at Canossa for the following reasons EXCEPT
   A. Henry had been excommunicated
   B. Henry had been taken prisoner by the Pope
   C. Henry's subjects had been freed from allegiance to him
   D. Henry's nobles were rebelling against him

____ 25. Chivalry was a code of behavior
   A. Which dedicated the knight to service to all mankind
   B. Which applied only to the knightly class
   C. Which obliged the knight to obey his king without question
   D. Which appeared only in the mythical Court of King Arthur

*____ 26. The Age of Commercialism was in part the result of the following EXCEPT
   A. The break-up of feudalism
   B. Geographic development which opened the world to exploration and expansion
   C. The rapid development in industrial inventions and techniques
   D. The effects of the Renaissance and scientific thinking

*____ 27. The position of the Church was threatened by the following EXCEPT
   A. Its use of the interdict against Kings
   B. Its interference with what people regarded as national affairs
   C. Its use of the Seven Sacraments
   D. Differences of opinion regarded as heresies

____ 28. During the period of the Mogul Empire in India all the following occurred EXCEPT
   A. Religious toleration was permitted
   B. Two cultures and religions developed in India
   C. India was divided into India and Pakistan
   D. The Taj Mahal was built

_____ 29. Under British administration in India this benefitted India
   A. The importation of British textiles
   B. The payment of taxes in money
   C. The participation of Indians in local government
   D. The introduction of centralized government

*_____ 30. Locke's _Treatise of Civil Government_ was of great interest to the American colonists because it advocated the following EXCEPT
   A. Men had the right to select their own government
   B. The colonists should revolt against king and parliament
   C. When a government does not carry out the wishes of the people they may remove it
   D. A government is a trustee charged with carrying out certain duties

*_____ 31. The middle class of France criticized the _ancien regime_ because of the following EXCEPT
   A. They had no political rights
   B. The clergy and nobility were not taxed
   C. The king and his nobles ruled exactly as they pleased
   D. France had lost prestige in foreign affairs

*_____ 32. Writs of Assistance were opposed by the American colonists for the following reasons EXCEPT
   A. Search warrants had never before been used
   B. They did not specify what premises were to be searched
   C. Any petty British official could use them as he saw fit
   D. They contained no expiration date

_____ 33. The Jacobins were
   A. A religious order living in a monastery
   B. French citizens who lived around Bordeaux
   C. Politicians supporting a constitutional monarchy
   D. Advocates of a republic

*_____ 34. The emancipation of the serfs by Alexander II benefitted the peasants for the following reasons EXCEPT
   A. Peasants were no longer the personal possession of landowners
   B. Each peasant now became the proprietor of his own piece of land
   C. Peasants were represented in local government
   D. The peasants were encouraged to grow more food

*_____ 35. Social Darwinism supported the following beliefs EXCEPT
   A. Government controls in economic life
   B. In general, the fittest people and nations survive
   C. Governments may use force to achieve their objectives
   D. Strong nations have the right to overcome weak nations

*____ 36. Germany became a member of the following EXCEPT
   A. The Three Emperors' League
   B. The Reinsurance Treaty
   C. The Dual Entente
   D. The Triple Alliance

____ 37. The major factor which enabled Germany to attempt a break-through on her western front in 1918 was
   A. The success of her submarine warfare in weakening the Allies
   B. French exhaustion after more than three years of warfare
   C. Germany's determination to capture Paris before United States troops arrived in France in large numbers
   D. The Treaty of Brest-Litovsk

*____ 38. The Three People's Principles included the following EXCEPT
   A. Liberation of China from foreign domination
   B. Elimination of trade relations with foreign nations
   C. Democracy for China
   D. Economic rights and security for the Chinese

*____ 39. The Covenant of the League of Nations included the following EXCEPT
   A. Members agree to consider what action to take against an actual or potential aggressor
   B. The Council shall order other nations to use force against an aggressor
   C. Members may decide to cut off all trade relations with an aggressor
   D. The Council may recommend the use of force

*____ 40. Five-Year Plans were designed to do the following EXCEPT
   A. Nationalize and organize all industrial and agricultural production
   B. Increase the production of consumer goods
   C. Move industrial plants into the interior as a defensive measure
   D. Conduct foreign policy aggressively so as to expand Russia's frontiers

*____ 41. The supporters of Marxism-Leninism advocated the following EXCEPT
   A. Complete and total dictatorship
   B. Co-existence with other nations wherever possible
   C. World-wide communist conspiracy under Moscow's leadership
   D. Class warfare

_____ **42.** Israel faces the following problems EXCEPT
  A. The refusal of the Palestine Arabs to accept officially resettlement outside Israel
  B. The refusal of the Arabs to recognize the Republic of Israel
  C. The announced intention of Arabs to drive the Israelis into the sea
  D. The unwillingness of the Israelis to join Israel's armed forces

*_____ **43.** Problems facing France after World War II were the following EXCEPT
  A. The Third Republic was blamed for defeat and had to be replaced
  B. In post-war elections the large number of political parties prevented a clear majority for a single party
  C. France was distracted by wars in Indo-China and Algeria
  D. De Gaulle was elected President of the Republic

*_____ **44.** The free enterprise democratic system may be delayed in African nations for the following reasons EXCEPT
  A. Insufficient capital may oblige them to introduce socialism
  B. Africans may generally favor accepting Russian assistance
  C. Africans prefer Russian domination to that of their former colonial rulers
  D. The democratic process and ideas are difficult to adopt in recently-independent African nations

*_____ **45.** The Twenty-One Demands by Japan upon China included the following EXCEPT
  A. No foreign power could lease any Chinese harbor or bay without Japan's permission
  B. China must allow Japan to acquire German rights in Shantung Province
  C. China must cede Manchuria to Japan
  D. China must permit Japan to share in the police administration of China

Questions 46 to 55 refer to the following types of governments

A. Constitutional Monarchy	C. Republic
B. Democracy	D. Dictatorship

Here are five countries, *each* of which can be properly classified under *two* of the above types. In order of the appearance of each country, list it as *two* of the above types.

The United States	Canada
U.S.S.R.	Great Britain
France	

_____ **46.**
_____ **47.** United States

_____ 48. U.S.S.R.
_____ 49.

_____ 50. France
_____ 51.

_____ 52. Canada
_____ 53.

_____ 54. Great Britain
_____ 55.

Associate the person in Column II with the appropriate statement in Column I.

COLUMN I	COLUMN II
_____ 56. I wanted Carthage destroyed	A. Champollion
_____ 57. I was assassinated in the forum	B. Hammurabi
_____ 58. I deciphered the Rosetta Stone	C. Schliemann
_____ 59. I discovered the ancient city of Troy	D. Caesar
_____ 60. A famous code was named after me	E. Cataline
	F. Cato

Put the men in their chronological order

_____ 61.	A. Metternich
_____ 62.	B. Hannibal
_____ 63.	C. Ben-Gurion
_____ 64.	D. Charlemagne
_____ 65.	E. Chaucer

Put the following wars in their chronological order

_____ 66.	A. Boer War
_____ 67.	B. Russo-Turkish War
_____ 68.	C. Crimean War
_____ 69.	D. Greek War of Independence
_____ 70.	E. Franco-Prussian War

71-85   For the following three topics indicate by T or F whether each statement is True or False.

The Counter Reformation

_____ 71. Was commenced by the Society of Jesus
_____ 72. Was a 16th century movement by the Catholic Church
_____ 73. Was an attempt of the Church to redefine Catholic doctrine
_____ 74. Was the name given to Luther's attempt to reform the Church
_____ 75. Included the Inquisition as a means to stamp out heresy

The Stamp Act

_____ 76. Threatened the power of the purse of the colonists
_____ 77. Had very little effect upon the average colonist
_____ 78. Made every business document illegal unless a stamp was affixed

_____ 79. Was the actual cause of the Battle of Lexington

_____ 80. Was not repealed before the actual fighting began between the British troops and the colonists

The Statute of Westminster

_____ 81. Gave Ireland its first government for the entire island

_____ 82. Established the British Commonwealth of Nations

_____ 83. Prohibited the British government from vetoing any laws passed by the Parliaments of the former British dominions

_____ 84. Established the British monarch as the ruler of all parts of the Commonwealth

_____ 85. Established the independent nation of Rhodesia

Associate the correct dates in Column II with the terms in Column I.

COLUMN I	COLUMN II
_____ 86. Alsace-Lorraine transferred to the German Empire	A. 1517
	B. 1848
_____ 87. Establishment of the Polish Corridor	C. 1871
_____ 88. The Ninety-Five Theses publicly exhibited	D. 1878
	E. 1915
_____ 89. The Tanaka Memorial supposedly announced	F. 1919
	G. 1928
_____ 90. The Sudetenland transferred to Germany	H. 1931
	I. 1938
_____ 91. The Oder-Neisse boundary line established	J. 1945
_____ 92. Serbia obtained its independence	
_____ 93. The Twenty-One Demands made by Japan	
_____ 94. The Manchurian Incident	
_____ 95. The Communist Manifesto issued	

Test V

Associate the lettered item or person in Column II with the appropriate numbered statement in Column I.

COLUMN I

_____ 1. The name of the God of the Nile

_____ 2. The barbarian who plundered Rome in 410 A.D.

_____ 3. They carried the alphabet throughout the Mediterranean

_____ 4. Describes the bestowing of leadership by Christ upon his first disciple

_____ 5. The agency of the Church to suppress heresy

_____ 6. The ability to levy and to decide how to spend taxes

_____ 7. Architecture typified by pointed arches

_____ 8. Name for the science of religion

_____ 9. This led to the separation of the Roman Catholic and the Greek Orthodox Churches

_____ 10. The succession of an estate to an eldest son

_____ 11. Paper money issued by the Directory

_____ 12. Conflict in Germany between Bismarck and the Catholic Church

_____ 13. The term sometimes used to describe a guarantee of Belgium's neutrality

_____ 14. The complete absence of government restrictions

_____ 15. This agreement of the Washington Conference of 1921 recognized the independence and territorial integrity of China

_____ 16. The name for modern descendants of Dutch settlers in Africa

_____ 17. The man who was the first president of Israel

_____ 18. Russian term for a local collective farm

_____ 19. An agreement signed in 1954 by France and the Viet Minh dividing Vietnam at the 17th parallel

_____ 20. Place in the U.S.S.R. where India and Pakistan engaged in negotiations

COLUMN II

A. Inquisition
B. Tashkent
C. Geneva Accord
D. Alaric
E. "Scrap of Paper"
F. Power of the Purse
G. Nine Power Pact
H. Phoenicians
I. Theology
J. Laissez-faire
K. Petrine Theory
L. Assignats
M. Iconoclastic Controversy
N. Kolkhoz
O. Afrikaners
P. Kulturkampf
Q. Osiris
R. Primogeniture
S. Gothic
T. Chaim Weizmann
U. Romanesque
V. Cretans

In the following multiple choice questions, place the appropriate letter in the blank space in front of the question.

_____ 21. In Egypt all land

    A. Belonged to the upper classes, who rented it out

    B. Was divided up between families

    C. In theory belonged to the Pharoahs

    D. Was owned exclusively by the priestly class

_____ **22.** The Olympic Games were
   A. Athletic contests only
   B. Contests held in commemoration of the Battle of Marathon
   C. Athletic contests and literary contests established in honor of the gods
   D. Memorial contests in honor of the Delphic Oracle

_____ **23.** The term "dyarchy" describes the administration of Augustus as
   A. Joint rule by Augustus and the Senate
   B. The system of two equally powerful consuls
   C. The system of checks by the tribunes on government actions
   D. Government by the aristocracy

_____ **24.** The Punic Wars were
   A. Civil wars among the various Phoenician colonies
   B. Waged between Phoenicia and Carthage
   C. Waged against Carthage by Rome
   D. General punitive wars waged by Rome against any enemy

*_____ **25.** The Crusades were stimulated by the following factors EXCEPT
   A. The desire of the Church to reduce fighting among local nobles
   B. The hopes of material rewards on the part of the Crusaders
   C. The threat of the Church to excommunicate those who did not go on a crusade
   D. The blessing of the Church on those who did go

*_____ **26.** The rise of banking contributed to the following EXCEPT
   A. The rise of a middle class
   B. The development of capitalism
   C. The establishment of feudalism
   D. The encouragement of European trading in general

_____ **27.** England's American colonies differed from those of other nations because
   A. The people sent to her colonies were carefully selected
   B. The colonists were expected to contribute to the wealth of the mother country
   C. The mother country regulated their trade
   D. The mother country claimed political authority over them

*_____ **28.** The Renaissance appeared first in Italy for the following reasons EXCEPT
   A. Venice brought in new ideas through its trading operations
   B. Italy had the wealth to pay for learning and intellectual pursuits
   C. Italy was the first country to develop a centralized monarchy
   D. Merchant princes encouraged painters and architects to produce masterpieces

*_____ 29. The Golden Age of medieval China was typified by the following EXCEPT
A. A good system of civil servants in government administration
B. The division of land among many
C. The encouragement of any contact with foreigners
D. The encouragement of agriculture

*_____ 30. John Locke's arguments included the following EXCEPT
A. Men have the right to life, liberty and property
B. The government they set up must act as their trustee
C. In an emergency the government has the right to decide policy, regardless of the people's wishes
D. Under certain conditions men have the right of revolution

_____ 31. The Physiocrats were
A. Scientists who resented royal interference
B. Supporters of restrictions of mercantilism
C. Advocates of the abolition of business regulation by the state
D. Politicians who demanded the abolition of the monarchy

_____ 32. The *assignats* became worthless because
A. They were paper money
B. The people would not accept and use them as money
C. Louis XVI warned the people that to use them would be sacrilegious
D. Too many were issued on the basis of land that was overvalued

_____ 33. The Revolutions of 1830 resulted in only one change in the settlements of the Congress of Vienna
A. The French forced Charles X to abdicate
B. Switzerland became an independent nation
C. Belgium achieved her independence
D. The German Confederation invaded and occupied Belgium

*_____ 34. The terms of the Triple Alliance included the following EXCEPT
A. Germany and Austria would assist Italy against France
B. Italy would assist Germany against France
C. Italy would assist Germany against Russia
D. Italy would assist Germany if France and Russia attacked her

_____ 35. Government in the United States and Great Britain differs in that
A. Two or more parties contest elections
B. All registered voters may participate in elections
C. The party with the majority of votes wins the election
D. The majority party in the legislature chooses the executive

_____ **36.** The Communist Party is not strictly a political party because it denies the essential right
    A. Of allowing people to vote
    B. Of holding periodic elections
    C. Permitting the minority party to become the majority by peaceful means
    D. Of allowing people to have any representation in the government

_____ **37.** The peace term which Germany was obliged to accept in 1919 and which she particularly criticized was
    A. Surrendering Alsace-Lorraine to France
    B. Full responsibility for the war
    C. The loss of her African colonies
    D. The limitation of her armed forces

_____ **38.** Italy joined the Dual Alliance partners in 1882 because
    A. She was afraid of French aggression
    B. She believed that this was the way to achieve unification
    C. She was angered at French seizure of Tunisia
    D. She opposed Russia's desire to get influence in the Balkans

*_____ **39.** Communism includes the following beliefs EXCEPT
    A. The state owns all means of production and distribution
    B. Periodic elections interfere with efficient administration
    C. Competing political parties are not permitted to exist
    D. Dictatorship of one party is necessary

*_____ **40.** The United States policy of neutrality in the 1930's was gradually abandoned by the following EXCEPT
    A. The Destroyer-Base Deal
    B. The establishment of U.S. bases in Greenland and Iceland
    C. The passage of the Selective Service Act of 1940
    D. The enactment of the Lend-Lease Act

_____ **41.** The leader of the U.S.S.R. wields his real power as
    A. Chairman of the Council of Ministers
    B. Prime Minister of the Supreme Soviet
    C. Chairman of the Presidium
    D. Marshall of the Red Army

_____ **42.** One of the following agencies of the United Nations attempts to encourage education and training in home economics
    A. WHO
    B. UNICEF
    C. UNESCO
    D. ILO

_____ 43. Japan initiated the Sino-Japanese War of 1894–95 because she
     A. Wanted to control a territory which would be a threat to her interests if it were held by Russia
     B. Wanted to see Korea become completely independent
     C. Needed more territory
     D. Believed this would be a way to gain prestige

_____ 44. The European communist nation which has criticized the U.S.S.R. and loudly supported Communist China is
     A. Yugoslavia
     B. Bulgaria
     C. Albania
     D. Poland

*_____ 45. The Alliance for Progress hopes to accomplish the following EXCEPT
     A. Assist political reform in Latin America without violence
     B. Bring about useful economic changes for the people
     C. Extend the operation of the Roosevelt Corollary
     D. Help raise the standard of living of the continent

Associate the persons in Column II with the statements in Column I.

COLUMN I	COLUMN II
_____ 46. I practiced civil disobedience	A. Nicholas II
_____ 47. I was elected for a second 7-year term	B. Alexander II
_____ 48. I took a piece of Poland for my country	C. Ben Gurion
_____ 49. I became prime minister of Israel	D. Chaim Weizmann
_____ 50. I abdicated and was later shot	E. Shastri
	F. Gandhi
	G. de Gaulle
	H. Louis Philippe
	I. Catherine the Great
	J. Peter the Great

List the following in chronological order.

_____ 51.	A. de Valera
_____ 52.	B. Metternich
_____ 53.	C. Cromwell
_____ 54.	D. Cavour
_____ 55.	E. Philip II of Spain

In the following definitions, choose for each what is the Most appropriate definition and mark it following the M, and choose the Least appropriate definition and mark it following the L.

Socialism

_M_ 56. A. An economic system in which the means of production and distribution are owned and operated by the state
     B. An economic system in which government regulation may determine minimum wages and maximum hours

___L___ 57. C. An economic system in which the state owns the means of production and distribution, but which the voters may change by majority choice
     D. An economic system in which the citizens own no private property whatever

Capitalism Today

___M___ 58. A. An economic system in which a few persons own all the means of production and distribution
     B. An economic system in which people are able to invest money in order to make a profit, even though there may be government regulations as to minimum wages

___L___ 59. C. A system in which the government decides how much income goes to wages, and how much to profits
     D. An economic system in which a man operates a business without any government restrictions whatever

Appeasement

___M___ 60. A. The attempt to resolve differences between nations by agreement to compromise
     B. The insistence that each side in a disagreement make a concession

___L___ 61. C. The willingness of one nation to make a concession, even though it is not obliged to do so
     D. The making of concessions by one side in the hopes of avoiding trouble, without taking a stand upon a matter of principle

Place the following in chronological order

_____ 62.	A.	Decembrists
_____ 63.	B.	Bolsheviks
_____ 64.	C.	Emancipation of the serfs in Russia
_____ 65.	D.	Brezhnev
_____ 66.	E.	October Manifesto

Associate the persons in Column II with the appropriate statements in Column I.

COLUMN I   COLUMN II

_____ 67. The leader of this country was forced to leave it

A. Indonesia
B. China

_____ 68. The leader of this country was obliged to surrender his title of President for Life

C. Germany
D. Ghana

_____ 69. The leader of this country was reduced to a private citizen

E. Russia

_____ 70. The leader of this country committed suicide

_____ 71. The leader of this country was deposed while he was on a foreign trip

Associate the person with his country or place associated with him.

_____ **72.** West Irian   A. Jinnah
_____ **73.** Austria   B. Ian Smith
_____ **74.** Rhodesia   C. Harold Wilson
_____ **75.** Egypt   D. Ben Bella
_____ **76.** Pakistan   E. Nasser
       F. Dolfuss
       G. Sukarno

For the following three topics, indicate by T or F whether each statement is True or False.

Peace of Westphalia
_____ **77.** It ended the Hundred Years War
_____ **78.** It included the recognition of the independence of the Dutch Netherlands
_____ **79.** It included the recognition of the independence of Switzerland
_____ **80.** Was one of the first of the significant post-war conferences to attempt to settle the problems of peace
_____ **81.** Re-established the Catholic Church throughout Europe

The Washington Conference, 1921–22
_____ **82.** Resulted in permitting Japan to have the strongest one-ocean navy
_____ **83.** Was the beginning of successful disarmament
_____ **84.** The conference members participating in the naval limitations were the United States, Great Britain, Japan, France, China
_____ **85.** Prohibited British fortifications east of Singapore, and American fortifications west of Hawaii

The Marshall Plan
_____ **86.** Offered economic aid to any nation in Europe, including the communist bloc
_____ **87.** Was designed as a military alliance against the U.S.S.R.
_____ **88.** Was organized partly as retaliation for the communist take-over of Czechoslovakia
_____ **89.** It later developed into NATO
_____ **90.** It provided economic aid to nations on condition that they assist in their own recovery

Associate the correct dates with the following treaties.

_____ **91.** Treaty of Nanking   A. 1648
_____ **92.** Treaty of Paris   B. 1713
_____ **93.** Treaty of Westphalia   C. 1783
_____ **94.** Treaty of Versailles   D. 1842
_____ **95.** Treaty of Utrecht   E. 1919

Test VI
Associate the lettered item or person in Column II with the appropriate numbered statement in Column I.

COLUMN I	COLUMN II
_____ 1. An official state priest of Roman times	A. Pontifex Maximus
_____ 2. A revived interest in classical writers	B. Fashoda Incident
_____ 3. The sacrament commemorating the death and sacrifice of Christ	C. Corvee
_____ 4. Invaders of early India	D. Turgot
_____ 5. The sun god of the Aztecs	E. Civil disobedience
_____ 6. The place where an emperor submitted to a Pope	F. Canossa
_____ 7. The term meaning the integration of Austria and Germany	G. Manchester School
_____ 8. The man who deciphered the Rosetta Stone	H. The Eucharist
_____ 9. Forced labor in France under the Old Regime	I. Catherine the Great
_____ 10. She acquired a large part of Poland for Russia	J. Aryans
_____ 11. A French finance minister who proposed "Taxation by the ability to pay"	K. Leipzig
_____ 12. A battle where Russia assisted in the defeat of Napoleon	L. Hanse
_____ 13. The Latin American who did a great deal to free the southern area from Spain	M. Anschluss
_____ 14. Advocates of free trade in Europe in the 19th century	N. Champollion
_____ 15. A north European association of trading towns	O. Economics
_____ 16. The study of how people and nations make a living	P. Quetzalcoatl
_____ 17. Anglo-French confrontation on the Nile river in the late 19th century	Q. Iraq
_____ 18. A 20th century nation which was once Mesopotamia	R. The Chartists
_____ 19. A document which favored a national home for the Jewish people	S. San Martin
_____ 20. A policy in India of refusing to recognize British laws and official edicts	T. Scholasticism
	U. Humanism
	V. Balfour Declaration

In the following multiple choice questions, place the appropriate letter in the blank space in front of the question.

_____ 21. Civilization developed along the Fertile Crescent because
    A. It was a "bridgehead" between Egypt and Mesopotamia
    B. The land could support large numbers of people
    C. The Assyrians wished to obtain copper from Egypt
    D. Civilization naturally spread eastwards from Egypt

_____ **22.** The name given to the architectural device used to give the visual impression of a perfectly cylindrical column is
    A. Architrave
    B. Frieze
    C. Entasis
    D. Doric

_____ **23.** Sparta was a military society because
    A. Its people preferred fighting to peaceful pursuits
    B. Its young men were trained as fighters
    C. The Spartans simply believed in a harsh, disciplined life
    D. The slave population heavily outnumbered the Spartan citizens

*_____ **24.** The decline of the Roman Empire was accelerated by the following EXCEPT
    A. Giving the army many of the rights of senators
    B. Admittance of barbarians into the empire
    C. Higher taxes and rising prices
    D. Strengthening the central authority of Rome over all parts of the Empire

_____ **25.** Feudalism developed because
    A. Central government had collapsed and men needed protection
    B. Serfs needed land
    C. Kings organized it after the collapse of the Roman Empire
    D. The middle classes wanted an opportunity to further their own interests

*_____ **26.** During the administration of Pope Gregory I the Church assumed all the following duties EXCEPT
    A. Feeding the poor and the indigent
    B. Participating in the election of the emperor
    C. Establishing farm prices
    D. Helping in the administration of the empire

*_____ **27.** Chinese guilds resembled European guilds for the following reasons EXCEPT
    A. They acted as liaison between local government and the community
    B. They regulated prices for their members and prevented competition
    C. They consisted of separate groups such as tailors, shoemakers and other crafts
    D. They fixed standards of work in order to maintain high standards of production

_____ **28.** The Counter-Reformation was
   A. The removal of the contemporary Pope
   B. The decision of the Church to change its basic religious beliefs
   C. The decision of the Church to reform its own abuses and to fight actively in its own behalf
   D. The successful overthrow of faiths other than Catholicism

* _____ **29.** Luther was excommunicated by the Church for the following reasons EXCEPT
   A. His criticism of indulgences directly challenged the authority of the Pope
   B. He taught that sincere faith alone could achieve salvation
   C. He taught that religion was simply a means to give the Church political control over countries
   D. He taught that the purchase of an indulgence without sincere penance could do no good

* _____ **30.** The Renaissance contributed the following EXCEPT
   A. Writing in the vernacular languages
   B. The increased use of Latin as the universal language
   C. Scientific enquiry about the universe
   D. An advance in the study of medicine

* _____ **31.** Louis XVI dismissed three finance ministers because they proposed the following EXCEPT
   A. Taxation based upon the ability to pay
   B. No further "pensions" to aristocrats from public funds
   C. That the clergy and nobility make financial contributions
   D. That money be raised by increasing the taille and the gabelle

_____ **32.** The best government, said one of the following, is achieved by the separation of powers
   A. Locke   C. Rousseau
   B. Voltaire   D. Montesquieu

_____ **33.** The Thermidorean Reaction was
   A. Robespierre's introduction of a new calendar
   B. The arrest and execution of Robespierre
   C. Robespierre's appeal for "purification" of the government
   D. The institution of the 9-day work week

* _____ **34.** Napoleon's determination to extend French domination in Europe was received in the following ways EXCEPT
   A. Accepted with sympathy by the middle class groups in Europe
   B. Opposed by kings whose thrones were threatened
   C. Supported by Great Britain which wished to see Napoleon expand eastwards
   D. Strongly opposed by Great Britain, which believed her balance of power to be threatened

*_____ 35. Southern Ireland has had the following names EXCEPT
    A. Irish Free State   C. Eire
    B. Ulster   D. Republic of Ireland

_____ 36. The "domestic system" of production was one which
    A. Supplied goods for domestic or home consumption
    B. Produced goods made by workmen in their own homes, using hand tools
    C. Which supplied raw materials to workmen in their homes through business corporations
    D. Organized new methods of raising capital through joint-stock companies

*_____ 37. A British dominion after 1867 had the following rights EXCEPT
    A. Its own freely elected legislature
    B. It could select its own executive for domestic affairs
    C. It could determine its own voting procedure
    D. It could operate all departments of government, including foreign affairs and defense

*_____ 38. World War I was precipitated by the following EXCEPT
    A. Germany gave Austria a "blank check" regarding Serbia
    B. Russia called for general mobilization
    C. Germany declared war on France
    D. Britain dared Germany to attack through Belgium

_____ 39. General Francisco Franco was
    A. The popularly-elected leader of Spain
    B. Appointed by the Spanish king as dictator
    C. Technically a successful rebel who became ruler of Spain
    D. Leader of the famous Fifth Column in Madrid

_____ 40. Czechoslovakia's most serious problem in the 1930's was
    A. That it had a minority of 25% of Germans
    B. That it consisted of Bohemia, Silesia, and Moravia
    C. That it was a republic
    D. That it was independent and no longer a part of Austria-Hungary

*_____ 41. Each of the following statements is true of the Russian Constitution of 1936 EXCEPT
    A. The Supreme Soviet consists of two houses
    B. The Presidium is the title of the dictator in power
    C. The Soviet of the Union represents the people of Russia
    D. The Soviet of Nationalities represents the several racial groups

_____ 42. During World War II the U.S.S.R. and Great Britain jointly occupied this Middle East nation for the duration of the war
    A. Egypt   C. Iran
    B. Syria   D. Iraq

_____ 43. The North Atlantic Treaty was designed
  A. As a military threat to Russia
  B. To encourage Eastern European satellites of the U.S.S.R. to break away
  C. To give the United States control of European foreign policy
  D. As a deterrent to Russian expansion westwards

*_____ 44. Radical movements in Latin America may be given impetus by the following EXCEPT
  A. The general antagonism to what is labelled U.S. imperialism
  B. Land and wealth are owned by a small percentage of the population
  C. The acceleration of the "revolution of rising expectations"
  D. United States program of the Alliance for Progress

*_____ 45. General Wedemeyer criticized the Kuomintang Party for the following EXCEPT
  A. The Kuomintang treated the peasants ruthlessly in grain collections
  B. It had no popular program of reform
  C. The Kuomintang had accepted $2 billion in United States aid
  D. The nation faced economic collapse

Associate the persons in Column II with the statements in Column I.

COLUMN I	COLUMN II
_____ 46. I challenged the Pope and was excommunicated	A. King John
_____ 47. Barons forced me to grant rights	B. Sukarno
_____ 48. I challenged the Pope and submitted to him	C. Henry IV
_____ 49. I was responsible for the execution of a king	D. Henry VIII
_____ 50. I was forced into temporary exile	E. Haile Selassie
	F. Luther
	G. Cromwell

Put the following in chronological order.

_____ 51.	A. Triple Alliance
_____ 52.	B. Delian League
_____ 53.	C. Hanseatic League
_____ 54.	D. Nine Power Pact
_____ 55.	E. Baghdad Pact

Put the following in chronological order.

_____ 56.	A. Battle of Trafalgar
_____ 57.	B. Battle of Midway
_____ 58.	C. Spanish Armada
_____ 59.	D. Dien Bien Phu
_____ 60.	E. Boxer Rebellion

For the following three topics, indicate by T or F whether each statement is True or False.

Quadruple Alliance

_____ 61. It consisted originally of Great Britain, Russia, Prussia, France
_____ 62. It consisted originally of Great Britain, Russia, Prussia, Austria
_____ 63. It proposed to encourage a policy of nationalism and democracy
_____ 64. It was organized to meet regularly to discuss common problems
_____ 65. It was strongly opposed to the extension of nationalism

Roosevelt Corollary

_____ 66. It announced the intention of the United States to intervene in Latin American affairs if necessary
_____ 67. It was simply another name for the Monroe Doctrine
_____ 68. It was another way of saying, "Walk softly but carry a big stick"
_____ 69. Simply restated the Monroe Doctrine more emphatically
_____ 70. Was ended by another Roosevelt in his announcement of the Good Neighbor Policy

Kellogg-Briand Pact

_____ 71. It was a bilateral pact between the United States and France
_____ 72. It was a multilateral pact of more than fifty nations
_____ 73. It successfully outlawed war
_____ 74. It was a useless agreement because it had no means of preventing war
_____ 75. It provided for joint action by the signatories if a member was attacked

Associate the correct dates with the topics.

_____ 76.	Poland finally partitioned	A.	476
_____ 77.	The end of the Roman Empire in the West	B.	622
_____ 78.	The flight of Mohammed to Medina	C.	800
_____ 79.	Charlemagne crowned Holy Roman Emperor	D.	1271
_____ 80.	Start of Marco Polo's visit in Asia	E.	1682
_____ 81.	Beginning of the reign of Peter the Great	F.	1762
_____ 82.	The beginning of the Boer War	G.	1795
_____ 83.	Beginning of the reign of Catherine the Great	H.	1814
_____ 84.	First meeting of the Congress of Vienna	I.	1823
_____ 85.	End of the Russo-Japanese War	J.	1870
_____ 86.	Beginning of the Sino-Japanese War	K.	1878
_____ 87.	The Congress of Berlin	L.	1894
_____ 88.	Monroe Doctrine announced	M.	1899
_____ 89.	Unification of Italy accomplished	N.	1905
_____ 90.	Germany's attack on Russia in World War II	O.	1941

Associate the appropriate country with the persons listed.

_____ 91.	Kosygin	A.	India	E.	Spain
_____ 92.	Gandhi	B.	Yugoslavia	F.	Finland
_____ 93.	Ebert	C.	Russia	G.	Germany
_____ 94.	Princip	D.	Serbia		
_____ 95.	Franco				

Test VII   Associate the lettered item or person in Column II with the appropriate numbered statement in Column I.

COLUMN I	COLUMN II

_____ 1. This was the form of temple built by the Assyrians

_____ 2. The place to which the emperor moved the capital of the Roman empire

_____ 3. The Moslem term meaning "Submission to God"

_____ 4. A Church order which denied the sacraments to an entire country

_____ 5. A characteristic which applied to the Pope in his official position

_____ 6. The Viceroyalty of Peru was formerly this country

_____ 7. A term meaning the language of a country or people

_____ 8. A system of investment to make a profit for personal use

_____ 9. The Englishman whose writings influenced the American Revolution

_____ 10. This announced an official British policy which annoyed the American colonists

_____ 11. A slogan expressing Germany's plan to extend its influence into and beyond the Balkans

_____ 12. A term meaning the restoration of monarchs entitled by heredity to their thrones

_____ 13. A military commander in 19th century Japan

_____ 14. An attempt in the 1920's to overthrow a government in Germany by force

_____ 15. A belief denouncing all government, tradition, and religion

_____ 16. An Israeli collective farm unit

_____ 17. The site of an Afro-Asian conference in 1955

_____ 18. A world organization of communist parties

_____ 19. Describes Italy as a government-controlled economy

_____ 20. The policy of permitting a native African to become a Portuguese citizen

COLUMN II

A. Blood and Iron
B. Putsch
C. Infallibility
D. Assimilation
E. Kibbutz
F. Byzantium
G. Hobbes
H. Proclamation of 1763
I. Nihilism
J. Bandung
K. Vernacular
L. Comintern
M. Interdict
N. Legitimacy
O. Kingdom of the Incas
P. Shogun
Q. Corporative State
R. Locke
S. Ziggurat
T. Capitalism
U. Drang Nach Osten
V. Islam

In the following multiple choice questions, place the appropriate letter in the blank space in front of the question.

*_____ **21.** All Greek citizens in an Athenian city-state, whether property-holders or not, could do the following EXCEPT
    A. Vote in the Ecclesia
    B. Serve on panels of juries
    C. Be appointed as a dictator in an emergency
    D. Cast a ballot to ostracise a man

_____ **22.** The first "scientific" historian who attempted to be historically accurate was
    A. Livy   C. Herodotus
    B. Thucydides   D. Plato

_____ **23.** The Roman latifundias were
    A. Large landed estates given to successful Roman generals
    B. Landed estates run by slave labor during the late Republic
    C. Roman colonies which produced grain for Rome
    D. Administrative districts organized during the Roman empire

*_____ **24.** The functions and purposes of guilds were the following EXCEPT
    A. To guarantee that the Crown received its proper share of taxes
    B. To serve the interests of its members
    C. To develop codes of business behavior with other guilds
    D. To buy a town its freedom from the owner of the land upon which it was built

*_____ **25.** The French kings established their authority by the following EXCEPT
    A. The system of primogeniture
    B. A system of seneschals for revenue collection
    C. The establishment of the Curia Regis
    D. Avoiding all conflict with the Popes

_____ **26.** The discovery of gold and silver in the Spanish colonies affected Spain adversely because
    A. The money was taken by force from the Indians
    B. Spain did not need the gold and silver
    C. The money was not invested in trade and commerce to develop Spain's economy
    D. It cost more than it was worth to bring to Spain from the colonies

*_____ **27.** Mercantilism contained the following beliefs EXCEPT
    A. A country should attempt to become self-sufficient
    B. The government should not interfere in the development of business and trade
    C. The government should regulate tariffs and some business methods
    D. Exports should exceed imports, with the balance paid in money

_____ **28.** Calvinism was a theocratic religion because
    A. It allowed complete freedom of worship
    B. It believed in predestination
    C. It permitted only members of its Church to hold political office
    D. It believed in simple worship, a sermon, prayers, and hymns

_____ **29.** The author of *Leviathan*, which advocated absolutism, was
    A. Diderot   C. Hobbes
    B. Locke   D. Rousseau

*_____ **30.** The Congress of Vienna decided upon the following conditions for France EXCEPT
    A. The ruling royal family was restored
    B. The empire of Napoleon was retained under his son as Emperor
    C. Frontier barriers were erected on her boundaries to prevent her future expansion
    D. She was obliged to pay a large indemnity

_____ **31.** The Writ of Habeas Corpus
    A. Orders a jailer to bring a person to proper trial
    B. Does not guarantee that a prisoner be charged with a crime
    C. Is a procedure in which a prisoner does not need a trial
    D. Safeguards the jailer from any penalty when he receives a prisoner

_____ **32.** The Brunswick Manifesto was
    A. The French declaration of war on England
    B. The order issued for the arrest of Louis XVI
    C. A warning that Frenchmen who resisted Austria and her allies would be treated as rebels
    D. The order issued by Danton suspending the monarchy

*_____ **33.** The Statute of Westminster did the following EXCEPT
    A. Established the British Commonwealth of Nations
    B. Granted independence to the dominions
    C. Established Ireland as a dominion
    D. Denied the British parliament the right to veto any law of a member of the Commonwealth

_____ **34.** The basic belief of Karl Marx was that
    A. A class struggle existed between property owners and workers
    B. Communism was not historically inevitable
    C. Economic factors were of slight importance in history
    D. The middle class would share their profits with the workers

*_____ **35.** The "opening" of China included the following EXCEPT
    A. Giving nations trading rights in treaty ports

   B. The "most-favored nation" clause to foreign powers
   C. The right of foreign powers to intervene and participate in China's government
   D. Territorial concessions in which foreign law, not Chinese, operated for the foreign nationals

_____ **36.** Self-determination meant
   A. The right of victors to determine the amount of reparations the vanquished shall pay
   B. The right of the victor nation to take whatever territory she claims belongs to her
   C. The right of Austria to handle her subject people as she wished
   D. The right of racial groups to decide their own future government

*_____ **37.** At the time of the Yalta Conference the advantage lay with the U.S.S.R. for the following reasons EXCEPT
   A. United States and British troops had not yet crossed the Rhine river
   B. The Germans had already made peace with Russia
   C. Russia occupied part of Eastern Europe including Poland
   D. The western allies had not yet defeated Japan

*_____ **38.** After the abdication of the Czar, necessary political reforms were not initiated for the following reasons EXCEPT
   A. The government was concerned chiefly with conducting the war
   B. There was no provision for any sort of representative legislature
   C. Radical groups were determined to use force rather than parliamentary means
   D. Lenin demanded a "revolutionary-democratic dictatorship"

_____ **39.** The Manchurian Crisis of 1931 was a set-back for collective security because
   A. The League appointed a Commission to investigate the facts
   B. Japan changed the name Manchuria to Manchukuo
   C. Japan, in effect, challenged the League to take action
   D. The League proposed a settlement making Manchuria an autonomous state under Chinese sovereignty but under Japanese control

*_____ **40.** As President of the Fifth Republic, de Gaulle had the following powers EXCEPT
   A. He could appoint all cabinet ministers
   B. He could dissolve the National Assembly at will
   C. He could re-appoint himself as President when his term expired
   D. He could appoint all military and civil officials

_____ 41. A possible dispute between nations would first be referred to this body of the United Nations
   A. The Assembly
   B. The International Court of Justice
   C. The Security Council
   D. The Secretary-General's office

_____ 42. Gandhi's civil disobedience campaign was an obstacle to Britain's long-range plans for India because
   A. Britain wished to continue to obtain income from her salt monopoly in India
   B. Gandhi embarrassed the British government by his hunger strikes
   C. Britain's plans for eventual Indian self-government depended upon cooperation from all groups in India
   D. The Hindus outnumbered the Moslems

* _____ 43. Probable causes of disturbances in African nations today are the following EXCEPT
   A. Tribal loyalties were broken down and not replaced with native government
   B. Colonial possessions had been acquired without regard to tribal or geographic boundaries
   C. African nationalism has been anti-colonialism rather than a constructive force with a positive program
   D. Africans are motivated by the general desire for independence

_____ 44. One of the following persistently attempted to prevent the development of nationalism in the 19th century
   A. Great Britain   C. Austria
   B. Italy   D. Russia

* _____ 45. Each of the following EXCEPT ONE was under British rule until it achieved independence
   A. Burma   C. Laos
   B. Ghana   D. Ceylon

Associate the persons in Column II with the statements in Column I.

COLUMN I	COLUMN II
_____ 46. "Peace Without Victory"	A. Hitler
_____ 47. "Peace in Our Time"	B. Churchill
_____ 48. "We shall last for a thousand years"	C. Woodrow Wilson
_____ 49. "An iron curtain has descended across Europe"	D. Napoleon
	E. Chamberlain
_____ 50. "We must be the arsenal of democracy"	F. Truman
	G. F. D. Roosevelt

Put the following in chronological order.

_____ 51.		A.	Darwin
_____ 52.		B.	Charles Martel
_____ 53.		C.	Luther
_____ 54.		D.	Turgot
_____ 55.		E.	Constantine
_____ 56.		F.	Copernicus
_____ 57.		G.	Mohammed
_____ 58.		H.	Plato
_____ 59.		I.	Newton
_____ 60.		J.	Hannibal

For the following three topics, indicate by T or F whether each of the statements is true or false.

The French Revolution

_____ 61. Began as a revolt of French peasants against their feudal lords

_____ 62. Was begun by the middle class as a protest against unfair taxation

_____ 63. Was originally the establishment of a constitutional monarchy

_____ 64. Should be called a coup d'etat rather than a revolution

_____ 65. Was called a revolution only after the reign of terror

The Third International

_____ 66. Was founded by Karl Marx

_____ 67. Was founded by Lenin in 1919

_____ 68. Was an international peace movement

_____ 69. Was designed to further world communism

_____ 70. Was a genuine organization of workingmen who denounced war

The North Atlantic Treaty Organization

_____ 71. Was designed as a defensive alliance against Russian expansion in Europe or North America

_____ 72. All members of it are countries whose coastlines are on the Atlantic

_____ 73. West Germany is a member

_____ 74. Spain is a member

_____ 75. All the Scandinavian countries are members

Associate the items in Column II with the appropriate nations in Column I.

COLUMN I	COLUMN II
_____ 76. Ireland	A. The Directory
_____ 77. Russia	B. Domesday Book
_____ 78. England	C. October Manifesto
_____ 79. Austria	D. Bandung Conference
_____ 80. Germany	E. Easter Rebellion
	F. Zollverein
	G. Dual Monarchy

From the following definitions, choose for each what is the Most appropriate definition and mark it following the M, and choose the Least appropriate definition and mark it following the L.

Self-Determination

M 81. A. Is the right of a nation to decide for itself whether to become involved in a war

B. The right of members of an alliance to decide individually whether to take action against an aggressor

L 82. C. The right of a racial group to decide whether it shall become independent or not

Collective Security

M 83. A. Any sort of defensive alliance between two or more nations

B. The willingness of nations to disarm in order to avoid the danger of war

L 84. C. An agreement between nations that an attack upon one is an attack upon all and shall be met by joint action against the aggressor, even if war results

D. An agreement to act collectively against an aggressor, but only if war can be avoided

Communism

M 85. A. An economic system in which the state owns all means of production and distribution

B. An economic system in which the state owns all means of production and distribution and in which only one political party is allowed to exist

L 86. C. An economic system in which the state owns all means of production and distribution, but one which may be changed by the voters whenever a majority so wishes

Totalitarian

M 87. A. A political system in which the state takes over the economy of a country in an emergency

B. A system of government in which every aspect of life of the citizens is controlled by the government

L 88. C. A temporary system of government control of the economy and politics of a country, subject to change at the request of the citizens

Imperialism

M 89. A. The acquisition of a colony to be used for the benefit of the colonizing nation

B. The acquisition of a colony in order to teach the natives self-government

L 90. C. Intervention in the internal affairs of a colony, such as United Nations action in the former Belgian Congo

Associate the appropriate country in Column II with each statement in Column I.

COLUMN I	COLUMN II
_____ 91. Incorporated into the U.S.S.R. in 1940	A. Switzerland
_____ 92. Became an independent nation in 1919	B. Iran
_____ 93. Officially recognized as independent in 1648	C. Iraq
	D. Estonia
_____ 94. Finally absorbed in 1795 by Russia, Prussia, and Austria	E. Finland
	F. Greece
_____ 95. Jointly occupied by the U.S.S.R. and Great Britain during World War II for the duration of the war	G. Poland

Test VIII

Associate the lettered item or person in Column II with the appropriate numbered statement in Column I.

COLUMN I	COLUMN II
_____ 1. The meeting place of the Greek Assembly	A. Episcopus
_____ 2. Lydia was the home of this fabulously wealthy ruler	B. Gabelle
	C. Zionism
_____ 3. An overseer of the early Christian Church	D. Kublai Khan
_____ 4. Writings of India concerned with the mystery of life	E. Medina
	F. Croesus
_____ 5. The city to which Mohammed fled	G. Roosevelt Corollary
_____ 6. He believed that the earth revolved around the sun	H. Totalitarian
	I. Hacienda
_____ 7. An association of artisans within a town	J. Pnyx
_____ 8. An Italian mathematician-astronomer, who lived in the 16th and 17th centuries who insisted that judgement be based upon experimentation	K. Kolkhoz
	L. Guild
	M. NEP or New Economic Policy
_____ 9. An economic belief in self-sufficiency as a method of increasing a nation's wealth	N. Galileo
	O. Monroe Doctrine
_____ 10. The compulsory purchase of government-taxed salt in France	P. F. D. Roosevelt
	Q. Mercantilism
_____ 11. A self-sufficient agricultural unit in Latin America	R. Copernicus
	S. Upanishads
_____ 12. A term indicating government control of all aspects of a citizen's life	T. Durham Report
	U. Dien Bien Phu
_____ 13. A community set up to produce goods for community use	V. New Harmony
_____ 14. A 19th century document advocating home rule for Britain's white colonies	
_____ 15. A famous Mongol ruler of China	
_____ 16. The term indicating United States intervention in Latin America	
_____ 17. He advocated the Good Neighbor policy toward Latin America	
_____ 18. The battle marking the end of French authority in French Indo-China	
_____ 19. Belief in an independent Jewish nation	
_____ 20. Limited capitalism permitted in Russia by Lenin in the 1920's	

In the following multiple choice questions, place the appropriate letter in the blank space in front of the question.

_____ 21. The caste system in India developed from
   A. The divisions of classes originating with the Dravidians
   B. The distinct groups of priests, warriors, and farmers
   C. The conquest of India by the British
   D. The war captives and slaves who belonged to no caste

_____ 22. The Delian League was the
   A. League formed by Athens and Sparta against Darius during the Persian wars
   B. League of all Greek city-states to defend their nation
   C. League of several Greek sea-states contributing ships for common defense
   D. Organization of Greek city-states opposed to Athenian leadership

_____ 23. Two famous generals in the Punic Wars were
   A. Cato and Hannibal
   B. Hannibal and Fabius Cunctator
   C. Caesar and Hannibal
   D. Mesinissa and Fabius Cunctator

_____ 24. The Athenians administered their city-state through
   A. A town-meeting type of government
   B. A carefully selected body of officials given complete authority
   C. The Council of Five Hundred
   D. A dictator appointed periodically

_____ 25. Scholasticism was
   A. A system of scientific enquiry into the origins of the world
   B. A system of teaching the relationships between God and Man
   C. The name given to a system of public education
   D. An organization of monks devoted to teaching

_____ 26. Charlemagne was a well-known historical figure because
   A. He was the last of the Roman Emperors
   B. He brought most of western Europe under his control
   C. He was badly defeated by the Franks
   D. He established the Byzantine Empire

*_____ 27. Louis XIV of France was a powerful monarch for the following reasons EXCEPT
   A. He said "I am the State"
   B. Law courts did not protect the interests of the ordinary people
   C. The King was above the Law
   D. The Fronde was successfully crushed

_____ 28. The Holy Roman Empire in the 16th century was
   A. The several Church lands under the administration of the Pope
   B. The area of Europe whose ruler was designated by the Pope
   C. A traditional area whose ruler had formerly been chosen by the Pope, but now by the German Electors
   D. A vast empire that included the whole of Europe

_____ 29. The term Balance of Power means
    A. The maintenance of greater exports than imports
    B. The development of power in the hands of one large nation in order to maintain peace
    C. The attempt to maintain an equal division of power between rival nations or groups
    D. The rise of powerful monarchs in England, Spain, and France in the 16th century

*_____ 30. Necessary conditions for nationalism are normally the following EXCEPT
    A. The growth of a middle class
    B. A strongly organized system of feudalism
    C. A strong central government
    D. A common heritage and common aspirations for the future

*_____ 31. The Jacobins wanted the following EXCEPT
    A. The execution of Louis XVI
    B. Peace with Britain while they established their power at home
    C. Rigid price controls
    D. The arrest and execution of the Girondists, their political opponents

*_____ 32. Terms decided upon at the Congress of Vienna included the following EXCEPT
    A. Austria was deprived of her Austrian Netherlands
    B. The former Holy Roman Empire was restored
    C. Russia received a large part of Poland
    D. Austria became the dominant state of the German Confederation

*_____ 33. The Intolerable Acts did the following EXCEPT
    A. Denied ships the right to use the port of Boston
    B. Closed down all the colonial ports on the eastern seaboard
    C. Interfered with colonial government of Massachusetts
    D. Made "justice" increasingly difficult for the colonists to receive

*_____ 34. On the fateful night of August 4, 1789 the nobility agreed to the following EXCEPT
    A. Fair taxation in France
    B. To give up their titles
    C. To renounce all feudal dues without any compensation whatever
    D. To open all official positions to all citizens

*_____ **35.** The Industrial Revolution began in England for the following reasons EXCEPT

    A. England had ample capital for investment

    B. An abundant source of power was available

    C. She was an island nation safe from invasion

    D. She had the necessary conditions for a factory system

*_____ **36.** The economic theory of laissez-faire supported the following EXCEPT

    A. Moderate regulation of business and the establishment of minimum wages by the government

    B. Wages should depend upon the supply and demand of available labor

    C. No regulations of hours of labor or conditions of work in factories

    D. Complete absence of any government interference

*_____ **37.** Causes of World War I were the following EXCEPT

    A. Shift in the European balance of power

    B. The growing antagonisms of the rival alliances

    C. Germany's and Russia's rival interests in the Balkans

    D. The dangerous situation arising from the Fashoda Incident

_____ **38.** The system of collective action

    A. Prevented the outbreak of war

    B. Prohibited the formation of local alliances

    C. Hoped to localize a war if one should break out

    D. Guaranteed that no nation would be attacked by any other

_____ **39.** The main difference between the local (kolkhoz) collective farm and the state (sovkhoz) collective farm was that

    A. The land was collectively owned in one, not in the other

    B. The peasants could retain a small garden plot in one, not in the other

    C. In one the government bought the crops, and in the other the peasants sold all their produce on the market

    D. The peasants had the choice of belonging to one, but no choice of belonging to the other

*_____ **40.** The reaction to Italy's attack on Ethiopia suggested a policy of appeasement for the following reasons EXCEPT

    A. England and France were unwilling to place an embargo on oil against Italy

    B. England and France did not close the Suez Canal to Italian troop and munitions ships

    C. Italy had no difficulty in defeating the ill-organized, primitively-armed Ethiopians

    D. By the Hoare-Laval Agreement England and France agreed that Italy could acquire part of Ethiopia

_____ 41. The North Atlantic Treaty Organization was in theory more effective than the United Nations because
    A. All signatory nations of NATO agreed to protect each other in the event of an attack upon one
    B. NATO was the smaller organization
    C. The veto power could be exercised in the Security Council
    D. NATO included only Atlantic nations originally

*_____ 42. The Four D's of the Potsdam Agreement regarding Germany were the following EXCEPT
    A. Disarmament
    B. Destruction
    C. Demilitarization
    D. Democratization

*_____ 43. The Sino-Soviet conflict arose from the following EXCEPT
    A. China wishes to become the dominant power in Asia
    B. China prefers its own program of peaceful coexistence to Russia's
    C. China challenges Russia for leadership as the dominant communist power
    D. Russia does not believe that war with capitalist nations is inevitable

*_____ 44. By 1932 Japan had acquired the following EXCEPT
    A. Korea
    B. Indo-China
    C. Manchuria
    D. The Liaotung Peninsula

_____ 45. A modern example of nationalism is
    A. The creation of the Common Market
    B. The Bandung Conference of 1955
    C. The separation of Pakistan from India
    D. The province of Kashmir, claimed by both India and Pakistan

Associate the countries in Column II with the people in Column I.

COLUMN I	COLUMN II
_____ 46. Eduard Benes	A. France
_____ 47. Walter Ulbricht	B. Italy
_____ 48. General Boulanger	C. Austria
_____ 49. San Martin	D. Yugoslavia
_____ 50. Dolfuss	E. Czechoslovakia
	F. Latin America
	G. German Democratic Republic

Associate the people in Column II with the appropriate statements in Column I.

COLUMN I	COLUMN II
_____ 51. I opposed the Church as chancellor of my country	A. Sun Yat-sen
_____ 52. I started the Young Italy movement	B. Hegel
_____ 53. I used the dialectical method	C. Mao Tse-tung
_____ 54. I said that population grows faster than food supply	D. Malthus
_____ 55. I established the Three People's Principles	E. Luther
	F. Mazzini
	G. Bismarck
	H. Cavour

For the following three topics, indicate by T or F whether each statement is True or False.

Congress of Vienna

_____ 56. It restored the Bourbon monarchs to the thrones of Europe

_____ 57. It established Napoleon III as the successor to Napoleon Bonaparte

_____ 58. It favored the spread of democratic ideas throughout Europe

_____ 59. It attempted to establish a balance of power in Europe

_____ 60. It is sometimes credited with preventing a major European war for a century

Twenty-One Demands

_____ 61. They were the peace terms demanded by Japan after the Sino-Japanese War

_____ 62. They were the demands made upon China by Japan during World War I

_____ 63. Had they been implemented, they would have made China a satellite of Japan

_____ 64. China's refusal to accept them led immediately to the Manchurian Crisis

_____ 65. They were the cause of the Chinese Revolution of 1911

Security Council of the United Nations

_____ 66. All matters of controversy are first referred to this body

_____ 67. It consists of 11 members, of whom any seven can form a majority

_____ 68. A majority of seven must always include the Big Five

_____ 69. It is charged with considering action in the event of aggression or the threat of aggression

_____ 70. As part of the United Nations it was officially engaged in war against North Korea

Questions 71-73 refer to the following statements, each of which represents a different religious belief. From the choices listed, select the country or region in which this belief was first current.

A.	India	C.	Egypt
B.	Palestine	D.	Middle East

Speaker I
A man is the creator of his own faith . . . he gets in life what he is fated to get, and even a God cannot make it otherwise . . .

Speaker II
All that we are is the result of what we have thought . . . If a man speaks or acts with an evil thought, pain follows him

Speaker III
I believe in individual resurrection, and I shall buy spells and charms to accompany me on my journey to the afterworld.

_____ 71. The country or region to which Speaker I refers
_____ 72. The country or region to which Speaker II refers
_____ 73. The country or region to which Speaker III refers

Questions 74-75 refer to the following statements, each of which represents a philosophical belief from Chinese or Indian history.

The four philosophies from which these two are to be selected are:

A.	Jainism	C.	Confucianism
B.	Buddhism	D.	Taoism

Speaker I
Behave away from home as though you were in the presence of an important guest . . . Never do to others what you would not like them to do to you.

Speaker II
A life given to pleasures . . . is degrading. A life given to mortification is profitless . . . I have gained the Middle Path . . . the Noble Eightfold Path

_____ 74. Which is the belief of Speaker I
_____ 75. Which is the belief of Speaker II

Put the following in chronological order.

_____ 76.		A.	Moroccan Crises
_____ 77.		B.	Weimar Republic
_____ 78.		C.	Sarajevo Affair
_____ 79.		D.	Fashoda Incident
_____ 80.		E.	Treaty of Brest-Litovsk

Questions 81-90 refer to the following statements.

Speaker I
After World War II, I was forced to leave my country and live elsewhere. However, I still regard myself as the legitimate ruler of the country I was forced to leave.

Speaker II
By not cooperating with the official government of my country I was largely responsible for ultimately winning independence for my country.

Speaker III
I was an underground leader in my country during the Second World War. Perhaps my success at that time enabled my country, although assisted by the U.S.S.R., to remain completely independent and be so recognized by the U.S.S.R.

Speaker IV
My country became independent after the Second World War, and the site some years later of a conference of Afro-Asian nations. At the conference the delegates expressed their opinion that Communism was a threat because it was "super-Imperialism."

Speaker V
In 1936 I was forced into exile because my country was conquered, but I came back again as Emperor in 1945.

_____ 81. Speaker I is   _____
_____ 82. The country to which Speaker I refers   _____
_____ 83. Speaker II is   _____
_____ 84. The country to which Speaker II refers   _____
_____ 85. Speaker III is   _____
_____ 86. The country to which Speaker III refers   _____
_____ 87. Speaker IV is   _____
_____ 88. The country to which Speaker IV refers   _____
_____ 89. Speaker V is   _____
_____ 90. The country to which Speaker V refers   _____

Put the following in chronological order.

_____ 91.   A. San Martin
_____ 92.   B. Franco
_____ 93.   C. Darwin
_____ 94.   D. Sun Yat-sen
_____ 95.   E. Mazzini

Test IX

COLUMN I

COLUMN II

_____ 1. A Roman who repeatedly demanded that Carthage be destroyed

_____ 2. The rectangular building in Mecca containing the sacred Black Stone

_____ 3. These lived in monasteries

_____ 4. A member of a high caste in India

_____ 5. These Greek philosophers stressed reason as a guide to conduct

_____ 6. Member of feudal society who paid for the use of his land but was not free to leave the manor

_____ 7. He first raised Prussia to the rank of a first-rate power

_____ 8. He became the emperor of Mexico in the 1860's with French help

_____ 9. A state ruled by a church

_____ 10. In France of the Old Regime this was the collective name for the clergy

_____ 11. These men served as priests in churches

_____ 12. This Latin American enunciated a doctrine condemning the collection of debts by force

_____ 13. He claimed that reason was the final authority

_____ 14. The term used to designate territory not yet brought under a nation's control

_____ 15. The name given to the problem caused by the attempted expansion of Russia through Turkish possessions in the Balkans

_____ 16. The island which officially became Nationalist China after 1949

_____ 17. The official title given to Hitler's Germany

_____ 18. The Soviet Union's equivalent of the Marshall Plan

_____ 19. An organization for group living for farm villages in Communist China

_____ 20. Name given to an area of Indo-China controlled by Ho Chi Minh before 1954

_____ 21. This gave Khrushchev the excuse to build the Berlin Wall

_____ 22. The name given to West Germany when it became independent

_____ 23. The Protestants of Ulster called themselves this

_____ 24. Willy Brandt's foreign policy as chancellor included this

_____ 25. The smallest country in the Middle East

A. Drago
B. Orangemen
C. Villein
D. Sadat
E. Commune
F. German Federal Republic
G. Brahmin
H. Ostpolitik
I. K'abah
J. Cuban Missile Crisis
K. Voltaire
L. Vietnam
M. U-2 Incident
N. Comecon
O. Diaspora
P. Cato
Q. Arafat
R. Maximilian
S. Lebanon
T. Nicholas II
U. Nasser
V. Regular Clergy
W. First Estate
X. Hussein
Y. Faisal
Z. Sophists
AA. Aliyot
BB. Irredenta
CC. German Democratic Republic
DD. OPEC
EE. Theocracy
FF. Third Reich
GG. Taiwan
HH. Secular Clergy
JJ. Frederick the Great
KK. Near East Question
LL. Stoics

_____ 26. The ruler of the Kingdom of Jordan
_____ 27. The leader of the Al Fatah guerrillas
_____ 28. The name for the waves of Jewish migrations
_____ 29. The symbol for the organization of oil-producing countries
_____ 30. The name of Egypt's president at the time of the Yom Kippur War

In the following multiple choice questions, place the appropriate letter in the blank space in front of the question.

_____ 31. The Egyptians built the pyramids
    A. As a monument to heroic leaders
    B. To propitiate the gods
    C. As tombs for their rulers
    D. To provide work for the unemployed

_____ 32. The Marathon race commemorates
    A. The defense of Thermopylae by the Spartans
    B. The victory of Miltiades against Darius and the Persians
    C. Religious festivals held annually in Greece
    D. The runner who brought the news of the naval victory at Salamis

_____ 33. The Greek building erected as a temple to Athena was the
    A. Parthenon
    B. Erechtheum
    C. Acropolis
    D. Agora

_____ 34. Throughout most of the Roman Republic, the government was
    A. An aristocracy
    B. A democracy
    C. A dictatorship
    D. Totalitarian

_____ 35. One of the following emperors proclaimed Christianity as the official religion of the Roman Empire
    A. Diocletian
    B. Trajan
    C. Theodosius
    D. Nero

*_____ 36. Venice lost its predominance in the trading world for the following reasons EXCEPT
    A. Attacks by the Turks on overland routes supplying Venice with goods
    B. People objected to buying goods carried in foreign ships
    C. The discovery by other nations of sea routes to the Indies
    D. Venice lost its monopoly on trade with the Far East

*_____ 37. Ivan the Terrible's achievements included the following EXCEPT
   A. The institution of serfdom
   B. The doubling of Russia's territory
   C. The acquisition of warm-water ports for Russia
   D. The obligation of military service by the peasants

_____ 38. The New Monarchs of Europe were called by this name because they
   A. Supported the aspirations of their nobles and barons
   B. Restricted the power of their nobles
   C. Refused to support hereditary monarchs against parliaments
   D. Worked closely with the Church in order to advance their power

_____ 39. The three contestants for election as Holy Roman Emperor in the 16th century were
   A. Francis I of France, Henry VII of England, Charles I of Spain
   B. The Duke of Saxony, Charles I of Spain, Maximilian
   C. Henry VIII of England, Charles I of Spain, Francis I of France
   D. Charles I of Spain, Frederick the Great of Prussia, Francis I of France

*_____ 40. The following resulted from the Peace of Westphalia EXCEPT
   A. Switzerland was recognized as the independent Swiss Confederation
   B. Holland became the independent United Provinces
   C. Protestantism became the acknowledged religion of Europe
   D. Prussia became more powerful in the German states

*_____ 41. Basic issues facing the representatives at the Congress of Vienna included the following EXCEPT
   A. Whether or not prewar boundaries should be replaced
   B. How to extend the democratic principles of the French Revolution to other countries
   C. Should the former types of government be restored?
   D. Should the former ruling families be restored?

*_____ 42. The Second Republic of France resulted from the following EXCEPT
   A. The banning of labor unions by Louis Philippe
   B. The demand of the "legitimatists" for a divine-right monarchy
   C. The abdication of Louis Philippe
   D. The new constitution inaugurated by the National Assembly

*_____ 43. The Treaty of Paris, 1783, resulted in the following EXCEPT
   A. The acquisition of Canada by England
   B. The cession of Florida to Spain
   C. The acquisition of New Orleans and Louisiana by England
   D. The loss of all territory east of the Mississippi by France

_____ **44.** One of the following books contains political ideas most closely re-
sembling those of John Locke

    A. The *Encyclopedie*
    B. The *Social Contract*
    C. The *Leviathan*
    D. The *Spirit of the Laws*

*_____ **45.** Utopian Socialists believed in the following EXCEPT

    A. State ownership of the means of production
    B. Free elections
    C. That the country would best be served by a dictatorial
government once an election had been held
    D. That common sense and reason should be applied to all
industrial problems

*_____ **46.** These objectives of Russian political parties are correct EXCEPT

    A. Social Revolutionaries believed in the elimination of the czar
by violence
    B. Christian Democrats advocated the abdication of the czar
    C. Social Democrats supported strikes as a means of removing
the czarist regime
    D. Constitutional Democrats advocated constitutional
monarchy

*_____ **47.** The Chinese Rebellion of 1911 was caused by the following EXCEPT

    A. Heavy indemnities paid to Japan after the Sino-Japanese War
    B. Resentment at the loss of territory to foreign nations
    C. The astute leadership of Mao Tse-tung
    D. Economic famine and deprivation unrelieved by the
Manchu government

*_____ **48.** Examples of self-determination are the following EXCEPT

    A. Poland in 1919
    B. Czechoslovakia and Yugoslavia freed from German
occupation in 1945
    C. Polish boundary changed to include West Prussia
    D. The creation of the Baltic States in 1919

*_____ **49.** Hitler defied the Versailles Treaty when he did the following
EXCEPT

    A. Occupied the demilitarized Rhineland
    B. Secured the Munich Agreement in 1938
    C. Effected anschluss with Austria
    D. Built up his armed forces in the early 1930's

*_____ **50.** The Washington Conference benefitted Japan in the following ways
EXCEPT

    A. It became the strongest one-ocean naval power in the Pacific
    B. It gained strategic islands in the Pacific
    C. It officially recognized China's independence and
territorial integrity
    D. The United States and Great Britain agreed to build no forti-
fications west of Hawaii and east of Singapore, respectively

_____ 51. The Kellogg-Briand Pact was not effective because
    A. More than 50 nations agreed not to use war as national policy
    B. It officially outlawed war
    C. It permitted war for self-defense
    D. The signatories agreed not to use force against each other

*_____ 52. The European Recovery Program proposed to carry out its objectives by the following EXCEPT
    A. Requesting nations to show how they could help themselves economically
    B. Providing whatever economic assistance European nations needed
    C. Providing nations with armed forces to protect themselves
    D. Offering to assist all nations, including the communist bloc

*_____ 53. The following statements EXCEPT ONE are true regarding Algeria in the 1950's
    A. The native Algerians demanded independence
    B. Algerians were regarded as citizens of France
    C. The French settlers were prepared to negotiate with the Algerians on the issue of independence
    D. The French army was generally opposed to independence

*_____ 54. Japan's attempt to industrialize in the 19th century had limited success for the following reasons EXCEPT
    A. Industry was developed for military rather than for consumer goods
    B. Low-paid workers could not afford to buy consumer goods
    C. Japan failed to develop modern political parties
    D. Japan had to compete on the world market to sell its goods

*_____ 55. Foreign investors have been reluctant to invest capital in Latin America for the following reasons EXCEPT
    A. Governments are too unstable in Latin America
    B. Some countries fail to meet their financial obligations
    C. Latin Americans do not want to industrialize
    D. Sometimes Latin American governments take foreign enterprises without compensating their owners

_____ 56. The usefulness of the United Nations is threatened because
    A. There are too many nations in the Assembly
    B. Yassir Arafat was allowed to address the Assembly
    C. The Middle East Crisis threatens it
    D. It is located in New York City

_____ 57. The Cuban Missile Crisis developed because
    A. Castro threatened nuclear attack
    B. The Bay of Pigs was a disaster
    C. The Soviet Union placed missiles in Cuba
    D. The United States threatened Cuba with missiles

_____   **58.** The Suez Canal Crisis was
      A. The withdrawal of British troops from the Canal
      B. Israel's attack on the Canal
      C. The closing of the Canal by Nasser
      D. The occupation of key points in Egypt by British and French troops

*_____   **59.** The problem of Ulster includes all of the following EXCEPT:
      A. Serious shortages of food and fuel in Northern Ireland
      B. Discrimination in jobs and housing against Catholics
      C. The violence of the IRA and the Ulster Vanguard
      D. The fear by Protestants that Ulster could be absorbed by the Republic

_____   **60.** Czechoslovakia was occupied by the Soviet Union in 1968 because
      A. It threatened to invade East Germany
      B. It wanted its own brand of socialism
      C. Khrushchev was threatened while visiting there
      D. It refused to supply finished goods to the Soviet Union

_____   **61.** The 1975 fighting in Beirut was caused by
      A. Opposition to the presence of Al Fatah in the city
      B. Resentment at Israel's guerrilla attacks on Lebanon
      C. Boundary disputes between Lebanon and Israel
      D. Rivalry between Moslems and Christians

_____   **62.** The "revolution from the throne" was
      A. The assassination of King Faisal of Saudi Arabia
      B. Economic changes in Iran instituted by the Shah
      C. The removal of the Shah of Iran by the military
      D. The change from democracy to dictatorship in Iran

_____   **63.** The purpose of the Balfour Declaration was to
      A. Create a completely independent Israel
      B. Encourage immigration into Palestine
      C. Create a homeland for Jewish people
      D. Denounce the British mandate of Palestine

*_____   **64.** The United Nations proposed the following for Palestine EXCEPT
      A. The expulsion of all Jews from Palestine
      B. The division of Palestine into Jewish and Arab communities
      C. A federal government for the two communities
      D. Some sort of partition of Palestine

*_____   **65.** The Israeli-Arab War of 1967 resulted in the acquisition by Israel of all of the following EXCEPT
      A. The Golan Heights
      B. Part of southern Lebanon
      C. The Gaza Strip
      D. The West Bank of the Jordan

Associate the people in Column II with the statements in Column I.

COLUMN I

COLUMN II

_____ 66. I demanded independence for Pakistan

_____ 67. I was once President for Life

_____ 68. I was a leader of the Sinn Fein

_____ 69. I was crowned the first Holy Roman Emperor

_____ 70. I was the first man to sail around the Cape of Good Hope

_____ 71. I was the U.S. President who decided to "contain" the Soviet Union

_____ 72. I was the U.S. secretary of state who proposed "brinkmanship"

_____ 73. I was the British prime minister who proposed the "social contract"

_____ 74. I was the leader in East Germany from 1945

_____ 75. I am the Protestant Ulsterite who threatened force against Britain

_____ 76. I proposed Ostpolitik

_____ 77. I wanted more rights for Czechoslovakia

_____ 78. One of my titles is "King of Kings"

_____ 79. I was the third prime minister of Israel

_____ 80. I am the leader of the Popular Front for the Liberation of Palestine

A. Truman
B. Charlemagne
C. Kissinger
D. Jinnah
E. Dulles
F. Heath
G. Henry IV
H. Wilson
I. Sukarno
J. Craig
K. O'Casey
L. Rabin
M. Meir
N. Pahlevi
O. Dubcek
P. Magellan
Q. Habash
R. de Valera
S. Ulbricht
T. Nehru
U. Suharto
V. Faisal
W. Brandt
X. Diaz
Y. Adenauer

Put the following in chronological order.

_____ 81.
_____ 82.
_____ 83.
_____ 84.
_____ 85.
_____ 86.
_____ 87.
_____ 88.
_____ 89.
_____ 90.
_____ 91.
_____ 92.
_____ 93.
_____ 94.
_____ 95.

A. Yom Kippur War
B. Independence of Ghana
C. Lend-Lease Act
D. Truman Doctrine
E. Suez Canal Crisis
F. Balfour Declaration
G. Alliance for Progress
H. Independence of Mozambique
I. Munich Agreement
J. Projected Angolan Independence
K. Potsdam Conference
L. Outbreak of Violence in Ulster
M. Cuban Missile Crisis
N. Independence of Israel
O. Moscow Summit Conference

For the following topics, indicate with T or F whether each statement is True or False.

The Monroe Doctrine

_____ 96. Was actually a joint declaration of policy by the United States and Great Britain

_____ 97. Was never actively enforced by the United States

_____ 98. Was designed to protect the Western Hemisphere from European intervention

_____ 99. Was invoked to protect Venezuela from European intervention

_____ 100. Denounced existing European colonies in Latin America

The Boer War

_____ 101. Broke out because diamonds were discovered in the Dutch Republics

_____ 102. Was largely caused by Cecil Rhodes' attempt to make the Dutch Republics British territory

_____ 103. Led the German Kaiser to express his sympathy for the Boers

_____ 104. Involved almost all of Africa before it was ended

_____ 105. Led eventually to dominion status and to independence for South Africa

The Atlantic Charter

_____ 106. Was an agreement between the United States and Great Britain on specific postwar settlements

_____ 107. Was an agreement between the United States and Great Britain announcing basic principles for a peace settlement based upon democracy

_____ 108. Was accepted by all the allied nations in the war, and became the basis for the United Nations

_____ 109. Included the Lend-Lease operation

_____ 110. Was the basis for NATO

Associate the appropriate countries in Column II with the statements in Column I.

COLUMN I	COLUMN II
_____ 111. Was taken over by the communists in 1948	A. Czechoslovakia
_____ 112. Became independent in 1919	B. Canada
_____ 113. Was recognized as independent in 1839	C. India
_____ 114. Became independent in 1931	D. Eire
_____ 115. Became an independent republic in 1947	E. Burma
	F. Belgium
	G. The Dutch Netherlands
	H. Yugoslavia

Indicate for each of the following statements the appropriate peace treaty or settlement from which it is taken.

A. Potsdam Conference
B. Treaty of Portsmouth
C. Peace of Westphalia
D. Treaty of Paris
E. Congress of Berlin
F. Yalta Conference
G. Treaty of Versailles
H. Treaty of Brest-Litovsk

_____ 116. Since the nation could not continue the war and its people were demanding "Peace, Bread, and Land," the government accepted a peace which included the so-called "independence" of Poland, the Ukraine, Finland, and an area later known as the Baltic States.

_____ 117. Serbia was given its independence, and Bulgaria was divided into three parts, although nominally remaining under the control of the Ottoman Empire. Germany took nothing, since Bismarck said he was the "honest broker," with interest in nothing except the peace of Europe.

_____ 118. The new American President, Harry S. Truman, represented the United States, and Clement Attlee replaced Winston Churchill as prime minister. The Conference did agree to disarm, demilitarize, and denazify Germany, but final peace terms could not be agreed upon. Meanwhile, German territory east of the Oder-Neisse rivers was given to Poland in exchange for Russian occupation of eastern Poland.

_____ 119. It renewed the Peace of Augsburg, granting each German state the right to decide its religion. It granted independence to the United Provinces and to the Swiss cantons, and the many German states became virtually sovereign and independent.

_____ 120. All French territory on the mainland east of the Mississippi became British. Thus Canada became British, and the thirteen colonies no longer had to face the threat of attacks from the French and their Indian allies.

Associate the appropriate persons in Column II with the statements in Column I.

COLUMN I	COLUMN II

_____ 121. European Recovery

_____ 122. The first president of the new China after the 1911 revolution

_____ 123. Arranged a peace treaty for Russia

_____ 124. Tried to guarantee perpetual peace

_____ 125. Thought he had gained lasting peace for his nation

_____ 126. Made his official sovereign the emperor of a nation he conquered

_____ 127. Said that foreign policy was determined by deed, not words; hence his motto, "Blood and iron"

_____ 128. Believed that world revolution was essential for his country's safety

_____ 129. Support for any nation asking for assistance against internal or external communism

_____ 130. Said that in politics the end justified the means

COLUMN II

A. Bismarck
B. Briand
C. Chamberlain
D. Churchill
E. Machiavelli
F. Mao Tse-tung
G. Marshall
H. Montesquieu
I. Mussolini
J. T. Roosevelt
K. Stalin
L. Sun Yat-sen
M. Trotsky
N. Truman

Test X

Associate the lettered item or person in Column II with the appropriate numbered statement in Column I.

COLUMN I

_____ 1. Natives of India

_____ 2. Personal inspectors sent out by Charlemagne

_____ 3. A leaning arch to keep walls from pushing outwards

_____ 4. A group of teachers and students in medieval society

_____ 5. He attempted to modernize Russia

_____ 6. A type of architecture typified by the rounded arch

_____ 7. President Wilson sent an expeditionary force after him

_____ 8. This document became the basis for the United Nations

_____ 9. The belief that economic factors change the course of history

_____ 10. These were examples of German diplomatic pressure upon France

_____ 11. Russian czars who ruled for three centuries

_____ 12. Agreement between the Consulate and the Pope regarding the Church in France

_____ 13. The founder of Methodism

_____ 14. Political belief advocating the use of force to eliminate any form of government

_____ 15. State Planning Commission in the U.S.S.R.

_____ 16. The Israeli Confederation of Labor

_____ 17. The policy committee of the Communist Party

_____ 18. A Roman general who restored power to the Optimates

_____ 19. A country with an elected ruler

_____ 20. The legislature in early 20th-century Russia

_____ 21. This ended French control of French Indo-China

_____ 22. This committed U.S. troops to full-scale fighting in Indo-China

_____ 23. These were expected to drive out the "four olds"

_____ 24. This started the modernization of Japan

_____ 25. The nation of Bangladesh was formerly this

COLUMN II

A. Geneva Accord
B. Romanovs
C. Universitas
D. Dravidians
E. Red Guards
F. Atlantic Charter
G. Hacienda
H. Zemstvo
I. Nicholas I
J. Biafra
K. Politburo
L. Histadrut
M. Caudillo
N. Missi Dominici
O. Gosplan
P. East Pakistan
Q. Duma
R. Economic Determinism
S. Ghana
T. Pancho Villa
U. Peter the Great
V. West Pakistan
W. Anarchism
X. Concordat
Y. Zaire
Z. Flying Buttress
AA. Sulla
BB. John Wesley
CC. Republic
DD. Meiji Restoration
EE. Tonkin Gulf Resolution
FF. Romanesque
GG. Tanzania
HH. Moroccan Crises

_____ 26. The Republic of the Congo was
renamed this

_____ 27. The first British colony in Africa to
become independent

_____ 28. The part of Nigeria which declared
itself independent

_____ 29. The name given to the political boss in
Latin America

_____ 30. The self-sufficient landed estate in
Latin America

In the following multiple choice questions, place the appropriate letter in the
blank space in front of the question.

_____ 31. The believers in reincarnation were
  A. The Brahmins   C. The Confucians
  B. The Egyptians   D. The Buddhists

_____ 32. The Socratic Method refers to
  A. A natural explanation for creation and existence
  B. A study of the human mind
  C. Teaching based upon challenging every idea
  D. A study of men and their relationship with one another

_____ 33. The Greek philosophy which taught that a simple life led to happi-
ness was
  A. Stoicism   C. Cynicism
  B. Platonism   D. Epicureanism

*_____ 34. Excommunication deprived a person of the following EXCEPT
  A. The right to receive Mass
  B. The right to ever regain admittance as a full Church member
  C. Burial in consecrated ground
  D. The right to receive any other of the Sacraments

*_____ 35. Feudalism declined for the following reasons EXCEPT
  A. As monarchs became more powerful, local law was replaced
     with centralized government
  B. Traders and middle-class groups wanted protection
     against lawlessness
  C. National security and defense depended upon a well-
     organized state
  D. Serfs revolted against their lords of the manor

*_____ 36. In the War of the Austrian Succession Frederick the Great did the
following EXCEPT
  A. Acquired Silesia for Prussia
  B. Built up Prussia's prestige through his successes
  C. Effected a "diplomatic revolution" by siding with Maria
     Theresa
  D. Fought against Great Britain which sided with Maria Theresa

*_____ 37. During the Thirty Years' War all of the following occurred EXCEPT
   A. France supported Philip in his attempts to restore Catholicism
   B. France supported the Protestants against Philip
   C. Bohemia chose a Protestant ruler
   D. The Swedish people supported the German Protestants

*_____ 38. According to the mercantile theory the following were true EXCEPT
   A. Colonies were to be run for the benefit of the mother country
   B. Colonies should be left alone to develop according to their ability
   C. Colonies were to be an important source of raw materials
   D. Colonies were to be an important market for the goods of the mother country

*_____ 39. The Monroe Doctrine was the following EXCEPT
   A. A joint British-American warning to other nations to leave Latin America alone
   B. A statement by the United States that Europe was not to interfere in the Western Hemisphere
   C. A warning by the United States against further colonization by European powers in Latin America
   D. A policy of the United States to prevent Spain from recovering its former Latin American colonies

_____ 40. President Theodore Roosevelt invoked the Monroe Doctrine in
   A. The Mexican War
   B. The Venezuela Crisis
   C. The acquisition of the Panama Canal
   D. The Good Neighbor Policy

_____ 41. Napoleon's Continental System was
   A. His plan to conquer the continent of Europe
   B. The Treaty of Tilsit signed with Russia
   C. A plan to close the continent of Europe to British trade
   D. His intention of spreading French culture throughout Europe

*_____ 42. The following statements regarding Karl Marx's beliefs are all true EXCEPT
   A. Labor theory of value: the value of a product equals the amount of labor put into it
   B. Surplus Value: the difference between the selling price and the wages paid for an article was fair profit for the employer
   C. Economic Determinism: economic issues determine changes in history
   D. Communism is inevitable because history so determines

_____ **43.** This Italian was the person most responsible for the attainment of Italy's unification
   A. The Pope
   B. Mazzini
   C. Count Cavour
   D. Garibaldi

_____ **44.** Of Wilson's Fourteen Points the following were impossible to carry out because of national interests EXCEPT
   A. No secret agreements or treaties
   B. Complete freedom of the seas
   C. Establishment of an international organization to discuss common problems
   D. Free trade between nations

_____ **45.** The "Father" of the Chinese Revolution of 1911 was
   A. Chiang Kai-shek
   B. Mao Tse-tung
   C. Sun Yat-sen
   D. Ho Chi Minh

_____ **46.** The Curzon Line was
   A. The western boundary of Poland
   B. The line agreed upon by Russia and Poland as Poland's eastern boundary
   C. The proposed eastern boundary of Poland determined by racial factors
   D. The eastern boundary which Poland finally acquired by force

*_____ **47.** In the corporative state the following controls operated EXCEPT
   A. Capitalism was completely eliminated
   B. Trade unions were forbidden to operate freely according to the wishes of the members
   C. The state organized corporations consisting of workers' and employers' groups
   D. Prices, wages, and working conditions were subject to government control

_____ **48.** The Atlantic Charter was
   A. An agreement between the United States and Great Britain on the joint conduct of the war
   B. An agreement by the United States to supply Britain with weapons
   C. An appeal to the belligerents to state their war aims
   D. A statement by the United States and Great Britain which set down their objectives for future peace

_____ **49.** The Balfour Declaration proposed to
  A. Give Palestine to Great Britain as a mandate
  B. Create the independent nation of Palestine
  C. Establish the Republic of Israel
  D. Find a place for the Jews to live together

_____ **50.** The Suez Canal Crisis of 1956 was caused originally by
  A. The establishment of the Canal Users' Association
  B. British and French armed attack upon Egypt
  C. The nationalization of the canal by Nasser
  D. Israel's invasion of Egypt

_____ **51.** The policy of apartheid operates in
  A. Zambia
  B. Congolese Republic
  C. Ghana
  D. Republic of South Africa

*_____ **52.** In Communist China the Marxist philosophy of reshaping society in the communist image was partly achieved by the following EXCEPT
  A. The elimination of traditional village independence
  B. Collectivizing the land and organizing communes
  C. Eliminating traditional ancestor worship and the guilds
  D. Attempting to raise the country's standard of living by encouraging some free enterprise

_____ **53.** One of the following does not belong in the group because it lacks a characteristic common to the other three
  A. The Baghdad Pact
  B. The Warsaw Pact
  C. North Atlantic Treaty Organization
  D. Southeast Asia Treaty Organization

_____ **54.** The Inner Six is
  A. A customs union which includes Norway and France
  B. A defensive alliance which includes the Benelux nations
  C. Another name for the Common Market
  D. A proposal for a new organization to replace NATO

_____ **55.** Malagasy is the name of an independent nation which was formerly called
  A. Malawi   C. Mauretania
  B. Mali   D. Madagascar

_____ **56.** Sri Lanka was formerly
  A. Bangladesh   C. Laos
  B. Ceylon   D. Lesotho

_____ 57. By the Geneva Accord, Vietnam was divided at the
   A. 38th parallel
   B. 25th parallel
   C. 17th parallel
   D. 19th parallel

_____ 58. The president of South Vietnam when it fell to the communists in 1975 was
   A. Diem
   B. Sihanouk
   C. Bao Dai
   D. Thieu

_____ 59. He allegedly attempted to assassinate Mao Tse-tung
   A. Chou En-lai
   B. Ho Chi Minh
   C. Lin Piao
   D. Le Duc Tho

*_____ 60. The following are all political parties in Japan EXCEPT
   A. Socialist Party
   B. Liberal-Democratic Party
   C. Komeito
   D. Soka Gakkai

_____ 61. The leader of the Awami League was
   A. Rahman
   B. Ayub Khan
   C. Bhutto
   D. Yahya Khan

*_____ 62. The former Portuguese colonies are the following EXCEPT
   A. Angola
   B. Cabinda
   C. Mozambique
   D. Guinea-Bissau

_____ 63. Of the 34 black African nations, those under military rule number
   A. 10
   B. 15
   C. 18
   D. 24

_____ 64. UDI refers to an incident in the following country
   A. Zaire
   B. Tanzania
   C. South Africa
   D. Rhodesia

*_____ **65.** The following refer to the actions or beliefs of Chile's president Salvador Allende EXCEPT

    A. He could lead the country to "Chilean socialism"
    B. He won only 36 percent of the popular vote
    C. He nationalized some Chilean businesses
    D. He tried to keep himself in power by a military coup

Associate the dates in Column II with the appropriate fact in Column I.

COLUMN I		COLUMN II	
_____ **66.**	Intolerable Acts	A.	1050–1100
_____ **67.**	Third French Republic	B.	1150–1200
_____ **68.**	Treaty of Tordesillas	C.	1200–1250
_____ **69.**	The First Crusade	D.	1450–1500
_____ **70.**	Magna Carta	E.	1500–1550
		F.	1750–1800
		G.	1800–1850
		H.	1850–1900

Associate the people in Column II with the statements in Column I.

COLUMN I		COLUMN II	
_____ **71.**	I am the world's first woman prime minister	A.	Bhutto
		B.	Bandaranaike
_____ **72.**	I led Bangladesh to freedom	C.	Smith
_____ **73.**	I proposed independence for Portugal's colonies	D.	Macmillan
		E.	Rahman
_____ **74.**	I announced UDI	F.	Spinola
_____ **75.**	As prime minister I vigorously supported apartheid	G.	Vorster
		H.	Pinochet
		I.	Mobutu

From Column I select the probable source of each statement in Column II.

COLUMN I

    A. Bismarck's attack on the Church
    B. The Lytton Commission on the Manchurian Incident
    C. Khrushchev denouncing United Nations' action in the Congo
    D. Hitler's denunciation of England and his announced intention to invade England
    E. The Fuhrer principle of the Nazi party
    F. The movement for *Italia Irredenta*
    G. Criticism of Rhodesia by Prime Minister Harold Wilson
    H. Napoleon's announcement of his Continental System
    I. The formation of the Young Italy movement

COLUMN II

_____ **76.** I meditated deeply upon the principles upon which to base the organization of the group, the aims of purpose of its labors ... We were few in number, young in years ... but I believe the whole problem to consist in appealing to the true instincts and tendencies of the Italian heart . . . I was led to prefix Unity and the Republic as the aim of the proposed association.

_____ 77. The Leader principle rests upon unlimited authority . . . and the Leader-order depends upon the responsibility of the followers, just as it counts on the responsibility and loyalty of the Leader . . . The Leader can summon all members of the people to a plebiscite on a certain question, but the Leader does not, of course, surrender his power to the voters.

_____ 78. England never recognizes the international law followed by all civilized people . . . She extends to unfortified towns and commercial ports the right of blockade . . . and she declares places under blockade before which she has not a single vessel of war . . . We have consequently decreed the British Isles to be in a state of blockade . . . All commerce with the British Isles is forbidden . . . Trade in English goods is prohibited and all goods belonging to England are declared lawful prize.

_____ 79. Tense feeling undoubtedly existed between the Japanese and Chinese military forces . . . The military operations of the Japanese troops during this night cannot be regarded as measures of legitimate self-defense . . . After careful study of the evidence presented to us . . . we have come to the conclusion that there is no general Chinese support for the Manchukuo government.

_____ 80. Of course, it was not concern for the life of Belgian citizens but the more tangible interests of the powerful monopolies which have taken root . . . to bring the people of this young state to their knees, to tear away by force its richest province of Katanga . . . It has been and always will be our position that the people of Africa, who strive for freedom from colonialism, should be allowed to set up their own governments without interference from the forces of imperialism.

Put each of the terms in the following three groups in chronological order.

GROUP I

_____ 81.	A.	Boxer Rebellion
_____ 82.	B.	Opium War
_____ 83.	C.	Sino-Japanese War
_____ 84.	D.	Sun Yat-sen
_____ 85.	E.	Chiang Kai-shek

GROUP II

_____ 86.	A.	Brussels Pact
_____ 87.	B.	Warsaw Pact
_____ 88.	C.	NATO
_____ 89.	D.	Geneva Accord on Vietnam
_____ 90.	E.	Kellogg-Briand Pact

GROUP III

_____ 91.	A.	Cease-fire in Vietnam
_____ 92.	B.	Independence of Ghana
_____ 93.	C.	Meiji Restoration
_____ 94.	D.	Independence of Mozambique
_____ 95.	E.	The Great Leap Forward

In the following three topics, indicate by T or F whether each statement is True or False.

Second French Empire

_____ 96. Was established immediately after Napoleon was sent into exile

_____ 97. Was voted into existence by the people of France

_____ 98. Was the result of a coup d'etat by Louis Napoleon

_____ 99. Ended with the defeat of France in the Franco-Prussian War

_____ 100. Lasted until World War I

The Crimean War

_____ 101. Resulted in the prohibition of warships in the Black Sea in peace time

_____ 102. It gave the Russians control over the Balkan states

_____ 103. At the subsequent peace conference the signatories agreed to guarantee the independence of Turkey

_____ 104. France supported Russia against England and Turkey

_____ 105. Napoleon III joined England against Russia

The Munich Agreement

_____ 106. Was between England, France, Germany, and Italy

_____ 107. Was between England, France, Germany, and Czechoslovakia

_____ 108. Resulted in "Peace in our Time"

_____ 109. Was the outstanding example of the policy of appeasement

_____ 110. Satisfied Germany's demand for the Sudetenland

For each definition which follows, write the one word which it defines.

111. It opposes all forms of government, religion, and tradition _____

112. Government by an unlimited ruler, from Roman to modern times _____

113. Investment of money to make a profit _____

114. The policy of giving in under pressure by another nation, in the hopes of avoiding trouble _____

115. A term which includes all types of state economic ownership, whether it be socialism, communism, or the Italian corporative state _____

116. An economic condition in which there is less money in relation to available goods _____

117. Type of reasoning from general statements to the particular application _____

118. A nation's policy of remaining uncommitted, of not joining any alliance or side _____

119. The giving of information in such a manner that the listener, from whom vital information is withheld, will be persuaded to accept what the speaker wants him to believe _____

120. The right of a group to decide for itself whether or not to become independent _____

For each statement which follows, write the place, the person, or the event to which it applies.

121. Unilateral Declaration of Independence _____
122. The "Homelands Policy" _____
123. The name of the North Vietnam negotiator who agreed to a cease-fire _____
124. The attack on the "disease of bourgeois ideology" and "evidences of the past" _____
125. The title given to General MacArthur during the occupation of Japan _____
126. The territory which the U.S. returned to Japan in 1972 _____
127. The man who insisted that East Pakistan remain an "inseparable part of Pakistan" _____
128. The native name for Rhodesia _____
129. The "vast effort . . . to satisfy the basic needs of the people for houses, work, and land" _____
130. The first freely elected Marxist president in Latin American history _____

Test XI
A Chronological
Factual Test

The following test consists of 200 matching questions, divided, as previously, into groups of 20. Therefore, the answers to each group of 20 numbered questions will be found in the lettered column which accompanies or immediately follows it. Associate the persons or terms in Column II with the phrases or sentences in Column I.

COLUMN I	COLUMN II
_____ 1. They refined and used iron	A. *Aeneid*
_____ 2. Book of the Dead	B. Alaric
_____ 3. Site of defeat of Darius by the Athenians	C. Caesar
_____ 4. Destruction of Athens resulted	D. Carthage
_____ 5. The ideal State here depicted	E. Cato
_____ 6. The Father of Medicine	F. Concordat of Worms
_____ 7. Reason as a guide to conduct	
_____ 8. Nation involved with Rome in Punic Wars	G. Diocletian
	H. Egypt
_____ 9. He said repeatedly, "Delenda est Carthago"	I. Episcopus
	J. Hegira
_____ 10. He crossed the Rubicon	K. Hildebrand
_____ 11. He divided the Roman Empire	L. Hippocrates
_____ 12. He captured and sacked Rome in 410 A.D.	M. Hittites
	N. Iconoclastic Controversy
_____ 13. A collection of Roman laws	
_____ 14. Depicts the mythical origin of Rome	O. Justinian Code
_____ 15. Name for an overseer of the Church	P. Marathon
_____ 16. Established Peter as leader	Q. Peloponnesian Wars
_____ 17. Involved in the Investiture Contest	
_____ 18. Arranged for election of bishops by Pope, and homage to the king	R. Petrine Theory
	S. *Republic*
_____ 19. The flight of Mohammed to Medina	T. Stoics
_____ 20. Separation of the Church into the Roman Catholic and Greek Orthodox Churches	

	COLUMN I	COLUMN II

_____	**21.** Resulted in the destruction of Constantinople	A. Aquinas
_____	**22.** The formal grant of a fief by a lord to a vassal	B. Aztec
_____	**23.** An association of Northern European trading towns	C. Babylonish Captivity
_____	**24.** He attempted to prove that all scientific knowledge agreed with Church beliefs	D. Calvinism
_____	**25.** The founder of modern astronomy	E. Colbert
_____	**26.** Discovered the circulation of blood	F. Copernicus
_____	**27.** This was a defense of power politics of the 16th century	G. Fourth Crusade
_____	**28.** The name given to the period when Popes lived in Avignon	H. Gupta Empire
_____	**29.** By this agreement the rulers of German states were to determine the religion of their subjects	I. Hanse League
_____	**30.** According to this belief, some men will be saved, some damned eternally	J. Harvey
_____	**31.** The founder of the Society of Jesus	K. Inca Kingdom
_____	**32.** An economic belief in national self-sufficiency	L. Induction
_____	**33.** An Indian civilization practicing human sacrifice	M. Investiture
_____	**34.** This was renamed by the Spanish the Viceroyalty of Peru	N. Kublai Khan
_____	**35.** He encouraged mercantilism in France	O. Loyola
_____	**36.** He acquired a "window on the Baltic"	P. Mercantilism
_____	**37.** Marco Polo served this ruler	Q. Peace of Augsburg
_____	**38.** This was the high classical period in India, between 321 and 535 A.D.	R. Peter the Great
_____	**39.** Opinion based on reason	S. Rationalism
_____	**40.** Reasoning from the particular to the general	T. *The Prince*

COLUMN I	COLUMN II

COLUMN I

_____ 41. His remedy for political insecurity was absolutism

_____ 42. This publication supported ideas which were the basis for democracy

_____ 43. His name associated with the dialectical method

_____ 44. An English document which laid down some of the basic principles of constitutional government

_____ 45. This prevented the American colonists from settling west of the Appalachians

_____ 46. The name for this form of government signified divine right

_____ 47. In pre-revolutionary France the nobles were so classified

_____ 48. These were 18th century critics of mercantilism and government regulation

_____ 49. His dismissal as finance minister was partly responsible for the French Revolution

_____ 50. These were collections of complaints presented to the Third Estate

_____ 51. These were paper money whose decline in value helped Bonaparte to power

_____ 52. Their Headquarters were a former monastery which gave them their name

_____ 53. This was a local government set up in Paris

_____ 54. This was the arbitrary government headed by Robespierre

_____ 55. This established a working week of nine days

_____ 56. This Englishman predicted the rise of an outstanding military leader in France

_____ 57. The "whiff of grapeshot" assisted his rise to power

_____ 58. This became the basis of law in Louisiana

_____ 59. The doctrine of restoring monarchs to their hereditary thrones

_____ 60. The desire of people with common interests to become independent

COLUMN II

A. Ancien regime
B. Assignats
C. Legitimacy
D. Bonaparte
E. Burke
F. Cahiers
G. Calonne
H. Code Napoleon
I. Committee of Public Safety
J. Commune
K. Nationalism
L. French Revolutionary Calendar
M. Hegel
N. Hobbes
O. Jacobins
P. Petition of Right
Q. Physiocrats
R. Proclamation of 1763
S. Second Estate
T. *Treatise of Civil Government*

<table>
<tr><td colspan="2" align="center">COLUMN I</td><td align="center">COLUMN II</td></tr>
</table>

	COLUMN I	COLUMN II
_____	**61.** This document said, in effect, "Hands Off."	A. Jeremy Bentham
_____	**62.** Supported Charles X of France in his claims to be divine right monarch	B. Simon Bolivar
_____	**63.** These started out to be worker-owned but became relief projects	C. Clark Memorandum
_____	**64.** He was called the Liberator of Northern Latin America	D. Decembrists
_____	**65.** This Latin American leader wanted a monarchy, and resigned his command when he was opposed	E. Economic Determinism
_____	**66.** This Latin American country was protected by the implementation of the Monroe Doctrine	F. Laissez-faire
_____	**67.** This extended the Monroe Doctrine into active intervention by the United States	G. Malthus
_____	**68.** An American expeditionary force went across the frontier after him	H. J.S. Mill
_____	**69.** Complete freedom from government interference	I. Monroe Doctrine
_____	**70.** This author pointed out that mercantilist ideas were outdated	J. National Workshops
_____	**71.** He believed that population would outrun food supply	K. Robert Owen
_____	**72.** He advocated more equitable distribution of wealth, without changing the principle of private ownership	L. Roosevelt Corollary
_____	**73.** He advocated "The greatest good for the greatest number" — the theory of utilitarianism	M. San Martin
_____	**74.** They believed that all problems of industrialization could be resolved by applied reason	N. Adam Smith
_____	**75.** He supported communities which would support themselves and share the products of their work	O. Third International
_____	**76.** This theory claimed that history was affected chiefly by material changes	P. Treaty of Paris, 1856
_____	**77.** This organization was founded to destroy capitalism	Q. Ultras
_____	**78.** This document, issued during the Hoover administration, repudiated the Roosevelt Corollary	R. Utopians
_____	**79.** These early 19th century reformers advocated a constitutional monarchy	S. Venezuela
_____	**80.** By this agreement the Danube river was opened to ships of all nations	T. Pancho Villa

COLUMN I	COLUMN II

<table>
<tr><td>_____ 81. During his reign the serfs were emancipated</td><td>A. Anarchists</td></tr>
</table>

COLUMN I   COLUMN II

_____ 81. During his reign the serfs were emancipated

_____ 82. They were supporters of the philosophical idea denouncing all government, religion, and tradition

_____ 83. These men advocated the elimination of government by violence

_____ 84. At this meeting the British received the right to control Cyprus

_____ 85. This group wished to remove the Czarist regime by strikes

_____ 86. By this agreement Russia was obliged to give back Liaotung Peninsula to China

_____ 87. In 1871 he was crowned at Versailles

_____ 88. By this document a duma or legislative body was chosen by universal male suffrage

_____ 89. They wanted decentralized local governments in France

_____ 90. This was said to be partly responsible for the Franco-Prussian War

_____ 91. By this document, representation was given to industrial towns

_____ 92. These men advocated political democracy in England

_____ 93. They wanted a separate parliament for Ireland

_____ 94. These men staged the Easter Rebellion in Ireland

_____ 95. This part of Ireland did not want to separate from the United Kingdom

_____ 96. Eamon de Valera changed the Irish Free State to this

_____ 97. This eliminated customs barriers between German states

_____ 98. He organized the North German Confederation with the King of Prussia as its president

_____ 99. This was the alliance of Germany, Austria, and Russia

_____ 100. This was formed by Germany, Austria, and Italy

COLUMN II

A. Anarchists
B. Bismarck
C. Chartists
D. Communards
E. Congress of Berlin
F. Dreikaiserbund
G. Eire
H. Ems Dispatch
I. Home Rulers
J. King of Prussia
K. Alexander II
L. Nihilists
M. October Manifesto
N. Reform Bill of 1832
O. Sinn Feiners
P. Social Democrats
Q. Treaty of Portsmouth
R. Triple Alliance
S. Ulster
T. Zollverein

COLUMN I

____ **101.** This was waged by Bismarck against the Catholic Church

____ **102.** He organized the group called Young Italy

____ **103.** This was a patriotic movement for the resurrection of Italy

____ **104.** He was the founder of Italian unification

____ **105.** He succeeded in taking over the Kingdom of the Two Sicilies

____ **106.** This historian said, "In war the chaff is winnowed from the wheat"

____ **107.** This advocated Home Rule for Canada

____ **108.** By this, the provinces of Canada were united and given dominion status

____ **109.** This belief supported colonization which would in time give colonial areas back to the natives

____ **110.** A term which means the acquisition of strategic bases for political objectives

____ **111.** He wanted to take over the Boer Republics for Great Britain

____ **112.** He was the intellectual leader of the Chinese Revolution of 1911

____ **113.** This was the Nationalist Party of China

____ **114.** The attempt of Russia to gain influence in the Balkans, and Great Britain's opposition to it was called this

____ **115.** The attempted organization of Slavs in the Balkans

____ **116.** He was the 19th century leader of nationalists in Hungary

____ **117.** The reorganization of the Empire of Austria and Hungary

____ **118.** This antagonized Russia and caused the collapse of the Three Emperors' League

____ **119.** Germany's actions at Tangier and Agadir resulted in these

____ **120.** This was an attempt by one nation to get economic advantage and political influence in Turkey

COLUMN II

A. Augsleich
B. British North America Act
C. Cavour
D. Congress of Berlin
E. Drang Nach Osten
F. Durham Report
G. Garibaldi
H. Geopolitics
I. Kossuth
J. Kuomintang
K. Kulturkampf
L. Mazzini
M. Moroccan Crises
N. Near East Question
O. Pan-Slavism
P. Cecil Rhodes
Q. Risorgimento
R. Sun Yat-sen
S. Treitschke
T. Trusteeship

	COLUMN I		COLUMN II
_____ 121.	The collective name given to former German colonies and Turkish possessions to be governed by specified nations responsible to the League of Nations	A.	Anschluss
		B.	Balfour Declaration
_____ 122.	This 1919 settlement was one reason for the outbreak of war in 1939	C.	Chairman of Council of Ministers
_____ 123.	The communication which promised to support a National Home for the Jewish people	D.	Conquest of Ethiopia
		E.	Kellogg-Briand Pact
_____ 124.	German foreign minister in the Republic	F.	Kerensky
_____ 125.	The League of Nations was weakened and humiliated by this action of Italy	G.	Kolkhozy
		H.	Kulaks
_____ 126.	His real name was Vladimir Ulianov	I.	Marxism
_____ 127.	He was a leader of the provisional government after the abdication of the Czar	J.	Leninism
		K.	Locarno Agreement
_____ 128.	The permission by Lenin of limited capitalism was known as this	L.	Mandates
		M.	Lenin
_____ 129.	These were relatively well-off Russian landowners	N.	NEP
		O.	Nine Power Pact
_____ 130.	The existence of a class struggle	P.	Polish Corridor
_____ 131.	The organization and use of a group dedicated to the actual class struggle	Q.	Stalin
		R.	Stresemann
_____ 132.	He believed in consolidating Russian communism before embarking upon a program of world communism	S.	Sudetenland
		T.	Trotsky
_____ 133.	He believed in world revolution as a protection for Russian communism		
_____ 134.	These were local farm collectives in Russia		
_____ 135.	This is the official title of the head of state in Russia		
_____ 136.	Japan was a signatory to this document which guaranteed the territorial and political integrity of China		
_____ 137.	This document of the 1920's guaranteed only the western boundaries in Europe		
_____ 138.	This document outlawed war		
_____ 139.	This was the annexation of Austria by Germany		
_____ 140.	This area was used as political blackmail for further expansion by Hitler		

COLUMN I   COLUMN II

_____ 141. This is perhaps the outstanding   A. Atlantic Charter
           example of appeasement   B. Attlee

_____ 142. The capital of the part of France not   C. Battle of the
           occupied by the Germans   Coral Sea

_____ 143. Assistance to any nation whose   D. Ralph Bunche
           defense was vital to the interests of   E. China
           the United States   F. Colons

_____ 144. This document became the basis for the   G. de Gaulle
           United Nations   H. Dien Bien Phu

_____ 145. The defeat of Japanese forces headed   I. Greece
           toward Australia   J. Iran

_____ 146. American and British forces here   K. Korea
           captured 300,000 German troops   L. Lend-Lease

_____ 147. It was at this city that the turning-point M. Marshall Plan
           in the war came for the U.S.S.R.   N. Munich Agreement

_____ 148. This promised free elections for   O. Stalingrad
           liberated European nations   P. Truman Doctrine

_____ 149. He replaced Churchill as Britain's   Q. Tunisia
           representative at Potsdam   R. Vichy

_____ 150. The other member of the Big Five of   S. Western European
           permanent members on the Security   Union
           Council — United States, Great Britain,   T. Yalta Agreements
           U.S.S.R., France

_____ 151. Here the United Nations used its
           influence to secure the removal of
           Russian troops in 1946

_____ 152. An American appointed as United
           Nations mediator in the Palestine-Israeli
           controversy

_____ 153. Here the United Nations created a
           unified command to protect a country

_____ 154. In this country, one of two, the Cold War
           was commenced by the U.S.S.R.

_____ 155. Support for people resisting attempted
           subjugation by armed minorities or
           outside pressure

_____ 156. Criticized by opponents as "Operation
           Rathole"

_____ 157. This became the basis for NATO
           subsequently

_____ 158. He was elected the first president of
           France after World War II

_____ 159. Here the French lost French Indo-China

_____ 160. These were Frenchmen to whom Algeria
           was home

<table>
<tr><td colspan="2">COLUMN I</td><td>COLUMN II</td></tr>
</table>

COLUMN I   COLUMN II

_____ **161.** This was the name of the revolutionary French government in Algeria

_____ **162.** This government commenced in 1958

_____ **163.** A social security measure for all citizens from "cradle to grave"

_____ **164.** Attempted to set up a radical government in Hungary after World War I

_____ **165.** This is the real name of the head of state in Yugoslavia

_____ **166.** This nation hoped to be a "bridge" between western democracy and Russian communism

_____ **167.** He became the leader of Eastern Germany

_____ **168.** This was communism's counterpart of the Marshall Plan

_____ **169.** He replaced Khrushchev as leader in the U.S.S.R.

_____ **170.** He proclaimed the Republic of Turkey and became its president

_____ **171.** He nationalized the Suez Canal

_____ **172.** This former French mandate became independent in 1945

_____ **173.** Great Britain and the U.S.S.R. took possession of this country for the duration of the war in order to get military supplies to the U.S.S.R.

_____ **174.** This one country is still known as the United Arab Republic

_____ **175.** In 1965 this broke away from the Federation of Malaysia to become an independent state

_____ **176.** He became Israel's first president

_____ **177.** He was elected the first prime minister of Israel

_____ **178.** This country today uses proportional representation in elections

_____ **179.** This is the Indonesian name for western New Guinea

_____ **180.** He replaced Sukarno as the actual leader in Indonesia

A. Bela Kun
B. Ben-Gurion
C. Brezhnev
D. Josip Broz
E. Comecon
F. Committee of Public Safety
G. Czechoslovakia
H. Egypt
I. Fifth Republic
J. Iran
K. Israel
L. Mustafa Kemal
M. Nasser
N. National Health Act
O. Singapore
P. Suharto
Q. Ulbricht
R. Syria
S. West Irian
T. Weizmann

<table>
<tr><td colspan="2" align="center">COLUMN I</td><td align="center">COLUMN II</td></tr>
</table>

_____ **181.** He was deprived of his life-time title	A. Afrikaners
_____ **182.** This was the only other signatory with France of the Geneva Accord of 1954	B. Apartheid
	C. Assimilation
_____ **183.** Once a member of the United Arab Republic, this nation later withdrew to form its own independent government	D. Colombo Plan
	E. Gandhi
	F. Gold Coast
_____ **184.** He was sent on a mission to China in an attempt to achieve collaboration between Chiang Kai-shek and Mao Tse-tung	G. Guyana
	H. Hacienda
	I. Kanagawa
	J. Korea
_____ **185.** He became the leader in 1949 of the People's Republic of China	K. Mao Tse-tung
	L. Marshall
_____ **186.** Here the first formal treaty by Japan with a foreign country was signed	M. Nehru
	N. Nyasaland
_____ **187.** This area was wanted in 1894 by Russia for its ice-free ports, and by Japan for its strategic position	O. SEATO
	P. Sukarno
	Q. Syria
_____ **188.** He supposedly advised the Emperor of Japan to conquer Manchuria as the first step in conquering Asia	R. Tanaka
	S. Viet Minh
	T. UNICEF

_____ **189.** His policy of civil disobedience helped to win independence for his country

_____ **190.** He succeeded to the leadership of India after Gandhi's assassination

_____ **191.** This was the announced policy of Portugal permitting Africans to become Portuguese citizens

_____ **192.** This British colony became the independent nation of Ghana

_____ **193.** This is the policy of complete racial segregation in South Africa

_____ **194.** This is the collective name for the present Dutch descendants in the Republic of South Africa

_____ **195.** This former British colony in Africa became the independent state of Malawi

_____ **196.** This was a former British colony in South America, which became independent in 1966

_____ **197.** This Latin American agricultural unit resembles a European feudal entity

_____ **198.** This was originally a scheme to raise capital in the West for the assistance of Asian nations

_____ **199.** The headquarters of this organization is in Bangkok, Thailand

_____ **200.** This is an organization to assist children throughout the world

Answers to Tests

Test I

1. C	11. N	21. A	31. C	41. D
2. I	12. S	22. B	32. B	42. A
3. F	13. M	23. A	33. C	43. C
4. E	14. L	24. C	34. D	44. D
5. K	15. W	25. B	35. B	45. C
6. B	16. Q	26. D	36. D	46. C
7. T	17. V	27. C	37. D	47. B
8. J	18. U	28. B	38. C	48. A
9. H	19. A	29. C	39. C	49. C
10. P	20. D	30. D	40. D	50. D

51. G	61. T	71. B	81. C	91. H
52. A	62. F	72. A	82. B	92. B
53. H	63. F	73. A	83. A	93. E
54. B	64. T	74. C	84. D	94. G
55. F	65. T	75. D	85. E	95. I
56. T	66. F	76. B	86. B	
57. F	67. F	77. C	87. E	
58. T	68. T	78. A	88. G	
59. F	69. T	79. E	89. B	
60. F	70. F	80. D	90. E	

Test II

1. F	11. R	21. D	31. C	41. D
2. I	12. G	22. A	32. D	42. C
3. U	13. C	23. C	33. B	43. C
4. A	14. S	24. C	34. B	44. B
5. N	15. L	25. B	35. A	45. B
6. E	16. D	26. A	36. B	46. B
7. J	17. T	27. A	37. C	47. C
8. P	18. K	28. D	38. C	48. E
9. B	19. Q	29. C	39. B	49. A
10. M	20. H	30. D	40. C	50. D

51. C	61. F	71. D	81. D	91. D
52. A	62. T	72. F	82. E	92. D
53. E	63. F	73. C	83. A	93. B
54. B	64. T	74. B	84. C	94. B
55. D	65. T	75. A	85. B	95. C
56. F	66. F	76. C	86. D	
57. F	67. T	77. A	87. D	
58. T	68. T	78. B	88. B	
59. T	69. F	79. E	89. B	
60. F	70. T	80. D	90. C	

Test III

1. H	11. E	21. D	31. D	41. D
2. I	12. K	22. C	32. B	42. C
3. U	13. G	23. C	33. C	43. C
4. N	14. O	24. B	34. C	44. D
5. P	15. C	25. D	35. B	45. B
6. L	16. S	26. B	36. C	46. C
7. B	17. Q	27. B	37. C	47. B
8. R	18. J	28. C	38. D	48. C
9. F	19. M	29. D	39. B	49. A
10. A	20. D	30. B	40. C	50. K

51. A	61. F	71. F	81. D	91. G
52. L	62. T	72. T	82. G	92. E
53. J	63. T	73. F	83. H	93. D
54. N	64. F	74. T	84. F	94. C
55. D	65. T	75. F	85. C	95. F
56. C	66. F	76. B	86. J	
57. M	67. T	77. D	87. A	
58. F	68. T	78. A	88. B	
59. E	69. F	79. E	89. E	
60. G	70. T	80. C	90. I	

Test IV

1. N	11. L	21. C	31. D	41. B
2. T	12. O	22. D	32. A	42. D
3. G	13. R	23. B	33. D	43. D
4. I	14. F	24. B	34. B	44. C
5. M	15. C	25. B	35. A	45. C
6. D	16. B	26. C	36. C	46. B/C
7. Q	17. J	27. C	37. D	47. B/C
8. P	18. H	28. C	38. B	48. C/D
9. K	19. E	29. C	39. B	49. C/D
10. A	20. S	30. B	40. D	50. B/C

51. B/C	61. B	71. F	81. F	91. J
52. A/B	62. D	72. T	82. T	92. D
53. A/B	63. E	73. T	83. T	93. E
54. A/B	64. A	74. F	84. F	94. H
55. A/B	65. C	75. T	85. F	95. B
56. F	66. D	76. T	86. C	
57. D	67. C	77. F	87. F	
58. A	68. E	78. T	88. A	
59. C	69. B	79. F	89. G	
60. B	70. A	80. F	90. I	

Test V

1. Q	11. L	21. C	31. B	41. A
2. D	12. P	22. C	32. D	42. C
3. H	13. E	23. A	33. A	43. A
4. K	14. J	24. C	34. C	44. C
5. A	15. G	25. C	35. D	45. C
6. F	16. O	26. C	36. C	46. F
7. S	17. T	27. A	37. B	47. G
8. I	18. N	28. C	38. C	48. I
9. M	19. C	29. C	39. B	49. C
10. R	20. B	30. C	40. C	50. A

51. E	61. B	71. D	81. F	91. D
52. C	62. A	72. G	82. T	92. C
53. B	63. C	73. F	83. F	93. A
54. D	64. E	74. B	84. F	94. E
55. A	65. B	75. E	85. T	95. B
56. C	66. D	76. A	86. T	
57. D	67. B	77. F	87. F	
58. B	68. A	78. T	88. F	
59. D	69. E	79. T	89. F	
60. D	70. C	80. T	90. T	

Test VI

1. A	11. D	21. B	31. D	41. B
2. U	12. K	22. C	32. D	42. C
3. H	13. S	23. D	33. B	43. D
4. J	14. G	24. D	34. C	44. D
5. P	15. L	25. A	35. B	45. C
6. F	16. O	26. B	36. B	46. F
7. M	17. B	27. A	37. D	47. A
8. N	18. Q	28. C	38. D	48. C
9. C	19. V	29. C	39. C	49. G
10. I	20. E	30. B	40. A	50. E

51. B	61. F	71. F	81. E	91. C
52. C	62. T	72. T	82. M	92. A
53. A	63. F	73. F	83. F	93. G
54. D	64. T	74. T	84. H	94. D
55. E	65. T	75. F	85. N	95. E
56. C	66. T	76. G	86. L	
57. A	67. F	77. A	87. K	
58. E	68. T	78. B	88. I	
59. B	69. F	79. C	89. J	
60. D	70. T	80. D	90. O	

Test VII

1. S	11. U	21. C	31. A	41. A
2. F	12. N	22. B	32. C	42. C
3. V	13. P	23. B	33. C	43. D
4. M	14. B	24. A	34. A	44. C
5. C	15. I	25. D	35. C	45. C
6. O	16. E	26. C	36. D	46. C
7. K	17. J	27. B	37. B	47. E
8. T	18. L	28. C	38. B	48. A
9. R	19. Q	29. C	39. D	49. B
10. H	20. D	30. B	40. C	50. G

51. H	61. F	71. T	81. C	91. D
52. J	62. T	72. F	82. B	92. E
53. E	63. T	73. T	83. C	93. A
54. G	64. F	74. F	84. B	94. G
55. B	65. F	75. F	85. B	95. B
56. F	66. F	76. E	86. C	
57. C	67. T	77. C	87. B	
58. I	68. F	78. B	88. C	
59. D	69. T	79. G	89. A	
60. A	70. F	80. F	90. B	

Test VIII

1. J	11. I	21. B	31. B	41. A
2. F	12. H	22. C	32. B	42. B
3. A	13. V	23. B	33. B	43. B
4. S	14. T	24. A	34. C	44. B
5. E	15. D	25. B	35. C	45. C
6. R	16. G	26. B	36. A	46. E
7. L	17. P	27. A	37. D	47. G
8. N	18. U	28. C	38. C	48. A
9. Q	19. C	29. C	39. B	49. F
10. B	20. M	30. B	40. C	50. C

51. G	61. F	71. D	81. Chiang Kai-shek	89. Haile Selassie
52. F	62. T	72. A	82. China	90. Ethiopia
53. B	63. T	73. C	83. Gandhi	91. A
54. D	64. F	74. C	84. India	92. E
55. A	65. F	75. B	85. Tito	93. C
56. T	66. F	76. D	86. Yugoslavia	94. D
57. F	67. F	77. A	87. Sukarno	95. B
58. F	68. T	78. C	88. Indonesia	
59. T	69. T	79. E		
60. T	70. T	80. B		

Test IX

1. P	11. HH	21. M	31. C	41. B
2. I	12. A	22. F	32. B	42. B
3. V	13. K	23. B	33. A	43. C
4. G	14. BB	24. H	34. A	44. B
5. LL	15. KK	25. S	35. C	45. C
6. C	16. GG	26. X	36. B	46. B
7. JJ	17. FF	27. Q	37. C	47. C
8. R	18. N	28. AA	38. B	48. C
9. EE	19. E	29. DD	39. C	49. B
10. W	20. L	30. D	40. C	50. C

51. C	61. D	71. A	81. F	91. L
52. C	62. B	72. E	82. I	92. O
53. C	63. C	73. H	83. C	93. A
54. C	64. A	74. S	84. K	94. H
55. C	65. B	75. J	85. D	95. J
56. B	66. D	76. W	86. N	96. F
57. C	67. I	77. O	87. E	97. F
58. D	68. R	78. N	88. B	98. T
59. A	69. B	79. M	89. G	99. T
60. B	70. P	80. Q	90. M	100. F

101. F	111. A	121. G
102. T	112. H	122. L
103. T	113. F	123. J
104. F	114. B	124. B
105. T	115. D	125. C
106. F	116. H	126. I
107. T	117. E	127. A
108. T	118. A	128. M
109. F	119. C	129. N
110. F	120. D	130. E

Test X

1. D	11. B	21. A	31. A	41. C
2. N	12. X	22. EE	32. C	42. B
3. Z	13. BB	23. E	33. D	43. C
4. C	14. W	24. DD	34. B	44. C
5. U	15. O	25. P	35. D	45. C
6. FF	16. L	26. Y	36. C	46. C
7. T	17. K	27. S	37. A	47. A
8. F	18. AA	28. J	38. B	48. D
9. R	19. CC	29. M	39. A	49. D
10. HH	20. Q	30. G	40. B	50. C

51. D	61. A	71. B	81. B	91. C
52. D	62. B	72. E	82. C	92. B
53. B	63. C	73. F	83. A	93. E
54. C	64. D	74. C	84. D	94. A
55. D	65. D	75. G	85. E	95. D
56. B	66. F	76. F	86. E	96. F
57. C	67. H	77. E	87. A	97. F
58. D	68. D	78. H	88. C	98. T
59. C	69. A	79. B	89. D	99. T
60. D	70. C	80. C	90. B	100. F

101. T	111. Nihilism	121. Rhodesia OR Smith
102. F	112. Dictatorship	122. South Africa
103. T	113. Capitalism	123. Le Duc Tho
104. F	114. Appeasement	124. Great Proletarian Cultural Revolution
105. T	115. Collectivism	125. Supreme Commander for the Allied Powers
106. T	116. Deflation	126. Okinawa
107. F	117. Deductive	127. Bhutto
108. F	118. Neutralism	128. Zimbabwe
109. T	119. Propaganda	129. Alliance for Progress
110. F	120. Self-determination	130. Allende

Test XI

1. M	11. G	21. G	31. O	41. N
2. H	12. B	22. M	32. P	42. T
3. P	13. O	23. I	33. B	43. M
4. Q	14. A	24. A	34. K	44. P
5. S	15. I	25. F	35. E	45. R
6. L	16. R	26. J	36. R	46. A
7. T	17. K	27. T	37. N	47. S
8. D	18. F	28. C	38. H	48. Q
9. E	19. J	29. Q	39. S	49. G
10. C	20. N	30. D	40. L	50. F

51. B	61. I	71. G	81. K	91. N
52. O	62. Q	72. H	82. L	92. C
53. J	63. J	73. A	83. A	93. I
54. I	64. B	74. R	84. E	94. O
55. L	65. M	75. K	85. P	95. S
56. E	66. S	76. E	86. Q	96. G
57. D	67. L	77. O	87. J	97. T
58. H	68. T	78. C	88. M	98. B
59. C	69. F	79. D	89. D	99. F
60. K	70. N	80. P	90. H	100. R

101. K	111. P	121. L	131. J	141. N
102. L	112. R	122. P	132. Q	142. R
103. Q	113. J	123. B	133. T	143. L
104. C	114. N	124. R	134. G	144. A
105. G	115. O	125. D	135. C	145. C
106. S	116. I	126. M	136. O	146. Q
107. F	117. A	127. F	137. K	147. O
108. B	118. D	128. N	138. E	148. T
109. T	119. M	129. H	139. A	149. B
110. H	120. E	130. I	140. S	150. E

151. J	161. F	171. M	181. P	191. C
152. D	162. I	172. R	182. S	192. F
153. K	163. N	173. J	183. Q	193. B
154. I	164. A	174. H	184. L	194. A
155. P	165. D	175. O	185. K	195. N
156. M	166. G	176. T	186. I	196. G
157. S	167. Q	177. B	187. J	197. H
158. G	168. E	178. K	188. R	198. D
159. H	169. C	179. S	189. E	199. O
160. F	170. L	180. P	190. M	200. T

Index

Acropolis, 19
Act of Supremacy-1534, 71
Aden, 250
Adenauer, Konrad, 238
Administration of Justice Act, 112
Aeneid, 41
Aeschylus, 27
Africa, 287-299
Afrikaner, 294
Age of Metals, 2
Age of Reason, 105-109
Agencies of the United Nations, 224
Aids, Feudal, 55
Akhenaton (Ikhnaton), 5
Al Fatah, 256
Albania, 226, 240
Alaric, 38
Alcestis, 27
Alexander the Great, 29
Alexander II of Russia, 146
Alexander III of Russia, 148
Alfonso XIII of Spain, 191
Algeciras Conference, 180
Algeria, 232-233
Algiers, 217
Aliyot, 252
Allende, Salvador, 303
Alliance for Progress, 302
Allied Airlift, 238
Alvarado, 79
Amenhotep III, 5
American Revolution, 110-113
Amun-Ra, 6
Anaxagoras, 26
Ancien Regime, 114
Angola, 292-293
Ankara, 190
Anschluss, 194, 212
Antigone, 27
Antioch, Kingdom of, 54
Antisthenes, 31
Apartheid, 294
Apella, 22
Appeasement, 209
Aquinas, Thomas, 61
Arab League, 251
Arab-Israeli War-1967 (Six-Day War), 255
Arafat, Yassir, 223, 256
Arameans, 10
Archimedes, 30
Architrave, 28
Archon, 21
Areopagus, 21

Argentina, 302
Aristarchus, 30
Aristophanes, 28
Aristotle, 27
Articles of Confederation, 112
Assignats, 117
Assimilation, 291
Assyria, 10
Asty, 20
Ataturk (Mustafa Kemal), 190
Athens, 21
Atlantic Charter, 216
Aton, 6
Attlee, Clement, 234
Augsleich, 177
Australia, 166
Austria, 95, 130, 174-177
Awami League, 284
Aztecs, 76

Baath Party, 249
Babylon, 9-11
Babylonia, 8-10
Babylonian Captivity, 68, 252
Bacon, Francis, 105
Baghdad Pact, 306
Bakunin, Mikhail, 146
Balfour, Arthur, 253
Balfour Declaration, 253
Balzac, Honore, 163
Bandaranaike, Mrs. Sirimavo, 267
Bandung Conference, 261-262, 306
Bangladesh, 284-286
Banking, 60
Bao Dai, 262
Batavian Republic, 122
Batista, Fulgencio, 304
Battle of:
    Britain, 215
    Coral Sea, 216
    Cynoscephalae, 35
    Dien Bien Phu, 232, 262
    Granicus, 25
    Issus, 25
    Leipzig, 125
    Marathon, 22
    Marengo, 122
    Midway, 216
    Mylae, 34
    Nations (Leipzig), 125
    Nile, 122
    Salamis, 23
    Trafalgar, 124

Ulm, 124
Waterloo, 125
Bay of Pigs, 230, 305
Behistun Inscription, 11
Bela Kun, 194, 240
Belgian Congo, 290-291
Belgium, 168
Benes, Eduard, 240
Ben-Gurion, David, 254
Benelux Nations, 193-194
Bentham, Jeremy, 140
Berlin Blockade, 227-228, 238
Berlin Decree, 125
Berlin Wall, 229
Bernadotte, Count, 222
Bessemer Converter, 139
Bhutto, Zulfilcar Ali, 285
Biafra, 293
Bill of Rights, 104
Bismarck, Otto von, 158
Black September, 256
Blockade System, British, 125
Boer War, 167
Bolivar, Simon, 132
Bonaparte, Napoleon, 121-125
Book of the Dead, 6
Boris, King of Bulgaria, 195
Bosnia-Herzegovina, 177, 181
Boston Port Act, 112
Boulanger, General, 151
Boule, 21
Bouteflika, Abdelaziz, 223-224
Boxer Rebellion, 169
Brahma, 17
Brandt, Willy, 238-239
Brazil, 80-81, 303
Brezhnev, Leonid, 245
Brinkmanship, 229
Britain, see Great Britain
British Commonwealth, 156
British Guiana-Venezuela Boundary Dispute, 135
British North America Act, 165
Broz, Josip (Tito), 240
Brunswick Manifesto, 118
Brussels Pact (Western European Union), 228
Buddhism, 98
Bulgaria, 226, 240
Burma, 266
Bundesrat, 159
Burke, Edmund, 120-121
Burschenschaften, 158
Burundi, 291
Byzantium, 50-52

Cabinda, 293
Cabot, John, 76
Caesar, Julius, 35-36, 41
Cafuso, 81

Cahiers, 117
Caliph, 53
Calonne, 117
Calvin, John, 71
Cambodia, 265
Canaan, 10
Canada, 165-166
Canterbury Tales, 62
Capetians, 86
Carlsbad Decrees, 158
Carbonari, 161
Carol II, King of Rumania, 195
Carranza, Venutiano, 136
Carthage, 33
Cartier, Jacques, 76
Cartwright, Edmund, 139
Casablanca, 217
Castro, Fidel, 229, 304-305
Catherine II the Great of Russia, 94
Catholic Emancipation Act, 155
Cato, Marcus, 34
Cavour, Count Camillo, 161
Censor, 32
Center Party (Germany), 160
CENTO (Central Treaty Organization), 306
Ceylon, 235, 267
Chamberlain, Neville, 212
Champollion, Jean, 7
Chanson de Roland, 62
Charlemagne, 47-50
Charles I of England, 103
Charles I of Spain, 82
Charles V, Holy Roman Emperor, 71, 82-83
Chartists, 153
Chaucer, Geoffrey, 62
Chiang Kai-shek, 172, 268
Chiaroscuro, 65
Chile, 303-304
Chiliastic, 43
China, 96-99, 168, 170-173
    Ch'in Dynasty, 14
    Chou Dynasty, 14
    Han Dynasty, 14
    Long March, 172, 269
    1911 Revolution, 171
    Opium War, 168, 170
    People's Republic of, 268-273
Chivalry, 56
Chou En-lai, 172, 269-270
Christos, 43
Church, Protestant, 70-71
Church, Roman Catholic, 42, 68-71
Churchill, Sir Winston, 218, 234
Cicero, 41
Cientificos, 305
Clark Memorandum, 136
Class Struggle, 142
Cleisthenes, 21

Clemenceau, Georges, 151
Clerestory, 6
The Clouds, 28
Clovis, the Merovingian, 47
Cnossus, 20
Code of Hammurabi, 9
Code of Lubeck, 59
Code Napoleon, 123
Cold War, 225-230
Colbert, 88
Coleridge, Samuel Taylor, 162
Collective Action, Security, 185, 209
Colombo Plan, 306
Coloni, 38
Colonialism, 289-294
Columbus, Christopher, 75
Comecon, 241
Cominform, 143, 242
Comintern, 242
Comitia Curiata, 32
Commercial Age, 73-74
Committee of Public Safety, 119
Common Law, 90
Common Market (EEC), 306
Common Sense, 112
Commonwealth of Australia, 166
Commonwealth of Nations, 235
Communards, 151
Commune, China, 270
Communism, 141-143, 205
Communist Manifesto, 141-142
Concordat, 123
Concordat of Worms-1122, 49
Confucianism, 14-15
Confucius, 14-15, 272
Congo Free State, 223
Congress of Berlin, 147, 177
Congress of Vienna, 126-128
Constable, John, 163
Constantine, Emperor of Rome, 38, 44
Constantinople, 51
Constitutional Democrats, Russia, 148
Consubstantiation, 70
Consul, 32
Consulate, see France
Continental System, 125
Cook, Captain, 166
Copernican Theory, 66
Copernicus, Nicholas, 66
Corporative State, 201
Cortes, Hernando, 76, 79
Council of Ancients, 120
Council of Constance, 68
Council of Ministers, U.S.S.R., 207
Council of Mutual Economic Assistance (Comecon), 241
Counter-Reformation, 71
Courts of King's Bench, Exchequer, Common Pleas, 90

Craig, William, 237
Crete, 20
Crimean War, 145-146, 175
Critique of Pure Reason, 109
Croesus, 10
Cro-Magnon, 2
Cromwell, Oliver, 104
Crusades, 53-54
Cuba, 304-305
Cuban Missile Crisis, 229-230
Cuneiform, 9
Curia Regis, 86
Curzon Line, 192
Cynics, 31
Cynoscephalae, Battle of, 35
Cyrus the Great, 22
Czechoslovakia, 195, 226, 240-241

D-Day, June 6-1944, 217
D'Estaing, Valery Giscard, 234
Da Gama, Vasco, 75
Da Vinci, Leonardo, 65-66
Dail Eireann, 156
Danish War, 158-159
Dante, Alighieri, 62
Darius, King of Persia, 22
Darwin, Charles, 163
Das Kapital, 142
Dawes Plan, 197
Decembrists, 129, 145
Declaration of Independence, 112
Declaration of the Rights of Man, 117
Deductive Reasoning, 107
Défaute de droit, 86
De Gaulle, Charles, 231-233
Deism, 107
Delian League, 23
Demesne, 56
Democratic Republic of Vietnam, 263
Democritus, 26
De Montfort, Simon, 90
De Rivera, 191
De Spinola, Antonio, 291-292
Destroyer-Base Deal, 215
De-Stalinization, 243
Détente, 230, 246
De Valera, Eamon, 156
Dialectic, 109, 142
Dialogues, 27
Diaz, Bartholomew, 75
Diaz, Porfirio, of Mexico, 305
Diaspora, 10, 252
Dicastery, 24
Dickens, Charles, 163
Dictatorship of the Proletariat, 142
Diderot, Denis, 107
Diem, Ngo Dinh, 263
Dien Bien Phu, 262

Diocese, 44
Diocletian, 38
Diretory, The, 120
Disraeli, Benjamin, 153
Divine Comedy, 65
Document 21, 272
Dogma, 61
Dolfuss, Engelbert, 194
Domesday Book, 89
Dominion of Canada, 165
Dom Pedro of Brazil, 81
Draco, 21
Drago Doctrine, 135
Drang Nach Osten, 180
Dreikaiserbund, 159
Dreyfus, Alfred, 151
Dual Alliance, 160
Dubcek, Alexander, 241
Dulles, John Foster, 229
Duma, 149
Dunkirk, Evacuation of, 215
Durham Report, 165
Dyarchy, 37

East Indies, 261
Easter Rebellion, 155
Ebert, Friedrich, 198
Ecclesia, 21
Economic Determinism, 142
Economics, 74
Eden, Anthony, 225
Edessa, 54
Egypt, 3-7, 168, 189-190, 247
Eire, 156
Eisenhower, Dwight D., 229, 263-264
Ems Despatch, 150
Encyclopedie, 107
England:
    Henry II, 1154-1189, 90
    Henry VII, 1485-1509, 91
    Henry VIII, 1509-1547, 91
    Elizabeth I, 1558-1600, 91
    James I, 1603-1625, 103
    Charles I, 1625-1649, 103
    Charles II, 1660-1685, 104
    James II, 1685-1688, 104
    William III, 1689-1702, 104
Engels, Friedrich, 141
England, for events see Great Britain
Entasis, 28
Ephor, 22
Epicureans, 30
Episcopus, 44
Erasmus, Desiderius, 65
Eratosthenes, 30
Erechtheum, 28
Escheat, 56
Eshkol, Levi, 255

Essay of Civil Government, 112
Estates-General, 116-117
Esterhazy, Major, 151
Estonia, 192, 226
Ethics, 27
Euclid, 30
Euripedes, 27
European Coal and Steel Community, 306
European Defense Community, 306
European Economic Community (Common Market), 306
European Free Trade Association, 306
European Security Agreement, 273
Excommunication, 46
Explorations, 72-76

Fabian Society, 143
Fabius Cunctator, 34
Factory Acts, 154
Factory System, 139
Faisal, King, 250
Fasci di Combattimento, 201
Fascist Party, 201
FAO, Food and Agricultural Organization, 224
Fashoda Incident, 179
Fazenda, 81
Fedayeen, 256
Fertile Crescent, 4, 8-9
Feudalism, 55-57
Fief, 55
Finland, 191, 226
First International, 143
Five Power Pact, 210
Five-Year Plans, 207
Fluvial, 4
Flying Buttress, 63
Ford, Gerald R., 234
Fourier, Francois, 141
Four Power Pact, 210
Fourteen Points, 183-184
France, 85-89, 114-125, 129, 150-152, 168, 231-234
    Louis VI, 1108-1137, 86
    Philip II, 1180-1223, 86
    Louis IX, 1226-1270, 86
    Louis XI, 1461-1483, 87
    Louis XIV, 1643-1715, 88
    Louis XVI, 1774-1793, 116
    National Assembly, 1789-1791, 117
    Legislative Assembly, 1791-1792, 117-118
    National Convention, 1792-1795, 119
    First Republic, 1792-1804, 119
    The Directory, 1795-1799, 120
    The Consulate, 1799-1804, 122
    The First Empire, 1804-1814, 123-124
    Napoleon, Emperor, 1804-1814, 123-124
    Second Republic, 130
    Second Empire, 130, 150
    Third Republic, 150-152

Fourth Republic, 231-232
Fifth Republic, 233
Franco, Francisco, 191
Franco-Prussian War, 150, 159
Frankfurt Assembly, 158
Frankish Empire, 47
French Guinea, 290
French Indo-China, 232, 265
French Revolution, 114-121
French Revolutionary Calendar, 120
French Second Republic, 1848-1852, 130
French Somaliland, 290
Frieze, 28
The Frogs, 28
The Fronde, 88
Fulton, Robert, 139

Gandhi, Indira, 286-287
Gandhi, Mohandas K., 282-283
Galileo, 66, 105-106
Garibaldi, Guiseppe, 161
Gaza Strip, 256
Geneva Accord-1954, 232, 262-263
Geopolitics, 167
George II of Greece, 195
Georgics, 41
Germany, 131, 157-160, 168, 196-200
    Frankfurt Assembly, 158
    Danish War, 158-159
    Seven Weeks' War, 158-159
    Bismarck, Otto von, 158-160
    Franco-Prussian War, 159
    Dreikaiserbund, 159
    Triple Alliance, 160
    Kulturkampf, 160
    William II, 160
    African Colonies, 168
    Anglo-German rivalry, 180
    Moroccan Crises, 180
    World War I, 181-182
    Treaty of Versailles, 184-185
    Weimar Constitution, 196
    Weimar Republic, 196-197
    Hitler, Adolf, 198-199
    National Socialist Party, 198-199
    Stresemann, Gustav, 198
    Mein Kampf, 198
    Hindenburg, 198
    Re-occupation of Rhineland, 200
    Anschluss with Austria, 200, 212
    Munich Pact, 212-213
    Non-aggression pact with U.S.S.R., 213
    Yalta Conference, 218-219
    Potsdam Conference, 218-219
    Berlin Blockade, 227-228
    German Federal Republic (West Germany), 228, 238-239, 241

German Democratic Republic (East Germany), 228-229, 239, 241
Geronsia, 22
Ghana, 235, 293
Ghibellines, 49
Giereck, Edward, 240
Girondists, 118
Goebbels, Josef, 199
Gomulka, Wladyslaw, 240
Gosplan (U.S.S.R. State Planning Commission), 207
Gottwald, Klement, 240
Government of Ireland Act, 156
Government of Massachusetts Act, 112
Good Neighbor Policy, 136
Granicus, Battle of, 25
Great Britain, 89-91, 102-105, 152-156, 234-237
    Reformation, 71
    Early colonial settlements, 76
    Hundred Years' War, 87
    Treaty of Utrecht, 89
    Magna Carta, 90
    Model Parliament, 91
    Tudor monarchs, 91
    Stuart monarchs, 103
    "Glorious Revolution", 104
    Colonial rivalry with France, 110-111
    Treaty of Paris-1763, 110
    American Revolution, 110-113
    Proclamation of 1763, 111
    Stamp Act, 111
    Intolerable Acts, 112
    Treaty of Amiens, 122
    Blockade vs France, 124-125
    Quadruple Alliance, 127
    Greek War of Independence, 129
    Venezuela Boundary dispute, 135
    Industrial Revolution, 137-143
    Crimean War, 145-146, 175
    Congress of Berlin, 147
    Reform Bills, 1832-1946, 152-153
    Social Security legislation, 154
    Ireland, 155
    Canadian Revolts, 165
    Dominion Status for colonies, 165
    Triple Entente, 179-180
    World War I, 182
    Munich Agreement, 212-213
    World War II, 215
    Labor Government of 1945, 234-235
    Balfour Declaration, 253
Greater East Asia Co-Prosperity Sphere, 216
Great Leap Forward, 270
Great Proletarian Cultural Revolution, 270-271
Greece, 19-31, 195-196
Greek Orthodox Church, 44
Greek War of Independence, 129
Gregory VII (Hildebrand), 49
Guelphs (Welfs), 49

Guild, 58-59
Guinea-Bissau, 292

Habeas Corpus, 104
Hacienda, 300
Haganah, 253
Haile Selassie, 202
Hammerskjold, Dag, 222
Hammurabi, 9
Hannibal, 34
Hanseatic League, 59
Harappa, 16
Hargreaves, James, 138
Harvey, William, 66
Hausa, 293
Heath, Edward, 236
Hegel, Georg, 108-109, 142, 163
Hegira, 52
Heliaea, 21
Hellas, 19
Helot, 22
Helvetian Republic, 122
Henlein, Konrad, 195
Henry IV, Holy Roman Emperor, 49
Henry the Navigator, 75
Heraclitus, 26
Heresy, 45
Herodotus, 28
Hidalgo, Father Miguel, 133
Hieroglyphics, 7
Hinduism, 16-17
Hippocrates, 29
Hiroshima, 217
Histadrut, 254
Hitler, Adolf, 198-199
Hittites, 9-10
Hobbes, Thomas, 107-108
Ho Chi Minh, 232, 262
Hohenlinden, Battle of, 122
Holy Alliance, 127
Holy Roman Empire, 47-48
Homage, 56
Homelands Policy, 296
Home Rule, 155, 165
Horace, 41
Hortensian Law, 33
Horthy, Admiral, 194
Hua Kuo-Feng, 270
Huerta, Victoriano, 136
Hugo, Victor, 163
Humanism, 65
Hundred, Hundred Moot, 90
The "Hundred Days," 125
Hundred Years' War, 87
Hungary, 194, 226, 240, 244
Hussein, King of Jordan, 248-249, 256
Hwang Ho (Yellow) River, 13
Hyksos, 5
Hypostyle, 6

Ibn Saud, 250
Ibo, 293
Iceland, 193
Iconoclastic Controversy, 51-52
Icons, 51-52
Ideogram, 7
ICAO, International Civil Aviation Organization, 224
ILO, International Labor Organization, 224
Iliad, 20
Il Risorgimento, 161
Imperium, 32
Incas, 76, 79
India, 15-17, 99-101, 282-287
Indian Mutiny, 101
Indigena, 291
Indonesia, 261-262
Inductive Reasoning, 107
Indulgences, 69
Industrial Revolution, 137-143
Inflation, 187
Initiative, 197
Inner Six (Common Market), 304
Inquisition, 72
Interdict, 46
International Bank for Reconstruction & Development, 224
International Court of Justice, 221
International Geophysical Year, 307
International Monetary Fund, 224
ITU, International Telecommunication Union, 224
International Workingmen's Associations, 143
Intolerable Acts, 112
Investiture, 49, 56
Iran, 222, 249-250
Iraq, 190, 249
Ireland, 154-156
Irian, (Western New Guinea), 261
Irish Free State, 156
Irish Republican Army, IRA, 156, 237
Iron Curtain, 242
Iron Law of Wages, 140
Islam, 50-53
Israel, 222, 252-259
Issus, Battle of, 25
Italian (Cisalpine) Republic, 122
Italy, 160-162, 168, 200-203
    Triple Alliance, 160
    Mazzini, Giuseppe, 161
    Risorgimento, 161
    Young Italy, 161
    Il Risorgimento, 161
    Garibaldi, Giuseppe, 161
    Kingdom of the Two Sicilies, 161
    Victor Emmanuel, 162
    Fascist Party, 201
    Mussolini, 201
    Corporative State, 201
    Ethiopia, 202
    Albania, 202
    Locarno Agreements, 210

Munich Agreement, 212-213
Iturbide, Augustin de, 133
Ivan the Terrible, 93

Jacobins, 118
Jainism, 17
Japan, 274-281
    Washington Conference, 210
    Nine Power Pact, 210
    Five Power Pact, 210
    Pearl Harbor, 216
    Battle of the Coral, 216
    Battle of Midway, 216
    Solomon Islands campaign, 216
    Hiroshima & Nagasaki, 217
    Capitulation-1945, 217
    Sino-Japanese War, 276
    Russo-Japanese War, 276
    Twenty One Demands, 276-277
    War against China, 276
    Since 1945, 278-281
Jinnah, Mohammed Ali, 283
Joan of Arc, 87
Johnson, Lyndon B., 263-264
Jordan, 248-249
Judah, 10
Justinian, 40
Juvenal, 41

K'abah, 52
Kadar, Janos, 240, 244
Kamikaze, 274
Kant, Immanuel, 108-109
Karma, 17
Karnak, 6
Kashmir, 284
Kay, John, 138
Kellogg-Briand Pact, 211
Kemal, Mustafa (Ataturk), 190
Kennedy, John F., 229-230, 263-264
Kenya, 294
Kenyatta, Jomo, 294
Kepler, Johann, 66
Kerensky, Alexander, 204
Khan, Ayub, 284
Khann, Yahya, 284-285
Khmer Rouge, 265
Khrushchev, Nikita, 229, 243-244
Kibbutz, 253
Kiev, 93
Kingdom of Jerusalem, 54
King's Messengers, 47
Kingsley, Charles, 143
Kismet, 53
Kissenger, Henry, 264
Kitchener, General Herbert, 179
Knesset, 254
Koch, Robert, 163
Kolkhoz, 206-207

Korea, 222
Kossuth, Louis, 176
Kosygin, Aleksei, 245
Kubla Khan, 162
Kulak, 206
Kulturkampf, 160
Kuomintang, 172, 268
Kuwait, 250

Labor Party, British, 154
Labor Theory of Value, 142
Laissez-faire, 139
Laos, 265
The Last Supper, 66
Latifundia, 35
Latin America, 77-81, 131-136, 299-305
Latvia, 192, 226
Lay Investiture, 49
Le Duc Tho, 264-265
League of Nations, 185, 209-210
Lebanon, 247
Legitimacy, 127
Leipzig, Battle of, 125
Lend-Lease-1941, 215
Lenin (Vladimir Ulianov), 204, 206
Leonardo da Vinci, 65-66
Leviathan, 108
Lie, Trygvie, 222
Lin Piao, 172, 269
Lister, Joseph, 163
Lithuania, 192, 226
Livy, 41
Locarno Agreements-1925, 210
Locke, John, 107, 112
Lon Nol, 265
Long Parliament, 1640-1660, 103
Louis Philippe (Philip Equality), 129-130
Loyola, Ignatius, 71
Lumumba, Patrice, 291
Luther, Martin, 69-71
Luxembourg, 194
Lvov, Prince George, 204
Lydia, 10
Lyrical Ballads, 162

Macedonian Wars, 215-168 B.C., 35
Machievelli, Niccolo, 66-67
Mackenzie, William, 165
Macmillan, Harold, 295
Magna Carta, 90-91
Malawi, Republic of, 296
Malay Peninsula, 261
Malaysia, 266
Malthus, Thomas, 140
Manchu Dynasty, 1644-1912, 97
Manchurian Incident-1931, 211, 277
Mao Tse-tung, 172, 268-269
Marathon, Battle of, 22
Marchand, Jean-Baptiste, 179

March on Rome-1922, 201
Marco Polo, 97
Marengo, Battle of, 122
Marshall Mission, 268
Marshall Plan, 227
Martel, Charles, 47
Marx, Karl, 141-143
Marxism, 206
Marxism-Leninism, 206
Masaryk, Thomas, 195
Masinissa, 34
Massive Retaliation, 229
MauMau, 294
Maximilian of Mexico, 134-135
Mayas, 78
Mazzini, Guiseppe, 161
Medina, 52
Mein Kampf, 198
Meir, Golda, 255-256
Memphis, 5
Menes, 5
Mercantilism, 74-75
Mesopotamia, 8-12
Mestizos, 80
Metamorphoses, 41
Metics, 23
Metternich, Prince von, 127
Mexicanidad, 305
Mexico, 133-136
Mexico, Intervention by U.S., 136
Michelangelo, 65
Middle East, 247-251
Midway, Battle of-1942, 216-217
Mill, John Stuart, 140
Miltiades, 23
Ming Dynasty, 1368-1644, 97
Miranda, Francisco de, 132
Missi Dominici, 47
Mobutu, Joseph, 291
Model Parliament-1295, 91
Mohammed, 52
Mohammedanism, 52
Mohenjo-Daro, 16
Moldavia & Wallachia, 146
Mona Lisa, 66
Monroe Doctrine, 129, 135
Montenegro, 147
Montesquieu, Charles, 107, 115
Montezuma, 79
Montgomery, General, 216
Moots, 90
Moroccan Crises, 180
Moscow Summit, 246
Moshav, 253
"Mountain," The, 119
Mozambique, 292
Mulatto, 81
Munich Pact-1938, 212-213

Mussolini, Benito, 201
Mustafa Kemal, 190
Mylae, Battle of-260 B.C., 34

Nagasaki, 217
Nagy, Imre, 240, 244
Napoleon, 121-125
Nasser, Gamel Abdel, 223, 235, 247
National Assembly, 117
Nationalist China (Taiwan), 173, 271
National Covenant, 247
National Health Act, 235
National Insurance Act, 234
National Socialists, 198-199
"Natural Rights of Man," 112
NATO, North Atlantic Treaty Organization, 228, 307
Neanderthal, 2
Near East Question, 145, 175
Nebuchadrezzar, 10
Necker, Jacques, 116
Nehru, Jawaharlal, 262, 283
Neolithic, 2
Netherlands, 129
New Babylonia, 10-11
New Economic Policy, NEP, 205
New Harmony, Indiana, 141
Newton, Isaac, 66
New Zealand, 166
Nguyen van Thieu, 264
Nietzche, Friedrich, 163
Nigeria, 293
Nihilism, 147
Nile, Battle of-1798, 122
Nine Power Paact-1922, 210
Nineveh, 10
Ninety-Five Theses, 70
Nixon, Richard M., 246, 264
NLF, National Liberation Front, 263
North Atlantic Treaty Organization, NATO, 228
Northern Ireland, 155
Northern Rhodesia, 296
Norway, 193
Nyasaland, 296

OAS, Organization of American States, 307
Octavian, (Augustus), 37
October Manifesto, 149
Oder-Neisse Line, 239
Odes of Horace, 41
Odyssey of Homer, 20
Oedipus the King, 27
O'Higgins, Bernardo, 133
Oligarchy, 24
Olympic Games, 29
OPEC, Organization of Petroleum Exporting Countries, 250, 257
Opium War, 1840-1842, 168, 170
Orange Free States, 167

Orations, 41
Oresteia, 27
Organization of American States, OAS, 306
Orthodoxy, 45
Osiris, 6
Ostpolitik, 238-239
Ostracism, 23
Otto the Great, 48-49
Ovid, 41
Owen, Robert, 140-141

Paderewski, Ignace, 192
Pakistan, 283-285
Paleolithic, 2
Palestine, 190, 222
Palestine Liberation Organization (PLO), 223, 256
Panama Canal, 135
Pancho Villa, 136
Panther, 180
Papineau, Louis, 165
Paracelsus, 66
Parliament Acts-1911, 1946, 153
Parnell, Charles, 155
Parthenon, 24, 28
Pasteur, Louis, 163
Pax Romana, 40
Peace of Augsburgh 1555, 70
Peace of Ryswick 1697, 88
Peace of Westphalia 1648, 83
Peaceful co-existence, 243-244
Peace Terms 1919, 184-185
Peloponnesian Wars, 431-404 B.C., 24-25
People's Republic (Communist) of China, 173, 268-273
Pepin, 47
Pericles, 23
Peron, Juan, 302-303
Perry, Commodore Matthew, 275
Persepolis, 25
Persia, 12
Persian Wars, 492-479 B.C., 22-23
The Persians, 27
Peter the Great, 94
Petition of Right, 103
Petrarch, 65
Petrine Theory, 44
Phalangist Party, 247-248
Philadelphia Convention, 113
Philip of Macedon, 25, 29
Philip II of Spain, 82-83
Philippines, 261
Philosophes, 107, 115
Phoenicia, 10
Philosophy, 26
Physiocrat, 116
Pictogram, 7
Pietism, 108
Pilsudski, Marshal, 192
Pisistratus, 21

Pizarro, Francisco, 76, 79
Plataea, Battle of, 478 B.C., 23
Plato, 27
Pnyx, 23
Point Four (Colombo) Program, 295
Poland, 191, 226, 240, 244
Polis, 20
Polish Corridor, 185
Politics, 27
Polytheism, 6
Pompidou, Georges, 234
Pontifex Maximus, 32
Popular Front for the Liberation of Palestine (PFLP), 256
Popular Republican Movement, MRP, 232
Portugal, 168
Potsdam Conference, 218-219
Praetor, 32
Prehistory, 1
Presidium, 207
Primogeniture, 86
The Prince, 66-67
Princeps, 36
Princip, Gabriel, 181
Principles of Political Economy, 140
Principles of Population, 140
Proclamation of 1763, 111
Propylaea, 28
Proportional Representation, 197
Prussia, 95
Prytaneum, 23-24
Ptolemaic Theory, 66
Ptolemy, 30
Punic Wars, 264-146 B.C., 33-34
Putsch, 197
Pyrrhus of Epirus, 33

Quadruple Alliance, 127
Quaestor, 32
Quintuple Alliance, 127

Ra, 6
Rabin, Yitzhak, 257
Rahman, Mujibur, 284
Rationalism, 106
Recall, 197
Red Guards, 271
Referendum, 197-198
Reform Bills-1832, 1867, 1884, 1918, 1928, 152-153
Reformation, 68-71
Regular Clergy, 45
Reichstag, 159
Re-Insurance Treaty, 179
Reliefs, 55
Renaissance, 64-67
Republic, 27
Republic of Ireland-1949, 156
Republic of Liguria (Genoa), 122

Republic of Parthenopea (Naples), 122
Republic of South Africa, 294-296
Republic of (South) Vietnam, 263
Revolutions of 1820, 128
Revolutions of 1830, 129
Revolutions of 1848, 130
Rhodes, Cecil, 167
Rhodesia, 296-297
Ricardo, David, 140
Richelieu, Cardinal, 83
Risorgimento, 162
Robespierre, Maximilien, 119-120
Romanesque, 62
Rome, The Republic, 32-36
Rome, The Empire, 37-41
Romanticism, 162-163
Rommel, Erwin, 216
Roosevelt Corollary, 135
Roosevelt, Franklin D., 216
Rosetta Stone, 7
Rousseau, Jean Jacques, 108, 115
Rumania, 226, 240
Russia & U.S.S.R., 92-95, 145-149
Russia, Emperors
    Ivan the Terrible, 1533-1583, 93
    Peter the Great, 1682-1725, 94
    Catherine the Great, 1762-1796, 94
    Nicholas I, 1825-1855, 145
    Alexander II, 1855-1881, 146
    Alexander III, 1881-1894, 148
    Nicholas II, 1894-1917, 148
Russo-German Non-Agression Pact-1939, 200
Russo-Japanese War, 1904-1905, 148, 276
Russo-Turkish War, 1877-1878, 147, 176
Rwanda, 291

Sacraments, 45-46
Sadat, Anwar, 265
Saint-Simon, 140-141
Salamis, Battle of, 23
SALT (Strategic Arms Limitation Conference), 230, 246
San Martin, Jose de, 132-133
Sarajevo Affair, 181
Saud, Ibn, of Arabia, 250
Saudi Arabia, 190, 250
Schleswig-Holstein, 158-159
Schliemann, Heinrich, 20
Schmidt, Helmuth, 239
Scholasticism, 61
Schuman Plan, 307
Scott, Sir Walter, 163
Scutage, 56
SEATO, South East Asia Treaty Organization, 266, 307
Second International, 143
Secular Clergy, 45
Self-determination, 183
Selective Service Act-1940, 215-216
Serbia, 174-175

Serf, 56
Seven Sacraments, 45-46
Seven Weeks War-1866, 158-159
Seventeenth Parallel, 232
Severus, Emperor of Rome, 38
Shah Reza Pahlavi, 249-250
Shelley, Percy Bysshe, 162
Shire, Shiremoot, 90
Shiva, 17
Shogun, 274
Sihanouk, Norodom, 265
Simony, 68
Singapore, 266
Siniticism, 15
Sinn Fein, 155
Sino-Japanese War, 1894-1895, 171, 173-174, 276
Sino-Soviet Breach, 244-245
Sino-Soviet Treaty of Friendship, 243
Smith, Adam, 140
Smith, Ian, 296
Social Contract, 108, 115
Social Democrats, Russia, 148
Social Democrats, Germany, 160, 239
Social Darwinism, 163, 166
Social Revolutionaries, Russia, 148
Society of Jesus, 71-72
Socrates, 27
Solon, 21
Somaliland, 202
Sophistry, Sophists, 27
Sophocles, 27
South East Asia Treaty Organization (SEATO), 296
South Africa, 167, 294-296
Southern Rhodesia, 296
Southern Yemen, 250-251
Soviet of Nationalities, 207
Soviet of the Union, 207
Sovkhoz, 207
Spain, 191
Sparta, 21-22
Spencer, Herbert, 163
Spirit of the Laws, 107, 115
Sputnik, 229
Sri Lanka (Ceylon), 235, 267
Stalin, Josef, 206-207, 219
Stamp Act-1765, 111
Stahrenburg, Prince, 194
Statute of Westminster-1931, 156
Stephenson, George, 139
Stoics, 30
Stone Age, 2
Stresa Front-1934, 200
Stresemann, Gustav, 198
Strategoi, 21, 24
Sub-infeudation, 55
Sudetenland, 212
Suez Canal Crisis-1956, 223, 235
Suharto, General, 262

Sukarno, Achmed, 261-262
Sumerians, 9
Summa Theologica, 61
Sun Yat-sen, 171
Supreme Soviet, 207
Surplus Value, 142
Susa, 12
Sweden, 193
Switzerland, 193-194
Syria, 248

Tacitus, 41
T'ai P'ing Rebellion, 1850-1864, 171
Tamerlane, 99
Tanaka Memorial, 277
T'ang Dynasty, 618-907, 96-97
Taiwan (Nationalist China), 173, 271
Tanzania, 294
Taoism, 15
Tarquin, 32
Tashkent Conference, 307
Tea Act-1773, 112
Ten Lost Tribes, 252
Tennis Court Oath, 117
Tenochtitlan, 78
Tetzel, 69
Thailand, 265-266
Thales, 26
Thalassic, 19
Themistocles, 23
Theocracy, 71
Theology, 61
Thermidorian Reaction, 120
Thermopylae, 22
Third International, 143
Thousand Red Shirts, 161
Third Reich, Germany, 199
Third Republic, France, 151
Third World, 223-224
Thirty Years' War, 1618-1648, 83
Three Emperors' League, 159, 179
Thucydides, 28
Tito, Josip Broz, 240
Tokugawa, 275
Tonkin Gulf Resolution, 264
Townshend Acts, 111
Trafalgar, Battle of, 124
Transept, 63
Transjordan, 190
Trans-Siberian Railroad, 148
Transubstantiation, 45, 70
Transvaal, 167
Treatises of Civil Government, 108
Treaty of:
    Andrianople-1829, 175
    Amiens-1802, 122
    Brest-Litovsk-1918, 182
    Frankfurt-1871, 150
        Kanagawa, 275
        Lausanne-1923, 190
        Nanking 1842, 168, 170
        Paris 1763, 110
        Paris 1856, 146
        Portsmouth 1905, 148
        Riga 1921, 192
        San Stefano 1877, 147, 176
        Sevres 1920, 247
        Shimonoseki, 276
        Tilsit 1807, 94
        Tordesillas 1494, 75
        Utrecht, 89
        Versailles 1919, 184-185
Treitschke, Heinrich von, 163
Tribune, 32
Triennial Act, 104
Triple Alliance, 160, 179
Triple Entents, 179-180
Tripoli, 54
Trireme, 33
Trojan Women, 27
Trotsky, Leon, 205
Truman Doctrine, 226-227
Tunisia, 168
Turgot, Baron, 116
Turkey, 174-177, 190, 247
Turner, William, 163
Tutankhamen, 5
Twelve Tables, 33
Twenty-One Demands, 276-277

UDI, Unilateral Declaration of Independence, 296
Ulbricht, Walter, 241
Ulm, Battle of, 1805, 124
Ulster Vanguard, 237
Ultras, 129
Union of Soviet Socialist Republics, see Russia and U.S.S.R., 204-208
United Arab Republic, 251
Union of South Africa, 167
United Nations, 220-224
Universitas, 61-62
Upanishads, 16
UPU, Universal Postal Union, 224
UNESCO, United Nations Scientific and Cultural Organization, 224
UNICEF, United Nations International Children's Emergency Fund, 224
UNRRA, United Nations Relief and Rehabilitation Administration, 307
Utopian Socialists, 143
Urban II, Pope, 54
U.S.S.R., Constitution 1936, 204-208
U Thant, 222

Vassal, 55
Vedas (Rigvedas), 16

Venetian Empire, 59-60
Vergil, 41
Vesalius, 66
Viceroyalty of La Plata, 79
    New Granada, 79
    New Spain, 79
    Peru, 79
Viet Minh, 232, 262
Viet Nam, 262-265
Villein, 56
Villeneuve, Admiral, 136
Vishnu, 17
Voltaire, 107, 115

Waldheim, Kurt, 222
Wallachia and Moldavia, 146
Wars:
    Austrian Succession, 114
    Boer, 167
    Crimean, 145-146, 175
    Franco-Prussian, 150, 159
    Greek Independence, 175
    Hundred Years', 87
    Opium, 168, 170
    Russo-Japanese, 148, 276
    Russo-Turkish, 147, 176
    Seven Weeks', 158-159
    Seven Years', 95
    Sino-Japanese, 171, 173-174, 276
    Spanish-American, 135
    Thirty Years', 83
    World War I, 178-182
    World War II, 214-219
    Yom Kippur, 223, 256-257
Warsaw Pact, 241, 307
Washington Conference 1921, 210

Waterloo, Battle of, 1815, 125
Watt, James, 138-139
Wealth of Nations, 140
Week Work, 56
Weimar Republic, 196-197
Western European Union (Brussels Pact)-1948, 228
White Man's Burden, 289
Whitney, Eli, 138
WHO, World Health Organization, 224
Wilson, Harold, 236
WMO, World Meteorological Organization, 224
Wordsworth, William, 162
Wyclif, John, 69

Xanthippus, 34
Xerxes, 22

Yalta Conference, 218-219
Yangtze-kiang River, 13
Yemen, 250
Yoruba, 293
Yuan or Mongol Dynasty, 1279-1368, 97
Young Italy, 161
Young Turks, 176
Yugoslavia, 195, 240

Zaire, 291
Zamora, 191
Zemstvos, 146
Zeno, 30
Ziggurat, 11
Zionism, 253
Zola, Emile, 151
Zollverein, 131

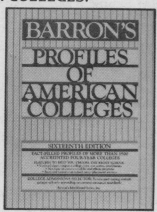
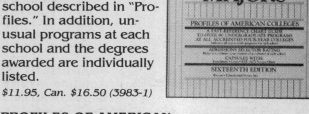

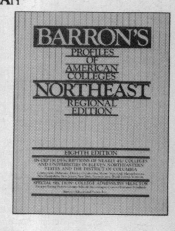

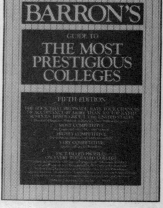